PRINCIPLES OF COMMUNITY PSYCHOLOGY

Principles of Community Psychology

PERSPECTIVES AND APPLICATIONS

Murray Levine

and David V. Perkins

New York   Oxford
OXFORD UNIVERSITY PRESS
1987

Oxford University Press

Oxford   New York   Toronto
Delhi   Bombay   Calcutta   Madras   Karachi
Petaling Jaya   Singapore   Hong Kong   Tokyo
Nairobi   Dar es Salaam   Cape Town
Melbourne   Auckland

and associated companies in
Beirut   Berlin   Ibadan   Nicosia

Library of Congress Cataloging-in-Publication Data
Levine, Murray.
Principles of community psychology.
Bibliography: p.   Includes index.
1. Community psychology.   I. Perkins, David V.   II. Title.
RA790.55.L48   1987   616.89   86-23812
ISBN 0-19-503946-7

5 7 9 8 6

Printed in the United States of America

To Seymour B. Sarason, and the spirit of the Psychoeducational Clinic—
ever since, I have been living off the intellectual capital I stored there;
and to the memory of Susan L. Shackman, who left us all too soon.

M. L.

To Linda, whose enduring support and understanding made my contribution
to this book possible.

D. V. P.

ACKNOWLEDGMENTS

The following material was used with permission of the author and publisher.

Figure 2-1 from B. S. Dohrenwend (1978), Social stress and community psychology. *American Journal of Community Psychology, 6,* 1–14. Used with permission of the journal and the author's estate.

Figure 4-1 from R. H. Price and R. H. Moos (1975), Toward a taxonomy of inpatient treatment environments. *Journal of Abnormal Psychology, 84,* 181–188. Used with permission of the journal and the authors.

Figure 4-2 from R. G. Barker and P. Schoggen (1973), *Qualities of community life.* San Francisco: Jossey-Bass. Used with permission of the publisher.

Table 4-1 from G. W. Fairweather, D. H. Sanders, H. Maynard, and D. Cressler (1969), *Community life for the mentally ill.* Chicago: Aldine. Used with permission of the authors.

Figure 5-1 from T. J. Scheff (1984), *Being mentally ill: A sociological theory* (2d ed.). New York: Aldine. Used with the permission of the publisher and the author.

Figure 6-1 from S. Cohen and T. A. Wills (1985), Stress, social support, and the buffering hypothesis. *Psychological Bulletin, 98,* 310–357. Used with permission of the publisher and the authors.

Figure 7-1 from D. Guerin and D. P. MacKinnon (1985), An assessment of the California child passenger restraint requirement. *American Journal of Public Health, 75,* 142–144. Used with permission of the journal and the authors.

We also appreciate the efforts of countless students, both undergraduate and graduate, who read these chapters and offered numerous critiques and suggestions for revision. An additional note of thanks goes to Lee Gordon, whose cheerful support and handling of many details helped to see the book to completion.

CONTENTS

PRINCIPLES OF COMMUNITY PSYCHOLOGY

Introduction
An Overview of Community Psychology

This book is about community psychology. Community psychology is based on a way of thinking. Our intention in this book is to develop that way of thinking and to show how the perspective is applicable to a wide range of problems in contemporary society.

A starting point for understanding the broader elements that have come to be known as community psychology is the community mental health movement. The community movement is characterized by its efforts to deliver services in the local community, to emphasize services other than long-term hospitalization, and to use outpatient services as much as possible. The community movement is also dedicated to the development of innovative services and to working with other agencies in the community for the client's benefit. The goals of care are also different. We no longer follow the policy of isolating the repulsive deviant in pursuit of some chimerical goal of cure. Those adopting the community mental health perspective work to support people in the local community. When hospitalization does occur, the goal of treatment is not cure of illness, but to restore the individual's equilibrium so that he or she may be returned to the community as rapidly as possible.

This preference for community-based treatment in contrast to institution-based treatment constitutes a perspective and an ideology (Baker, 1974), or a set of beliefs that characterize a group of professionals. The new perspective, in contrast to the clinical perspective, draws much more direct attention to the conditions of life for the person who is the client. The clinical perspective leads us to be primarily concerned with the person's inner life and perhaps with characteristics of his or her relationships, as in family group treatment. The community mental health perspective may incorporate such concerns and interests, but it also leads the helping person to be concerned about living conditions—the availability of housing, employment, recreation, medical care, and transportation. Once the concerns extend that far, to looking at the network of support for the client, the community mental health worker is focusing on the community, a larger unit than the individual or the family. Note that the new perspective requires us to use theoretical conceptions that extend beyond those useful in understanding an individual (e.g., diagnostic categories, psychodynamics, traits) and that incorporate larger units of analysis.

One important characteristic of the community field is an emphasis on what textbook authors have come to call the ecological viewpoint. It is characterized by some as the study of the fit between persons and environments (Rappaport, 1977). Mann (1978) characterizes the ecological viewpoint as requiring "a concern with the relationships of individuals to each other as a community; as a differentiated social grouping with elaborate systems of formal and informal relationships" (p. x). Heller and Monahan (1977) agree that the community perspective includes a "focus on broader ecological levels than the level of the exclusive treatment of the individual" (p. 16). Korchin (1976) lists 13 themes which he believes characterize the field; these include the emphasis on socioenvironmental factors and the emphasis on system-oriented as against person-oriented interventions (pp. 474–475). Graziano and Mooney (1984) offer a similar thoughtful discussion of the difference between the community and the clinical orientation in terms of the choice of point of intervention (pp. 371–373).

If we examine the concept of a point or level of social intervention beyond the individual, a great many lines become fuzzy. Interventions in the name of mental health or community mental health at any ecological level beyond that of the individual imperceptibly shade into social and political action. Because so much of our discourse in the public arena takes on a rational character with resort to quantitative evidence, scientific endeavors become part of the social action and the political process.[1] By political process, we do not necessarily mean electoral politics; instead, we refer to the effort to influence the allocation of public resources. Korchin's (1976) list of themes is in agreement with the view that social intervention is intimately connected with political action and social reform.

Most of those who espouse the theme of social and political action have not departed from the scientific values reflected in their original training in psychology or other social sciences. Most emphasize the necessity to develop sound research bases for informed intervention. Many also note, however, that new emphases if not new models of research will be required. Rappaport (1977) is explicit in stating that a paradigm shift has occurred. He believes that both the questions asked and the methods used to obtain answers have changed. Sarason (1974, 1981, 1982) has argued vigorously and effectively that if psychology and social science are to be relevant and useful for the solution of social problems, the conceptual and research approaches will have to broaden to take into account the historical, social, economic, and political contexts within which policies are developed and implemented.

Most psychologists following the community perspective accept the broader society as it is and see it as their mission to help create or change service organizations and other institutions and agencies to become more effective in achieving the goals of providing humane, effective care and less stigmatizing services to those in need, and of enhancing human psychological growth and development. One can have less than radical aims and remain within the community orientation. No matter the aim, and no matter the predilection to social action or to engaging in conflict as a mode of inducing change, academically based community psychologists are in agreement with the necessity to develop stronger research and conceptual bases for social action and social change. In the absence of useful theory and a sound empirical base, social action will achieve its purposes inefficiently and capriciously, if at all.

Given the less radical aim of working to make human service organizations more effective and more humane, community-oriented psychologists are interested in creating new services consistent with the ecological perspective. The medical model, in which the person in need defines his or her own problem and then seeks out help from a professional helper, most often on a fee-for-service basis, is useful for many people and for many problems. The medical model is unable to provide for all in need, however. Some argue that certain forms of care may contribute to the perpetuation of problems because of the way problems are defined as residing exclusively within the boundaries of an individual. For many problems, it is necessary to seek out and develop alternatives.

In the ecological perspective, human behavior is viewed in terms of the person's adaptation to resources and circumstances. From this perspective, one may correct unsuccessful adaptations by altering the availability of resources. Thus new services may be created, or existing strengths in social networks may be discovered and conditions created to enhance the use of such resources. From this perspective, solutions to problems in living do not necessarily require more professional therapists; instead, one may seek to work through other agencies and institutions and with people who may not have advanced training in the mental health professions. The ecological perspective encourages a search for resources instead of a search for psychopathology. It encourages us to view others as having strengths that may be put to good use in the service of their own development if resources are available. The perspective urges us to believe that one need not necessarily first undo psychopathology.

Crisis theory also provides a useful model that can be integrated with an ecological perspective. Crisis theory argues that as a result of either failures of past socialization or present circumstances, a person may respond with transient distress. In attempting to come to terms with the circumstances and the feelings of distress, the person may return to a point of equilibrium, may worsen and need further care, or may come to terms with the distress and emerge strengthened. Crisis theory states that the difference in outcome is some function of the environmental supports and psychological mediators available to the person who is coping.

Crisis theory is helpful because it points to possibilities for intervention at different points in the process of coping with distress. It also directs attention to the necessity of resources, personal or social, in the coping process. Crisis theory has similarities to the theory of neurosis, but crisis theory directs attention to the possibilities for improvement. In that sense, the theory leads us to view the potential for growth and development as more important than the underlying psychopathology. One should not overestimate the power of our theories, but on the other hand neither should one underestimate it. Our concepts can serve as blinders or as guides. A combination of crisis theory and the ecological perspective directs us to explore new territory in ways that the psychopathological viewpoint and the medical model do not.

Community psychologists have also rallied around the theme of prevention. The concept of prevention has been taken over from the field of public health. Public health professionals argue that no disease has ever been truly conquered by treatment. The greatest advances have been made when we have been able to prevent disease. Deadly scourges have been all but wiped out by inoculations and modern sanitary methods. Our increased average length of life, and our better health throughout a longer fraction of that life span, are more attributable to preventive than to therapeutic measures. The public health model leads us to seek out the causes of pathology and to act to prevent them either by modifying environmental conditions (e.g., cleaning out the swamps to prevent yellow fever, keeping the water supply from becoming contaminated) or by strengthening the organism against disease (e.g., immunization). Efforts to improve the quality of life and efforts that help us to become better people— efforts that strengthen us all—also contribute to prevention. The public health model evidently cannot be adopted whole hog when we deal with social and mental health problems, but it does provide a set of goals and a way of thinking that direct our attention to different issues than does the individual model, which focuses on psychopathology and its treatment.

The concept of prevention offers a different time perspective and suggests different loci for intervention. It asks us to think about whether and how one might take action before the undesirable behavior actually appears, or alternately to learn to position assistance—resources—so that an attempt at problem resolution can occur early in the history of the manifestation of a problem. Our experience as clinicians has taught us to work at the endpoint of the history of a problem. We are generally called in after an intolerable situation has developed for an individual or a family. In the preventive perspective, we are encouraged to think systematically about the beginnings of the process that results in a person defining himself or herself, or being defined by others, as a "case."

Preventive approaches also require us to function in new organizational settings. As mental health professionals, we have become accommodated to our workplaces— the clinic, the hospital, the private practice office—and we generally pay little conscious attention to the social organization that supports our efforts. We do not recognize the invisible structure supporting us until something interferes with that structure. In preventive work, and utilizing the community perspective, we must leave familiar settings and learn to live in, work with, and adapt to environments that are at best unfamiliar or uncongenial, and at worst may be actively hostile to strangers and to change efforts, no matter how benignly intentioned. We must work with and through schools, welfare departments, recreation facilities, the mass media, the legislative and the political process, and people representing many varied interests and values. If we are to do something different, in fact, we face the problems of change and the problems related to the creation of new settings. We are working in a more complex environment and in a different time frame.

Community psychology directs attention to the larger context within which plans are developed and implemented. The possibilities for gaining resources must be carefully evaluated. The political climate supporting one type of programming at one time and another at another time must be understood. Levine and Levine (1970) noted many years ago that during more conservative periods, person-centered interventions tend to predominate, while during periods of reform, the focus of attention is less on the deficient person and more on the inadequacies of societal institutions in meeting needs. What is feasible at one time is sometimes approached only with great difficulty at another time. Competition among agencies and groups for the same pool of limited resources becomes a factor. When we adopt the community perspective, in other words, our professional concerns necessarily broaden.

Prevention activities and community orientation raise many new and difficult questions of values and ethics. The professionally trained individual who lays claim to the mantle of science and who enters the difficult field of social intervention has special problems. Sarason encourages academically based social scientists to get involved in the solution of real-world problems because he believes the disciplines within the social sciences will benefit by taking advantage of the opportunity to test theory in the public arena. Sarason (1978) has also argued there can be no "final" answers to such problems because the nature of problem solving in the social and the physical realms is different. These value questions place limits on what may be accomplished by purely rational analysis or reliance on fact or scientific method.

Those interested in influencing policy are interested in influencing more than our understanding. They are interested in influencing how we allocate resources and toward what issues we allocate resources. Deciding the allocation of resources is, of course, a function of the public political process, and policy-oriented research is designed to influence that process. A moment's consideration will bring realization that when scarce resources are allocated, winners and losers result, and we cannot expect the process of collecting scientific information to go on as if nothing were at stake but disinterested knowledge or as if the solutions were so obvious that everyone would agree on them. The use of scientific studies and data-based arguments in public policy discourse has alerted us as nothing else did to the fact that scientific effort is not value-free and that it is also influenced by its social context. Both scientists and the public have new problems when science enters into decision making in the public arena (see A. Levine, 1982). It is sometimes said that if you are not part of the solution, you are part of the problem. In this instance, research workers and professionals are both part of the problem and part of the solution by virtue of their embeddedness in the social context. In this book we take the position that we need to understand the place and role of social scientists and their work if we are to understand how problems are defined and how we choose among possible solutions.

This brief discussion is meant to underscore that everything is connected to everything else and can be broken into little pieces for analysis only at the hazard of misunderstanding the larger, complex, interconnected structure. We have no role in American society such as the one August Comte envisioned for his scientist-priest. We should recognize, however, that social science research, concepts, theories, and technologies are more and more affecting our lives. As we study these relatively early attempts at social intervention, and even as we recognize that most such attempts are comparatively feeble, we should not overlook the larger philosophical questions raised by work in this field.

In what follows we will examine some of the theories and programs in community psychology and some of the research related to them. We are as much interested in showing the interrelationships among problems and theories and in trying to develop something of a systematic framework as we are in teaching specifics of method or theory. At this point in the development of the field, the best we can hope to convey is an orientation and a way of thinking, rather than tightly tested propositions and hard knowledge. Hard knowledge does not yet exist, and perhaps it never will, but the problems the field looks at will persist, and we will continue our efforts to develop better—if imperfect—approaches. When those of us working in this field in the early 1960s began, we were innocent of the questions as well as of the answers. Now at least we are beginning to develop an intellectual framework within which diverse experiences make some sense, and we can at least ask questions that are more meaningful than the ones we were able to ask 20 years ago.

The content of the book is organized as follows. The first two chapters establish a philosophical and temporal context for community psychology. Chapter 1 examines the nature and scope of issues and problems facing the field and discusses the implications of a view that asserts that the definition of a problem involves its situational context. Chapter 2 reviews the historical background of this perspective and presents a unified model of the community psychology field and the many activities it endorses. Chapters 3 through 6 describe and assess the major conceptual foundations of community psychology, including principles of ecology, conceptions of behavior in a social context, and the increasingly useful concepts of stress and support.

The remainder of the book gives somewhat more attention to applications of community psychology principles while maintaining the focus on concepts. Chapter 7 outlines and discusses community psychology's perspective on prevention in mental health. The chapter pays particular attention to interventions involving individual competence building and interventions in important social settings such as schools. Some of the ideas derived from prevention are applied in Chapter 8 to the condition of people who need help on a more chronic, long-term basis. Self-help groups offer an important alternative to traditional clinical services in the way they conceptualize problems and the nature of their approach to overcoming a problem. The breadth of self-help is further illustrated in Chapter 9, which examines women's consciousness raising groups as they existed during the late 1960s and early 1970s.

The remaining chapters elaborate on the various issues cited. Chapter 10 considers the problem of change at the level of individual settings and organizations. Creating new settings and changing existing settings are both discussed, along with several illustrative case studies. Perspectives in community psychology also offer insights into the process of change at larger levels. For example, school desegregation, the focus in Chapter 11, was a change of nationwide proportions in which psychologists and other social scientists played a relatively important role. Chapter 12 concludes the book by examining the nature of problem definition in a community context and some of the alternative interventions that follow from different definitions. A community perspective on scientific research and the ethics of intervention completes the book. We hope the person who reads this book will learn from it, but as long as we stimulate the reader to think about these issues, our most essential objective will have been accomplished.

Note

1. Because the shift to community mental health resulted from federal policy and raised questions about how public money was being spent, administrators', politicians', legislators', and citizens' concerns led to the development of research evaluating the effectiveness of new programs and services. Such research was initially directed toward evaluating specific projects, but eventually the cumulation of data produced an evaluation of the public policy of supporting community-based treatment. Although a research base underlay the development of community mental health policy (see Mechanic, 1980; Levine, 1981), social scientists became more interested in the contributions of social science research to the development of public policy. (See Kiesler, 1980, 1982; Kiesler et al., 1983; Shadish, 1984, and any recent issue of *American Psychologist,* the major journal of the American Psychological Association, which routinely carries articles on public policy issues in many fields in addition to community mental health.) During the 1960s, social programs proliferated under President Lyndon B. Johnson's vision of a Great Society; social scientists participated in the development and evaluation of many of them. Mental health is obviously not the sole source of social scientists' interest in policy-relevant research.

References

Baker F. (1974). From community mental health to human service ideology. *American Journal of Public Health, 64,* 576–581.

Graziano, A. M., & Mooney, K. C. (1984). *Children and behavior therapy.* New York: Aldine.

Heller, K., & Monahan, J. (1977). *Psychology and community change.* Homewood, IL: Dorsey Press.

Kiesler, C. A. (1980). Mental health policy as a field of inquiry for psychology. *American Psychologist, 35,* 1066–1080.

Kiesler, C. A. (1982). Public and professional myths about mental hospitalization: An empirical reassessment of policy-related beliefs. *American Psychologist, 37,* 1323–1339.

Kiesler, C. A., McGuire, T., Mechanic, D., Mosher, L. R., Nelson, S. H., Newman, F. L., Rich, R., & Schulberg, H. C. (1983). Federal mental health policy making: An assessment of deinstitutionalization. *American Psychologist, 38,* 1292–1297.

Korchin, S. J. (1976). *Modern Clinical Psychology. Principles of intervention in the clinic and the community.* New York: Basic Books.

Levine, A. G. (1982). *Love Canal: Science, politics and people.* Lexington, MA: Lexington Books.

Levine, M. (1981). *The history and politics of community mental health.* New York: Oxford University Press.

Levine, M., & Levine, A. (1970). *A social history of helping services.* New York: Appleton-Century-Crofts.

Mann, P. A. (1978). *Community psychology. Concepts and applications.* New York: Free Press.

Mechanic, D. (1980) *Mental health and social policy* (2d ed.). Englewood Cliffs, NJ: Prentice-Hall.

Rappaport, J. (1977). *Community psychology. Values, research, action.* New York: Holt, Rinehart & Winston.

Sarason, S. B. (1974). *The psychological sense of community.* San Francisco: Jossey-Bass.

Sarason, S. B. (1978). The nature of problem solving in social action. *American Psychologist, 33,* 370–380.

Sarason, S. B. (1981). *Psychology misdirected.* New York: Free Press.

Sarason, S. B. (1982). *Psychology and social action. Selected papers.* New York: Praeger.

Shadish, W. R., Jr. (1984). Policy research: Lessons from the implementation of deinstitutionalization. *American Psychologist, 39,* 725–738.

1

Life Is a Soap Opera

A number of years ago there was a popular television program called *Queen for a Day*. Contestants competed by listing a catalog of personal miseries, tragedies, and catastrophes which they and their families had endured. The show was considered a vulgar, if not obscene, display pandering to the morbid curiosity of the general public; its popularity was embarrassing if not puzzling. *Queen for a Day* was but one manifestation of the same deep interest in the plight of individuals and families who struggle with personal, familial, medical, psychiatric, legal, and economic problems that leads millions to read Ann Landers and similar columns every day. The ever-popular soap operas, first on radio and now on television, chronicle for the American public the impact of death, disease, accident, divorce, crime, and sundry tragedies in the everyday lives of the characters.

The popularity of soap operas is not explained by lonely homemakers filling drab lives by experiencing vicariously the excitement in the lives of the beautiful, glamorous figures who populate televisionland. Soap operas do more than dispel boredom. The myths that are the staple fare of the soap opera touch on universal themes, provide an opportunity for catharsis, and teach, as all good myths do, that the tragedies of life are inevitable and, if not surmountable, then at least endurable with dignity.

One ought to entertain the hypothesis that soap operas are popular not only because they are entertaining but precisely because they are a way of understanding life. Life itself is the soap opera. The popularity of the television version simply reflects that fact. By looking at life as a soap opera, we can develop a better understanding of our cultural concern with psychological well-being, the rapid growth of demand for psychological services, the emphasis on crisis and coping in the contemporary professional literature, and the recent proliferation of self-help and social-support groups. We may well come to a different view of what is "normal," in the sense of typical or widely prevalent.

An important theme of this book is that problem definitions themselves offer insights into social phenomena. For example, does a mental or emotional problem reside entirely inside a person's skin, or does it also become tangled in the specific events and situations immediately surrounding him or her? Given this latter definition, if many individuals and families feel lonely, isolated, overwhelmed, and beset by problems, the simple statistics suggest that such feelings are readily understandable. Multitudes are struggling with critical problems in living. Struggle with life's problems is the rule, not the exception. That the struggle and sense of isolation may be exacerbated by characteristics of twentieth-century American society does not take away from the fact that most if not all Americans regularly face emotionally demanding, critical problems affecting psychological well-being.

Our understanding that struggles with critical problems are more to be considered normative than exceptional goes a long way toward explaining why public services built on the conception that serious problems in living are the exception have no chance of serving the full public need. Critical problems of living are not the exception at all; any such conception does a disservice to the people living through the events and is a definition of the problem that inevitably leads to ever-increasing frustration. To understand why alternate forms of service, alternate personnel, and prevention are necessities, we have only to turn to statistics describing the frequency of problems in living. We will present data from several different vantage points, including statistics concerning persons receiving psychiatric treatment and other prevalence estimates for mental disorders, epidemiological and survey estimates of certain maladaptive behavior patterns (e.g., alcohol abuse), and disadvantaged social conditions (e.g., widowhood, poverty), and also the implications for mental health of several contemporary social and cultural trends. The knowledgeable reader will recognize that many items in the catalog of problems reviewed here resemble those listed on measures of "stressful life events" (cf. Holmes & Rahe, 1967; life-stress constructs and scales are discussed formally in Chapter 6). To appreciate fully the impact of the figures we will cite, keep in mind that the average household in the United States in 1980 consisted of 2.75 individuals (U.S. Bureau of Census, 1981, Table 60).[1] Thus for each individual affected by a given condition, nearly two other people were affected to some degree.

Institutionalized Population

For an estimate of the crude demand for service and the number of people whose lives are influenced by critical and traumatic events, we first look at the institutionalized population. Table 1-1 shows that over 2 million people a year live in institutions, not counting halfway houses, group homes, board and care homes, and similar facilities in the community. An overall figure of approximately 2.5 million is probably a conservative estimate of the number of people who are institutionalized at any moment. In addition to these, using our multiplier of 2.75 persons per household, approximately 4,375,000 more persons are living with the fact that some household member has been institutionalized.

In 1977 there were 1,817,000 patient care episodes in mental hospitals (Table 186). In 1980 there were 1,746,000 additional patient care episodes in general hospitals (Kiesler, 1982). A patient care episode is defined as an individual who is admitted and discharged during the year. Some of these are obviously repeated admissions. Using our multiplier and including the patients, we can say that about 9.8 million persons are affected by an episode of psychiatric hospitalization during any given year. (See Chapter 2 for a further discussion of these issues in relation to community mental health practice.)

Outpatient Mental Health Care

Let us now examine estimates of the number of persons who have problems that could be treated with formal mental health services on an outpatient basis and of the total number affected by each person's problem.

Table 1-1. Institutionalized Population of the United States

Population	No. Persons in Institution	Year
Adult patients, state and county mental hospitals	122,073	1981[a]
Public facilities for the mentally retarded	131,721	1980[b]
Nursing homes for elderly	1,303,000	1977[c]
Dependent, neglected children, residential treatment centers, emotionally disturbed, and other juveniles	152,000	1976[d]
Physically handicapped	22,739	1970[e]
Correctional institutions	314,272	1980[f]
Jails	158,394	1978[g]
Total institutionalized	2,278,157[j]	
Patient care episodes in mental hospitals	1,802,000	1979[h]
Patient care episodes in general hospitals	1,746,000	1980[i]
Patient care episodes in outpatient facilities	4,602,000	1979[h]

[a]Redick & Witkin, 1984.

[b]U.S. Bureau of Census, 1981, Table 188.

[c]U.S. Bureau of Census, 1981, Table 184.

[d]Kadushin, 1980.

[e]U.S. Bureau of Census, 1981, Table 78.

[f]U.S. Bureau of Census, 1981, Table 330.

[g]U.S. Bureau of Census, 1981, Table 332.

[h]U.S. Public Health Service, 1982.

[i]Kiesler, 1982.

[j]These figures do *not* include residents of halfway houses, group homes, board and care homes, and similar institutions in the community.

One index of the demand for services is the utilization rate as provided in standard reports to government agencies. In 1977 there were 4,823,000 episodes of outpatient care in outpatient facilities (Table 186). These figures exclude all care in private-sector facilities, all psychiatric care in federal facilities other than community mental health centers, and all partial care and outpatient care in Veterans Administration hospitals. Using our multiplier of 2.75, we can state that the lives of more than 10 million persons were affected by participation in outpatient mental health care.

We obtain similar figures on utilization by looking at data gathered with a different method. A sampling survey conducted in 1980–1982 in three communities revealed that 6–7% of the adult, noninstitutionalized population visited either a general medical care provider or a mental health specialist for a mental health problem in the 6 months prior to the interview. Between 2% and 4% of the population visited a mental health specialist in the 6 months prior to the interview (Shapiro, et al., 1984). Extrapolating to the population at large, we estimate from their data that between 4.5 and 9.0 million visited a mental health specialist. Using our multiplier, between 7.8 and 15.75 million more were affected by that visit.

Another sampling survey of households reported that 9,574,660 persons had one or more visits for ambulatory mental health care in 1980. About half were seen in clinics and about half in private-practice offices. This estimate includes only those seen for a specific mental disorder. If visits for "nerves" are included, the survey estimated that the number of persons actually using services may be 50% higher. That would mean that as many as 14,361,990 persons were seen at least once by specialty mental health providers (Taube, Burns, & Kessler, 1984). These figures do not include the untold millions with psychological components to their complaints who visit general practitioners.

The Shapiro et al. study (1984) used a survey instrument that sorted respondents into selected DSM-III diagnoses (Myers et al., 1984). They also asked their respondents whether they had visited a doctor or a mental health service in the previous 6 months and the reasons for the visit. Utilization figures from a door-to-door survey in three communities showed that approximately 67% of those with recent classifiable disorders (i.e., they had symptoms within the previous 6 months) made one or more visits to either a physician or a mental health provider in the previous 6 months. Only 18% made the visit for mental health reasons. That means 80% or more of persons with classifiable disorders did not consider the visit to a service provider a visit for a mental health reason. Approximately 10% of those with a recent DSM-III diagnosable disorder went to see a mental health specialist for mental health reasons. If we take that figure (approximately 10% of those with disorders), the actual prevalence of outpatient mental health care for those with disorders based on utilization is about 3 million persons in any 6-month period.

Only part of the total utilization is accounted for by DSM-III diagnosable conditions. Approximately 4% of the population *without* DSM-III diagnosable conditions also made one or more visits for mental health reasons in the previous 6 months. That figure means that another 5.2 million persons sought outpatient care for mental health reasons in the previous 6 months. The total using services is about 8.2 million (Shapiro et al., 1984). Using the 8.2 million estimate of utilization and using our multiplier, the number affected by an episode of mental health care is 22,550,000. Using the Taube et al. (1984) 14.4 million estimate of utilization and our 2.75 multiplier, the affected population is 39,495,000. Given that Shapiro et al. (1984) are reporting utilization in the previous 6 months, and Taube et al. (1984) for the previous year, the figures are reasonably close to each other. Another door-to-door survey taken in 1976 revealed that 26% of the adult noninstitutionalized population had sought professional help for a problem at some time in their lives (Veroff, Kulka, & Douvan, 1981).

The number utilizing services is far under the number identified in the survey as having a DSM-III diagnosable disorder. The prevalence rate for adults living in the community with any of the DSM-III diagnoses that were tabulated is about 16.8% (Myers et al., 1984). That means about 26,880,000 adults have a diagnosable disorder. Using our multiplier for household size, we arrive at a figure of 47,040,000 additional persons affected by the person with a diagnosable condition. The survey instrument excluded such conditions as generalized anxiety disorders and posttraumatic stress disorders. The prevalence rate is systematically underestimated.

The 6-month prevalence rate, as determined in three communities, ranged from 14.8% to 22.5%. Extrapolating to the population aged 18 and over, and using the 14.8% figure, we arrive at a potential number of 23,680,000 persons with problems. Using the 22.5% figure, the number becomes 36,000,000 persons. Keep in mind that the estimates are only for selected DSM-III diagnoses, excluding transient conditions, generalized anxiety states, and posttraumatic disorders and excluding the institution-alized population. Using our multiplier, we estimate that 99 million persons are affected by having or by living with someone with symptoms severe enough to warrant a DSM-III diagnosis. Even if we use the 2-week prevalence rate (an episode within the previous 2 weeks), the study provides a prevalence estimate of about 12%. That rate translates into approximately 19.2 million persons (Myers et al., 1984). Using our multiplier, we arrive at a total of 52.8 million affected persons in any 2-week period. The surveyors interviewed adults over age 18 and provided no estimates for children and adolescents.

Looked at in this way, these data indicate that as much as half the population is affected by mental health problems. Is that large a percent of the population sick? We don't think so. We believe that the definition of subjective distress as a mental health problem, or as a "diagnosable disorder," reflects the influence on the field of the medical model (see later). We also believe that such a definition limits our vision because it directs us to think in terms of treating disorders, instead of understanding what in fact are ubiquitous problems in living. Later in this chapter, we will provide some figures showing the prevalence of problems in living. In anticipation, we ask the reader to consider how the possibilities for intervention change when we conceive of the issues in a different way.

Substance Abuse

A 1983 monograph from the U.S. Congress Office of Technology Assessment esti-mates that 10–15 million U.S. adults have serious problems related to alcohol and that 35 million Americans are indirectly affected by alcohol problems (Office of Tech-nology Assessment, 1983a). Even if we cut the estimate of alcohol abusers by one-third, we would still face the fact that between 9 and 14 million Americans and their families are struggling with relatively severe problems related to alcohol. A recent sur-vey of 27,000 randomly sampled high school students in New York (Barnes, 1984) indicates that 10% of such students abuse alcohol at least once per week, 26% abuse alcohol six or more times per year, and 11% report being "hooked" (dependent) on beer, wine, or liquor.

Defined more narrowly, in 1980 there were 1,289,000 arrests on charges of driving while intoxicated and 1,048,000 arrests for drunkenness (Table 312). In 1980 some 181,500 persons were under treatment for drug abuse in the country (Table 201), and there were 532,000 arrests for violation of narcotic drug laws (Table 312). Again, we do not know the overlap and have no idea of how many repeaters are among those arrested. If we consider only those arrested and their families, we can say that the lives of about 7.5 million persons are affected by substance abuse leading to some contact with the law. Table 1-2 shows that a substantial percent of youth and young adults are current users of marijuana, cocaine, or hallucinogens. Not all have drug-related diffi-culties, but each one is potentially a problem user.

Crime and Victims of Crime

In 1980 some 13,295,000 offenses were known to the police; of these 1,309,000 were for murder, forcible rape, robbery, or aggravated assault (Table 1-3). Victimization estimates based on house-to-house surveys show that 35 per 1,000 of population over

Table 1-2. Substance Abuse

Condition	Number	Year
Alcohol abuse and dependence	10–15,000,000	1983[a]
Arrests, driving while intoxicated	1,300,000	1980[b]
Arrests, drunkenness	989,000	1980[b]
Arrests, violation of narcotics laws	533,000	1980[b]
Percent current users of marijuana		
Youth, 12–17	16.7	1979[c]
Young adults, 18–25	35.4	
Adults, 26+	6.0	
Percent current users of cocaine		
Youth, 12–17	1.4	
Young adults, 18–25	3.1	
Adults, 26+	.9	
Percent current users of hallucinogens		
Youth, 12–17	2.2	
Young adults, 18–25	2.5	
Adults, 26+	<.5	
Clients, drug abuse treatment units	181,500	1980[d]

[a]Office of Technology Assessment, 1983a.

[b]U.S. Bureau of Census, 1981, Table 311.

[c]U.S. Bureau of Census, 1981, Table 199.

[d]U.S. Bureau of Census, 1981, Table 201.

age 12 reported being the victim of a crime against one's person. Translated into total population figures, in 1979, about 6.5 million individuals experienced at least one episode as a victim of *violent* crime (Table 298). These figures indicate that some 18 million Americans coped with an episode of violent crime in which some household member was a victim. The U.S. Department of Justice (1985) estimated there were 154,000 rapes or attempted rapes in 1983. There are approximately 2.2 attempted rapes for each completed rape. Almost half of the total of 338,800 attempted rapes were never reported to the police, and 40% of the completed rapes were not reported either. Twenty-nine percent of victims of attempted rape were physically injured, as were 58% of victims of completed rapes. Eleven percent of all rape victims were between the ages of 12 and 15, and another 25% were between 16 and 19.

Table 1-3. Crimes and Victims of Crimes

Problem	No. Persons	Year
Offenses known to police	13,295,000	1980[a]
Arrests, all causes	9,700,000	1980[b]
Arrests, sex offenses	51,000	1980[a]
Arrests, crimes against family	50,000	1980[a]
Victimization, over age 12		
Violent crime	6,441,500	1979[c]
Nonviolent crime	15,459,600	1979[c]

[a]U.S. Bureau of Census, 1981, Table 311.

[b]U.S. Bureau of Census, 1981, Table 252.

[c]U.S. Bureau of Census, 1981, Table 298.

In addition, over 16 million individuals reported being the victim of a *nonviolent* crime in 1979. Probably 20% of the population, or well over 40 million persons, were affected by some household member or themselves becoming a victim of a crime. In 1977 some 45% of the population said they feared walking around in neighborhoods within a mile of their homes (U.S. Bureau of Census, 1980, Table 5/1). The experience of criminal victimization can have important psychological consequences ranging from discomfort for a short period to a long-term posttraumatic stress disorder that may be disabling (APA Task Force on the Victims of Crime and Violence, 1984; Riger, 1985). Based on a telephone survey of women 18 years of age and older, Kilpatrick et al. (1985) report that 21% said they had been a victim of a completed or an attempted rape, of sexual molestation, or robbery, or of aggravated assault. Victims experienced nervous breakdowns, thought of suicide, and made suicide attempts at a far higher rate than nonvictims. Those who were victims of a crime reported most often that their symptoms appeared after the episode of victimization, not beforehand.

A large number of persons are arrested for crimes and experience stress for that reason. (Serving a term in jail is in fact the fourth most stressful event on the Holmes and Rahe scale.) In 1980 some 9.7 million persons were arrested for some crime (Table 311). In addition, 63,000 individuals were arrested for sex offenses not listed elsewhere, and 50,000 more for crimes against family or children (Table 311). Including household members, 26,675,000 persons are affected annually by an arrest for a crime. Assuming victims and perpetrators are nonoverlapping populations (not a wholly safe assumption), perhaps a third of the population is directly affected by crime each year.

Problems of Children and Adolescents

The problems of children and adolescents should be considered separately; they are not included in most of the figures cited previously. The prevalence of diagnosable problems in children and youth has been found in different surveys to be between 5 and 23% of the population (Namir & Weinstein, 1982). In addition, of the nearly 10 million people arrested and charged with crimes, 20.9% were under age 18 (Table 311). Juvenile courts handled 1,374,000 cases in 1979 (Table 327).

Children's problems emerge in educational settings and involve intellectual competence as well as issues of adjustment to classrooms (see Table 1-4). Schools reported that 2,807,000 children were enrolled in public special-education facilities in 1978 (Table 228). This figure probably underestimates the number who may have special educational needs but who are mainstreamed pursuant to Public Law 94-142. Seventeen percent of all children are rated by their teachers as poorly adjusted (National Health Survey, 1972). Other studies report comparable maladjustment rates (e.g., Glidewell & Swallow, 1968; Joy, 1973). Based on the number of children under age 14, we estimate that 5.9 million children are considered maladjusted by their teachers. In 1980 approximately 80,629,000 individuals were under age 21. By definition, some 3% of all children, or 2,429,000, are considered mentally retarded, and most of those are in need of special services. Problems of delinquency and education are intimately intertwined. Surveys provide estimates indicating that perhaps 30% of all juvenile delinquents are learning disabled.

Table 1-4. Problems of Children and Adolescents

Problem	No. Persons	Year
Arrested under age 18	2,027,000	1980[a]
Juvenile court cases	1,374,000	1979[b]
Enrolled in public or private special-education facility	2,807,000	1978[c]
Maladjusted in school, under 14	5,900,000	1980[d]
Mentally retarded, under 21	2,429,000	1980[d]

[a]U.S. Bureau of Census, 1981, Table 311.

[b]U.S. Bureau of Census, 1981, Table 327.

[c]U.S. Bureau of Census, 1981, Table 228.

[d]See text.

If examined from the perspective of formally recognized children's disabilities, and from the perspective of having had a formal encounter with the law, as many as 15 million individuals and their families may be coping with whatever special class placement or juvenile court contact entails. If we consider just the children who are considered maladjusted and those considered mentally retarded, and we use our multiplier, we estimate that over 22.8 million persons are involved in a school-related problem.

The problem of the sexual abuse of children has recently come to public attention. Surveys produce estimates that over 300,000 children may be sexually abused each year. Younger children are likely to be repetitively abused, and by someone the child knows; substantially less than a majority of the sexual assaults on children are perpetrated by strangers (Pettis & Hughes, 1985). The victimized child may be interviewed repeatedly about the offense and may be required to testify subject to cross-examination. We know little about the emotional sequelae of these events (Goodman, 1984). Browne and Finkelhor (1985) interpret the available research to indicate that a high proportion of victims suffer short-term emotional upset, and a smaller number, perhaps 20%, suffer long-term damage.

Medical Problems and Chronic Illness

We now turn to the myriad of other problems of living with which people cope on an everyday basis (Table 1-5). Personal injury or illness was the sixth most stressful life event on the Holmes and Rahe list. How common is this event? In 1981 there were about 38 million hospital admissions. Over 100 million individuals and their families were affected by an illness requiring hospitalization. In 1979, based on a house-to-house survey, 69.1 million individuals reported an injury sufficiently severe to lead the individual to cut down on usual activities for at least one entire day, including missing work or school and/or seeking medical attention for the injury (Table 190).

Examining the major killers and cripplers, we see that: 20.2 million persons require medical care for arthritis; 9.6 million are visually impaired, 1,306,000 so impaired that they cannot read; more than 1 million persons were under treatment for cancer in 1975 (with improved treatment, many more now survive for 5 years, but survivors, especially children, are faced with lifelong problems of adaptation); 750,000 are afflicted with cerebral palsy; 2 million lack sufficient hearing to understand speech;

Table 1-5. Medical Problems and Chronic Illness

Condition	No. Persons	Year
Hospital admissions		
General medical	38,417,000	1981[a]
Injuries leading to one or more days of lost work or school	69,100,000	1974[b]
Arthritis	20,200,000	1975[c]
Visual impairment, cannot read	1,306,000	
Cancer, under treatment	1,000,000	
Cerebral palsy	750,000	
Hearing impairment, cannot understand speech	2,000,000	
Epilepsy	3,000,000	
Birth defects, varying severity	15,000,000	
High blood pressure	23,000,000	
Multiple sclerosis	500,000	
Muscular dystrophy	200,000	
Cardiac conditions	10,300,000	
First heart attack	800,000	
First stroke	400,000	
Asthma	6,000,000	
Diabetes	4,200,000	
Limitation in major activity due to chronic illness	24,700,000	1979[d]
Venereal disease		
Gonorrhea, reported cases	1,004,000	1979[e]
Syphilis, reported cases	67,000	1979[e]
Genital herpes, new cases per year	500,000–1,000,000	1979[f]

[a]U.S. Public Health Service, 1983, Table 41.

[b]U.S. Bureau of Census, 1981, Table 190.

[c]See text for sources.

[d]U.S. Bureau of Census, 1981, Table 194.

[e]U.S. Bureau of Census, 1981, Table 192.

[f]Department of Health, Education and Welfare, 1979, p. 31.

between 2 and 4 million have epilepsy; about 15 million have birth defects of varying severity; 23 million have high blood pressure; over 500,000 have multiple sclerosis; and about 200,000 have muscular dystrophy (National Health Education Committee, 1976). Six million had asthma in 1970; 10.3 million had heart conditions in 1972; 4.2 million had diabetes in 1973 (Health, 1976). In 1973 some 800,000 individuals suffered their first heart attacks and 400,000 their first stroke (Health, 1976).

A house-to-house survey taken in 1979 estimated that 31.5 million persons have some limitations as a result of heart conditions, arthritis and rheumatism, visual impairments, hypertension without cardiac involvement, and mental or nervous conditions. Fourteen percent of the population has some limitation due to one or another of these particular chronic conditions, and 10.9% of the noninstitutional population, or 24.7 million persons, suffer a limitation in a major activity due to the chronic disorder (Table 194). That estimate should probably be increased by some factor to account for those who have other limitations consequent to injuries, amputations, and other sources of chronic problems not specified in the selected group of disorders in the table. We may safely say that 75 million persons are coping with their own chronic physical limitations or with a member of the household who is limited in some significant degree by a chronic problem.

Venereal disease may no longer be the social disgrace it once was, but it remains embarrassing at least and seriously disabling at worst. In 1979 one million cases of gonorrhea and 67,000 new cases of syphilis were reported (Table 192). It was estimated that another 450,000 individuals were in need of treatment for syphilis (Health, 1976). Genital herpes is so prevalent that some say the sexual revolution has been slowed because of fear of contracting this painful and troublesome sexually transmitted disorder. There are estimates of between 500,000 and 1 million new cases annually, with several million recurrences each year. Because of complications following from sexually transmitted diseases, many women suffer pelvic inflammatory disease (the condition is also caused by using some birth control devices). Sterility due to pelvic inflammatory disease affects over 50,000 women annually creating emotional distress in those who may wish to conceive but cannot (DHEW, 1979). The sexually transmitted disease AIDS (Acquired Immune Deficiency Syndrome) is afflicting an increasing number. Because it leads to death within a few years and is untreatable at present, AIDS is frightening. The condition has ramifying consequences. Children who have been exposed to the AIDS virus present a problem for school districts. Despite the evidence that AIDS is only readily transmitted sexually (or by exchange of body fluids, such as by a hypodermic needle), parents in some communities have protested the presence in school of children with AIDS or children who have been exposed to the AIDS virus. These issues are currently working their way through the courts. These disorders are correlated with psychological distress and present problems of adaptation to the millions who are afflicted. Moreover, in the absence of medical means of preventing the disorders, prevention depends on behavioral change and life-style change. Although the manifestations are primarily medical in nature, the problems of prevention and adaptation are social and psychological.

Disasters

Natural disasters do not take many lives, comparatively speaking, but many individuals are affected (see Table 1-6). In 1979, tornadoes, hurricanes, cyclones, and floods accounted for only 195 lives, but 73 tornadoes each left property losses in excess of $500,000, while floods resulted in property losses of over $4 billion (Table 368). The American Red Cross provided emergency care for 689,000 individuals in disasters in 1980 (Table 590). In 1980 there were 758,000 residential fires, which resulted in property losses totaling $3.042 billion (Table 895). Fires killed 6,163 persons in 1978. Catastrophic fires in which five or more persons are killed account for an average of 270 lives each year. Nineteen percent of these mass deaths take place in hotels, boarding houses, rooming houses, and facilities for the aged (Table 120). Hundreds of thousands of people each year are affected by a natural disaster resulting at least in inconvenience and some degree of fear, but potentially resulting in death or severe injury, the necessity to change living arrangements or to start one's life anew, and in some cases enduring psychological distress (Gleser, Green, & Winget, 1978; Green, Grace, Crespo da Silva, & Gleser, 1983; Zusman & Simon, 1983).

Technological advances have created the possibility of new technological disasters. The Three Mile Island nuclear plant accident made real the danger of an accidental

Table 1-6. Disasters

Condition	No. Episodes	Year
American Red Cross disaster services, persons served	689,000	1980[a]
Residential fires	758,000	1980[b]
Tornadoes, floods, hurricanes with five or more deaths	91	1971–1979[c]
Toxic-waste dump sites	80,000+	1983[d]

[a]U.S. Bureau of Census, 1981, Table 590.

[b]U.S. Bureau of Census, 1981, Table 895.

[c]U.S. Bureau of Census, 1981, Table 120.

[d]Office of Technology Assessment, 1983b.

nuclear disaster (Perrow, 1984) as did the accident at Chernobyl. The former incident, with a temporary evacuation of the area, led to acute anxiety; the long-term effects are debatable. A large number of nuclear plants are on-line in the nation. Fear of the possibility of a nuclear accident, whether exaggerated or not, crosses the minds of many children and adults (Schwebel & Schwebel, 1981).

The Love Canal episode (A. Levine, 1982; see also Chapter 12), in which a leaking, abandoned toxic-waste dump site threatened the safety of a residential area brought that hazard to public attention. More than 80,000 hazardous waste sites have been identified in the United States. Ninety percent pose a threat of contamination to the water supply of nearby communities. Although a clear relationship to adverse health effects remains to be fully documented, untold thousands live with a threat to health and safety (Office of Technology Assessment, 1983b; Epstein, Brown, & Pope, 1982). Many communities are now organizing to get rid of toxic-waste dump sites, to close them down, or to prevent the opening of new ones.

These new disasters are different from floods or hurricanes. Their impact is as much psychological as it is physical. We do not minimize the real danger to health and safety posed by these technologically related disasters, but they can have an impact on our minds and on our emotions well before we see a detectable impact on our health. A community's problems are every bit as real in the technological as in the natural disaster.

Marriage and Parenting

Marriage (the seventh most stressful of Holmes and Rahe's 43 events) and parenthood (the fourteenth most stressful event) both affect large numbers of people (see Table 1-7). Both events also represent major life transitions posing myriad problems of adjustment. Most people in U.S. society eventually marry at least once; by age 35, some 95% of women and men have married (Table 52). The likelihood of marriage for those who have not married by age 40 is much lower, posing a different problem of adaptation for those who have not married and thus have not attained the most commonly expected status in American life. In 1983 there were 2,444,000 marriages involving 4,888,000 individuals (National Center for Health Statistics, 1984).

Many people who marry (and many who don't) have children, another important life transition. In 1983 there were 3,614,000 live births (National Center for Health Statistics, 1984). Of the 1979 births, 17% or 593,980 occurred out of wedlock, and

Table 1-7. Marriage and Parenthood

Condition	Number	Year
Marriages	2,444,000	1983[a]
Divorces	1,180,000	1983[a]
Live births	3,614,000	1983[a]
Out of wedlock	593,980	1979[b]
To mothers under 19	262,700	1979[c]
Fetal deaths	32,330	1978[d]
Deaths of infants under 1 year	31,663	1978[d]
Births with diagnosis of retardation	126,000	1975[c]
Births with diagnosis of cerebral palsy	15,000	
Births with some genetic defect	158,000	
Legal abortions	1,297,000	1980[f]
To unmarried women	972,750	1980[f]
Unwanted children		
Percent of all births	12.0	1976[g]
Adoptions	169,000	1971[h]
Foster care, total in care	395,000	1980[i]
Children involved in a divorce, each year	1,118,000	1979[j]

[a]National Center for Health Statistics, 1984.

[b]U.S. Bureau of Census, 1981, Table 85.

[c]U.S. Bureau of Census, 1981, Table 98.

[d]U.S. Bureau of Census, 1981, Table 111.

[e]Health, U.S., 1976.

[f]U.S. Bureau of Census, 1981, Table 101.

[g]U.S. Bureau of Census, 1981, Table 99.

[h]U.S. Bureau of Census, 1976, Table 506.

[i]Kadushin, 1980.

[j]U.S. Bureau of Census, 1981, Table 124.

262,700 were to unmarried mothers under 19 (Tables 85 and 98). Whatever value position one adopts, clearly a young mother who has a child out of wedlock will be coping with considerable stress. Postpartum reactions are not uncommon whether or not the mother is married. Some new mothers require psychological intervention or support to deal with the stresses and adaptations that arise in the immediate postpartum period.

Not all pregnancies are desired. A 1976 household survey (Table 99) reported that 12% of all children born to women between the ages of 15 and 44, in and out of wedlock, were unwanted. In 1980 there were 1,297,000 legal abortions; 75% involved unmarried women (Table 101). Any legal change, whether a decision of the U.S. Supreme Court or legislation making it still more difficult to fund or to obtain abortions, promises to complicate this situation in the future (*Spokeswoman*, 1977). A study of the effects of a change in Massachusetts law affecting the ability of minors to obtain abortions showed that the number of minors' abortions in the state decreased, but the number of out-of-state abortions increased (Cartoof & Klerman, 1986).

Not all pregnancies are healthy or happy events. In 1978 there were 32,330 fetal deaths (stillbirths under 5 months). We have no idea of the number of miscarriages not counted in the fetal death figure. As many as 16% of pregnancies result in miscarriages that the mother can report (Warburton & Fraser, 1964). Having a child is no guarantee the child will live and grow up. In 1978 there were 31,663 deaths of infants under 1 year, most of which occurred within 28 days of birth (Table 111).

Having a live child does not mean one will have a healthy infant. About 5% of all infants born alive have some genetic defect. Approximately 126,000 children born every year are diagnosed as retarded. About 15,000 infants, or roughly 1 per 200 live births, are born with cerebral palsy. Although the annual incidence is not high, about 200,000 persons are afflicted with muscular dystrophy. Two-thirds of these are children between the ages of 3 and 13. For some sizable number of families, the birth of a live child may signal the beginning of an enduring struggle with a chronic disorder, requiring an emotional adaptation on the part of the family and long-term planning for coping with the special problems that will inevitably arise (Health, U.S., 1976).

In addition to childbirth, there were 175,000 adoptions in 1970, although the numbers of adoptions have been declining over the years (Kadushin, 1980). Adoptions solve the problem of childlessness for some couples—and increasingly for single parents who desire a child—and of parentlessness for the children who are adopted. Adoption, however, brings its own problems of adaptation. Of children referred for psychiatric treatment, anywhere from 1.5 to 13.3% (with an average of 4.8%) are adopted (Kadushin, 1980). Herskovitz, Spivack, and Levine (1959) report that 12.5% of all nonbrain-damaged children in residence at a private residential treatment center were adopted, while fully 25% who had a history of acting out or delinquency were adopted. Private schools serving the same socioeconomic class report rates of adoption of under 1%. Kadushin (1980) also indicates that the adopted children in the population total about 1%. Of course, the vast bulk of adoptions work out well.

Kadushin (1980) estimates that some 395,000 children are in foster care. A smaller but growing number are in group homes. Most of them were removed from their homes by the courts because of neglect or abuse by their parents or the incapacity of a parent. In other words, about 500,000 children a year are in, or enter, new families, many after having endured some kind of stress or trauma in their natural families. Forming a relationship with such children provides new and special problems for the adopting parents or the foster parents.

Divorce and separation are the second and third, respectively, most stressful events on the Holmes and Rahe scale. In 1979 there were 1,181,000 divorces, with an average of one child per divorce. Divorce is a stressful life event correlated with many physical and psychological difficulties (Bloom, Asher, & White, 1978). Divorce is also a stressful life event for the 1.2 million children who are involved in divorces each year, although it is not clear whether there are long-term consequences for the psychological development of children of divorce (Luepnitz, 1978). About 10% of divorces involve custody fights that may continue for years and may involve repeated encounters with the legal system (Clingempeel & Reppucci, 1982). Children's adjustment is poorer when former spouses are in conflict (Emery, 1982; Luepnitz, 1982).

Available statistics do not reveal the number of children per year who enter into a stepparent relationship. About half of all widowed and divorced women remarry within 5 years (Blane, 1976). About half a million women of childbearing years remarry each year (Table 124). Thus a large number of persons face the problem of becoming a parent to someone else's partially grown child, a problem that can be difficult for at least some of those involved in the relationship.

In sum, entering the parenting role is a frequent event in the United States. In a large number of instances, the role is entered in ways that deviate from the idealized norm of a happily married couple eagerly expecting a healthy child. This recital of dreary statistics is not meant to discourage parenthood; if one emphasizes the positive side of the parenting role, the overall prospects favor having a child. The point here is simply to emphasize that problems in living associated with marriage and parenthood occur with great frequency in our society, affecting many millions of people each year.

Economic Issues and Employment

Several events involving financial problems are in the top half of Holmes and Rahe's list. In general, a great many people regularly struggle with inadequate incomes (Table 1-8). The Social Security Administration developed a poverty index (based in large part on the amount of income necessary to provide a nutritionally adequate economical food plan adjusted by family size and farm versus nonfarm place of residence) for individuals or for families. The index is adjusted annually based on changes in the cost of living. In 1980 some 27.4 million persons had incomes below the poverty line, and an additional 37.5 million had incomes below 125% of the poverty line (U.S. Bureau of Census, 1980, Table 304). The probability of a black family falling below the poverty line is three times that of a white family (U.S. Bureau of Census, 1980, Table 304).

The situation is still more difficult for families headed by women. In 1980 about 25,137,000 persons were in families headed by women. Among white families with female heads, 24.7% or 3,812,410 persons had incomes below the poverty line. Among blacks, 49.8% or 4,069,000 persons were in female-headed families with incomes below the poverty line (U.S. Bureau of Census, 1980, Table 304). Many women who are in poverty are divorced. Harrington (1984) points out that in present-day America women and children make up the poorest group. Poverty has been both feminized and "childrenized."

Large numbers of people are on welfare or other forms of public support. In 1980, aid to families with dependent children went to 11,102,800 recipients. Of those who received the aid, 7,600,800 were children. The mean monthly payment per individual was $100 (Table 559).

In 1980 an additional 4,142,000 persons were receiving Supplemental Security Income (SSI) payments because they were aged, indigent, blind, or otherwise disabled. Of this number 2,256,000 were disabled. Many were former mental patients or retarded. Disabled persons received an average monthly payment of $198 (Table 559).

Poor people live in less desirable residences than do wealthier people. Zahner et al. (1985) report a correlation between the presence of vermin in the home, particularly rats, and measures of psychological well-being in minority women. Those who reported a decrease in rat infestation at a repeat survey a year later reported a significant decrease in psychophysiological symptoms associated with anxiety—dizziness, palms sweating, headaches, and similar reactions. Conditions associated with poverty were associated with psychological symptoms of a kind that are measured in epidemiological surveys. Had the research team just measured anxiety, they would have reported high levels, but in all likelihood the anxiety would have been interpreted as a disorder instead of a response to unhealthy living conditions.

In 1981 about 7.9 million persons were unemployed (Table 569). Unemployment

Table 1-8. Economics and Employment

Condition	Number	Year
Income below poverty line	27,400,000	1980[a]
Income between poverty line and 125% of poverty line	37,500,000	1980[a]
Number of persons in female-headed families below poverty line	8,981,410	1980[a]
Aid for Dependent Children recipients	11,102,800	1980[b]
Supplemental Security Income for disability	4,142,000	1980[b]
Unemployed	7,900,000	1981[c]
Involved in strike	1,727,000	1979[d]
Business failures	11,742	1980[e]
In arrears on installment debt	7,500,000 (est.)	1980[f]
Bankruptcy petitions filed	361,000	1980[g]
Bankruptcy cases pending	421,000	1980[g]

[a]U.S. Bureau of Census, 1980, Table 304.

[b]U.S. Bureau of Census, 1981, Table 559.

[c]U.S. Bureau of Census, 1981, Table 569.

[d]U.S. Bureau of Census, 1981, Table 695.

[e]U.S. Bureau of Census, 1981, Table 908.

[f]U.S. Bureau of Census, 1981, Table 865.

[g]U.S. Bureau of Census, 1981, Table 911.

insurance cushions the economic shock for many, but for others unemployment triggers depressive reactions or feelings of worthlessness and requires some adaptation to unaccustomed free time. Some seek new positions, putting themselves under the stress of evaluation of their qualifications and competence by others, while others relocate to obtain work. Plant closings affecting entire communities present new problems of adaptation not only to those who lose jobs, but also to those whose communities are affected because of new social problems or because people move away (Buss, Redburn, & Waldron, 1983). Besides unemployment, others lose time at work because of strikes or other work stoppages. In 1979 some 1,727,000 workers were involved in a work stoppage or strike, for a median period of 54 days per worker (U.S. Bureau of Census, 1979, Table 695). In some instances, as in recent teacher strikes, a residue of bitterness and difficult interpersonal relationships can persist for months, if not years. The striking workers, even if covered by unemployment insurance or union benefits, lose money during the strike period.

Over and beyond unemployment and strikes, 11,742 businesses failed in 1980 (Table 908). Most were small businesses, but each one represented the dashed hopes of individuals and their families, affected their livelihoods, and forced some rethinking of a major life activity.

As might be expected from the numbers of people with low incomes and our credit economy, a high number have debts they cannot easily repay. In 1980 about 361,000 bankruptcy petitions were filed in the federal courts, and an additional 421,000 cases were pending (Table 911). In 1981 American consumers were in debt for the amount of $389 billion. Of this amount, $315 billion was in installment credit; of the installment debt, 2.37% was delinquent 30 days or more (Table 865). In other words, bills amounting to about $7,465,500,000 were chasing delinquent borrowers. If we assume the average debt is $1,000, about 7.5 million persons are coping with bill collectors who are after them because they haven't paid the installment on a loan. Using our multiplier for household size, we estimate that 20.6 million people are affected by a delinquent debt.

Taking on mortgage debt is another item on the Holmes and Rahe scale. In 1979 some 26,400,000 owner-occupied dwellings were mortgaged (Table 1396). The median mortgage loan was in excess of $42,000 (Tables 1399, 1400). In 1980 the average monthly mortgage payment was $599, which constituted 32.4% of income (Table 1395). Because of high prices for homes and the high mortgage interest rates then in effect, many homeowners may be "house poor."

For many reasons, including the necessity to make ends meet, women are entering the labor market in larger numbers. In 1980 women constituted 42.4% of the labor force. Of these, 56% were married and living with their spouses (Tables 638; 640). Married women with children are entering the labor force at an ever-increasing rate, and on the average their incomes represent nearly 30% of family income (Cymrot & Mallan, 1974). Working mothers with husbands present number 13.5 million (Table 653). In addition to those who work because they are the sole source of support for themselves and their families, a large number of married women work out of economic need. Many others work to provide their families with a better standard of living or to provide college educations for their children. An additional 3.1 million divorced and separated women with children under 17 work (Table 653).

Contemporary research in marital happiness and stability links marital dissatisfaction with low socioeconomic status and low income (Hicks & Platt, 1971). We may assume that financial problems are associated with unstable marriages. If financial stability is helpful for marital stability, working wives help to ease financial stresses. Income rises regularly with the number of earners in a family. Two-earner families have more than two times the income of one-earner families (Table 727). Married women contribute a large share of family income these days, though, leading to changing relationships within the family and to new problems of accommodation to differing views of what constitutes appropriate sex role behavior. A certain amount of marital conflict has always been related to financial issues. The attempts by many families to solve financial problems by having women work have led to new problems and conflicts around sharing household tasks and around authority and responsibility within the family (A. Levine, 1977a).

The Changing Nature of Work and of Work-Related Values

The nature of work in American society is changing. That change is bringing new problems and new opportunities. The nineteenth and early twentieth centuries saw a change from an agricultural to an industrial economy. Change in life-style related to the shift of population from rural to urban centers brought its own problems. Levine and Levine (1970) showed how many of the contemporary social and clinical services for children were created around the turn of the century to help solve problems related to those social changes. Since the end of World War II, the United States has been changing from an industrial to a service economy. In 1929 about 20% of the work force was employed in agriculture and 40% in industry (see Table 1-9). About 40% of the labor force was employed in service industries. By 1965 only 5.7% of the work force was in agriculture, 40% was in industry, and nearly 55% was in the service industries (Fuchs, 1968). By 1980 agriculture accounted for 3.2% of the work force, industry

Table 1-9. Changing Work Force and Changing Values

Work force	1929 (%)[a]	1975 (%)[b]
Agriculture	20.0	3.2
Industry	40.0	35.9
Services	40.0	60.9

Dissatisfaction with current employment (1980[c])	Number
Men	8,404,128
Women	7,011,122

Personal expenditures on recreation	
1950[d]	$11,147,000,000
1980[e]	$106,414,000,000

[a]Fuchs (1968).

[b]U.S. Bureau of Census, 1981, Table 658.

[c]U.S. Bureau of Census, 1981, Table 649.

[d]U.S. Bureau of Census, 1976, Table 359.

[e]U.S. Bureau of Census, 1981, Table 396.

35.9%, and service industries 60.9% (Table 658). Moreover, Fuchs (1968) points out that within the industrial classification, service jobs have also been increasing. There has been relatively high growth in professional and managerial occupations relative to line workers: "In the future, the large corporation is likely to be overshadowed by the hospitals, the universities, research institutes, government agencies, and professional organizations that are the hallmarks of a professional service economy" (Fuchs, 1968, p. 10).

These changes in the distribution of employment can have profound effects socially and culturally. As Fuchs (1968) put it: "Changes in the industrial distribution of employment have implications for where and how men live, the education they need, and even the health hazards they face. Indeed it has been written that when man changes his tools and his techniques, his ways of producing and distributing the goods of life, he also changes his gods" (p. 184).

In the service industries, work tasks change from person-to-thing relationships, as in industrial production, to person-to-person relationships, as in the delivery of services. The work is more personalized and requires greater interpersonal skills. Work in a service setting might therefore reduce alienation. Thus people have possibilities for greater personal satisfaction, but new problems also emerge. For one, many of the women entering the labor market enter the service industries. They account for 50% of the work force in services, in contrast to 20% of the work force in industry (Fuchs, 1968). The presence of large numbers of women working has led to renewed concern about sexual attitudes and to renewed attention to sex role problems and relationships on the job (A. Levine, 1977a). We now see problems of sexual harrassment emerging in the workplace. The nature of work in service industries—relating to other people— emphasizes interpersonal skills and makes different demands on the ability to express and control emotions. More opportunity for the stimulation of libidinal and aggressive motives is present in the daily working situation because of increased interaction between people on the job and increased daily contact between men and women in the work setting.

The changing nature of work, including an increasing emphasis on leisure time away from work (a factor discussed later), has important implications for the organization of psychological defenses in relation to aggressive and sexual drives (Levine & Levine, 1971). New kinds of challenges at work may well reduce the repression of libidinal and aggressive expression and the strictures of conscience against such expression. In other words, the controls of guilt may lessen, and norms for appropriate behavior may also change. Changes in our economy produce new challenges to our psychic economies.

Our impression is that one rarely encounters a work setting devoid of interpersonal conflicts, animosities, and feuds. Some conflicts concern organizational problems and the difficulty of defining productivity in service settings, which results in greater emphasis at work on ideology and relationships (Hasenfeld & English, 1974). Other problems stem from a contemporary state of "normlessness" about work behavior and the failure of our institutions of socialization to prepare us adequately for interpersonal work tasks. The sensitivity training movement had its early important impact on managers who were dealing with interpersonal relationships on the job.

At any rate, many people in all occupations, including the professions (Sarason, 1977), are dissatisfied with their jobs. In 1980 a national opinion research survey revealed that 15% of the male work force and 17% of the female work force were less than "somewhat satisfied" with their jobs (i.e., some 8,404,128 men and 7,011,122 women expressed dissatisfaction with their current employment) (Table 649). Although the reasons for job dissatisfaction were not reported, we can safely say that large numbers of employed Americans derive considerably less than full satisfaction from their jobs. That kind of dissatisfaction must certainly undermine their overall sense of well-being.

Another characteristic of the service industries is that the individual employee's workweek is shorter. In 1929 the average workweek in industry was 47.2 hours, and it declined to 39.7 by 1965 (Fuchs, 1968). It has since stabilized. In 1981 the average workweek in industry was 40.1 hours (Table 666). In 1929 the average workweek in service industries was 50.8 hours, and by 1965 it had declined to 40.1 hours (Fuchs, 1968) and to 32.8 hours by 1981 (Table 666). Many women and older workers work part-time in the service industries, and that may account for some of the differential. Sometimes the distinction between work and play is blurred when managers entertain customers, when staff go to sales conferences, or when intellectuals such as college professors spend their work time reading. Overall, workers are putting in less time at work, and many may invest themselves more in other activities.

In the United States, the use of leisure time is emphasized. Many in the service industries (hotels, restaurants, entertainment, sports, and so on) cater to those with leisure time. A few figures are illustrative. From 1950 to 1980 the population increased from 152,271,000 to 226,505,000, a change of 48.8% (Table 26). If we take prices in 1967 as 100, the consumer price index has changed from 72.1 in 1950 to 269.0 in 1981 (Table 779). Expenditures on personal consumption for recreation have increased from $11,147,000,000 in 1950 to $106,414,000,000 in 1980 (Table 396). In other words, while population increased by 48% in that period and the consumer price index nearly quadrupled, recreational expenditures have increased 9.3 times in the same period. People are spending much more of their personal resources on recreational and leisure-time activities. In the urban population in recent years, the average number of hours per week spent in work has decreased from 33.0 to 32.5 hours, and the number of leisure hours has increased from 34.8 to 38.5 hours per week (U.S. Bureau of Census, 1980, Table 11/13).

Not only are hours in all employment shorter, but vacations have also increased in length. Many have the opportunity to retire early. One can retire from the military or the police with a pension while still in the 40s, or in the 50s in civil service positions, if one has worked a sufficient number of years. Early retirement has been proposed as a solution for chronic unemployment, although at present fiscal pressures on federal Social Security funds have led to discussion of extending the age of retirement. Shortening the workweek is another possible solution to chronic unemployment that is proposed from time to time. The long-range trend may well move us toward greater leisure-time availability in the future. With shorter hours, increased vacation time, and a shorter lifetime work span, the average person today has an estimated 45,000 more free hours available during a lifetime than a counterpart 100 years ago (De Grazia, 1962).

These figures reflect a normative change, which must be accompanied by a change in the value system. Precisely those changes in values—changes in the Protestant ethic emphasizing work, saving, and sacrifice—were involved in the sexual and cultural revolutions of the 1960s. Reich's (1970) best-seller *The Greening of America* defined the new levels of consciousness characteristic of the youth of the 1960s. Roszak's (1969) well-received *The Making of a Counterculture* spoke to exactly the same issues. The problems of value change are important in making cultural conflict on the one hand, and in creating a state of anomie for many individuals on the other. The widely heralded generation gap is one example of cultural conflict attributed to value shifts. The sense of uncertainty about values and goals and the changing norms of behavior make it difficult for many to take action with a sense of surety and to find satisfaction in what they do. The young bride-to-be who apologized to a confidant for getting married when so many of her peers simply lived together is a small example of an internalized conflict based on changing values. Levine and Levine (1971) suggested that the apparently increasing prevalence of character disorders, in contrast to the classical neuroses of an earlier day, could be attributed to the unevenness of change in different segments of society and to a lag in the rate of change of stated values when compared with changes in behavioral norms.

Value changes aside, increasing leisure time is not an unmitigated blessing. Increasing leisure time requires the ability to use that leisure time satisfactorily. More satisfying use of leisure time means that people need to be educated to decide how to use time for themselves, in contrast to the external discipline of the clock in the workplace. Blind obedience and dependence on authority figures will necessarily decline as people decide for themselves how to use time. Until new explicit norms, values, and expectations develop, people will feel uncertain about the proper relationship to authorities.

Greater enjoyment of many activities depends on mastery of skills. A good tennis player enjoys the game more than an unskilled, indifferent player. Mastery of skills requires time, effort, and the opportunity to learn. Increasing leisure interests have already influenced, and will continue to influence, the school curriculum, to the consternation of "back-to-basics" advocates. In other words, our increasing emphasis on leisure will likely have long-range effects on other basic institutions as well.

Some have spoken of the harried leisure class, in which a compulsive drive to make good use of leisure time leads to financial overextension with a consequent need to work additional time to pay for the motorboat, mobile home, beach buggy, or four-wheel-drive recreational vehicle. Twenty-six percent of the urban population said they always feel rushed to do the things they have to do (U.S. Bureau of Census, 1980, Table 11/2). We need not overevaluate the problems associated with leisure. We simply note that the changing nature of work and of leisure has led to new problems, including the development of behavioral norms appropriate for today's world. The problem is to develop a version of the good life that is well articulated, well internalized, and supported by other social and financial resources.

We have sketched some of the major problems that beset contemporary Americans with great frequency. Having problems and having to cope and struggle with problems in living is more the rule than the exception. The problems documented in regularly kept statistics are similar to those that appear in stressful-life-events scales (see Chapter 6). At any given moment, a large number of Americans are affected by acute and chronic illness and accidents, by disasters of one sort or another, or by problems related to crime, delinquency, drug addiction, and alcoholism. Parenthood has its own special problems, and large numbers of Americans have serious financial problems as well. The work setting has introduced new problems and new opportunities, and increasing leisure also poses problems.

In a 1978 household survey, 36% reported one or more traumatic events (hospitalization or disability, death of someone close to the respondent, divorce, unemployment, etc.) in the previous year (U.S. Bureau of Census, 1980, Table G). In that year 14% of Americans characterized their lives as "hard" (U.S. Bureau of Census, 1980, Table B). The indications that we obtain from examining individual incidents, or summary data concerning the quality of life, and the indications obtained from examining epidemiological data on the prevalence of DSM-III disorders lead to similar conclusions about the number of Americans coping with psychologically distressing problems in living.

Aloneness in American Society

Many Americans face their problems in relative isolation (see Tables 1-10 and 1-11). Slater (1970) suggests that American culture deeply frustrates three basic human desires—for community, for engagement, and for dependence. By these terms, he means the desire to live "in trust and fraternal cooperation with one's fellows in a total and visible collective entity" (p. 4), the desire to come to grips with social and interpersonal problems, and the wish to share with others responsibility for the direction of one's life. Sarason (1974) emphasizes much the same set of desires in his concept of the psychological sense of community, defined as "the sense that one was part of a readily available, mutually supportive network of relationships upon which one could depend and as a result of which one did not experience sustained feelings of loneliness that impel one to actions or to adopting a style of living masking anxiety and setting the stage for later and more destructive anguish" (p. 1).

Slater and Sarason sense and describe a key problem in American life. The figures bear out their contentions. Many, many Americans face myriad problems in living alone. Separations occur with great frequency. In 1983 there were over 2 million deaths and about 1.2 million divorces (National Center for Health Statistics, 1984).

Table 1-10. Aloneness in American Society

Condition	Number	Year
Separations		
Deaths	2,060,000	1983[a]
Divorce	1,180,000[b]	1983[a]
Residential change within one year		
Homeowners	13,177,000	1974[c]
Renters	27,712,440	
Live alone	20,682,000	1980[d]
Female-headed families	8,440,000	1980[e]
Male-headed families	1,499,000	
Divorced		
Men	3,871,000	1980[f]
Women	5,831,000	
Widowed		
Men	1,972,000	1980[f]
Women	10,104,000	

[a]National Center for Health Statistics, 1984.

[b]The number divorced does not include the number separated but not divorced.

[c]U.S. Bureau of Census, 1976, Table 1283.

[d]U.S. Bureau of Census, 1981, Table 56.

[e]U.S. Bureau of Census, 1981, Table 62.

[f]U.S. Bureau of Census, 1981, Table 49.

We have no comparable figures of emotionally trying breakups of relationships among those who are not married. In our own unpublished survey of life events in college students, we found that almost 20% were involved in the breakup of a heterosexual relationship each year.

We have already noted that divorce and separation are among the most emotionally trying events. The loss of a loved one also stands high on the scale of stressful events and is followed by consequences similar to those involved in the loss of a relationship in divorce or separation. On the list of stressful events rated by adults in studies by Holmes and Rahe (1967), death of one's spouse was the single most stressful event one could experience, while death of a family member was among the top five most stressful events, and death of a close friend was in the top half. A recent study by the National Academy of Sciences points out that these events are relatively common (1984).

> For most people bereavement is a fact of life. Only those who themselves die young escape the pain of losing someone they love through death. Every year an estimated eight million Americans experience the death of an immediate family member. Every year there are 800,000 new widows and widowers. There are at least 27,000 suicides in this country annually, and probably many more, since suicide is underreported. Each year approximately 400,000 children under the age of 25 die. Just as each type of relationship has special meaning, so too does each type of death carry with it a special kind of pain for those who are left behind. (p. 4)

Also noted in this comprehensive study are the many adverse health effects of bereavement, including increased mortality, depression, drug and alcohol abuse, cardiovascular disease, and accidents.

Table 1-11. Number of Widowed Persons by Sex and Age, 1980[a]

By Age	Male	Female	Ratio Female/Male
Under 24	2,000	26,000	13.00
25–29	8,000	33,000	4.12
30–34	11,000	102,000	9.27
35–44	45,000	292,000	6.49
45–54	176,000	821,000	4.66
55–64	397,000	2,082,000	5.24
65–74	557,000	3,444,000	6.18
75 and over	776,000	3,677,000	4.74
Total	1,972,000	10,104,000	5.56

[a]U.S. Bureau of Census, 1981, Table 49.

Americans move frequently. Between 1975 and 1980 about 47.0% of the population 5 years old and over had moved at least once, and 45.6% of the moves were relatively long distance (Table 18). Among those who owned their own homes, 9.8% had lived in those homes for less than 12 months in 1974. Among renters, 37.6% had lived at their current addresses for 12 months or less (U.S. Bureau of Census, 1976, Table 1283). Geographic mobility in and of itself is not necessarily associated with increased risk of psychological disorder (Levine, 1966), but many people move every year, disrupting existing networks of relationships and requiring the development of new networks. Children who move even short distances must often face the problem of adapting to a new school (Felner, Ginter, & Primavera, 1982).

In 1980 some 20,682,000 people lived alone. The number of persons living in single-person units has increased by 60% since 1970 (Table 56). Of 79,108,000 households counted in 1980 in the United States, 48,180,000 or 60.9% were husband-and-wife units, while 39.1% consisted of other living arrangements (Table 61). Of the remaining household units, 8,440,000 were female-headed families and 1,706,000 were male-headed families (Table 62). More women than men lived alone (12,088,000 versus 8,594,000) (Table 57). Not all were necessarily isolated, but no one was sharing the household from whom they could receive support in time of need.

When we examine the distribution of widowed and divorced adults, the inference that more women than men are alone is strongly supported. In 1980 some 3,871,000 men said they were divorced and were not, at the time they were asked, remarried; 5,831,000 women also so characterized themselves. In that year 1,972,000 men characterized themselves as widowers, not remarried, as did 10,479,000 women (Table 49).

The figures on widowhood deserve closer attention. In 1980 women constituted 52.5% of the population 18 years and older. There were 7,953,000 more adult women than men (Table 49). The differential in the population begins to show itself relatively quickly. Although there are more males than females under age 24, in the age range 25–44 there are 974 males per 1,000 females, 907 males per 1,000 females at 45–64, and over 65 years 676 males per 1,000 females (Table 27). The figures on widowhood are particularly striking, as Table 1-11 (adapted from Table 49) shows.

At every age the odds of a widowed woman finding a widowed male to marry are poor, and they are poorest in the middle years of life. The same holds true for the divorced population. At every age there are at least 1.5 divorced women who have not yet remarried for every divorced male who has not yet remarried (Table 49). There are more single males than single females at every age until one reaches age 65 and above, but a substantial proportion of those males over 35 who have never married are probably not in the marriage market, for whatever reason. The sex ratio may well have important implications for the way we live and for determining changes in relationships between the sexes (Guttentag & Secord, 1983).

Because women live longer than men, women cannot count on developing another monogamous heterosexual relationship once having experienced a loss of relationship because of a death or a divorce that might have occurred when the woman was as young as 30. These figures confirm that substantial numbers of women will face the vicissitudes of life relatively alone. Of course, divorced and widowed women have friends and can turn to their parents and relatives or to their children for emotional support, companionship, and other aid. These figures confirm, however, that the ideal image of a married couple coping with the problems of life together does not fit the picture for substantial numbers of Americans, and particularly for substantial numbers of women.

Some laws meant to support married women have not caught up with contemporary realities. The Social Security laws provide survivors' benefits for minor children but they provide no widows' pensions for women under age 60. Therefore many women who were homemakers during a large portion of their adult lives may find themselves without any source of income after their children come of age and before they reach age 60 (Hoskins & Bixby, 1973). Because many will not have had other work experience during the years they were homemakers, they will also find it hard to reenter the employment market. Services for displaced homemakers to provide job training, placement, and counseling for women who are ineligible for existing health, retirement, or unemployment benefit programs have been developing in recent years (*Spokeswoman,* 1977).

Gove (1976) examined a number of indices to attempt to determine rates of mental illness in males and females. He reviewed community surveys, first admissions to mental hospitals, psychiatric admissions to general hospitals, psychiatric care in outpatient clinics, private outpatient psychiatric care, and surveys of the prevalence of mental illness in the patients of physicians in general practice. By every index, in just about every study Gove reviewed, more women than men were found to have psychological problems. Gove limited himself to studying the neuroses and functional psychoses. His method eliminated from consideration many diagnostic categories such as mental retardation, alcoholism, and organic brain syndromes.

Guttentag et al. (1974) reviewed utilization rates at state and county mental hospitals, at community mental health centers, and in epidemiological studies. Their review showed that women are more often depressed than men and that women have higher rates of neurotic disorders than do men, as inferred from utilization data. Men show higher rates of alcoholism, drug abuse, personality disorders, and transient situational and behavioral disorders than do women. Myers et al. (1984) confirmed that general line of findings in their door-to-door survey. They found that affective disorders and phobias were more prevalent among women than men; alcohol and drug abuse and antisocial personalities were diagnosed more often in men than in women. Guttentag et al. further reported that single men and separated and divorced men and women showed the highest rates of mental illness. Persons with low household incomes who are unhappy with their jobs or their marriages, or who have experienced life-event losses in the previous year, were among the high-risk groups for depression.

Gove (1976) and Guttentag et al. (1974) explored several hypotheses related to sex roles that might account for the differences between men and women. We will not join that debate but will point out that because they live longer, more women than men are likely to be struggling with problems in living, and they are more likely to be struggling with those problems alone (a conclusion whose implications will be explored further in Chapter 6). One consequence of aloneness may be a heightened tendency to reach for professional care when experiencing distress related to frequently occurring life events.

The Availability of Professional Care

Understood in terms of stressful events, "normal" life is indeed a soap opera for most people. To what extent is formal help available to those who need it? Albee's (1959) work for the Joint Commission on Mental Health and Mental Illness alerted us to the problems of providing sufficient personnel if treatment is delivered by professionally trained staff through designated mental health organizations. Budget cuts may have tightened the job market, but that should not lead us to believe that we have produced enough trained people to meet the needs of the population. Table 1-12 shows the numbers of professional personnel employed in mental health facilities in 1974. Looking at professional staff only, and defining the staff to include the types of workers listed, 152,402 individuals provided direct patient-care services, although in total they made up only 127,160 full-time equivalent positions. About 22% of all professional staff in mental health facilities are part-time. Nearly a third of the part-time workers are psychiatrists.

Assume a 2000-hour work year (i.e., 40 hours × 50 weeks). Assume further that 80% of that time is devoted to patient care, including record keeping and staff conferences, but excluding in-service training, administrative meetings, and research that does not involve direct patient care. Multiplying the 127,160 full-time equivalent (FTE) positions by 1600 hours yields a figure of 203,456,000 hours a year devoted to direct patient care. Because these figures do not take into account private-practice hours, let us take the total number of patient-care staff available, 152,402 individuals, instead of the full-time equivalent positions to generate the number of hours available. That number is 243,843,200 hours of patient care available from some professional annually, very likely a liberal estimate.

We get a lower estimate of the number of hours available by accepting Klerman's (1982) figure that there are about 100,000 practitioners of psychotherapy including psychologists, psychiatrists, social workers, marriage and family counselors, psychiatric nurses, and pastoral counselors. If we assume 1600 patient-care hours are available per year per professional person, about 160,000,000 hours of psychotherapeutic time are available each year. For illustrative purposes, we will use the higher estimate of available hours.

The hours are not available to all equally. There are important regional differences in the distribution of mental health services. Trained personnel tend to be concen-

Table 1-12. Mental Health Personnel Working in 1974[a]

Profession	Number	FTE Positions[b]
Psychiatry		14,947
Child psychiatrists	2,362	
Neurologists	3,741	
Office practice	11,900	
Institutional, full-time	4,900	
Residents, full-time	3,700	
Administration, research, teaching	2,800	
Total	27,041	
Other physicians	27,000	3,548
Psychologists	27,000	22,577
Social workers	33,800	22,147
Specialized rehabilitation services	11,050	39,832
Vocational rehabilitation counseling	17,000	
Registered nurses in mental health care	36,511	34,089
Total professional patient-care staff	152,402	127,160
Total time available (see text)	203,456,000 hours per year	

[a]Figures adapted from Table 24, National Health Education Committee (1976, p. 172); Health, U.S. (1975); Table 118, Statistical Abstract of the U.S. (1976). We did not find comparable figures to those available for the earlier period. Redick and Witkin (1984) report an 11% increase in all FTE staff in all mental health organizations between 1972 and 1982. They do not provide a breakdown of professional and other staff for other than state and county mental hospitals. The overall population increased by about 11% between 1972 and 1982. The increase in mental health staff is about the same as the increase in the population. Thus if the number of personnel was inadequate in 1972, the situation had not improved by 1982.

[b]NIMH, Staffing of Mental Health Facilities (1974).

trated in urban areas. Many areas of the country are almost totally without specialized mental health services. The shortage of personnel trained to work with children and the elderly is extreme. In some places minority and bilingual persons may go without treatment because insufficient numbers of trained personnel speak the language (Task Panel on Mental Health Personnel, 1978; Snowden, 1982).

Personnel are by no means distributed evenly throughout all types of mental health facilities. State and county mental hospitals and Veterans Administration psychiatric services account for 55.1% of all full-time equivalent positions (Redick & Witkin, 1984). Staff:patient ratios, one index of quality of service, are also distributed quite differently depending on the facility. Psychiatric units in general hospitals have a ratio of 69.1 professional staff per 100 resident patients. The ratio in private mental hospitals is similar, 66.1 per 100. Residential treatment centers for emotionally disturbed children show a ratio of 49.7 per 100. Veterans Administration hospitals have 33.4 professionals per 100 resident patients. State and county mental hospitals have an average of 18.1. In recent years, there has been some improvement in the availability of professional staff in state and county mental hospitals, even though the overall number of patient-care staff decreased with the decline in the number of patients in residence. The professional staff increased from 38,516 in 1972 to 48,224 in 1982 (Redick & Witkin, 1984).

The greatest number of the full-time equivalent professional positions (65%) were in inpatient-care facilities (NIMH, 1974). The data in Tables 17 and 18 in Redick and

Witkin (1984) show that close to that same percentage of the approximately 107,000 professionals employed by all mental health organizations were in inpatient settings in 1981 and 1982.

If the entire number of patient-care hours were devoted to the care of the individuals involved in the 1,680,000 inpatient care episodes and the 3,569,000 outpatient-care episodes reported for 1974, an average of about 46.5 hours of some professional's time was spent per patient-care episode. Kiesler (1982) states that when we take into account psychiatric units in general hospitals and episodes of hospitalization for mental illness in general hospitals without psychiatric units, the total is 3,012,500 inpatient episodes. If we add the additional inpatient-care episodes to the total, the professional time per patient-care episode is reduced to 37.1 hours. If we multiply the number of patient-care episodes by two to include only one of the household members who might have an interest in seeing a professional person during a patient-care episode, the time available is reduced to 18.5 hours per person involved in a patient-care episode in an inpatient or outpatient mental health facility. The number of outpatient-care episodes has been growing in recent years, so this number of hours per patient-care episode is undoubtedly an overestimation.

These figures, of course, would leave no time at all for the more than 1 million residents of nursing homes, where up to 75% are estimated to have some degree of mental illness, nor could any services be provided to the 1 million or more who reside in other institutions. Add the 2 million who are not in mental hospitals but are in other institutions, and double the number to account for one household member who might wish to see some professional person. We arrive at a figure of about 16.8 hours of *some* professional person's time devoted to each individual, or to some family member, who was *institutionalized* or who was seen in a formal mental health facility. Rosenhan's (1973) observation that his pseudopatients rarely saw doctors on the wards of the hospitals in which they stayed makes perfect sense in this context, as do Scheff's (1966) and Miller's (1976) observations that psychiatric interviews for purposes of determining the need for involuntary hospitalization averaged just a few minutes.

Depending on the assumptions, we can arrive at figures of minutes or even seconds per year available to those who might be dealing with crises of living consequent to chronic and acute illness, employment and financial problems, or problems of death, divorce, and other separations. We have said nothing about the nearly 8 million children estimated to be in need, nor have we considered at all the problems in living consequent to transitions in adult life. Sheehy's (1976) best-selling popularization of psychological problems of adult development, whatever its inadequacies as a text (Levine, 1977b), touched on the feelings of a great many people, and we have not provided for those millions either.

On numbers alone it is apparent that professionally trained personnel will never be available in sufficient numbers to meet even a fraction of the *potential* demand for psychological services. The *actual* demand, based on Shapiro et al.'s (1984) estimates of those with DSM-III diagnoses who actually sought help is a third or less of the potential demand. That fact somewhat tempers our conclusion. We do not need to modify radically the basic point that we would have to increase professional personnel several times, an extremely unlikely occurrence, to provide adequate hours of treatment in the present mode of service delivery.

Problems of the Medical Model

Availability aside, the form in which services are delivered is also a problem. The term *medical model* has several meanings, as Zax and Specter (1974) point out. The fee-for-service medical model is built on the assumption that most problems can be handled by acute, episodic interventions limited in time and with an enduring effect. As we readily see by looking only at the 22.4 million noninstitutionalized individuals who suffer some limitation in a major life role due to a chronic disability, help provided with those assumptions misses the need. Even when treatment for the physical disorder is stabilized, the patient and the family have to work out their adaptations to the limitations imposed by the condition. When we look at those involved with the criminal justice or the welfare system, we must concede that a sizable proportion of the problems are chronic and will not readily give way to acute, episodic interventions. In the words of Stanton Coit (1891), one of the founders of the American settlement house movement:

> If we consider the vast amount of personal attention and time needed to understand and deal effectively with the case of any one man or family that has fallen into vice, crime or pauperism, we shall see the impossibility of coping with even these evils alone, unless the helpers be both many and constantly at hand. (p. 19)

The medical model also implies a passive help giver who waits for the client to define his or her own need and then to request help. That model of service is in keeping with American ideals of individuality and self-determination. It does, however, assume that help seekers know the kind of help available, find the help acceptable, and that they are acceptable clients to the help givers. Hollingshead and Redlich (1958) point out that the help-giving system sorts clients by social class and provides different treatment to people of different class origins.

The U.S. Congress recognized the problem of the appropriateness of services in the Community Mental Health Centers Amendments of 1975 (PL 94-63) by requiring that:

> (D) in the case of a community mental health center serving a population including a substantial proportion of individuals of limited English-speaking ability, the center has (i) developed a plan and made arrangements responsive to the needs of such population for providing services to the extent practicable in the language and cultural context most appropriate to such individuals, and (ii) identified an individual on its staff who is fluent in both that language and in English and whose responsibilities shall include providing guidance to such individuals and to appropriate staff members with respect to cultural sensitivities and bridging linguistic and cultural differences. (PL 94-63, Sec. 206)

Giordano and Giordano (1976) review the issues of service delivery in mental health not only for those who speak different languages within the United States, but also for those of varying ethnic backgrounds. They point out that attitudes toward help seeking vary among different groups, which often have different preferences for the kinds of help they find acceptable. Cultural characteristics of either the provider or the recipient can be barriers preventing the use of help that might be available (Snowden, 1982).

Fuchs (1968) argues that the service industries are "consumer intensive" in the sense that worker productivity is in part a function of the "quality" of the user of the services. Thus productivity in a bank is partly dependent on how well customers fill out deposit slips, or a physician's productivity is improved by the patient's ability to give a good history. In educational settings, a teacher's productivity is partly dependent on how good the student is. Garvey and Levine (1977) report that faculty ratings of how much faculty time and effort are involved in working with a graduate student on the student's Ph.D. qualifying paper are negatively correlated with ratings of the quality of the student's work. The productivity of psychotherapists is improved by clients who are ready and willing to use the psychotherapy that is offered. Some have experimented with pretherapy training for clients in how to assume the client role (Hastrup, 1974). The consequence is that in the free-market system provided by the fee-for-service model, the YAVIS (young, attractive, verbal, intelligent, successful) client is preferred. Ryan's (1969) demonstration that a substantial proportion of the case load of private psychiatrists in Boston consisted of college-educated women between the ages of 25 and 35 who lived in a few census tracts in Boston is a case in point. Contemporary services are not equally available to all who might need them, and some clients are better prepared to use the services that are offered.

The picture may be changing. We have some reason to believe that with greater availability of health insurance coverage for mental health services, a broader segment of the socioeconomic spectrum is seeking out mental health care (Taube et al., 1984). We also have reason to believe that some mental health practitioners are learning how to treat clients from differing backgrounds (Snowden, 1982). Overall, however, mental health care as we know it is probably most effective with those who are best prepared to use it. Too many in need are probably still filtered out of treatment by their encounters with the kind of therapist who considers them unsuitable for the therapy he or she prefers to offer.

We mention a further issue in a medical model in which responses to problems in living are called *disorders* and professional services *treatment* for those disorders. The subtle implication may be that because help is provided through professional services, the events that have led the individual to seek help are unusual and should not have occurred. There is even some implication that feelings of anxiety, tenseness, or depression in relation to problems in living should not occur. Certainly that implication might exist for the 13% of males and the 29% of females over 18 who said they used some type of prescribed psychotherapeutic drug in the past year (Parry et al., 1973). Given that psychotherapeutic drugs accounted for 17% of all prescriptions filled in American drugstores (Parry et al., 1973), striking numbers of people have difficulty in living with the emotions that are generated day by day. One could argue that the existence of help reinforces the belief that the event and the associated emotions are unusual, if not pathological.

Wilensky and Lebeaux (1965) described two conceptions of social welfare, the *residual* and the *institutional*. The *residual* concept holds that welfare, or other helping services, should come into play only when the normal structures of supply—the family and the market—do not function adequately to meet a need. Because of their residual, temporary, substitute character, helping services thus conceived carry with them the implication of an isolated individual or familial failure that should not have occurred. The *institutional* view recognizes the complexity of modern social life and accepts it as a legitimate function of modern society to provide aid to individuals to move toward self-fulfillment. This view recognizes that in today's interdependent society, institutional arrangements are necessary to help people solve problems of living; there is no implication that the distressing event should not have happened. The institutional view is preferable because it minimizes any stigma or secondary reaction that one has failed because one has problems that need help.

To the degree that either view emphasizes the responsibility of the state to provide the services, and emphasizes the necessity for a special class of professional helpers, the definition of the problem may add to the problem. For instance, an emphasis on professional assistance may undermine one's confidence in one's own ability to cope, or in one's ability to cope with the assistance of a friend, a neighbor, or a relative. Or the conception that professional help should be available for problems in living may undermine the sense of responsibility one person feels for another, or that a network or a face-to-face community might feel for one of its members. If someone is available to take care of the problem, then send the problem to someone who is paid to do the job.

Having said that, we want to back away from that position slightly, for we do not mean to give credence to some romantic notion that any nonprofessional is for that reason alone a more effective person than any professional, or that professionals do not have valuable knowledge, experience, and special services to offer. Moreover, the alert reader will note that we have been emphasizing the essential aloneness of much in American society, which in and of itself should limit the utility of the concept that one can rely on friends,[2] neighbors, or relatives, or even on the local bartender or hairdresser (cf. Cowen, 1982). We mean to emphasize the sense of responsibility that one person who is not paid feels for another. As Jane Addams (1910) put it, too many seem to have "lost that simple and almost automatic response to the human appeal, that old healthful reaction resulting in activity from the mere presence of suffering or helplessness" (p. 71). We believe that some new helping forms are being built and will be built precisely out of the responsibility one person feels for another and the iden- tification and sympathy one person feels for another. The self-help movement, so prominent in the present day (see Chapters 8 and 9), is an example of a person-to- person, nonprofessional, nonstate-supplied service.[3]

Dohrenwend and Dohrenwend (1969) argue that most life crises and associated emotions are transient in nature and that serious (in the sense of chronic) mental health problems do not emerge until some additional secondary gain is associated with the initial distress (see Chapters 2 and 6). We do not believe the Dohrenwends mean to imply that the stressful feelings accompanying life crises are to be dismissed or that their transience makes them less worthy of our attention. On the contrary, the resources available to the individual to help mediate life crises can make the difference between a favorable outcome in which a preexisting balance is restored and one in which the individual is a better, stronger person for having coped successfully with distress.

As the Dohrenwends and many others point out, there are severe, chronic disor- ders in all countries and in widely varying cultures. Some of these chronic disorders may well fit a medical disease model. The care of some problems requires highly spe- cialized resources, trained personnel, and special facilities. The problem for the field is to distinguish among the problems that are amenable to one solution and those that require other solutions. The concept of mental disorder, implying a unitary phenom- enon, is itself misleading. Although it is certainly true that a great many people have problems, it is not true that all of their problems are the same or that all problems will yield to or be ameliorated by the same solutions. Even in the case of a chronic disorder with a physical cause, the degree of social disability will vary with the available solutions to the social problem and the modes of care provided.

Attitudes and Ideologies

One further issue is the attitude with which we face the vicissitudes of life. Perhaps it is a myth, and perhaps it was never so, but in the "good old days" when religious beliefs were strongly held, many could accept or at least find some sense of relief from the pain of outrageous fortune by seeing it all as the will of a god whose ways were unclear to mortals but whose eventual purposes were beneficent. Natural disaster and social and economic inequality could be rationalized in the same terms. A church or a religious institution not only provided the ideology to make the sea of troubles bearable, but it also provided rituals to help in coping and a sense of shared fellowship by the participation of members of the religious group in both the suffering and the joys of the individual member. The influence of the religious institution waned over the years, Christianity having lost to science in a fair contest of miracle working, as the late Paul Goodman once put it. But the need to have an ideology with which to interpret life and to give meaning to it has not waned at all.

The recent revival of fundamentalist religious groups and the powerful attraction among youth of the "Moonies," the Hari Krishnas, and religiously tinged cults is testimony to the continuing attraction of social movements with strong ideologies. The degree to which we discuss alienation, anomie, and existential crises is the degree to which we recognize a void in our lives.

At one time, when much seemed beyond our reach, an ideology that taught tolerance of life's troubles made sense. In today's world, given our activist problem-solving values and our faith that all problems indeed have solutions, such a theology seems passive and unworthy. Moreover, we are now willing and eager to commit a good part of our economic resources to the pursuit of our own pleasures. A retarded child, an aged and sick parent, the death of a loved one, economic uncertainty, and our personal limitations in achieving the wherewithal to pursue pleasures all become frustrations which we wish we could put away from ourselves; we fault ourselves for feeling the associated complex of anger, guilt, depression, and helplessness that accompanies frustrations emerging from seemingly uncontrollable forces.

We are not sure that we know in a cultural sense how to face the soap opera of life, or that appropriate social institutions have evolved to help us to do that as fully as we might wish. There is probably a substantial overlap between the functions professional psychotherapists fulfill and the functions our religious institutions fulfill. Professional psychotherapists are groping toward providing the ideology, but the professional therapist cannot provide the social institution within which an ideology is lived out day by day.

We probably do not prepare ourselves and our children well enough to cope with life's difficulties. Rossman (1976) points out that the best-selling self-help books are in those areas in which our socializing institutions have grossly failed us—marriage, giving birth, parenting, divorce, living with illness, sexuality, and the like. There is a clue to prevention in the situation. Those who look to education and preparation for coping to provide some additional personal resources to reduce the worst consequences of life's stresses may have much to tell us. Graziano's (1977) work showing that parents can be taught to treat their children's problems offers a related method, which suggests a change in role for professionals and a way of "giving away" psychology on a broad basis.

These particular directions—providing public resources in such a fashion as not to undermine person-to-person responsibility and caring, encouraging face-to-face mutual assistance, teaching people to cope, helping to develop meaningful and satisfying life views that can be lived out in a supportive social organization—offer important possibilities for dealing with the soap opera of life, in addition to relying exclusively on specialized professional institutions.

Summary

To recapitulate, professional mental health personnel are not now, and never will be, available in sufficient numbers to provide assistance for the tens of millions who are daily coping with stressful problems in living. Moreover, our medical-model delivery system will be available in a psychological and social sense to relatively few people. Whatever position we take on the effectiveness of psychotherapy—and good arguments can be made that psychotherapeutic efforts are helpful (Meltzoff & Kornreich, 1970; Bergin, 1971; Smith & Glass, 1977; Kendall & Norton-Ford, 1982)—services provided in only that modality will be available in limited quantities. Psychoactive drugs may relieve symptoms of anxiety and depression, but do little to help individuals cope with ongoing problems in life. For some, relief from affective distress, or a reduction in pathological thinking consequent to the relief of distress, may be sufficient to enable them to adapt. For others, chemical relief of distress may be only a small step in helping them deal with day-to-day problems.

In any event, large numbers of people cope with significant problems in living on a daily basis. Many cope alone, living in relative isolation from others who might provide emotional support, an opportunity to see problems differently, or more concrete assistance. Furthermore, broad social and cultural changes continuously add to the difficulties confronting many segments of the population. As we have noted, the problems in living discussed here appear on stressful-life-events scales, which are correlated with psychiatric symptoms and with physical illness (Rabkin & Streuning, 1976; Gersten, et al., 1977). We can arrive at similar estimates of the potential psychological need whether we use epidemiological studies of DSM-III diagnoses or a problems-in-living and stressful-life-events perspective. We have a different focus when we look at an epidemiology of "cases" as against an epidemiology of events. Cases lead us to treatment of individuals. An epidemiology of events offers broader possibilities for thinking about helpful or preventive interventions. We obviously need to think our way through alternative analyses of the problems before us. In our opinion, an individual psychological orientation and the medical model seriously limit our thinking, while the view that life is a soap opera opens new vistas for the development of therapeutic and preventive services. In the following chapters we will be examining some alternatives and the concepts and the research related to them. As a group these topics comprise our view of what is called community psychology.

Notes

1. If only a table number is given, the source is U.S. Bureau of the Census, 1981.

2. We know an apocryphal story about a famous experimental psychologist who attended a symposium considering the impact of psychoanalysis. The symposium was unusual in that it consisted of patients and their analysts. The experimental psychologist commented that he didn't think he had gotten much more out of his analysis than he would have gotten by spending the same time talking to a good friend. His analyst replied: "But Eddie, at the time you didn't have a friend!"

3. We agree with aspects of Kropotkin's (1902) position that the state's efforts undermine the feeling for mutual assistance, and we believe that Sarason's (1976) paper describing the anarchist insight says much of importance, but we also believe that public resources should be generously available to those in need. The problems of the aged, the mentally retarded, the chronically mentally ill, and many who are alone will not be dealt with satisfactorily, if at all, without the ample availability of public funds and resources. Our concern is with how the purposes of the funds are distorted when made available through the complex of fragmented governmental agencies and with how resources can be made to serve human rather than institutional needs.

References

Addams, J. (1910). *Twenty years at Hull House*. New York: Macmillan.

Albee, G. W. (1959). *Mental health manpower trends*. New York: Basic Books.

American Psychological Association Task Force on the Victims of Crime and Violence. (1984). *Final Report*. Washington, DC: American Psychological Association.

Barnes, G. M. (1984). *Alcohol use among secondary school students in New York State*. Buffalo: New York State Research Institute on Alcoholism.

Blane, M. J. (1976). *Here to stay: American families in the twentieth century*. New York: Basic Books.

Bergin, A. (1971). The evaluation of therapeutic outcomes. In A. Bergin & S. Garfield (Eds.), *Handbook of psychotherapy and behavior change: An empirical analysis*. New York: Wiley.

Bloom, B. L., Asher, S. J., & White, S. W. (1978). Marital disruption as a stressor: A review and analysis. *Psychological Bulletin, 85*, 867–894.

Browne, A., & Finkelhor, D. (1985). Impact of child sexual abuse: A review of research. *Psychological Bulletin, 99*, 66–77.

Buss, T. F., Redburn, F. S., & Waldron, J. (1983). *Mass unemployment. Plant closings and community mental health*. Beverly Hills: Sage.

Cartoof, V. G., & Klerman, L. V. (1986). Parental consent for abortion: Impact of the Massachusetts law. *American Journal of Public Health, 76*, 397–400.

Clingempeel, W. G., & Reppucci, N. D. (1982). Joint custody after divorce: Major issues and goals for research. *Psychological Bulletin, 91*, 102–127.

Coit, S. (1891). *Neighborhood guilds: An instrument of social reform*. London: Swan Sonnenschein.

Cymrot, D., & Mallan, L. B. (1974). *Wife's earnings as a source of family income* (DHEW Publication No. (SSA) 74-11701, Note No. 10). Research and Statistics Note. Washington, DC: HEW Office of Research and Statistics.

DeGrazia, S. (1962). *Of time, work and leisure*. New York: Twentieth Century Fund.

Department of Health, Education & Welfare. (1979). *Promoting health, preventing disease. Objectives for the nation*. Washington, DC: Author.

Dohrenwend, B. P., & Dohrenwend, B. S. (1969). *Social status and psychological disorder.* New York: Wiley.

Emery, R. E. (1982). Interparental conflict and the children of discord and divorce. *Psychological Bulletin, 92,* 310–330.

Epstein, S. S., Brown, L. O., & Pope, C. (1982). *Hazardous waste in America.* San Francisco: Sierra Club Books.

Felner, R. D., Ginter, M., & Primavera, J. (1982). Primary prevention during school transitions: Social support and environmental structure. *American Journal of Community Psychology, 10,* 277–290.

Fuchs, V. R. (1968). *The service economy.* New York: National Bureau of Economic Research.

Garvey, C. F., & Levine, M. (1977). *Myth and reality: An evaluation of a reform in graduate education.* Unpublished paper, Department of Psychology, SUNY at Buffalo.

Gersten, J. C., Langner, T. S., Eisenberg, J. B., & Simcha-Fagan, O. (1977). An evaluation of the etiologic role of stressful life-change events in psychological disorders. *Journal of Health and Social Behavior, 18,* 228–243.

Giordano, J., & Giordano, G. P. (1976). Ethnicity and community mental health. *Community Mental Health Review, 1,* No. 3.

Gleser, G. C., Green, B. L., & Winget, C. N. (1983). Quantifying interview data on psychic impairment of disaster survivors. *Journal of Nervous and Mental Diseases, 166,* 209–216.

Glidewell, J. C., & Swallow, C. S. (1969). *The prevalence of maladjustment in elementary schools: A report prepared for the Joint Commission on the Mental Health of Children.* Chicago: University of Chicago.

Goodman, G. S. (Ed.). (1984). The child witness. *Journal of Social Issues, 40,* 1–175.

Gove, W. R. (1976). Adult sex roles and mental illness. In F. Denmark & R. Wesner (Eds.), *Women* (Vol. 1). New York: Psychological Dimensions.

Graziano, A. M. (1977). Parents as behavior therapists. *Progress in Behavior Modification, 4,* 251–298.

Green, B. L., Grace, M. C., Crespo da Silva, L., & Gleser, G. C. (1983). Using the Psychiatric Evaluation Form to quantify children's interview data. *Journal of Consulting and Clinical Psychology, 51,* 353–359.

Guttentag, M., Salasin, S., Legge, W. W., Bray, M., Dewhirst, J., Goldman, N., Phegley, T., & Weiss, S. (1974). *Sex differences in the utilization of publicly supported mental health facilities: The puzzle of depression* (Final Report, MH26523-02). Collaborative Grant, Mental Health Services Branch. Washington, DC: National Institute of Mental Health.

Guttentag, M., & Secord, P. F. (1983). *Too many women? The sex ratio question.* Beverly Hills: Sage.

Harrington, M. (1984). *The new American poverty.* New York: Holt, Rinehart & Winston.

Hasenfeld, Y., & English, R. A. (1974). *Human services organizations.* Ann Arbor: University of Michigan Press.

Hastrup, J. (1974). *Issues and methods in training clients for therapy.* Unpublished doctoral qualifying paper, Department of Psychology, SUNY at Buffalo.

Health: United States, 1975. (1976). (DHEW Publication No. [HRA] 76-1232.) Washington, DC: Department of Health, Education and Welfare.

Herskovitz, H. H., Spivack, G., & Levine, M. (1959). Anti-social behavior of adolescents from higher socioeconomic groups. *Journal of Nervous and Mental Disease, 129,* 467–476.

Hicks, M. W., & Platt, M. (1971). Marital happiness and stability: A review of the research in the sixties. In C. Broderick (Ed.), *A decade of family research and action.* Minneapolis: National Council on Family Relations.

Hollingshead, A. B., & Redlich, F. C. (1958). *Social class and mental illness.* New York: Wiley.

Holmes, T. H., & Rahe, R. H. (1967). The social readjustment rating scale. *Journal of Psychosomatic Research, 11,* 213–218.

Hoskins, D., & Bixby, L. E. (1973). *Women and Social Security: Law and policy in five countries*

(Research Report No. 42. DHEW Publication No. (SSA) 73-11800). Washington, DC: DHEW, SSA, Office of Research and Statistics.

Joy, A. (1972). *Deviant behavior in school children.* Unpublished doctoral qualifying paper, Department of Psychology, SUNY at Buffalo.

Kadushin, A. (1980). *Child welfare services* (3d ed.). New York: Macmillan.

Kendall, P. C., & Norton-Ford, J. D. (1982). Therapy outcome research methods. In P. C. Kendall & J. N. Butcher (Eds.), *Handbook of research methods in clinical psychology.* New York: Wiley.

Kiesler, C. A. (1982). Public and professional myths about mental hospitalization: An empirical reassessment of policy-related beliefs. *American Psychologist, 37,* 1323–1339.

Kilpatrick, D. G., Best, C. L., Veronen, L. J., Amick, A. E., Velleponteaux, L. A., & Ruff, G. A. (1985). Mental health correlates of criminal victimization: A random community survey. *Journal of Consulting and Clinical Psychology, 53,* 866–873.

Kropotkin, P. (1972). *Mutual aid.* New York: New York University Press. (Original work published 1902.)

Levine, A. G. (1977a). Women at work in America: History, status and prospects. In H. Kaplan (Ed.), *American minorities and economic opportunity.* Itasca, IL: Peacock.

Levine, A. G. (1977b). Growing (and reading) can be painful [Review of G. Sheehy, *Passages: Predictable crises of adult life*]. *Contemporary Psychology, 22,* 284–285.

Levine, A. G. (1982) *Love Canal: Science, politics, people.* Lexington, MA: Lexington Books.

Levine, M. (1966). Residential change and school adjustment. *Community Mental Health Journal, 2,* 61–69.

Levine, M., & Levine, A. (1970). *A social history of helping services.* New York: Appleton-Century-Crofts.

Levine, M., & Levine, A. (1971). Social change and psychopathology: Some derivations from *Civilization and its discontents.* In D. Milman & G. Goldman (Eds.), *Psychoanalytic contributions to community psychology.* Springfield, IL: Charles C Thomas.

Luepnitz, D. A. (1978). Children of divorce: A review of the psychological literature. *Law and Human Behavior, 2,* 167–179.

Luepnitz, D. A. (1982). *Child custody. A study of families after divorce.* Lexington, MA: Lexington Books.

Meltzoff, J., & Kornreich, M. (1970). *Research in psychotherapy.* New York: Atherton.

Miller, K. S. (1976). *Managing madness: The case against civil commitment.* New York: Free Press.

Mnookin, R. H. (1973). Foster care—In whose best interests? *Harvard Educational Review, 43,* 599–638.

Myers, J. K., Weissman, M. M., Tischler, G. L., Holzer, C. E. III, Leaf, P. J., Orvaschel, H., Anthony, J. C., Boyd, J. H., Burke, J. D. Jr., Kramer, M., & Stoltzman, R. (1984). Six-month prevalence of psychiatric disorders in three communities: 1980–1982. *Archives of General Psychiatry, 41,* 959–67.

Namir, S., & Weinstein, R. S. (1982). Children: Facilitating new directions. In L. R. Snowden (Ed.), *Reaching the underserved: Mental health needs of neglected populations.* Beverly Hills: Sage.

National Academy of Sciences. (1984). *Bereavement: Reactions, consequences, and care.* Washington, DC: National Academy Press.

National Center for Health Statistics. (1979). *Vital statistics of the United States, 1979. Volume II—Mortality.* Washington, DC: U.S. Department of Health and Human Services.

National Center for Health Statistics. (1984, September 21). Annual summary of births, deaths, marriages and divorces, United States, 1983. *NCHS Monthly Vital Statistics Report, 32.*

National Health Education Committee. (1976). *The killers and cripplers: Facts on our major diseases in the United States today.* New York: McKay.

National Health Survey. (1972). *Behavior patterns of children in school* (DHEW Publication No.

(HSM) 72-1042). Rockville, MD: Public Health Service and Mental Health Administration, National Center for Health Statistics.

National Institute of Mental Health. (1974). *Staffing of mental health facilities, United States, 1974* (Series B, No. 8). Rockville, MD: Alcohol, Drug Abuse, and Mental Health Administration.

Office of Technology Assessment. (1983a). *The effectiveness and costs of alcoholism treatment.* Washington, DC: U.S. Congress.

Office of Technology Assessment. (1983b). *Technologies and management strategies for hazardous waste control.* Washington, DC: U.S. Congress.

Parry, H. J., Balter, M. B., Mellinger, G. D., Cisin, I. H., & Manheimer, D. I. (1973). National patterns of psychotherapeutic drug use. *Archives of General Psychiatry, 28,* 769–783.

Perrow, C. (1984). *Normal accidents. Living with high-risk technologies.* New York: Basic Books.

Pettis, K. W., & Hughes, R. D. (1985, February). Sexual victimization of children: A current perspective. *Behavioral Disorders,* 136–144.

Rabkin, J. G., & Streuning, E. L. (1976). Life events, stress and illness. *Science, 194,* 1013–1020.

Redick, R. W., & Witkin, M. J. (1984, September). State and county mental hospitals, United States, 1980–81 and 1981–82. *Mental Health Statistical Note, No. 166.* Washington, DC: NIMH Division of Biometry and Epidemiology, Survey and Reports Branch.

Reich, C. A. (1970). *The greening of America.* New York: Random House.

Riger, S. (1985). Crime as an environmental stressor. *Journal of Community Psychology, 13,* 270–280.

Rosenhan, D. L. (1973). On being sane in insane places. *Science, 179,* 250–258.

Rossman, M. (1976). Self-help marketplace. *Social Policy, 7,* 86–91.

Roszak, R. (1969). *The making of a counterculture.* Garden City, NY: Doubleday.

Ryan, W. (1969). *Distress in the city.* Cleveland: Press of Case Western Reserve University.

Sarason, S. B. (1974). *The psychological sense of community.* San Francisco: Jossey-Bass.

Sarason, S. B. (1976). Community psychology and the anarchist insight. *American Journal of Community Psychology, 4,* 243–261.

Scheff, T. J. (1966). *Being mentally ill.* Chicago: Aldine.

Schwebel, M., & Schwebel, B. (1981). Children's reactions to the threat of nuclear plant accidents. *American Journal of Orthopsychiatry, 51,* 260–270.

Sheehy, G. (1976). *Passages: Predictable crises of adult life.* New York: Dutton.

Shapiro, S., Skinner, E. A., Kessler, L. G., Von Korff, M., German, P. S., Tischler, G. L., Leaf, P. J., Benham, L., Cottler, L., & Regier, D. A. (1984). Utilization of health and mental health services. *Archives of General Psychiatry, 41,* 971–978.

Slater, P. (1970). *The pursuit of loneliness.* Boston: Beacon Press.

Smith, M. L., & Glass, G. V. (1977). Meta-analysis of psychotherapy outcome studies. *American Psychologist, 32,* 752–760.

Snowden, L. R. (Ed.) (1982). *Reaching the underserved. Mental health needs of neglected populations.* Beverly Hills: Sage.

The Spokeswoman. (1977, August 15). *8,* No. 2.

Task Panel on Mental Health Personnel. (1978). *Report of the Task Panel on Mental Health Personnel, Submitted to the President's Commission on Mental Health.* Vol. II, Appendix. Washington, DC: U.S. Government Printing Office.

Taube, C. A., Burns, B. J., & Kessler, L. (1984). Patients of psychiatrists and psychologists in office-based practice: 1980. *American Psychologist, 39,* 1435–1447.

Taube, C. A., & Witkin, M. J. (1976). *Staff-patient ratios in selected mental health facilities, January 1974* (Mental Health Statistical Note No. 129. DHEW Publication No. (ADM) 76-158). Rockville, MD: Alcohol, Drug Abuse, and Mental Health Administration.

U.S. Bureau of the Census. (1976). *Statistical abstract of the United States, 1976* (97th ed.). Washington, DC: U.S. Department of Commerce.

U.S. Bureau of the Census. (1979). *Social indicators. Selected data on social conditions and trends in the United States.* Washington, DC: U.S. Department of Commerce.

U.S. Bureau of the Census. (1980). *Detailed population characteristics. United States Summary. Section A: United States.* Washington, DC: U.S. Department of Commerce.

U.S. Department of the Census. (1981). *Statistical abstract of the United States, 1981* (102d ed.). Washington, DC: U.S. Department of Commerce.

U.S. Department of Justice Statistics Bulletin. (1985). *The crime of rape.* Washington, DC: U.S. Department of Justice.

U.S. Public Health Service. (1982). *Health. United States.* Washington, DC: U.S. Department of Health and Human Services.

U.S. Public Health Service. (1983). *Health and prevention profile. United States.* Washington, DC: U.S. Department of Health and Human Services.

Veroff, J., Kulka, R. A., & Douvan, E. (1981). *Mental health in America. Patterns of help-seeking from 1957–1976.* New York: Basic Books.

Warburton, D., & Fraser, C. (1964). Spontaneous abortion risks in man: Data from reproductive histories collected in a medical genetics unit. *Journal of Human Genetics, 16,* 1–25.

Wilensky, H. L., & Lebeaux, C. N. (1965). *Industrial society and social welfare.* New York: Free Press.

Zahner, G. E. P., Kasl, S. V., White, M., & Will, J. C. (1985). Psychological consequences of infestation of the dwelling unit. *American Journal of Public Health, 75,* 1303–1307.

Zax, M., & Specter, G. A. (1974). *An introduction to community psychology.* New York: Wiley.

Zusman, J., & Simon, J. (1983). Differences in repeated psychiatric examinations of litigants to a lawsuit. *American Journal of Psychiatry, 140,* 1300–1304.

2

The Social and Historical Context
of Community Psychology

Community psychology is best understood as an ideological perspective as well as a branch of scientific psychology. Viewed only as a scientific subdiscipline, community psychology's historical and ideological aspects are easy to overlook, yet an essential characteristic of this field is the fact that it arose at a particular time and place. Its past was prologue for the kind of psychology and mental health practiced today. Reviewing the social and historical context of community psychology also prepares us for the extended discussions of ecology, social labeling, stress, and prevention in the chapters that follow. The present chapter examines the recent social and historical context of community psychology and the important place of community concepts in contemporary mental health practice. We conclude the chapter by returning to the scientific question in terms of a formal model for theory and research in community psychology. This model articulates similarities and differences between the clinical and community perspectives and thus provides a "road map" of the community approach leading to important conceptual issues developed in later chapters of the book.

The Climate of Change Preceding Community Psychology

Community psychology and community mental health emerged in the mid-1960s during a period of great ferment not only in the mental health fields but also in society at large. The successful civil rights movement of the 1950s and 1960s (Brooks, 1974), having begun with the profound stimulus to social change provided by the Supreme Court's desegregation decision in *Brown v. Board of Education,* 347 U.S. 483 (1954), became a model for others to use in attacking social inequities in many areas of society. The Kennedy–Johnson War on Poverty (Levitan, 1969; Levitan & Taggart, 1976; Mann, 1978; Klein, 1981) stimulated assaults on a wide variety of social problems, including poverty, crime, delinquency, unemployment, poor education, mental retardation, welfare inequities, and troubles in prisons. New kinds of questions regarding social problems and their solutions, such as those posed in Chapter 1, were being raised. Social change was so rapid and far-reaching that the limits of the social science concepts used to understand change were reached, making it difficult for science to keep up with the conditions it was studying.

In the field of mental health, a real impetus to the community approach was John F. Kennedy's address to Congress in 1963, in which he announced a bold new approach to the care of the mentally ill.[1] This approach advocated the reintegration of mental patients into the community; it also called for the prevention of personal waste and misery and the promotion of positive mental health.

Kennedy's radical approach to mental health policy emerged as a consequence of post-World War II developments. Military psychiatry had demonstrated that with early treatment, provided by psychologists, nurses, and nonprofessional personnel, it was possible to restore a great many individuals to full duty. Community-based care in the new mental health centers was modeled conceptually after methods and approaches developed in the military. For example, mental health needs were seen to include "normal" distress in reaction to "abnormal" situations (i.e., as in combat). Also, the idea that help should be located strategically to the stressful situation and provided as quickly as possible was a forerunner to the popular current notion of social support (Mangellsdorf, 1985). Furthermore, the military's success with crisis-oriented methods of intervention sharply challenged the hopeless attitude toward mental illness that had prevailed in the prewar years.

The extensive prevalence of mental-health-related problems recognized today (see Chapter 1) was first brought to public attention by the war. A distressingly high proportion of the men called up for service were rejected for neuropsychiatric reasons, and neuropsychiatric conditions ranked high among medical reasons for discharge from service. Because mental illness was a prominent public health issue and because the government's partnership with science had been successful during World War II, postwar federal policy supported the development of a research capability in mental health. In addition, the disastrous condition of state mental hospitals, the mainstay of our system of care, came to light after the war and produced a call for reform. The National Institute of Mental Health thus came into being in 1946 to develop a research capability and to produce trained clinical personnel in all of the mental health professions. Psychoactive drugs came into use in the mid-1950s and led to the view that many patients could be maintained outside of hospitals. If patients were to be maintained outside of hospitals, community-based services were necessary.

The need for mental health services was evaluated by the Joint Commission on Mental Health and Mental Illness, a commission appointed by Congress to study this problem and develop a comprehensive mental health plan. The joint commission reported in 1960, just as Kennedy took office.[2] Among other things, the joint commission emphasized that current patterns of care could provide for only a tiny fraction of those in need of help for mental and emotional problems. This report was the stimulus for Kennedy's 1963 address to Congress and for passage of the Community Mental Health Centers Act that year. The Swampscott Conference on Community Psychology (Bennett et al., 1966) gave formal recognition to the emergence of a new field of psychology, as did other volumes trying to define the new field and specify appropriate training for it (Iscoe & Spielberger, 1970). Similar views were expressed in all of the helping professions (see Bindman & Spiegel, 1969).

The community mental health thrust was based on more than optimism that a new approach would help. Change of this magnitude usually reflects both hope and frustration (see Chapter 10), and alongside hope for the new approach was considerable frustration with the status quo. Critics of mental hospitals asserted that such institutions created more problems than they solved (see Goffman, 1961). Aftercare facilities for adults released from mental hospitals were almost nonexistent, and institutions for the care of the retarded were in scandalous condition (Blatt & Kaplan, 1966).

Szasz (1961) went so far as to attack the very concept of "mental illness," calling it a myth. He urged that we attend to the moral, legal, and social norms that produce our definitions of abnormal behavior, and to what kind of person becomes a patient. His argument directed attention less to the patient and the patient's condition and more to the social conditions under which illness and patienthood were defined. Epidemiological studies had consistently shown an inverse relationship between social status and psychological disorder (Dohrenwend & Dohrenwend, 1969). Srole et al. (1962) and Leighton et al. (1963) showed not only that emotional problems are more frequent and more severe in low-income populations, but also that such problems occur in areas noted for social disorganization. Surveys of children's problems revealed much the same situation (White & Harris, 1961). Knobloch and Pasamanick (1961) argued that low-income populations show higher rates of prematurity, problems associated with low birth weight, probable brain damage, and a variety of childhood disturbances including behavior disorders and learning problems. The Coleman (1966) report confirmed on a national level that low-income children and adolescents had educational deficits that presaged a disastrous social and economic adjustment for many of them. Moynihan (1965) pointed to a state of disorganization in lower-class black families that he believed would perpetuate social and psychological problems.[3] Considered as a whole, these data pointed to the need for social reform as well as better mental health care.

Hollingshead and Redlich (1958) showed that the existing system of service delivery provided one kind of care for middle- and upper-class individuals and another kind for lower-class patients. Middle- and upper-class patients more often received less severe diagnoses and were treated with outpatient therapy. Lower-class patients more often were treated in a public system using inpatient custodial care, shock treatment, and lobotomies.

To this criticism of the service-delivery system were added questions concerning the effectiveness of the services being offered. Eysenck (1952, 1961) led the attack by marshaling evidence challenging psychotherapists to show that their efforts produced more change than did no help at all, or no special help over an equal length of time. Others summarized similar evidence for psychotherapy with children and issued similar challenges to the profession (Levitt, 1957; Levitt, Beiser, & Robertson, 1959). Studies showed significant rates of dropout from treatment (Tuckman & Lavell, 1959; Furman, 1965; Reiss & Brandt, 1965), suggesting that a great deal of therapeutic and diagnostic time was wasted.[4] The psychologist's testing function also came under attack. Meehl (1954, 1960) argued that clinicians' predictive validity was no better, and in many instances was much poorer, than simple regression equations based on standard mechanical psychometric research. Moreover, he pointed out that the diagnostic appraisal rarely influenced a therapist's specific approach to treatment. Research also accumulated attacking the validity of tests themselves (Rickers-Ovsiankina, 1960; Murstein, 1963; Zubin, Eron, & Schumer, 1965; Levine, 1966).

In addition to criticism regarding service delivery and the adequacy and relevance of the services provided, problems arose as a consequence of new sociological thinking that characterized mental illness as social deviance, and mental health facilities as agencies of deviance control (these concepts are examined in detail in Chapter 5).

Critics asserted that the mental health professions in general, and psychiatry in particular, contributed to the incidence of mental health problems by confirming and helping to enforce existing social norms. Some critics claimed that by defining mental illness in isolation from social conditions, the profession distracted attention from social issues that were at the root of abnormal behavior in the first place. Less radical thinkers suggested that at the very least it was necessary for the mental health professions to work more closely with the people staffing community agencies—schools, courts, welfare departments, churches, police departments—to encourage handling of problems through means other than referral to formal mental health agencies, and perhaps through new programs using different personnel.

Kennedy's new approach to mental health practice not only involved the reintegration of recovered mental patients into the community; it also called for the *prevention* of mental, emotional, and behavioral disorder and the promotion of positive mental health. Positive mental health meant more than the absence of symptoms; it included the state of well-being that enables an individual to pursue personal fulfillment. These are bold and broad objectives for community mental health programs. Once the field targets positive mental health as a goal, the mental health professional necessarily studies and attempts to influence those major institutions of society that contribute to the creation, perpetuation, or exacerbation of personal waste and misery. In a sense, all of the soap opera that is life becomes the mental health professional's concern. He or she retains an interest in the distressed individual, but as a helper the professional now wishes to influence families, schools, social agencies, courts, industrial organizations, and perhaps even the overall economic order. The role model changes from that of physician and healer to that of educator, social critic, reformer, and social planner. The expansion in the scope of problems defined as mental health issues and the advocation of social intervention by mental health workers were viewed by some articulate critics as a dangerous professional imperialism (Dunham, 1965).

The War on Poverty, which began in the early 1960s, spewed forth a great variety of programs designed to ameliorate problems of the poor. In addition to direct services, training, education, and assistance with housing and welfare, the community action programs under the Office of Economic Opportunity were designed to influence existing service systems and existing social institutions (e.g., welfare, medical care, schools, clinics, employment services, police, housing authorities) to improve services to the poorer population (Levitan, 1969; Moynihan, 1969; Plotnick & Skidmore, 1975).

The War on Poverty had as a goal social change as well as the provision of direct assistance to the poor. It mandated the "maximum feasible participation" of those to be served by the programs, an idea that was translated into the concept of community control, which in turn led to a great deal of conflict in many places (Moynihan, 1969; Kellam, Branch, Agrawal, & Grabill, 1972; Zax & Specter, 1974). Community control became an ideology and came to symbolize much more than making programs relevant to the people in the neighborhoods served.

The concept of community control had important economic implications. For example, it meant the paid employment of people indigenous to the neighborhoods being served. This strategy was justified on the grounds that white middle-class professionals had little ability to understand those living in poverty. Community control was also offered as a strategy to meet the labor shortage in the human services and to create permanent jobs for those who would otherwise not enter the middle class (Pearl

& Reissman, 1965). The use of paraprofessionals proliferated in many service agencies (Sobey, 1970; Alley & Blanton, 1978), and evidence began to accumulate on the effectiveness of programs employing paraprofessionals (Alley, Blanton, Feldman, Hunter, & Rolfson, 1979).

The climate of change encouraged experimentation with different approaches to providing service in an effort to reach populations that were underserved, poorly served, or did not voluntarily use the existing service system. Some mental health professionals became involved not only in the new community mental health center programs, but also in alternative service settings (e.g., Sarason, Levine, et al. 1966). Given attacks on the validity of conventional professional practice, the reform-minded rhetoric of the time, and the accumulating evidence that alternative personnel and alternative services were viable, a great variety of programs emerged, some more conventional than others. Some programs developed with the assistance of mental health professionals, while many developed without such assistance.

Both mental health professionals and other activists, taking as their model the successful civil rights movement of the 1950s and 1960s, adopted similar ideologies, rhetoric, and strategies to achieve social and economic change. Their goals were not limited to material gains; they included rejecting the socially imposed view of one's self as a deservedly despised deviant. Activists and the social groups they created provided socially shared bases for maintaining self-esteem and encouraging social action to change one's situation (Ryan, 1971; Goldenberg, 1978). Activism in the social arena paralleled and was intertwined with the culturally profound antiwar movement and the sexual revolution, both of which entailed distrust of constituted authority and tradition (Roszak, 1969; Reich, 1970; Slater, 1970). Because many programs and interventions were directed toward relieving psychological misery and enhancing self-esteem, some mental health professionals came to believe that almost any social action and almost any intervention could be legitimately viewed as falling within the province of mental health. Empowering the powerless was worthwhile in and of itself in the quest for a more perfect democracy through the attainment of political, social, and economic equality (e.g., Cloward & Piven, 1971). It could also be justified as treatment for, and prevention of, a range of mental health problems which some observers understood to be direct consequences of psychological apathy and helplessness (Rappaport, 1977).

The great expansion in programs and activities during this time was confusing. Community psychology seemed to cover everything from "showing Szondi plates to ghetto residents in an inner-city storefront, to engineering new communities" (Cowen, 1973, p. 423). Ideologically as well as scientifically driven, the new thrust seemed to shoot off in all directions at once, with little coherence in its activities and little conceptual clarity. Critics committed to traditional practice under the medical model of person-centered illness looked askance at the social activism of the new movement. Those committed to the viewpoint elsewhere termed "intrapsychic supremacy" (Levine, 1969)—that problems in living depend on people's internal psychological structures, which in turn dictate perceptions, feelings, and actions in everyday situations—viewed the activists as misguided romantics who had foolishly strayed from proper professional roles and activities. Community-oriented critics of traditional practice were equally firm in their convictions, but had little to offer by way of alternate theoretical conceptualizations.[5] Levine (1973) justified novel activity on the basis of necessity, calling for a "responsible chutzpah," that is, doing the best one could even though the scientific base supporting novel activity was rather thin.

For the most part, the new thrust developed along highly pragmatic lines. For example, Emory Cowen, an early proponent of prevention programs and a practitioner skilled at delivering alternative services in the schools, operated in terms of what worked. His efforts were directed less by theory than by seat-of-the-pants experience, judged against research as thorough as circumstances would allow (Cowen, Trost, Izzo, Lorion, Dorr, & Isaacson, 1975). Seymour Sarason, a leader in the movement toward acting on the basis of "responsible chutzpah" (Sarason, Levine, et al., 1966; Sarason, 1982), was well aware of the theoretical and empirical problems facing psychologists. He understood the limits he was facing in his own experience and thinking in exploring new ground. Sarason asserted that psychology and other social sciences were not prepared to offer much to policymakers (Sarason, 1981), a position that would have been well received by Moynihan (1969). Moynihan attributed losses in the War on Poverty to the innocence of social scientists whose theories were too simple to encompass the complexity of social action, and who sent brave programs into the wild blue yonder, naively unaware that many would be shot down by the flak of politics, limited resources, and cultural impatience with the pace and nature of change.

A case in point is the Welfare Rights Organization. Welfare workers were initially successful in pushing for changes in the system by urging clients to apply for all possible benefits, thus driving up costs to intolerable levels. Workers hoped that this tactic would promote reform of the welfare system. The movement was soon defeated, however, by the simple expedient of changing the rules the workers had used to bedevil the system (Cloward & Piven, 1971). Once the organization was no longer able to provide immediate concrete benefits for its members, its power to organize and to sustain its efforts diminished sharply. We may fairly say that the failure was at least in part attributable to the then-prevalent romanticized notion of social change, to an inadequate appreciation of cultural and social problems in organizing the poor, and to misapprehension of the nature of power in society.

The limited accomplishments of the welfare rights movement and other interventions should give us pause for thought, not about the motives or intelligence of their designers but about the limits of the theoretical propositions with which we work. Sarason (1981) is instructive because he discussed more than the problems encountered in the attempt to be "relevant." He argues for adopting a viewpoint that goes beyond the person-centered psychology dominant in our definitions of social and psychological problems. The universe of alternatives in which problems are defined and solutions are proposed can be severely limited by the cultural-theoretical blinders imposed by the narrow disciplinary perspectives from which we view and define problems.[6]

Sarason went further in arguing that among the relevant variables is the social scientist's place and stake in the world. Gouldner (1968) made a similar point about the role of sociologists as partisans in a welfare state. In addition to understanding a problem as it exists "out there," we must include in our thinking the particular perspective from which the social scientist is defining the problem, from which solutions are proposed, and from which the values guiding action are derived.

Sarason (1978) does not claim that answers will come from better science alone.

He argues that the nature of problem solving in social action is different from that in the physical sciences. Because social problems may be deeply rooted in the human condition, they may be intractable and will not yield to once-and-for-all solutions. Sarason writes:

> There will be no final solutions, only a constantly upsetting imbalance between values and action; the internal conflict will not be in the form of "Do I have the right answer?" but rather of "Am I being consistent with what I believe?"; satisfaction will come not from colleagues' consensus that your procedures, facts, and conclusions are independent of your feelings and values, but from your own conviction that you tried to be true to your values. (p. 379)

Our experiences have led us to understand that we need to develop theoretical perspectives and concepts that take us beyond individual psychology and that allow us to go beyond the limits imposed by psychology's reliance on experimental methods. Our excursions into the community have opened our minds to new possibilities and pointed us in directions that may provide new insights into the human condition and the ability of the social sciences to illuminate that condition. Out of the chaos that Cowen (1973) describes, we see another direction. As Gergen (1982) points out in his review of Sarason's *Psychology Misdirected,* "the grounding rationale for the new psychology, the character and function of inquiry and its relationship to the social order, remain as provoking challenges" (p. 361). At least we are now thinking of such issues, and that is helpful in and of itself. We are now more aware than ever that we are inevitably dealing with matters of value and that action is inevitably intertwined with value considerations.

To summarize, community psychology emerged during a period of change in many institutions of society. The field had a name, and to some extent an ideology, but it was unclear what community psychology encompassed, what its methods were, what its goals were, or what its scientific theories were. Because one could justify so many diverse activities in the name of "community mental health," this concept appeared to have little real meaning and led to much soul-searching (Iscoe, Bloom, & Spielberger, 1977). A rough division emerged between rehabilitative and restorative efforts on the one hand and preventive-prophylactic efforts on the other (Cowen, 1973), a distinction others have called community mental health and community psychology, respectively (Rappaport, 1977).

Although some programs failed, and others have yet to demonstrate fully their effectiveness, the community movement has had profound effects on the field of mental health and on our thinking about psychological issues. In fact, in our opinion maintaining a sense of uniqueness is a contemporary problem for community psychology. So many of its general concepts and programs have been taken over in clinical settings that the community perspective can no longer claim novelty and innovation. In many areas of programming the community perspective has become the conventional wisdom! Furthermore, if indeed the past is prologue for what is to come, as we suggested in introducing this chapter, then today's conventional wisdom provides the historical context for the next generation of perspectives and practices in psychology and mental health. The question of community psychology's scientific foundations is important, and we return to it in the final section of this chapter. Before examining those issues, however, let us survey briefly the contemporary situation in community mental health.

Current Issues in Community Mental Health

The community movement of the past two decades has had a far-reaching impact on mental health services, going well beyond the establishment of some 750 federally funded community mental health centers (about half the number originally envisioned for the program) under the 1963 Community Mental Health Centers Act. In addition to these new centers, the emphasis on treatment in the community has led to noticeable changes in the mix of services available. A greater variety of services and of service deliverers also reflects the community thrust. In this section we discuss several aspects of current mental health practice, including the recent deinstitutionalization movement, the range of community alternatives to inpatient care now available, the situation with respect to mental health services for minority groups and other traditionally underserved populations, and the recent history of mental health services for children.

Deinstitutionalization

Since the 1950s the decline in the patient population in state and county mental hospitals has been drastic. The inpatient census of these institutions has been reduced from nearly 600,000 to about 200,000 today. Over the same period the population residing in institutions for the retarded has also declined, although less steeply, from over 200,000 to approximately 150,000. These reductions in institutional populations fulfilled one goal of the community mental health centers program—to halve the institutional population within 10 years of the program's inception. The decline is only partly attributable to treatment philosophy, however. It also reflects changes in funding and reimbursement practices and changes in law that make it more difficult to hospitalize involuntarily or to retain persons in the hospital involuntarily (Levine, 1981).

Benefits attributed to the deinstitutionalization movement must be weighed against the increased numbers of older persons in nursing homes and the problems of providing adequate community-based services for the chronically mentally ill (see Lamb, 1984). Providing such services is an important challenge today (President's Commission on Mental Health, 1978; Shinn & Felton, 1981), and not all commentators hold a benign view of the deinstitutionalization movement (see Scull, 1977). Early in the deinstitutionalization process, patients were discharged from hospitals to single-room-occupancy hotels or to board-and-care homes. The level of care in many of these facilities was exceedingly poor. Elderly patients were simply discharged to nursing homes where, in too many instances, the care provided was scandalous. The scandals may have resulted in greater regulation of the facilities, and conditions may have improved somewhat in recent years, but we would not be overly surprised if newspaper headlines exposed continuing patient-care scandals in these facilities. Segal and Baumohl (1982) and Bachrach (1984) argue further that deinstitutionalization policy has created a new underserved population of vulnerable individuals, who are younger than formerly, disinclined to use the formal mental health system, resist the appellation of "mental patient," and use drugs and alcohol to the point of complicating their social statuses and conditions.

The state hospital provided a full array of services from cradle to grave. The community mental health system cannot readily supply the same range of services. Moreover, without involuntary commitment, the community-based system depends on voluntary participation by prospective clients, although in some states it is possible to commit patients to outpatient care and perhaps to alternative treatment facilities such as day care or halfway houses (Peele, Gross, Aronse, & Jafri, 1984). Many former patients, for whatever reasons, do not use the formal system of care. The large number of homeless street people reflects the rate of unemployment as well as the conversion of former low-rent properties to high-rent properties. Not all of the homeless are former mental patients, but a great many are, and they represent visible signs of the problems in deinstitutionalization policy (Bachrach, 1984). The slogan "problem creation through problem solution" is apt in this context. Positive effects of deinstitutionalization have been noted (Beiser et al., 1985), and studies uniformly report that patients feel more satisfied in community settings than in the hospital. The overall consequences of deinstitutionalization pose new challenges to the service system, however (Lamb, 1984; Thompson, 1985).

Since 1963 the proportion of inpatient-care episodes to outpatient episodes has changed drastically. Twenty years ago, 75% of all patient-care episodes took place in state and county mental hospitals. Today, only 25% take place there. Kiesler (1982) notes that the figures may be deceptive, for they do not account for episodes in general hospitals, both with and without psychiatric units. Taking these into account and keeping in mind that a large number of people with diagnosable disorders are in nursing homes, the estimate of the number of inpatient-care episodes doubles. The shift in proportion of inpatient to outpatient care is still there, but it is not as sharp. These figures show that the locus of much inpatient care has shifted from the isolated mental hospital to new sites such as community-based hospitals and nursing homes. One might question whether resources in mental health have been adequately reallocated to take into account the shift in locus of patient care, especially for community-based services designed to avoid hospitalization. Funds for inpatient care in state and county mental hospitals still absorb the lion's share of state mental health budgets (Goldsmith, 1984).

Kiesler (1982) reports that the length of stay in mental hospitals has decreased drastically in comparison with 30 or even 15 years ago. He reports a mean length of stay for state and county mental hospitals of 421 days in 1969 and 189 days in 1978. The mean length of stay for psychiatric conditions in general hospitals is only 8 days. Some argue that these shorter stays have produced a "revolving-door" phenomenon in which patients are in, out, and then in again. Kiesler believes the revolving-door hypothesis is reasonable given that a high proportion of all those hospitalized had previous histories of hospitalization. Kiesler concludes that the data are not yet sufficient to support fully the revolving-door thesis.

A shortened mean length of stay reflects the community thrust of dealing with episodes of distress by restoring the person's equilibrium as rapidly as possible and then returning him or her to the community. It may also reflect legal problems in holding those who are not dangerous to themselves or others (Levine, 1981). Although mean-length-of-stay data are important in understanding the financial costs of care, standing alone they do not tell us much about the meaning of short stays to patients and their families. If patients improve as much in short stays as they do in longer ones, shorter stays have benefits for the patient and for society. If patients do not improve sufficiently to allow resumption of relatively peaceful and independent living, however, short stays may not be greeted with much enthusiasm, especially by families who felt relieved when hospitalization lifted a burden from their shoulders. One implication of short hospital stays is the necessity for aftercare and for prepared environments, whether the patient returns to the family or to some community residence. Once again, a reallocation and reorientation of mental health resources is required to keep up with the changes in practice. The trend toward privatization of the health care system may have important effects on mental health care in the future. Panzella (1985) suggests that as private, for-profit corporations expand in the mental health field, community mental health centers may accommodate the needs of the poor and the chronically mentally ill, while the private institutions, in an effort to be cost effective and profitable, an effort fostered by third-party payers, will adopt community mental health practices for their middle-class clientele. These trends are important and deserve careful scrutiny.

Community Alternatives to Hospitalization

We have seen a substantial increase in the number of group homes and other alternative community living facilities for former mental patients, the retarded, and other populations such as delinquent or neglected youth who in the past might have been sent to large, isolated institutions. We have also seen an increase in congregate living facilities for the elderly. New organizations now provide social, medical, and recreational services for the elderly. In-home care plans, in which services are delivered to the elderly person's home in an effort to avoid institutionalization, have also developed (see generally Shinn & Felton, 1981). In noting the increase in alternative care programs, we must also state that we know very little about how extensive they are, which segments of the population they serve, and how effective they are in serving those groups. The many examples of new services provide conceptual and research challenges to the mental health community. Are they fads, or is there substance to these programs? Are they therapeutically effective, or simply designed to save money at the expense of the recipients of care and their families? Are there as yet unrecognized and unanticipated effects of these new programs, and if so, what are they? Can we learn to measure humane values in care as well as such outcomes as rehospitalization or employment?

Kiesler (1982) reviewed a number of studies with reasonably good methodologies comparing alternatives such as day hospitalization, or the delivery of crisis services, with hospitalization for mental illness. "Alternative care always is as good [as] or better than hospitalization regarding outcomes, and almost always is less expensive" (p. 1327). That conclusion holds for services provided within the formal system of mental health care and for those who would have been hospitalized. It cannot be generalized to cover all alternative services for all populations.

Alternative services operating outside the formal mental health care system have increased in number. Many cities now have shelters for battered women and homes for runaway youths. There are treatment and residential facilities for persons with substance-abuse problems, peer counseling programs, street-work projects, and healing and birthing centers. Often such facilities are staffed not by mental health professionals but by persons who themselves have suffered with the problem or who have a personal aptitude for the work instead of professional credentials. The staffs of alternative facilities believe they offer different services than do traditional mental health services and serve clients who would not use traditional services (Gordon, 1978).

Abortion clinics grew rapidly after *Roe v. Wade,* 410 U.S. 113 (1973), and many of them offered counseling along with abortion services. Antiabortion groups do not just protest abortion clinics and abortion laws. Some offer counseling and assistance either in placing infants for adoption or in keeping them. Rape counseling programs have also developed, as have victim assistance programs. Community action programs, originally established during the War on Poverty, still exist and provide a variety of neighborhood services, including counseling, training, advocacy for clients, and referral to other agencies.

Suicide prevention services developed during the 1960s and grew rapidly. Many expanded from their initial missions of suicide prevention to provide broadly defined crisis services. Many crisis services use volunteers who are trained to staff telephone "hotlines" (McGee, 1974). Now other specialized services offer such hotlines as well. This concept of anonymous services, readily available whenever the person feels the need, represents a different orientation from that reflected in weekly 50-minute appointments at a service provider's office.

In some places church-affiliated or lay counseling centers developed. Volunteers were trained in counseling methods and supervised by professionals. Volunteers (NIMH, 1970), along with the paraprofessionals found widely in many mental health centers (Sobey, 1970), expanded the base of personnel available to deliver services. Self-help groups also proliferated (see Chapters 8 and 9), in part because professional services did not, in the view of members, provide adequately for their needs, and also because of the general recognition that professional training is not the sine qua non for the delivery of psychotherapeutically effective care. This proposition became identified with the community movement.

We emphasize that the knowledge we have of these alternative services is usually based on small-scale studies of programs whose representativeness is unknown, and that these studies are rarely followed up. We know little about who uses the services or who drops out after having made some contact. These are questions that remain for research if we are to understand which needs the proliferation of community-based alternatives is actually serving.

Providers of outpatient psychotherapy services have also proliferated. Klerman (1982) estimates there are about 100,000 psychotherapy practitioners in the United States, counting psychiatric nurses trained at the M.A. level, marriage and family counselors, and pastoral counselors and clergy trained in psychotherapy or counseling, as well as psychologists, psychiatrists, and psychiatric social workers. This increase in numbers and types of psychotherapists is consistent with the extensive needs for service identified by the Joint Commission on Mental Health and Illness in its 1961 report. We do not know whether the nonprofessional alternatives are competing with the professionals for the same pool of clients. Obviously not everyone with problems seeks help, so the effective market for services is far less than the potential demand. One might even speculate that the psychotherapy market is oversaturated in some areas. The deficiency may reside in the geographic distribution of practitioners, not in their overall numbers.

Although many professional practitioners work in public clinics and agencies, a large number are in private practice (Taube et al., 1984). Growth in private practice has been supported by growth in insurance coverage for outpatient mental health services. Because there is insurance support, more persons who might not ordinarily use psychotherapy can avail themselves of it. Taube et al. (1984), for example, report that males comprise about 40% of the case loads of private practitioners in psychology and psychiatry. Males are somewhat underrepresented compared to their 48% share of the general population, but not badly underrepresented. Although psychologists in private practice see a disproportionate number of college graduates compared to the number of college graduates in the population, patients seen by psychiatrists are no different in educational level from the general population. Both psychiatrists and psychologists see disproportionate numbers of upper-income clients, but 42% of psychiatrists' patients and 32% of psychologists' patients have incomes under $15,000. Persons over 55 years of age are underrepresented in the practices of both groups. Taube et al. (1984) do not describe the racial or ethnic characteristics of persons seeing psychologists and psychiatrists.

Even though the distribution of client characteristics does not precisely match those of the population as a whole, the mismatch may not be as great as some believe. The degree to which YAVIS (young, attractive, verbal, intelligent, successful) clients once monopolized outpatient psychotherapy services may have changed. Expanded outpatient services, insurance coverage, and cultural change in our attitudes toward mental health services may lead to use of traditional outpatient services by clients from a broader segment of the social spectrum. This trend may be reversed if mental health coverage is reduced or eliminated from health insurance policies and health maintenance organizations, especially those covering blue-collar workers and their families.

Minorities and Other Underserved Groups

The President's Commission on Mental Health (1978) identified rural populations and ethnic and racial minorities as unserved or underserved populations. Some arguments for a new mental health policy were based on the observation that lower-class populations were not well served by the mental health care then available. The data on private practice suggest that patterns of service delivery may have changed. Has the community thrust resulted in improved services to groups formerly less well served?

Blouch (1982) evaluated epidemiological studies concerning the mental health of persons in rural areas compared with urban areas. He concludes that there was no real advantage to rural living in avoiding mental health problems and, based on the distribution of mental health workers, that rural populations continue to be underserved. Barrera (1982) notes that more recent studies, in contrast to earlier ones, have tended to show that underutilization of mental health services by Mexican-Americans has lessened and in some cases is proportional to their numbers in the population. The availability of bilingual/bicultural therapists may be an important factor in determining utilization rates. Manson and Trimble (1982) claim that service delivery to American Indian and Alaskan native communities has increased greatly in quantity, but they raise questions about the appropriateness of the services that are available. Cross-cultural therapy presents many problems of differences in "shared assumptions, experiences, beliefs, values, expectations and goals" between the service provider and the service recipient. Thus there are barriers to service, and underutilization continues despite availability. Service systems should perhaps be redesigned to meet needs as they exist. Similar conclusions hold for Asian-American and Pacific-American populations (Wong, 1982).

Data on the utilization of services by blacks are less well developed. Based on a national sampling survey of blacks, Neighbors (1985) finds that blacks tend not to use the formal mental health system to aid in coping with stress. They are more likely to turn to informal networks, including their ministers. Shapiro et al. (1984) do not find differences between blacks and whites in their reported use of mental health services, and a survey by Myers et al. (1984) finds few racial differences in the prevalence of DSM-III categories. Those data must be considered in relation to the finding that blacks have higher hospitalization rates than do whites (Task Panel, President's Commission on Mental Health, 1978). Moore (1982) documents the many inequities in American society between blacks and whites that may be related to the prevalence of mental health problems and stress in the black populations. A more salient question for blacks than utilization of mental health services may be: "What social changes are likely to promote the involvement and participation of black Americans as full and equal citizens?" (Moore, 1982, pp. 178–179). The question does not mean we should ignore the problems of service delivery in relation to blacks, but that other matters should be addressed as well.

Jones and Matsumoto (1982) and Zane, Sue, Castro, and George (1982) challenge the assumption that lower socioeconomic level clients are not amenable to psychotherapy. Recent research, they argue, shows that the attitudes of blacks and whites toward mental illness and toward treatment services differ very little (Gordon, 1982). Moreover, evidence now suggests that dropout rates from therapy by lower-class clients may have diminished over the last 20 years. Jones and Matsumoto assert that there is no formal outcome study showing lower rates of success in psychotherapy with economically disadvantaged groups and that patient preparation for treatment may reduce dropout rates and improve treatment outcomes. They express some reservations about the trend toward using less trained paraprofessional service providers for low-income populations and professional providers for upper-income populations. Korchin (1980) quotes a black psychologist friend in making this same point: "I'll send my mother to a paraprofessional when the people in [a fashionable San Francisco suburb] go to one!" (p. 266).

We still have the problems of trying to understand how to design services that are more responsive to the needs of various populations. Zane et al. (1982) offer six principles to help produce service-delivery systems responsive to the needs of ethnic minorities.

1. *Match or fit of services* to the particular needs and help-seeking patterns of the client population with a particular emphasis on addressing the impact of social problems (such as alcohol abuse, truancy, or unemployment) on adaptive social functioning.
2. *Integration and linkage of relevant services,* namely mental health services and other health-related and social services.
3. *Efficient utilization of services,* primarily by focusing on primary prevention efforts that incorporate natural support systems.
4. *Comprehensive services* at the four levels of intervention—individual, family, organizational, and social system.
5. *Community control* by means of advisory board and administrative representation and service accountability.

6. *Knowledge development and utilization* with an emphasis on promoting the adoption and implementation of innovative service system models (Zane et al., 1982, p. 232).

As these comments show, the six principles incorporate much of the community orientation. Zane et al. concur that there have been advances in experimentation with new service models and that some experiments appear to have been successful. They argue that the experience of the last 20 years can now be distilled and used to overcome the problems that still exist—problems that are not readily overcome by an exclusively individual orientation to problems in living.

The community movement has undoubtedly had a strong impact on our thinking and on how we approach problems. This assertion should be tempered by the fact that most mental health services continue to offer primarily individual, group, and family therapy and psychotropic medications. Furthermore, most new service thrusts have developed piecemeal and sporadically, often out of largely pragmatic considerations. Because each program often has its own distinct source of funds, the piecemeal approach has produced a crazy-quilt pattern of funding and eligibility requirements. Frequently these requirements are written into legislation and end up determining program considerations. The New York Governor's Select Commission identified 19 federal and state sources of funds for mental health programming, each with its own requirements. Sometimes the requirements are such that different levels of government work at cross-purposes to each other. Thus local and state governments may be at odds over who will pay for services to certain clients. Such confusion has also led to the anomaly of the state government participating as a plaintiff in a suit against the federal government to help those who have disabilities for mental disorders or mental retardation retain their federal disability status. If they lost that status, responsibility for income maintenance would fall on state welfare programs (Goldsmith, 1984). These problems are evidence that we cannot pay attention to program ideas alone. At every step, our thinking must take into account the political, social, and economic contexts of ideas and the programs they inspire.

From a scientific perspective this diversity of approaches and problems challenges community psychology to articulate and test new concepts. This challenge was recently heightened by a renewed emphasis on preventive services, an emphasis attributable to the President's Commission on Mental Health (1978). Programs in prevention are the only mental health services that received new funding under the first Reagan administration. In the absence of a viable theoretical paradigm, however, community psychology's response to the challenge of prevention may fail. We will examine some promising theoretical concepts generated by the community thrust later in this chapter. Before doing so, we will review the situation concerning services for children and adolescents.

Children and Adolescents

Mental health problems of children and adolescents have received far less attention than the problems of adults. Neglect of children's services has been chronic, despite evidence of overwhelming need. In 1962, school-based surveys revealed that 7–12% of children under 14 had emotional problems requiring professional help. In the early

1960s, four-fifths of all counties in the United States had no mental health clinic. About one-quarter of the 1800 clinics then in existence served children exclusively, and the rest accepted both child and adult clients. Most clinics had long waiting lists. Children from low-income populations were generally underrepresented in child guidance clinics (Furman et al., 1965; Harrison et al., 1965). The juvenile and family courts, originally created with a broad mandate for child welfare, rarely had adequate treatment facilities, although some had diagnostic clinics. The courts were castigated both for providing inadequate care and for neglecting children's rights [*In re Gault*, 387 U.S. 1 (1967)]. Welfare programs, administered through social service departments in local communities, rarely provided more than administrative supervision to families (May, 1964). Case reports of problems related to welfare agencies and to the juvenile court may be found in Sarason, Levine, et al. (1966). School-based services were available, but generally only in better neighborhoods (Sexton, 1961). In the early 1960s, when the adult population of state hospitals was declining, the number of children between 10 and 14 entering state hospitals increased (American Psychiatric Association, 1964). In other words, existing services were neither sufficient in quantity to meet existing need nor successful in reaching the populations at greatest risk.

The Joint Commission on Mental Illness and Health (1961) noted the number and severity of problems in the field of child welfare, including children on welfare, broken homes, children in institutions, problems of foster care, issues in adoption, and the increasing number of children and adolescents who were being institutionalized. The Joint Commission's report criticized as inadequate the services available through most juvenile courts and noted the dearth of school-based services for exceptional children. It called for an expansion of children's services, a recommendation that had little effect at the time.

Congress appointed a Joint Commission on the Mental Health of Children (1969) in 1965, which issued a report in 1969. This commission characterized services as grossly inadequate, poorly coordinated, and limited in scope. For a short period of time, special funds were made available to federally funded community mental health centers to develop services for children. In 1980, however, block granting with no strings attached replaced the funding of specific mental health programs. The block grant program allowed each individual state to allocate the funds, and thus no special funds were designated for children and adolescents.

The President's Commission on Mental Health (1978) designated the population of children and adolescents as "underserved." The commission described the problem in these words:

> As the Commission traveled throughout America, we saw and heard about too many children and adolescents who suffered from neglect, indifference and abuse, and for whom appropriate mental health care was inadequate or nonexistent. Too many American children grow to adulthood with mental disabilities which could have been addressed more effectively earlier in their lives through appropriate prenatal, infant and early child development care programs.
>
> Troubled children and adolescents, particularly if they are from racial minorities, are too often placed in foster homes, special schools, mental and correction institutions without adequate prior evaluation or subsequent follow-up. Good residential facilities specializing in the treatment of special problems are in short supply.

During the past two decades, many adolescents have struggled to adapt to rapid social changes and conflicting, often ambiguous social values. There has been a dramatic increase in the use and misuse of psychoactive drugs, including alcohol among young people and nearly a three-fold increase in the suicide rate among adolescents.

Services that reflect the unique needs of children and adolescents are frequently unavailable. Our existing mental health services system contains too few mental health professionals and other personnel trained to meet the special needs of children and adolescents. Even when identified, children's needs are too often isolated into distinct categories, each to be addressed separately by a different specialist. Shuttling children from service to service, each with its own label, adds to their confusion, increases their despair and sets the pattern for adult disability. (pp. 6–7)

Namir and Weinstein (1982) reviewed epidemiological studies and conclude that the prevalence of diagnosable disorders among children and adolescents under age 18 ranges between 5% and 23%. The variation in estimates stems from different methods and sampling procedures employed by different studies. Adopting the soap-opera vantage point of Chapter 1, we note further that these figures may not include adolescents who abuse alcohol or drugs, the estimated 1 million children each year who are physically abused, children and adolescents in institutions for juveniles, or the mentally retarded. Mentally retarded children, who are not usually included in counts of mental health problems, constitute 3% of all children and adolescents by definition. Also not included are the hundreds of thousands of adolescents who have out-of-wedlock children, a situation with severe consequences for both the mothers and their children. A report by the Children's Defense Fund (1974) indicates that probably more than 2 million children and adolescents of school age are not in school. The reasons vary, but included are those who are suspended or expelled for disciplinary reasons. These surveys may also fail to include the half-million children who have been removed from their own homes, with responsibility for them given over to our system of public child care (Children's Defense Fund, 1978).

Obtaining accurate figures on the number of children and adolescents in need who actually receive services is difficult. Some estimate that about one in three such children is served (Knitzer, 1984), but as many as 90% of children and adolescents in need may not receive mental health services (Namir & Weinstein, 1982).[7] Namir and Weinstein (1982) also indicate that there are social-class, racial, and ethnic barriers to delivering services to children and adolescents. Knitzer (1984) summarizes studies indicating that as many as 40% of children and adolescents who are hospitalized are there merely because more suitable alternatives were not available. She believes that while many problems are identified early enough, appropriate services generally are not.

Knitzer (1984) states that the groups most likely to be inappropriately served or underserved are:

Disturbed adolescents (particularly older adolescents with multiple problems who are hospitalized or at risk of hospitalization); seriously disturbed children and adolescents who are in state custody under child welfare or juvenile justice auspices (some states report that such children account for as many as 60% of the psychiatrically hospitalized population); and children from poor, disorganized, and troubled families who do not use or benefit from traditional mental health services.

Despite research evidence of their vulnerability, children of mentally ill or sub-
stance-abusing parents are also likely to be poorly served. (p. 906)

Problems in designing new services are compounded by our lack of knowledge
concerning child development and psychopathology. Difficulties in separating developmental from psychopathological effects, and in understanding environmental and
social-setting influences on children's behavior and on definitions of disorder, have
resulted in inadequate classification systems and correspondingly weak research. Graziano and Mooney (1984) have reviewed applications of behavior therapy techniques
to a variety of childhood disorders. They conclude that the research shows promising
developments in many areas, but behavior therapy is not yet the standard treatment.
In any event, as they note, the problem of transferring gains made in the therapeutic
milieu to other environments has not yet been solved. Thus, aside from our limited
knowledge of disorders of childhood and adolescence, our treatment technologies
leave much to be desired. The social and political problems complicating the picture
might be easier to overcome if our treatment technologies were more powerful.

Political, social, and professional problems hampering the reform of children's
services have also been identified. Knitzer (1984) finds that state departments of mental health often lack clear statutory mandates to serve children and adolescents, lack
organizational units primarily concerned with that population, and have limited
information about how children are or are not being served. She also finds that state
nonmental health agencies are most likely to have responsibility for the most seriously
disturbed children, yet are least likely to serve them well. Namir and Weinstein (1982)
point to the fragmented nature of children's services, children's lack of political clout,
and cultural attitudes emphasizing family responsibility for children as factors limiting reform in this area. Change will require greater cooperation and collaboration
among agencies responsible for child welfare, including the schools, health services,
and mental health services. Growing concern over sexual and physical abuse of children is bringing mental health workers into more intimate contact with police, prosecutors, judges, lawyers, and social service agencies. The problems of interagency
cooperation are difficult, but a good start in coordinating services has been made in
some communities. How to make the service system both more attractive and more
responsive to the needs of atypical families (e.g., those with a single parent) and families from different social and ethnic backgrounds is an urgent problem. We cannot
approach lightly the task of integrating services, for in the past others have recognized
the critical issues and developed promising solutions, only to encounter insurmountable difficulties (Levine & Levine, 1970).

Knitzer (1984) and Namir and Weinstein (1982) believe that good examples of
responsive service systems have been developed during the past 20 years and that they
follow many of the principles used in similar programs for adults (see, for example,
Kriechman, 1985). Services are delivered in alternative settings, using educational and
rehabilitative as well as therapeutic modalities, and are staffed by others in addition
to traditional mental health personnel. These programs often have a preventive thrust
and appear to be cost-effective as well as clinically effective. Observers generally seem
to agree, however, that mental health services alone are not enough. Policies and programs governing nutrition, health, prenatal care, day care, help for single-parent families, and family policy generally need reconsideration. Some studies of early childhood education, such as the Head Start program, have demonstrated remarkable

success in preventing educational disability and later social disability (Berrueta-Clement et al., 1984; Darlington et al., 1980; see chapter 7). Such large-scale programs, even those holding out the promise of prevention, are not likely to receive favorable attention in today's political climate, however. As Iscoe and Harris (1984) note: "If the priorities of a nation are mirrored in its SCIs [social and community interventions], the welfare of children and youth [is] clearly not uppermost in the minds and intentions of policymakers" (p. 354). Knitzer (1984) states that continued cooperation between citizen advocates and professionals will be necessary to move ahead in solving critical problems and gaining new resources.

If anything, the community perspective is even more important as far as programs for children and adolescents are concerned. Opportunities for prevention may be more favorable with children than with adults, although that is an arguable proposition (see Chapter 7). Moreover, children and adolescents are less likely to bring themselves to treatment settings, and many of the more vulnerable children do not have parents who are likely to use traditional services. Therefore, services with an outreach component, and efforts to influence the natural community settings within which children and adolescents are found, are at least as important here as in work with adults.

Contemporary mental health practices thus entail a considerable amount of community-oriented thinking and activity. As we noted earlier, the primary scientific shortcoming of community psychology has been its lack of a well-articulated, widely shared conceptual model or set of theoretical principles. From the preceding review, we see that a useful characteristic for any contemporary model would be comprehensiveness. In that way both person-centered (e.g., drugs, skill training) and environment-centered (e.g., Head Start, welfare rights) activities, and also services aimed at different kinds of problems and subgroups in the community, can be understood in relation to one another.

One activity useful to include, for example, would be traditional clinical work. Although important differences exist between clinical and community psychology, they also share important similarities. For example, primary prevention has as its aim a reduction in the overall incidence of target conditions, and in that sense it is considered a community intervention, the goals of which differ from the aim of treating psychological "casualties." A moment's reflection will reveal that defining disorders, delivering services, dealing with the social, historical, and political contexts, and all of the issues in changing social organizations are no different in preventive efforts than in treatment. In that sense the two branches of the field have much in common and much to learn from each other.[8] The concluding section of this chapter describes a comprehensive framework useful in defining community psychology and distinguishing it from clinical psychology; it introduces several of community psychology's central concepts.

A Conceptual Road Map to Community Psychology

In her presidential address to the Division of Community Psychology of the American Psychological Association, Barbara Dohrenwend (1978) proposed a conceptual model to help answer two questions: "What do community psychologists do?" and "What's the difference between community psychology and clinical psychology?" (One could ask the same questions in psychiatry, social work, nursing, and any of the helping professions that have developed a community orientation in their literature, if not in their practices.) These questions had become pertinent, as we have noted, because of diffuse activities all unified under the label *community psychology,* implying differences between this and other fields sufficiently great to warrant separate professional identities. Dohrenwend's conceptual model is helpful for several reasons. It is built around a unifying concept of psychosocial stress (the kinds of problems we describe as the soap opera of life), includes a temporal dimension, and enables us to focus in a more or less unified and systematic manner on both person-centered and environmental issues in behavior and mental health.

Her model is based on the connection between psychosocial stress and psychopathology. She differentiates psychosocial stress from psychopathology and does not view the immediate emotional reaction to a stressful event as pathology. In her words, the model "provides a framework within which the apparently disparate activities of community psychologists . . . are . . . uniformly directed at undermining the process whereby stress generates psychopathology but, given the complexity of this process, vary because they tackle it at different points" (Dohrenwend, 1978, p. 2). We show her conceptual model in the following paragraphs.

Let us follow her argument. "The process . . . starts with a proximate rather than distant cause of psychopathology, with recent events in the life of an individual rather than with distant childhood experiences. It describes an episode that is initiated by the occurrence of one or more stressful life events, and is terminated by psychological change, for good or ill, or by return to the psychological *status quo ante*" (pp. 2–3). "Stressful life events vary in the extent to which they are determined by the environment or by psychological characteristics of the central person in the event" (p. 3). The model enables one to focus on the person or the social setting and allows for the possibility "that an individual may take part in creating the very events that appear later to cause him to undergo psychological change" (p. 4).

Regardless of the source of the stress response, "a common characteristic of all of these forms of stress reaction is that they are inherently transient or self-limiting, . . . most people who are exposed to these stressful events develop psychological symptoms, and . . . these symptoms are almost always transient, unless perpetuated by secondary gains. . . . What follows after the immediate, transient stress reaction depends on the mediation of situational and psychological factors that define the context in which this reaction occurs" (p. 4).

In this model, both situational and psychological mediators of the stress-pathology relationship are important. "Other things being equal, an individual whose financial or other material resources are strained by the demands of a stressful life event is likely to have a worse outcome than a person with adequate material resources. Similarly, lack of social support is hypothesized to increase the likelihood of a negative outcome. . . . These mediators . . . include 'values' . . . and 'coping abilities'" (p. 5).

Transient stress reactions and situational and psychological mediators interact in some complex fashion to produce one of three classes of outcomes; the person (a) may grow and change positively as a result of mastering the experience, (b) may essentially return to some state normal for that person, or (c) may develop psychopathology, defined by Dohrenwend as a persistent, apparently self-sustaining dysfunctional reaction. The utility of that definition of psychopathology aside, the model forces attention to much more than the psychological and emotional reaction of the individual person. (In Chapter 6 we will contrast the concept of an acute neurotic reaction, based on a failure of defenses and the return of repressed emotions, to the stressful-life-events or crisis model to show the differences in focus.) Note that the concept of psychosocial stress requires attention to life circumstances and to the individual's resources—psychological, material, and social—available to meet the demands posed by life circumstances. It is insufficient in this model to focus only on the person and to ignore all else, as the model of individual psychopathology leads us to do.

By following the three outcomes (the boxes at the far right of the model in Figure 2-1), we see that the bulk of clinical effort has been directed toward providing treatment at the endpoint of the process, the outcome box labeled psychopathology. We cannot doubt that people in difficulty need help and, in a caring society, deserve help. Some (e.g., Scheff, 1966; Graziano & Fink, 1970) have argued, however, that the treatment of pathology may contribute to the problem of "secondary gain" that Dohrenwend mentions.[9] For example, Hankin and Locke (1982) found that contrary to expectations, initially depressed patients who continued to be depressed at follow-up were *more* likely to have had a psychiatry visit than were patients no longer depressed at follow-up. These differences were observed even after controlling for patients' initial levels of depression. Patients whose symptoms persisted also averaged more visits to psychiatry than did patients whose symptoms remitted.[10]

Whether or not one accepts the view that treatment contributes to secondary gain, the finding that receiving psychiatric treatment was associated with worse outcomes than not receiving treatment is certainly paradoxical. Furthermore, even if we agree that psychotherapeutic interventions have been effective (Meltzoff & Kornreich, 1970; Bergin, 1971), we still face practical limitations in the provision of psychotherapeutic services. If life is a soap opera, for example, the costs of services for all may be overwhelming, although costs might be relieved by using paraprofessionals and volunteers (see McGee, 1974).

Dohrenwend raises the possibility that the timing of help be moved to the earliest point in the stress reaction in the form of "crisis intervention" services. She has several criticisms of this strategy. She questions whether enough people in need would seek out the preferred help or whether crisis services could be positioned to reach persons soon enough during acutely stressful episodes. Compared with the population that might be served, crisis services tend not to be used very much, with telephone services tending to draw the same chronic callers. A thorough evaluation of these services as implemented through crisis centers fully bears out Dohrenwend's judgment (Auerbach & Kilmann, 1978). One recent study (Miller et al., 1984) examined the effectiveness of suicide prevention services, finding that these programs may have an effect in reducing successful suicides among young white females. No statistically significant effect could be detected in other age and sex groups. Although young white females are among the most frequent callers to crisis lines, successful suicide is lowest in this age and sex group. Rates of completed suicide are 20 or more times higher among white males over age 65, and these men are not frequent callers to suicide prevention services. In other words, in depending on voluntary use of a single service modality, the crisis hotline reaches the group at lowest risk, albeit with some success, and fails to reach the group at highest risk. Crisis hotlines clearly have a "marketing" problem regarding the groups in greatest need for their services.

The life-stress concept does provide certain advantages in guiding the positioning of services (e.g., in relation to predictable, so-called milestone events), and it suggests the possibility of prevention (see Chapters 6 and 7). Recognizing that not everyone

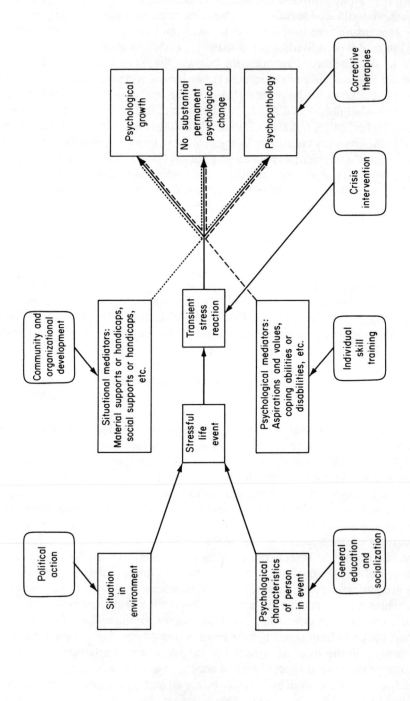

Figure 2-1. A model of the process whereby psychosocial stress induces psychopathology and some conceptions of how to counteract this process (from Dohrenwend, 1978).

will use a particular service raises a number of social issues, such as where, when, how, and to whom a given service might be offered. Developing a treatment technology to cope successfully with transient reactions is not the only concern. Many other social variables are involved. We still need to learn how to market our services—to package, advertise, price, and sell—to different groups. A given service offered in a particular way will reach some in need, but characteristics of the service will likely result in a mismatch with the needs of others, effectively screening them out. How to tailor services, be they preventive or rehabilitative, to take into account the characteristics of the target "consumer," remains a problem for the mental health field.

In theory, psychological mediators such as values or coping skills play an important role in determining the outcome of a transient stress reaction. Dohrenwend (1978) notes that strengthening a person's psychological mediators may help him or her "develop a high level of ability to face and solve complex social and emotional problems" (p. 8). One way of looking at these issues may involve early intervention to help children cope with emotional stresses or the challenges of growing up. The original child-guidance clinics of the 1920s were based on a similar concept (Levine & Levine, 1970). Cowen's Primary Mental Health Project (Cowen et al., 1975) is an updated, school-based version of child guidance designed to help children who have already been identified as vulnerable in order to prevent the development of more serious problems later in life (see Chapter 7).

In an approach that deviates still more from traditional helping sevices, Spivack and Shure (1974) and Spivack, Platt, and Shure (1976) have demonstrated that social adjustment may be enhanced by programs explicitly designed to teach social and interpersonal problem-solving skills—that is, psychological mediators. These programs are not offered only to children in difficulty or even only to those at high risk. Instead, the programs are designed to be integrated directly into the educational curriculum to help provide children with styles or means of coping with problems they encounter day by day. The strategy in such programs is to improve the child's overall coping ability by teaching him or her skills needed to master or to avoid occupational and interpersonal crises. Preschool programs designed to enhance children's abilities to adapt to elementary school are variants of this approach.

Another example of such a program, although little studied in the context of prevention, is sex education within the school curriculum. Sex education has among its aims the provision of greater knowledge and healthier attitudes and values to help adolescents cope with sexuality and its demands (see Valerio, 1985). Presumably, greater comfort with sexuality has important ramifications for each individual's interpersonal relationships and personal satisfaction throughout life. Nothing in the theory restricts such education to the schools. The development of psychological mediators could follow from the efforts of parents, peers, or, for that matter, the mass media. Dohrenwend (1978) notes that such programs reach "back to the very origin of the stress process and have, therefore, moved as far as possible from the treatment of individual cases of psychopathology into the realm of primary prevention" (p. 9).

The psychosocial stress perspective holds that the outcome of a stressful life event also depends on situational mediators. When an individual's resources are insufficient for coping with a problem, the outcome may be poorer than if adequate resources are available. For many, the resources provided by friends and relatives are sufficient to assist in coping. In fact, the family and the various functions it fulfills in an individual's psychic and social economy provides a useful model for social support (Caplan,

1976; Gottlieb, 1981; see Chapter 6). For many people and many purposes, however, the resources of family and friends are insufficient. Public services are necessary in lieu of family support. Levine (1982) points out that in the Love Canal emergency, blue-collar families simply did not have the financial resources to support a move away from the neighborhood threatened by toxic wastes. Government assistance was necessary. In many other problems, individual resources are insufficient, and collective resources are necessary. Some form of welfare is necessary for income maintenance for those who cannot provide for themselves. Unemployment insurance keeps many from despair when they lose their jobs.

Public services are aids to coping, and in their absence community and organizational development efforts are necessary to provide that help. As Kelly (1966) points out, one of the aims of the community movement is to produce the resources a community needs to cope with its problems. Thus the activities of community-oriented mental health professionals in helping to develop respite care so that families may maintain retarded children at home, or a shelter for battered wives, or a service to help widows with inadequate financial resources and with no recent work histories reenter the labor force are all examples of the creation of situational mediators. The availability of such mediators supplements and extends individual and family resources; in their absence, the outcomes of a stressful life event might be worse. Dohrenwend's (1978) model helps us see how such activity is comprehensible within a single conceptual framework.

Some preventive programs aim to eliminate the circumstances that produce stressful life events in the first place. Thus programs to develop housing, recreation, and employment opportunities may prevent life events related to inadequate housing, inactivity or boredom, and unemployment. Nutrition and prenatal care may reduce the incidence of low-birth-weight babies who prove to be at risk for several other disorders. The means necessary to attain such ends are political in nature. Because they are, some (e.g., Dunham, 1965) have said that if mental health professionals wish to influence the political system they should enter politics directly and run for office. One answer is that there are many means of influencing political action in addition to running for office. Harrington's (1962) book on poverty is said to have influenced John F. Kennedy's thinking about his political program and social objectives. Social scientists work as advisors to government and testify to congressional committees based on their research and its implications. There are many professional roles, in addition to that of officeholder, through which social scientists and mental health workers may exercise influence within the political system. A model for such activity was provided by the settlement house workers at the turn of the century. These early social workers were researchers, community organizers, lobbyists, and interpreters of the needs of poor immigrants to the middle class. Because of their knowledge some headed governmental departments at state and federal levels. Later, some joined the Franklin D. Roosevelt administration and influenced many of its social policies. This tradition of social and political activism was forgotten because of the emphasis on individual psychology that permeated the social work field beginning in the 1920s (Levine & Levine, 1970). Dohrenwend's (1978) model restores political and social activism to the mental health professional's methods for working to reduce psychopathology.

The space we have devoted to Dohrenwend's model should not be taken to indicate that we endorse all of its propositions. The various situational contributions to stress and recovery are not described in detail, and the model fits discrete life events much better than more chronic, enduring stresses. We believe it is a useful conceptualization, however, that helps us get our bearings by asking us to view problems in a more holistic light. It includes a temporal dimension suggesting when, where, and why certain interventions might help in reducing pathology. The model directs our attention to the way in which human problems are embedded in a total context. Its inclusion of situational as well as psychological mediators pushes us beyond the study of the isolated individual. It tells us we need to develop theories that take into account the "person-in-a-situation." (The hyphens are meant to underscore the oneness of that concept.) The words *holistic,* and *embedded* in a total context are nothing more than truisms unless developed in greater detail. The purpose of this chapter is to describe how community psychology moved toward accepting a notion like psychosocial stress as an organizing concept. The purpose of subsequent chapters will be to elaborate other theoretical propositions that are more detailed in their own realm, but are compatible with the ideas contained in the psychosocial stress viewpoint. Much of the rest of this book will be directed toward examining theories and examples of interventions that move us a little bit further in the direction of a more sophisticated person-in-a-situation concept.

Summary

One important basis for understanding the field of community psychology involves its connections to specific social and historical conditions of the past four decades. World War II, the struggle for civil rights, and other events wrought great changes in American society, to a point where an ideological and scientific perspective such as community psychology could gain credence. Community psychology was also a response to specific deficiencies some perceived in the traditional medical model of mental illness and treatment.

Community-based helping alternatives proliferated during the 1960s and 1970s as social change continued. The foundations of the community perspective in ideology, more than in well-validated scientific concepts, were not always recognized, however, leading many to be disappointed in the results of initial efforts at change from a community perspective. Nevertheless, the changes wrought in contemporary mental health practice have been considerable, such that community approaches now represent the conventional wisdom in such areas as long-term rehabilitation of the chronically mentally ill, programs for minorities and other underserved groups, and prevention of social problems in young children.

Why does practice in the community continue? One explanation may be that the scientific aspects of community psychology remain relevant to contemporary problems. From a scientific vantage, the sundry community interventions are understandable when organized around a unifying perspective on psychosocial stress. A model of this sort proposed by Barbara Dohrenwend (1978) provides a useful framework for integrating the disparate activities pursued under the aegis of community psychology with more traditional interventions such as psychotherapy and crisis intervention. This model directs attention to the relationship between stress and behavior, including processes very early in the sequence of events leading to pathology or to recovery.

This view raises a greater variety of options, based on either person-centered or environment-centered interventions, and particularly prominent in Dohrenwend's model are strategies aimed at prevention.

As it stands, however, the Dohrenwend model is little more than a heuristic explanation and outline of a comprehensive field and its many activities. Considerably more theoretical detail is needed, as is empirical research. In the next four chapters we develop a number of theoretical and empirical details in preparation for a careful examination of prevention in mental health.

Notes

1. The issues discussed in the next few paragraphs are developed in greater detail by Levine (1981) and Mechanic (1980).

2. During that period our economic high priests cast their statistical equivalents of dry bones and prophesied that growth in the gross national product (GNP), the sacred portent that the gods were looking favorably upon the nation, would depend on massive spending in the public sector. They argued that growth depended on redistributing wealth and encouraging consumption of the goods and services produced in the private sector. Arguing further that public services and facilities required refurbishing, economists pressed for a policy of public spending for education, welfare, youth services, mental health, correctional services, urban renewal, and the construction of public buildings, roads, and other facilities (Galbraith, 1958). The Community Mental Health Centers Acts of 1963 and 1965, the Economic Opportunity Act of 1964, and subsequent legislation supporting community-oriented programs followed from this philosophy.

3. Critics of the Moynihan (1965) report attacked it impolitely by calling it racist and politely by asserting that it failed to consider the effect of racial prejudice on family structure and neglected the strengths of 75% of black families in focusing on the 25% that were female-headed families. (See Carper (1970), Payton (1970), and Tumin (1970) for commentary on the Moynihan study.) The Moynihan study may have stimulated black scholars to redefine some of the research issues, enriching our understanding of black families and their needs (Special Populations Subpanel on Mental Health of Black Americans, 1978; Moore, 1982; Zane, Sue, Castro, & George, 1982). On the other hand, criticism of the Moynihan study may have created barriers to studying problems in black families. Cummings (1983) reports data showing that the proportion of black female-headed households has nearly doubled since Moynihan's original report. Cummings indicates that leaders in the black community are now expressing more concern about the issue of female-headed households. This episode provides an excellent case study of the interplay among research, social values, and political considerations.

4. Although many clinics have since streamlined their intake procedures, the dropout rate is still probably fairly high. Taube, Burns, and Kessler (1984) report that the median number of visits to psychiatrists and psychologists in private practice is 4.0 and 5.0, respectively. They do not indicate what percentage of the cases were planned terminations. Bloom (1984) has summarized evidence indicating that clients may benefit from as few as one or two visits. As a problem the dropout rate may be more apparent than real.

5. Gerald Caplan's (1959, 1970) writings on consultation had become influential by this time. The theory of consultation, however, was simply an extension of clinical theory, in many ways not terribly different from the supervision of psychotherapy and perhaps not much more efficient (Levine, 1972). Consultation and education became a core service in community mental health centers and a major claimant on the imaginations, if not on the time, of professionals (D'Augelli, 1982). Consultation theory did not go very far in providing a guide to theory, strategy, or practice.

6. Because a university is divided into psychology, sociology, anthropology, economics, political science, law, philosophy, and English departments is no reason to believe that problems in the world are so divided. Unfortunately, those organizational divisions tend to compartmentalize knowledge in our minds as well. A personal incident is illustrative. Levine was fortunate to encounter Scheff's (1966) elegant, disarmingly simple, and therefore persuasive book, *Being Mentally Ill,* shortly after publication. He was much taken with the presentation in propositional form of labeling theory, a viewpoint not represented in his education in clinical psychology. At the time, he was introducing a community perspective into his teaching. While preparing a reading list for his course, he found himself in a quandary about whether to include Scheff's book, not because he doubted its value or its pertinence for his course, but because the subtitle of the book was *A Sociological Theory.* He debated with himself whether it was proper for a psychologist to include a sociological work as part of a course in psychology! Concluding that that way lay madness, he did include the book. The incident may reveal as much about the person as it does about the university. It may reflect his concerns about criticism from colleagues within psychology or a misguided respect for intellectual turf. The critical point is that a conceptual label, the distinction between psychology and sociology (a meaningless distinction if we think about intervention in the social world), affected his thought process and his feelings and might have influenced his actions.

7. The figures on numbers of children served do not take into account children receiving special educational services through the public schools. The Education for All Handicapped Children Act (PL94-142) requires that all identified handicapped children, including those with physical, developmental, intellectual, emotional, or learning problems, be evaluated. Individual educational plans must be drawn up with the participation of the children's parents; services are then delivered in accordance with those plans. Sarason and Doris (1979) express reservations about the impact of this law on schools and on services. A great deal of litigation has taken place regarding what services the law requires schools to provide (and to pay for), and the impact of the law on the provision of services remains to be evaluated.

8. Because we will devote a section of this book to issues in prevention, we will simply note here that everything we have said about the limits of our conceptualizations applies to problems in prevention. The field has not yet transcended its individually oriented biases to understand fully some of the constraints the person-environment conceptualization imposes on the very concept of prevention (Levine & Perkins, 1980).

9. That view is also oversimplified, but in raising the issue we can see that what is apparently benign may serve other, latent political purposes. The treatment process calls for adaptation to the existing culture, the emphasis on pathology from this perspective is a form of social control, and thus mental health treatment is inherently conservative in a social sense.

10. The results might have been different had the therapists used more effective methods for treating depression. It is also possible that the persistently depressed population is somehow a more seriously disturbed population. The interpretation that therapy results in a fixation of symptoms for some clients is ours and obviously is not the only plausible one.

References

Alley, S., & Blanton, J. (Eds.). (1978). *Paraprofessionals in mental health: An annotated bibliography from 1966 to 1977.* Berkeley: Social Action Research Center.

Alley, S., Blanton, J., Feldman, R. E., Hunter, G. D., & Rolfson, M. (1979). *Case studies of mental health paraprofessionals. Twelve effective programs.* New York: Human Sciences Press.

American Psychiatric Association. (1964). *Planning psychiatric services for children in the community mental health program.* Washington, DC: Author.

Auerbach, S. M., & Kilmann, P. R. (1978). Crisis intervention: A review of outcome research. *Psychological Bulletin, 84,* 1189–1217.

Bachrach, L. L. (1984). The homeless mentally ill and mental health services. An analytical review of the literature. In H. R. Lamb (Ed.), *The homeless mentally ill.* Washington, DC: American Psychiatric Association.

Barrera, M., Jr. (1982). Raza populations. In L. R. Snowden (Ed.), *Reaching the underserved: Mental health needs of neglected populations.* Beverly Hills: Sage.

Beiser, M., Shore, J. H., Peters, R., & Tatum, E. (1985). Does community care for the mentally ill make a difference? A tale of two cities. *American Journal of Psychiatry, 142,* 1047–1052.

Bennett, C. C., Anderson, L. S., Cooper, S., Hassol, L., Klein, D. C., & Rosenblum, G. (1966). *Community Psychology. A report on the Boston conference on the education of psychologists for community mental health.* Boston: Department of Psychology, Boston University.

Bergin, A. E. (1971). The evaluation of therapeutic outcomes. In A. Bergin & S. Garfield (Eds.), *Handbook of psychotherapy and behavior change.* New York: Wiley.

Berrueta-Clement, J. R., Schweinhart, L. J., Barnett, W. S., Epstein, A. S., & Weikart, D. P. (1984). *Changed lives.* Ypsilanti, MI: High/Scope Press.

Bindman, A. J., & Spiegel, A. D. (Eds.). (1969). *Perspectives in community mental health.* Chicago: Aldine.

Blatt, B., & Kaplan, F. (1966). *Christmas in purgatory.* Boston: Allyn & Bacon.

Bloom, B. L. (1984). *Community Mental Health: A general introduction* (2d ed.). Monterey, CA: Brooks/Cole.

Blouch, R. G. (1982). Rural people. In L. R. Snowden (Ed.), *Reaching the underserved: Mental health needs of neglected population.* Beverly Hills: Sage.

Brooks, T. R. (1974). *Walls come tumbling down.* Englewood Cliffs, NJ: Prentice-Hall.

Caplan, G. (1959). *Concepts of mental health and consultation. Their application in public health social work.* Washington, DC: Social and Rehabilitation Service. Children's Bureau.

Caplan, G. (1970). *The theory and practice of mental health consultation.* New York: Basic Books.

Caplan, G. (1976). The family as a support system. In G. Caplan & M. Killilea (Eds.), *Support systems and mutual help.* New York: Grune & Stratton.

Carper, L. (1970). The Negro family and the Moynihan report. In P. I. Rose (Ed.), *Slavery and its aftermath.* New York: Atherton.

Children's Defense Fund. (1974). *Children out of school in America.* Washington, DC: Author.

Children's Defense Fund. (1978). *Children without homes.* Washington, DC: Author.

Cloward, R. & Piven, F. F. (1971). *Regulating the poor: The function of public welfare in America.* New York: Random House.

Coleman, J. S., Campbell, E. Q., Hobson, C. J., McPartland, J., Mood, A. M., Weinfeld, F. D., & York, R. L. (1966). *Equality of educational opportunity.* Washington, DC: U.S. Government Printing Office.

Cowen, E. L. (1973). Social and community interventions. *Annual Review of Psychology, 24,* 423–472.

Cowen, E. L., Trost, M. A., Izzo, L. D., Lorion, R. P., Dorr, D., & Isaacson, R. V. (1975). *New ways in school mental health.* New York: Human Sciences Press.

Cummings, J. (1983, November 20). Breakup of black family imperils gains of decades. *The New York Times,* pp. 1, 56.

Darlington, R. B., Royce, J. M., Snipper, A. S., Murray, H. W., & Lazar, I. (1980). Preschool programs and later school competence of children from low income families. *Science, 208,* 202–204.

D'Augelli, A. R. (1982). Historical synthesis of consultation and education. In D. R. Ritter (Ed.), *Consultation, education and prevention in community mental health.* Springfield, IL: Charles C Thomas.

Dohrenwend, B. S. (1978). Social stress and community psychology. *American Journal of Community Psychology, 6,* 1–14.

Dohrenwend, B. P., & Dohrenwend, B. S. (1969). *Social status and psychological disorder.* New York: Wiley.

Dunham, H. W. (1965). Community psychiatry: The newest therapeutic bandwagon. *Archives of General Psychiatry, 12,* 303–313.

Eysenck, H. J. (1952). The effects of psychotherapy: An evaluation. *Journal of Consulting Psychology, 16,* 319–324.

Eysenck, H. J. (1961). The effects of psychotherapy. In H. J. Eysenck (Ed.), *Handbook of abnormal psychology.* New York: Basic Books.

Furman, S. S. (1965). Suggestions for refocusing child guidance clinics. *Children, 12,* 140–144.

Galbraith, J. K. (1958). *The affluent society.* Boston: Houghton-Mifflin.

Gergen, K. J. (1982). [Review of S. B. Sarason, *Psychology misdirected.*] *Contemporary Psychology, 27,* 36–61.

Goffman, E. (1961). *Asylums.* New York: Doubleday.

Goldenberg, I. I. (1978). *Oppression and social intervention.* Chicago: Nelson-Hall.

Goldsmith, J. M. (1984). *Final report of the Governor's Select Commission on the Future of the State-Local Mental Health System.* Albany, NY: Governor's Select Commission.

Gordon, J. S. (1978). Final report to the President's Commission on Mental Health of the special study on alternative mental health services. *Task Panel Reports Submitted to the President's Commission on Mental Health,* Appendix, Vol II. Washington DC: U.S. Government Printing Office.

Gordon, M. (1982). Attitudes toward mental illness held by two disadvantaged inner city ethnic groups. Unpublished doctoral dissertation, Department of Psychology, SUNY at Buffalo.

Gottlieb, B. (1981). *Social networks and social support in community mental health.* Beverly Hills: Sage.

Gouldner, A. W. (1968). The sociologist as partisan: Sociology and the welfare state. *American Sociologist, 3,* 103–116.

Graziano, A. M., & Fink, R. (1973). Second order effects in mental health treatment. *Journal of Consulting and Clinical Psychology, 40,* 356–64.

Graziano, A. M., & Mooney, K. C. (1984). *Children and behavior therapy.* New York: Aldine.

Hankin, J. R., & Locke, B. Z. (1982). The persistence of depressive symptomatology among prepaid group practice enrollees: An exploratory study. *American Journal of Public Health, 72,* 1000–1007.

Harrington, M. (1963). *The other America. Poverty in the United States.* New York: Macmillan.

Harrison, S. I., McDermott, J. F., Wilson, P. T., & Schrager, J. (1965). Social class and mental illness in children: Choice of treatment. *Archives of General Psychiatry, 13,* 411–417.

Hollingshead, A. B., & Redlich, F. C. (1958). *Social class and mental illness.* New York: Wiley.

Iscoe, I., Bloom, B., & Spielberger, C. D. (1977). *Community Psychology in transition.* New York: Halsted Press.

Iscoe, I., & Harris, L. C. (1984). Social and community interventions. *Annual Review of Psychology, 35,* 333–360.

Iscoe, I., & Spielberger, C. D. (Eds.). (1970). *Community psychology: Perspectives in training and research.* New York: Appleton-Century-Crofts.

Joint Commission on Mental Illness and Health. (1961). *Action for mental health.* New York: Basic Books.

Joint Commission on the Mental Health of Children. (1969). *Crisis in child mental health: Challenge for the 1970's.* New York: Harper & Row.

Jones, E. E., & Matsumoto, D. R. (1982). Psychotherapy with the underserved: Recent developments. In L. R. Snowden (Ed.), *Reaching the underserved: Mental health needs of neglected populations.* Beverly Hills: Sage.

Kellam, S. G., Branch, J. D., Agrawal, K. C., & Grabill, M. E. (1972). Woodlawn Mental Health Center: An evolving strategy for planning in community mental health. In S. E. Golann

& C. Eisdorfer (Eds.). *Handbook of community mental health.* New York: Appleton-Century-Crofts.

Kelly, J. G. (1966). Ecological constraints on mental health services. *American Psychologist, 21,* 535–539.

Kiesler, C. A. (1982). Public and professional myths about mental hospitalization. An empirical reassessment of policy-related beliefs. *American Psychologist, 37,* 1323–1339.

Klein, D. N. (1981). The community action program: Its origins, implementation, decline and accomplishments. Unpublished doctoral preliminary paper, Department of Psychology, SUNY at Buffalo.

Klerman, G. L. (1982). The psychiatric revolution of the past twenty-five years. In W. R. Gove (Ed.), *Deviance and mental illness.* Beverly Hills: Sage.

Knitzer, J. (1984). Mental health services to children and adolescents: A national view of public policies. *American Psychologist, 39,* 905–911.

Knobloch, H., & Pasamanick, B. (1961). Some thoughts on the inheritance of intelligence. *American Journal of Orthopsychiatry, 31,* 454–473.

Korchin, S. J. (1980). Clinical psychology and minority problems. *American Psychologist, 35,* 262–269.

Kriechman, A. M. (1985). A school-based program of mental health services. *Hospital and Community Psychiatry, 36,* 876–878.

Lamb, H. R. (Ed.). (1984). *The homeless mentally ill.* Washington, DC: American Psychiatric Association.

Leighton, D. C., Harding J. S., Macklin, D. B., Macmillan, A. M., & Leighton, A. H. (1963). *The character of danger: Psychiatric symptoms in selected communities.* New York: Basic Books.

Levine, A. (1982). *Love Canal: Science, politics and people.* Lexington, MA: Heath.

Levine, M. (1966). Psychological testing of children. In M. Hoffman and L. Hoffman (Eds.), *Review of child development research.* New York: Russell Sage Foundation.

Levine, M. (1969). Some postulates of community psychology practice. In F. Kaplan & S. B. Sarason (Eds.), *The Psycho-Educational Clinic papers and research studies.* Springfield, MA: Department of Mental Health.

Levine, M. (1972). The practice of mental health consultation. Some definitions from social theory. In J. Zusman & D. L. Davidson (Eds.), *Practical aspects of mental health consultation.* Springfield, IL: Charles C Thomas.

Levine, M. (1973). Problems of entry in light of some postulates of practice in community psychology. In I. I. Goldenberg (Ed.), *Clinical psychologists in the world of work.* New York: Heath.

Levine, M. (1981). *The history and politics of community mental health.* New York: Oxford University Press.

Levine, M., & Levine, A. (1970). *A social history of helping services.* New York: Appleton-Century-Crofts.

Levine, M., & Perkins, D. V. (1980). Social setting interventions and primary prevention. *American Journal of Community Psychology, 8,* 147–158.

Levitan, S. A. (1969). *The Great Society's poor law.* Baltimore: Johns Hopkins Press.

Levitan, S. A. & Taggart, R. III. (1971). *Social experimentation and manpower policy.* Baltimore: Johns Hopkins Press.

Levitt, E. E. (1957). The results of psychotherapy with children: An evaluation. *Journal of Consulting Psychology, 21,* 189–196.

Levitt, E. E., Beiser, H. R., & Robertson, R. E. (1959). A follow-up evaluation of cases treated at a community child guidance clinic. *American Journal of Orthopsychiatry, 29,* 337–349.

Mangellsdorf, A. D. (1985). Lessons learned and forgotten: The need for prevention and mental health interventions in disaster preparedness. *Journal of Community Psychology, 13,* 239–257.

Manson, S. M. & Trimble, J. E. (1982). American Indian and Alaska native communities: Past efforts, future inquiries. In L. R. Snowden (Ed.), *Reaching the underserved: Mental health needs of neglected populations.* Beverly Hills: Sage.

May, E. (1964). *The wasted Americans.* New York: Harper & Row.

McGee, R. K. (1974). *Crisis intervention in the community.* Baltimore: University Park Press.

Mechanic, D. (1980). *Mental health and social policy* (2d ed.) Englewood Cliffs, NJ: Prentice-Hall.

Meehl, P. E. (1954). *Clinical versus statistical prediction.* Minneapolis: University of Minnesota Press.

Meehl, P. E. (1960). The cognitive activity of the clinician. *American Psychologist, 15,* 19–27.

Meltzoff, J., & Kornreich, M. (1970). *Research in psychotherapy.* New York: Atherton.

Miller, H. L., Coombs, D. W., Leeper, J. D., & Barton, S. N. (1984). An analysis of the effects of suicide prevention facilities on suicide rates in the United States. *American Journal of Public Health, 74,* 340–343.

Moore, T. (1982). Blacks: Rethinking service. In L. R. Snowden (Ed.), *Reaching the underserved. Mental health needs of neglected populations.* Beverly Hills: Sage.

Moynihan, D. P. (1965). *The Negro Family: The case for national action.* Washington, DC: Office of Planning and Research, U.S. Department of Labor.

Moynihan, D. P. (1969). *Maximum feasible misunderstanding. Community action in the War on Poverty.* New York: Free Press.

Murstein, B. I. (1963). *Theory and research in projective techniques.* New York: Wiley.

Myers, J. K., Weissman, M. M., et al. (1984). Six month prevalence of psychiatric disorders in three communities. *Archives of General Psychiatry, 41,* 959–967.

Namir, S., & Weinstein, R. S. (1982). Children: Facilitating new directions. In L. R. Snowden (Ed.), *Reaching the underserved: Mental health needs of neglected populations.* Beverly Hills: Sage.

National Institute of Mental Health. (1970). *Volunteers in community mental health.* Washington, DC: U.S. Government Printing Office.

Neighbors, H. W. (1985). Seeking professional help for personal problems: Black American's use of health and mental health services. *Community Mental Health Journal, 21,* 156–166.

Panzella, A. F. (1985). Whatever happened to community mental health: Portents for corporate medicine. *Hospital and Community Psychiatry, 36,* 1174–1179.

Payton, B. F. (1970). New trends in civil rights. In P. I. Rose (Ed.), *Slavery and its aftermath.* New York: Atherton.

Pearl, A., & Reissman, F. (1965). *New careers for the poor: The nonprofessional in human services.* New York: Free Press.

Peele, R., Gross, B., Arons, B., & Jafri, M. (1984). The legal system and the homeless. In H. R. Lamb (Ed.), *The homeless mentally ill.* Washington, DC: American Psychiatric Association.

Plotnick, R. D., & Skidmore, F. (1975). *Progress against poverty. A review of the 1964–1974 decade.* New York: Academic Press.

President's Commission on Mental Health. (1978). *Report to the President* (Vol I). Washington, DC: U.S. Government Printing Office.

Rappaport, J. (1977). *Community psychology. Values, research and action.* New York: Holt, Rinehart & Winston.

Reiss, B. F., & Brandt, L. W. (1965). What happens to applicants for psychotherapy? *Community Mental Health Journal, 1,* 175–180.

Rickers-Ovsiankina, M. A. (Ed.). (1960). *Rorschach psychology.* New York: Wiley.

Reich, C. A. (1970). *The Greening of America.* New York: Random House.

Roszak, T. (1969). *The making of a counter culture.* New York: Doubleday.

Ryan, W. (1971). *Blaming the victim.* New York: Random House.

Sarason, S. B. (1978). The nature of problem solving in social action. *American Psychologist, 33,* 370–380.

Sarason, S. B. (1981). *Psychology misdirected.* New York: Free Press.

Sarason, S. B. (1982). *Psychology and social action. Selected papers.* New York: Praeger.

Sarason, S. B., & Doris, J. (1979). *Educational handicap, public policy, and social history.* New York: Free Press.

Sarason, S. B., Levine, M., Goldenberg, I. I., Cherlin, D. L., & Bennett, E. M. (1966). *Psychology in community settings; clinical, educational, vocational, social aspects.* New York: Wiley.

Scheff, T. J. (1966). *Being mentally ill: A sociological perspective.* Chicago: Aldine.

Scull, A. T. (1977). *Decarceration: Community treatment and the deviant—A radical view.* Englewood Cliffs, NJ: Prentice-Hall.

Sexton, P. C. (1961). *Education and income.* New York: Viking.

Segal, S. P., & Baumol, J. (1982). The new chronic patient: The creation of an underserved population. In L. R. Snowden (Ed.), *Reaching the underserved: Mental health needs of neglected populations.* Beverly Hills: Sage.

Shapiro, S., Skinner, E. A., et al. (1984). Utilization of health and mental health services. *Archives of General Psychiatry, 41,* 971–978.

Shinn, M., & Felton, B. J. (Eds.) (1981). Institutions and alternatives. *Journal of Social Issues, 37,* 1–176.

Slater, P. (1970). *The pursuit of loneliness.* Boston: Beacon Press.

Sobey, F. (1970). *The nonprofessional revolution in mental health.* New York: Columbia University Press.

Special Populations Subpanel on Mental Health of Black Americans. (1978). *Task Panel Reports Submitted to the President's Commission on Mental Health* (Appendix, Vol III). Washington, DC: U.S. Government Printing Office.

Spivack, G., & Shure, M. (1974). *Social adjustment of young children.* San Francisco: Jossey-Bass.

Spivack, G., Platt, J. J., & Shure, M. B (1976). *The problem-solving approach to adjustment.* San Francisco: Jossey-Bass.

Srole, L., Langner, T. S., Michael, S. T., Opler, M. K., & Rennie, T. A. C. (1962). *Mental health in the metropolis: The midtown Manhattan study.* New York: McGraw-Hill.

Szasz, T. S. (1961). *The myth of mental illness.* New York: Dell.

Task Panel, President's Commission on Mental Health. (1978). Mental Health—Nature and scope of the problems. *Task Panel Reports Submitted to the President's Commission on Mental Health* (Vol. II, Appendix). Washington, DC: U.S. Government Printing Office.

Taube, C. A., Burns, B. J., & Kessler, L. (1984). Patients of psychiatrists and psychologists in office-based practice: 1980. *American Psychologist, 39,* 1435–1447.

Thompson, C. M. (1985). Characteristics associated with outcome in a community mental health partial hospitalization program. *Community Mental Health Journal, 21,* 179–188.

Tuckman, J., & Lavell, M. (1959). Attrition in psychiatric clinics for children. *Public Health Reports, Public Health Service, 74,* 309–315.

Tumin, M. M. (1970). Some social consequences of research on racial relations. In P. I. Rose (Ed.), *Slavery and its aftermath.* New York: Atherton.

Valerio, A. M. (1985). Sex education program evaluations: A review and analysis. Unpublished doctoral preliminary paper, Department of Psychology, SUNY at Buffalo.

White, M. A., & Harris, M. W. (1961). *The school psychologist.* New York: Harper & Row.

Wong, H. Z. (1982). Asian and Pacific Americans. In L. R. Snowden (Ed.), *Reaching the underserved: Mental health needs of neglected populations.* Beverly Hills: Sage.

Zane, N., Sue, S., Castro, F. G., & George, W. (1982). Service system models for ethnic minorities. In L. R. Snowden (Ed.), *Reaching the underserved: Mental health needs of neglected populations.* Beverly Hills: Sage.

Zax, M., & Specter, G. A. (1974). *An introduction to community psychology.* New York: Wiley.

Zubin, J., Eron, L. D., & Schumer, F. (1965). *An experimental approach to projective techniques.* New York: Wiley.

3

The Ecological Analogy

"Ecology" is a fundamental metaphor in community psychology, embodying both the structure of a scientific paradigm and a specific set of values (Slotnick, Jeger, & Trickett, 1980). Among ecological values, for example, is the belief that environments exert significant effects on human behavior and that people can therefore explain and perhaps control their behavior through greater understanding of specific environmental influences. Another ecological value is that to the extent understanding of these influences is achieved, one has an obligation to apply the understanding in *actions* that improve people's lives.

The previous chapter noted how fixation on a single intervention such as psychotherapy has sometimes left us in the paradoxical situation where some people who receive therapy are later *worse* off than are those who do not. The clinical view explains this paradox in terms of some hypothetical individual characteristic that differentiates the two groups (e.g., the people receiving treatment were unable to use it effectively). In contrast, the ecological perspective, because it values individual diversity, deals with a paradox like this by developing a greater variety of problem definitions and solutions, one or another of which will serve the needs of different segments of the population (Rappaport, 1981).

Implications of the ecological analogy for scientific work are also important. Any intervention in the social environment is predicated on a particular understanding of what that environment is like—that is, a point of view. From a scientific standpoint, conceptualizing and measuring the environment of human behavior are relatively recent developments in psychology; at present there is no single coherent and comprehensive theory. Several approaches offering a variety of heuristic constructs are regularly cited (e.g., Moos, 1973). In general, however, the empirical foundations of these concepts are less thoroughly developed than are the theoretical proposals.

This chapter first presents the ecological analogy as a paradigm for thinking and research and then outlines four fundamental ecological principles to guide the community psychologist. These principles are illustrated with detailed examples involving interplay between the mental health and law enforcement systems, and the unforeseen consequences of deinstitutionalizing the mentally retarded. The chapter concludes by discussing the nature of values embodied in the ecology perspective and five principles of community psychology practice inspired by the metaphor of ecology. The next chapter will present three other conceptions that are more thoroughly operationalized than the principles outlined here and will discuss the nature of systematic empirical research on each. (A detailed example applying these views concludes that chapter.)

Ecology as a Paradigm

Ecology is the field of environmental biology. The term *ecology* derives from the Greek root *oikos,* meaning "house." Ecology, then, is the study of "houses" within which organisms live or, more broadly, their environments. The modifier *social,* or *human,* is attached to indicate the specific interest in studying the environments in which people live.

Although biological ecologists consider their field a basic division within biology, they see it as an integral part of the studies of other divisions as well. In general, ecologists study units larger than individual organisms, including populations, communities, ecosystems, and the biosphere. A *population* is a group of similar individuals; *community* refers to the populations within a defined area. The community and the inanimate environment constitute the ecosystem, while *biosphere* refers to the larger inhabited environment. Although ecologists do not ignore the rest of biology by any means, they believe that explanatory concepts should be appropriate to the level of organization studied. While concepts from another level can be helpful in understanding the phenomena under study, the more reductionist concepts can never fully account for phenomena at other levels of organization. In Odum's (1963) words, "to understand a tree, it is necessary to study both the forest of which it is a part as well as the cells and tissues that are part of a tree" (p. 4).

Most community psychologists who use the language of ecology have not adopted this perspective completely, but find a useful analogy in its outline and general principles. In adopting the metaphor of ecology, proponents are trying to say both what they are for and what they are against. For example, they use the scientific language of ecology to assert that an individually oriented psychology is less than fully helpful in thinking about many problems, limits the range of options for intervention (see previous chapter), and may distract attention from important issues. Proponents find ecological concepts attractive because they transcend individual psychology. Just as biological ecology directs attention to the intimate interrelationship between organisms and resources, the concept of the visible organism as a product of its built-in properties and its competitive adaptation to available or changing resources directs attention to more than the individual person.

Those who call for a new paradigm in psychology (e.g., Sarason, 1981; see Chapter 2) assert that problem definitions, research methods, ideological values, and the researcher's (or intervenor's) social position are inseparable. In what follows we will show how those issues mesh with the ecological perspective.

Psychology is one of the few sciences that has no branch devoted to the observation of phenomena in their natural states. Psychology leaped from the armchair to the laboratory, omitting the study of people in natural settings.[1] As consequences of this leap, psychology's concepts are concerned with "inside" properties of organisms and treat the outside as alien. Even Kurt Lewin (1935), the field theorist who developed the formula $B = f(P,E)$ (Behavior is a function of Person and Environment) and the concept of a life space that incorporates an external world, primarily examined the responses of single organisms to the inner-defined life space. Roger Barker (1965), one of Lewin's students, pointed out that an individual's behavior may make little sense when viewed in isolation. One would understand little about a baseball game by observing the behavior of the first baseman alone; his or her actions have meaning only as part of the surrounding game. In adhering to the idea that knowledge is best obtained through the momentary experiment, moreover, psychological research lost a time perspective and created the problem of ecological validity—that is, the questionable external validity or generalizability of its findings (Barker, 1965).

The markedly different nature of scientific research from the ecological viewpoint is described well by Trickett, Kelly, and Vincent (1985):

> Community research is an intervention into the ongoing flow of community life and should be approached as such. While community inquiry—like all research—is designed to generate knowledge, it also can serve as a primary vehicle for the development of a setting. By its very nature, it cannot help but have impact on the place where it occurs. (p. 284)

According to Trickett et al., research activities exemplify resource exchanges involving persons, settings, and events, the goal of which is to create products that benefit the community as a whole (i.e., not just the researcher or funding source). No distinction is made between setting and method. The method is part of the setting, and vice versa (see the principle of interdependence in the next section). All those who are affected by research, including community residents who serve as subjects, are considered formal participants in it.

Because it is part of the community and is affected by the community, ecological research is much more flexible and improvisational than laboratory research. Unplanned events and "side effects" are expected. Research inevitably changes the community and its residents in important ways, and so the whole enterprise of research must be understood *longitudinally*. A longitudinal focus on research as a catalyst for creating and maintaining resources makes it more likely that any products of the research will endure over time. All research is in fact longitudinal, regardless of the stated design in a particular case, since there is always a preexisting context of relationships among participants, and the research activity itself inevitably changes the subsequent nature of that context (e.g., for future research activities).

One complication is that from its longitudinal vantage, the ecological perspective generally does not understand human behavior as the linear effect of some single, isolatable cause. This "noncausal" way of understanding behavior marks a sharp break with the dominant traditions and philosophies in psychology built on the testing of causal hypotheses.

Given our new view of its research and its new methods, we may speak of ecological psychology as a paradigm shift, or revolution, in the Kuhnian sense (Kuhn, 1962). Social ecologists continue to use the language of science, however (after all, as a branch of biology ecology is one of the natural sciences). By retaining the language of science, social ecologists confirm their endorsement of the values of science—objectivity, in the sense of requiring findings to be public and replicable, and empiricism, meaning that all concepts are open to modification in light of new evidence.

This continuing identification with science is important in establishing certain boundaries for the field of ecology. Its intellectual products must not be too discontinuous with other products of scientific endeavor. Identification with other sciences is important in another respect. Although the ecological critique of traditional individual psychology is intellectually grounded, it is also a political statement to the degree that it generates a basis for competing for resources necessary for the ecologist to thrive—research funds, jobs, and recognition within the community of science. The previous chapter showed how historical events and other changes over time affected the popularity of various ideological and theoretical perspectives and thus the opportunities of those who advocated one particular view over another. In this sense, social ecologists can be viewed as a variant population competing for resources with existing populations in the same community.

We note in passing that to the degree methods change, other aspects of the research enterprise will change. One does not need laboratory space, for example, but one does need the resource of time away from the laboratory to study the natural setting. The requirement that one study natural settings raises the issue of access to these settings, and a host of ethical and value questions follow. Does a social ecologist, or any other social scientist, have automatic right of access to such settings as schools, courts, or hospitals? To what degree does the process of observing disrupt or alter phenomena in the natural setting? A study of the civil commitment process in California, for example, reported that a 76% rate of commitment by judges in the month before the study fell to 43% during the course of the study (Miller, 1976). Assuming a cause-and-effect relationship, the difference between 43% and 76% for civil commitments implies a substantial effect on the lives of many people. In that instance, mere observation for purposes of research was far from neutral. One could resort to cost-benefit analysis in these cases, weighing the benefit of the knowledge gained against the impact of research on people's lives, but value problems arise that are not easily resolved (e.g., what specific worth does one assign to a person's being in or out of a mental hospital?).

The methods of ecological psychology raise additional issues. Ecological psychologists rely on multiple measures, including unobtrusive techniques, to collect data in the field. These measures are designed to preserve the complexity of the phenomena under study and to maximize generalizability in the sense that the research studies phenomena as they are found in "nature." Ecological investigators prefer this kind of ecological validity over the tight control and internal precision of the laboratory experiment.

What are the standards of quality for such research? Presumably, we know what these standards are for the laboratory experiment. What implications follow our assertion that the standards we strive to meet in the laboratory are less important for judging products in this new tradition?

The issue of quality standards in research is related to competition for resources. We need standards of goodness if we are to assert entitlement to societal resources and to claim special status in society as professionals. If we relax our preference for control and internal precision, which standards replace those? Sarason (1976) struggled with this issue in trying to answer a student who asked how such research was anything more than "common sense." Sarason answered that such research was Everyman's common sense but, quoting the historian Becker, was "more consciously and expertly applied." Levine (1980a, 1982) suggested that self-conscious discipline is what distinguishes the professional worker from the layperson. Nonetheless, the standards of quality that are to be met if we or others are to rely on research findings emerging from such perspectives remain to be articulated.

This issue of standards is not idle when viewed in relation to the competition for resources. To survive, a new population must have access to resources. One such resource might be a base within a university, for example, where research and scholarship may be conducted and the results disseminated by teaching. Standards for the goodness of research influence the award of grants and other funds and publication in journals, and those in turn influence tenure and appointment decisions—in a word, survival. New journals may proliferate because the standards of excellence as well as the substance of new work differ from the traditional. In other words, the effects of a given change radiate. Where and how one may obtain funds for research and where and how one might get work published influence the thinking of research workers. Fortunately, the overall system does allow for diversity. A viable new population may find a niche and compete successfully for resources with other populations in the same community.

Principles of Ecology

James G. Kelly (1966) was an early proponent of the ecological analogy in community psychology. He articulated four principles, adapted from ecology, that he believed were useful in approaching problems in community intervention. The first of these principles states that components within a social unit are *interdependent.* Changes in one component of an ecosystem will produce changes in other components of that system. As we explain later, for example, the deinstitutionalization of patients from psychiatric hospitals had important effects on other systems besides mental health, such as justice and law enforcement. Interdependence refers not only to the existence of mutual influence among community components, but also to their dynamic interaction over time. In research, for example, the relationship between the investigator and the setting under study becomes part of the community system. Investigator and setting are assumed to have significant effects on each other during all stages of the research (Vincent & Trickett, 1983).

In Kelly's view, the principle of interdependence not only alerts us to the complexity of change, but also directs us to deal with the community as the unit of analysis for some interventions. It directs our attention to a different level of analysis from the internal characteristics of an individual patient. A further implication of interdependence, moreover, is that mental health professionals intervening in the community-oriented mode will adopt different roles and work in different environments than where professionals are normally found. It is one thing to see patients in a clinic. It is quite another to consult with teachers in a classroom, and still another to participate in a communitywide coordinating council, as the short-lived Mental Health Systems Act of 1980 would have required. If effective coordination requires additional legislative authority, for example, mental health professionals must know how to operate in the appropriate environments. As a caution, we should note that the principle of interdependence warns us in general that we should attend to the relationships that comprise the community system, but it does not tell us precisely to what we should attend in any specific case.

How does one get a handle on the specific interdependent connections in a given community? Kelly's second principle, referred to as the *cycling of resources,* suggests that in a biological system the transfer of energy reveals the individual components that comprise the system and also their relationship to each other. A larger animal feeding on a smaller one, which fed on a plant, which derived energy from the sun,

leaves fertilizer for another plant. Energy is transferred throughout the cycle; one creature's waste is another's raw material. An intervention represents a change in the way
resources are cycled, and thus this principle concerns the way resources are created
and defined as well as how they are distributed. Furthermore, Kelly states that before
intervening to change the distribution of resources (e.g., creating situational mediators
that ameliorate crisis reactions), one ought to know how a community cycles resources
on its own. To change a community, one must know something about how it works.

The difficulties encountered in transferring resources from the psychiatric hospital
to the community at large in support of deinstitutionalization provide a good example
of an intervention or policy undertaken without full cognizance of how communities
distribute resources. The expectation that resources would follow patients from the
hospital into the community was not always fulfilled. As long as hospitals remained
open, basic costs and overhead remained high. It costs almost as much to maintain
relatively few patients in the hospital as it does to care for many more patients, if one
has to maintain a 24-hour staff and a physical plant. More important, perhaps, hospitals provide employment and are often the main economic resource for small
communities.

A case history presented by Levine (1980b) demonstrates that closing a hospital is
not easy, even when there is little need for it in the state system. The policy that
resources should *precede* the patient into the community is more effective in implementing the goals of deinstitutionalization. Substantial effort is required to provide
outpatient care, however, and the introduction of hospital-sponsored services into the
community often creates conflict between the population of state hospital staff and
the population of local agency staff (Levine, 1980b; see Chapter 10 for a fuller description of the case and the process of change).

Kelly's third principle is *adaptation.* Environments are not behavior-neutral:
through the specific resources it provides, an environment effectively constrains some
behaviors and facilitates others. Adaptation describes the process by which organisms
vary their habits or characteristics to cope with available or changing resources. In the
absence of adaptation, a change in resources may threaten survival. For example, the
federal government during the Reagan administration decided to stop providing funds
for graduate training in clinical psychology. In the past, those resources were important for stimulating the growth of clinical training in psychology. Training grants were
resources for universities in providing teaching costs and for students in providing
tuition and stipends to underwrite full-time study. In the absence of those funds, clinical training faculties are rethinking their programs. Programs may shrink in size to
compensate for reduced resources, for example, although that alternative has other
long-range implications for survival. Programs may change to accommodate student
need for support (e.g., part-time study or the development of a professional school
model with a time-limited course of study and all costs borne by the student). Other
features of training may change to help produce additional resources. The faculty ani-
mals, presumably with greater adaptive skills, may forage over a wider turf to bring
back new resources. They may start selling their services (e.g., psychotherapy, consultation) to produce the funds needed to maintain graduate education.

The concept of adaptation is related to the concepts of *niche* and *niche breadth.*
Niche refers to the habitat within which a given creature can survive. The broader the
range of habitats within which creatures of the same type are found, the greater the

niche breadth. Humans, by virtue of their great ability to adapt behaviorally and culturally, are found at the North Pole and at the equator, in oxygenless space and underwater. In that sense, humans may be said to have a wide niche breadth.

As Mills and Kelly (1972) point out, the concept of niche leads us to think about the development of functional roles within a new social organization (niche) and the provision of resources appropriate for characteristics of the population occupying this niche. We can also contemplate teaching adaptive skills so that a population's niche breadth can be extended. Consider the chronic mental patients found in psychiatric hospitals, for example. The behavioral characteristics of these patients are to some extent a reflection of limited situational resources and adaptation to the custodial nature of hospital care. By training such patients in skills of daily living and providing other resources (e.g., group homes, income under the Supplemental Security Income program), their niche breadth widens and the likelihood they will adapt to normal community life increases. Kruzich and Berg (1985) found that the self-sufficiency of chronic mentally ill clients depends on the organizational characteristics of the long-term care facilities in which they live. The attitudes of staff, and their willingness to allow some flexibility in their routines while maintaining a moderate degree of scheduling of activities, predict client self-sufficiency. Even within the hospital, Zusman (1967) reports changes in patient appearance when services adopt a therapeutic instead of a custodial orientation to care.

A great many individuals appear "mentally retarded" only with respect to their ability to cope with the intellectual demands of schools. Follow-up studies indicate that at least within the upper ranges of mental retardation, such individuals fare no worse occupationally and socially than other persons of similar social-class background (see Sarason & Doris, 1969, pp. 86–89; Bloch, 1984). The identification of some individuals as retarded is a reflection on the schools and how they are organized as much as on the characteristics of the individuals themselves. School curricula teach verbal-cognitive skills. The curricula are organized by grade levels, in part because we recognize that children of different ages are different intellectually, but also because the needs of a mass education system have demanded such age grading (Levine, 1976). Once the man-made (not god-given) standard is in place and a limited fare is offered, those whose characteristics mesh with the standard and with that fare will thrive, while those who cannot use what is offered will languish. Alternative school programs (i.e., different niches allowing for different rates of development, teaching through varied methods and acknowledging varied accomplishments) might go a long way toward preventing many instances of individual "retardation."

As another illustration, we note that the mobility of physically disabled people has been greatly improved by wheelchairs and other technological devices. Until well into the 1970s, however, the physical architecture of many buildings, including restroom facilities, made access by people in wheelchairs difficult, producing a lack of fit and a difficult adaptation to work and school settings by handicapped individuals. To a degree, however, one can say that the behavioral handicap of the person in the wheelchair is as much a function of the staircase or the curbstone as it is of the person's nonfunctional limbs. Thus, following the passage of regulations requiring wheelchair access ramps and restroom modifications, the adaptation of such individuals to key community settings improved. The concepts of niche and adaptation are useful because they teach us to think about alternatives and lead us to think about the resources necessary to provide an alternative. They also help us to accept differences among individuals and, if necessary, to consider political solutions such as environmental regulation to problems of poor person-environment fit.

Kelly's fourth principle is *succession*. Environments are not static; they change. A change in the environment may create conditions more favorable to one population and less favorable to another. Eventually a more favored population will squeeze out the others, or at least dominate a given area, or some new level of homeostasis will develop among populations sharing the same area. Thus, while interdependence teaches us to understand the community before trying to change it, succession implies that change, both natural and artificial, can contribute to our understanding in the first place.

A good example of this principle is the succession of populations in urban neighborhoods. Psychiatric ghettos take root more readily in transient neighborhoods where anonymity is widespread, other populations have little rootedness, and the neighborhood has little formal organization. Such ghettos developed where properties were not profitable for other use, as in the old residential hotels on Manhattan's Upper West Side. As property values increased and tax benefits were made available to developers, "gentrification" took place, and these hotels were converted to condominiums. Many former patients and welfare clients living in the hotels were evicted, sometimes ruthlessly, helping to create the troublesome phenomenon of homelessness. The economically and politically stronger middle class was better able to compete with the poor for housing niches.

Sometimes a neighborhood organization welcomes newcomers to the community because of resources the newcomers may bring. A YWCA residence with which we are familiar, dedicated to serving women but unable to attract young businesswomen as residents, opened its doors to female ex-patients. Its buildings were resources for the former patients, and their rental payments were resources to keep the building functioning and to pay for necessary staff. Convents in New York State, emptying because of the declining number of persons entering religious life, were put to new use as group homes for retarded individuals deinstitutionalized under court order. Church organizations took in the deinstitutionalized persons, fulfilling the religious value of service, and received money for their care. Unused for their original purposes, convents became resources not only for the retarded living in them, but also for administrators charged with carrying out the deinstitutionalization order. The church, with a stake in providing service, often used its influence to restrain neighborhood resistance (competition from still other popoulations) to the invasion of the new population (Rothman, 1982).

In addition to alerting us to some issues of change, the principle of succession teaches that some resources otherwise discarded may be put to use by other populations. The principles of succession and the cycling of resources both tell us to search broadly through the universe of alternatives for new resources. The self-help movement provides a case in point: a "useless" individual, a drain on resources, may become a therapeutic resource within the context of a self-help organization such as Alcoholics Anonymous (see Chapter 8). Self-help movements, able to use different resources from those that professionals require, are to a certain extent succeeding the population of professional service providers. The literature on how self-help organizations and mental health professionals can relate to each other may be taken as an example of the development of a new homeostasis between populations, based on the possibility of exchanging resources to meet mutual needs.

Illustration: Mental Health and the Law

The ecological principles of interdependence, cycling of resources, niche, and adaptation are well illustrated in the problem that Teplin (1983) calls the criminalization of the mentally ill. As we noted in Chapter 2, the inpatient census of state mental hospitals has declined dramatically since the 1950s. Whatever the merits of the argument that incarcerating patients in "total" institutions was harmful, unnecessary, and expensive, the fact was that federal policies, reflected in reimbursement formulas, made it advantageous to shift patients from in-hospital niches to other niches—nursing homes, board-and-care homes, or similar facilities. The patient's adaptation to the community was to have been assisted by the provision of resources in the form of supervised medication, day care, rehabilitation services, and outpatient psychotherapy. Those resources were not always forthcoming, however, nor were they forthcoming in forms many persons could use (Levine, 1981).

Levine (1981) described how litigation in the 1960s and 1970s, designed to correct abuses in the hospital system, led to a tightening of legal standards for involuntary commitment. Committing a person involuntarily to a mental facility for more than brief emergency care required evidence that the person was not just mentally ill but was dangerous to himself or herself or to others or was unable to survive even with assistance from family or friends. In many states these court decisions imposed restrictions on the process of commitment that were translated into statutory standards affecting everyone concerned with the problem of deviant behavior. The person at risk for involuntary hospitalization was entitled to a number of procedural due-process protections to ensure that the commitment and loss of personal liberty occurred for good reason. On paper, at least, it became more difficult to hospitalize someone involuntarily. Relationships among the hospital as a resource, professional mental health workers as a population, prospective patients' families, and other community agencies as populations changed with ramifying effects.[2]

Although outpatient services have grown, those services would not necessarily have been directed to persons who formerly would have been served as inpatients. General hospital psychiatric services and outpatient clinics restrict the types of cases they believe are suitable for service in their facilities. A prospective patient may be denied care because he or she doesn't have the financial resources and is not eligible for welfare or other insurance that will pay the costs of care. Other institutions may not have secure facilities to manage excited, aggressively acting-out clients. Teplin (1983, p. 60) reports that some mental hospitals will not accept a patient who has any criminal charge pending, even if it is a minor one. Patients can thus face barriers to gaining access to niches and the resources they contain.

These two sets of forces, mental health litigation and legislation regarding funding, make it more difficult to hospitalize people. The principle of interdependence would lead us to predict that policies that keep patients out of the hospital will influence the working environments of two important populations in the community—persons working in the criminal justice system and mental health workers. If these changes are potent, we would expect to see adaptations by members of these populations, and also some change in the niches in which members of these populations are found.

Let us first examine the mental health professionals and their situations. Jacoby (1983) studied the implementation of a 1976 statute reforming Pennsylvania mental health law (Mental Health Procedures Act, 1976). This act, similar to many passed by other states in recent years, had as its purpose to decrease long-term mental hospitalization, provide greater procedural due process in commitment proceedings, provide for periodic judicial review of commitment, and ensure that appropriate treatment was provided in the least restrictive setting.

Although the formal leadership of the state psychiatric association favored the new law, Jacoby notes, a great many front-line mental health professionals were not at all happy with its provisions. One source of opposition was the substitution of a legal standard—dangerousness to self or others—for a professional judgment of the need for treatment. As Jacoby puts it, bureaucratic norms were set in opposition to professional norms of making judgments about what is or is not in a patient's best interests. Jacoby describes two forms of adaptation by mental health professionals to this turbulence in the ecosystem. One is simply a failure to comply by continuing to admit patients, especially for emergency care, and then asserting in subsequent hearings that the patient met legal standards for commitment. Because in many places judicial examination of psychiatric evidence is perfunctory (see Levine, 1981, pp. 148–153), patients may end up being retained for extended care even if they do not meet legal criteria. More often, however, mental health workers probably adapt in the opposite way, such as by defining the legal criteria very narrowly and refusing service to persons who do not clearly meet the standards for inpatient care.

Mental health advocacy tends to be vigorous in the city of Philadelphia, according to Jacoby's observations, in contrast to other communities where it is considerably less so. (Philadelphia has an active public-interest bar. Its attorneys have brought several important suits asserting the rights of the mentally retarded in particular—e.g., *PARC v. Commonwealth of Pennsylvania,* 343 F. Supp. 279 (1972); *Halderman v. Pennhurst,* 49 LW 4363 (1981). The presence of an active bar may encourage more vigorous advocacy.) Jacoby notes that the public defender in Philadelphia specialized in mental health work, developed some expertise in it, and seemed to define the lawyer's professional role as requiring vigorous advocacy.

The combination of a new law and vigorous advocacy led to the perception that it was difficult to hospitalize people in Philadelphia. The local newspaper attributed the large number of all-too-visible "street people," "vent men," and "bag ladies" to rigid hospital policies and the refusal of the courts to hospitalize those in need. Jacoby claims that although mental health workers also believed it difficult to get a commitment order in Philadelphia, the facts do not support this belief. For example, the overall rate of commitment on hearings after an emergency commitment was about 80% in Philadelphia, the same rate as in the state at large. Jacoby attended 20 commitment hearings and observed that despite vigorous advocacy for release, all 20 persons were committed. Although these facts do not support the perception that commitment was difficult to obtain, Jacoby believes that this perception nevertheless affected the actions of workers before cases got to hearings.

Given the perception that getting a commitment is difficult, Jacoby believes that mental health workers adapted by screening the cases they brought to court and by releasing patients for whom they were less certain of successful commitment. He cites data showing that 33% of those hospitalized on an emergency basis statewide were subject to a petition for extended emergency treatment, an action that occurred in only 19% of the cases in Philadelphia. In Philadelphia, moreover, 58% of patients committed for extended emergency treatment were subject to petitions for continued involuntary treatment. In the rest of the state, this figure was 71%. Similarly, 58% statewide were subject to petitions for an extension of the period of involuntary treatment, while in Philadelphia that was true for only 16%.

In other words, although an equal proportion were committed when the case went to a hearing, a smaller percent of cases apparently went to a hearing in Philadelphia than in the rest of the state. Because mental health workers believed it was a hassle to get a commitment in Philadelphia, Jacoby argues, they systematically screened people for hearings, releasing some who were troubled and troublesome. (Gupta (1971) described a similar process of negotiated out-of-court "settlements" when attorneys were part of the work environment of mental health professionals.)

We should not make a value judgment as to whether the informal screening is a positive consequence of the enforcement of patient rights, or instead harms people who would be better off if they were subject to extended involuntary treatment. What Jacoby describes is simply the adaptation of mental health workers to a change in their community, or their ecosystem, assuming that the statutory provisions for due process are considered part of the inanimate environment.

The police represent another population in this community faced with the problem of adapting to changes in the working environment. Police can take into emergency custody people involved in a disturbance of some kind. Police cannot take a person into custody without either having a warrant for arrest, based on a complaint from someone that the person has done something wrong or, in the absence of a warrant, witnessing the infraction themselves or having other probable cause to act. In theory, police act under a complex set of rules designed to protect citizens against the abuse of police power.

In the case of persons exhibiting signs of disturbance, the standards of the American Bar Association (ABA) state that police authority to take such persons into custody should be defined by statute[3] and should be limited to the standards of dangerousness to self or others, or to the appearance of being unable to survive alone. The police role, the ABA says, should be strictly limited to transporting the person in custody to an appropriate facility for examination and treatment (ABA, 1984, Part II).

In general, police have a great deal of authority to take into custody those who are overtly dangerous to themselves or others. They have less authority, however, to detain someone apparently unable to care for his or her own basic needs (and whose life or health is in danger for that reason), or someone who seems disoriented and confused but is sufficiently alert to decide that he or she does not wish to receive care. As the ABA standards note, police must make an on-the-spot determination in such cases, weighing the state's interest in protecting an individual from harm against the individual's constitutionally based interest in being free to manage his or her own affairs. A moment's reflection on the inherent complexity of this decision helps to explain why police may be reluctant to become involved in noncriminal situations.

Both the availability of facilities in the community and the policies and attitudes of mental health workers affect police willingness to take someone into custody for mental-health-related purposes. The ABA standards (1984, 7–37) cite research indi-

cating that police become cynical about mental health services if the admission procedure is tedious or uncertain. On occasion the mental health worker may refuse
admission to someone who later attempts suicide or engages in violence. Such episodes may enter into folklore, not as the exceptional case but as the general rule, helping to shape police attitudes toward the use of mental health facilities as an alternative
disposition in cases where the police have discretion in taking the person to a lockup
or a hospital.

Police do not necessarily view symptoms of mental disorder with indifference.
Based on observations of police-citizen encounters, Teplin (1984) found that if there
was some indication of mental disorder, independent of the severity of the episode,
the police were twice as likely to make an arrest as when such indication was absent.
Most prospective patients who come to police attention have probably committed at
least a violation, if not a more serious crime. Even if the violation is disorderly conduct, once convicted the person can receive a jail sentence of up to 15 days. If the
charge is sufficiently serious, the arraigning magistrate can set bail at a level the
accused person may not be able to meet, requiring him or her to be held in custody
until trial. If someone raises a good-faith doubt as to the accused person's mental or
emotional competence to stand trial, he or she may be held for an examination to
determine competency or be admitted to a hospital for that purpose[4] (ABA, 1984, Part
IV). This combination of factors, including police preference for the criminal justice
system over the mental health system, leads to the hypothesis that many persons formerly served in a mental hospital, during an era of less rigid standards for admission
and more rigid standards for discharge, now will be found in new niches: jails and
prisons.

If more disturbed persons are now found in jails and holding centers, and in prisons after sentencing on criminal charges, we face a societal problem of reallocating or
redistributing professional resources to new institutional settings. For one thing, any
right to treatment probably extends to a person with a history of mental or emotional
disturbance who is being held on criminal charges. That issue aside, arrest and jailing
constitute a distinctively stressful experience, often triggering fear, anxiety, and
depression. The suicide rate among inmates in county jails is 16 times greater than
among adults of comparable age in the population at large. For youths held in adult
jails, the rate is three to five times higher than the rate in the general population
(Hayes, 1983; Fox, 1981, p. 671). A heightened state of arousal may precipitate excited
aggressive acts toward both custodial personnel and other prisoners, especially in individuals prone to such behavior. Custodial personnel in holding centers and short-term
correctional facilities may need training in the day-to-day management of disturbed
persons and, if medication is used, to understand its nature and side effects (see ABA,
1984, Standard 7–2.8).

Teplin's (1983) review points up the difficulty in answering the question of
whether as a result of deinstitutionalization policies more persons with mental and
emotional disorders are now being cared for in the criminal justice system and in
correctional facilities than was true before. Certainly, very disturbed individuals are
being arrested, arraigned, and jailed. In one study of cases referred for forensic evaluation, 80% exhibited severe psychopathology. Of those 94% were recommended for
hospitalization; 90% of the group had had histories of psychiatric hospitalization.
Nearly half the individuals were charged with misdemeanors. Although the police

could have screened this group at the time they took the individuals into custody, the study noted that police feel that hospitalization is too time consuming if not unpredictable (Lamb & Grant, 1982). Callahan and Diamond (1985) studied a random sample of 949 jail inmates in five California jails with a mental health assessment to determine the presence of mental illness. In this study, 67% were found to have some mental disorder. Only 7.7% were diagnosed as psychotic. The rest were classified as personality disorder, substance abuser, neurotic, and either mentally retarded or suffering from an organic brain syndrome. Guy, Platt, Zwerling, and Bullock (1985) report similar findings for psychiatric examinations of new admissions to a county jail.

One hypothesis that seems to have solid support in the research literature is that formerly hospitalized persons have higher arrest rates than those without such histories (Teplin, p. 57). Interpreting the existing data is complicated, as she notes. A simple "hydraulic" hypothesis (i.e., that overflow from the mental hospitals because of deinstitutionalization accounts for the increase in the prison population) cannot be sustained.

If police do prefer the criminal justice route, however, more disturbed persons would now be in jails (presentencing holding facilities) than was formerly true. Although the epidemiology is difficult, Teplin reads the evidence to conclude that the jail has indeed become the poor person's mental health facility as a consequence of changes in the admission of persons to mental hospitals.It would indeed be ironic if that were the case, for Dorothea Dix's mid-nineteenth-century crusade to build mental hospitals was based in part on her observations that too many mentally ill persons were being held in jails (Levine, 1981, p. 24).

This excursion into the complex interrelationships among systems and the rules governing their operation should adequately illustrate the implications of interdependence when community change occurs. Change requires adaptations on the part of existing populations in the ecosystem, in this instance the police, mental health workers, jailers, and court personnel. Moreover, we see that adaptation by some populations can force another population (mental patients) into new niches (jails). Furthermore, such a change also requires reallocation of resources to populations and niches (e.g., mental health personnel more active in criminal justice niches).

Note that none of these events can be understood in terms of individual psychopathology, nor from examining clinical treatment or diagnostic processes. The mental health worker is presumably trained to evaluate problems according to clinical criteria, but an understanding of clinical criteria alone (e.g., behaviors that enter into a determination of diagnosis under the categories of DSM-III) will not explain the decisions mental health workers make. Similarly, examining the formal rules under which they operate will not fully explain the behavior and attitudes of police in exercising discretion when arresting and charging persons they encounter. Moreover, Jacoby's and Teplin's research required field study and an analysis of data that could not possibly have been generated in a laboratory. This complex example indicates that mental health workers cannot fully appreciate their own behavior and the behavior of their clients without stepping back and looking at the system of which they are a part. The concepts of ecology, crude as they may be when applied in this context, are useful because they direct our attention to important issues that affect us every day and that we cannot understand without examining the larger system around us.

Illustration: Deinstitutionalization of the Retarded

Willer and Intagliata (1984) provide an excellent review of deinstitutionalization policy as it affects services for the retarded. Problems similar to those occurring with the deinstitutionalization of the mentally ill are apparent, suggesting that the principles of social ecology have general application. The policy of deinstitutionalizing the mentally retarded arose in the optimistic social and economic climate of the 1960s and early 1970s (see Chapter 2). Dramatic exposures of poor institutional conditions, development of the ideology of "normalization," court decisions enunciating the concept of care in the least restrictive setting, and a willingness to use public resources to attempt to solve the problems all led to a general policy of providing care for the mentally retarded in the community. The policy was implemented at the federal level by amending the Social Security Act (Title XIX) to make resources available for intermediate-care facilities, by supplying funds for the construction of group homes and similar new niches through Housing and Urban Development legislation, and through the Supplemental Security Income (SSI) disability program, which provided incomes (resources) for retarded individuals. The policy led to a decline in the institutional population.

The policy also had several unintended consequences, however. Because less severely impaired persons were discharged to the community, the institutional population now has a higher density of persons who are older, are more profoundly retarded, possess serious behavioral problems, and carry diagnoses of organic damage. Although staff:patient ratios have improved as a result of deinstitutionalization, a problem of adaptation has arisen involving employee satisfaction in working exclusively with a more difficult population. Staff turnover has been high, and morale problems related to promotion and other economic rewards have cropped up. A sharp increase in the number of community residences has created other problems. Community opposition to the placement of group homes (i.e., competition among populations for resources) can be intense, although it usually dies down over time (Lubin, Schwartz, Zigman, & Janicki, 1982). Some communities have attempted to introduce zoning restrictions on group homes, however, which has led to litigation.[5]

As Willer and Intagliata (1984) point out, even though the number of retarded individuals in public institutions has declined, the total number in residential care facilities (new niches) has increased. Formerly, parents were encouraged to place retarded children in institutions. Although public policy is now ostensibly directed toward maintaining retarded individuals in the community, increased placement in residential facilities appears to be coming from those who were previously cared for in their natural family homes, a form of succession. The group-home population tends to be middle-aged and mildly impaired or borderline.

Changes in institutional admission policies have restricted the admission of younger, more severely handicapped individuals, who now tend to remain in their own homes. Willer and Intagliata question whether families who keep younger, more severely retarded children in the home are adequately helped by existing services. These more severely handicapped children are eligible for public school services through mainstreaming legislation (PL 94-142, Education for All Handicapped Children Act), placing new demands on the public school system.

Willer and Intagliata also point out that the interests of parents of the retarded may differ from the interests of public policymakers. Parents are concerned about the adequacy of community-based services and the permanence of funding for these services and do not entirely agree with the goals of institutional programs to make their retarded children more independent. These policies thus created some parental opposition, which has led to parents lobbying against deinstitutionalization and becoming more involved in the deinstitutionalization decision (Frohboese & Sales, 1980).

These ramified and unintended consequences of policy implementation must be weighed against the still developing but as yet ambiguous evidence regarding benefits of deinstitutionalization policy for the retarded. The widespread effects on so many different actors and social institutions indicate that the ecological principle of interdependence cannot be ignored. Even though its precise effects cannot be predicted, as we noted with respect to both the mentally ill and the retarded, the principle of interdependence leads us to expect effects that have an impact well beyond the problem receiving our immediate attention.

We can easily offer post-hoc examples of concepts. Such an exercise should not be mistaken for solid evidence of the validity of the concepts nor of their utility in providing predictive guidelines. New concepts enable us to depart from conceptual ruts and to explore the universe of alternatives more thoroughly by encouraging us to roam over many different terrains in search of resources.

New concepts also ask us to view our research problems in a different way. Ecology requires us to look not only at the person, but also at the environment, and to think of behavior as a form of adaptation between persons and environments. At an individual level, we are likely to miss a lot when we study a "specimen" in our psychological laboratory or in the clinic, especially when we use instruments that measure the person alone. The ecological viewpoint tells us that the behavior we observe may be at least in part an adaptation to a specific situation, and thus that the behavior we see in the clinic or the laboratory may work itself out in quite a different fashion in another setting.

The ecological perspective poses different questions: How do members of different populations adapt to their environments? When a deviant (variant) individual comes to our clinical attention, is that an isolated aberration, or are we perforce directed toward examining the environment to see what other populations share the same space, what nutrients are missing, and what toxins are present that might be removed? In this perspective, each variant case represents a class of phenomena that challenges our current level of understanding.

Ecology and Values

We noted earlier that the ecological perspective asks us to examine the researcher's (or intervenor's) social values and perspective as well as his or her methods and concepts. Textbook writers in community psychology clearly believe the field's purpose is to serve the underdog. This desire reflects compassion and a sense of social justice. Goldenberg (1978) is outspoken in his view that oppression is the target of any intervention and that oppression is not personal but structural and institutional in nature. More than others, he is willing to relate his views of social science to memories of his father, whom he movingly describes as having succumbed to circumstances. Rappaport (1977) writes that the professional work of community psychology is directed toward the implementation of "a more equitable, just and fair society."

Those aims are frankly political. Viewing mental health issues in terms of the redistribution of power and money provides congruence between those writers' scientific interests and their personal and political values, and is also congruent with community psychology's origins in the Kennedy–Johnson War on Poverty. During that period, public resources were allocated for the benefit of the underdog. The social-justice concept underlying the Kennedy–Johnson programs attracted many social scientists whose values resonated with that concept. They saw an opportunity to fulfill, in professional roles, their personal social and political values.

Environmental explanations for the causes of social misery were then prominent (see Levine & Levine, 1970). President Kennedy (1963) articulated that message in his address to Congress on the needs of the mentally ill and the mentally retarded in discussing the necessity for preventive programs. It was easy to accept the argument that poverty and the evils attendant on poverty were associated with lack of opportunity and the failure of social agencies to serve those in the poverty group. According to this viewpoint, schools, welfare agencies, employers, landlords, and police acted in concert to deny or to minimize opportunity.[6] Chronic mental illness was attributed, at least in part, to hospitals that were inadequate to their task of healing and structured in a manner designed to perpetuate maladaptation. Goffman (1961), calling hospitals "total institutions," saw patient behavior as not entirely the result of psychosis but instead as an adaptation to life in the oppressive hospital. Szasz's (1963) attack on psychiatry as a threat to civil liberties added to the climate of the time. Championing social justice and the cause of the underdog could be accomplished through applications of science and enabled social scientists to fulfill in professional roles the values they held as persons and citizens.

As Rappaport (1977) notes, the ecological analogy is consistent with the values of democracy and equality, for it directs us to value diversity. It asserts that while populations may be different from each other in appearance, culturally speaking, they are not different when viewed as products of adaptation. Consciousness raising among such populations as blacks, women, and gays led members of those groups to create social environments (niches) within which individual self-images changed from despised failures to persons with valued traits (see Chapter 9). Members of such groups then acted aggressively to change the views and actions that members of other populations displayed toward them. The aim of such social and political action can be characterized as an effort to extend niche breadth and command new resources (e.g., jobs, housing, education, social esteem), enabling its members to thrive in a greater number of environments.

The concept of adaptation to available resources leads us to think not of inferior persons, but of persons whose characteristics must be understood in relation to the resources available in a niche, to the persons' ability to extend niche breadth by adapting, and to barriers to extending niche breadth because of competition from members of other populations. The ecological perspective stands in contrast to a hereditarian position that attributes variance in human behavior primarily to immutable genetic characteristics of individual organisms. Social ecology accepts that organismic characteristics set certain limits for development. Within those limits, however, the variance among organisms is strongly related to available resources and to necessary adaptations. A potted houseplant may be small while its brother in a tropical rain forest is huge. A pine tree subjected to offshore winds grows scrubby at the seashore or small at the low-oxygen tree line on a mountain peak, but in a valley forest it grows tall and straight. The ecological analogy suggests that the person in one setting, nurtured in one way and competing for resources, may be very different in another setting if nurtured differently or if given different cultural tools for adaptation. The problems and limitations we face reside not in people but in the capacity of our imagination to envision and create new settings. Scientific principles thus blend with personal values in a political argument for resource redistribution and with an ideology that at once does not blame the victim (Ryan, 1971) and expresses hope for a brighter future.

Ecology and Practice

The ecological analogy led Levine (1969) to propose five principles of practice in community psychology.

I. *A problem arises in a setting or in a situation: Factors in the situation cause, trigger, exacerbate, and/or maintain the problem.* This first principle indicates that we cannot direct our diagnostic efforts exclusively toward describing the characteristics of the individual person. We have to learn to understand the characteristics of settings as well. We need to look for a lack of fit between persons and environments, for environmental "toxins," and for the possibility that with different resources in the setting, the individual's behavioral adaptation would be different. The principle also implies that we must leave our offices and learn to appreciate how problems are actually manifested in a given setting.

II. *A problem arises because the problem-resolving (i.e., adaptive) capacity of the social setting is blocked.* The ecological notion of interdependence implies that persons and settings function as parts of the same integrated system. A second principle implies that the adaptive capacity of people in a setting is limited in some ways by the nature of its social organization or its access to resources. One can illustrate the concept by asking workers in any human-service setting to describe problems they face in providing service to their clients. A number of problems will be described. If one then asks for solutions to the problems, a number of creative ones will be suggested. If one asks further why the solutions are not implemented, problems with the system will emerge. In effect, the principle states that a problem is that for which you do not have a solution. When you have a solution, adaptation will occur. Problems are thus understood differently using an ecological perspective. Because a problem requires adaptation, it is essentially an opportunity for short- and long-term change in the system.

III. *To be effective, help has to be located strategically to the manifestation of the problem.* The third principle also emphasizes the situational approach inherent in the ecological analogy. It suggests that we should alter our view of how help is to be delivered. Instead of sending the person to help, the principle suggests that we should bring help to the person, or more precisely to the setting in which the person is defined as a problem. The term *strategically* can have temporal as well as spatial referents, which helps us to think of *when* in the course of the development of a problem it would be useful to deliver assistance. The ecological analogy suggests that we examine environmental circumstances, while Dohrenwend's model (Chapter 2) introduces the dimension of time. This principle suggests that the design of helping services should make use of both the spatial and the temporal dimensions of a problem.

IV. *The goals and values of the helping agent or service must be consistent with the goals and values of the setting.* The fourth principle brings us face-to-face with the value issues in intervention. Settings have both latent and manifest purposes. If the goals of change are consistent with the latent and manifest purposes of the setting, the change process will not stimulate resistance on those grounds. If the essential values of the change agent conflict with values in the setting, the agent can expect opposition, including efforts to block the change or to extrude the agent. For example, a change agent may be able to justify on mental health and prevention grounds a course on sex education and the art of love, including supervised laboratory experiences. No high school in the country would allow such a program, however, because of the conflict in values and goals that would be introduced. A change agent proposing such a project would undoubtedly be extruded from the setting, if not worse.

Values and goals different from those that characterize the setting may be pursued, but not without conflict. Some argue that conflict is essential to change and that conflict should be used consciously to induce change. That may be so. The error is in *not* anticipating conflict or in misunderstanding its basis. This principle calls attention to the issue.

The principle also requires the change agent to confront the potential conflict between his or her values and the values of those in a setting. Ira Goldenberg once illustrated this problem by a hypothetical situation he presented to a seminar at the Yale Psychoeducational Clinic. Goldenberg asked staff members how they would react if the clinic were approached by a klavern of the Ku Klux Klan for assistance with organizational problems. Suppose, for example, that the KKK wanted help in improving communications among its members so that they could more efficiently carry out attempts to terrorize or to intimidate various minority groups. Staff members might have the technical skills to help the KKK improve communication and develop as an organization. Should the clinic accept the assignment? Essentially the same problem is posed if the change agent is asked to help improve the adjustment of prisoners to an oppressive institution or schoolchildren to a rigid or sterile school program, or to help develop methods to uncover welfare mothers who may earn some extra money doing housework without reporting the income to the welfare worker. Change may be accomplished using knowledge and methods that appear to be value-free, but not all changes are equally desirable, and a request for help in achieving change may force the change agent to confront his or her own values (Sarason, 1978).

V. *The form of help should have potential for being established on a systematic basis, using the natural resources of the setting or through introducing resources that can become institutionalized as part of the setting.* The fifth principle suggests that one should strive to understand the nature of resources and how a community cycles its resources. Moreover, the principle implies that one would prefer introducing a change that endures and continues to help resolve problems in a particular setting. For the change to endure, one must understand how the new component will fit in the old niche and how the ecosystem will be affected by the change. Using the ideas of interdependence and succession in this manner is the key to achieving truly long-term preventive effects through programs (e.g., Head Start) that take permanent niches in their communities (e.g., so that parents and other citizens become full participants—see the extended discussion of Head Start in Chapter 7).

These principles establish a framework for conceptualization and action in community psychology and foreshadow a number of important issues to be taken up in the following chapters, including assessment, intervention, community change, and research.

Summary

Community psychology is founded on a point of view that is perhaps best represented by what we have called the *ecological analogy*. This analogy is explicit in its endorsement of certain values and raises important implications regarding the conduct of scientific research. As a conceptual paradigm, ecology deals with units larger than the single individual, emphasizes natural settings instead of laboratories or clinics as the most valid and appropriate locus of intervention and research, and conceptualizes research as an ongoing, longitudinal collaboration among the researcher, the residents, and the settings of the community.

Four principles are fundamental to the ecological perspective. The first is that because the people and settings within a community are interdependent, change occurs in a social system, not just in an individual, and thus a variety of different problem definitions and solutions are possible in any situation. A second principle states that community systems are defined by resource exchanges among persons and settings involving commodities such as time, money, and political power. The third principle is that the behavior we observe in a particular individual always reflects a continuous process of adaptation between that individual, and his or her level of competence, and the environment, with the nature and range of competence it supports. Adaptation can thus proceed by changing the environment as well as the person. The fourth principle states that change occurs naturally in a community, as well as by intentional design, and that change represents an opportunity to redefine and reallocate resources in ways that facilitate adaptation by all populations in the community.

We illustrated these principles by describing how the deinstitutionalization of psychiatric patients from hospitals to community settings forced law enforcement and justice officials to work alongside mental health professionals in unexpected ways and with unanticipated results. All parties concerned were affected, including the patients and their families. The generality of the principles was suggested by a second illustration concerning consequences that followed the deinstitutionalization of mentally retarded people. The chapter closed by summarizing the values embodied in the ecological analogy and presenting five principles of practice derived from the metaphor of ecology.

We conclude with the point that the ultimate usefulness of the ecological analogy for theory, research, or intervention remains to be demonstrated. It is an analogy useful only at the most general level, and it has not yet been employed in rigorous study, even within its own terms. Not much has yet been done to design interventions using ecological principles, although some research (e.g., Kelly et al., 1971) has been reported on issues relevant to general questions in this field. Other concepts and the research associated with them are examined in the next chapter. Although in sum ecology remains largely a metaphor, it is a metaphor that may yet open our minds to new approaches to a variety of problems.

Notes

1. Psychology broke away from philosophy in the late nineteenth century after the natural sciences had succeeded theology and the humanities as the dominant populations in the university community. The victory was so complete that the ideology and language of science were adopted even by traditional fields. At Harvard, for example, law was to be transformed into a science by means of studying appellate decisions, arriving at rules of law inductively, and then applying those to new problems deductively. As a consequence of that decision, the study of legal institutions, the law in action, lagged (Auerbach, 1976). Moreover, focusing on the disembodied principle meant that the moral significance and the political advantage a rule of law offered to one group as against another was not studied. The justification for separating psychology from philosophy was likely that its mission, methods, and needs for laboratory space and scientific equipment differed from those in philosophy. By going into the laboratory and modeling their field on the physical sciences, psychologists concentrated on the individual and failed to study the individual in context.

2. Arnhoff (1975) suggests a number of other unintended ecological consequences of mental health policies supporting care in the community. These include the effects on children of being reared by a psychotic parent in varying degrees of remission controlled by drugs. Children of psychotic parents are a population at increased risk of maladjustment, and Arnhoff suggests that deinstitutionalization may increase that risk. He also notes that persons who are hospitalized have low rates of reproduction and cites evidence that the policy of deinstitutionalization has resulted in an increase in both the in- and out-of-wedlock birth rates among mentally ill people. Moreover, if one accepts the concept of genetic risk, the overall risk of mental illness is increased by having a larger number of individuals with a predisposition to mental illness reproducing. Arnhoff cites studies indicating that the policy of deinstitutionalization increases the amount of stress experienced by family members who are forced to cope with a disturbed person.

3. Although most states do give police such statutory authority, in its absence police may be vulnerable to civil suits if they intervene in mental illness cases without evidence of a crime. In general, the police and the municipalities that employ them are protected by statute and by "good-faith immunity" in damage actions. In recent years, the courts have limited the vulnerability of officials and municipalities to damage suits based on civil rights violations, so that may not be a serious problem (e.g., *Wood v. Strickland,* 420 U.S. 308 (1975); *Monell v. Department of Social Services of the City of New York,* 435 U.S. 658 (1978)).

4. The courts have an obligation to determine a defendant's competence to stand trial anytime the defense counsel, the prosecutor, or the judge raises a good-faith doubt about such competence (ABA, 1984, Standard 7-4.2). We have no recent evidence on the point, but in the past the process of ascertaining competence was used as an alternate disposition to criminal charges. Some critics believed that prosecutors used incompetence as a pretext to hold against their will persons on whom the evidence to convict was weak (see *Jackson v. Indiana,* 406 U.S. 715 (1972)).

One study did report a doubling in pleas of incompetence to stand trial in the year following the passage of a California statute implementing patient rights to due process in hospitalizations (Abramson, 1972). In addition to ascertaining competence, this procedure allows the person who has created a public disturbance to be taken off the streets, at least briefly. If the person is found competent to stand trial and the offense is not serious, the plea-bargaining process may result in a dismissal of charges conditional on the person seeking treatment, or to outright release, with the sentence being limited to the amount of time the person was held in pretrial custody.

5. Proponents of group homes have generally been successful in gaining protective legislation and in overcoming restrictive legislation. The U.S. Supreme Court addressed the issue in 1985 and balanced the wishes of community members against the benefits to retarded individuals of residing in community residences in favor of the retarded. (See *Cleburne Living Center v. City*

of Cleburne, Texas, 726 F. 2d 191 (5th Cir. 1984); *City of Cleburne, Texas v. Cleburne Living Center,* 53 LW 5022 (1985).

6. Gouldner (1968), looking at the long-term battle between cosmopolitans (standing for centralization at the federal level) and locals (interested in maintaining local control of agencies and institutions) argues that research on the underdog perspective often emphasizes the inadequacies of locally controlled institutions. Noting that such research is often funded by cosmopolitans, he argues that the research results support the political aims of the sponsors to weaken local control. This issue is discussed further in Chapter 12.

References

Abramson, M. F. (1972). The criminalization of mentally disordered behavior: Possible side effects of a new mental health law. *Hospital and Community Psychiatry, 23,* 101–105.

American Bar Association. (1984). Standing Committee on Association Standards for Criminal Justice. Proposed Criminal Justice Mental Health Standards. Washington, DC: American Bar Association.

Arnhoff, F. N. (1975). Social consequences of policy toward mental illness. *Science, 188,* 1277–1281.

Auerbach, J. S. (1976). *Unequal justice.* New York: Oxford University Press.

Barker, R. G. (1965). Explorations in ecological psychology. *American Psychologist, 20,* 1–14.

Bloch, A. (1984). Twenty-year follow-up of pupils in a special class for the mentally retarded: A study of a complete school community. *American Journal of Orthopsychiatry, 54,* 436–443.

Callahan, L. A., & Diamond, R. J. (1985). *Mad, bad, or both? A survey of the mentally ill in jail.* Paper presented at the meeting of the Law and Society Association, San Diego.

Fox, S. J. (1981). *Cases and materials on modern juvenile justice* (2d ed.). St. Paul: West.

Frohboese, R., & Sales, B. D. (1980). Parental opposition to deinstitutionalization: A challenge in need of attention and resolution. *Law and Human Behavior, 4,* 1–87.

Goffman, E. (1961). *Asylums.* New York: Doubleday.

Goldenberg, I. I. (1978). *Oppression and social intervention.* Chicago: Nelson-Hall.

Gouldner, A. W. (1968). The sociologist as partisan: Sociology and the welfare state. *American Sociologist, 3,* 103–116.

Gupta, R. K. (1971). New York's Mental Health Information Service: An experiment in due process. *Rutgers Law Review, 25,* 405–435.

Guy, E., Platt, J. J., Zwerling, I., & Bullock, S. (1985). Mental health status of prisoners in an urban jail. *Criminal Justice and Behavior, 12,* 29–53.

Hayes, L. M. (1983). And darkness closes in .... A national study of jail suicides. *Criminal Justice and Behavior, 10,* 461–484.

Jacoby, J. E. (1983, August). Securing compliance of mental health professionals to changing commitment laws. Paper presented at the meeting of the Society for the Study of Social Problems, Detroit.

Kelly, J. G. (1966). Ecological constraints on mental health services. *American Psychologist, 21,* 535–539.

Kelly, J. G., Edwards, D. W., Fatke, R., Gordon, T. A., McClintock, S. K., McGee, D. P., Newman, B. M., Rice, R. R., Roistacher, R. C., & Todd, D. M. (1971). The coping process in varied high school environments. In M. J. Feldman (Ed.), *Buffalo Studies in Psychotherapy and Behavior Change.* No. 2, Theory and Research in Community Mental Health. Buffalo: SUNY at Buffalo.

Kennedy, J. F. (1963, February 5). Mental illness and mental retardation. Message from the President of the United States relative to mental illness and mental retardation. House of Representatives, 88th Congress, 1st Session, Document No. 58.

Kruzich, J. M., & Berg, W. (1985). Predictors of self-sufficiency for the mentally ill in long-term care. *Community Mental Health Journal, 21,* 198–207.

Kuhn, T. S. (1970). *The structure of scientific revolutions* (2d ed.). Chicago: University of Chicago Press.

Lamb, H. R., & Grant, R. W. (1981). The mentally ill in an urban county jail. *Archives of General Psychiatry, 39,* 17–22.

Levine, M. (1969). Some postulates of community psychology practice. In S. B. Sarason & F. Kaplan (Eds.), *The Psycho-Educational Clinic. Papers and research studies.* Springfield: Massachusetts Department of Mental Health.

Levine, M. (1976). The academic achievement test: Its historical context and social functions. *American Psychologist, 31,* 228–238.

Levine, M. (1980a). Investigative reporting as a research method. An analysis of Bernstein and Woodward's *All the President's Men. American Psychologist, 35,* 625–638.

Levine, M. (1980b). *From state hospital to psychiatric center: The implementation of planned organizational change.* Lexington, MA: Lexington Books.

Levine, M. (1981). *The history and politics of community mental health.* New York: Oxford University Press.

Levine, M. (1982). Method or madness: On the alienation of the professional. *Journal of Community Psychology, 10,* 3–14.

Levine, M., & Levine, A. G. (1970). *A social history of helping services.* New York: Appleton-Century-Crofts.

Lewin, K. (1935). *Principles of topological psychology.* New York: McGraw-Hill.

Lubin, R. A., Schwartz, A. A., Zigman, W. B., & Janicki, M. P. (1982). Community acceptance of residential programs for developmentally disabled persons. *Applied Research in Mental Retardation, 3,* 191–200.

Miller, K. S. (1976). *The case against civil commitment.* New York: Free Press.

Mills, R. C., & Kelly, J. G. (1972). Cultural adaptation and ecological analogies: Analysis of three Mexican villages. In S. E. Golann and C. Eisdorfer (Eds.), *Handbook of community mental health.* New York: Appleton-Century-Crofts.

Moos, R. H. (1973). Conceptualizations of human environments. *American Psychologist, 28,* 652–665.

Odum, E. P. (1963). *Ecology.* New York: Holt, Rinehart & Winston.

Rappaport, J. (1977). *Community psychology. Values, research and action.* New York: Holt, Rinehart & Winston.

Rothman, D. J. (1982). The courts and social reform: A postprogressive outlook. *Law and Human Behavior, 6,* 113–119.

Ryan, W. (1971). *Blaming the victim.* New York: Random House.

Sarason, S. B. (1976). Community psychology, networks, and Mr. Everyman. *American Psychologist, 31,* 317–328.

Sarason, S. B. (1978). The nature of problem solving in social action. *American Psychologist, 33,* 370–380.

Sarason, S. B. (1981). *Psychology misdirected.* New York: Free Press.

Sarason, S. B., & Doris, J. (1969). *Psychological problems in mental deficiency* (4th ed.). New York: Harper & Row.

Slotnick, R. S., Jeger, A. M., & Trickett, E. J. (Eds.). (1980). Social ecology in community psychology. *Division of Community Psychology Newsletter, 13,* 1–19.

Teplin, L. A. (1983). The criminalization of the mentally ill: Speculation in search of data. *Psychological Bulletin, 94,* 54–67.

Teplin, L. A. (1984). Criminalizing mental disorder: The comparative arrest rate of the mentally disordered. *American Psychologist, 39,* 794–803.

Trickett, E. J., Kelly, J. G., & Vincent, T. A. (1985). The spirit of ecological inquiry in community research. In E. C. Susskind & D. C. Klein (Eds.), *Community research: Methods, paradigms, and applications* (pp. 283–333). New York: Praeger.

Vincent, T. A., & Trickett, E. J. (1983). Preventive interventions and the human context: Ecological approaches to environmental assessment and change. In R. D. Felner, L. A. Jason, J. Moritsugu, & S. S. Farber (Eds.), *Preventive Psychology: Theory, research and practice in community intervention* (pp. 67–86). New York: Pergamon Press.

Willer, B., & Intagliata, J. (1984). An overview of the social policy of deinstitutionalization. *International Review of Research in Mental Retardation, 12,* 1–23.

Szasz, T. S. (1963). *Law, liberty and psychiatry.* New York: Macmillan.

Zusman, J. (1967). Some explanations of the changing appearance of psychotic patients. *International Journal of Psychiatry, 3,* 216–237.

4

Three Psychological Conceptions
of the Environment

The previous chapter concluded that the ecological perspective on human behavior has important theoretical and political implications for community psychologists. The five principles of intervention we used in summarizing the ecological analogy, however, are more abstract than they are specific. The metaphor of ecology tells us to recognize and attend to alternatives, for example, without directly helping us identify what those alternatives are. Scientific advances and effective practical applications will require sharper conceptualization of the operational units making up human environments than was provided by Kelly's pioneering work.

What kinds of details are left out of the orientation provided by the five principles of intervention? To review briefly, Principles I and II propose that problems and their solutions be defined in situational terms. What this implies is a need to identify explicitly the specific characteristics of situations that are relevant to problems of adaptation. By what mechanisms do settings facilitate changes in behavior? By what processes does a person adapt to a setting (or vice versa)? Theoretical conceptions are needed that offer more detailed descriptions of these effects.

Consider in this light the conclusions of Landesman-Dwyer's (1981) review of the literature on community-based programs and residences for the mentally retarded. Despite an obvious commitment to environmental intervention, whether institutional or community based, the mental retardation field has had little in the way of a well-validated conceptual foundation on which to base its policies. For example, different labels applied to the various alternative residential environments (e.g., "foster homes," "group homes") in reality indicate nothing about important differences among residences in size, staffing, rehabilitative focus, quality of care, or client outcome. Environments may represent powerful interventions, but like other powerful interventions such as psychoactive drugs, environments are complex, multidimensional stimuli having unwanted as well as wanted effects. Landesman-Dwyer (1981), for example, concludes that a behavioral emphasis on education and training of the retarded has overshadowed the important social needs these individuals have. That is, although moving a retarded person abruptly from one intensive training program to another may make sense from the viewpoint of helping him or her learn a wide variety of specific vocational skills, such a policy may seriously disrupt his or her ability to maintain supportive social relationships and skills.

The presence of multiple effects from the same environment suggests that one conceptual limitation we must overcome is the myth of setting uniformity. Schools, for example, are not the uniformly interchangeable settings many psychologists assume they are—schools vary across important social, cultural, and behavioral dimensions (Sarason & Klaber, 1985). Without adequate conceptual attention to differences among settings, research on schools has by default been directed primarily at the individual characteristics of students. If overall results for Head Start preschool intervention are mixed, for example (Sarason & Klaber, 1985; see also Chapter 7), what factors might explain the inconsistency of these results? Surely, not all of it is attributable to individual differences among the children involved. What do we understand to have been the key differences among Head Start settings?

One need we have is the creation of useful typologies for key community settings (Cowen, 1973; Landesman-Dwyer, 1981), and more than one kind of approach may be necessary here. Principle III, for example, says that the key settings to understand are those that are spatially and temporally most immediate to the problem of maladaptation. One basis for a typology might thus be the way in which settings are organized spatially and temporally in relation to individuals and their behavior. Initial efforts at taxonomy development (e.g., Price & Blashfield, 1975), while important, have tended to group environments in general categories (e.g., business settings, religious settings) instead of in terms of spatial or temporal relationships as related to the lives of community residents.

Principle IV equates psychological environments with the expression of specific human values and goals, suggesting that a conceptual system should help us understand the purposes, both manifest and latent, that a given setting serves (i.e., the values it expresses). Bear in mind that the different constituencies represented in a setting (e.g., leader, members, and researchers) may perceive and describe the purposes of a setting differently. Theoretically, the ecological analogy supports diversity in the service of freedom of choice by consumers, and thus citizen empowerment (see Chapter 12), yet adequate diversity in residential and program settings has not always been available to groups such as the mentally retarded and their families (Landesman-Dwyer, 1981).

Principle V, which is related to Kelly's notion of succession, urges us to understand the principles and mechanisms of setting change to the point where adaptive change not only occurs, but can also be maintained. Dohrenwend's (1978) model of stress and community psychology (see Chapter 2) introduces a time dimension to our thinking in suggesting that adaptation and maladaptation are episodic kinds of responses that do not necessarily endure over time. How well does a given concept capture the temporal aspects of situations and of behavior?

Finally, given that fully half of Dohrenwend's model involves person-centered influences on behavior, where does the person fit into a given conception of adaptation to the environment? Are there commensurate dimensions (i.e., involving the same kinds of units) to use in linking persons with environments? Landesman-Dwyer (1981), for example, points out that a significant degree of diversity characterizes the mentally retarded and that what we lack are well-validated person-environment dimensions involving specific environmental characteristics as well as differences among retarded individuals.

These questions are useful in setting the stage for a review of some current conceptions of the psychological environment. Rudolf Moos (1973, 1976; Moos & Insel,

1974) has surveyed a variety of different theoretical conceptions of the human environment in terms of their relevance to psychological thinking and practice. The present chapter focuses on three of the best known conceptions, Moos's own "perceived social climate" approach, Roger Barker's "ecological psychology," and Theodore Sarbin's "role theory." Each perspective is reviewed in turn, after which a specific example is presented and used to illustrate the perspectives in practical terms.

Perceived Social Climates

Henry Murray's seminal work on personality theory (Murray, 1938) presented a model of behavior based on relative degrees of fit between what he called individual *needs* (e.g., to achieve or to affiliate) and environmental *presses* (the analogous pressures most settings exert on their occupants to express various personality needs). Considerable effort has gone into developing instruments such as the Personality Research Form (Jackson, 1965) that measure the individual personality needs identified by Murray. It remained to Moos and his associates (Moos, 1976), however, to develop a corresponding set of scales assessing the behavioral presses of key community environments.

The underlying assumptions of Moos's approach are that (1) we can think of environments as having "personalities" (as being achievement oriented, interpersonally supportive or controlling, and so on), just as people do, and (2) these personalities can be measured using the same methods used to assess the personalities of people. That is, in Moos's approach one simply asks the participants in a given setting to respond "true" or "false" to a set of declarative statements describing what it is like to be a participant in that setting. The responses of all participants are then averaged to obtain a single profile (generally presented in terms of standard scores) describing the "perceived social climate" of the setting. These measures thus provide a cognitive "bridge" between the objective stimulus configuration presented by the environment and the characteristic responses people make to that environment (Kiritz & Moos, 1974).

Recognizing that such quantitative information would be useful for a broad range of natural community settings, Moos and his colleagues have developed specific social-climate scales for psychiatric wards, community-oriented programs, family environments, work settings, classrooms, residence halls, military organizations, correctional facilities, and sheltered-care settings for the elderly. The specific subscales, or dimensions of environmental press, vary somewhat from one instrument to another (relevant situational presses in a work setting, for example, could easily be different from those present in a family environment). All perceived social climate scales, however, have the same three *kinds* of dimensions represented in their subscales: relationship-oriented dimensions (e.g., affiliation, cohesiveness), personal-development dimensions (e.g., achievement, moral-religious emphasis), and system-maintenance and change dimensions (e.g., order and organization, control). These three broader categories are assumed to encompass the key psychological dimensions of any human environment.

Considerable data have been accumulated on the construct validity of Moos's scales (see Moos, 1976; Kiritz & Moos, 1974). For example, settings high in relation-

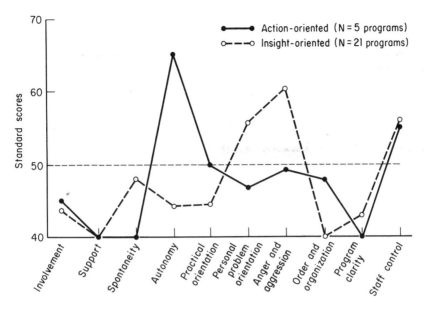

Figure 4-1. Mean Ward Atmosphere Scale profiles for action-oriented and insight-oriented treatment program clusters (from Price & Moos, 1975).

ship-oriented dimensions have been found to show high satisfaction and self-esteem among the occupants, low anxiety, depression, and irritability (Moos, 1976), and also low physical complaints (Moos & Van Dort, 1979). Settings high in personal-development dimensions involve more positive attitudes and higher skill acquisition among members, but in some cases they are also characterized by greater tension (Trickett & Moos, 1974). As we noted earlier, a complex stimulus such as a school classroom can have unwanted as well as wanted effects. In terms of system-maintenance and change dimensions, high order and clarity are associated with high satisfaction, while high degrees of control are associated with dissatisfaction and other negative outcomes.

The various social-climate scales have several useful applications in community psychology. One of these is clearly setting description and classification. Price and Moos (1975), for example, cluster analyzed Ward Atmosphere Scale profiles from 144 different inpatient psychiatric wards in 44 hospitals across the country, identifying six relatively homogeneous clusters or types of wards ("therapeutic relationship-oriented," "control-oriented," and so on). Figure 4-1 compares the profiles for two of these six kinds of wards, identified by Price and Moos as "action-oriented" and "insight-oriented," respectively. The mean climate provided by the action-oriented wards is average or below average on all dimensions except autonomy and control, indicating that these programs primarily emphasize the personal responsibility that individual patients have to assume in recovering from their problems. Given the relatively low degrees of support, involvement, and program clarity present, the action-oriented climate appears to minimize the likelihood that patients will become excessively dependent on the treatment program. In contrast to this picture, the insight-oriented type of ward places more emphasis on the individual problems patients have and also appears to facilitate patients' expression of anger and aggression, albeit in a context of moderately high staff control. The emphasis here is thus on achieving individual insight more than on the quality of staff-patient relationships or the program's overall degree of order and organization.

An intriguing implication of the Price and Moos (1975) findings is that the psychological environments of thousands of different inpatient wards all over the country are reducible to only six general types, which is an important contribution to research in general. Investigators conducting clinical trials of new psychotropic medications, for example, might now be able to control for important psychological characteristics of the inpatient milieu in which the drug is tested simply by sampling representatively from each of the six basic types of wards.

A second practical application of the perceived social-climate approach is in evaluating the effects of consultation services or other interventions provided to participants in a given setting. A useful tactic at the outset of consultation, for example, is to have setting participants complete the relevant social-climate scale twice, once as they currently perceive the setting and again as they would ideally like it to be. The two profiles can then be compared, with any disparities between them assumed to indicate characteristics of the psychological environment needing attention. Consultation sessions can then be devoted to specific issues influencing those dimensions. Later the scale can be readministered as a method of evaluating the outcome of consultation. If both real and ideal forms are again used, any remaining real-ideal discrepancies can form the basis for further consultation.

DeYoung (1977), for example, administered real and ideal forms of the Classroom Environment Scale (CES) to an undergraduate social science class. Discrepancies between the real and ideal profiles indicated that students wanted to be more involved in the class, experience more innovative teaching methods, and understand more clearly the organization of the course and the instructor's expectations. The next term DeYoung modified the course to include more individual contact with students, a more explicit grading policy, and group projects and other innovative forms of classroom participation by students. Readministration of the real and ideal forms of the CES found that although the ideal climate had not changed noticeably from one term to the next, students' perceptions of the actual classroom environment more closely resembled the ideal profile on each of the specific dimensions targeted for intervention. Furthermore, these changes during the second term were associated with greater student interest, participation, and attendance.

A third use of Moos's scales is in setting selection to maximize person-environment fit. For example, suppose that the residents of every foster home in a given county completed the Family Environment Scale (FES), so that an "atlas" of profiles from all of the homes was available to caseworkers planning the placement of foster children.[1] A caseworker might then work with a child and the child's parents in filling out the FES as it would ideally exist for that child. This information might then be used in conjunction with the atlas of FES profiles in deciding on the optimum placement for that child.

Finally, perceived social-climate scales can be used in the planning and creation of new settings in the community. Those responsible for developing a new mental health center program, for example, could use the Community-Oriented Programs Environment Scale (COPES) to develop a shared conception of what the optimum social climate in the new setting would be. The ecological prescription that all points of view be represented in the data used to understand a setting could be addressed by obtaining separate mean profiles from line workers, supervisors, members of the administrative support staff, and so on. Structural characteristics necessary to achieve a particular ideal profile might then be built into the setting at the start. If staff "burn-out" is anticipated to be a problem, for example, so that a high degree of interpersonal support among staff members would be desirable, regular meetings of a peer support group made up of program staff might be planned for the program right from the start. Once the new program is under way, the COPES might then be readministered as a means of evaluating the various dimensions of social climate present in the setting, and indicating where adjustments in the structure or process of the program might be needed.

Moos's perceived social-climate concept of the environment thus has many practical applications, and its chief advantage over other approaches is probably the ease with which the relevant information can be collected and interpreted (i.e., the 90-item full-length scales require only about 20 minutes to complete). Two restrictions to bear in mind, however, are that: (1) to answer the items meaningfully, the respondents in the setting under study must have regular face-to-face contact with each other; and (2) the number of respondents must not be too large (i.e., no more than 20–25), so that the group profile is not attenuated by excess error variance. One should also keep in mind that profiles generated by these instruments are not objective descriptions of the environment per se, but instead describe the social climate of that setting as perceived by its current participants.

Moos's conception adequately addresses several of the specific questions raised earlier in this chapter. The mechanism of behavior change implied in this view is the process of fit between individual personality needs on the one hand and commensurate environmental presses on the other. Changing a setting to improve the degree of fit is not done directly using this approach, however (except perhaps by changing the individual people in the setting). Instead, as indicated in the example involving social support in a work setting, a more concrete behavioral prescription (regular meetings of a support group) is necessary. Maintaining changes in social climate may also be difficult in view of the heavy turnover of people in some settings, although regular administration of the appropriate social-climate scale would certainly help in monitoring the effects of turnover and other ongoing events.

Setting taxonomies are being developed using this concept, although the focus thus far has been on limited types of settings such as psychiatric wards (Price & Moos, 1975) and high school classrooms (Trickett, 1978), instead of on the spatial and temporal distribution of setting climates as they occur in people's lives. Diversity in the goals and purposes of settings is clearly acknowledged in this concept, as is the importance of individual needs in adapting to a setting. In general, this view presents one of the clearest illustrations available of how psychologists can take seriously the need to assess and understand characteristics of key community environments as well as those of the people inhabiting them. It assists people in "tuning in" to the social climates surrounding them (Moos, 1979) and, from an ecological perspective, helps empower people to participate more widely in the process of community assessment and change (Vincent & Trickett, 1983).

Behavior Settings[2]

If Moos conceives of the psychological environment much as a traditional personality theorist does, Roger Barker might be said to view it more as a behavioral psychologist does—that is, with an emphasis on physical and behavioral characteristics that are directly observable and objectively definable. Barker's (1978) informal observations of human behavior in its natural context led him to the realization that most of human behavior is not randomly distributed across space and time but instead occurs in consistent patterns of regularly scheduled activities he called "behavior settings." Everyday examples of such settings include school classrooms, stores, government offices, playgrounds, and even sidewalks. For Barker, an important characteristic of every setting is the set of "standing" behavior patterns that define the nature and meaning of that setting, regardless of who its occupants are (e.g., praying in a church, sunbathing at the beach). In fact, the essence of any behavior setting is seen to reside in the relationship between these behaviors and characteristics of the setting's physical and temporal milieu (Barker, 1968). In most classrooms, for example, the chairs, desks, blackboards, and open spaces are uniquely constructed and arranged to facilitate performance of the standing behaviors in that setting—speaking, listening, sitting, and writing.

Two key assumptions of ecological psychology are also worth noting. First, the individuals who perform in a given setting are thought to be more or less interchangeable with each other and with people outside of the setting, in that even a complete turnover in participants does not change how the requisite behaviors are performed at the prescribed time and place. In Barker's conception, then, the psychological environment is defined independently of the people in it, which is not the case in Moos's approach, as we noted earlier.

This idea that behavior settings exist independent of particular individuals leads to the second key assumption of ecological psychology: that settings themselves generate the forces necessary for their own maintenance and survival (Barker, 1968). Behavior settings are seen to possess "forces" that, in the interest of internal homeostasis, impel their occupants to perform the standing behavior patterns and conform to setting programs. These homeostatic forces are organized into

1. *Program circuits,* which represent the agenda connecting people to the required sequence of behavior patterns. In a church service, for example, the congregation stands or sits in unison at the appropriate times (e.g., for singing or prayer), as indicated by the organized ceremony of worship.
2. *Goal circuits,* which represent the confluence of participants' individual needs with specific experiences or products provided by the setting. The motivations of those attending a church service, for example, are typically congruent with the specific kinds of social and spiritual satisfactions such a setting provides.
3. *Deviation-countering circuits,* which reduce or eliminate behavior that deviates from the program. A baby crying loudly during a wedding ceremony elicits prompt efforts by those nearby to quiet him or her.
4. *Veto circuits,* which result in the ejection of a nonconforming occupant from the setting. The crying baby who cannot be quieted during a solemn ceremony will usually be ushered quickly away from the setting (see Barker, 1968, pp. 167–185).

Consider the following example. Customers at a 24-hour bank machine enter the correct information in the proper sequence because they wish to make a transaction and because the setting program requires it, not because that specific pattern of behavior is naturally spontaneous or familiar to them. Up to a point, the bank machine's program will direct the customer to correct any errors he or she makes, but under some conditions (e.g., the identification code is entered incorrectly on three successive tries) the program in many machines keeps the card and dismisses the customer with no business being transacted. Thus theoretically a setting's internal control circuits are the reason for the striking uniformity in behavior by its occupants. Because of the uniformity of behavior within a setting, most people attribute noticeable deviations from a setting's program to significant person-centered deficits such as "mental illness" (e.g., drunkenness, psychosis, mental retardation). This kind of active, even coercive influence of settings on behavior is known as "behavior-environment congruence," and is believed to have important practical and theoretical implications for eliciting and maintaining specific changes in human behavior (Barker, 1968; Wicker, 1972).

The processes or mechanisms by which settings coercively influence participants' behavior are not well understood, although one kind of internal homeostatic mechanism operating within program circuits is thought to be the degree of "manning" present (Barker & Gump, 1964; Wicker, 1979). Manning theory deals with the effects of various numbers of occupants in a setting relative to the optimal number for that setting; it grew out of Barker and Wright's (1955) behavior-setting survey of a town in Kansas (pseudonym "Midwest"). Barker and Schoggen (1973) subsequently extended the survey to a town in Yorkshire, England (pseudonym "Yoredale"). In 1953–1954, Midwest (population 830) was found to have 884 settings, while Yoredale (population 1310) contained only 758 settings.

Barker and Schoggen (1973) interpreted these differences to indicate that settings in Midwest, facing greater overall threats to their existence, strengthened their program and goal circuits, relaxed their deviation-countering and veto circuits, and in the process effectively "pulled" more behavior from their occupants than did the settings in Yoredale. What this means is that with more settings, the smaller number of people residing in Midwest of necessity participated more often and for longer lengths of time in the town's public activities. Another consequence inferred by Barker and Schoggen was that with the greater importance and responsibility given each resident of Midwest, the amount of attention paid to social distinctions was less in that community than in Yoredale.

Subsequent comparisons among several small (presumably undermanned) and large (presumably overmanned) high schools in Kansas indicated that on the average, students from small schools participated in more school settings, assumed more positions of responsibility, and expressed a greater "sense of obligation" to their schools than did students from large schools (Barker & Gump, 1964). Other research supported manning theory's predictions in churches of different sizes (Wicker, McGrath, & Armstrong, 1972) and in several laboratory-based experiments (Arnold & Greenberg, 1980; Perkins, 1982; Wicker, Kirmeyer, Hanson, & Alexander, 1976).

This dimension of manning may provide new insights into how environments can be described and their effects on behavior understood. Landesman-Dwyer's (1981) review of community care for the mentally retarded, for example, concludes that no relationship exists between size of residence and client outcome. The problem with this analysis is that overall number of residents may be too crude as a measure of residence size. From Barker's viewpoint, the relevant characteristic is number of residents per setting or activity. The lower this ratio (i.e., the more undermanned the settings are), the higher will be the average level of satisfaction reported by residents. Manning theory thus offers a basis for specific quantitative predictions concerning direct environmental effects on behavior, although at this point the durability of these effects is not known because little or no longitudinal research has been done.

One problem with manning theory, however, is that for some settings fewer than the optimal number of occupants apparently does not produce greater satisfaction. Whyte (1980), for example, found that certain public settings in smaller communities (i.e., those considered more undermanned by Barker) are generally less successful psychologically than similar settings in large cities, and that the best solution would be for the smaller communities to "compress" or "concentrate" public spaces and the people in them to a much greater degree (p. 92)—that is, to make them more *over*manned.

Manning effects are not universal even in high school settings. Baird (1969), for example, found that students in small high schools showed no higher achievement compared with students in large schools in settings involving art and science (e.g., science fair projects and awards). Morgan and Alwin (1980), moreover, found that in extracurricular activities that are peripheral in importance to the school, and also flexible in the number of participants they allow (e.g., hobby clubs), manning influences seem to operate in reverse (i.e., higher rates of participation in larger schools).

In the long run, the optimal number of participants in a setting may have less to do with specific structural factors like the number of roles and more to do with the overall purpose of the setting for its occupants. Thus for some settings (e.g., parades, political conventions) whose purpose is to bring together large numbers of people, the optimal number of participants may be quite large, regardless of the number of different roles available.

Ecological psychology has made two fundamental contributions to community psychology. First is the environmental "unit of analysis" ecological psychology provides for the description and assessment of human behavior on situational and community levels. That is, behavior settings are assumed to represent naturally occurring units of the environment, phenomena that are discrete, relatively stable, and "objective in the sense that they exist independent of anyone's perception of them" (Barker & Schoggen, 1973, p. 9). These units are the most "immediate" human environments (Wicker, 1979, p. 9) and in this sense are the most commensurate with individual human beings and their behavior.

Furthermore, although any individual setting may have only limited impact on a given person or community, Barker and Schoggen (1973) defined two superordinate levels at which settings can be aggregated systematically to measure the psychological character of a community. The first, called the "genotype," includes all the settings of a given type in the community (e.g., all the elementary school basic classes, all the grocery stores, all the telephone booths). The second level of aggregation, called a "habitat," is much broader in that each represents a class of settings related to each other by their contribution to some general aspect of community life (e.g., formal education, medical care, government). The habitat concept is rather broad, but using it the community psychologist can accomplish the behavioral assessment of an entire community by cataloging its settings and distributing their behavioral contributions among the various habitats (e.g., commercial, recreational, educational, entertainment).

Consider Figure 4-2, for example, which is reprinted from Barker and Schoggen (1973). The top part of this figure compares the respective sizes of various habitats in Midwest and Yoredale in 1963–1964. The behavioral opportunities provided by Midwest involving nutrition, business, and professional activity are noticeably fewer than those available in Yoredale, while those concerning religion, government, and education are slightly greater in Midwest. The bottom half of Figure 4-2 depicts the changes in habitat sizes in the two towns between 1954 and 1963. The greatest change was a tripling in size of the education habitat in Yoredale caused by the addition of a large new school. Midwest doubled the size of its religion habitat, but at the same time lost about 20% of its business habitat.

The methods of ecological psychology thus make possible a systematic, comprehensive assessment of the specific behavioral opportunities provided in a given community. Furthermore, the settings available to particular subgroups, such as children, the elderly, and deinstitutionalized psychiatric patients, can be compared with the specific behavioral needs of these groups (e.g., for health care, social services) to provide sharper and more detailed assessments of how habitable a given community is for specific groups. Ecological psychology thus provides a range of progressively inclusive units of analysis, from a single activity (setting), a specific kind of activity (genotype), and a general sphere of community life (habitat), to an entire community (a collection of habitats).

The second contribution of ecological psychology is that behavior-environment congruence and undermanning provide conceptual mechanisms for describing how environmental settings may directly facilitate permanent changes in behavior (Price, 1974; Wicker, 1972). That is, because behavior is a property of settings as well as of people, it provides a basis for direct examinations of person-environment fit, including the process by which people acquire new behaviors when participating in new settings. For example, focused vocational training of psychiatrically disabled clients in a sheltered-workshop setting helps them develop the interpersonal behaviors, manual skills, and punctuality necessary to have any hope of later competitive employment. Similarly, preschool children develop preventive "interpersonal cognitive problem-solving skills" by actively participating in gamelike settings where the specific behavior pattern emphasizes *how* to think, not *what* to think, in solving interpersonal problems (Spivack & Shure, 1974; see Chapter 7). Furthermore, the stability or instability of changes in behavior can be seen as predictable responses to the continuity or discontinuity in behavior patterns across different settings in the person's life (Levine & Perkins, 1980).

Practical applications of the behavior-setting approach have focused on such problems as (1) assessing the range of therapeutic behavioral opportunities available to high-risk populations like the chronically mentally ill (Perkins & Perry, 1985) and the residents of inner-city housing projects (Bechtel, 1977); (2) intervening to reduce problems of overcrowding in popular national parks (Wicker, 1979); and (3) evaluating the behavioral and environmental effects on a community of creating an artificial lake nearby (Harloff, Gump, & Campbell, 1981). The approach has some limitations in this regard, because it is much more complicated and time consuming to conduct a behavior-setting analysis of an environment than, for example, to administer one of Moos's perceived social-climate scales.

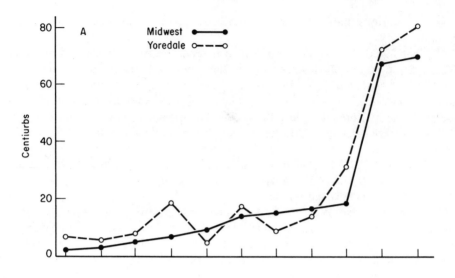

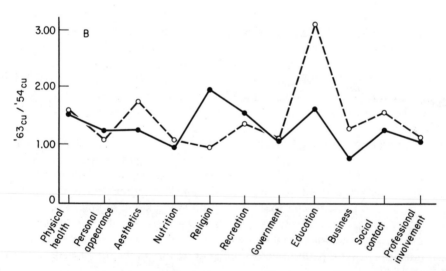

Figure 4-2. Sizes of various "action pattern" habitats (values for the centiurb unit presented on the ordinate are determined by the number of settings in a given habitat and how often each occurs). Top: Midwest compared with Yoredale in 1963–1964. Bottom: Changes in habitat sizes (1963 size divided by 1953 size) (from Barker & Schoggen, 1973).

Another problem with ecological psychology involves the assumption inherent in the principle of behavior-environment congruence that the reported occurrence of a setting is always equivalent to the performance of certain discrete, precise quantities of behavior by its occupants. This assumption is critical to ecological psychology's conception of environmental settings as universal agents of behavior change. The actual degree of constraint that settings exert over behavior varies substantially, however (Price & Bouffard, 1974), and little ecological psychology research, save the laboratory studies (Perkins, 1982; Wicker et al., 1976), has specifically estimated how much behavioral effort is generated under different setting conditions. Given some of the implications drawn regarding ecological psychology's potential applications to large-scale preventive and therapeutic behavior change (cf. Schoggen, 1978), more attention should be directed to the relationship between setting characteristics and the specific quantity and quality of occupants' behavioral responses.

Where do individual people fit into Barker's view of the community? One possible angle is Barker and Schoggen's (1973) concept of "habitat-inhabitant bias" (pp. 381–397). The degree of bias for any population subgroup in the community (e.g., infants, blacks, women) is the extent to which the mean occupancy time of that subgroup in a given habitat varies from that of the population as a whole. This latter value is arbitrarily taken to be 100, and subgroup bias is expressed as a percentage of it. Thus the bias for females in Midwest's "primary business habitat" was 87 in 1963–1964, while that for males was 103 (Barker & Schoggen, 1973, p. 387). Although systematic and quantitative, this concept implies nothing about the process of person-environment selection or the psychological significance of such a difference. As a result, ecological psychology has yet to integrate meaningfully any individual difference factors, even those based solely on overt behavior, into a working model of the community.

What about the process of setting evolution or succession? Understanding community change in the form of setting creation or termination has long been an issue central to community psychology (Sarason, 1972). Ecological psychology is of limited use for this purpose because it handles community change only descriptively—that is, without providing a formal basis for analyzing and interpreting changes. For example, Barker and Schoggen (1973, p. 424) reported that between 1954–1955 and 1963–1964 the education habitat in Midwest grew by 54% and that of voluntary associations increased 89%, while settings devoted to private enterprise declined 7%. The comparable figures for Yoredale were increases of 289% for schools and 4% for private enterprise, with a decline of 7% for voluntary associations.

Ecological psychology is unable to explain why changes in these patterns occur because of its fundamental assumption that settings (and by extension communities) are driven entirely by the forces of internal homeostasis; that is, Barker's conception is fundamentally *ahistorical* in the way it ignores external forces responsible for change. Starting, stopping, and maintaining a setting cannot even be fully described, let alone understood, without reference to factors external to it and without formal consideration of the purposes that setting serves.

Perhaps its most significant limitation in the present context is that ecological psychology is largely devoted to the structural form settings take instead of to the goals, purposes, and values they express. That is, beyond their structural features (i.e., boundaries and standing behaviors) the information ecological psychology provides for creating new settings is meager. As it stands, this concept would be of little use in helping us disseminate a subjective experience like Sarason's (1974) "psychological sense of community."

The potential for understanding and disseminating such an experience may exist, however. Consider in this light ecological psychology's concept of community "focal points," an idea originated by Barker and Wright (1955) and later elaborated by Bechtel (1977). The behavioral focal point of a community is the one setting accessible to the largest number of different resident groups (e.g., a town square or park). Research presented by Bechtel (1977) suggests that a focal point should: (1) be centrally located at a crossroads point in the community's traffic pattern (i.e., to serve among other things as a conduit to and from other settings); (2) be richly endowed with voluntary behavior patterns (i.e., be low in constraint); (3) be free of visual barriers (to maximize visual stimulation and ease of recognizing others); and (4) provide seating for participants. Whyte's (1980) observations of urban plazas and other focal points also pointed to the importance of easy access, movable seating, good lighting, opportunities to eat and drink, and also the aesthetic value of trees and water (e.g., a fountain).

So far these qualities remain largely structural in nature, although we can at least speculate on the important psychological and behavioral purposes the successful community focal points serve. Their central purpose is to foster participation by the largest number of different community groups in such a way that the major pattern of behavior is simply unstructured, informal contact among people (i.e., visual and/or verbal, with no particular commitment to any strictly defined setting program). The structure and behavior patterns of these settings thus facilitate communication (e.g., news, gossip), social support, and ultimately the establishment and maintenance of a strong sense of community. Interestingly, Bechtel found that the presence (versus absence) of a successful focal point was associated with increased support and morale among community residents and that residents will often create their own focal point when a satisfactory one does not yet exist (e.g., in a dormitory corridor or a vacant city lot).

One theme of this chapter, and the preceding one, is that preventive and therapeutic changes in individual behavior reflect processes of person-setting interaction and fit. In the case of ecological psychology, for example, the hypothesized mechanism by which individual behavior change occurs and is maintained is behavior-environment congruence. Barker (1968), however, argues that persons and settings are incommensurate—that is, they obey different kinds of laws (i.e., biological and ecological, respectively). In some respects this point seems valid, while in other respects it does not. For example, one underdeveloped concept in ecological psychology has been the idea of "goal circuits," which concern the values and purposes expressed by settings. Greater attention to this notion might help to answer why there are so many different kinds of settings.

What may prove more fruitful for community psychology than Barker's descriptive concept of habitat-inhabitant bias may be to look for ways to link persons and settings systematically using dimensions that are directly comparable to each other, such as the behavioral repertoire of the person and the set of standing behaviors required of that person by key community settings. Perkins and Perry (1985), for example, empirically derive several dimensions of behavioral "demandingness" for use in assessing the settings of a community residence for deinstitutionalized psychiatric patients. When combined with similar information on behavioral capacities and skills of the residents themselves, such information yields estimates of the fit or lack of fit between patients and settings having significant implications for patients' long-term adaptation to community life (Anthony, Cohen, & Vitalo, 1978).

Barker also overlooks characteristics of the setting program as a possible basis for commensurate person-environment dimensions. As an organized behavior-environment entity, for example, a setting is not just "out there" in the environment; in a sense its program also resides inside the heads of its occupants. Some kind of mental representation regarding settings thus seems useful. Understanding the interaction of setting characteristics with the cognitive scripts or schemas held by occupants may help to shed light on the process of setting creation and change.

In terms of taxonomic issues, the kinds of interrelationships that connect different settings are also important to understand. Much of the research on ecological psychology, for example, has been done in schools (cf. Barker & Gump, 1964). Schools are not isolated settings, however. A given classroom influences, and is influenced by, a host of other educational, administrative, governmental, and family settings (Sarason & Klaber, 1985). Setting taxonomies developed to date group settings by content instead of by their spatial and temporal characteristics, although the focal-setting concept is a move in the latter direction. In general, however, the natural life cycles of settings are not well understood, although recent thinking by Wicker (in press) regarding settings as "open" instead of "closed" systems offers a promising start (see also Chapter 10).

Although its potential usefulness to community psychology is thus considerable, ecological psychology remains in need of further development (Perkins, Burns, Perry, & Nielsen, in press). Barker and his colleagues have pushed for extreme degrees of quantification in all the phenomena under study (cf. Barker & Schoggen, 1973), and at this point we may not understand well enough which are the important *qualities* making up human environments, let alone what quantities of environmental experience are optimal for community life. In addition, given that the concept of goal circuits remains undeveloped, the human occupant as an individual person is essentially absent from Barker's system. Still needed at this point are units of analysis that fit both the individual and the surrounding social context. Such a unit is the basis of role theory, the concept we consider next.

Social Roles

The concept of a role provides another heuristic basis for defining the relationship between an individual person and his or her social environment. Sarbin (1970) has argued that the concept of role may be more useful in diagnosing problems of adaptation and in designing interventions other than those centered on individuals. An examination of role theory also forms a useful bridge between discussion of the basic ecological analogy in community psychology and our analysis of labeling theory in the next chapter.

Sarbin introduces his role-theory concept by arguing that *environment* is too vague a construct to be useful for community psychologists. The concept of *setting* is somewhat more defined, but lacks a social dimension. In Sarbin's view the environment can best be regarded as a set of differentiated "ecologies" within which people must correctly locate themselves to survive and to thrive. He identified four such ecologies: self-maintenance, social (or the role system), normative, and transcendental.

To survive as a biosocial organism, an individual must recognize the difference between friend and foe, between the edible and the poisonous, between potentially hostile and potentially benign circumstances. Upon encountering a new object or person, an individual quickly runs through such questions as: Should I run from, attack, or ignore this new object? Can I play with it, eat it, have sex with it, or make use of it in some other fashion? Aside from this cognitive and perceptual reality testing, social questions are asked in determining action, such as: Are the social conditions appropriate for the activity I would like to select? Am I the appropriate person to engage in such activities in this situation? Incorrect answers to these questions result in dysfunctional conduct and, if sufficiently severe, result in some segregation of the individual—to a mental hospital, an institution for the retarded, or a prison. We believe that correct answers to these questions depend on appropriate socialization and education and on an intact, or at least not too severely impaired, organism.

The second ecology, related to the first, is the social ecology or role system. The question to be answered is, "Who am I in relation to you, in this situation?" A man is king if others bow down and recognize his authority. If he calls himself king and others do not recognize his authority, under many circumstances he is considered a madman. Role relationships are reciprocal. It takes at least two to tango. The variety of relevant answers to the question, "Who am I in relation to you?" or the question, asked by another, "Who are you?" define one's social identity. Failures (in terms of one's behavior) to answer these questions properly (that is, in accord with mutual expectations) lead to conflict and breakdown in social relationships. Entrance into and recognition of appropriate roles depend on adequate socialization and also on adequate opportunity. For example, social rules—gender, racial discrimination, or stigma—may prevent some individuals from entering some roles or from receiving acceptance in those roles. Changing social rules, by changing laws, by engaging in conflict and confrontation, or by changing incentives, can open up a greater variety of roles for those who were formerly denied them. In addition to examining the socialization of people for particular roles, Sarbin's position allows us to examine the opportunities for entering into given roles as well and to work to change those rules.

The third ecology is the normative. Here one asks how *well* one is meeting the particular requirements of a given role. The answer, "Not too well" is often accompanied by low self-esteem, and the answer, "Pretty good" by a more positive sense of satisfaction. The answers to these questions are based partly on self-evaluations and partly on the feedback received from others. Attributions of the "cause" of failure may vary. Under some circumstances, people engage in self-blame, and under others the cause of failure is seen to reside in factors beyond the individual's control. At one and the same time, an individual may believe that the cause of failure (or success) resides in his or her own efforts, while an external observer views the cause as situational in nature. The reverse may also be true, of course. We must recognize the implications of different perspectives, for the solution chosen will depend on how the problem is defined. How we perceive and value our accomplishments, or devalue ourselves for real or perceived failures, depends in part on the normative framework we adopt. It may also depend on the system of values we hold, and our system of values depends in substantial part on our participation in social relationships with others who share those values.

Sarbin's fourth ecology, called transcendental ecology, consists of abstractions that give meaning to life. For some people, the important abstraction is the relationship to a deity. For others, it may be an existential issue: Given that death is inevitable, how am I spending my life? For still others at different ages, the question may be one of integrity, to use Erikson's (1950) term—the acceptance of one's life-style and the willingness to defend it against attack by others or by the vicissitudes of life. In other words, we need to achieve and maintain a sense of order, meaning, and continuity to our experiences. We gain that sense through a set of beliefs that help us come to terms with ourselves and with events in the world. These beliefs are best developed and maintained by our participation in social groups, and to be part of a group means one has a role within that group. One may be born into the role, as a family member, one may choose to participate in it, as a member of a political party, or one may earn a position within a group through accomplishment and effort.

Sarbin assumes that people continuously strive to locate themselves within these varied ecologies. Everyone has many roles, for example, and participates with many different social groups. Furthermore, the nature of most behavior in a social setting is much more a function of the given roles being performed than of the individuals performing them (Katz & Kahn, 1966). Over the sum of their behavior as members of a given psychology class, for example, individual students are much more alike than they are different; each will go through the complicated process of registering for the course within the time specified, buying the required books, reading and studying the various assignments, attending class meetings, and completing tests, papers, and any other requirements for the course (i.e., roles can involve multiple settings). The instructor's role has a similarly constraining effect on the nature and range of his or her behavior. The most efficient way to describe any person's behavior in the context of this course is thus based on the role he or she occupies, not the person's individual characteristics.

As with behavior settings, we can even think of roles as coercive in their influence on behavior, because people exert considerable behavioral effort in many cases to maintain their eligibility for certain roles (e.g., medical students study hard, athletes spend long hours in training). Loss of roles is a serious threat to people, because most communities require their members to maintain stable role performance or run the risk of being labeled some sort of deviant. Minor criminal offenses such as loitering and vagrancy, and psychiatric diagnoses such as depression and mental retardation, are applied at least in part on the basis of the individual's failure to perform adequately a sufficient number of socially required roles.

In practice every adult is called on to perform many different roles, and not all of them are necessarily compatible. Roles conflict with each other when they limit the person's behavioral choices in a mutually exclusive way. For a woman who is strongly career oriented, for example, the birth of a first child, with its intense and anxiety-producing demands, can seriously divide her attention and lead to strongly mixed emotions. If performance of a given role limits choices in some cases, it also protects them in many others. People whose roles bring them substantial incomes, for example, can qualify for mortgages and loans to purchase homes and other expensive possessions even when they have little or no money currently on hand.

One issue for the community psychologist is thus the availability of adequate numbers of roles (e.g., jobs) in a community, given the number of people who live there. Beyond mere availability, however, the ecological perspective directs us to examine the degree of fit between the available roles and each individual's behavioral propensities, social aspiration, beliefs, and other role-related characteristics. Does a small college town have a sufficient number of suitable jobs for the professionally trained spouses of new faculty? Does an inner-city neighborhood have an adequate number of organized athletic programs for the interested young people there? Does a community have enough organized opportunities for newcomers to meet other residents and learn about the community?

Not all roles have equal importance, either to the individual holding them or to others. Sarbin proposes that the relative contribution of different roles to an individual's social identity can be determined by examining each role along three dimensions: status, value, and involvement. Status refers to one's position in a social structure. Value refers to the positive or negative evaluations attached to performance, or failure to perform, in a role. Involvement refers to the degree of participation in the role as measured both by time spent in it and by energy expended in performing it.

Sarbin further differentiates the status dimension into ascribed and achieved. Ascribed statuses are those that are biosocial in nature. We enter those statuses with little contribution on our parts, and we can do little about changing them (e.g., age, sex, kinship, or race). Achieved statuses are those about which we have some degree of choice, often a great deal. For most people the most important achieved status is their occupation.

At a minimum, each individual is granted the status of a person, which means the individual is entitled to certain minimum rights no matter what his or her circumstances are. We see this principle operate in the way incarcerated individuals, no matter how disturbed, at least in theory are granted certain minimum rights regarding the way others may treat them. With achieved statuses, on the other hand, the individual is granted a great deal of power and social esteem. The president of the United States or the chairman of the board of a major corporation can exercise a great deal of power and receive a great deal of esteem from others.

Sarbin points out that we receive little positive valuation for minimally adequate performance in ascribed roles such as mother or father, male or female, for such performance is expected. To fail in such roles brings considerable social opprobrium, however. A neglectful mother may have her children taken away from her and under some circumstances may be prosecuted for criminal behavior. A good mother may be lucky to receive a Mother's Day card in some families. In contrast, no matter how poorly it is performed, an achieved role constitutes a basis for some esteem. Accepting a U.S. president's denigration of the accomplishments of his predecessor, for example, might lead us to consider the predecessor a complete failure in his role as president. Yet a former president receives many "perks" and is accorded the greatest respect when he arrives at a public gathering. The same is true for almost any occupation. Having had an occupational title earns some social points, almost no matter what else is true of your performance in that occupation. If you have a job, you are someone. If you don't and you should (i.e., you are not disabled, the beneficiary of a trust fund, or excused in some other fashion), you are considered a loafer or a bum. Sarbin also says that the degree of involvement will vary with the type of status. We are always involved in our ascribed statuses, whereas we can more easily step in and out of other statuses. In some roles, such as prisoner or "bag lady," we might have great difficulty escaping from the role, even for brief periods.

Sarbin argues that persons with degraded social identities are those with few opportunities to enact roles that are entered by choice. The best such a person can hope for is to attain a neutrally valued social identity if he or she meets all the expectations for whatever makes up his or her predominant ascribed status. In a sense, one can say that the best an individual with a degraded social identity can expect is to be ignored. The social relationships of persons with degraded social identities are often limited to those with similar identities, and in many cases their networks include a large proportion of persons who are paid to take care of them—doctors, nurses, social workers, jailers.

Sarbin's analysis is interesting, for it suggests additional avenues for diagnosis and intervention. In treating persons with degraded social identities, for example, role theory suggests increasing the variety of roles and social relationships available to such persons and working to promote positive social esteem and value for all roles, including ascribed ones (e.g., such as "old" people). The creation of jobs, even within sheltered settings, may be an important means of helping to undo a degraded social identity. Organizing patient clubs, with roles such as president, secretary, or committee chairperson, also helps to upgrade social identities. Such clubs may even provide, if not a full ideology, at least a partial ideology to serve as a guide to behavioral conduct, to articulate some values, and to support the individual's self-esteem. Participation in self-help groups that admit to membership persons who are otherwise isolated helps to undo social degradation. Some people are able to find important positions of leadership in such organizations and can, to some extent, rebuild their social identities around participation in such groups (see Chapter 8). All of these efforts have as their goal an increase in the number of role choices available to community residents and a decrease in the amount of role conflict taking place.

In terms of issues raised at the start of this chapter, role theory apparently relies on a mechanism of "role congruence" (presumably analogous to Barker's concept of behavior-environment congruence) in explaining how individual behavior changes and how changes are maintained over time. Some recognition of the importance of person-environment fit (i.e., that the available roles need to match the individual's goals and values) is also present. Like Barker, however, Sarbin's conception makes little use of person-centered factors. It does not explain, for example (if the position stated by Alcoholics Anonymous is correct), why the alcohol abuser begins the process of recovery at the very moment he or she accepts what is otherwise an extremely ascribed and degraded role: that of alcoholic (see Chapter 8).

Role theory also leaves unanswered the question of how a community psychologist participates directly in the creation of jobs and other achieved roles. Role theory suggests a problem for the community psychologist: in what types of roles and in which settings can the community psychologist participate in creating roles for others? Role theory offers a conception complementary to those of Moos and Barker, however, in defining a unit commensurate with the individual person that can also encompass many different settings at the community level.

Illustration: The Fairweather Lodge

An excellent example applying social ecology to community intervention is the lodge program developed by Fairweather and his associates (Fairweather et al., 1969, 1974; Fairweather, 1980). Beginning as a "milieu treatment" program inside the walls of a psychiatric hospital, this intervention involved small, self-governing patient groups operating under an unusually limited degree of staff authority. Within the hospital this program was highly successful in helping patients recover from acute psychiatric episodes. The major difficulty encountered was that once patients were discharged from the program and away from the daily support of their peers, they had difficulty assuming or maintaining the kinds of roles and responsibilities that would help to ensure their adaptation to the community.

Clinically, the traditional explanation for this kind of problem focuses on the characteristics of chronically mentally ill people and attributes their failure to adapt to independent living to the behavioral deficits that are perceived to set them apart from other people. As we noted in the previous chapter, however, adaptation is not a person-centered trait but a process of fit involving both person and environment. Maladaptive responses usually occur episodically over time (see Morell, Levine, & Perkins, 1982) and tend to involve certain situations more often than others. Fairweather's explanation for the poor adaptation shown by patients focuses on the community, particularly its intolerance of patients' psychotic symptomatology (e.g., delusions and hallucinations).

Table 4-1, taken from Fairweather et al. (1969), elaborates this explanation in some detail, and the bottom row indicates the essential problem. Prior to Fairweather's development of the community lodge concept, the two psychiatric statuses available to individuals were "sick person," entailing supervised living in an institution with limited rights and duties, and "well person," requiring completely independent living with full adult rights and obligations.[3] The lightly supervised group work-living situation in the community, described in the right-center column, initially was not available to patients at release from the hospital.

Reasoning, much as Kelly did, that adaptation to the community needs to occur in the community instead of inside patient's heads (in some metaphorical sense, anyway), Fairweather worked with a group of patients to develop a new kind of community setting. This "small-group" unit was designed to be a transitional step bridging the successful inpatient treatment program and the less receptive community settings outside. Fairweather draws an analogy between the lodge concept and the "melting-pot" role attributed to ethnic ghettos—that is, protective and tolerant of the in-group's characteristic behavioral idiosyncrasies, yet at the same time providing an important and challenging interface with the larger society.

Patients themselves decided who would be members of the lodge, and those chosen were assisted in developing small commercial enterprises (i.e., gardening and janitorial services). Professional mental health personnel designed the lodge program and initially took a great deal of responsibility for it. These professionals later reduced their participation to consulting roles and eventually turned over full responsibility for the operation of the residence and businesses to the residents.

All members of the lodge attended regular meetings designed to handle problems, review procedures, plan activities, and maintain the group-oriented focus of the lodge program. Many positions of responsibility came with the residential and commercial operations of the lodge. Each of the two businesses had three levels of responsibility—crew chief, worker, and "marginal" worker— and support services at the lodge residence required a cook, dishwasher, housekeeper, medication distributor, bookkeeper, and truck driver. In what Fairweather (1980) describes as a "principle of substitution," every resident performing a given job was backed up and could be replaced by another resident with little or no forewarning.

Several principles of Barker's ecological psychology are clearly evident in the Fairweather lodge. For example, participation in the meetings, commercial activities, and

TABLE 4-1. Autonomy of Mental Patients' Social Status

	Dimension of Autonomy							
	None		**Supervised community situations**			**Unsupervised community group situations**	**Partially autonomous individual status**	**Complete**
	Supervised institutional situation: mental hospital							Autonomous individual status
	Closed locked ward	Open unlocked ward	Living situations (home care, day-care centers, day hospitals)	Work situations (sheltered workshops)	Combination of work-living situations			
Social Situation						Discharged ex-patient-led group work-living situations—work in reference groups	Counseling or psychotherapy	No treatment
Status Situation	Very limited adult rights and duties		Some adult rights and duties			Otherwise, full adult rights and duties	Otherwise, full adult rights and duties	Full adult rights and duties
Available Social Statuses	Sick person					(Unavailable)	Well person	

Reprinted with permission from G. Fairweather et al., *Community Life for the Mentally Ill* (Chicago: Aldine), 1969.

other settings helped patients to recognize, model, and rehearse key behavioral skills necessary to community life. As Fairweather (1980) describes it,

> Each member of the crew had a particular task; the usual composition of such a crew was a leader (crew chief), worker, and a marginal worker. It was the marginal worker whose work was constantly brought up to acceptable standards by the working example of the supervisor and the worker. Without the framework of the group and the supervision and help of the crew chief, the marginal worker often failed. (p. 29)

Lodge members thus carefully managed the "program," with "deviation-countering" and "veto" circuits operating as part of its settings. That these circuits sometimes operated differently here than in other settings is illustrated in another passage from Fairweather (1980);

> It is difficult, if not impossible, for individuals who have been hospitalized continuously to discard aberrant behaviors immediately upon entry into a community if, indeed, such behavior can be totally extinguished at all. The members of the subsystem must be tolerant of these behaviors. In the Lodge, for example, members often hallucinated while talking with other members within the confines of the Lodge itself. To take an extreme example of such tolerance, one member who openly hallucinated within the Lodge and on the way to work was informed by his crew chief upon arrival at the work site that no talking was permitted on the job. Usually he was silent during work hours, but upon entry into the truck for the trip back to the lodge he began hallucinating again—an acceptable behavior to his peers. (p. 27)

In addition, movement back and forth between jobs and levels of authority was used to assist a member in reaching the maximum level of participation he was capable of during a given period of time. Barker's principle of behavior-environment congruence, which focuses attention on the spatial and temporal regularities of behavior and not on the internal state of a specific performer (and assumes that individual performers are in fact interchangeable), was clearly a useful mechanism of therapeutic change here.

From Sarbin's viewpoint, the Fairweather lodge worked because it entailed roles other than that of "mental patient," and two key characteristics were that the new roles were (1) achieved instead of ascribed and (2) flexible in the degrees of involvement they entailed, both of which served to increase the value or esteem given residents and enhance their social identities. Moos's interest would be drawn to the social-group format of the lodge and to characteristics of the social climate that residents provided to one another on a day-to-day basis. From Fairweather's description, this climate appears high in such "relationship-oriented" dimensions as support, cohesiveness, and involvement, and also high in "personal development" dimensions such as autonomy and responsibility. Also consistent with Moos's conception, Fairweather suggests that the program not exceed a certain overall size to keep it on a human scale. The maximum size ever reached by the lodge was 33 members.

The important thing to note here is that the lodge intervention was not directed toward changing individuals, per se. Instead, a setting was created that exerted the therapeutic influence—if not for all, at least for many. Some patients were unable to adapt to the setting demands, and they left or returned to the hospital. Not all responded, illustrating a limit to the effort to treat a heterogeneous population like the chronically mentally ill using only an environmental setting. The lodge persisted, however, and exerted its influence as new members entered.

Fairweather and his associates (Fairweather et al., 1974) also demonstrated that the lodge program could be replicated in other communities. In keeping with the experience that introducing change is not easy (see Chapter 10), however, they reported that considerable effort was necessary to interest other hospitals in adopting their program. From the ecological position taken by Kelly, a paradox of sorts is present in Fairweather's description of the lodge, which by definition had to be *in* the community in certain respects (i.e., in providing legitimate "nondeviant" social statuses) and also *not in* the community in other respects (e.g., in exerting special controls over members' conduct). In other words, while it may have been physically located in the community, the lodge was also tied to the hospital in some ways. This paradoxical position may have been a source of stress to the most vulnerable residents, contributing to their inability to succeed as members of the lodge.

Postscript: What Role Remains for Individual Differences?

The strong emphasis given in this chapter to environmental effects on behavior may seem unsettling to some in light of the widely held assumption that personality traits and other individual characteristics are important precisely because they dominate behavioral responding across time and place. Indeed, the issue of cross-situational consistency and specificity in behavior has been a major focus of debate in psychology. Epstein and O'Brien (1985) reviewed the history of this controversy. In their view, the debate exists largely because investigators have mistakenly assumed that traits should accurately predict individual episodes of behavior, when traits are actually much broader constructs related instead to large aggregates of behavior sampled across situations and over time. Although Epstein and O'Brien argue persuasively for consistency in person-centered traits at this aggregate level, we note that their approach treats differences among individual situations as simple measurement error. The work reviewed earlier in this chapter suggests that such differences have considerable practical importance. For example, intervention to change behavior is based on changing a specific setting, an action that has little significance for aggregate behavior, in the view of Epstein and O'Brien.

A more useful conceptualization by Mischel (1973) presents several person-centered characteristics he believes show significant consistency across time and place. We examine two of them at this point to offset somewhat the relentlessly "situationist" position advanced earlier and to pave the way for the attention we give in later chapters to preventive and rehabilitative interventions involving person-centered factors. One of those most relevant for our purposes Mischel calls "cognitive and behavioral construction competencies." This characteristic represents the individual's ability to construct and put into operation adaptive, effective cognitive and behavioral responses to specific situations (for example, being able to generate any number of potentially successful responses to a situation of interpersonal conflict). For Mischel, it is not the responses already available in the individual's repertoire (i.e., its "content") which are of major interest, but instead the *process* by which information is handled during the search, retrieval, and organizational operations that direct the individual's construction of a behavioral response. As an example he cites the varying degrees of fidelity with which children are able to reproduce on request a complex behavior that has only been modeled for them previously (i.e., that is not currently in their repertoire). Accurate modeling in this case appears to be based on an active synthesis of the response out of relevant domains of information, not some sort of "mechanical" duplication of what was modeled. Situationally based construction or synthesis of a response is thus determined by the individual's competence in handling information as much or more than by the responses he or she already knows. Mischel suggests that competence in cognitive and behavioral constructions is a form of intellectual aptitude and is related to such familiar constructs as intelligence, cognitive and social maturity, ego strength, and social and intellectual achievements. His earlier review (Mischel, 1968) established that this kind of characteristic is indeed one of the most stable across situations.

This construct is of use to the community psychologist in anticipating certain limits to an individual's degree of adaptation in response to purely environmental changes. A chronically and severely impaired psychiatric client, for example, may not automatically thrive and prosper when deinstitutionalized to the community if his present ability to construct effective cognitive and behavioral responses to the new settings is deficient in some respect. On the other hand, adoption of this construct also points the way toward possible person-centered interventions that would build competence and foster positive mental health by explicitly facilitating the development of cognitive and behavioral construction competencies in high-risk individuals (see Chapter 7).

A second person-centered characteristic with reasonably high cross-situational consistency is called "encoding strategies and personal constructs." Mischel points out that the same information can be evaluated differently by different individuals and will thus have different meanings for them, because they attend to different aspects of the information (e.g., the content versus the emotional meaning of verbal statements) and/or because they use different "personal constructs" (Kelly, 1955) to structure their perception of it. Personal constructs include ideological beliefs about oneself and the meaning of one's experiences and have important implications for such actions as attributing blame for one's problems and evaluating the relative desirability of different solutions to problems (e.g., psychotherapy versus self-help). Consistency across situations in an individual's cognitive and behavioral responses can thus occur simply because the individual, through his or her idiosyncratic encoding strategies and personal constructs, perceives these situations (e.g., relationships with wife and with mother) to be similar, regardless of how different they might appear to another observer. Thus adaptive changes in the personal constructs or encoding strategies of certain individuals (e.g., belief in one's power to make choices and to reject emotionally arousing stimuli, by members of Recovery, Inc., a self-help group for chronic mental patients) will help these people maintain their adaptive responses across different situations precisely because this characteristic is generally so resistant to change. This relatively stable difference among people is one reason why, for example, implicit assessments of the mental health needs of a community by a professional may not agree with an explicit needs assessment based on the reports of indigenous community residents, and why these discrepant views may be difficult to reconcile. The view each constituency has of the world is simply different. Although they are more stable than overt behavior from one situation to another, however, personal constructs and ideological beliefs are amenable to change, a phenomenon used with considerable success by many self-help groups (Antze, 1976; see Chapters 8 and 9).

In spite of evidence for these and other consistently generalizable characteristics, we believe that the relevant perspective for the community psychologist is still one of the "person-in-context." For efficiency and comprehensiveness, the smallest unit we choose to take is still larger than the single individual considered in isolation. Furthermore, virtually all of the experimental research on the cross-situational consistency and specificity of behavior has concluded that the largest effects are a result of person-situation *interactions,* not of "main effects" of persons or situations alone (Bowers, 1973; Endler & Magnusson, 1976). What we mean here is that individuals are consistent within themselves over time, and different from other individuals, in their patterns of behaving in given types of situations. For this reason, we have stressed that differences among individuals are most usefully conceptualized in units commensurate with those of the social ecology around them. Mischel (1973) points out in this connection that even though cognitive and behavioral construction competencies, for example, are generally consistent across situations, they still fluctuate somewhat depending on the specific incentives present in the immediate situation. Finally, consideration of both components, person and situation, opens up a much wider avenue of potential solutions to mental health problems, including environmentally facilitated changes alone, individual competence building alone, and strategies that unite both components in the pursuit of stable change, such as teaching high-risk individuals how to recognize and select personally optimal environments (Levine & Perkins, 1980).

Summary and Conclusions

This chapter began by raising a number of potential limitations to the ecological metaphor in psychology. For example, what specific mechanisms of behavior change does this analogy provide? How are changes in behavior maintained over time? To what extent have taxonomies of environmental settings been developed, particularly with respect to the often overlooked spatial and temporal dimensions of behavior? Finally, what place is given by specific ecological concepts to individual differences in the expression of values, goals, and purposes using environmental settings? Moos's concept of perceived social climates, Barker's ecological psychology, and Sarbin's role theory were reviewed in some detail as important theoretical systems community psychologists have used in developing answers to these questions.

Each of these concepts is essentially descriptive and ahistorical. The mechanism of behavior change each articulates is more intuitive than it is precise and complete. Moos's notion of fit between individual needs and environmental presses, for example, still depends on a concrete behavioral prescription to achieve and maintain individual change. The complexity of environmental influences, which often produce unwanted as well as wanted effects, has not been fully examined using these concepts. Furthermore, the issues of how current environmental conditions came to be and what conditions are likely to follow them are not readily answerable. Relatively little research has been longitudinal or otherwise focused on long-term changes using these concepts.

We illustrated some of the ideas generated by these concepts using Fairweather's community lodge program for chronic schizophrenics. Interpreted from the vantage of the three concepts reviewed here, membership in the lodge community provided patients with a supportive network of relationships, gave them regular opportunities to rehearse adaptive behavioral responses to key community settings, and created respectable roles for them that helped to compensate for their erstwhile status as mental patients. We closed the chapter by concluding that a place remains for individual differences in the community psychology field, noting that "cognitive and behavioral construction competencies" and "encoding strategies and personal constructs" (Mischel, 1973) are two important person-centered characteristics showing relative stability across situations and over time.

In conclusion, the social context of behavior helps to define its nature, and in so doing gives us an important perspective on individual and community change. Increased understanding of environmental contexts will help in empowering individuals to recognize and control important aspects of their environment. There are limits to what a single individual acting alone can do, however. Important restrictions can be imposed by others in the social context, as we will see in the next chapter.

Notes

1. We are indebted to Richard H. Price for providing this example.
2. The material in this section is based on Perkins, Burns, Perry, & Nielsen, in press.
3. The person in the mental hospital loses many rights associated with personal liberty when committed by a court. Following discharge, the person in the community has all the rights that every other person has, including the right to refuse to participate in any aftercare program. The problem of treating chronic mental patients in the community stems in part from their right to refuse treatment. Patients who are merely on "parole" from the hospital can be rehospitalized readily, but those who are discharged have full liberty to decide for themselves about treatment. In some jurisdictions it is possible to "commit" a person to outpatient treatment, thus creating an intermediate legal status between those of sick person and well person. The roles are a function not only of custom but also of legal regulation.

References

Anthony, W. A., Cohen, M. R., & Vitalo, R. (1978). The measurement of rehabilitation outcome. *Schizophrenia Bulletin 4*, 365–383.

Antze, P. (1976). The role of ideologies in peer psychotherapy organizations. *Journal of Applied Behavioral Science, 12*, 323–346.

Arnold, D. W., & Greenberg, C. I. (1980). Deviate rejection within differentially manned groups. *Social Psychology Quarterly, 43*, 419–424.

Baird, L. L. (1969). Big school, small school: A critical examination of the hypothesis. *Journal of Educational Psychology, 60*, 253–260.

Barker, R. G. (1968). *Ecological psychology: Concepts and methods for studying the environment of human behavior.* Stanford, CA: Stanford University Press.

Barker, R. G. (1978). *Habitats, environments, and human behavior.* San Francisco: Jossey-Bass.

Barker, R. G., & Gump, P. V. (1964). *Big school, small school; High school size and student behavior.* Stanford, CA: Stanford University Press.

Barker, R. G., & Schoggen, P. (1973). *Qualities of community life: Methods of measuring environment and behavior applied to an American and an English town.* San Francisco: Jossey-Bass.

Barker, R. G., & Wright, H. F. (1955). *Midwest and its children.* New York: Harper & Row.

Bechtel, R. B. (1977) *Enclosing behavior.* Stroudsburg, PA: Dowden, Hutchinson & Ross.

Bowers, K. S. (1973). Situationism in psychology: An analysis and a critique. *Psychological Review, 80,* 307–336.

Cowen, E. (1973). Social and community interventions. *Annual Review of Psychology, 24,* 423–472.

DeYoung, A. (1977). Classroom climate and class success: A case study at the university level. *Journal of Educational Research, 70,* 252–257.

Endler, N. S., & Magnusson, D. (1976). Toward an interactional psychology of personality. *Psychological Bulletin, 83,* 956–974.

Epstein, S., & O'Brien, E. J. (1985). The person-situation debate in historical and current perspective. *Psychological Bulletin, 98,* 513–537.

Erikson, E. H. (1950). *Childhood and society.* New York: Norton.

Fairweather, G. W., Sanders, D. H., Maynard, H., & Cressler, D. L. (1969). *Community life for the mentally ill.* Chicago: Aldine.

Fairweather, G. W., Sanders, D. H., & Tornatzky, L. G. (1974). *Creating change in mental health organizations.* New York: Pergamon.

Fairweather, G. W. (1980). *The Fairweather lodge: A twenty-five year retrospective.* San Francisco: Jossey-Bass.

Harloff, H. J., Gump, P. V., & Campbell, D. E. (1981). The public life of communities: Environmental change as a result of the intrusion of a flood control, conservation, and recreational reservoir. *Environment and Behavior, 13,* 685–706.

Jackson, D. N. (1965). *Personality research form.* Goshen, NY: Research Psychologists Press.

Katz, D., & Kahn, R. L. (1966). *The social psychology of organizations.* New York: Wiley.

Kelly, G. A. (1955). *The psychology of personal constructs.* New York, Norton.

Kiritz, S., & Moos, R. H. (1974). Physiological effects of social environments. *Psychosomatic Medicine, 36,* 96–114.

Landesman-Dwyer, S. (1981). Living in the community. *American Journal of Mental Deficiency, 86,* 223–234.

Levine, M., & Perkins, D. V. (1980). Social setting interventions and primary prevention: Comments on the Report of the Task Panel on Prevention to the President's Commission on Mental Health. *American Journal of Community Psychology, 8,* 147–158.

Mischel, W. (1968). *Personality and assessment.* New York: Wiley.

Mischel, W. (1973). Toward a cognitive social learning reconceptualization of personality. *Psychological Review, 80,* 252–283.

Moos, R. H. (1973). Conceptualizations of human environments. *American Psychologist, 28,* 652–665.

Moos, R. H. (1976). *The human context: Environmental determinants of behavior.* New York: Wiley.

Moos, R. H. (1979). Social climate measurement and feedback. In R. Munoz, L. Snowden, & J. Kelly (Eds.), *Social and psychological research in community settings.* San Francisco: Jossey-Bass.

Moos, R. H., & Insel, P. (1974). *Issues in social ecology.* Palo Alto, CA: National Press Books.

Moos, R. H. & Van Dort, B. (1979). Student physical symptoms and the social climate of college living groups. *American Journal of Community Psychology, 7,* 31–43.

Morell, M. A., Levine, M., & Perkins, D. V. (1982). Study of behavioral factors associated with psychiatric rehospitalization. *Community Mental Health Journal, 18,* 190–199.

Morgan, D. L., & Alwin, D. F. (1980). When less is more: School size and student social participation. *Social Psychology Quarterly, 43,* 241–252.

Murray, H. A. (1938). *Explorations in personality.* New York: Oxford University Press.

Perkins, D. V. (1982). Individual differences and task structure in the performance of a behavior setting: An experimental evaluation of Barker's manning theory. *American Journal of Community Psychology, 10,* 617–634.

Perkins, D. V., Burns, T. F., Perry, J. C., & Nielsen, K. P. (in press). Ecological psychology and community psychology: An analysis and critique. *Journal of Community Psychology.*

Perkins, D. V., & Perry, J. C. (1985). Dimensional analysis of behavior setting demands in a community residence for chronically mentally ill women. *Journal of Community Psychology, 13,* 350–359.

Price, R. H. (1974). Etiology, the social environment, and the prevention of psychological dysfunction. In P. Insel & R. Moos (Eds.), *Health and the social environment.* Lexington, MA: Heath.

Price, R. H., & Blashfield, R. K. (1975). Explorations in the taxonomy of behavior settings: Analysis of dimensions and classification of settings. *American Journal of Community Psychology, 3,* 335–351.

Price, R. H., & Bouffard, D. L. (1974). Behavioral appropriateness and situational constraint as dimensions of social behavior. *Journal of Personality and Social Psychology, 30,* 579–586.

Price, R. H., & Moos, R. H. (1975). Toward a taxonomy of inpatient treatment environments. *Journal of Abnormal Psychology, 84,* 181–188.

Sarason, S. B. (1972). *The creation of settings and the future societies.* San Francisco: Jossey-Bass.

Sarason, S. B. (1974). *The psychological sense of community: Prospects for a community psychology.* San Francisco: Jossey-Bass.

Sarason, S. B., & Klaber, M. (1985). The school as a social situation. *Annual Review of Psychology, 36,* 115–140.

Sarbin, T. R. (1970). A role theory perspective for community psychology: The structure of social identity. In D. Adelson & B. Kalis (Eds.), *Community psychology and mental health: Perspectives and challenges.* Scranton, PA: Chandler.

Schoggen, P. (1978). Utility of the behavioral settings approach. In D.Forgays (Ed.), *Primary prevention of psychopathology (Vol. 2).* Hanover, NH: University Press of New England.

Spivack, G., & Shure, M. B. (1974). *Social adjustment of young children.* San Francisco: Jossey-Bass.

Trickett, E. J. (1978). Toward a social-ecological conception of adolescent socialization: Normative data on contrasting types of public school classrooms. *Child Development, 49,* 408–414.

Trickett, E. J., & Moos, R. H. (1974). Personal correlates of contrasting environments: Student satisfactions in high school classrooms. *American Journal of Community Psychology, 2,* 1–12.

Vincent, T. A., & Trickett, E. J. (1983). Preventive interventions and the human context: Ecological approaches to environmental assessment and change. In R. Felner, L. Jason, J. Moritsugu, & S. Farber (Eds.), *Preventive psychology.* New York: Pergamon.

Whyte, W. H. (1980). *The social life of small urban spaces.* Washington, DC: Conservation Foundation.

Wicker, A. W. (1972). Processes which mediate behavior-environment congruence. *Behavioral Science, 17,* 365–377.

Wicker, A. W. (1979). *An introduction to ecological psychology.* Monterey, CA: Brooks-Cole.

Wicker, A. W. (in press). Behavior settings reconsidered: Temporal stages, resources, internal dynamics, context. In D. Stokols & I. Altman (Eds.), *Handbook of environmental psychology.* New York: Wiley.

Wicker, A. W., Kirmeyer, S. L., Hanson, L., & Alexander, D. (1976). Effects of manning levels on subjective experiences, performance, and verbal interaction in groups. *Organizational Behavior and Human Performance, 17,* 251–274.

Wicker, A. W., McGrath, J. E., & Armstrong, G. E. (1972). Organization size and behavior setting capacity as determinants of member participation. *Behavioral Science, 17,* 499–513.

5

Labeling Theory:
An Alternative to the Illness Model and Its Limitations

The two previous chapters introduced and examined from different perspectives the idea that behavior is usefully understood not as a specific sign of health or disease but as the product of human adaptation to specific situations. The basic ecological analogy (Chapter 3), however, while comprehensive and elegant, is rather abstract and thus difficult to use in specific predictive applications. The conceptions offered by Moos, Barker, and Sarbin (Chapter 4) are more concrete and practical for many problems, but do not explicitly integrate a view of human individual differences into the perspective they provide on behavior. In the present chapter we examine a theoretical perspective that does make an effort to explain behavior in terms of a dynamic interaction between the person and his or her social context.

This perspective is known as "labeling theory." Like other developments that led during the 1960s to the founding of community psychology (see Chapter 2), labeling theory was a product of new thinking about abnormal behavior and of criticism directed at traditional mental health practices regarding diagnosis and treatment. As we will see, an important tenet of labeling theory is that what gets formally diagnosed as psychopathology is not the deviant behavior that occurs, but merely the behavior that is officially *noticed.* Whether a deviant episode is noticed or not, moreover, is determined by factors other than the behavior itself, such as the individual's social identity and position, and also the discretionary actions of professionals engaged in diagnostic and treatment activities. Labeling theory's explanation for the coercive effects of role congruence in changing behavior (see the previous chapter) is thus that other people actively interpret and respond to a person's behavior by imposing and maintaining the boundaries defined by a role.

The labeling theory alternative to the view of abnormal behavior as a disease contained largely within the skin of the suffering individual was first provided by sociologists and represents a true interpersonal theory of deviance. It places abnormal behavior in a social context and shows how a systems approach can illuminate issues in mental health. In this theory, for example, deviance is a property of an individual's actions and is also "in the eye of the beholder." Beholders include all those who interact with the person who exhibits deviant behavior, including those who are in professional helping roles. The deviance perspective, as developed by sociologists Lemert, Becker, and others (see Gove, 1980), was refined by Scheff (1966, 1984) into an elegant alternative to the illness model. Scheff's presentation of deviance theory in propositional form set the terms of debate for the decade following its appearance.[1]

This chapter begins with a review of social and historical factors that attended the development of labeling theory and then presents the central concepts this view has provided. We continue by examining the issue of stigma in abnormal behavior, and we close the chapter by illustrating how the successful *management* of deviant behavior can also be explained and understood using principles from labeling theory.

The Social Context for the Development of Labeling Theory

Aside from Scheff's lucidity in presenting it, the labeling position took hold at a time when many people were seeking alternatives to the medical model. During the 1950s and 1960s, the reality of terrible institutions became an impetus for reform. Goffman's (1961) widely acclaimed *Asylums* was an important book that argued persuasively that mental hospitals were inherently oppressive and acted to disable patients as much as or more than did the conditions that brought them to the hospital in the first place.

This attack on what was characterized as an oppressive social institution came during the same period the Kennedy–Johnson reforms were taking hold and when the ideals of social justice and the plight of the underdog were moving us to action. Moreover, an alternative to institutional care had emerged from experience in military psychiatry during World War II (Levine, 1981). The labeling viewpoint fit well with the thrust toward deinstitutionalization and provided an intellectual rationale for that policy (e.g., Bachrach, 1976).

Szasz (1961, 1963), using strong language, added to the criticism of hospitals and mental health professionals by stating that mental illness was a myth and that psychiatrists working in the mental hospital were not healers.

> Most of the legal and social applications of psychiatry, undertaken in the name of psychiatric liberalism, are actually instances of despotism. To be sure this type of despotism is based on health values, but it is despotism nonetheless. Why? Because the promoters of mental health do not eschew coercive methods but, on the contrary, eagerly embrace them. Just as in democracy there lurks the danger of tyranny by the majority, so in mental-health legislation there lurks the danger of tyranny by therapy. (Szasz, 1963, pp. vii–viii)

Szasz (1961) worked independently of labeling theorists. He asserted that problematic behavior was not a medical illness based on known physical pathology, but instead was simply behavior that violated social, ethical, moral, and legal norms. Deviance was not an illness, but a social status created in response to our demands for social conformity. If deviant behavior was defined by acts violating social norms, moreover, the psychiatrist (and by implication other mental health professionals), with formal responsibility for certifying that norms had been violated, was as much an agent of social control as an agent of healing. Morse (1978) arrived at a similar conclusion based on a careful review and analysis of the legal, psychiatric, psychological, and sociological literature.

Szasz's attack fit well with several other trends of that day. First, because Szasz's position implied that "illness" was a culturally relative concept, it supported by impli-cation the criticisms of existing social norms. His position attracted those who felt disaffected with the state of life in America, for it fed into the distrust of constituted authority (including psychiatric authority) that was to become so prominent later in the decade (Sedgwick, 1982).

Second, his attack on the medical aspect of mental health was welcomed by those groups competing with the medical establishment for dominion in the delivery of mental health services. The mental health revolution, as Klerman (1982) calls it, was just beginning. We were fast becoming aware of the size of the market for mental health services. Professional battles about who would be included and who would be regulated out of that market were just heating up. World War II had shown that psy-chologists, social workers, nurses, and paraprofessionals could provide competent services. If mental illnesses and similar disorders were determined socially and psy-chologically, not medically, other professional groups could argue that there was no necessity for medical training to provide psychotherapeutic services in the private sec-tor, nor to hold positions of authority within public-sector institutions.

In addition to the effort to reform inferior institutions provided for the mentally ill, the modes of psychiatric practice prevalent in the 1950s came under scientific attack as well. Hollingshead and Redlich (1958) showed that both diagnoses and treat-ment rendered were correlated with social class, a point initially disputed bitterly by clinicians. Hollingshead and Redlich's data challenged the social neutrality of the practice of psychiatry. Research psychologists revealed the many inadequacies of the diagnostic system and its lack of predictive validity for clinical judgments (Meehl, 1954). Academic psychologists rediscovered Watson and behaviorism after they were shown the way by the psychiatrist Wolpe (1958). Psychologists began developing their own versions of behavior modification, based on psychology's long suit at that time—learning theory (Graziano & Mooney, 1984). The ability to modify behavior thera-peutically without first undoing complex psychodynamic and unconscious problems undermined the authority of psychoanalysis, in that day practiced largely by medically trained psychiatrists. Valid or not, Eysenck's (1952) attack on the efficacy of psycho-therapy created an intellectual climate within which alternatives could be examined.

This assault on the medical model opened the field to new thinking and to new models. That we can identify ideological positions and battles over professional turf does not deny the existence of problems the critics of the mental health system were noting. We should recognize, however, that a theory gains currency for many more reasons than its fit with data. The debate between Schacht (1985a, 1985b) and Spitzer (1985) about the interplay between political and scientific issues in the development and adoption of the DSM-III diagnostic system illustrates that the point is also appl-icable today, for instruments as well as for theories.

Caveat

Labeling theory is designed to account for the presumed "amplification" of acts of *primary* deviance (violations of norms) into *secondary*, or "career" deviance. Labeling theory seeks to answer this question: If deviant behavior is merely a norm violation, why do so many deviants become chronic mental patients, unable to assume other than ascribed roles?

A caveat is in order at the outset. The labeling position in its strong version (i.e., that under given conditions, a chronic mental patient can be created out of nothing more than the violation of a social norm) is almost certainly wrong, as Gove (1980, 1982) has diligently and persuasively shown. The weaker version, that social disability (i.e., career deviance) based on an initial episode of rule breaking may vary depending on treatment, is a more viable position. That version is unable to account for variations in outcomes after the initial deviant episode, however. Not all who are treated become chronic patients, and diagnosis does have some predictive significance for long-term outcomes. Persons who receive diagnoses of schizophrenia, for example, are more likely to become chronic patients than those who receive diagnoses of depressive reactions. Since all patients are affected by the same diagnostic and treatment system, labeling theory must account for the fact that outcomes differ systematically by diagnostic category. Its present version has no theoretical constructs that explain the variations in outcome. Labeling theory is at best incomplete, and at worst wrong.

Labeling theory is worth considering because of its analytic strength. The reader, however, should take Scheff (1966, 1975, 1984) along with a full dose of Gove (1980, 1982), a proponent of the medical model and labeling theory's chief critic. The usefulness and attractiveness of the theory as an analytic device should not be mistaken for the truth of its every detail.

A second caveat is also in order. Because labeling theory pays less attention to the behavior triggering the labeling process and more to the labeling process and its consequences, its adherents may well overlook that difficult behavior does exist, and not only in the eyes of the beholder. Because labeling theory argues that the social reaction is critical does not mean that behavior that triggers the labeling process is objectively "harmless." Rule-breaking behavior can be difficult to bear, both for the person exhibiting it and for those around him or her. Such behavior may understandably elicit reactions of fear, anger, loathing, helplessness, or weariness.

Scheff's (1966, 1984) exposition depicts deviance as a social status or role within the larger culture, but a role whose characteristics are closely related to the way in which mental hospitals and mental health professionals work. Perforce, labeling theory extended our vision to include among the variables of interest the individual's social position and the professional care system. Even if wrong in its details, and if it did nothing else, labeling theory made it more difficult for us to think about psychopathology in isolation from the social context and the system of care.

Principles of Labeling Theory

Primary and Secondary Deviance

Scheff, following other theorists of his school, differentiates *primary* deviance, the specific act that violates one or more social norms, from *secondary* deviance, a term applied to the role of a career deviant or a chronic patient. Using the systems concept of a feedback loop and applying the analogy of an amplification device, Scheff hypothesizes that under certain circumstances the act or acts of rule breaking (the primary deviance) may bring a person to public attention. In the absence of public attention, the act of primary deviance is transitory, and if unrecorded there is no "illness."

Following an act of primary deviance, the single most important event in determining entrance into the role of career deviant is the societal response to the primary deviance, in particular the public labeling of the individual as mentally ill. Labeling theory asserts that the individual is culturally prepared to accept a self-definition of mental illness, first because the individual can apply the label of "crazy" to his or her own behavior, and second because the definition of self as mentally ill is reinforced by powerful others in the hospital. Once the person is released, after having been in the role of "good patient," the stigma associated with the mental illness label will keep the person in that role.

Labeling theory does not address the *cause* of the act of primary deviance in any explicit way. Primary deviance may originate from four sources—an organic deficit, psychological dynamics, external stress, or volitional acts in defiance of social rules. The theory implies that an intact person is capable of producing a much greater variety of behavior than we ordinarily believe, especially when we consider the labeling theory assumption that most pathological behavior is transitory in nature. In this view, less behavior is genuinely "abnormal" or "sick" than most of us believe.

An act of primary deviance occurs when a social norm has been violated or when some social rule has been broken. Depending on the class of rules broken, the individual will be referred to and processed by a specialized agency of social control (i.e., oriented to helping, punishing, containing, or isolating). Criminals who have broken rules affecting property or who have harmed others "normally" are handled by the criminal justice system. Children who cannot function adequately in school may be characterized as mentally retarded and treated by the special education system, or they may be admitted to an institution for the retarded (Mercer, 1974). Juveniles are treated differently, depending on the offense. Status offenses are acts that would not be criminal if committed by an adult, but they subject the juvenile to the court's jurisdiction. Therefore they are less serious in society's view than delinquent acts, which would be crimes if committed by adults. Juveniles who have committed delinquent acts are less often referred for psychiatric and social services than juveniles who commit status offenses (e.g., running away, incorrigibility, sexual activity, truancy). Status offenders are more likely to be referred to a social service agency under diversion programs, while juvenile delinquents will receive probation or will be sent to secure facilities (Murray, 1983; Handler & Satz, 1982).

Persons who are processed through the psychiatric system have broken what Scheff calls "residual rules." These are the remaining social norms, so taken for granted that the violation of "goes-without-saying" assumptions regarding proper and decent conduct or the nature of social reality immediately leads to a perception of the individual as bizarre, strange, and perhaps frightening. An individual biting his nails in public might strike an observer as tense or nervous, but would elicit no other reaction. A person who bit his hand, sucked his fingers, nervously twisted his hair into braids, and then chewed the braids would seem bizarre to the observer. Ordinarily we do not expect an individual to walk down the street smiling vacantly, gesticulating, talking to himself, apparently tuned to inner space, unless the person happens to be carrying a Sony Walkman. Smiling at no one in particular, talking aloud to one's self, and gesticulating with no one to receive the communication are acts that so violate our assumptions about how people ought to act socially that we immediately question the person's sanity. You can test this proposition by violating the rule about how near one should stand to another while conversing. If you stand too close, the other person will immediately feel uncomfortable; that person, if a stranger, will think you are odd, to say the least.

Because labeling theory postulates that residual rule breaking is transitory in nature, it assumes that an intact organism is capable of a far greater repertoire of behaviors than theories of abnormality allow. Moreover, what are taken as symptoms of mental illness can be interpreted as violations of "culturally particular normative networks." Thus interpreted, the "symptoms" should be studied by methods designed to analyze behavior in social contexts, not by methods suitable for the study of individual psychopathology.

The norm-violating behavior alone does not elicit the effort at social control, Scheff argues. Social control is exerted whenever a "socially unqualified person" engages in the norm-violating act. In this viewpoint, who is behaving where, when, and in whose presence are more important questions than what behavior was actually performed. A soldier on the battlefield killing an enemy is not committing murder, but one civilian shooting another is. A mime in a store window holds his body in an awkward position for a long time, completely unresponsive to those around him who may try to make him flinch or smile, but no one would consider him a catatonic. A medium may talk to spirits or claim to be influenced by unearthly forces, yet is not considered a paranoid schizophrenic. Distinguishing the properties of that person's thoughts from those of a paranoid schizophrenic would be difficult, however. A patient in a psychiatric hospital claimed she was possessed by a devil, yet the priest who tried to exorcise the devil was not committed.[2] A person who isolated him or herself, refused to speak, practiced self-flagellation, dressed in a strange costume, refused to eat for long periods, kept odd hours, rose at dawn, and went to bed at a child's hour might well compel the anxious attention of friends or relatives, but not if that person belonged to a religious order.

The overt acts and expressed thoughts or feelings are not the only determinants of the outcome. The reactions of others to the actor are critical. Note that this position has something in common with Dohrenwend's model (Chapter 2). The disruptive experience associated with a stressful life event is not considered pathological, but a normal reaction to an abnormal event. The outcome in Dohrenwend's model depends on some combination of the individual's psychological strengths and available social supports. In neither Scheff's nor Dohrenwend's model does the stressful experience inevitably proceed to a pathological reaction.

In labeling theory, the reactions of others may determine whether or not the individual enters into a career deviant role. Consider the example of becoming a shaman or healer. Murphy (1964) describes the process as one in which the candidates for shamanship "go crazy" for a period of time. The person might wander alone, go without sleep or food, suffer physical hardship, and exhibit severe agitation, all of which are instances of primary deviance. Shamans report that they feel "sick and perplexed" during this period. Not all prove to be acceptable candidates, but once the acute phase of distress passes, those who do enter the role are received with honor and enrolled in the profession for further training.

One could argue that entry into shamanship represents a favorable outcome of some unknown stressful life event, with the favorable outcome determined by the reactions and support of the prospective shaman's community. This scenario seems plausible, yet Murphy claims that few of the shamans enter that role after having been considered mentally ill by their fellows, although she cites other scholarly opinion that shamans may be recruited differentially from among the mentally ill.

Murphy's (1982) informants distinguish the shaman's behavior from mental illness. "When the shaman is healing, he is out of his mind, but he is not crazy" (p. 64). The fact that he is not crazy afterward (Murphy, 1976) does not contradict the possibility that had his crisis been treated differently, he might not have come through so well.

Murphy (1982), an anthropologist, advocates the illness model, especially for conditions such as schizophrenia. She notes that all groups have members who do not function normally and that some are considered crazy. The symptoms considered crazy are similar from one group to another. Some of those considered crazy respond to native treatment, to Western treatment, or to a combination of therapies, and some become chronically disabled whether or not they receive care. Murphy's observations suggest that labeling theory has distinct limits. In her view, entry into career deviance occurs for certain persons without regard to the care they received. The process of entry into shamanship, however, reveals that a socially *qualified* individual who exhibits deviant behavior will not necessarily be labeled a deviant and will not perforce enter a deviant career.

Cultural Stereotypes and Labeling

Labeling theory requires that the rule breaker and others in the rule breaker's social field be able to recognize manifestations of mental illness. Scheff and Gove disagree about the nature of the stereotypes of mental illness held by the public and whether societal and individual reactions to acts of primary deviance are in keeping with cultural stereotypes of mental illness. The argument between them depends in part on whether cultural stereotypes are measurable using the survey instruments we have available. Tebes (1983) points out that results of studies using survey instruments are so method bound (that is, the results differ greatly depending on the wording and presentation in the survey instrument) that generalization is difficult.

Whatever the outcome of the debate on public stereotypes, today a whole range of behaviors other than serious mental illness have fallen within the domain of the mental health professions. That fact prompted Klerman (1982) to note that the drastic expansion in the market for mental health services has been accompanied by a mushrooming growth in the numbers and kinds of mental health service providers (see Chapter 1). The burgeoning market for mental health services has been apparent for quite a while. Oltman and Friedman (1965) reviewed first-admission data over a 20-year period in a state mental hospital that had had little turnover in senior psychiatric staff. First-admission diagnoses of alcoholism, neuroses, character disorders, and addictions were proportionately much higher later than earlier in the period studied, and the numbers increased at a rate faster than could be accounted for by the increase in population in their catchment area. First admissions of schizophrenia and other major mental disorders remained relatively constant compared to the increase in population. In other words, a greater number of people were being hospitalized in the mid-1960s than could be accounted for by the overall increase in population, and the increase fell into categories other than major mental disorders. Writing from another perspective, Kittrie (1971) discussed the growth of the "therapeutic state." Alcohol and drug problems, sex offenses, and the behavior problems of juveniles were more and more being treated as mental health problems than as criminal offenses. Responsibility for controlling and regulating a large variety of deviant behavior shifted from the criminal justice system to the mental health system.

Because the behavior patterns now coming to the mental health system are so diverse, the argument over public stereotypes of serious mental illness is less relevant. Just about every day, Ann Landers tells us that a great variety of personal idiosyncrasies ought to be referred to some professional agency for care. It is very easy for present-day observers of deviant behavior (including self-observers) to apply the label of "sick" and for individuals to be psychologically ready to receive confirmation of that judgment from professionals who, as Scheff pointed out, are only too ready to find pathology.

Gove (1980, 1982) also argues that the increasing proportion of voluntary-to-involuntary admissions to mental hospitals and the fact that most referrals for service are voluntary in all types of mental health agencies are difficult for labeling theory to explain. The increase in voluntary admissions and voluntary seeking of services argues against Scheff's claim that society exacerbates acts of primary deviance. Although the increasing numbers of voluntary compared to involuntary commitments reflect changes in law (Levine, 1981), the numbers may be deceptive. Lewis et al. (1984) systematically observed negotiations between public defenders and mental health personnel about whether a patient should be admitted involuntarily or released after an emergency commitment. They noted that so many persons accepted voluntary commitment under conditions that could only be considered coercive that doubts might be raised about the meaning of the overall statistics showing an increase in voluntary admissions.

Moreover, understanding and acceptance of services are now more widespread. Attitudes toward seeking and accepting mental health services may have relaxed. Gordon (1981) reports that the attitudes toward mental illness and mental health services of lower-class blacks and lower-class whites are not very different from each other, nor from attitudes reported as characteristic of middle-class individuals. Although it may be easier to *accept* treatment now, it does not follow that the consequences of having been labeled are different.

Instead of being an argument against labeling theory, the increase in voluntary help seeking can be seen as an argument for extending the premises of labeling theory to a broad range of problems in living. Encouragement in the media to seek help, the sympathetic portrayal of mental illness on the screen (Gove, 1982), the availability of ordinary health insurance for psychotherapeutic and psychiatric care, and the wide prevalence of care providers in contemporary society are evidence of social support for seeking help. Those same social structures encourage self-definitions that include a "sick" part, having "unresolved issues," or being in need of help. For some, that aspect of self-definition may come to play a central part in their lives. It may be useful to break the concept of career deviant into several subclasses that reflect different consequences of participation in mental health care. A socially functioning therapeutic "addict" may be as much a career deviant, in one sense, as the chronic schizophrenic is in another. Of course, the rapid rate at which people define all kinds of problems in living as related to mental health may eventually result in a normalization of such conditions and some degree of destigmatization. The argument may not revolve around the cultural stereotype so much as the types of behavior and the conditions under which behavior patterns create sufficient social concern to elicit coerced intervention.

When Is Residual Rule Breaking Labeled?

Scheff states that most instances of residual rule breaking are ignored, denied, or ratio- nalized away. Lacking a societal reaction, these episodes do not lead to illness, but just fade away. Scheff's position is rooted in positivism to the degree that it assumes that illness does not exist unless the illness has social consequences. If most primary devi- ance is ignored, making the episode transitory, unrecorded, and of no particular social consequence, why in other cases does the same behavior lead to social control and public labeling? The outcome is essentially determined by five sets of variables (See Figure 5-1).

1. Irrespective of cause, the degree, amount, and visibility of the rule breaking are determinants of whether or not there will be any public reaction and efforts at social control. As an extreme illustration, if an individual was capable of exhibiting crazy behavior but engaged in residual rule breaking only when alone, that behavior would never come to the attention of others, would pass, and would not be recorded as ill- ness. Those who work with chronic mental patients understand this principle when they encourage clients to suppress symptoms when in public. Thus patient members of Fairweather's community lodge (see the previous chapter) were told they were not allowed to act crazy while interacting with customers of their janitorial and gardening service, and most were able to suppress norm-violating behavior (Fairweather et al., 1969). Patients were allowed to act crazy while at home in the lodge. This form of treatment recognizes that societal reaction has consequences for continued living in the community. In Scheff's view, to the degree that symptoms are "invisible," there is no illness.

Many persons suffer from anxiety, depression, strange thoughts, or bizarre, fright- ening, or embarrassing fantasies but are able to meet everyday responsibilities and conceal their symptoms from all but themselves. Their conditions may wax and wane without attracting the notice of others. In a study we mentioned in Chapter 2, Hankin and Locke (1982) evaluated a group of adults on the rolls of a health plan who all had scores on a depression scale that fell well within the pathological range. A year later, the initial scores of those who had improved on a readministration of the same depres- sion scale were compared to those whose scores remained in the depressive range. Let us assume that invisibility means there was no formal diagnosis and treatment of the depressive conditions. Twice as many of those whose depression did *not* remit (23.9%) had one or more visits to the Psychiatry Department of the health service, compared with those whose depressions did remit (12.3%). A greater number of the illnesses in the former group may have become "visible" by virtue of treatment. Hankin and Locke interpret the difference as a difference in type of depressive illness. One may view their findings as a reflection of the visibility of the treated conditions, however, thus showing a labeling effect.

Hankin and Locke do not make the interpretation that for some patients the per- sistence of depressive symptoms may have an iatrogenic component. Note that 76% of those whose conditions did not remit had no visit to a mental health professional,

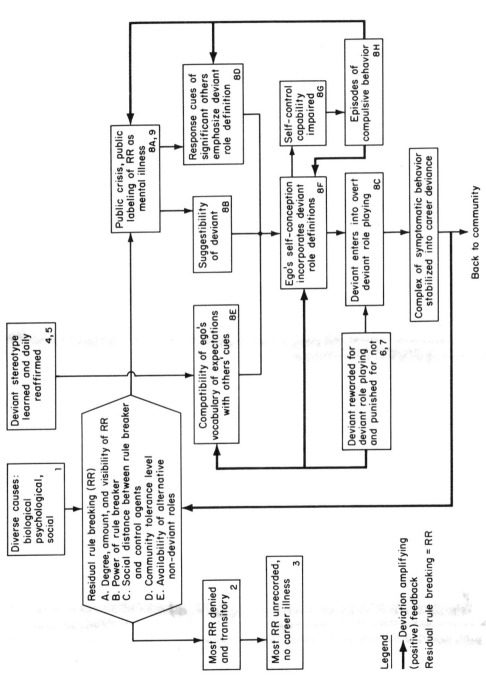

Figure 5-1. Flowchart—stabilization of deviance in a social system (from Scheff, 1984).

Diverse causes: biological psychological, social 1

Deviant stereotype learned and daily reaffirmed 4, 5

Residual rule breaking (RR)
A. Degree, amount, and visibility of RR
B. Power of rule breaker
C. Social distance between rule breaker and control agents
D. Community tolerance level
E. Availability of alternative non-deviant roles

Most RR denied and transitory 2

Most RR unrecorded, no career illness 3

Public crisis, public labeling of RR as mental illness 8A, 9

Response cues of significant others emphasize deviant role definition 8D

Suggestibility of deviant 8B

Self-control capability impaired 8G

Episodes of compulsive behavior 8H

Compatibility of ego's vocabulary of expectations with others' cues 8E

Ego's self-conception incorporates deviant role definitions 8F

Deviant enters into overt deviant role playing 8C

Deviant rewarded for deviant role playing and punished for not 6, 7

Complex of symptomatic behavior stabilized into career deviance

Back to community

Legend
Deviation amplifying (positive) feedback
Residual rule breaking = RR

137

at least none that was noted on the health plan's records. That means that the bulk of persons whose condition did not improve were not labeled. The data support labeling theory to some degree, but the theory cannot fully account for the majority of cases. Hankin and Locke's data on the persistence of depression do not support the view that only the more seriously ill enter treatment, because all started at the same level on the depression scale. The depression scale used may not measure all of the critical features of depressive illness, of course, and the study was limited to an outpatient treatment context.

The intensity, frequency, and duration of the rule-breaking episode may present primary conditions for the initiation of treatment and efforts at social control. Gove (1980, 1982) cites literature indicating that those who enter treatment have more severe symptoms than those who do not. Whitt and Meile (1985) find that people are not likely to label behavior as mental illness even when the label is suggested to them. Gove notes that families tolerate a great deal of disturbed behavior before they act to hospitalize a member of the family. Herz and Melville (1980) report that the overwhelming majority of patients and their families were aware of changes in thoughts, behavior, and feelings for at least one week, and in many cases for more than one month, before rehospitalization occurred. Morrell, Levine, and Perkins (1982) reviewed the daily logs kept by staff in a proprietary home for adult mental patients located in a city neighborhood. Those patients who were later rehospitalized had many more episodes that brought the residents to the attention of staff recorded in the log book than did comparable patients who were not rehospitalized. This difference in number of behavioral incidents was noticeable for many weeks before rehospitalization. Because both groups were chronic patients, these data suggest that greater frequency and visibility of disturbed behavior is associated with rehospitalization and not just the condition of mental illness.

Outcomes also vary by initial symptom picture and diagnosis. Not all who are publicly labeled become career deviants, a fact that labeling theory does not explain. Nor does it explain why those who may not have been labeled also have symptoms that persist or they develop chronic conditions. It does not explain why the prognosis for those with depressive disorders is on the whole better than the prognosis for those with schizophrenic disorders. Moreover, other longitudinal studies have revealed perplexing problems for labeling theory. Robins (1974) showed that antisocial behavior in childhood predicts antisocial behavior in adult life among those who were treated (labeled) in a child guidance clinic. Most children with antisocial behavior patterns do not grow up into antisocial adults, whether or not they were treated. Moreover, those children who presented neurotic complaints and were treated (labeled) were no different at follow-up than untreated controls. These two categories of behavior show that outcome does vary by initial symptom picture, and labeling theory cannot account for that fact.

2 and 3. Scheff's second and third variables deal with the power and social status of the rule breaker vis-à-vis the agent of social control. If the power differential favors the rule breaker, he or she may not be readily subject to social control. During his last days as president, Richard M. Nixon is said to have exhibited some bizarre behavior (Woodward & Bernstein, 1976). Although many expressed concern over the state of his mind, no one did anything to bring the president to the attention of a mental health professional. Taking another example closer to the everyday experience of people in the mental health field, we note that untold numbers of neophyte psychother-

apists have been urged if not ordered by therapy supervisors to work out some personal problem interfering with therapy or supervision by entering treatment. Although any number of neophyte therapists may well have entertained serious doubts about the mental health of some of their supervisors, it is a rare student or intern who would have the courage to urge the supervisor to seek treatment. The student certainly could not order the supervisor to enter treatment and enforce the order with a threat of dismissal or a poor recommendation or letter of reference.

Gove has examined the argument that lower-class individuals, a relatively powerless group, draw more serious diagnoses and tend to be treated in state facilities with more drastic therapies because of their powerlessness. A Task Panel of the President's Commission on Mental Health reported that nonwhites were admitted to psychiatric facilities at a rate approximately 1.3 times greater than whites (Task Panel, 1978). We can assume that nonwhites as a group are more powerless and of lower social class than are whites as a group. Gove agrees that blacks and lower-social-class individuals have a higher rate of hospitalization, but he believes it reflects the higher degree of stress in the lives of lower-class persons. Although Gove (1980) acknowledges that well-controlled studies do not appear in the literature, he believes the available evidence indicates that controlling for social class washes out nonwhite-white differences in hospitalization rates.

Looking at still another index of social power, Gove notes that persons who occupy more central roles in families and who presumably have greater social power are hospitalized sooner than those occupying more peripheral roles. If a mother is unable to meet her obligations, the household soon falls apart, and others will seek help for mother. If grandmother wanders and is forgetful or incoherent, however, she may not be hospitalized for a much longer time after symptoms have been noted.

Gove (1980) points to other relationships between social class and aspects of mental illness that do not support predictions from labeling theory. For example, members of lower social classes tend to define indices of mental illness much more narrowly in terms of aggressive or antisocial behavior. Much that would be recognized as "sick" in persons of higher social class would be ignored in lower social classes, thus reducing the vulnerability to labeling in a relatively powerless group. In fact, Gove believes that the theory of labeling should postulate *greater* vulnerability to the effects of labeling among the upper classes (the more powerful group) who view a wider range of behaviors and expression of feelings as indicative of mental illness. Hollingshead and Redlich (1958) reported that upper-class individuals do seek treatment, but tend to receive it as outpatients and tend to receive less serious diagnoses. The vulnerability to labeling may work itself out in a different fashion among the middle and upper social classes. If lower-class individuals turn out to be more subject to pejorative public labeling, the difference in attitude toward mental illness held by members of different social classes may not be relevant to labeling theory.

The social distance between the rule breaker and the agent of social control may also be a factor in determining whether the agent of social control will act in relation to an episode of primary deviance. Keil et al. (1983) found that persons of higher socioeconomic status were better able to avoid rehospitalization for excessive drinking than persons of lower status, even when drinking patterns were controlled. Consider the following example. A police officer seeing a drunk who is obviously a homeless street person may arrest the person or consider emergency hospitalization. The same officer seeing a disheveled but well-dressed drunk vomiting and staggering down the street may find a cab and send him home. Gove (1980), however, claims that the scenario is not accurate for mental disorder. He believes police are quite discerning in selecting the circumstances in which to intervene and are more likely to ignore primary deviance among lower-class citizens, intervening only when violence threatens or at the behest of a relative of a prospective patient. In Gove's view, the facts do not support predictions from the social-distance factor of labeling theory. Teplin (1984), on the basis of an observational study of police on the streets, found that police are more likely to arrest a person who is showing signs of psychological disturbance than a person who has come to police attention and is not showing signs of disturbance. Teplin reports no data on the social-class characteristics of those who were or were not arrested. Her data do not provide a test of labeling theory except to indicate that the violation of some norms is more likely to call forth acts of social control than violations of other norms.

4. Scheff's fourth factor is the level of tolerance for deviance within a community. A psychiatrist on an admitting service of a large urban receiving hospital reported a conversation with a newly arrived, itinerant, streetwise patient who desired to be admitted to the psychiatric facility in a city unfamiliar to him. The patient inquired seriously about what he had to do to be admitted—break a window or run down the street with his clothes off. In that particular city, the better choice would have been nudity. In 1982 the city's mayor and many leading citizens threatened to close down the play *Oh Calcutta,* because in their view the nudity in it was obscene. Yet in San Francisco's Golden Gate Park it would not have been unusual during the height of the flower child years to see an adult male, stark naked, happily listening to a concert in the park. That community's tolerance for personal oddity was much greater. In a more bohemian neighborhood more tolerant of personal idiosyncrasy, a former mental patient dancing in the streets and disrupting traffic would elicit only the amusement of neighbors. The same person dancing in the parking lanes of a surburban shopping center and disrupting traffic would bring the police.

Geel, Belgium, has been a haven for mental patients for over 700 years (Roosens, 1979). The community has unusual tolerance for deviant behavior. The citizens of Geel earn money by boarding patients from the nearby mental hospital. The patients wander the streets freely. Roosens observes that citizens quietly but effectively engage anyone who is disruptive and stop the disruptiveness. Everyone in the city accepts it as an obligation to work with patients, and otherwise patients are tolerated. More overtly troubled and troublesome patients are returned to the hospital, of course, but the citizens of Geel accept a great deal of oddity without special notice. According to Roosens, patients find appropriate niches in Geel. In many community settings patients are segregated (e.g., the balcony of the movie theater; patients are permitted in some bars, but not in all), and in many community settings patients are not found at all. Apparently the level of tolerance may be enhanced by a tacit understanding of whose turf is whose. Geel is an important example; Roosens's observations indicate what the limits are to the integration of persons with deviant characteristics into a community. There can be great tolerance and substantial integration, but by no means is either tolerance or integration complete.

5. Scheff's fifth factor regarding the labeling of residual rule breaking is the availability of alternative nondeviant roles. He describes several examples of primary deviance interpreted in such a fashion that the person's status was elevated. One example

is the entrance into shamanship following a period of agitation. A second is that of religious prophets who report extraordinary extrasensory communications, but normalize that communication by putting it into a religious context. Such persons sometimes emerge as respected members of a community. John Humphrey Noyes, founder of the religiously based Oneida commune, went through a "dark night of the soul" and emerged strengthened from the experience after his friends assisted him and continued to accept him as their spiritual leader (Levine & Bunker, 1975). A third example Scheff offers is of a woman who experienced hallucinations while in church at a time when her personal problems seemed overwhelming. Although she was startled by her hallucinations, her chance encounter with a stranger who identified herself as a psychic helped the woman to reinterpret her hallucinations as manifestations of psychic powers. The encounter led her into a career as a psychic.

The best known example of the creation of niches and roles for mental patients as forms of treatment is the Fairweather et al. (1969) creation of roles for patients as managers of residential lodges and businesses (see Chapter 4). In contemporary society, an alternative nondeviant role is often provided to those who participate in various self-help groups and become deeply involved as senior members or as more formal leaders. In these cases, it is necessary to have experienced the primary deviance (the alcoholism or the "nervous breakdown") and to have overcome it by active participation in the self-help group. Krizan (1982) describes a small religious sect that evidently had success with some disturbed individuals who found personal havens and missions for themselves by joining the congregation and proselytizing for it. In both of these examples, people entered existing social organizations while under great stress. Whether prepared niches could be created as therapeutic devices for persons who are experiencing great personal problems and who are acutely disturbed remains to be seen. In a later section we will discuss how deviant behavior may be managed to avoid the undesirable effects of the labeling process and of social control.

Diagnosis and Labeling Theory

The diagnostic process is an important element within labeling theory. After a person goes (or is brought by someone else) for care, a mental health professional uses a diagnostic process to certify whether or not the person has a disorder suitable for treatment in that particular facility. The U.S. Supreme Court based its decision in *Parham v. J. and J.R.* (1979) on the assumption that a child's personal rights when brought for hospitalization by a parent are sufficiently safeguarded by the integrity of the diagnostic process that additional safeguards of due process are unnecessary[3]. Can we depend on the validity and integrity of the diagnostic process to identify and label only those who are ill and in need of care?

Scheff notes that the diagnostic process itself occurs within a social context that has implications for the outcome. In the cultural attitudes of physicians, it is more important to avoid failing to diagnose pathology when it exists than to suspect pathology when it doesn't exist. It is more harmful to miss a diagnosis and fail to institute treatment than to continue to observe and test in order to rule out pathology. The medical assumption that it does less harm to observe further than to miss illness may not be appropriate for mental illness, because the *social* costs for the prospective patient of hospitalization to diagnose mental illness are greater than the costs of hospitalization for diagnosing physical illness. Admission to a hospital for laboratory tests and X-rays doesn't have the same implication for the person's social identity as admission to a psychiatric service.

Scheff believes that mental health professionals, by virtue of their position in the social system providing care, are biased toward finding pathology and holding people for care. His argument is important for the "deviance amplification" position of labeling theory, in that any behavior pattern is potentially subject to labeling. The ability of those in the mental health system to differentiate between those whose problems are best characterized as manifestations of illness and those who have other problems in living is important.

This problem turns on two issues: the social context within which mental health professionals make professional judgments and the inherent unreliability of the diagnostic procedures and systems in use. Scheff shows that in the commitment context, psychiatric interviews were often brief, legal hearings were often perfunctory, and the necessary evidence regarding the criteria for commitment (e.g., dangerous to self or others) was often not clearly brought out in the record or the psychiatric testimony. His observations match those of Albers et al. (1976), Warren (1977), and Hiday (1977), who also note that the necessary evidence to support commitment was not carefully evaluated in commitment hearings.

Scheff argues that the commitment system encourages findings of illness because mental health professionals who are not well paid for public work of this sort often increase their rates by reducing the amount of time they spend per case. Moreover, judges, who face dispositions for troubled people who have been brought to public attention, and face the possible political repercussions of releasing someone who would then harm himself or herself or others, are prone to favor commitment. Judges may encourage mental health professionals in subtle and not so subtle fashion to produce findings supporting commitment. Ennis and Litwack (1974) note that mental health personnel are at risk for liability in a civil suit if they release someone who harms another, but they are far less likely to be found liable if they hold someone in a hospital for further treatment.[4]

In part, the issue is the reliability of psychiatric diagnosis. Spitzer and Williams (1982) agree that in the past such reliability left much to be desired. They claim that the situation has improved substantially with the development of DSM-III, however. Be that as it may, the weakness of psychiatric diagnosis and clinical methods has been exposed in many adversary hearings, such as the trial of would-be presidential assassin John Hinckley. Levine (1985) has summarized evidence showing that psychiatric judgments are highly unreliable, especially within the adversary process. The degree of reliability that may emerge in research tests of the diagnostic system may not hold for other contexts. Moreover, psychiatric judgments are difficult to support when they are subject to question. Theoretical abstractions applied with minimal rules of inference from shaky evidence are easy to dispute. The evidence that patients who are represented by attorneys more often win dismissal of petitions to retain them than do unrepresented patients underscores the point (Wenger & Fletcher, 1969).

The nature and degree of the patient's presenting condition are not the only (and may not even be the primary) considerations in the decision to hospitalize and thus to assign a diagnostic label for the record. Many other variables affect the decision to admit. On admission services, the family's desire for the individual to be hospitalized tends to be a stronger factor in the admission decision than is the clinician's judgment of degree of disorder, although some parents who have unsuccessfully sought the hospitalization of an adult family member may dispute that conclusion. Many factors beyond the patient's presenting condition influence admission decisions—fear of being manipulated by a patient, research needs for a certain kind of patient, or the need for certain cases for teaching or training purposes (Baxter et al., 1968; Hogarty et al., 1968; Richart & Milner, 1968; Tischler, 1966).

Those who are selected for labeling may have some social or clinical characteristics that make it easier for some labels to stick. Lindsay (1982) demonstrates that subjects could readily detect first-admission schizophrenics from nonpatients when observing interviews on the topic of schooling, even when given false labels. The stringency of the decision-making process leaves much to be desired under ordinary working conditions, however, as Rosenhan's (1973) classic study demonstrates. Rosenhan showed that pseudopatients (researchers who presented themselves to a mental hospital admitting service as ill but who acknowledged only the most minimal symptoms) were readily admitted on their own application, and their deception went undetected. The diagnostic process is sufficiently unreliable under ordinary working conditions that labels can readily be misapplied. This body of evidence supports one component of the labeling theory model, although it by no means confirms the major proposition of labeling theory that anyone thus mislabeled could be made a career deviant.

Behavior Is Assimilated to the Label

Few rules govern observation and inference in the psychiatric setting. Clinicians are unaware of the limits of inferences drawn from clinical observations. Any behavior observed in the hospital may be assimilated to the initial diagnosis, or to the patient's status as a deviant individual. Patients are observed and diagnosed based on an important unstated assumption of the clinical enterprise stemming from the pervasive influence of Freudian thinking on clinical workers. In the Freudian system, surface appearances are distrusted and situational factors are discounted. The important factor is not what is apparent, but what lies underneath the apparent. Because there are no or few explicit rules relating observed behavior to the unobserved construct, anything can be related to anything else. One can accept the surface behavior or reinterpret it to fit whatever construct the worker has in mind.

Observing psychiatric residents in training, Light (1982) notes that they were often bewildered by the intangible nature of psychiatric symptoms and complaints. He believes they were subject to doctrinaire instruction, with little review of the research literature to foster an appreciation of the weakness of the methods and theories they were being taught. He argues that the process of psychiatric interviewing leads to accentuating the neurotic characteristics of everyone concerned, including the psychiatric interviewer. Consequently, interviewers feel a need to distance and to differentiate themselves from patients.[5] Light argues that all of the uncertainties lead to quick assimilation of the psychiatric culture, including uncritical use of diagnostic labels. We have no reason to believe that clinical psychologists or psychiatric social workers training in medical settings are any more immune to this culture than are psychiatric residents. We have some evidence that psychologists trained in behavioral approaches may be less inclined to resort to inferences about unobservable causes and may be more immune to labeling effects in observing patients (Langer & Abelson, 1974).

Once a tentative diagnosis is developed, many aspects of patient behavior are assimilated to the diagnosis. Rosenhan (1973) reports that perfectly normal behavior of his pseudopatients was recorded as symptoms of disturbance. Light (1982) also reports that the psychiatrists he observed were unaware of the degree to which their own personal styles in dealing with patients contributed to patient reactions. There was an uncritical assumption that the way the patient appeared in the clinical interview with that doctor was predictive of the patient's behavior in all other circumstances and that all behavior was a function of the patient's psychopathology.

Psychiatric training, centering as it does on the classification of disorders into mutually exclusive categories and on the assumption that environmental circumstances do not matter very much, fails to sensitize practitioners to the situationally determined character of much behavior. Braginsky, Braginsky, and Ring (1969) demonstrate that patients can manipulate their presentation of themselves in psychiatric interviews depending on their goals. Blind ratings of psychopathology from tape recordings of interviews showed that when patients wanted to achieve a valued goal (e.g., move to a more desirable ward), less psychopathology was found than when patients believed the interview would have a result they wished to avoid (e.g., for these chronic patients, to be discharged from the hospital).

Many studies have shown the limited predictability of clinical assessments to behavior in other settings. Ratings of psychopathology based on psychiatric interviews, for example, do not predict work competence (Lipton & Kadin, 1965; Olshansky, 1968). Quite a number of studies have shown that professional prediction of adjustment in the community, based on knowledge of behavior in the institution, is poor (Ellsworth et al., 1968; Stack, Lannon, & Miley, 1983). Tuckman and Lavell (1962) showed that patients discharged against medical advice did just as well in the community as those discharged with medical approval. The only difference was that patients discharged against medical advice had somewhat shorter hospital stays. Even if the use of DSM-III criteria results in more reliable applications of clinical labels, we have no reason to believe that judgments predicated on those labels will have any greater validity. The mental health world-view simply does not take situational influences sufficiently into account, and so it is all too easy to assume that any behavior that is observed is related to pathology.

In labeling theory, staff within institutions assimilate patient behavior to patient diagnosis and find reasons why the patient is "sick." Patient complaints and objections are likely to be treated as manifestations of resistance or as part of the patient's illness. The patient's suggestibility during a period of crisis and the patient's distress at treatment in the hospital may lead to behavior that appears both to the observer and to the patient as out of control.

A patient may refuse medication for any number of reasons, for example, including the fear that medication will produce untoward side effects. The patient's resistance to taking medication is sometimes termed "paranoid." Hospital personnel may insist that the patient accept the medication. If the patient continues to refuse and loses his or her temper or cries when pressed, the patient may be considered to be hostile and aggressive or in a labile emotional state. The patient, noting the emotional behavior in himself or herself, may feel out of control. At that point, self-observation coupled with reinforcement from powerful others feeds into the formation of the person's identity as "sick."

Once the self is viewed as "sick," the next step is to accept the role of good patient and to play it out until discharge. During a hospital stay, much of a patient's life is regimented. Patients lose a great deal of autonomy and are encouraged to rely on the advice and direction of treating personnel. A "good" patient accepts the therapeutic regime without question. One who disputes the professional's view of his or her intentions, motives, feelings, or behavior is judged resistant. Rosenhan (1973) reports that a pseudopatient who was bored by the lack of activity in the hospital paced the dayroom. When questioned by a nurse, the pseudopatient said that he was bored. The nurse insisted that the pseudopatient was anxious and persisted in getting the pseudopatient to accept the "true" nature of his "symptom" of pacing. If the pseudopatient expressed annoyance at the nurse, in all likelihood he would have been characterized as resistant and hostile. If he accepted her interpretation of his state, he would have been characterized as having "gained insight" and thus was improving. In other words, powerful social forces are at work to encourage the patient to accept and to internalize the hospital's and the professional's views of the patient's conditions and capabilities.

Gove is willing to admit that in bygone days, chronicity may have been fostered in total institutions that kept patients for long periods. He believes the situation has changed drastically in recent years, however (see Kiesler, 1982). Given modern clinical practices, most patients are released relatively quickly, with little time for chronicity to set in. In addition, the removal of a patient from a stressful life setting has ameliorative effects in and of itself. The hospital experience provides a retreat during which the person may recover. Moreover, active therapy does help a great many individuals. Gove argues that far from keeping patients in the patient role, adequate treatment frees patients. He points out that in the absence of treatment, many deinstitutionalized patients quickly deteriorate.

Methods of diagnosis and observation are probably not very good. We do not have powerful theories and constructs that allow us to predict accurately to new circumstances (see the previous chapter). We can too easily assume that once sick, always sick, or that everything we observe in a person reflects his or her sickness. Mental health personnel probably convey such attitudes to their patients, and to some degree patients tend to accept that view of themselves. Present-day conditions of treatment surely are not sufficient to produce the kind of chronic condition that is implied in the concept of a career deviant. Nonetheless, labeling theory's emphasis on the undesirable side effects of care should be taken seriously, if only to cause us to reexamine our attitudes and practices with an eye toward understanding their consequences and limitations. Not all that is done in the name of doing good in fact does good.

Stigma

The final factor aiding in the formation of a deviant career is the stigma attached to the role of mental patient or ex-mental patient. In Scheff's view, once the patient returns to the community, the stigma of having been a mental patient continues to follow him or her. Opportunities for employment may be affected, and, equally important, others will tend to interpret the individual's behavior in light of the history of mental illness. Thus it is easier for the individual to be rehospitalized because he or she has never been fully rid of the taint to social identity. The stigma attached to mental illness serves to keep the released patient in the tainted role, thus creating the role of career deviant or chronic mental patient. The disagreement between Scheff and

Gove revolves around the role of stigma in creating chronic mental patients. Labeling theory places a great deal of emphasis on this issue, while Gove claims that the primary determinant of any social reaction to a former mental patient is the person's current behavior.

Aside from whatever informal social sanctions followed commitment, in an earlier day the individual was placed under a number of formal constraints. His or her liberty to engage in a great many activities was restricted. A committed mental patient, regardless of his or her competence, might lose a driver's license, be unable to contract for goods and services, be disqualified from marrying, or be barred from military service. In recent times, the rights of mental patients have been better protected (Ennis & Siegel, 1973). In addition to formal disabilities, occupational and social stigmas also resulted. The President's Commission on Mental Health (Task Panel, 1978) indicated that in its view, stigma was still a critical factor in the contemporary mental health scene.

In labeling theory, stigma helps to keep the person in the patient role. Significant others may interpret the individual's behavior in light of their knowledge of the person's history. Anger, dislikes, disagreements, moods, or failure to achieve may all be read as continued manifestations of disorder or as prodromal to another episode, even after a period of normality. Recall Rosenhan's (1973) report that the normal behavior of his pseudopatients was interpreted as pathological by nurses and attendants and recorded in case files as symptoms of disorder (e.g., pacing out of boredom was characterized as anxiety, note taking for purposes of research became compulsive writing). Even after discharge, the diagnosis was not changed, but the person continued to carry the label—Schizophrenia, Chronic Undifferentiated Type, in Remission. To use Goffman's (1963) term, the patient's social identity was "spoiled."

If we have any question concerning the power of stigmatization, we need only look at Senator Thomas Eagleton, who was forced to withdraw from candidacy for the vice-presidency in the 1972 election campaign after it was revealed that he had been treated for a depressive disorder many years before. Even though he had functioned visibly and responsibly in positions of public leadership for many years following the episode, the stigma of mental disorder was sufficient to disqualify him from running for that office.

Not only public figures suffer. One of us was psychotherapist for a boy of about 14 who had been having more than the usual share of growing-up difficulties. Several years later the young man joined the navy. He completed basic and specialist training successfully and performed competently in the navy. Despite the navy's experience with him over several years, when his promotion required an additional security clearance, a naval intelligence officer contacted his therapist wanting to know about the nature of problems for which the boy was treated several years earlier.

The ordinary person is also concerned about stigma. Lois Gibbs (1983), president of the Love Canal Homeowners Association, reported that blue-collar families actively avoided the eager mental health worker on the scene during the initial days of the community's crisis. They avoided the table labeled Mental Health, not because people were not under emotional strain, but because they feared their neighbor's reactions if they openly accepted help. "I'm not crazy!" they would say.

Is stigma a potent factor in producing career deviants? One body of studies using surveys and questionnaires suggests that Americans have become more tolerant of mental illness over the years. The procedure often makes use of vignettes portraying various types of disorders; it measures social distance in terms of a scale that asks questions such as: Would you accept such a person in your community? Would you work with such a person? Would you rent a room in your home to such a person? Would you want such a person to marry into your family? Studies using these methods have reported very mixed results. Brockman, D'Arcy, and Edmonds (1979) note that most of the studies used two different methods of collecting data. In one group of studies, subjects completed paper-and-pencil social-distance scales using vignettes describing patients. The second group of studies employed face-to-face interviews and asked about a hypothetical mental patient. They found that researchers coming from medical backgrounds and institutions favored the face-to-face interview using the hypothetical mental patient as the stimulus. These investigators said that public attitudes toward the mentally ill were improving. Social science researchers preferred using the former method of self-response questionnaires and vignettes as the stimulus material. These studies consistently reported negative attitudes toward mental patients. Therefore, results reporting the degree of optimism or pessimism attributed to the public may be a function of method and discipline of the investigator more than of the public's real attitude.

At an attitudinal level, at least as measured by scales and self-report, the stigma attached to the former mental patient may have been reduced from former times. Data also show that families are more tolerant toward the mentally ill than is the general public. Family members report experiencing little stigma despite expectations that stigma would be great (Clausen, 1981). We really know very little about the relationship between expressed attitudes and behavior. Public education on questions of mental illness may have influenced what people are willing to say on questionnaires, but it does not necessarily follow that people always act in complete consistency with those expressed attitudes.

Family members do report concealing to some degree the family member's history of hospitalization for their own social comfort. A body of literature summarized in Tebes (1983) suggests that family members often reduce the frequency of their visits to mentally ill persons and that many are reluctant to accept the person back into the home. Distinguishing between rejection that results from stigma and rejection that results from the strain of dealing with a mentally ill person is difficult. Tebes believes the explanation that family members reject the mental patient because of the physical, economic, and psychological burdens of care is more plausible than the theory that rejection is based on stigma.

The situation of family members may differ from that of potential neighbors, employers, landlords, and others dealing with the former mental patient. Many court cases have challenged zoning ordinances that exclude group homes for the mentally ill and the mentally retarded from residential neighborhoods. (The U.S. Supreme Court decided such a case in 1985: *City of Cleburne, Texas v. Cleburne Living Center*, 53 LW 5022, 1985) The existence of zoning ordinances reflects community attitudes. People fear being harmed or they fear property values will decrease. Both of those fears appear to be overly exaggerated. In the case of the mentally retarded, studies show that there is little or no impact on any measurable aspect of neighborhood property value attributable to the presence of a group home (Dolan & Wolpert, 1982). Studies also show that mentally retarded individuals living in group homes in the community have a far lower rate of contact with the police than does the average citizen in that community (Lubin, Janicki, Zigman, & Ross, 1982). When a group home is proposed for a neighborhood, there is often vocal community opposition. Plans to open some group homes may have been changed because of local opposition. If such a home does open, however, follow-up studies show that neighbors become positive or indifferent toward it after a while. We would assume that if undesirable consequences actually followed the opening of a group home, neighborhood opposition would increase with time. The initial attitude thus appears to be prejudiced and is based on stigma, not on the actual events that follow the opening of a group home.

Employers may stigmatize persons with a history of mental illness, making it difficult for the former mental patient to obtain employment. Brand and Claiborn (1976) sent four undergraduates and two graduate students to answer ads for job openings in retail sales. Each student participated in six interviews, two in which they gave histories as ex-tuberculosis patients, two as ex-convicts, and two as ex-mental patients. They were coached to dress and to act the same in each role. In the role of former tuberculosis patient, 75% received job offers. The roles of ex-convict and ex-mental patient drew 58% job offers. These results indicate that although employers will hire ex-patients for some jobs, ex-patients are still at some handicap when being considered for employment. That this handicap is no worse than that for ex-convicts does not change the conclusion. Note that Scheff's model should apply to any form of deviance. These were also entry-level jobs. We don't know what would happen if the experiment were repeated with positions requiring more responsibility.

Once the former mental patient has a job, the degree of disability associated with a history of hospitalization is relatively small. Ratings by work supervisors were somewhat poorer for those who had had a schizophrenic diagnosis than for those who had had a neurotic diagnosis, but the latter were rated much the same as those who had no psychiatric history. Persons with diagnoses of schizophrenia showed lower rates of promotion and higher rates of demotion or of leaving the job, but the majority (78%) had no such difficulties. It was not clear in that study (Cole, McDonald, & Branch, 1968) whether work supervisors were "blind" to the former patient's history of treatment. If they were blind to this fact, the differences between patients and others can be attributed to patient behavior and not to the label.

Gebhard and Levine (1985) constructed résumés of persons already employed and asked management students to say whether they would promote the person described to a more responsible position. The résumés were identical, except that in one the individual had lost time from work 3 years earlier due to a gall bladder operation; in the second, the person was described as having lost time from work due to alcoholism; in the third, the person was described as having lost time from work due to alcoholism and was a member of Alcoholics Anonymous. The label of alcoholism significantly reduced the person's chances of being considered for promotion, even though the résumés all indicated very good job performance and no indication of alcohol problems over 3 years. The study was designed to test the hypothesis that membership in Alcoholics Anonymous would be destigmatizing. That hypothesis could not be confirmed.

Former patients are probably subject to labeling effects in social relationships. Page (1977, 1983) called landlords who had advertised the availability of rental units in the classified section of a daily newspaper. If the person calling identified himself as having been a mental patient, the response from the landlord was immediately less positive. In one study, the simple fact that the caller stuttered was sufficient to reduce the number of positive responses to the call (a positive response being that the rental quarters were still available and the person was encouraged to make an appointment to see them). In other words, any deviant condition may be sufficiently stigmatizing to reduce opportunities for the person so stigmatized.

The courts have noted that stigma can be a problem. For example, it is not necessary that a claimant for disability under Social Security or under the Supplemental Security Income (SSI) program be represented by an attorney. In *Cullison v. Califano* (1980), however, the court noted that claims for disability on the basis of mental or psychological symptoms are likely to lead to highly prejudiced determinations by the administrative officials who review these claims. The court stopped short of requiring that counsel be provided to ensure that these claims are reviewed thoroughly and impartially. The claimant's credibility is at stake in such instances, and persons with histories of mental disorder, having spoiled identities, may be much less able to speak for themselves because their identities lead others to discount what they say. In speaking as it did, the court was recognizing a consistent problem in the cases that had been reviewed on appeal.

Tebes (1983) reviewed a large number of field and laboratory studies testing the effects of stigmatization. He concludes:

> The results from studies of labeling effects reveal that, in social interactions, both the perceptions and behaviors of persons carrying a mental disorder label and those responding to them are significantly affected by the pejorative impact of the label. This impact predisposes the labeled person to feel and be rejected by others. On the one hand, there is the situation where the non-labeled social participant is aware of the person's deviant history. In many such cases, the person can expect social responses of rejection and/or avoidance especially if the participant is male. On the other hand, if the former patient believes his deviant history is known to others in his immediate social situation, the problem is further compounded by the likelihood that he will act in a way which alienates those around him, thus predisposing him to rejection. Clearly, the former mental patient would do well to conceal his status if at all possible, a practice which, ironically in itself requires considerable social agility, as Goffman (1963) has described. (pp. 70–71)

The question of whether stigma is sufficiently powerful to prevent a person who is otherwise behaving normally from reentering normal life must be restated. For some persons, some occupations, and some relationships, stigma may operate forcefully, while in other cases it will not. The available evidence does support labeling theory's emphasis on the force of stigma in maintaining a person in a deviant role. The proposition is stated too simply in labeling theory, however, and this oversimplified form cannot be supported. To have continued viability, labeling theory needs to be modified to take into account data that are inconsistent with its tenets. The labeling hypothesis is simply too crude in its present form, as Scheff recognizes. Whatever the validity of its specific propositions, labeling theory is still useful as an analytic device, providing one does not overlook that the behavior of many who do come to the attention of some system of social control may indeed be difficult to tolerate, burdensome, repulsive, or dangerous. The flaw of labeling theory is that it feeds too neatly into an antiauthority stance in favor of any underdog. Nonetheless, the theory points out areas of interest for research, for service, and for prevention. As a model, it helps us pay attention to a broader set of variables than individual psychology includes.

Group Sex: An Example of the Management of Deviance[6]

Conducting systematic research on the phenomena of "swinging," "wife swapping," and group-sex orgies is difficult. The available information shows that what in many circles would be considered deviance can be managed and limited successfully. Those who participate in these activities encourage their mates to have sex with other persons regularly. Many participants report taking pleasure in knowing that their mates are having full sex lives. Others participate in open orgies where all engage in sex as a group or, at some parties, where couples go off to private rooms to have sex. Many people have extramarital affairs, but these are recognized almost as normative departures from a normative ideal. The marital pattern among swinging couples certainly deviates drastically from the normative relationship that most of us would recognize. Observers claim that a subculture has developed with its own values, beliefs, and norms of behavior. Although group sex is statistically infrequent, some sources estimate that as many as a million adults participate in it. It is interesting to note that we have not had calls for action against these activities as an epidemic of disorder. How do participants manage their deviance so successfully?

First, the married members of this subculture tend to be white, middle class, reasonably well educated, and suburban dwellers. They earn above-average salaries and tend to be in professional, sales, and managerial occupations. Few blue-collar workers are involved. Swingers tend to be political conservatives and, during the days when the studies were done, anti-"hippie" and antiradical. Their religious distribution is roughly in proportion to that in the general population. Participants tend not to go to church, but they do send their children.

Second, the members of this subculture are discrete. They tend not to discuss their experiences except with those who accept or share them, and then such discussion is very open. Participants will talk more openly about techniques for performing oral sex than they will talk about religion, politics, or income, but they do not openly proselytize.

Third, their social status enables them to conceal their practices readily. They can protect themselves from unwanted intrusions. Bartell (1971) reports an incident in which a young child had discussed some of the occurrences of the previous weekend in a share-and-tell session in school. The school called the mother in. She was neatly dressed and was known to be conservative. The family lived in a desirable suburban neighborhood. The mother's social standing was at least as high as, if not higher than, the teacher's. The mother simply denied everything. The social distance between the deviant and the agent of social control was probably unequal and favored the deviant. The teacher accepted the story as the child's fantasy and discussed with the mother whether her child ought to enter treatment. Because of her social standing, the mother was able to escape labeling.

Parenthetically, we ask the reader to imagine what would ensue had the child of a welfare mother in an inner-city school reported a similar incident. The child's mother, as a person lower in social status than the teacher or the principal, in all likelihood would have been much more vulnerable to investigation, social control, and labeling by social welfare authorities than was the middle-class surburban mother that Bartell describes.

Group-sex participants have developed a socially shared ideology to justify their behavior. Sexual expression is viewed as a form of recreation, and participants value others who are able to express themselves fully. They see their practices as a means of enriching marriage by providing sexual variety and preserving marriage by increasing communication. An extramarital affair may threaten a marital relationship, but in this form the extramarital affair is presumably co-opted, socialized, and controlled. A number of other rules have been established to preserve the basic marital relationship. For example, couples will engage in sex with other couples only with the consent of both partners. At a party, if the man fails to have an erection or the woman is having her period, neither will engage in sex.

Swinging is pursued in organized social forms. There are organized means of contact through advertisements in certain periodicals or through referrals from friends. People with common interests may congregate in swinger bars. Members accept a great variety of sexual expression, and acting out sexual fantasies is encouraged. The subculture sanctions sexual experimentation and takes away from any feeling that the behavior may be shameful, wrong, or "sick."

There are additional rules to preserve order. A participant who contracts a venereal disease is obliged to inform others who were at the same party, to the degree that is possible. Sex is by mutual consent. Just because everyone is indulging is no license simply to join in. This rule probably limits the danger of charges of rape and the bad feelings that may arise when one person imposes on another. Because sex is readily available, participants claim that they can concentrate on getting to know the other person. In addition, certain taboos are respected. Homosexual contact between males is avoided, although sexual contact between females is common. Disorderly, noisy parties are frowned on, and members tend to be security conscious. Not infrequently, participants camouflage their identities.

We emphasize that research on this phenomenon is highly limited. Moreover, informants and active participants have a stake in making the activity appear attractive and trouble-free. We know little about those who indulged in group sex and then dropped out because of guilt or anxiety over their behavior. We know little about conflicts that may afflict those couples in which one spouse wants to participate and the other spouse refuses. We also know little about the adverse long-term consequences of participation in wife swapping or group sex. The idealized version recounted by its partisans is surely not the whole story.

Walshok (1971) concludes that the group-sex phenomenon illuminates important aspects of deviance theory. She notes, for example, that one can engage in a deviant subculture and still maintain a commitment to highly conventional roles in other spheres of life. In Scheff's terms, participants manage to keep the visibility of the deviant behavior low, thus avoiding contact with agents of social control. The participant's respectable social status also protects him or her against intrusion by social-control agents. In addition, the participants create a subcommunity within which deviance not only is tolerated but in effect becomes the norm. Finally, what would be deviance if isolated or infrequent is normalized by creating a social group with secure places for its members and valued roles for those who participate. If we believe the participants, socializing the deviance in the form of externally structured rituals also protects the participant's self-esteem. Thus this form of sexual deviance (deviance in the sense that it departs from most people's norms and ideals) does not get publicly labeled and bring trouble to its participants.

Summary and Conclusions

We have emphasized that labeling theory is to be valued more for the analytic perspective it offers than for the correctness of its details. The incorrect details are important. Failure to verify some of its predictions should not be overlooked in evaluating the merits and deficiencies of labeling theory. One strength of a scientific conception is that it leads us to seek out observations that will test its propositions. Labeling theory has done exactly that. It has asked us to look at data that we would have overlooked had we adopted the perspective that psychopathology resides solely within an individual's skin. Labeling theory encompasses individual differences in behavior. It does not say that any behavior or person is equally subject to labeling. The theory does direct our attention to the social setting within which the particular behavior pattern is manifested, however, and asks us to look at the relationships among the individual in his or her roles, the agents of social control, and the therapeutic system. If we recall the ecological lessons of Chapter 3, labeling theory alerts us to the consequences of diversity in status, values, and goals among different groups that happen to share the same community settings. It explains more thoroughly than did Sarbin's role theory how the behavior of others can limit one's opportunities in ways that cut across multiple situations and endure over time. A weakness of labeling theory is that it does not distinguish among the initial causes of abnormal behavior and thus provides no new insights into this aspect of the problem. Unlike the conceptions presented in the previous two chapters, however, labeling theory does consider the contribution the individual makes to the process. The theory provides a conceptual corrective for our exclusive reliance on the psychology of the individual.

Labeling theory has something in common with the Dohrenwend position discussed in Chapter 2 (and considered further in Chapter 6). Both are systems theories emphasizing the context within which behavior is studied. Both viewpoints also emphasize the transient nature of the initial deviant episode. Labeling theory focuses on the undesirable and unanticipated effects of the existing treatment system, which might be understood as society's effort to supply social support to the individual in need. Dohrenwend's position calls attention to the positive effects of existing social and personal resources for helping when an individual is experiencing a stressful life event.

In the next chapter we examine the concepts of adaptation, crisis, coping, and social support. We urge the reader to reflect on the similarities between those ideas and labeling theory. For example, primary deviance may be thought of as the initial emotional and behavioral reaction to a stressful life event. One may also draw a parallel between the social support available to a person and the system of care provided for mental health problems. In addition, one may consider how the societal reaction to an emotional response produced by acute stress (whether or not the person's problem comes to public attention) is influenced by psychological mediators the person uses as well as the social support that is available. Finally, when we propose alternative methods of providing assistance to the individual in distress, the reader should keep labeling theory in mind. Especially in its emphasis on the stigma associated with treatment under some conditions, labeling theory reminds us that interventions generally have multiple effects and directs us to examine the possibility that the newer forms of assistance, designed to assist the processes of coping and adaptation following a stressful event, may also have unintended consequences. Having noted the complementary features of the Dohrenwend and labeling viewpoints, we turn now to an elaboration of the Dohrenwend discussion and some concepts and research associated with it.

Notes

1. Although Scheff's model and the present discussion center on the problem of chronic mental illness, the model is applicable to any form of deviance.

2. We are indebted to attorney Sheila Graziano for this example drawn from her practice.

3. The U.S. Supreme Court held in *Parham* that a child is not entitled to a due-process hearing when a parent elects to commit a child to a mental hospital. The Supreme Court asserted that the diagnostic process preceding commitment and the independent determination by the admitting staff of the need for hospitalization provided sufficient safeguards against unwarranted intrusions on the minor's liberty. See Melton (1984) for a critique of the Supreme Court's decision. Melton's critique is based on empirical data assessing the validity and reliability of diagnosis. Berger (1985) raises many questions about the due-process implications of giving as much decision-making authority to mental health workers as Parham does.

4. The U.S. Supreme Court upheld the civil liability of a hospital superintendent who refused to discharge a patient who was not dangerous to himself or others. The decision (*O'Connor v. Donaldson*, 1975) adds to the problem a psychiatric decision maker faces. If a patient is released prematurely and injures someone, the decision maker may be held liable; if the patient is held unnecessarily, liability may also accrue.

5. As a personal anecdote, Levine notes that when he worked in a mental hospital he often found himself fingering the keys that differentiated him from the patients. These keys served as a security blanket.

6. The discussion in this section is based on Bartell (1971) and Walshok (1971).

References

Albers, D. A., Pasewark, R. A., & Smith, T. C. (1976). Involuntary hospitalization: The social construction of danger. *American Journal of Community Psychology, 4,* 129–132.

Bachrach, L. L. (1975). *Deinstitutionalization: An analytical review and sociological perspective* (DHEW Publication No. (ADM) 76–351). Washington, DC: U.S. Government Printing Office.

Bartell, G. D. (1971). *Group sex.* New York: Wyden.

Baxter, S., Chodorkoff, B., & Underhill, R. (1968). Psychiatric emergencies: Dispositional determinants and the validity of the decision to admit. *American Journal of Psychiatry, 124,* 1542–1548.

Berger, R. S. (1985). The psychiatric expert as due process decision maker. *Buffalo Law Review, 33,* 681–727.

Braginsky, B. M., Braginsky, D. D., & Ring, K. (1969). *The mental hospital as a last resort.* New York: Holt, Rinehart & Winston.

Brand, R. C., Jr., & Claiborn, W. L. (1976). Two studies of comparative stigma: Employer attitudes and practices toward rehabilitated convicts, mental and tuberculosis patients. *Community Mental Health Journal, 12,* 168–175.

Brockman, J., D'Arcy, C., & Edmonds, L. (1979). Facts or artifacts? Changing public attitudes toward the mentally ill. *Social Science and Medicine, 13A,* 673–682.

City of Cleburne, Texas v. Cleburne Living Center 53 LW 5022 (1985).

Clausen, J. A. (1981). Stigma and mental disorder: Phenomena and terminology. *Psychiatry, 44,* 287–296.

Cole, N. J., McDonald, B. W., Jr., & Branch, C. H. H. (1968). A two year follow-up study of the work performance of former psychiatric patients. *American Journal of Psychiatry, 124,* 1070–1075.

Cullison v. Califano, 613 F. 2d 55 (4th Cir. 1980).

Dolan, L. W., & Wolpert, J. (1982). *Long term neighborhood property impacts of group homes for mentally retarded people.* Unpublished report. Woodrow Wilson School of Public and International Affairs, Princeton University.

Ellsworth, R. B., Foster, L., Childers, B., Arthur, G., & Kroeker, D. (1968). *Journal of Consulting and Clinical Psychology Monograph Supplement, 32* (Part 2), 1–41.

Ennis, B. J. & Litwack, T. R. (1974). Psychiatry and the presumption of expertise: Flipping coins in the courtroom. *California Law Review, 62,* 693–752.

Ennis, B. J., & Siegel, L. (1973). *The rights of mental patients.* New York: Avon.

Eysenck, H. J. (1952). The effects of psychotherapy: An evaluation. *Journal of Consulting Psychology, 16,* 319–324.

Fairweather, G. W., Sanders, D. H., Cressler, D. F., Maynard, H., & Bleck, D. S. (1969). *Community life for the mentally ill.* Chicago: Aldine.

Gebhard, C, & Levine, M. (1985, March 22). Does membership in Alcoholics Anonymous reduce the stigma of alcoholism? Paper presented at the annual meeting of the Eastern Psychological Association, Boston.

Gibbs, L. M. (1983). Community response to an emergency situation: Psychological destruction and the Love Canal. *American Journal of Community Psychology, 11,* 116–125.

Goffman, E. (1961). *Asylums.* Garden City, NY: Doubleday.

Goffman, E. (1963). *Stigma.* Englewood Cliffs, NJ: Prentice-Hall.

Gordon, M. (1982). *Attitudes toward mental illness held by two disadvantaged inner-city ethnic groups.* Unpublished doctoral dissertation, SUNY at Buffalo.

Gove, W. R. (Ed.). (1980). *The labelling of deviance* (2d ed.). Beverly Hills: Sage.

Gove, W. R. (Ed.). (1982). *Deviance and mental illness.* Beverly Hills: Sage.

Graziano, A. M., & Mooney, K. C. (1984). *Children and behavior therapy.* New York: Aldine.

Handler, J. F., & Satz, J. (Eds.). (1982). *Neither angels nor thieves: Studies in deinstitutionalization of status offenders.* Washington, DC: National Academy Press.

Hankin, J. R., & Locke, B. Z. (1982). The persistence of depressive symptomatology among prepaid group practice enrollees: An exploratory study. *American Journal of Public Health, 72,* 1000–1007.

Herz, M. I., & Melville, C. (1980). Relapse in schizophrenia. *American Journal of Psychiatry, 137,* 801–805.

Hiday, V. A. (1977). Reformed commitment procedures: An empirical study of the courtroom. *Law & Society Review, 11,* 651–656.

Hogarty, G. E., Dennis, H., Guy, W., & Gross, G. M. (1968). Who goes there? Critical evaluation of admission to a day hospital. *American Journal of Psychiatry, 124,* 939–944.

Hollingshead, A. B., & Redlich, F. C. (1958). *Social class and mental illness.* New York: Wiley.

Keil, T. J., Usui, W. M., & Busch, J. A. (1983). Repeat admissions for perceived problem drinking: A social resources perspective. *Journal of Studies on Alcohol, 44,* 95–108.

Kiesler, C. A. (1982). Public and professional myths about mental hospitalization. An empirical reassessment of policy-related beliefs. *American Psychologist, 37,* 1323–1339.

Kittrie, N. N. (1971). *The right to be different. Deviance and enforced therapy.* Baltimore: Johns Hopkins Press.

Klerman, G. L. (1982). The psychiatric revolution of the past twenty-five years. In W. R. Gove (Ed.), *Deviance and mental illness.* Beverly Hills: Sage.

Krizan, L. (1982). *A descriptive study of the Niagara Falls Christian Fellowship from a social intervention perspective.* Unpublished manuscript, Department of Psychology, SUNY at Buffalo.

Langer, E. J., & Abelson, R. P. (1974). A patient by any other name. . . . Clinical group differences in labeling bias. *Journal of Consulting and Clinical Psychology, 42,* 4–9.

Levine, M. (1981). *The history and politics of community mental health.* New York: Oxford University Press.

Levine, M. (1985). The adversary process and social science in the courts: *Barefoot v. Estelle. Journal of Psychiatry and Law, 12,* 147–181.

Levine, M., & Bunker, B. B. (Eds.). (1975). *Mutual criticism.* Syracuse, NY: Syracuse University Press.

Lewis, D. A., Goetz, E., Schoenfield, M., Gordon, A. C., & Griffin, E. (1984). The negotiation of involuntary civil commitment. *Law & Society Review, 18,* 629–649.

Light, D. W. (1982). Learning to label: The social construction of psychiatrists. In W. R. Gove (Ed.), *Deviance and mental illness.* Beverly Hills: Sage.

Lindsay, W. R. (1982). The effects of labelling: Blind and nonblind ratings of social skills in schizophrenic and nonschizophrenic control subjects. *American Journal of Psychiatry, 139,* 216–219.

Lipton, H., & Kaden, S. E. (1965). Predicting the post hospital work adjustment of married male schizophrenics. *Journal of Consulting Psychology, 29,* 93.

Lubin, R. A., Janicki, M. P., Zigman, W., & Ross, R. (1982). *The likelihood of police contacts with developmentally disabled persons in community residences.* Unpublished report. Institute for Basic Research in Developmental Disabilities, Staten Island, NY.

Lubin, R. A., Schwartz, A. A., Zigman, W. B., & Janicki, M. P. (1982). Community acceptance of residential programs for developmentally disabled persons. *Applied Research in Mental Retardation, 3,* 191–200.

Meehl, P. E. (1954). *Clinical versus statistical prediction.* Minneapolis: University of Minnesota Press.

Melton, G. B. (1984). Family and mental hospital as myths: Civil commitment of minors. In N. D. Reppucci, L. A. Weithorne, E. P. Mulvey, & J. Monahan (Eds.), *Children, mental health and the law.* Beverly Hills: Sage.

Mercer, J. R. (1973). *Labeling the retarded.* Berkeley: University of California Press.

Morell, M. A., Levine, M., & Perkins, D. V. (1982). Study of behavioral factors associated with psychiatric rehospitalization. *Community Mental Health Journal, 18,* 190–199.

Morse, S. J. (1978). Crazy behavior, morals and science: An analysis of mental health law. *Southern California Law Review, 51,* 527–564.

Murphy, J. M. (1964). Psychotherapeutic aspects of shamanism on St. Lawrence Island, Alaska. In A. Kiev (Ed.), *Magic, faith and healing.* New York: Free Press.

Murphy, J. M. (1976). Psychiatric labelling in cross-cultural perspective. *Science, 191,* 1019–1028.

Murphy, J. M. (1982). Cultural shaping and mental disorders. In W. R. Gove (Ed.), *Deviance and mental illness.* Beverly Hills: Sage.

Murray J. P. (Ed.) (1983). *Status offenders. A sourcebook.* Boys Town, NE: Boys Town Center.

O'Connor v. Donaldson, 422 U.S. 563 (1975).

Olshansky, S. (1968). Some assumptions challenged. *Community Mental Health Journal, 4,* 152–156.

Oltman, J. E., & Friedman, S. (1965). Trends in admissions to a state hospital, 1942–1964. *Archives of General Psychiatry, 13,* 544–551.

Page, S. (1977). Effects of the mental illness label in attempts to obtain accommodation. *Canadian Journal of Behavioural Science, 9,* 85–90.

Page, S. (1983). Psychiatric stigma: Two studies of behaviour when the chips are down. *Canadian Journal of Community Mental Health, 2,* 13–19.

Parham v. J. R. and J. L., 442 U.S. 584 (1979).

Richart, R. H., & Milner, L. M. (1968). Factors influencing admission to a community mental health center. *Community Mental Health Journal, 4,* 27–35.

Robins, L. N. (1974). *Deviant children grown up.* Huntington, NY: Krieger.

Roosens, E. (1979). *Mental patients in town life. Geel—Europe's first therapeutic community.* Beverly Hills: Sage.

Rosenhan, D. L. (1973). On being sane in insane places. *Science, 179,* 250–258.

Schacht, T. E. (1985a). DSM-III and the politics of truth. *American Psychologist, 40,* 513–521.

Schacht, T. E. (1985b). Reply to Spitzer's "Politics-science dichotomy syndrome." *American Psychologist, 40,* 562–563.

Scheff, T. J. (1966). *Being mentally ill. A sociological theory.* Chicago: Aldine.

Scheff, T. J. (Ed.). (1975). *Labelling madness.* Englewood Cliffs, NJ: Prentice-Hall.

Scheff, T. J. (1984). *Being mentally ill. A sociological theory* (2d ed.). Chicago: Aldine.

Sedgwick, P. (1982). Antipsychiatry from the sixties to the eighties. In W. R. Gove (Ed.), *Deviance and mental illness.* Beverly Hills: Sage.

Spitzer, R. L. (1985). DSM-III and the politics-science dichotomy syndrome: A response to Thomas E. Schacht's "DSM-III and the politics of truth." *American Psychologist, 40,* 522–526.

Spitzer, R. L., & Williams, J. B. W. (1982). The definition and diagnosis of mental disorder. In W. R. Gove (Ed.), *Deviance and mental illness.* Beverly Hills: Sage.

Stack, L. C., Lannon, P. B., & Miley, A. D. (1983). Accuracy of clinicians' expectancies for psychiatric rehospitalization. *American Journal of Community Psychology, 11,* 99–113.

Szasz, T. S. (1961). *The myth of mental illness.* New York: Harper & Row.

Szasz, T. S. (1963). *Law, liberty and psychiatry.* New York: Macmillan.

Task Panel (1978). Report of the Task Panel on the nature and scope of the problems. *Task Panel Reports Submitted to the President's Commission on Mental Health* (Vol II. Appendix). Washington DC: U.S. Government Printing Office.

Tebes, J. A. (1983). Stigma and mental disorder: A review and analysis. Unpublished Ph.D. qualifying paper, Department of Psychology, SUNY at Buffalo.

Teplin, L. A. (1984). Criminalizing mental disorder: The comparative arrest rate of the mentally disordered. *American Psychologist, 39,* 794–803.

Tischler, G. L. (1966). Decision making in the emergency room. *Archives of General Psychiatry, 14,* 69–78.

Tuckman, J., & Lavell, M. (1962). Patients discharged with or against medical advice. *Journal of Clinical Psychology, 13,* 177–180.

Walshok, M. L. (1971). The emergence of middle class deviant subcultures: The case of swingers. *Social Problems, 18,* 488–495.

Warren, C. B. (1977). Involuntary commitment for mental disorder: The application of California's Lanerman-Petris-Short Act. *Law & Society Review, 11,* 629–650.

Wenger, D. L., & Fletcher, C. R. (1969). The effect of legal counsel on admissions to a state mental hospital: A confrontation of professions. *Journal of Health and Social Behavior, 10,* 66–72.

Whitt, H., & Meile, R. (1985). Alignment, magnification, and snowballing: Processes in the definition of "symptoms of mental illness." *Social Forces, 63,* 682–697.

Wolpe, J. (1958). *Psychotherapy by reciprocal inhibition.* Stanford, CA: Stanford University Press.

Wood, E. C., Rakusin, J. M., & Morse, E. (1965). Resident psychiatrist in the admitting office. *Archives of General Psychiatry, 13,* 54–61.

Woodward, B., & Bernstein, C. (1976). *The final days.* New York: Simon & Schuster.

6

Adaptation, Crisis, Coping, and Support

In Chapter 2 we introduced the useful perspective on stress and disorder presented by Barbara Dohrenwend (1978) as a more inclusive and comprehensive model of mental health than that provided by traditional clinical conceptions, and one offering a number of alternative solutions to mental health problems. Recall that the components of the Dohrenwend model comprise two broad factors: personal resources such as educational background and coping skills on the one hand, and situational qualities such as environmental support and political power on the other. Dohrenwend's model also depicts health or pathology as the product of a dynamic interaction between person and environment that occurs over time, suggesting that health and disorder are episodic states that can characterize the behavior of the same person at different times in his or her life.

In the preceding chapters we described various situational and interactive conceptions of behavior. The present chapter builds on these views in elaborating Dohrenwend's overall model. We begin by examining the concepts of adaptation and crisis in light of the traditional psychoanalytic conception of disorder, extend the idea of a psychological crisis to recent research on stressful life events, and then reevaluate the person-environment approach using what has come to be called the "vulnerability" model. This latter framework paves the way for a discussion of coping and social support.

One issue in which we will be particularly interested in this chapter is how individuals avoid developing psychopathology or, more positively, how individuals move to restore psychological equilibrium, or even achieve psychological growth, as a result of exposure to and mastery of a stressful life event. Although some community psychologists (e.g., Bloom, 1984) draw a distinction between the concepts of crisis and stress, one strength of Dohrenwend's model is that it allows these two constructs to be examined as part of the same conceptual framework.

Adaptation

Dohrenwend (1978) defines the aim of community psychology as "undermining the process whereby stress generates psychopathology" (p. 2). A useful starting point in understanding this process is the concept of "adaptation." Adaptation refers to improvements in the fit between an individual's behavior and the specific demands and constraints of settings making up his or her environment. As we have explained in the preceding chapters, adaptation is facilitated by widening the niche provided in the environment and/or increasing the behavioral competence of the resident person—that is, strengthening his or her "niche breadth." Recall, for example, that in Fairweather's lodge for chronic psychiatric patients (Chapter 4), patients' living and working conditions were modified somewhat to compensate for their lack of full autonomy and employability, and patients also worked to develop useful social and job-related skills as employees of patient-run businesses. Driven as it is by stressful events, Dohrenwend's model implies that change in the environment is an ongoing stimulus to behavior, and thus that any given state of adaptation is episodic and time limited, always subject to challenge by the next stressful event.

In addition to its meaning as the modification of one's behavior in response to altered conditions, adaptation has additional (dictionary) meanings that refer to conformity or adjustment. From perspectives that are more humanistic (i.e., "self-actualizing"), or alternatively more revolutionary, the concept of adapting or adjusting oneself to external conditions can be anathema. If one sees the social environment as oppressive, then encouraging adaptation to it is to act as an agent of oppression. In Goldenberg's (1978) terminology, one who encourages adaptation is no more than a "social technician" who identifies strongly with the institution's values, sees little need for any basic change, and encourages the adaptation of members to the system's needs through the application of a variety of techniques or tactics" (p. 21).

Helping a prisoner adjust to oppressive prison conditions or a mental patient adjust to a nontherapeutic hospital situation simply encourages adaptation to a fundamentally unsatisfactory, if not unhealthy, environment. Should disadvantaged, poverty-stricken, stigmatized, and other relatively powerless groups play the game of adaptation to the social world as it is, or are their interests better served by methods that raise consciousness and demand change in the environment?

Raising this question may alert us to a problem that has no absolute solution, because it is impossible to think of a criterion of mental health that does not refer to a social order of some kind. Freud, for example, defined the normal, healthy person as one who can love, work, and play. These seem like individual goals, but as soon as one says love, work, or play, one is necessarily involved with other people in some kind of social order. These terms also imply activity and cognition—knowing how to love, work, and play. Inevitably, even those change strategies that Goldenberg (1978, p. 17) terms fundamental or basic and meet his criteria for social intervention (i.e., "collective action, an institutional focus, and an orientation toward altering existing practices and priorities") have as their end result the adaptation of individuals to some social order. Although the term *social adaptation* seems to imply that individuals must adjust to a fixed social order and thus appears conservative in its orientation, in fact every individual adapts to some social order or another. Furthermore, nothing in the concept precludes adapting by changing social conditions.

Social adaptations imply socially structured transactions between person and environment. A stressful event may threaten the availability of resources, disrupt ongoing transactions, and require an adaptive response. The range of possible disruptions is broad, and the adaptive change required may be quite significant. To survive as a biosocial organism in the "self-maintenance" ecology, for example (see Chapter 4), the individual must correctly identify objects and events and define himself in relation to those objects and events. One might include under this category, as Hansell (1974) does, the necessity to identify correctly one's own need for food, oxygen, shelter, and the like, and to have the wherewithal to obtain those necessities. To have money, or purchasing power, is one such form of attachment to the social order; in the absence of having the means of participating in the exchange of goods and services, the individual is in serious difficulty.

Sarbin (1970) speaks of the "social" ecology, where through a variety of social roles one achieves a sense of self-worth and belongingness. Failure to locate oneself correctly within the social ecology violates others' expectations and leads to corresponding efforts to have expectations fulfilled. The threatened loss of an important achieved role may well put a person under stress. A recently retired judge, for example, accustomed to receiving deference from others, may be distressed by the experience of being treated like any other anonymous older person. Failure and disappointment with oneself or the reactions of others to oneself are critical to locating oneself within the "normative" ecology (i.e., to answering the question "How well am I doing?"). If the answer is "Not very well," the person may be forced to seek some other form of adaptation. Finally, the individual must locate himself or herself in what Sarbin calls the "transcendental" ecology, where the questions have to do with values. Hansell (1974) also recognizes the necessity for a comprehensive system of meanings that help clarify current experience and help define ambiguity in events and relationships. When one's gods fail and a state of meaninglessness threatens, one is greatly troubled and may seek new sources of meaning or a new kind of adaptation.

To summarize, adaptation can involve biological, social, self-reference, or value-laden dimensions. A given state of adaptation is also situation specific and temporary, not sweeping and permanent. It may be disrupted by new stressors and other changes in the external environment, so that periods of adaptation inevitably alternate with transient periods of disequilibrium. Let us now look more closely at how we conceptualize the disruptive state that signals the need for adaptation.

Crisis and Neurosis

Just as the individual deprived of oxygen or food experiences a physiological crisis or emergency, so too does the individual whose attachments (in Hansell's terms) or locations in the several ecologies (in Sarbin's terms) are disrupted enter a state of crisis. Hansell (1974) defines *crisis* as any rapid change or encounter that provides an individual with a "no-exit" challenge to alter his or her conduct in some manner.

The concept of crisis was very influential in the development of community mental health and preventive modalities of care. Crisis theory began with Erich Lindemann's (1944) follow-up study of people related to the many victims of a Boston nightclub fire. Lindemann observed that each survivor had to carry out "grief work" by detaching from the relationship with the deceased person, readapting to an environment no longer including the deceased, and then forming new attachments and relationships. Lindemann concluded that inevitable events in the life cycle generate emotional tension and require adaptation, an idea that represented a shift in emphasis from the dominant thinking in mental health at that time.

To understand fully the shift in orientation signaled by the crisis concept, we should contrast it with the psychoanalytic theory of neurosis. The "disease"-oriented model of psychoanalysis postulated that behavioral problems were the result of unresolved conflicts at earlier phases of development. These conflicts were repressed or otherwise defended against psychologically. As long as the defenses worked effectively, enabling the individual to avoid anxiety, all was reasonably well, except that the individual's life-style would be constructed to maintain the defensive pattern. Thus if the basic conflict stemmed from the "anal" period, with its conflicts around the task of toilet training, defenses would be related to orderliness, cleanliness, obeying or resisting, or withholding. Failure to solve developmental problems at a particular level would lead to fixation at that level and to a "complex." For example, one could solve the problem of messiness by being exceptionally clean and in this way continue to involve oneself with dirt. One is thus able to deal with the world while expressing forbidden desires by defending against awareness of the dangerous impulse. At some point something might happen to interfere with the effectiveness of the defense. If the temptation to be dirty or act sadistically then became too great, the defense would fail, and repressed energy would return in the form of great anxiety.

For psychoanalysis, "symptoms" are a means of controlling the intense anxiety associated with the return of a formerly repressed impulse. In the case of anal fixation, a hand-washing symptom might develop in an exaggerated attempt to be rid of dirt. Hand-washing in that case is a compromise formation that at once expresses something of the repressed impulse and also controls it; at the same time it is self-punitive and thus a way of dealing with feelings of guilt associated with the forbidden impulse. At times the individual debilitated by such a symptom achieves "secondary gain"— that is, others may organize their lives about the sick person, take care of him or her, or otherwise allow the symptom to control their relationships. The symptom is reinforced because it creates other benefits, but further disability may result. Other life tasks may not be accomplished, leading to further problems in adaptation.

The Freudian model recognizes as some precipitating event or state whatever it is that strengthens a drive or weakens a defense, with the result that the individual develops anxiety and then symptoms as means for controlling the anxiety. When the compulsive hand-washer is asked why that particular behavior occurs so frequently, he or she will report feeling compelled; any attempt to limit the hand-washing results in strong fear. The "arrest" in psychological development returns to disable or at least badly disturb the individual. Thus the focus is always on the individual instead of on the precipitating event.

One explanation for this focus may be that psychoanalytic theory was developed to deal with clinical observations of persons who had already become disabled. The theory developed in the context of a disease-oriented model of underlying disorder. Because it postulates that the basic cause of the disorder took place long ago and little of significance can be done in the present until the "original" problems are worked through, the psychoanalytic conception limits the possibilities for intervention. Furthermore, the specific events that precipitate disorder are not predictable because their meaning derives from the individual's unconscious interpretation. If a panic state is precipitated by taking a new job, for example, that event would have psychopathological significance only if the individual viewed the new position of authority as a displacement of his father, with the rearousal of Oedipal fears that father will castrate the upstart challenger.

In crisis-theory terms, accepting a new position can be seen as a challenge to the previous state of adaptation, thus requiring a new adaptation. Accepting a new position of authority may call for new, yet to be learned, or unpracticed coping skills.

Entering a position of authority also changes the individual's adaptation within a network of supportive relationships. After all, one can hardly get together with the boys to knock the boss when one *is* the boss.

The crisis concept is similar to that of "neurosis," except that the crisis concept does not make use of the "pathological disease" framework. The terms themselves express a difference in outlook. *Neurosis* comes from a Greek word meaning "sinew" or "tendon." The term was later extended to mean the condition of some object, in terms of its strength or vigor or energy—for example, a taut bowstring or, in the vernacular, "strung out." By Freud's time neurosis meant a functional derangement arising from disorders of the nervous system, especially when unaccompanied by organic change. In this medical model it is as if the underlying concept of "nervous" means that the nerves themselves are not functioning properly.

Crisis comes from a Greek root meaning "to decide." It is used to describe a point in the course of a disease that is decisive for either recovery or death. More generally, the term means a critical turning point in the progress of some state of affairs in which a decisive change, for better or for worse, is imminent. In this case, then, the idea that change can be for the better and not just for the worse leads one to think and act differently in relation to a problem; it implies a reserve of strength, a capacity to deal or cope with or master the distress.

While neurosis is defined as a failure of the defenses, crisis is said to occur when an individual faces an obstacle to important life goals that appears insurmountable through the use of customary methods of problem resolution. Using terms we introduced earlier, the individual is dislocated in one of the four ecologies within which he or she functions, or some vital attachments have been disrupted. A crisis is precipitated by some situation that disturbs prior adaptations and requires a new response. A state of crisis can occur in anyone, not only in those with some previous "fixation," and it is to be expected whenever some external event requires a change in customary ways of dealing with a problem.

Crisis theorists (Ewing, 1978; Golan, 1978; Parad, 1965; Slaikeu, 1984) postulate several essential features of a crisis. First is a stressful or hazardous event or events requiring change. The event presents a new problem to the individual, a problem which he or she may perceive as unsolvable in the present or the immediate future. Hazardous or stressful life events are classified as anticipated or unanticipated. In an unanticipated event is some loss (e.g., death in the family, lost job, illness resulting in disability or disfigurement) or threat (e.g., physical disaster, assault, rape, or assault to one's personal integrity, as in the case of a woman in a concentration camp who had to make a choice between her life and her mother's life) that is beyond the individual's control. Although unanticipated events are those whose timing cannot be predicted, in some cases (such as the death of a family member) the general class of events is predictable. Anticipated events generally refer to role transitions, changes in a way of life, new responsibilities, or the necessity to develop new social relationships. Entering school, getting married, retiring, becoming a parent, or moving to a new location are all examples. Because these events are predictable, one can seriously consider either preventive action or the positioning of assistance so that it is available when and where it is needed.

A second characteristic of a crisis is that the nature of the new problem taxes the material, physical, or psychological resources of the individual, his or her family, or others who might be part of the individual's social support network. Bereavement, loss of a parent or a spouse, having a premature child born into the family, becoming a parent for the first time, or becoming the boss all require people to take action, experience new emotions, and make decisions about certain matters for the first time. A crisis arises when one's methods of dealing with one's own emotions and the external problems are inadequate. One consequence is that a person in crisis may feel helpless, ineffective, anxious, fearful, and guilty, with the result that his or her behavior is less efficient than usual.

The crisis situation may awaken old personal problems as well. For example, a person rejected by all the graduate schools to which he or she applies faces two problems (see Silber et al., 1961). The person must decide what else to do in place of going to graduate school, a task that may bring back ambivalence and uncertainty about making choices or about growing up. Second, he or she will usually feel rejected, frustrated, and a failure, which may reawaken old feelings of rejection generally or of helplessness when someone else decides one's fate. (From a psychoanalytic viewpoint, this concept that the new problem may revive old problems is similar to the idea of the return of the repressed.) Once the individual is open and vulnerable, many memories and feelings from the past may return, adding to the problem of coping in the present.

The acute phase of the state of upset must last more than a day or two for it to qualify as a crisis. Some say that the acute phase rarely lasts longer than 6 weeks,[1] although other evidence questions this claim (e.g., Lewis, Gottesman, & Gutstein, 1979). Data on this point are not plentiful, but as a matter of definition we do not call the episode a crisis unless the state of upset persists for more than a relatively brief period. The acute phase is sometimes referred to as a state of heightened vulnerability and is further divisible into two periods, one of initial impact and a second of rising tension. Initial impact refers to the recognition that the individual faces a situation that demands some response. Sometimes the initial phase is accompanied by a state of shock or numbness, but shortly thereafter tension rises rapidly as one recognizes the need to act. With the rise in tension the individual initiates his or her habitual problem-solving responses, which can be as varied as depending on someone else to solve the problem, retreating, or actively seeking information or alternatives. Tension dissipates once the problem is solved. If the problem-solving device used was a new one, the person can be said to have grown or developed new knowledge or skills and now can command additional personal resources for dealing with the world.[2]

Research on Stressful Life Events

Not all crises are resolved successfully, of course, and one implication of both Dohrenwend's model and the ecological analogy is that environmental factors are involved in adjusting to stress as well as personal characteristics. In fact, Lindemann's seminal study of nightclub-fire survivors marked the beginning of a broad shift in attention away from pathological characteristics of certain individuals and toward the pathology-inducing aspects of stressful events. Similar investigations of otherwise ordinary people undergoing one kind of situational crisis or another soon followed his work, and evidence began to accumulate showing a higher than expected incidence of disorders following single, highly traumatic experiences such as marital disruption (Bloom, Asher, & White, 1978) and economic distress (Dooley & Catalano, 1980). A common theoretical explanation arose based on Selye's (1956) description of the "general adaptation syndrome." Selye's idea, developed in a psychophysiological context, was that any significant change in a person's life upsets the individual's equilibrium, creating stress and thus requiring a compensating, adaptive response of some sort. Large changes such as divorce or job loss, but also a series of smaller events in close succession, can overtax the individual's coping resources, threatening his or her physical or psychological well-being.

Subsequent investigators systematically pursued the idea that discrete, time-limited events requiring change or adaptation increase risk for a wide range of human disorders. An early list compiled by psychiatrists Thomas Holmes and Richard Rahe (1967), called the Schedule of Recent Experiences (SRE), contained 43 human events (e.g., marriage, change in residence, major personal injury or illness); an individual's life-stress score was simply the number of events he or she reported experiencing during some recent interval of time (usually between 6 and 24 months). Holmes and Rahe soon recognized that some of these events (e.g., death of spouse) required considerably more change and adaptation than did others (e.g., vacation), and so was born the Social Readjustment Rating Scale (SRRS), which *weighted* each event using a ratio scale to estimate the amount of change or readjustment required on the part of the individual experiencing the event. The estimate of total life stress experienced by a person thus became the sum of the weights, or "life-change units," for the events reported. Note that both events that represent positive experiences (e.g., Christmas) and those clearly negative in valence (e.g., fired from job) are seen to make adaptive demands on the individual and thus to produce stress.

Life-events scales have now been used with a wide variety of populations, and the massive empirical literature that has resulted leaves little doubt that a significant relationship exists between the cumulative experience of stress, as assessed by life-events scales,[3] and a host of adverse medical and psychological conditions (see Bloom, 1984, for a recent review). Critical reviews (e.g., Rabkin & Streuning, 1976), however, have pointed to the modest size of stress-disorder correlations identified in this fashion (typically .30 or less, accounting for under 10% of variance). Other critics (e.g., Dohrenwend et al., 1984; Dohrenwend & Shrout, 1985; Monroe & Steiner, 1986) have suggested that there is such overlap in the items on life-events scales and on measures of personality or disorder that the scales are not truly independent. These critics are suggesting that the reported relationships between life events and disorder may be largely artifactual. Lazarus et al. (1985), on the other hand, do not believe that the apparent confounding of stress measurement and adaptational outcomes is sufficient to account for the relationships reported between stress and outcome. This debate appears to turn on whether one assumes that the measurement of life events necessarily includes an individual's subjective appraisal of the event (see the later discussion of coping), or whether instead one should measure stressful events simply by describing the concrete event (e.g., death of a loved one; a flood or other natural disaster) without respect to subjective appraisal. This debate notwithstanding, the degree of risk (for virtually all outcomes studied) entailed by the kinds of life events found on the typical scale, no matter how many of them one reports experiencing, appears to fall short of the expectation created by the early studies.

Several conceptual and methodological issues are worth raising here. The methodological breakthrough provided by the life-events method was its quantification of what had been largely a qualitative area of study. That is, life events can provide a simple index of life stress. Several different life-stress constructs or dimensions have been quantified to date. The empirical limits to stress-disorder prediction may to some extent reflect construct validity problems in the life-events scales. For example, one implicit assumption is that the stress-disorder relationship is *linear,* in that while catastrophic events elicit much stress and high risk for disorder, everyday events also entail some stress and some risk, and some stress is always riskier than no stress. This assumption conflicts with intuitive notions that an *absence* of life events (boredom?) may entail just as much disequilibrium (and hence stress) as is created by some events. This view also assumes that individual events are independent and additive and that a given event always elicits the same amount of stress.

In the traditional Holmes and Rahe view, life events were seen as nonspecific stimuli that impact on different people from different situations to approximately the same degree (i.e., no significant role is played by other factors such as the individual's cognitive appraisal of the event or the degree of social support available to him or her), an idea that now seems limited and oversimplified. An alternative approach emphasizes not life change per se, but the psychological and emotional aspects of adapting to events. This alternative differentiates events in terms of the degree of undesirability or threat they entail and the individual's degree of anticipation or control over them. Life events are thus seen to interact with characteristics of the individual and the situation (e.g., cognitive appraisal, social support) in producing stress.

Another issue is that any single events list presents items that may or may not be relevant to a specific target population. For example, many of the Holmes and Rahe items (e.g., retirement from work, foreclosure on a mortgage or loan, son or daughter left home) would have little direct relevance for a population of college students, for whom the experience of many events *not* on that list (e.g., academic difficulties, relationship with parents) would more closely reflect their degree of exposure to stress. Recently investigators have paid more attention to tailoring events lists for specific populations. Representatives of the target group itself nominate events based on what has happened to them or to people like them (Levine & Perkins, 1980a).

Dohrenwend's view that various personal and situational factors interact with characteristics of life events to produce stress and influence outcome is becoming more widely accepted in at least its general outlines (Perkins, 1982). One class of personal factors with which the occurrence and the meaning of stress have been extensively associated is demographic background. Surveys at three contrasting colleges (Perkins et al., 1982), for example, indicated that at each school the student at greatest risk for both number of stressful events and total amount of stress was the freshman or sophomore female who lived off campus. In another study of 2,780 residents from two different communities, Goldberg and Comstock (1980) found that being younger, better educated, or separated/divorced increases a person's risk for experiencing life events like those on the SRRS. One explanation is that youth, education, and marital disruption increase one's opportunities to make changes in school or work activities or in one's place of residence. Note, however, that it can be difficult to separate personal factors from situation factors in identifying conditions of risk.

The evidence linking dimensions of personality with life events is also of interest. Such processes as individual perception, ego defense, psychophysiological responsiveness, and coping ability have all been hypothesized to mediate the effects of life events. Smith, Johnson, and Sarason (1978), for example, found in a study of college students that undesirable life change was significantly associated with psychological distress only among students who were low in "sensation seeking"; high-sensation-seeking students apparently were much more tolerant of undesirable life change.

The assessment of stress using simple life-events scales alone is probably destined to be replaced by multifactorial models encompassing individual differences and situational contexts as well. Some stressors are probably so severe that almost anyone would be at risk for disorder, and some people may be so "hardy" that no set of events would induce disabling stress in them, but the vast majority of situations lie somewhere in between these extremes.

Another recent development is the extension of the cumulative life-events model to more commonplace experiences. DeLongis et al. (1982), for example, found that the frequency and intensity of everyday "hassles" in work, family, financial, or social affairs were better predictors of overall health in a normal sample than was the incidence of nonhealth-related life events in this group. Progress in the near term, however, may require a measured return to interest in the qualitative aspects of life stress. Research will focus more explicitly on the individual, situation, and life-event correlates of specific outcomes. As Rahe and Arthur (1978) put it:

> Initial conceptions of the life changes and illness work were necessarily simple and straightforward, but as the evidence for the validity of the general concept has mounted, it has also become necessary to think in terms of the complexity of the social, psychological, and physiological variables involved. . . . The enormously difficult task awaits us of filling in the crucial steps in an all-encompassing model which takes into account not only environmental variables but the social, psychological, and physiological characteristics of the individual. (p. 13)

Vulnerability: An Integrative Perspective

To summarize, knowledge regarding the number and characteristics of recent stressful events is generally insufficient to predict with great accuracy a person's future level of well-being. Dohrenwend's model in fact suggests three possible outcomes to any transient stress reaction, wherein the person can return to the previous level of functioning, become a case of psychopathology, or resolve the experience to the point where he or she is even stronger than before. Furthermore, our review of contemporary social conditions in Chapter 1 suggested that stress is ubiquitous in life, yet clearly not everyone succumbs to disorder. Many authorities (e.g., Cassel, 1976) have concluded that while stressful events seem to increase a person's overall risk for disorder in a nonspecific way, no given external stressor is likely to be etiologically specific for any particular medical or psychological dysfunction.

Another tenet of Dohrenwend's model not observed in the simple life-events paradigm is that stress-related disorders, such as depression, alcohol abuse, and even schizophrenia, are usually *episodic* to at least some degree; their symptomatic manifestations come and go over time, alternating with periods of relatively normal behavior. One reason may be that people suffering from those conditions tend to seek relief in a variety of ways, including formal treatment and also self-directed "natural healing" and mutual support (see Chapter 8). Such efforts are frequently successful on a short-term basis, but in the long run may be followed by recurring episodes of difficulty. The simple dichotomy between traits, or even states (Spielberger, Gorsuch, & Lushene, 1970), of mental health and mental illness may in fact be misleading. We may more accurately assume that individuals who at a particular moment are dysfunctional will eventually recover to a greater or lesser degree and for some period of time, and that individuals currently in a normal state of mental health could conceivably become stressed to the point of succumbing to an episode of disorder.

For these reasons, we must distinguish between an individual's degree of predisposition to disorder on the one hand and the onset and course of a given episode of disorder on the other. In this sense, we assume that everyone has only a finite degree of resistance to stress. Stated another way, everyone is endowed with a specific degree of *vulnerability* to such episodes (somewhere from high to low) that under certain conditions will express itself in a time-limited crisis of adaptation. Thus no one has zero vulnerability, and vulnerability is distinct from psychological disorder per se. One's degree of vulnerability is determined partially by inborn or other "predisposing" factors such as genetic inheritance and prior coping competence; it is also influenced by environmental factors such as social support. When we use the term *vulnerability* we do not mean it to imply personality weaknesses alone. An episode of disorder occurs when the degree of disequilibrium brought by recent stressful experiences exceeds the threshold imposed by the individual's level of vulnerability.

Several advantages characterize this vulnerability perspective as an integrative replacement for the older person-centered view of psychopathology. Like Dohrenwend's model and the ecological analogy (Chapter 3), it relates both person-centered and environmental factors to time-limited episodes of mental health and disorder. Furthermore, the episodic nature of these experiences is explained by the fact that even with a relatively stable degree of initial vulnerability, one's levels of acute stress and environmental support fluctuate over time. In addition, many self-healing responses and formal treatment efforts produce short-term improvement by reducing the level of external stress. Sometimes more stable improvement may result from reduced vulnerability (e.g., the individual develops better coping skills, makes a permanent change in his or her environment, and so on). The model is also consistent with the observation that with nearly everyone experiencing the soap opera that is life, most people do not develop diagnosable pathology (i.e., both the degree of vulnerability and the amount of stress experienced vary widely, even within the same family or group). Finally, "vulnerability" is a less stigmatizing concept than "disease" (especially because everyone is vulnerable to some extent), yet is completely compatible with the other evidence for a stable individual difference factor—those at greatest risk all share a high degree of vulnerability, not a uniform pattern of environmental experience.

More attention is obviously needed to the two kinds of factors that both Dohrenwend and the preceding perspective suggest determine individual vulnerability to psychopathology. We now turn to a review of ideas and research on individual coping, followed by an examination of the concept of social support.

Coping

One characteristic that reduces vulnerability to stress is coping ability (Dohrenwend, 1978). Coping can be defined as "cognitive and behavioral effort made to master, tolerate, or reduce demands that tax or exceed a person's resources" (Kessler et al., 1985, p. 550). In this section we describe the general experience of coping with stressful events; we then discuss the evidence for important individual and situational differences in coping.

General Characteristics of Coping

The individual facing a stressful event has two problems. One is how to manage the internal stress, anxiety, tension, depression, anger, restlessness, difficulty in concentrating, sleeplessness, and fatigue—and the associated thought content, self-doubt, and self-blame. The second is how to take appropriate action. Although these two tasks, dealing with one's feelings and dealing with the external situation, are inseparable in the real world, conceptually they are separable. Separating the concepts is useful because distinctly different ameliorative and preventive approaches may follow.

Lazarus (1966) emphasizes the role of cognitive appraisal in coping. Folkman (1984) offers an extended version of Lazarus's early model, but one that retains the essential features of the earlier model. Lazarus defines two phases in the process of cognitive appraisal. The first phase, primary appraisal, is biologically designed to provide sufficient energy to respond to the problem at hand, and it involves a judgment by the individual about the meaning or possible significance of an event based on the nature of the event and the individual's psychological makeup. Secondary appraisal is a reaction to the intense feeling, and it underlies the actual coping responses that are subsequently made. For example, observing that one is aroused worsens the situation if the arousal is interpreted as bad, wrong, sick, or a sign of weakness or incompetence. Thus the individual may worry about worrying—adding tension.

From a preventive viewpoint, education may conceivably help one to understand, identify, and tolerate a range of feelings and thus to prevent the secondary reaction to primary arousal. Some preventive efforts consist of little more than preparation and warning. If the dentist tells you that you will feel pain or the surgeon tells you that you will have a certain kind and degree of discomfort following surgery, when the pain occurs later you tend not to worry about it as much because it was expected. Under those conditions discomfort is not a sign that something has gone wrong, but indicates that one's condition is "normal" under the circumstances. A large body of research has shown that prior to surgery such simple preparation and warnings can have a measurable effect on the postsurgical course of recovery (Mumford, Schlesinger, & Glass, 1982). For example, a meta analysis of 10 well-controlled studies showed that patients who received information and emotional support in brief preoperative sessions had a length of stay that was on the average 2.4 days less than the stay for untreated controls. Some of the studies showed that the effect of the intervention was enhanced if it was matched to the patient's coping style. Patients who cope with stress by denial may be less benefited or even burdened by too much explanation and warning, while those who cope with stress by seeking information and mastery may be more benefited by preoperative preparation. These interventions are inexpensive compared with the cost of a hospital day and are thus highly effective from a benefit:cost viewpoint.

Many people have learned how to modulate their feelings by talking to themselves, distracting themselves, or suppressing the feelings while it is necessary to act. We have little knowledge of techniques for modulating feelings. Most of what we know has been articulated in the context of psychoanalytic defense mechanisms. Although defenses have generally been discussed as detrimental to coping, Hartmann (1958) pointed out that they also have adaptive qualities, and we now are attending more to that hypothesis. Developing methods for teaching the modulation of feeling is an important area for research, since teaching these skills to everyone may represent a preventive program.

Another popular area of work in this vein is the use of individual training and workshops to teach stress management (see Meichenbaum & Jaremko, 1983). One such technique involves exposing the individual to "graded" doses of stress under conditions where he or she can rehearse effective responses in a repetitive fashion. Systematic desensitization is one example, where the phobic client imagines increasingly more anxiety-arousing experiences while sustaining the calming response of deep muscle relaxation. Another example involves providing presurgery patients with increasingly more detailed and explicit descriptions of the impending procedures and likely outcomes they will face. Often included in such coping-skills interventions are procedures that help the person anticipate and prepare for possible failures, and also the expectation that successful coping will be generalized by applying the specific techniques in new situations.

Once the acute stress is under control, the second major task is that of taking appropriate action (i.e., coping with the situation). One coping task is an emotional one and involves the arousal of hope or a sense that one may indeed be able to do something about one's situation. A not infrequent reaction after an initial psychotherapy interview, for example, is the sense that something good may come of it—there is some hope that one's desperate situation will be relieved. Consider as an example a woman with a new baby who moves to a new community and hasn't yet made any friends. Her husband is busy in a new and demanding job and doesn't have much time or energy to help at home. Finances are tight, and they can't afford household help. Their families live far away and cannot be counted on too much, for there are often petty squabbles when mother and daughter or son and mother-in-law are together for too long a time. One day the woman's husband disappoints her badly, and she considers leaving him to go home to her mother. She is greatly distressed, crying one moment and raging the next, and can't get over the episode, remaining tense and depressed. Finally she calls a psychotherapist who helps her work out a plan of action. After a few days she calls back to report that she is following through, and now says that she is *hopeful* something good will happen. That feeling of hope represents an important aspect of her belief that she will be able to deal with her circumstances.

We actually know very little about the emotion of hope. Under what circumstances is hope aroused? Does it require some support from another person? Can hope or something like it be generated from within by recalling other occasions when one has succeeded in overcoming adversity? Is the ability to generate hope an indication that one has been strengthened by overcoming adversity earlier? Is the emotion of hope a necessary part of what we call determination? Are there comparable motives such as a desire for revenge or a desire to prove something to another that can stimulate effort to overcome adversity? The latter motives may be less praiseworthy, but they nonetheless can be quite powerful. Frankl (1963) noted that many survivors of Nazi concentration camps managed to develop some transcendent goal—to tell the world about the experience or to finish some unfinished work—that aided them in coping with extreme adversity and helped them to avoid surrendering to seemingly insurmountable difficulties. Because much of our knowledge of personality derives from the study of persons who may be said to have succumbed to difficulty, we know all too little about those who have mastered difficulty and have become stronger for it.

While coming to terms with a crisis is in part an emotional task, solving the problem often requires additional thinking and action. Consider a widow in her late 40s or early 50s with grown children, who is not yet eligible for a Social Security pension, has only minimum resources from her husband's insurance for financial support, and has not been in the labor market for 20 or 25 years. Such a person can expect to live another 30 or more years. In addition to living with the complex emotion of grief following the loss of her husband, the widow faces the problem of making new friends, especially if she finds herself uncomfortable as a single person among friends who are married couples. She may have to cope with problems of dating, should she decide in a year or two she wants to develop a relationship with a man. She has many other problems to solve, including how to maintain or repair the house if she continues to live in it or how to find and manage workers who will do the work. She may have little experience in managing finances or investments and now has to decide what to do about what money she does have. Beyond home and social relationships, she has to decide how to spend her time. She has to assess her own resources, her assets on the job market, and she may have to find opportunities for training or education. Having decided on the course she will pursue, she may then have to take on new experiences of studying, taking examinations, and relating in an unaccustomed role to persons perhaps much younger than herself. Similar problems confront widowers and divorced men and women. Little wonder, when we review all of the adaptations that are necessary, that the death of a spouse and divorce are heavily weighted on life-events scales.

The widow's situation can be conceptualized in problem-solving terms: she must examine each problem, develop alternative strategies for solving it, assess the resources each solution requires, and then risk failure by acting in uncertain and unfamiliar territory. Psychologists (e.g., Spivack & Shure, 1974, 1985) have developed techniques and approaches to problem solving that, when taught to people, represent psychological mediators of the sort considered by Dohrenwend (1978). Whenever a person has taken new risks, engaged in new experiences, or mastered some new approach to living, he or she may be said to have grown psychologically. The crisis model directs us toward enhancing the individual's ability to solve problems by systematically providing such techniques to the individual. If the technique is taught before the problem arises, we have a preventive approach, in that the psychological mediator, the problem-solving approach, is made available in advance of the crisis.

Stages in Crisis Resolution

The crisis model offers an additional analytic advantage important in understanding the individual's situation and in providing services appropriate to his or her circumstances. The crisis model postulates stages in the resolution of crises that change over a long period of time. An important contribution made by Kubler-Ross (1969) to the field of death and dying was specifying the stages a person goes through in coming to terms with death. Lindemann (1944) had earlier specified stages in working through loss based on the reactions of people grieving over family members lost in a fire. Other crises may also have stages in their resolution that are important to understand. People may be ready to cope in one way at one stage and in another way at a different stage.

Resolving a crisis in the short term does not necessarily result in the assimilation of the event into the personality. If the event arouses strong feelings of fear, anger, or guilt, memory of the event may haunt the person from time to time. Thus men who had combat-related anxiety states sometimes report bad dreams and episodes of acute fear for years afterward (Atkinson et al., 1984). Follow-up studies of women who have been raped have identified three phases of response (Sutherland & Scherl, 1970; Burgess & Holmstrom, 1979). The first is simply getting through the trauma, fear, shame, and related concerns. The second phase includes efforts to return to normal and control or minimize the significance of the event for one's life. In the third phase, occurring weeks or sometimes months later, the experience returns to conscious attention, and the individual is once again faced with integrating and resolving it. This phase is often marked by depressive feelings or anxiety (Kilpatrick, Veronen, & Resich, 1979). In this last phase, the person works to integrate the experience into the self. The view of self as one who was once assaulted, violated, and subjected to sexual abuse has to be incorporated or assimilated within the general self-concept. Some rape counselors encourage their clients to think of themselves not as victims, but as survivors.

Even though self-blame may reflect the introjection of cultural values, or may reflect experiences with insensitive police, prosecutors, medical personnel, relatives, lovers, or friends, nonetheless, many blame themselves: "I shouldn't have been out at night alone," "I shouldn't have been hitchhiking," "I shouldn't have gone to his apartment," or "I should have screamed louder or fought harder." The truth of the matter is subordinated to the process of self-blame (Libow & Doty, 1979). There may be some adaptive value to this self-blame, in that the person might be saying, "If I had something to do with causing the event, perhaps I can prevent a repetition in the future." This last phase may contribute to reappraisals and to new learning. "Was I staying out late or hitchhiking because I wanted to, or was I running unnecessary risks to get back at my parents?" Coming to terms with the event might require rethinking one's own contribution to it, and that can be painful and depressing.

In the alternative, one might also direct attention toward circumstances (and toward the culturally determined attitudes of some males) that place a woman at risk simply because she was on the street. Such a rethinking may allow for participation later in groups that provide escort services, seek greater police protection, or promote more sensitive handling of persons who have been harmed by a rape or a rape attempt.

Included in the complex emotion is anger. In the earlier phases, the woman may have suppressed or denied the anger, viewing the rape impersonally as a social fault. In the third phase, however, the anger can become more personalized and in a sense more real: "That SOB! He used me! I could kill him!" Such feelings of rage after the event need to be worked through. This account has dealt with phases in the inner psychological development of the response to the experience of rape and has only touched on the complications introduced into relationships with lovers or husbands and on the subsequent frustrating if not humiliating encounters with the legal process (Silverman, 1978; Burgess & Holmstrom, 1979).

The reliving described here may not occur with all challenges to adaptation and may be more likely to occur when the strongest emotions of fear, rage, and guilt are engaged. Note, however, that casting the emotional experience into the conceptual terms of a phase in the restorative process enables one to look at the experience not as a permanent disability but as an emotional state natural to the experiences one has had. Viewed in this light, the emotions and thoughts need not be experienced as an unwanted manifestation of a neurotic illness, but more like the postsurgical discomfort one has been warned about. In this case it may simply be easier to live through, and may also be turned to personal advantage.

Individual and Situational Differences in Coping

Any life event potentially has positive as well as negative effects. Negative aspects are nearly always apparent almost immediately, while positive effects may take some time to emerge. Not everyone is able to benefit in a positive way from stress, however, and an interesting question is what accounts for this difference. From the vulnerability perspective, the concept of host resistance gives us an opportunity to shift our focus from personal and situational processes that damage a person's mental health to those that strengthen it. From this viewpoint the question is not what accounts for disorder in response to stress, but what accounts for strength. If one looks for stable person-centered strengths, the evidence suggests that one will find them.

Finkel (1974, 1975; Finkel & Jacobsen, 1977), for example, asked adults and college students to identify and describe previous significant life experiences that were either negative or positive and to indicate how these experiences changed their views of themselves and their lives. Unexpectedly, most of Finkel's subjects spontaneously described *three* kinds of experiences: negative events, positive events, and events that started out as negative but later became positive in their overall effect. He calls the third kind "trauma-stren conversions." Finkel, noting that we have no word in English that is an antonym for trauma, used the made up word stren to mean a personality-strengthening experience. Subsequent interviews with the subjects characterized the conversion experience as beginning with a sudden insight or "flash" that enabled them to reinterpret the traumatic event in a more positive light. The previous debilitating construction produced by the psychological trauma was replaced by a new construction that emphasized the individual's ability to cope, adapt, and learn from the trauma.

Among people reporting such a conversion experience, 60% performed the conversion spontaneously by themselves. Finkel concludes that conversion was not simply a defensive distortion of the experience, since the existence of pain, regret, and anger during the initial period of trauma was fully acknowledged by the person, and only in hindsight was the event thought to have positive value.

Most interesting of all perhaps was that for most converters, the first conversion produced a significant change in their subsequent experience of life events. That is, before their first conversion, converters did not differ from nonconverters in the proportions of traumas and growth-promoting experiences they reported. *Following* the first conversion, however, converters reported only half the proportion of traumas and 50% more positive events than did nonconverters, as well as additional conversion experiences (Finkel & Jacobson, 1977). Thus from a preventive standpoint, achieving one's first conversion appears to reduce the negative impact of subsequent life events, and perhaps the risk of stress-related psychopathology as well, although Finkel did not actually show that converting an event results in better mental health.

Is the conversion of life events generalizable—can even severe psychological trauma be converted? What are the psychological correlates of the conversion of stressful life experiences? Research on stressful life events with college students has shown that about 4% have a parent die during any given academic year, and that parental death is among the most highly stressful of student life events (Levine & Perkins, 1980a). Recent research by Tebes and Perkins (1984) found that between 4 and 22 months following the death of a parent, about half of the students experiencing this event converted the severe stress it entails into positive change. A comparison of the mental health of students who had converted the parent's death, students unable to convert this event, and normal nonbereaved students using Goldberg's (1972) General Health Questionnaire (a measure of nonpsychotic psychiatric impairment) showed that bereaved nonconverters were significantly more impaired than were either bereaved converters or normal controls, and that bereaved converters were actually *less* impaired than controls.

Better understanding of such stress-conversion experiences has implications for being able to facilitate conversions in individuals who would fail to do so on their own, and thus for the primary prevention of stress-related problems. Conceptually, however, the specific nature of a life-event conversion is not yet clear—particularly what roles are played by the individual's prior competence and current levels of social support and life stress and how these factors interact over time to influence cognitive appraisal. Is conversion an intuitive cognitive skill, as Finkel maintains? If so, why aren't converters able to convert all the stressful events they experience? From an ecological viewpoint, might conversion instead be understood as a fortuitous kind of adaptation assisted in important ways by specific situational resources?

Taylor (1983) provides another view of conversion experiences. She describes a process of self-enhancement by means of social comparisons that allows the person experiencing a stressful life event to feel better off than someone else. She illustrates the concepts in her study of women adapting to breast cancer. Taylor argues that women who make a positive adaptation to cancer develop and use what she calls beneficial illusions. Beneficial illusions are not denials; they represent constructions of reality that permit one to function with a degree of optimism and a sense of control over events. The cognitive mechanisms Taylor describes may also have utility for our understanding of the potential in stressful experiences for enhancing (or at least maintaining) growth and self-esteem under difficult circumstances.

Other researchers have taken the position that stable, traitlike psychological mediators play a central role in coping with a stressful experience. Kobasa (1979), for example, identifies what she terms a "hardy" personality style. Individuals with hardy personalities easily commit themselves to what they are doing, generally believe themselves to be in control of events, and consider life change a challenging and necessary impetus to development. In contrast, people low in hardiness often feel alienated and powerless and are threatened by change. Kobasa's research has involved middle- and upper-level executives with especially high levels of life stress who are typically divided into groups high and low on symptoms of illness. Results generally indicate that the high-stress/low-illness group shows significantly greater personality hardiness than do high-stress/high-illness subjects and that hardiness is particularly effective in reducing the risk of illness during high-stress periods.

Other psychological mediators of an individual's response to stress have also been suggested, including cognitive and behavioral construction competencies (Mischel,

1973; see Chapter 4), perceived personal control (Langer, 1983), self-esteem (Chan, 1977), social competence (Iscoe, 1974; Spivack & Shure, 1974; see following chapter), and self-efficacy (Bandura, 1977). Keep in mind, however, that from the perspective of crisis theory and Dohrenwend's model, adaptation is determined not by these personal characteristics alone, but by the relationship between psychological mediators and specific factors in the environment. We do not know how to produce hardiness or the other individual difference characteristics that have been studied. If hardiness and other traits are inborn, then as a preventive strategy we might look to approaches that would help people to enhance their fit with key environments (Levine & Perkins, 1980b).

In contrast to the primary emphasis given by many researchers to psychological mediators in the response to stress, a considerable amount of evidence to date suggests that strategies for effective coping may be situation specific instead of global. In a study of 2,300 adults, for example, Pearlin and Schooler (1978) found that not all coping responses are reported to be equally effective across all life situations (e.g., responses that are effective in resolving marital conflict are not necessarily successful at work). The fact that no single coping response was reported to be universally effective by this large sample suggests that research should be as careful in describing the specific stressful situation as in delineating the particular responses seen as successful or unsuccessful. Given the "soap opera" argument advanced in Chapter 1, an important aspect of the Pearlin and Schooler research is its focus on relatively commonplace events involving marriage, parenting, household management, and work.

More recent research by Folkman and Lazarus (1980) attempted to answer directly the question of how consistently people use specific coping behaviors across a sample of everyday situations. One hundred men and women aged 45 to 64 reported the specific coping thoughts and actions they used in response to recent stressful events. Both problem-focused and emotion-focused coping were used extensively and, contrary to cultural stereotype, women did not use emotion-focused coping more than men did. Furthermore, the situational context of the event and how the event was appraised were the strongest determinants of what kind of coping response was made. For example, events related to work, where some sort of constructive response was often possible, elicited more problem-focused coping. Health-related problems, on the other hand, which may have been appraised as offering fewer opportunities for constructive change, were more likely to elicit emotion-focused coping. These results support Dohrenwend's (1978) idea that the relationship between the person's individual appraisal of an event and the situational context in which it occurs determines the nature of the person's coping response.

At this point theory and research on coping remain in a relatively crude state (Kessler et al., 1985). Little of the research has examined "natural" coping by ordinary people in response to commonplace kinds of events, and an important question for research concerns the extent to which variations in coping strategies (direct action, cognitive reappraisal, etc.) are consistently associated with a particular outcome achieved in response to a stressful event. Because coping and appraisal probably exert a reciprocal influence on each other over time, longitudinal studies examining the dynamic aspects of coping also need to be done. As we come to understand the coping process better, we may learn how to teach coping skills in a timely fashion to prevent crises and maladaptations.

Social Support

Crisis theory assumes that a person enters a state of crisis because attachments are threatened *and* he or she lacks the immediate resources to respond adaptively. Some of these resources may come from others in the person's network of relationships. Consider the following example. A young woman goes off to another city with a man she does not know very well. Far from home, he suddenly and unexpectedly tells her he is tired of their relationship, and he leaves her there alone. She is shocked, frightened, and too ashamed to call home. Fortunately, she remembers an old friend of the family who lives nearby. This person takes her in, allows her to stay, and asks no unwanted questions until she is able to make plans to return home.

An individual in crisis may require material resources, emotional support, and guidance. As a second example, suppose a college woman becomes pregnant and does not have the money to pay for an abortion. She tells friends on her dormitory floor of her plight. They raise the money from among their friends, arrange for the abortion at a clinic, arrange for her to stay in another city with a college friend while she recovers from the abortion, and then have other friends meet her at the airport in her home city and take her to her parents' home. Although one may question the moral decision to have the abortion, one might well consider that the social, emotional, and economic consequences of teenage pregnancy are profound for both the teenage mother and her child (Phipps-Yonas, 1980).

Note that both young women were able to obtain something they needed from their respective social networks. How typical is this? Like stress, support is sometimes assumed to be ubiquitous in people's lives. Gottlieb (1983), for example, includes among his types of supportive networks one's family and friends, "natural care givers" such as family physicians, lawyers, and clergy, organized neighborhood associations, and self-help groups. In spite of these widespread sources of support, some people are still isolated, and isolated people may be restricted to seeking support only from formal agencies—welfare or the police—and bearing all the social costs of accepting such aid. Furthermore, people who are able to make use of the resources available through friends and relatives may have the social skills to develop good relationships in the first place (Heller & Swindle, 1983).

In both of these examples, the women felt free to ask for help, and they judged correctly who might best provide the assistance. Twenty or 30 years ago so much stigma would have been attached to each woman's conduct that each might have been reluctant to reveal her plight, thus cutting herself off from possible aid. Even today an individual may feel so guilty, have so little self-esteem, or for darker reasons feel so hopeless that he or she may not use support that is available. People who have been embedded in a close and supportive social network have been known to commit suicide despite the best efforts of friends, relatives, and professional therapists. Their difficulties in using support may reflect a maladaptive coping style that reduces the their ability to see or to generate alternatives (Ellis, 1986).

In both examples those asked were willing to help. Sometimes a person's needs are so great, and he or she has "gone to the well" so often, that the well turns up dry. In fact, some people may well be isolated precisely because they have exhausted others' goodwill and other interpersonal "credits." Tebes (1983) reviewed a body of literature showing that families of chronic schizophrenics tended to reject them, not so much because of the stigma associated with the condition but because of the burden of care the chronic patients imposed.

Knowing when and whom to ask for help may be a matter of judgment or skill, and not going to the well too often may also be a manifestation of skill. If the ability to utilize resources is a matter of interpersonal skills, those skills might be teachable. If they are teachable, as other interpersonal problem-solving skills appear to be (see the following chapter), and if having such skills aids adapting during a crisis or avoiding a crisis altogether, once again theory and analysis lead us toward the possibility of prevention.

In both examples the individuals from whom help was sought did things that were helpful. Some persons in a network of relationships might not be helpful and if approached would either not provide the support required or act in such a way as to make the problem worse. Perrotta (1982), studying middle-aged adults who were responsible for the care of their elderly parents, found that one factor contributing to the stressfulness of this experience was the caretaker's failure to receive the support of someone from whom support was expected. For example, if a brother or sister was not taking a fair share of the care or of the responsibility for spending time with the parent, the caretaking experience was more stressful. The sibling providing the care had to struggle with feelings of anger and disappointment, as well as with the problem of providing the care. Fiore, Becker, and Coppel (1983) report a similar correlation between perceived upset in the social networks of those taking care of Alzheimer's patients and the care givers' depression scores.

Those interested in research on natural support networks have a tendency to romanticize the "natural" strengths of families and friends and have overlooked the fact that conflict within the network may be frequent, or that the support provided may be insufficient or inappropriate. Luepnitz (1978), for example, found that children in divorced families were maladjusted to the degree that their divorced parents continued to be in conflict. In some divorced families the natural support network failed. As Turkington (1985) points out, membership in a network may expose the individual to stressors as well as buffer him or her against them.

Social support does not consist only of unconditional positive regard. Janis (1983) notes that clinical interventions for obesity, smoking or substance abuse, and assertiveness improvement appear to be effective during treatment, but studies regularly find "backsliding" after treatment ceases. Janis argues that a common feature in all of these interventions is the provision of social support during the period of treatment and the withdrawal of social support when treatment ends. Based on controlled field experiments of adherence to decisions to improve assertiveness, go on a diet, or stop smoking, Janis identifies 12 variables making up that support. The first set refers to the building up of referent power, by which he means that the helping person becomes a significant other, one whose approval or disapproval is highly rewarding to the client. The second group of variables refers to the use of referent power to enhance commitment to the stressful decision, to reward actions that promote the desired goals and to express mild disapproval of actions contrary to meeting the goals. The third group of actions are those that may be useful in retaining referent power after treatment ends by promoting internalization of the commitment and the rewards. The techniques are designed to help the client shift from other-directed to self-directed approval.

In the context of adherence to stressful decisions, an effective therapist clearly does more than just listen empathically. Janis points out that successful treatment requires unconditional acceptance most of the time. Once established, however, referent power is used to express mild criticism when the client departs from the agreed course of action. As we will see later, Janis's findings are consistent with the description of social support provided by Gerald Caplan.

Outside the therapeutic context, we do not know very much about what is helpful for one person to do for another. The way psychotherapists respond is not necessarily the best way to help someone under any and all circumstances. Listening and responding empathically are probably more helpful than other things one might do. Some authorities (Cowen, 1982) have suggested teaching these skills to such "natural care givers" as hairdressers, taxi drivers, and bartenders, all of whom often find themselves in the position of listening to other people's problems. Although these skills are undoubtedly teachable (D'Augelli & Vallance, 1982; Danish, D'Augelli, & Brock, 1976), we do not as yet have good evidence that they are helpful in resolving crises.[4]

Although the approaches that Janis describes may be helpful for the specific problems he studied, his approach is not necessarily useful for all problems. Taylor (1983) describes different cognitive approaches that women adapting to mastectomies developed for themselves. A person providing support to a woman coping with that problem might be effectively helping the struggling person develop and sustain "illusions" and helping the person to see setbacks not as evidence of the failure of the illusion but as a temporary frustration. As we will see in Chapter 8, Taylor's approach resembles the use of cognitive "antidotes" by the members of many self-help groups. Support is a complex concept, and the words, actions, and feelings that constitute support should be tailored to specific persons, problems, and circumstances.

The other side of the support coin, of course, is also of interest to the community psychologist. Isolated individuals, by definition not part of a social network, may be highly vulnerable for that reason alone (D'Augelli, 1983; Leavy, 1983). Work by Blazer (1982) and by Lynch (1977) has even suggested that loneliness and isolation are in fact lethal. Note here that the social networks of those whom we consider chronically dependent tend to consist of workers in agencies—the welfare worker, day-care counselor, aide in a social club for former patients, or police officer. This is in sharp contrast to the situation of most other people, who look to lovers, spouses, family, and friends or who can afford to hire the sort of private-sector professional helpers— doctors, lawyers, or tax accountants—whose help is not stigmatizing. Both groups— those who use a social network of professional public helpers and those who can call on a private and personal network—must possess certain skills and qualifications to gain access to the resources the network provides. Those who rely on a public network may need to have "bureaucratic competence," while those who rely on their families and the private marketplace may utilize other skills and approaches. We would be in serious error to confuse the skills necessary to function in one network with the skills necessary to function in another. It is one thing to be a good client and another to be a good friend.

Theory and Research Concerning Social Support

In the vulnerability model described earlier in this chapter, environmental factors such as social support generally act by increasing or decreasing, in some nonspecific way, a person's resistance to stress. In crisis theory the presence of social support changes the nature of the situational context of stress, with the consequence that not everyone who experiences high levels of stress is equally at risk for disorder. The role played by social support also illustrates the conceptual alternatives provided by Kelly's ecological principle of "adaptation" (see Chapter 3) and its analysis of behavior in terms of person-environment fit. Instead of being labeled "withdrawn" as a stable individual trait, for example, the chronic schizophrenic can also be described as a person who lacks a social support network (Leavy, 1983). In this way the search for specific drugs or other person-centered treatments for withdrawal can be supplemented by the potentially effective strategy of connecting the schizophrenic with others to form a network.

Reviews of the empirical literature (e.g., Broadhead et al., 1983; Cohen & Wills, 1985; Kessler et al., 1985) conclude that the presence of social support has consistently been associated with lower risk for psychological problems. Various clinical populatins such as depressives, for example, are reported to receive less support than do normal individuals. In addition, normal people experiencing high levels of stress are apparently at lower risk for disorder if they enjoy high levels of support than if they do not (i.e., the so-called buffering hypothesis). The mechanism hypothesized to operate here assumes that a lack of social support in the face of acute stress engenders negative psychological states such as anxiety, helplessness, and depression. These psychological states in turn will affect physical health either by directly influencing susceptibility to disease (involving the neuroendocrine or immune systems, for example) or by provoking certain behavioral responses (such as smoking, drinking, or failing to seek needed medical care) that actually increase risk of disease or mortality (Cohen & Wills, 1985). An interesting question that remains, however, concerns whether the amount of support and the degree of health are related in a direct monotonic fashion (i.e., where one variable increases smoothly and steadily as the other does across all of their respective values) or whether instead there is simply a "threshold" effect in which only those people who are lowest in support (i.e., those truly isolated) have a significantly elevated risk for disease or death (Blazer, 1982).

Keep in mind that as with coping, the relationship between high levels of support and successful adaptation to stressful circumstances can operate in either direction. Marital stability and a large circle of positive friendships may produce high self-esteem and competent coping, for example, but the latter assets may also explain why a particular person is able to attract and maintain many supportive relationships (Heller & Swindle, 1983). Monroe and Steiner (1986) make the following methodological point regarding studies of stress, support, and disorder:

> The measurement redundancy between stressors and support . . . may be more broadly based and pervasive than previously suggested. This is particularly so when it is recognized that a large number of the stressors in such lists are social in nature . . . and many forms of chronic stressors . . . are also essentially synonymous with certain indices of support. For instance, chronic marital difficulties, enduring problematic family relationships, poor relationships at work, and so on, all reflect chronic interpersonal discord that is not assessed as stress by the typical life event inventory yet is definitionally identical to certain procedures for quantifying social support. This problem is a complex one, and not easily resolved. (p. 33)

Broadhead et al. (1983) point out that a central problem in this literature is inconsistency among investigators in their conceptual and operational definitions of social support. In fact, as a scientific term, *social support* is probably too vague to have much value, and investigators have ended up adopting a variety of different approaches to defining the term (Mitchell & Trickett, 1980). In quantitative, or structural, terms, social support has been operationalized as the number of people in the person's "network" (i.e., family and friends with whom the person is frequently in contact), the frequency of contact with members in the network, the degree of demographic homogeneity of members, the proportion of redundant ties (sometimes called the "density" of the network), and/or the degree of reciprocity in supportive transactions among members (i.e., as givers as well as receivers of support). Qualitatively, social support is usually defined by the nature of the resources provided by one person to another, or by the specific content of social interactions (e.g., emotionally warm versus hostile and destructive). The two dimensions of support, qualitative and quantitative, are distinguishable empirically as well as conceptually, as indicated by their modest inter-correlation of .2 to .3 (Cohen & Wills, 1985).

A comprehensive review of this literature by Cohen and Wills (1985) concludes that support appears to influence well-being through both kinds of processes: (1) structural embeddedness in a network of human relationships, which may engender feelings of stability and predictability regarding one's social world, and (2) provision of the specific resources required to cope effectively with stressful situations. In this respect, Cohen and Wills argue that support has both a direct effect in enhancing the well-being of people in general and a buffering effect for people in specific high-stress situations.

The general model presented by Cohen and Wills (1985) is depicted in Figure 6-1. In this model, stress results when one appraises an event or situation as demanding a response that one is unable to make. Support is seen to mitigate the effects of stress in either of two ways. First, the presence of social support may reduce the probability that the event will be appraised as stressful in the first place. That is, the threat implied by an event, such as changing jobs, is reduced or eliminated by the perception that others can and will provide the resources necessary to adapt to this change. A second possibility is that even if the event is appraised as stressful, support may attenuate the stress reaction by offsetting the negative feelings (e.g., through increased esteem), by directly facilitating healthy coping (e.g., through material assistance), or by influencing the individual's self-perceptions (e.g., regarding self-efficacy) in a way that leads to more persistent coping efforts.

Social Support and the Model of a Family. The most significant issue in the social support literature, however, remains that of how to define this construct in valid, operational terms. One heuristic approach to definition taken by Gerald Caplan was to use the family as a prototypic source of social support. Caplan's (1976) writing about support systems depicts the *idealized* version of the family as fulfilling several functions for its members. (Note the description is of an idealized family. Caplan does not assert that every family functions in such a supportive fashion.)

First, the family collects and disseminates information about the world. Just as parents share their knowledge of the outside world with children, providing the basis for learning, even if vicariously, about various roles one might play in the world (mother, father, worker, etc.), so too people in supportive relationships share information with each other about characteristics of the world.

Second, the family serves as a feedback and guidance system to help its members

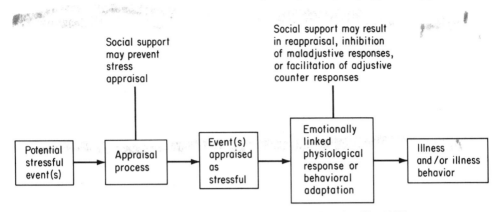

Figure 6-1. Social support and the buffering hypothesis (from Cohen & Wills, 1985).

understand their reactions to others and the reactions of others to them. Caplan notes how family members almost ritually discuss with each other the day's events. During these discussions family members help each other evaluate the significance of others' reactions and evaluate the family member's behavior in relation to the family's beliefs and values.

Third, Caplan notes that the family group is the major source for developing "the belief systems, value systems, and codes of behavior that determine an individual's understanding of the nature and meaning of the universe, of his place in it, and of the paths he should strive to travel in his life" (p. 23). Referred to as "encoding strategies and personal constructs" by Mischel (1973; see Chapter 4), this information comes from direct teaching within the family, from a deep—even if unverbalized—learning of the family's culture, and from the day-by-day living out of these values. By applying the tenets of the ideology to everyday problems, the ideology provides, as Caplan puts it, "prescriptions for wise conduct."

A fourth family function is that of serving as a guide and mediator in problem solving. Family members share each other's problems, offer each other advice and guidance, assist in finding external sources of aid, and may even make arrangements for such assistance. It is in the nature of family life for members to assist each other in dealing with the emotional and cognitive difficulties attendant upon role changes— entering school, becoming an adult, getting married, becoming a parent, experiencing loss, and the subsequent change in status when a spouse dies or a divorce takes place. Older members have gone through the changes and serve as models or transmit experience. Moreover, certain ceremonies mark the role transitions and help make the changes less ambiguous. Families share both joys and sorrows. Emotional sustenance comes from the shared experiences.

As Stanton Coit, one of the originators of the settlement house movement of the late nineteenth century put it:

> It is terrible when men draw together only in suffering; whereas those who have laughed and thought together, and joined in ideal aims, can so enter into one another's sorrow as to steal much of its bitterness away. (quoted in Levine & Levine, 1970, p. 101)

As a fifth function, family members provide material aid and concrete services to each other. Gifts, help with specific tasks, housing, financial aid, and dozens of other exchanges take place on a daily basis.

As a sixth function, the family is a haven for rest and recuperation. One can go home and lick one's wounds from the day, knowing that in the idealized family others will understand the need for peace and quiet. One can relax and be one's self within the family. There is no need to conceal or to explain the problem to anyone. All understand because all have experienced similar needs and emotions.

A seventh function of the family is to serve as a reference and control group. Family members are highly sensitive to each other's opinions about attitudes and behavior reflecting family values. As Caplan notes, family members are likely to be judgmental. Success in meeting the family's expectations is rewarded, and failing to live up to the family's expectations is punished in some fashion. Thus the family's standards are enforced, helping to maintain behavior in conformity with family standards. Whether or not the individual family member lives up to family ideals, he or she is still a family member and entitled to call on the family for assistance as a matter of right.

As an eighth function, the family provides the foundation for personal identity. As Caplan (1976) puts it:

> During the frustration and confusion of struggling with an at-present insurmountable problem, most individuals feel weak and impotent and tend to forget their continuing strengths. At such times, their family reminds them of their past achievements and validates their precrisis self-image of competence and ability to stand firm. (p. 30)

Caplan notes as a final function that family members assist each other with the task of emotional mastery. Family members ideally offer love, affection, and comfort to a member in need. By their constancy of support, family members help to counter feelings of despair or helplessness, and thus kindle hope that the difficult situation will be resolved. Moreover, in a time of crisis there may be a loss in the sense of personal worth. Family members shore up the sense of personal worth by continuing to treat the individual with love and respect and, if a loss is involved, by providing an alternative source of satisfaction.

The set of functions that Caplan specifies for the family may be thought of as dimensions of support that can be evaluated when studying support networks. His model may lead us to a more sophisticated and complex understanding of support than we have managed to achieve so far. It is also useful in understanding self-help groups, as we will see in Chapter 8.

Further Research on Social Support. Although enthusiasm for the role of social support in reducing individual vulnerability to stress-related problems remains high, research on this construct by community psychologists and others will need to address several critical substantive and methodological issues.

One of these is the problem of situational specificity. Kobasa and Puccetti (1983) report that the availability of social support from home and from work has a significant, although not always beneficial, relationship to the likelihood of stress-related illness. Perceived support at work seems to buffer the subjects from high-stress conditions in that situation, while for some executives (those low in hardiness) high family support is apparently detrimental to health. Since more stress arises at work than at home for most of these subjects, it should be no surprise that perceiving more support in the job situation is beneficial. Perhaps support at home is counterproductive because it is distracting and does not directly help the subjects adapt to their specific work situation. These findings raise new questions. Does the specific nature of support provided differ between such settings as work and home? If so, how specific must the match be between the needs elicited by particular stressful events and the supportive resources available? For example, does material aid represent the most useful form of support in response to loss of income, or can esteem or informational support be equally effective in maintaining well-being under these circumstances?

In contrast to Kobasa and Puccetti's (1983) findings of situational specificity, Kraus (1981) reports some degree of generality in the way people say they would use support in different situations. This difference in results may reflect a difference in research methods. Method-specific results present distinct problems for our understanding of process in this as well as in many other areas of psychology, and greater clarity in the methods used will likely improve our theoretical understanding of support (Cohen & Wills, 1985).

Other issues that need further study include differences involving the specific source of support (e.g., family member, natural care giver) and the extent of reciprocity within support networks. Most research to date has focused on the recipient of support, with much less known about what the phenomenon is like for the provider— for example, what the costs and benefits are to providing support for someone else. People involved in caring for elderly or ill relatives, for example, may invest hundreds of hours in this activity, with significant detrimental effects on other aspects of their lives (Perrotta, 1982). Does the ability to provide support have to be distributed symmetrically, or can different functions be "bartered" among the members of a network (e.g., informational support from one person exchanged for material aid from another)?

A further issue is our lack of understanding of the natural course of such supportive relationships and activities over time. The social-skills literature, for example, has concentrated more on the skills used in accessing support than on those useful in maintaining support, which may be different (Heller & Swindle, 1983). Furthermore, the optimal nature and amount of support provided may also vary at different times during a given stressful experience. In the case of bereavement, for example, a small, dense network may be more effective during the initial traumatic reaction, while for subsequent periods of transition to new roles a broader, looser network of relationships and sources of information is probably better (Walker, MacBride, & Vachon, 1977).

More sophisticated conceptualizations of support will be required to improve significantly our level of theoretical understanding. Heller and Swindle (1983), for example, present a comprehensive model in which social support and coping are dynamic processes that interact in a reciprocal manner over time. The possibility that support is situation-specific also suggests that, following Caplan, we might assess (independently, if possible) more than one aspect or component of support at a time (cf. Blazer, 1982) and specify the circumstances in which each component is useful. It may also lead to a better understanding of the specific mechanisms by which support operates.

Finally, most of the attention has been devoted to social support as an independent variable (i.e., what support itself hypothetically has direct causal effects on). Support as a dependent variable has not been so extensively studied. Broadhead et al. (1983)

suggest that community characteristics, social roles, coping skills, and so on, be inves-tigated prospectively for their potential contributions to the development of social support networks. We may add that there is probably a distinct advantage in studying these variables in relation to common stressors such as the death of a parent, rather than to examine the concepts globally. We have much to learn at a phenomenon level before we leap to a higher order of generality.

Summary Implications

The specific concepts of adaptation, crisis, coping, and support are very useful when we consider the "soap-opera" events affecting a significant number of Americans of all ages, in all walks of life, every day. The concepts of crisis and vulnerability open up a wider range of possible interventions and allow us to consider the possibility that a large proportion of human misery can be alleviated, even though we do not yet know whether the most serious and disabling mental illnesses can be prevented in this fashion.

We have reviewed the process of coping with the state of crisis that ensues when a person's state of adaptation is disrupted and he or she does not have the psycholog-ical, social, or material resources to produce a new adaptive response. From the per-spective outlined here, nearly everyone is assumed to be at risk for such experiences, and the ensuing affective state is not a sign of illness, but is a natural response to a specific set of circumstances. Dysphoric feelings are a signal that the individual is in a situation calling for some change in customary ways of dealing with demands or solving problems. We have noted, for purposes of analysis, that the crisis concept directs us to separate the issues into the management of affect on the one hand and solving the problem on the other. The concept of affective education and the possi-bilities for learning approaches to managing or modulating feelings are important both therapeutically and preventively.

The crisis concept also identifies two classes of crises, anticipated and unantici-pated. In general, we speak of anticipated changes when the network of relationships, the tasks to be accomplished, and the roles the individual occupies will change. Crises following such changes can be considered situational-transitional in nature, or they can be considered developmental. The important idea here is that if changes are antic-ipated, one can devise preventive strategies. Preparation, rehearsal, anticipation of feelings, warnings, preparation of resources beforehand, or practice with techniques for dealing with new problems all may be helpful in meeting anticipated challenges. A Peace Corps program created support groups before the volunteers left for a distant country. Members got to know each other, learned to discuss problems of cultural isolation and cultural shock, and were prepared to call on each other for assistance as necessary (Arnold, 1967). Sex education in high school, or training for parenting, might similarly prepare individuals for new relationships and new challenges.

In addition to preparing the individual to cope when crises can be anticipated, help can also be positioned so as to be available when the event occurs, or soon afterward. Much can be done to develop one's place in a social network when moving to a new community, for example, or when leaving an institution such as a prison or a mental hospital. Either temporary or ongoing groups can be developed, made up of people in the same situation who can support each other. Parents of retarded, diabetic, or crippled children can assist each other in coming to terms with the feelings of having a child with different needs, and in coming to terms with their own feelings about parenthood under such circumstances. In many tasks in everyday life, experienced parents can assist the less experienced in coping with the new crisis that emerges when a child is identified as having a serious, chronic disorder. Rape counseling centers dispatch workers to hospitals and police stations to help the rape victim come to terms with the problems of the different phases of this trauma. The police and hospital personnel are well positioned to be of assistance when a potential crisis is first revealed. Divorce lawyers deal with clients in crisis. Bartenders and beauticians are there when troubled people discuss their troubles (Cowen, 1982).

If general problem-solving skills exist, we can think about teaching such skills as part of the regular school curriculum. As we learn how people handle problems on an everyday basis, we can translate that learning into curricula and methods for teaching everyone. Spivack and Shure (1974), in fact, did precisely that when they created a curriculum in interpersonal problem solving that could be employed by nursery school teachers with preschool children (see the following chapter). Many other investigators have since adapted their methods for specialized populations. Intagliata (1978), for example, used the Spivack and Shure approach in teaching alcoholics who were about to be discharged from the hospital how to plan for their release and for immediate postdischarge adjustment.

The concept that crises have phases and that each phase is different is useful in devising helping strategies. It strongly suggests that the type of assistance that is useful varies at different phases in the crisis. Regarding Finkel's work, for example, if people are able on their own to convert traumatic events into growth-promoting experiences, it may be useful to consider how assistance can be provided in advance to help individuals cope effectively with problems. Alternatively, the stages of coping may themselves be understandable as adaptive responses to specific situations.

Although much of what we have said in regard to managing feelings and solving problems involves "psychological mediators," we also noted that individuals call on members of social networks to find the psychological, social, or material resources useful in achieving a new state of adaptation. The individual's ability to find and to call on members of a social network may depend on that person's understanding of reciprocity in social relationships, and it may also depend on having the social skills necessary to function in a social network. In this sense we have been discussing the interaction between psychological and situational mediators. While apparently separable at a conceptual level, they are in reality intimately intertwined (Folkman & Lazarus, 1980; Heller & Swindle, 1983; see also Holahan & Spearly, 1980).

We have contrasted the concept of neurosis with those of crisis and vulnerability to show how different concepts lead to different opportunities for intervention. The psychoanalytic view emphasizes unconscious conflict as the fundamental explanation of behavior disorder and emotional tension reduction as the primary objective of one's response to stressful circumstances. The psychoanalytic view seems to assume that effective problem solving follows automatically from mastering strong emotions. Research on natural coping by ordinary people, however, places just as much emphasis on the value of action-oriented, problem-solving responses in dealing with stress. Because we can draw these conceptual distinctions does not mean that they are empirically valid or that all of the propositions associated with crisis theory are well established. In fact, some persons, in certain conditions, by virtue of their experiences and their biological and psychological makeups, would find the types of interventions we point to here inadequate and insufficient to help them cope with their problems. Psychoanalyst Herbert Herskovitz used to distinguish between those clients who, he said, came by their problems "honestly" and those who could not be readily understood by examining their histories. The crisis concept and associated interventions may be meaningful only for those who come by their problems honestly. Our theoretical doubts, however, and the broad gaps in our knowledge should not prevent us from experimenting with different approaches when a reasonably interesting theory points the way.

Notes

1. The 6-week period calls to mind the number 40 associated with crises in the Bible (e.g., Noah on the waters for 40 days, Christ in the desert for 40 days, Moses wandering for 40 years). It also parallels the 40-week period of human gestation normally required to create and deliver, in a literal sense, a "new life."

2. It is also possible to solve a problem by redefining it. Members of Al-Anon, the organization for families of alcoholics, may join out of desperation over an inability to stop a spouse from drinking. Al-Anon teaches that one can only control one's own behavior, so that all the dysphoric feelings related to the inability to stop the other from drinking may fade. Another possible response to some crises is "need resignation." The person not admitted to graduate school, for example, may decide that he or she never really wanted to go anyway, thus divorcing the stressful event from one or more of the individual's ecologies or need states.

3. Initially researchers hypothesized that any life change, positive or negative, was sufficient to produce stress. The evidence clearly showed, however, that only negative life events predict later disorder and that, at least as measured, positive life events do not offset the effects of negative life events or correlate on their own with disorder. Dohrenwend (1978) agrees that positive life events do not correlate well with disorder, but she believes that positive life events may simply entail less life change and therefore less stress. Bloom (1984) believes the question is still an open one, and argues that it is worthwhile trying to assess the role of positive events in promoting the sense of well-being.

4. This question is researchable, however. Since the 1960s hundreds of thousands of volunteers have been trained to staff telephones in crisis centers. Most volunteers work for a few months and then leave, making room for still others to learn the skills. A huge pool exists of people with enough training to be helpful in crisis situations. Although no one has done the follow-up research to see if these people put their training to work in dealing with friends, relatives, spouses, and children, and whether or not the training and the skills are actually helpful, this research ought to be done.

References

Arnold, C. B. (1967). Culture shock and a Peace Corps mental health program. *Community Mental Health Journal, 3,* 53–60.

Atkinson, R. M., et al. (1984). Diagnosis of Post-Traumatic Stress Disorder in Viet-Nam veterans: Preliminary findings. *American Journal of Psychiatry, 141,* 694–696.

Bandura, A., (1977). Self-efficacy: Toward a unifying theory of behavioral change. *Psychological Review, 84,* 191–215.

Blazer, D. G. (1982). Social support and mortality in an elderly community population. *American Journal of Epidemiology, 115,* 684–694.

Bloom, B. L. (1984). *Community mental health: A general introduction* (2d ed.). Monterey, CA: Brooks-Cole.

Bloom, B. L., Asher, S. J., & White, S. W. (1978). Marital disruption as a stressor: A review and analysis. *Psychological Bulletin, 85,* 867–894.

Broadhead, W. E., et al. (1983). The epidemiologic evidence for a relationship between social support and health. *American Journal of Epidemiology, 117,* 521–537.

Burgess, A. W., & Holmstrom, L. L. (1979). Rape: Sexual disruption and recovery. *American Journal of Orthopsychiatry, 49,* 648–657.

Caplan, G. (1976). The family as a support system. In G. Caplan & M. Killilea (Eds.), *Support systems and mutual help: Multidisciplinary explorations.* New York: Grune & Stratton.

Cassel, J. (1976). The contribution of the environment to host resistance. *American Journal of Epidemiology, 104,* 107–123.

Chan, K. B. (1977). Individual differences in reactions to stress and their personality and situational determinants: Some implications for community mental health. *Social Science and Medicine, 11,* 89–103.

Cohen, S., & Wills, T. A. (1985). Stress, social support, and the buffering hypothesis. *Psychological Bulletin, 98,* 310–357.

Cowen, E. (1982). Help is where you find it: Four informal helping groups. *American Psychologist, 37,* 385–395.

Danish, S. J., D'Augelli, A. R., & Brock, G. W. (1976). An evaluation of helping skills training: Effects on helpers' verbal responses. *Journal of Counseling Psychology, 23,* 259–266.

D'Augelli, A. (1983). Social support networks in mental health. In J. Whittaker & J. Garberino (Eds.), *Social support networks: Informal helping in the human services.* Hawthorne, NY: Aldine.

D'Augelli, A. R., & Vallance, T. R. (1982). The helping community: Issues in the evaluation of a preventive intervention to promote informal helping. *Journal of Community Psychology, 10,* 199–209.

DeLongis, A., Coyne, J. C., Dakof, G., Folkman, S., & Lazarus, R. S. (1982). Relationships of hassles, uplifts, and major life events to health status. *Health Psychology, 1,* 119–136.

Dohrenwend, B. P., & Shrout, P. E. (1985). "Hassles" in the conceptualization and measurement of life stress variables. *American Psychologist, 40,* 780–785.

Dohrenwend, B. S. (1978). Stress and community psychology. *American Journal of Community Psychology, 6,* 1–14.

Dohrenwend, B. S., Dohrenwend, B. P., Dodson, M., & Shrout, P. E. (1984). Symptoms, hassles, social supports and life events: Problem of confounded measures. *Journal of Abnormal Psychology, 93,* 222–230.

Dooley, D., & Catalano, R. (1980). Economic change as a cause of behavioral disorder. *Psychological Bulletin, 87,* 450–468.

Ellis, T. E. (1986). Toward a cognitive therapy for suicidal individuals. *Professional Psychology: Research and Practice, 17,* 125–130.

Ewing, C. P. (1978). *Crisis intervention as psychotherapy.* New York: Oxford University Press.

Finkel, N. J. (1974). Strens and traumas: An attempt at categorization. *American Journal of Community Psychology, 2,* 265–273.

Finkel, N. J. (1975). Strens, traumas, and trauma resolution. *American Journal of Community Psychology, 3,* 172–178.

Finkel, N. J. & Jacobsen, C. A. (1977). Significant life experiences in an adult sample. *American Journal of Community Psychology, 5,* 165–177.

Fiore, J., Becker, J., & Coppel, D. B. (1983). Social network interactions: A buffer or a stress. *American Journal of Community Psychology, 11,* 423–439.

Folkman, S. (1984). Personal control and stress and coping processes: A theoretical analysis. *Journal of Personality and Social Psychology, 46,* 839–852.

Frankl, V. E. (1963). *Man's search for meaning.* New York: Washington Square Press.

Folkman, S., & Lazarus, R. S. (1980). An analysis of coping in a middle aged sample. *Journal of Health and Social Behavior, 21,* 219–239.

Golan, N. (1978). *Treatment in crisis situations.* New York: Free Press.

Goldberg, D. P. (1972). *The detection of psychiatric illness by questionnaire.* London: Oxford University Press.

Goldberg, E. L., & Comstock, G. W. (1980). Epidemiology of life events: frequency in general populations. *American Journal of Epidemiology, 111,* 736–752.

Goldenberg, I. I. (1978). *Oppression and social intervention.* Chicago: Nelson-Hall.

Gottlieb, B. H. (1983). Social support as a focus for integrative research in psychology. *American Psychologist, 38,* 278–287.

Hansell, N. (1974). *Enhancing adaptational work during service.* Paper presented at Conference on State Hospitals and Emerging Alternatives, Human Resource Institute of Boston, Newton, MA, January 17–19, 1974.

Hartman, H. (1958). *Ego psychology and the problem of adaptation.* New York: International Universities Press.

Heller, K., & Swindle, R. W. (1983). Social networks, perceived social support and coping with stress. In R. Felner, L. Jason, J. Moritsugu, & S. Farber (Eds.), *Preventive psychology: Theory, research and practice in community intervention.* New York: Pergamon Press.

Holahan, C. J., & Spearly, J. L. (1980). Coping and ecology: An integrative model for community psychology. *American Journal of Community Psychology, 8,* 671–685.

Holmes, T. H., & Rahe, R. H. (1967). The Social Readjustment Rating Scale. *Journal of Psychosomatic Research, 11,* 213–218.

Intagliata, J. (1978). Increasing the interpersonal problem-solving skills of an alcoholic population. *Journal of Consulting and Clinical Psychology, 46,* 489–498.

Iscoe, I. (1974). Community psychology and the competent community. *American Psychologist, 29,* 607–613.

Janis, I. L. (1983). The role of social support in adherence to stressful life decisions. *American Psychologist, 38,* 143–160.

Kessler, R., Price, R. H., & Wortman, C. (1985). Social factors in psychopathology: Stress, social support, and coping processes. *Annual Review of Psychology, 36,* 531–572.

Kilpatrick, D. G., Veronen, J. J., & Resick, P. A. (1979). The aftermath of rape: Recent empirical findings. *American Journal of Orthopsychiatry, 49,* 658–669.

Kobasa, S. C. (1979). Stressful life events, personality, and health: An inquiry into hardiness. *Journal of Personality and Social Psychology, 37,* 1–11.

Kobasa, S. C. O., & Puccetti, M. C. (1983). Personality and social resources in stress resistance. *Journal of Personality and Social Psychology, 45,* 839–850.

Kraus, S. (1981). A multidimensional approach to the assessment of social support. Unpublished doctoral dissertation, Department of Psychology, SUNY at Buffalo.

Kubler-Ross, E. (1969). *On death and dying.* New York: Macmillan.

Langer, E. (1983). *The psychology of control.* Beverly Hills: Sage.

Lazarus, R. S. (1966). *Psychological stress and the coping process.* New York: McGraw-Hill.

Lazarus, R. S., Delongis, A., Folkman, S., & Gruen, R. (1985). Stress and adaptational outcomes: The problem of confounded measures. *American Psychologist, 40,* 770–779.

Leavy, R. L. (1983). Social support and psychological disorder. *Journal of Community Psychology, 11,* 3–21.

Levine, M., & Levine, A. (1970). *A social history of helping services.* New York: Appleton-Century-Crofts.

Levine, M., & Perkins, D. V. (1980a). Tailor-making a life events scale. In D. Perkins (Chair), *New developments in research on life stress and social support.* Symposium presented at the American Psychological Association Convention, Montreal.

Levine, M., & Perkins, D. V. (1980b). Social setting interventions and primary prevention:

Comments on the Report of the Task Panel on Prevention to the President's Commission on Mental Health. *American Journal of Community Psychology, 8,* 147–158.

Lewis, M. S., Gottesman, D., & Gutstein, S. (1979). The course and duration of crisis. *Journal of Consulting and Clinical Psychology, 47,* 128–134.

Libow, J. A., & Doty, D. W. (1979). An exploratory approach to self-blame and self-derogation by rape victims. *American Journal of Orthopsychiatry, 49,* 670–679.

Lindemann, E. (1944). Symptomatology and management of acute grief. *American Journal of Psychiatry, 101,* 141–148.

Luepnitz, D. (1978). *Some problems and coping strategies of children of divorce: A retrospective study.* Unpublished doctoral dissertation, Department of Psychology, SUNY at Buffalo.

Lynch, J. J. (1977). *The broken heart.* New York: Basic Books.

Meichenbaum, D., & Jaremko, M. E. (1983). *Stress reduction and prevention.* New York: Plenum.

Mischel, W. (1973). Toward a cognitive social learning reconceptualization of personality. *Psychological Review, 80,* 252–283.

Mitchell, R. E., & Trickett, E. J. (1980). Social networks as mediators of social support: An analysis of the effects and determinants of social networks. *Community Mental Health Journal, 16,* 27–44.

Monroe, S. M., & Steiner, S. C. (1986). Social support and psychopathology: Interrelations with preexisting disorder, stress and personality. *Journal of Abnormal Psychology, 95,* 29–39.

Mumford, E., Schlesinger, H. J., & Glass, G. V. (1982). The effects of psychological intervention on recovery from surgery and heart attacks: An analysis of the literature. *American Journal of Public Health, 72,* 141–151.

Parad, H. J. (ed.). (1965). *Crisis intervention: Selected readings.* New York: Family Service Association of America.

Pearlin, L. I., & Schooler, C. (1978). The structure of coping. *Journal of Health and Social Behavior, 19,* 2–21.

Perkins, D. V. (1982). The assessment of stress using life events scales. In L. Goldberger & S. Breznitz (Eds.), *Handbook of stress.* New York: Free Press.

Perrotta, P. (1982). *The experience of caring for an elderly family member.* Unpublished doctoral dissertation, Department of Psychology, SUNY at Buffalo.

Phipps-Yonas, S. (1980). Teenage pregnancy and motherhood: A review of the literature. *American Journal of Orthopsychiatry, 50,* 403–431.

Rabkin, J. G., & Streuning, E. L. (1976). Life events, stress and illness. *Science, 194,* 1013–1020.

Rahe, R. H., & Arthur, R. J. (1978). Life change and illness studies: Past history and future directions. *Journal of Human Stress, 4,* 3–15.

Sarbin, T. R. (1970). A role theory perspective for community psychology: The structure of social identity. In D. Adelson & B. Kalis (Eds.), *Community psychology and mental health: Perspectives and challenges.* Scranton, PA: Chandler.

Selye, H. (1956). *The stress of life.* New York: McGraw-Hill.

Silber, E., Hamburg, D. A., Coelho, G. V., Murphy, E. B., Rosenberg, M., & Pearlin, L. I. (1961). Adaptive behavior in competent adolescents. *Archives of General Psychiatry, 5,* 354–365.

Silverman, D. C. (1978). Sharing the crisis of rape: Counseling the mates and families of victims. *American Journal of Orthopsychiatry, 48,* 166-173.

Slaikeu, K. A. (1984). *Crisis intervention: A handbook for practice and research.* Boston: Allyn and Bacon.

Smith, R. E., Johnson, J. H., & Sarason, I. G. (1978). Life change, the sensation seeking motive, and psychological distress. *Journal of Consulting and Clinical Psychology, 46,* 348–349.

Spielberger, C., Gorsuch, R., & Lushene, R. (1970). *The State-Trait Anxiety Inventory.* Palo Alto, CA: Consulting Psychologists Press.

Spivack, G., & Shure, M. B. (1974). *Social adjustment of young children*. San Francisco: Jossey Bass.

Spivack, G., & Shure, M. B. (1985). ICPS and beyond: Centripetal and centrifugal forces. *American Journal of Community Psychology, 13,* 226–243.

Sutherland, S., & Scherl, D. J. (1970). Patterns of response among victims of rape. *American Journal of Orthopsychiatry, 40,* 503–511.

Taylor, S. E. (1983). Adjustment to threatening events: A theory of cognitive adaptation. *American Psychologist, 38,* 1161–1173.

Tebes, J. A. (1983). Stigma and mental disorder: A review and analysis. Unpublished doctoral qualifying paper, Department of Psychology, SUNY at Buffalo.

Tebes, J. A., & Perkins, D. V. (1984). Converting stress to positive mental health: Evidence from students coping with parental death. Paper presented at the Eastern Psychological Association Convention, Baltimore.

Turkington, C. (1985). What price friendship? The darker side of social networks. *APA Monitor, 16,* 38–41.

Walker, K. N., MacBride, A., & Vachon, M. L. S. (1977). Social support networks and the crisis of bereavement. *Social Science and Medicine, 11,* 35–41.

7

Prevention in Mental Health

The current importance of prevention in mental health is due in no small part to the interest in the subject generated by the 1978 President's Commission on Mental Health. Professional interest in prevention arose during the deliberations of the earlier Joint Commission on Mental Health and Mental Illness. The need for preventive programs was apparent to the participants, but the need to revitalize and to restructure the state hospital system in the post-World War II period took precedence. Preventive thinking was represented in the requirement that federally funded community mental health centers have consultation and education units, but beyond that there was little professional and political interest in prevention. In the years between the Joint Commission's report (1961) and the formation of the President's Commission, however, the prevention enterprise had moved ahead largely as a result of dedicated professional advocates such as George Albee, Emory Cowen, and Gerald Caplan, among many others, and advocates within government such as Steven Goldston. In addition, as Goldston (1986) points out, respected investigators had made progress in conceptualizing issues in prevention and in demonstrating the feasibility of programs in prevention. The Task Panel on Prevention, working for the President's Commission, had a more solid base for developing its recommendations because of the work of a diverse group of researchers.

The Task Panel on Prevention (1978) contributed a report that defined the rationale for and evidence justifying primary prevention as a federal initiative in mental health. The recommendations of the report were adopted by the President's Commission and written into legislation by Congress during the last days of the Carter administration. Interest in prevention research and funding for new initiatives in prevention were continued under the Reagan administration. Several themes developed in the Task Panel report have become the linchpins of current thinking in prevention. We will refer to those ideas throughout this chapter.

As we noted in Chapter 2 (see also Levine, 1981), the history of efforts to reduce the prevalence of mental and emotional problems in this country is largely one of treating such problems in individuals after they have arisen. For the most part, there had been little interest in proactive, preventive efforts. Professional and governmental factors combined to produce incentives, monetary and otherwise, that encouraged treatment based on the medical model (Levine & Levine, 1970). Cowen (1980) notes that the history of psychology's efforts in this area might well have been different. Indeed, from time to time various authorities argued that prevention should be given more emphasis. Spaulding and Balch (1983) cite the work of Clifford Beers and the mental hygiene movement and the child guidance clinics of the 1920s and 1930s (see also Levine & Levine, 1970) as examples of earlier efforts with a preventive thrust. Crisis theory as developed by Lindemann and others as early as the 1940s (see the previous chapter) provided a beginning for contemporary thinking about prevention. The Joint Commission on Mental Illness and Health (1961) discussed the desirability, if not the necessity, for programs in prevention. More recently, both the 1963 Community Mental Health Centers Act (Bloom, 1977) and the *Report of the President's Commission on Mental Health* (President's Commission on Mental Health, 1978) highlighted prevention as a major strategy for dealing with mental health problems in this country.

A moment's reflection may suggest why prevention has had this appeal from time to time. One reason is certainly the "numbers" problem we examined in Chapter 1—given the way psychological problems have traditionally been defined, there are not now and presumably never will be enough trained professionals to meet the mental health needs of most communities. A second impetus for prevention, mentioned in Chapter 2, has been dissatisfaction with the effectiveness of traditional interventions (Heller & Monahan, 1977) that seek to remove pathology, and the growing appeal of strategies that increase competence, adaptiveness, and other positive states and conditions (Albee, 1980).

A third impetus toward prevention—for some the most compelling of all—is that prevention may be much more cost-effective than treatment. Consider an illustration provided by Swift (1980, pp. 233–234). In 1978 the cost of one year of inpatient care for a single mentally retarded individual in the state of Wisconsin was $24,000. That same $24,000 invested in prevention would have bought either (1) screening for lead poisoning for 414 children at $58 each, including two blood tests, medical treatment, and a check of the child's home environment, *or* (2) genetic consultation, ultrasonic scanning, amniocentesis, and chromosomal analysis for 80 "at-risk" pregnant women, at $300 each. If only a single case of mental retardation were prevented among the individuals screened, the prevention program would break even after just one year. If as many as two cases were prevented, the program would be $24,000 ahead after just one year. Over the 50–55-year lifetime of a retarded person, the savings would amount to over $1 million, even if only a single case of mental retardation were prevented.

Why, then, has prevention enjoyed only sporadic popularity among mental health professionals? Some critics (e.g., Lamb & Zusman, 1979) take the position that the existing knowledge base regarding the nature and causes of psychopathology is still inadequate for effective prevention. That the state of this knowledge base may also be insufficient to justify treatment apparently poses no paradox for these critics. They believe we are obligated to provide care for those in need, and that resources devoted to uncertain efforts at prevention will take away from the scarce pool of resources currently available for treatment.

Others believe that making an effort at prevention is worthwhile despite the uncertainty of the knowledge base. Bloom (1965) points out that we can learn from the eighteenth-century "miasma" theorists. During the 1700s and early 1800s, long before the development of germ theory, influential citizens successfully advanced their theory that a whole host of health problems were direct results of the foul-smelling air that permeated swampy, refuse-strewn areas of towns and villages. Draining the swamps and covering or removing the malodorous waste materials greatly reduced the prevalence of disease in those areas and lent great respect to the miasmatists and their theory of disease. That the theory was vague and inaccurate in terms of its understanding of cause and effect did not prevent it from being successful. The great progress made since then in all but eradicating cholera, typhoid fever, malaria, smallpox, and other diseases probably has more to do with general improvements in sanitation, nutrition, and overall standard of living than with advances in the treatment of these diseases (see Leavitt, 1982, for a discussion of the significance of social and political factors in the prevention of infectious diseases).

Mental health professionals are in a similar situation today, facing overwhelming numbers of people in need of help with no handy germ theory to guide and to maximize the effectiveness and efficiency of their efforts. We do have other theories with some empirical support that offer directions for preventive efforts. Bloom (1977) says that current efforts to reduce stress and increase coping are quite analogous to the work of the miasma theorists, and may have the same reasonable degree of success if put into practice in the same deliberate and conscientious way.

Another constraint on the practice of prevention has been the lack of formal training available to mental health professionals in this area (Cowen, 1977). Without the decisions made following World War II to train psychologists in Veterans Administration hospitals and other medical settings (Sarason, 1981), professional psychology might well have come to look more like education than medicine, and to specialize more in prevention than in treatment. Psychology's roots in the study of learning, cognition, social behavior, and normal development give its subject matter much more relevance to positive, growth-producing changes than to the treatment of "diseases" through a medical model.

Prevention has not been popular among professionals and the public because of the necessity to confront social and political factors in defining the solutions to social problems (Levine, 1981). A strategy of prevention generally implies environmental in addition to individual explanations for the causes of psychological disorders, and a firm belief in the value of large-scale, active intervention using public resources instead of more passive efforts by smaller private interests. Implementing preventive programs requires the mental health professional to take social and political action designed to achieve change. Many mental health professionals do not include such activities within their definition of a proper professional role, although historical precedent for an activist role in the mental health professions is found in the settlement house movement (Levine & Levine, 1970).

The general congruence of the assumptions of prevention with those of community psychology makes prevention a major focus of interest for us. In the rest of this chapter we review some of the basic concepts and research underlying the practice of prevention in mental health. We will give particular attention to examples of the many kinds of prevention programs aimed at elementary and preschool children.

Basic Concepts in Prevention

Many contemporary ideas regarding prevention are rooted in the public health movement that developed in this country during the nineteenth century (Bloom, 1977). We will continue to use the language of prevention that developed in public health, despite our misgivings that the disease model for which the concepts are most appropriate is not fully applicable to the problems of living that occupy the attention of workers in the fields of mental health and social problems. As yet, the field of prevention in mental health has not developed its own language and concepts, although we believe the field would be better off if it did. In our view, the core idea of prevention is to take action beforehand to limit or avoid an undesirable consequence or state of affairs in the future. The undesirable state of affairs does not necessarily have to be an illness.

In examining the public health model of prevention, we should understand what is meant by the *incidence* and the *prevalence* of a disorder. The incidence of a disorder is the number of new cases that arise in the population of interest during a specified interval of time, usually one year. Its prevalence is the number of cases in existence at a specified point in time, and reflects both the incidence rate and the duration of the disorder. Note that prevalence will be reduced if incidence is reduced, and it will also be reduced if treatment reduces the duration of an episode of disorder.

Gerald Caplan (1964) is widely credited with introducing the distinctions among primary, secondary, and tertiary prevention strategies in mental health. Tertiary prevention does not reduce the prevalence of a disorder; tertiary efforts are directed toward ameliorating its long-term symptoms and ramifications. A common example in medicine is fitting an amputee with a prosthetic device to alleviate his or her deficits in mobility, with consequent improvements in independence, self-esteem, and so on. The individual adapts better as a result of the prosthetic device and training in its use, but would continue to be counted in determining the prevalence of amputees. In teaching mentally retarded individuals to dress themselves, care for themselves physically, travel in the community, or learn some vocationally useful skills, the social disability associated with retardation will be reduced, even though the individual may still be counted as a case of mental retardation in an epidemiological survey. Perhaps the best example of tertiary prevention in mental health has been the large-scale deinstitutionalization of psychiatric inpatients to community settings (cf. Levine, 1981), which was accomplished in part as an effort to alleviate the "social breakdown syndrome" (Gruenberg, 1974) of apathy, withdrawal, poor hygiene, and lack of attention to personal appearance following many years of psychiatric hospitalization for psychosis and other chronic disorders. Many, but not all, who have been spared long years of hospitalization in custodial institutions do not show this extreme level of loss of social functioning, even though they may continue to show other symptoms of a diagnosed disorder. Tertiary prevention has otherwise not attracted much interest from mental health professionals interested in prevention, probably because in practice tertiary prevention activities are nearly impossible to distinguish from those involved in treatment and rehabilitation of psychiatric clients.

Secondary prevention is defined as reducing the prevalence of a disorder by drastically curtailing its duration, typically through early case finding and prompt intervention. Secondary prevention is common in medicine, and includes such tests as the "Pap smear" for cervical cancer, or the tuberculin test for tuberculosis, along with appropriate therapeutic steps when a "positive" diagnosis is made. In the mental health field, crisis intervention, juvenile delinquency diversion, employee assistance programs, and psychological screening of elementary school children (e.g., Cowen et al., 1975) are all throught to have secondary preventive effects. Programs like these are "preventive" in the sense that *prevalence* is reduced if a case is successfully treated early and the duration of the disorder is shortened. The rate of *new* cases (i.e., the incidence) presumably is not affected, however.[1]

Finally, when the effect of an intervention is actually to reduce the incidence of a disorder, the program is a primary preventive one. By definition, after the primary prevention intervention, the program's targets must show no overt signs of the disorder. Health care, vaccinations to prevent polio or measles, or fluoridation of water to prevent dental caries are clear examples of primary prevention. As yet, we do not have examples of preventive programs that have the power of vaccinations. By adopting the public health model and its language, however, we risk inadvertently over-promising results, with the consequence that prevention programs may lose public support when our interventions cannot deliver results as powerful as those implied in our analogy. In mental health we might consider social support groups for the newly widowed to prevent depression or training in cognitive problem solving to prevent school failure as examples of primary prevention. The goal of such programs is to act before the manifestation of an undesirable end-state to prevent its appearance.

As valuable as it is from the viewpoint of reducing social costs, tertiary prevention does not present the dramatic potential that many see in pimary prevention efforts. Historically, secondary prevention has had considerably more appeal to mental health professionals, but at the moment it is also hampered by some fundamental limitations. We can benefit from examining secondary prevention in some detail before reviewing the strategy drawing the greatest attention at present: primary prevention.

Secondary Prevention

The Primary Mental Health Project

The best known among secondary prevention programs in mental health is the Primary Mental Health Project (PMHP) conducted over the past 30 years in Rochester, New York, by Emory Cowen and his associates. The program has been widely praised because of its innovativeness, durability, and devotion to documenting its effects. It has successfully exported its approach to school systems all over the country. We will examine briefly the background of the PMHP and some of its most salient empirical findings. Because its developers have studied it carefully, their experience sheds considerable light on the practice of secondary prevention in mental health. This review is based largely on the information in the book by Cowen, Trost, Lorion, Dorr, Izzo, and Isaacson (1975) entitled *New Ways in School Mental Health.*

During the 1950s Cowen, a clinical psychologist, observed that existing services for mental health problems (i.e., treatment) did not seem adequately effective and were limited in the size and nature of the population they served. He saw that the early school histories of many children who later had problems in adapting to life presented clear signs of the trouble to come, which suggested that intervention might be possible during a child's elementary school years, prior to the onset of full-fledged disorder.

Cowen and his colleagues launched the PMHP as an early detection and intervention program for children in the primary grades of a Rochester elementary school. All first-graders in this school were assessed on the basis of classroom observations, psychological tests, and interviews with their mothers concerning the family's history and living situation. Based on this information, a clinical judgment was rendered by the PMHP team that resulted in each child being classified into one of two groups: those showing signs of psychological problems or potential problems (overall, about 33%), or those showing no problems and no specific indication of any future problems (about 67%). Children in the "incipient problem" group were identified to project staff by having a red tag clipped to their folders, thus accounting for the common reference to this project as the "Red Tag" study. The project is classified as secondary prevention because all of the children were already showing some signs of problems. Had the children been selected on the basis of characteristics that were not themselves considered problem behaviors, but nonproblem characteristics predictive of future problems (e.g., the children's parents were dropouts from school), the project would have been considered one in primary prevention. Two comparison schools, demographically similar to the target school, were selected for later use in evaluating long-term preventive effects on children in the target school (see later). PMHP staff did not do any formal preassessment of children nor did they provide any intervention in the other two schools, which were to serve as comparisons or controls.

The initial intervention included informal conferences, meetings, and educational efforts for parents, and teacher-led afterschool groups in baking, woodworking, and so on for children in the experimental school. An evaluation of this early phase of the PMHP reported by Cowen, Izzo, Miles, Telschow, Trost, and Zax (1963) found that as a group, the children in the experimental school had lower grades and poorer attendance, but less anxiety, than did those in the two control schools. Many other comparisons were not significant, and overall the results were essentially inconclusive.

Other analyses involving only those children in the experimental school found that the Red Tag children remained below the others in average achievement, teacher behavior rating, peer and self sociometric ratings, and overall adjustment as assessed by the PMHP team. The children labeled earlier were still doing worse, indicating that (1) it was possible to differentiate children who would later have adjustment difficulties as early as the first grade at a better than chance level, and (2) the intervention program as then implemented had not succeeded in eliminating this deficit, in the sense of bringing the Red Tag children to the same level as others at the point of follow-up several years later.

The program's designers and sponsors understood that even though results were equivocal, a period of research and development was necessary in order to develop more effective intervention. (We should recognize that we can expect to invest a great deal in research and development before a working product emerges. We often anticipate that the development of a weapons system will result in huge cost overruns. We should have similar expectations for innovative mental health interventions.) PMHP's staff reviewed the program's findings and how it had been operating. They developed a revised intervention program that pioneered the use of alternative mental health resources such as homemakers and college students. These paraprofessionals made it possible to provide much more direct help inexpensively to children in the experimental school on a 1:1 or small-group basis. By the next evaluation of PMHP (Cowen, Zax, Izzo, & Trost, 1966), children in the experimental school were doing significantly better on average than children in the control schools on about half the outcomes measured, including grades, achievement test scores, teacher ratings, and self-reported anxiety. On the other hand, within the experimental school the Red Tag children continued to fare more poorly than the others on nearly all measures. Ironically, although children who happened to be seen once per week did not differ initially from those seen twice per week, those seen less often were most improved at the time of a later follow-up study (Lorion, Cowen, & Kraus, 1974).

We cannot be sure what explanation for these results is most valid. Cowen and others have suggested that all children benefited from the presence of PMHP, including those who were competent and well adjusted to begin with, and that without PMHP the Red Tag children would have fallen even further behind. The study did not include a nontreated Red Tag group, so the latter conclusion cannot be assessed. Levine and Graziano (1972), on the other hand, raised the theoretical possibility that being singled out as "high risk" may not have been entirely to the benefit of the Red Tag children. Recall our discussion of labeling theory in Chapter 5; the Red Tag designation with all that followed may have heightened the sensitivity of teachers (and even other children) to the difficulties many Red Tag children were having in school, making the teachers and others uncomfortable and prone to make responses that exacerbated the situation. In addition, we must account for the paradoxical result that given equal levels of difficulty initially, children seen *least* often in the PMHP programs had improved the most by the time of follow-up. Possibly the children seen least often constituted a subsample of children with greater personal resources, or whose initial behavior pattern did not reflect disorder so much as normal developmental variation. The impact of PMHP was obviously complex; the data permit us to speculate about possible negative as well as positive effects on the children.

What relationship has been found to exist between the PMHP assessment of children in the first grade and the incidence of *treated* psychological disorder later? One of the most interesting studies in the lengthy series on PMHP (Cowen, Pederson, Babigian, Izzo, & Trost, 1973) used the psychiatric register of Monroe County (where Rochester is located) to determine the number of children in all groups who received psychiatric treatment in community clinics during the period up to 11–13 years following first grade. The proportions of children from the experimental and control schools in the register did not differ significantly (7–8% in each), indicating that PMHP did not noticeably prevent the occurrence of treated psychiatric conditions in the experimental school as a whole. One interesting difference between schools was that children from the experimental school who received treatment did so, on average, over two years earlier than did control schoolchildren who received treatment (12.59 versus 14.88 years of age, respectively), perhaps because of the sensitizing effect of PMHP's early case-finding and referral activities.

Originally one-third of the children who entered the experimental school were identified as members of the Red Tag group, for whom future problems of adjustment were predicted. Of the children from the experimental school who turned up on the psychiatric register, two-thirds were from the Red Tag group. Compared to their numbers in the overall population of the experimental school, Red Tag children were overrepresented on the roles of the psychiatric register. Only 19% of all Red Tag children turned up in the register, however, which means that 81% of those predicted to have problems were not treated. If we assume that those Red Tag children who later received treatment were "true positives" and those Red Tag children who did not receive treatment were "false positives" (see later), the false positive rate was 81%. Most of those who were identified as potentially having problems did not go on to receive (need?) treatment. (We are assuming now that the Red Tag treatment program did not result in so much improvement in the 81% that they did not need further treatment. It is more likely the predictor was in error than that the treatment program was highly effective.)

In sum, PMHP has definitely demonstrated statistically significant success in predicting high versus low risk for later maladjustment in children as young as the first grade of elementary school. The effectiveness of its various intervention programs at reducing the degree of maladjustment shown by the high-risk children is more open to debate. On a positive note, we would point out that the PMHP has continued to evolve over time in keeping up with advances in mental health intervention practices. It has adopted programs in competency training (Gesten et al., 1982), and it is studying children of divorce, a group at risk for emotional disturbance in the early years of a separation and divorce (Felner, Stolberg, & Cowen, 1975; Felner, Farber, Ginter, Boike, & Cowen, 1980; Pedro-Carroll & Cowen, 1985). PMHP's durability is testimony to the fact that it is perceived as helpful by those who sponsor it, despite the weaker formal evidence of its effectiveness. The voluminous record of publication by Cowen and his associates has been indispensable in clarifying the important issues in the practice of secondary prevention. We are now in a position to examine these issues more closely.

Limitations in the Practice of Secondary Prevention

Secondary prevention is often defined as "early detection and treatment." Both the method of early detection and the delivery of early treatment raise significant practical questions. We can also raise questions about the utility of secondary prevention efforts in mental health as prevention. We see problems with the degree of accuracy of detection currently achievable and the undesirable consequences of inaccurately labeling someone an incipient "case" of pathology. We rarely understand the natural course of a disorder over time well enough to identify its incipient stage, yet the incipient stage, assuming there is one, may be the crucial period for secondary prevention. What we think of as an incipient stage may actually be a "normal" variation in behavior. If so, the intervention at that point may be wasted, or worse. On the other hand, by the time we are able to identify an "early" case, the problem may already exist in a more entrenched and resistant stage. The intervention may thus come too late. With our lack of knowledge at the conceptual level, we should not be surprised that "early detection" of specific disorders is often fraught with difficulty.

Accuracy of detection is judged in terms of the rates of two types of errors in classification: "false positives" and "false negatives."[2] One false positive occurs when an individual is assessed as an incipient case of disorder when in fact he or she will never develop the disorder, even if left untreated (e.g., the 81% of Red Tag children who were never treated). Conversely, one false negative represents the *failure* to detect an incipient case when in fact that individual will eventually suffer the disorder. All those children from the experimental school who were *not* Red Tag and who were later treated would be counted as false negatives.

Aside from knowing the rates of these two types of errors, it is also relevant to know what *value* one assigns to each type of error in evaluating the usefulness of a detection procedure. Let us hypothetically assume that our intervention procedure is completely effective for 100% of cases in which it is applied, but is relatively costly and results in some degree of stigmatization of the individuals to whom it is delivered. The accuracy of detection in Table 7-1 is based approximately on data reported by

Table 7-1. Accuracy of Detection[a] and Costs per Individual for a Hypothetical Secondary Prevention Program

% / $1,000		Actual Classification		
		Case	Noncase	Total
	Case	6% +$452,000	27% −$48,000	33%
Predicted classification				
	Noncase	3% −$500,000	64% $0	67%
Total		9%	91%	100% −$84,000[b]

[a]Data on accuracy of detection from Table 1 of Cowen, Pederson et al. (1973, p. 442).

[b]Following Blumberg (1957), *Operations Research,* 351–360, the net value of any screening procedure equals $V_{tp}TP + V_{tn}TN + V_{fp}FP, + V_{fn}FN$, where TP is the number of true positives, TN the true negatives, FP the number of false positives, FN the number of false negatives, V_{tp} the value of one true positive, V_{tn} the value of one true negative, V_{fp} the value of one false positive, and V_{fn} the value of one false negative. In the hypothetical example, the net loss is $84,000 for each 100 individuals screened (see text).

Cowen, Pederson et al. (1973). Suppose we estimate that the occurrence of one "case" of disorder costs the community $500,000 in services and lost productivity over the individual's lifetime. One false negative, a case which our detection procedure misses, thus costs us the $500,000 we would have saved had we accurately detected the case and effectively treated the person. A true positive case, one we detect accurately and treat effectively, produces the savings and productivity of a healthy individual whose disorder was prevented, minus the cost of applying the intervention and of the stigma accrued by the individual. If we assume the latter two costs total $48,000, the value to the community of one true positive successfully treated is thus $452,000. A false positive case contributes no positive value, because the individual would not have become a case, and costs the community the value of the intervention and the associated stigma. Finally, a true negative costs nothing. No intervention is applied, but we gain nothing over what the value of a single healthy individual is anyway. Combining these hypothetical cost figures with the percentages in Table 7-1, we see that for each 100 individuals screened using this procedure, the community loses $84,000, even with the unrealistic assumption that the intervention is 100% effective.

A detection procedure only as good as the one presented is simply not adequate from a hypothetical cost-benefit point of view. As the cost of the detection procedure and the rate of false positives come down, however, the relative value of secondary prevention increases sharply as long as we continue to assume that the intervention is highly effective. The cost of administering a detection procedure can be reduced by integrating it within routine contacts with the target group (e.g., through schools, family physicians, and churches).

Reducing the rate of false positives is an empirical problem. It can be a difficult task when the base rate of a disorder is less than the rate of cases the identification procedure can reliably detect. Take the prevention of suicide, for example. The highest rate reported by Miller, Coombs, Leeper, and Barton (1984) was 52.8 per 100,000 of population of white males over the age of 65. Under these circumstances no detection procedure would improve the error rate (false positives plus false negatives) over simply predicting that no one would ever commit suicide. If we predicted no suicide for each white male over 65 coming to our attention, we would be wrong only 52.8 times in 100,000 and right 99,947.2 times. When the base rate is low, any predictor, unless perfectly valid, would always make a large number of false positive errors, and in addition would make some false negative errors. Even though a history of a previous suicide attempt is a valid predictor of subsequent suicide, the base rate for suicide attempters is still low. Of hospitalized suicide attempters, 2% committed suicide within 1 year after hospitalization and 10% committed suicide within 10 years (Weiss & Scott, 1974). Even restricting ourselves to the population of suicide attempters, we would have a high false positive rate if we used information about previous suicide attempts as the predictor. If the preventive treatment was drastic, such as hospitalizing involuntarily everyone we predicted would commit suicide, we would be hospitalizing many more people unnecessarily than we would save, and we would still miss some who would commit suicide when our predictor said they would not. Unfortunately, given our present state of knowledge, we would be unable to differentiate the true positives. Our inability to predict accurately creates important dilemmas, not only for prevention, but also for clinical decision making in contexts where predictions are important.

We should point out that the social costs of false positives and false negatives are not absolute, but depend on the particular disorder. A person would presumably rather be told he might have cancer when in fact he does not (i.e., be a false positive), for example, than *not* be told he might have cancer when in fact he does (false negative). That particular condition can be studied and ruled out with little social cost to the individual. If the diagnosis is missed, on the other hand, the person might lose the opportunity for effective treatment. The label *mental illness,* however, carries with it stigma and other social losses. The action of holding a person for further study of mental illness carries with it social costs that are not present with other medical diagnoses.

Leaving aside issues of assessment, there are also several requirements for an intervention if we are to justify secondary prevention. In presenting the detection example, we assumed the existence of a universally effective intervention. Obviously no such procedure is currently available in mental health. In fact, a serious ethical issue is raised if we can detect disorder but can do nothing about it. Should we inform the person with the disorder or the person at risk and thereby increase anxiety when we have no treatment to offer? Is it better to ignore the signs of incipient disorder and let nature take its course?

Even assuming that highly effective interventions are someday available, they will have to meet two further requirements. Because the *timing* of the intervention is crucial in secondary prevention (i.e., the target may be an "incipient" case for only a limited time before more entrenched pathology sets in), the intervention must be aggressively delivered to reach enough cases to have a measurable effect on prevalence. Although some authorities assert that crisis intervention has a secondary preventive effect, its typically "passive" format (i.e., where clients must locate the professional service provider, not vice versa) effectively prevents it from having an impact on very many people. In our survey of life events among college students, for example, we found that less than 1% of those who experienced stressful life events ever used a hotline or a crisis service (Levine & Perkins, 1980a). Many secondary prevention efforts (e.g., juvenile delinquency diversion or referrals to employee assistance programs for alcoholism) probably occur too late in the development of the disorder to test the benefits postulated for early intervention.

Table 7-2. Screening Procedures in Secondary Prevention

Criteria to be met before applying any screening procedure[a]

1. The condition in question should be an important health problem (i.e., should be sufficiently prevalent).
2. The natural history of the condition should be adequately understood.
3. There should be a recognizable latent or early symptomatic stage.
4. There should be a suitable test or examination (i.e., screening should validly and reliably discriminate cases from noncases and borderline cases, and the cost of screening should be reasonable).
5. The test should be acceptable to the population being screened and should not harm the individual being screened.
6. There should be an acceptable treatment for individuals diagnosed as having a latent or early symptomatic condition (i.e., prognosis should be improved if the disease is detected early and treated.)
7. Facilities for diagnosis and treatment should be available.
8. There should be an agreed-upon policy on whom to treat as patients.
9. The cost of case finding (including diagnosis and treatment) should be economically balanced in relation to health care expenditures as a whole.
10. Case finding should be a continuing process.

[a]Adapted from J. M. G. Wilson & G. Junger (1968), Principles and practice of screening for disease, *Public Health Papers, 34*, Geneva: World Health Organization.

The second requirement is that the intervention must be deliverable *economically* and in *quantity* if it is to make a serious dent in the prevalence of disorder. The limits of lengthy, costly 1:1 interventions should be obvious by now; simply too many potential cases are in existence for any kind of 1:1 approach to deliver a cost-effective secondary prevention service. Bloom's (1984) assertion that brief one- or two-session psychotherapy has positive lasting effects is interesting in this context, but we have seen no demonstration of its utility in early intervention and no follow-up to show any preventive effect. Secondary prevention suffers from some of the same conceptual and practical problems that limit the social utility of psychotherapy and other variants on the medical model (see Chapter 1).

Many of these issues regarding secondary prevention are summarized in Table 7-2. In light of them, we are not surprised that the present status of secondary prevention in mental health is unclear. We may find valid humanitarian arguments for making treatment readily available, and for making it available at the earliest indications that someone is having difficulties, but the promise of a systematic decrease in the prevalence of disorder is not one of the stronger arguments. Primary prevention, which we examine next, currently dominates the interest of prevention advocates (cf. Task Panel on Prevention, 1978).

Primary Prevention

The historical rationale supporting primary prevention is clear and widely acknowledged: disorders are not brought under control by training more professionals to treat individual cases, but by pursuing strategies that reduce the number of new cases to arise in the first place. Public health has accomplished the primary prevention of physical diseases through both specific (e.g., polio vaccines) and nonspecific (e.g., improved sanitation) measures. The broad success of large-scale improvements in sanitation, nutrition, and the overall standard of living has led authorities on prevention in mental health (e.g., Albee, 1980) to suggest that from a preventive viewpoint, extensive and lasting benefits might be expected from large-scale social system changes and improvements in the quality of life, even though such efforts are not specifically targeted at reducing the incidence of a specific disorder. Price (1974) has noted that while treatment is often more effective the more specific it becomes, prevention may be more effective the *less* disease-specific it is.

Primary prevention unquestionably has philosophical appeal. Actual implementation of preventive interventions is more complicated. The scope of possible targets and interventions is exceedingly broad, a dilemma faced by Kessler and Albee (1975) in preparing a chapter on primary prevention for the *Annual Review of Psychology.*

> We found ourselves constantly writing references and ideas on scraps of paper and emptying our pockets each day of notes on the primary prevention relevance of children's group homes, titanium paint, parent-effectiveness training, consciousness raising, Zoom, Sesame Street, the guaranteed annual wage, legalized abortion, school integration, limits on international cartels, unpolished rice, free prenatal clinics, antipollution laws, a yoghurt and vegetable diet, free VD clinics, and a host of other topics. Nearly everything, it appears, has implications for primary prevention, for reducing emotional disturbance, for strengthening and fostering mental health.

This surplus of relevant issues has helped to make "prevention" a construct that is very loosely and widely applied. Cowen (1983) has argued for a much tighter definition of primary prevention, which he would restrict to programs that (1) are directed at groups, not at individuals, who are (2) well, not disordered, and (3) receive an intervention that rests on a sufficient knowledge base to allow for specific goals to be articulated, for a useful evaluation plan, and so on.

Important though this definitional debate is, useful proposals such as Cowen's do not solve all the problems inherent in the concept of prevention. Any deliberate intervention into the lives of normal, healthy groups, for example, raises questions about priorities and values. Accepting that our resources are not limitless, money spent on preventing future problems is money that is not available to help people already in difficulty. The counterargument asserts that diverting resources to prevention is worthwhile because of the potential for great savings in human misery and in dollars.

Our concepts of privacy and freedom also enter into the discussion. Once we open the door to direct intervention in the lives of healthy individuals, where would such intrusions stop? How long would it be before any arbitrarily defined condition of "risk" could qualify a person for "preventive" correction? Consider, for example, the following "high-risk" groups targeted for preventive interventions in the 1880s: "children of the insane, isolated persons, dark-haired persons, and the idle rich" (Spaulding & Balch, 1983, p. 60). Our review of social labeling processes in Chapter 5 shows that assessments of risk can be influenced by social and political factors as much as by physiological and behavioral ones. The issue is far from idle. Ewing (1985) suggests that a recent U.S. Supreme Court decision, *Schall v. Martin* (1984), may provide a legal basis for involuntary preventive treatment for juveniles predicted to commit future acts of delinquency. We do abrogate some individual freedom in the name of public health when we require children to have vaccinations to enter school. How far do we wish to go in abrogating individual freedom or privacy by intervening in people's lives in the name of public mental health?

Furthermore, our intervention may well have unintended negative consequences, since procedures we believe to be powerful enough to permanently change a person's behavior in one direction are presumably capable of significant harmful effects as well. This kind of effect has been recognized in psychotherapy for some time (e.g., Bergin, 1971), yet is of even greater concern ethically in the case of prevention. Psychotherapy clients already have problems and have initially sought help voluntarily, whereas in prevention, by definition, the participants enter the program in a healthy condition and thus stand to be worse off than they otherwise would have been if the program turns out to be harmful. The specific risks and benefits of participating in a prevention program, whose effects are presumed to endure for the rest of one's life, are not always known to any great degree.

Where might prevention activities begin in a community? Goldston (1977) points out that we already possess sufficient understanding of the causes of many cases of mental retardation to speak realistically of incidence reduction as a goal. Among the known causes are poisoning of children or the unborn from chemical toxins, drugs, or alcohol, infections such as rubella or syphilis, nutritional deficiencies, accidents and injuries, genetic disorders, and, in general, prematurity and/or low birth weight. Assessment of many such conditions is possible in utero using amniocentesis and ultrasonic scanning, although the choices resulting from a positive diagnosis of retardation again raise difficult value issues.

Biological causes are certainly known, but a moment's thought will reveal the involvement of additional social and behavioral factors in implementing preventive programs. These social and behavioral factors call on our knowledge of community processes and require interdisciplinary effort. Although we now have a great deal of knowledge of the virus that causes the disease AIDS, for example, in the absence of a vaccine to prevent AIDS prevention "depends upon education and counselling. . . . Prevention efforts begin with providing up-to-date, accurate information and sound recommendations to individuals on how to prevent transmission. Community prevention programs must proceed now, before definitive evidence of their effectiveness is available" (Curran et al., 1985, p. 1357). The field of mental retardation presents similar problems of implementation, even when biological causes are ascertainable. The social and political problems are amplified greatly if, reasoning from the correlation between poverty and mental retardation, we advocate a nonspecific effort to improve the standard of living and quality of life in poverty-stricken communities. Do we choose the Kennedy–Johnson War on Poverty or Reagan supply-side economics as our route to an improved quality of life, and on what possible grounds could a mental health professional advocate for one or the other, or for that matter any other socioeconomic approach?

The major public health approaches may be classified into two groups. First is a set of methods directed at strengthening the organism. The model here is inoculation. The second group of strategies is directed at changing the social environment. Metaphorically, we may call that approach "cleaning out the swamps." A variant of this environmental approach may be termed "accident prevention" (Peterson & Mori, 1985). Before examining these general approaches in some detail, we explain several useful concepts currently guiding preventive efforts in mental health.

Promoting Positive Mental Health. Methods for improving the health of people in general (e.g., better nutrition and exercise) are directed toward producing a higher prevalence of generally healthy people. An analogous strategy in mental health is to increase the prevalence of positive mental health rather than reduce the prevalence of psychopathology (Albee, 1980; Cowen, 1980). The aim of such interventions is to increase the overall level of well-being and thus reduce the potential for undesirable outcomes. We would include improvements in prenatal care, dissemination of information regarding effective child rearing, the creation of mutual support systems, and individual and community competence building as examples.

Any strategy requires us to consider not only what may be done, but also how it may be done. Spaulding and Balch (1983) point out that primary prevention has never successfully proceeded from a base in the service delivery system (e.g., child guidance clinics, community mental health centers). Shifting the paradigm from "disease prevention" to "health promotion" may require a focus on prevention efforts in other settings (e.g., families, schools, the workplace, the mass media). If the model changes, the services change, the service deliverers change, and their base of operations also changes.

Promoting positive mental health is also consistent with a newer, more comprehensive conception of mental health as a *process* or way of life, definable not as the absence of disease, but as the successful mastery of developmental tasks across the life span. Recall from our discussion of the ecological analogy (Chapter 3) and crisis theory (Chapter 6) that people vary in their vulnerability. Developmental stages, environmental settings, and the tasks they impose differ in what they require of people, making "mental health" more a product of the individual's transactions with his or her environment than a static, fixed condition. Note that if our aim is to increase the rates of successful mastery of developmental life tasks across the life span, and if etiological factors such as stress are nonspecific, preventive effects will not always show up clearly in the incidence rates for a limited number of specific disorders. Instead, we will have to examine pre- and postintervention status of target populations on such indices as competence, achievement, and satisfaction. If, as we have suggested, many disorders that are diagnosed by the DSM-III reflect problems in living, the diagnoses most likely to reflect life stresses should be the ones that show decreases. If the measures confound appropriate emotional response to stress generated by inescapable life events with disorder, however, even those indices may not show change. One may still feel anxious when under stress even if one copes more effectively with stress.

High-Risk Strategies. Delivering an intervention, be it health promoting or disease preventing, to every member of the community is often a luxury the community cannot afford. Currently healthy individuals can, however, be differentiated in terms of the relative risk each of them has for a given disorder or for psychological disorder in general. The so-called risk factors can include all manner of genetic, prenatal, developmental, and experiential variables. Although the risk any randomly selected member of the population has for developing schizophrenia is about 1%, for example, this risk for the child of a schizophrenic person is 10% (Garmezy, 1971). Programs to prevent schizophrenia could be delivered more effectively if aimed at the children of schizophrenics than if administered to all children. "Risk" is still a somewhat vague concept, however. For the most part it is determined actuarially (i.e., not always with any clear theoretical basis), and most risks are nonspecific instead of specific. For example, being at increased risk for schizophrenia because you are the child of a schizophrenic could be due to genetic factors, environmental factors, or the interaction of both, but a child of schizophrenic parents is at risk for a host of other disorders as well, not just schizophrenia. In addition, the coefficient of prediction for any single risk factor is generally small. For example, 90% of the children of schizophrenics will *not* develop the disorder, and 90% of people who do become schizophrenic did not have a schizophrenic parent (Gottesman & Shields, 1972).

Another factor complicating the evaluation of high-risk strategies is that the time interval of interest in prevention is very long. Primary prevention of schizophrenia, to take an example, means a reduction in the incidence of the disorder over the entire duration of the period of risk (i.e., until every member of the cohort is at least 45–50 years of age). This expanded time perspective complicates our understanding of concepts such as risk, intervention, and change in the context of natural maturation and development across the life span. The vulnerability model suggests there may be no person- or situation-oriented, *early* intervention that has the power to overcome all possible future stressors or losses of support. There are also practical problems in evaluating preventive interventions when their effects must span a lengthy period of time (Heller, Price, & Sher, 1980).

One group of investigators is conducting long-range, prospective follow-up research using the high-risk paradigm (Mednick & McNeil, 1968). In their design a cohort of individuals who are initially at risk to an equivalent degree (e.g., all are children of schizophrenics) are followed prospectively until the period of risk for the disorder has passed (e.g., age 50 or so). By that time those who stood to become schizophrenic will have done so, and any factors differentiating them from those who do not develop the disorder will provide a basis for improving estimates of risk. Furthermore, the additional factors uncovered (i.e., above and beyond being the child of a schizophrenic) might suggest some basis for developing preventive interventions. Those conducting longitudinal high-risk studies seek to include not only the individual with no present disorder, but also the individual who is unlikely *ever* to develop a particular disorder, even one he or she is at risk for (Dawber, 1980). If stress during adolescence turns out to increase risk for schizophrenia beyond that from being the child of a schizophrenic, for example, one promising intervention might involve reducing the stress impacting on these individuals or increasing their ability to cope with stress.

To complicate the researcher's task, however, the cohort at risk does not necessarily split into two "clean" groups (i.e., cases versus normals) by the end of the risk period, but instead can fragment into several more or less distinguishable subgroups, including borderline cases, those with other kinds of disorders, and so on (cf. Mednick et al., 1979). A further problem is that many alternative explanations for the differences observed become plausible over so many years of follow-up. Long-term longitudinal research to date has generally not controlled for such important threats to validity as differential attrition between the intervention and control groups (Campbell & Kimmel, 1985). Nonetheless, the strategy is plausible and may be very effective in those instances in which the risk factors predict a high incidence of disorder among those identified as at risk. The strategy may be still more effective if research pinpoints specific points of vulnerability later in life that may yield to further timely intervention. We should not believe that we can depend on a one-time, forever effective intervention in our field because most problems have complex etiologies and are affected by many variables that change with time.

Multifactorial Etiologies. Bloom (1979) notes that the health problems for which effective treatment and prevention efforts have lagged (e.g., heart disease, cancer, the common cold, and mental illnesses) all can be characterized as having multiple rather than single causes, and also as including behavioral factors of one kind or another (e.g., habits, life-styles) among the contributing causes. The concept of a multifactorial etiology has thus been suggested to account for this observation that any single factor is usually not sufficient to produce a case of disorder, and furthermore that in some cases the symptomatic manifestation of a disorder can occur long after the individual risk factors are present and active. For example, evidence of exposure to the virus related to the disease AIDS places one in a higher risk category than if one has not been exposed. There is, however, "an annual attack rate of from 1 to 2 percent of those currently infected with the virus" (Curran et al., 1985, p. 1354). We have little knowledge of the reasons why few who have been exposed develop the disorder, and many, many others do not.

The complexity of the processes by which these multiple causes interact to produce disorder probably explains why progress in treating and preventing them has come so slowly. Few intervention programs ever deal directly with more than one of the possible risk factors, and few investigators can afford to follow their subjects for the number of years required to demonstrate conclusively that prevention was achieved. Multifactorial etiologies may complicate our conceptual understanding of cause and effect, but it is plausible that some degree of risk for the disorder, and perhaps incidence as well, can be reduced by intervening in relation to any of the etiological factors. Anthony (1977), for example, describes a potentially useful psychological intervention involving competence building for preventing schizophrenia even while acknowledging that much of schizophrenia's etiology may be genetic.

Precipitating Versus Predisposing Factors. The vulnerability model we discussed in Chapter 6 makes a useful distinction between predisposing and precipitating factors. Predisposing factors may be genetic in nature, or may reflect the individual's history and experiences. A predisposing factor for committing child abuse, for example, may well be the person's experience of having been abused as a child (Rosenberg & Reppucci, 1985). Precipitating factors occur close to the point when an episode of disorder begins. Exposure to severe battle conditions may be a precipitating factor in the development of a stress-trauma syndrome, for example. Being isolated with a crying child for a long period of time may precipitate an episode of child abuse (Rosenberg & Reppucci, 1985). The stressful life events we discussed in Chapter 6 are most often conceptualized as precipitating factors.

Perhaps on the assumption that predisposing factors are more readily discernible in the lives of children, and more important than anything that happens later in life for the development of disorder, primary prevention efforts have been directed more at children than any other age group (Spaulding & Balch, 1983). The Task Panel on Prevention (1978) of the President's Commission on Mental Health stated, for example: "it follows, virtually automatically, that primary prevention programs must be heavily oriented to the very young" (p. 1840). Kornberg and Caplan (1980) reviewed some 650 studies on risk factors and primary prevention approaches involving children. Most of the studies focused on very young children (e.g., infant stimulation programs, mother-infant bonding).

Some authorities (e.g., Bloom, 1979), however, have suggested that our emphasis on predisposing factors has not met with much success, whether in treatment or with respect to prevention. It might prove more fruitful to focus instead on proximal, precipitating factors such as stressful life events. Reviews by Kagan (1976) and Kohlberg, LaCrosse, and Ricks (1972) seriously question whether early childhood experiences have any irreversible consequences for the ultimate attainment of adolescent and adult competence. As we noted earlier, the natural history of many psychological disorders is not well understood, perhaps in part because of the lack of continuity in behavior over substantial lengths of time. Ecological conceptions of behavior (Chapters 3–5) and the vulnerability model (Chapter 6) teach us that an individual's vulnerability varies with circumstances throughout his or her life. Primary prevention should be effective at later life stages—adolescence, middle age, or even retirement—as well as during early childhood. Placing excessive importance on interventions in infancy and early childhood, in the absence of compelling evidence on their long-term benefits, may needlessly hamper the practice of prevention at other milestones. Focusing on precipitating factors, as in Dohrenwend's stressful-life-events model, allows us to think about reducing the occurrence of stressful life events (e.g., lowering unemployment) or creating resources that are well positioned in time and place to reduce vulnerability. The stressful-life-events model directs our attention to here-and-now events that are predictable and can be modified to prevent difficulties. We may also be able to prepare individuals to cope with such events. The breadth of alternatives provided by these new ways of thinking is shown in the following discussion.

Prevention through Stepwise Risk Reduction

A public health model not often considered in discussions of prevention in mental health is that of accident prevention. Accident prevention does not depend on a disease concept. Instead, we wish to prevent unwanted injuries to healthy persons, and we extend the concept of injury to include psychological damage as well as physical injury. Are some concepts analogous to accident prevention in mental health?

The vulnerability model we introduced in the previous chapter is based on the concept of a multifactorial etiology and on the distinction between predisposing and precipitating causes. Recall that level of vulnerability is a property of individual persons, while maladaptive behavior, occurring in time-limited episodes, is the product of the individual's level of vulnerability and various specific and nonspecific conditions in the environment. Nonspecific environmental conditions, such as the levels of chronic stress and social support, contribute to the likelihood of maladaptive behavior by affecting the person's acute level of resistance to periodic life crises and other disruptive events. The goal in the accident-prevention approach is to reduce the incidence of maladaptive episodes or traumatic accidents by reducing either individual vulnerability or the degree of risk added by conditions in the environment.

The various risks involved in a particular situation are often assumed to occur sequentially, an idea expressed in the distinction made earlier between factors that are proximal, or precipitating, and those assumed to be distal (remove in time, or predisposing). This sequential relationship can be depicted using what is called a Markov chain. In this approach, any given outcome (in our case a maladaptive condition) is understood as the end result of a particular sequence of steps, each of which is made up of two dichotomous alternatives defined in terms of "yes" versus "no" answers to a specific question. The concept of accident prevention describes this model. One may prevent accidents, or the injury associated with accidents, in any number of ways. The accident-prevention concept suggests that we examine the sequence of events that precede the undesirable end-state and attempt to identify promising points of intervention anywhere along the chain.

Consider the serious and growing problem of pregnancy among unwed teenagers. This condition had associated with it a high prevalence of seriously maladaptive outcomes such as school dropout and child abuse. Although teenage pregnancy has obvious biological aspects, thinking of this complex social and psychological problem as a "disease" leaves only a few limited options available for preventing its occurrence. From a biological standpoint, in other words, childbirth is preventable using contraception or abortion. Taking the longitudinal view depicted in the Markov chain allows us to consider other possibilities as well.

The sequence of steps that can produce maladaptive behavior as a result of unwanted pregnancy is depicted in Table 7-3 using a Markov chain. Depending on the answer to each of a series of questions, the risk of poor adaptation is either high or low. Aside from the biological statuses of pregnancy and abortion, there are alternative behavioral responses concerning amount of sexual activity, use of contraception, and compensating responses made after the child is born (the latter might include placing the child for adoption or making some other arrangement that prevents dropping out of school and other high-risk conditions). The important point is that choosing *any* one of the alternatives leading to the low-risk condition is sufficient to break the chain leading to poor adaptation. Valerio (1985) reports suggested evidence that sex education results in reduced pregnancy rates and increased birth control usage, based on self-reported data, in a national survey of children. Furstenberg et al. (1985) show that 15- and 16-year-olds exposed to sex education delay their initiation of sexual activity.

To summarize, part of the reason why teenage pregnancy is complicated and difficult to control is that it is not just one condition, but the culmination of several events and responses, some of which are social and behavioral instead of biological. Prevention can be conceptualized in social and behavioral terms for virtually any multifactorial problem, including heart disease, cancer, alcohol abuse, diabetes, and sexually transmitted diseases.

The stepwise risk-reduction approach thus uses the idea of multifactorial etiologies and proximal versus distal steps in the causal chain to increase the number of different opportunities for prevention. Some of these opportunities occur much earlier in time than the target condition itself, and when delivered on a communitywide or milestone basis (e.g., through sex education or through creating a social climate supporting premarital chastity), have a potentially wide impact. Furthermore, nearly everyone is subject to at least a slight degree of risk in this view, because risk is a function of events and circumstances as well as of people. Programs of prevention where everyone is at risk may be politically and socially acceptable and less stigmatizing than programs focused on people singled out as already at high risk.

The broadest preventive impact occurs when large segments of the population perform behaviors (e.g., contraception, exercise, safety precautions) consistent with

Table 7-3. Markov Chain for Problems Associated with Teenage Pregnancy

High-Risk Condition	Low-Risk Condition
Chaste?	
↓No	→ Yes
Contraception?	
↓No	→ Yes
Pregnant?	
↓Yes	→ No
Abortion?	
↓No	→ Yes
Compensating abilities?	
↓No	→ Yes
Poor adaptation School dropout Child abuse	

maintaining a low-risk status. Education is one approach used to induce large numbers of people to modify their behavior in a low-risk direction, although it is not always successful by itself. Use of seat belts and child safety restraints in automobiles is widely credited with preventing deaths and injuries, for example, yet under completely voluntary conditions many people do not consistently use seat belts or child restraints. On the other hand, evidence suggests that a large segment of adults will adopt such behaviors once they are legally prescribed. Consider the following example concerning the prevention of deaths and injuries in young children through the use of car seats for children.

An Example: Influencing Auto Safety Legislation. A study by Jason and Rose (1984) provides an interesting example of the interplay in the legal system of activism, prevention, and social science research. Jason and Rose noted that many of the 60,000 injuries and 1,000 deaths in children under 5 that occur annually because of car accidents could be prevented if parents used appropriate car safety seats. Working in cooperation with an advocacy group, they undertook a research project to provide data to help influence the passage of legislation that would mandate the use of safety seats with children under age 4 in Illinois.

The researchers selected two intersections to observe whether children in cars were in safety seats. Over a 19-month period they observed that on the average, less than 50% of infants under 1 year were in appropriate restraints. Approximately 10% of children between 1 and 4 were in proper safety seats. They conducted a telephone survey with a randomly selected sample of citizens in their area. They found that about half the respondents regularly transported children in automobiles. Nearly 80% agreed that using safety restraints was important, and 78% indicated they would support state legislation that would mandate the use of proper automobile safety restraints for children.

Legislation mandating seat belts had failed to pass when it was introduced during the previous legislative session in Illinois. Knowledgeable observers predicted that the Illinois House would pass the legislation in the next session, which in fact did happen. In the researchers' judgment, however, the vote in the state senate was much more doubtful.

Because the vote was doubtful, the investigators had the opportunity to test whether legislators would be influenced by scientific data. Nine days before the critical vote in the state senate, the investigators sent a personal letter to a randomly selected half of the state senators describing the data on seat restraint usage and the results of the citizen survey. The letter included Illinois statistics on deaths and injuries over a 5-year period and estimates of the lifetime dollar costs of rehabilitating a child who had sustained a serious injury. Written on university stationery and identifying the authors as faculty members, the letter asked the senators to consider the data when deciding how to vote on the pending bill.

Of 29 senators who received the letter, 23 or 79% voted yes. Of the 30 who were not sent the letter, 16 or 53% voted yes. The difference was statistically significant.

This study is probably the only one in the literature that attempted to trace the effect of a lobbying campaign on legislative votes using the experimental method. Special conditions were undoubtedly involved. The legislation would probably have passed anyway, judging from the rate of positive votes in the unsolicited half of the senate. The use of information contained in a single letter might have been influential because little active controversy had arisen about the legislation. It would probably be more difficult to demonstrate the effect of the letters if there was opposition presenting arguments against the proposed legislation or presenting data disputing the findings of the one study.

The facts do support the preventive benefits of safety seat legislation, however. Guerin and MacKinnon (1985) did a sophisticated time-series analysis of accidents in California resulting in injury to children under age 3 and between ages 4 and 7. California's statute required that children under 3 use safety seats, but there was no such requirement for children between 4 and 7. The data clearly showed a statistically significant *reduction* of 8.4% in injuries to children under 3 and a nonsignificant *increase* in injuries in the older group in the 12 months following passage of the legislation. The decrease in injuries among the youngest children in California could not

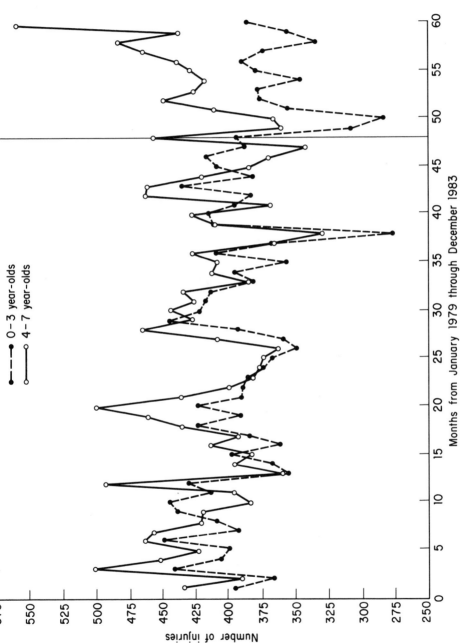

Figure 7-1. Time series showing change in injuries in California after passage of safety seat legislation in January 1982 (from Guerin & MacKinnon, 1985).

209

be explained by changes in the number of children that were born during the period of study. The investigators examined comparable data for Texas, which had no legislation requiring safety seats. Over the same time, the data showed a nonsignificant increase in injuries in Texas in children of comparable age to those in California.

Parenthetically, we may note that this brief example of the relationship between law and social science research indicates a mode of cooperation that will probably grow in the future. Legislatures often review pertinent facts in developing policy and when writing legislation to implement policy. Social scientists can provide some of the legislative facts not only by sending letters to legislators, but also by testifying before committees and by publicizing research in other forums in order to influence public opinion. Social science research can influence legal process in the interests of prevention or the amelioration of harm. (The relationship between science and politics is discussed further in Chapter 12.) The research shows that intervention at a distal point—the state legislature—had effects at a proximal point—in the car involved in an accident—that prevented physical injuries.

Implications of an Accident-Prevention Model. The paradigm of accident prevention directs our attention to different issues for research and for intervention than does a disease model. Research using the accident model focuses on the conditions under which undesirable events occur and what leads to those conditions, in addition to the nature of the reaction to the undesirable event and its characteristics. An ecological analogy is highly appropriate in an accident-prevention orientation.

An additional example may help in making the point. When parents with children divorce, a formal agreement is reached settling the custody of the children and the noncustodial parent's visitation rights. In most cases, the custody settlement is satisfactory, and problems that arise are resolved informally between the parties. In perhaps 10% of the cases, however, continuing conflict between the divorced spouses centers on their relationships with the children. The primary occasion for contact and for face-to-face conflict between divorced spouses occurs when one spouse arrives at the home of the other to pick up or to deliver a child for a visit. The reasons for the conflict are complex and need not detain us here, but they often result in the parents returning to court to seek modification or enforcement of the visitation order.

Stott, Gaier, and Thomas (1984) describe a program of court-ordered, supervised, neutral-site visitation conceived and funded as a delinquency-prevention program. The sponsors reasoned that intervention in disrupted families will reduce the "negativity and trauma" associated with the visit and therefore reduce the child's potential for future acting out. Supervised visitation was ordered by the court in families with multiple problems and long histories of involvement with the courts, social services, and mental health agencies. After an interview, a schedule was established for weekly 1–2-hour visits at a neutral site. Both parents signed a contract specifying the conditions of visitation. The custodial parent dropped the child off at the neutral site and left the child with a worker. Fifteen minutes later, the noncustodial parent arrived to pick up the child, thus avoiding the opportunity for face-to-face conflict with the former spouse. The worker participated actively in the visit if there was reason to suspect abuse or if a parent exhibited poor parenting skills. Records were kept on each visit, and the worker sent recommendations for future visitation based on these reports to the referring court.

No formal evaluation of this program has been conducted. According to Stott et al. (1984), however, the program has "the enthusiastic support of the family court judges, who are relieved of many hours of counterproductive courtroom time with noncompliant parents" (p. 216). The program provided safe visits for parents and children, when in the past there were no visits or the visits were stressful. It provided an opportunity for the noncustodial parent to continue a relationship with the child, and it offered both parties that opportunity to document allegations that the other was breaking agreements concerning visitation. Stott et al. reported that in an undetermined number of cases, parents worked out satisfactory arrangements between each other, if only because the court-imposed visitation was inconvenient.

Note that the intervention in no way depended on any measurement or evaluation of the personalities or any analysis of the relationship between the parents that resulted in the continuing conflict. The intervention depended on an analysis of the situational circumstances under which conflict emerged. Action was directed toward modifying the circumstances so that the manifest conflict did not emerge. Just as a safety seat prevents injury to a child wearing it in an accident, so this intervention reduced the sum total of overt conflict, and presumably the undesirable sequelae of the conflict as well. The accident-prevention model may have much to recommend it in preventing such phenomena as child abuse, spouse abuse, or driving while drunk. The success of Head Start in preventing social problems (see later) also yields to analysis with an event-avoidance model. Research on a variety of social problems undertaken from an ecological perspective may help us to define the chain of events leading to undesirable end-states and may offer us new and different strategies for intervention. The original Holmes and Rahe (1967) stressful-life-events scale (see the previous chapter) was stimulated by the observation that stressful life events occurred frequently in the histories of those who were treated for psychiatric disorder. An analysis built on the Markov chain concept may well demonstrate that many behavior patterns we now consider manifestations of illness might instead be understood as the outcome of a potentially breakable chain of events. One complication is that the accident-prevention model may require its own approach to evaluation, for the initial goal is primarily to control specified target behaviors, not final end-states. In sum, if we do not limit ourselves to the disease model, we may open other opportunities for prevention.

As a product of thinking from an ecological perspective, the accident-prevention model is largely directed at the situational factors that raise or lower risk. Do any individual difference factors exist that are stable across situations and over time? Recall the discussion in Chapter 4 concerning "cognitive and behavioral construction competencies" of the sort identified by Mischel (1973). In the following section we examine the theory and research relating this kind of characteristic to primary prevention in mental health.

Competence Building

By the early 1970s several streams of thought came together to form a primary prevention strategy known as "competence building" (Cowen, 1973; Task Panel on Prevention, 1978). In the years preceding this development, for example, White (1959) had argued that the motive to interact competently with one's environment was basic to human experience. Ojemann (Ojemann et al., 1955) developed a curriculum and teacher training methods to facilitate adoption of causal reasoning and other social competencies in elementary schoolchildren. "Ego psychology" emerged in the 1940s and 1950s from psychoanalytic enclaves to expand the focus of professional interest to include rational, conscious processes as well as irrational, unconscious ones (Hartman, 1958; Zax, 1980). Cognitive behavior therapists moved away from a focus on discrete situational reinforcements alone and toward a workable concept of central cognitive mediating processes. Concepts such as "positive mental health" (Jahoda, 1958) and psychological "invulnerability" (Garmezy, 1971) entered the literature on abnormal psychology and demanded theoretical attention. Ultimately, the zeitgeist of the 1960s may have been what gave rise to competence building as an intervention, based squarely on the then-popular assumption of the "plasticity" of intellectual and psychological structures (Hunt, 1968) and perhaps best exemplified by the Head Start program (reviewed later in this chapter).

Practical application of the competence-building paradigm in prevention has become straightforward. It starts with a theoretically or empirically based assumption that high-risk individuals within a given population (e.g., inner-city minority preschoolers) differ from low-risk individuals in the same population by their lack of some basic psychosocial skill or skills, and that individuals who lack these competencies can nevertheless acquire them under the right conditions. These skills are then taught directly to the groups at risk on the assumption that their acquisition eliminates the fundamental discrepancy between the high-risk and low-risk members of the population, thus reducing or eliminating the added risk.

Perhaps the best illustration of prevention through competence building is the work of George Spivack and Myrna Shure at the Hahnemann College Mental Health Center in Philadelphia (Spivack & Shure, 1974; Task Panel on Prevention, 1978). An assessment of the inner-city population served by their facility indicated that about half of the children in day care and kindergarten displayed behavioral problems, including impatience, overemotionality, aggression, or excessive shyness and fear. Studies of hundreds of 4- and 5-year-old children revealed that those with behavior problems were often distinguishable from those without by their lack of certain "interpersonal cognitive problem-solving" (ICPS) skills, including:

1. *Alternative thinking:* the ability to conceptualize alternative solutions to problems involving peers or adults.
2. *Consequential thinking:* the ability to foresee accurately the consequences of one's own actions.
3. *Causal thinking:* an appreciation of the role of antecedent events as causes of other events.
4. *Sensitivity:* to the existence of a problem as an interpersonal one.
5. *Means/ends thinking:* the ability to plan a course of action in pursuit of a goal, one that may involve several different steps.

How is it that some preschoolers acquire these competencies while others do not, and how are they related to prevention? Studying the interaction of mothers and their children, Spivack and Shure observed that girls who acquired these skills seemed to learn them directly from their mothers, while for boys the source of such knowledge was unclear. Shure and Spivack (1982) see the theoretical relevance of ICPS skills for prevention to reside in the facilitation of positive peer relationships, which in turn reduce the risk of pathology later during adolescence and adulthood (Cowen et al., 1975).

The prevention program designed by Spivack and Shure consists of some 40 or more "game" activities, each about 20 minutes long, designed to be used by preschool teachers in regular preschool classrooms or by parents at home to teach preschoolers the following kinds of skills: (1) *word concepts,* such as "not" or "same-different," which prepare children to understand the meaning of "*not* a good idea, try something *different*"; (2) *interpersonal skills,* such as listening, watching, and understanding the other person's feelings; and (3) *generating alternative solutions* to a problem situation, including conceptualizing the potential consequences of actions, analyzing the relationship between cause and effect, and so on. Spivack and Shure wish to teach the child *how* to think, not *what* to think, and thus instruct parents and teachers to avoid making evaluative judgments about a child's responses during the games. They claim the *process* of thinking is what is important, not its content. The games teach the process of thinking by posing interpersonal problems, however, not by using the puzzles studied in the laboratory. Spivack and Shure believe that once children learn to predict the likely consequences of their actions for themselves, short-sighted, ineffective responses will naturally drop out. Another skill taught to both teachers and mothers is "dialoging," or how to solve a problem interpersonally when it occurs in real relationships. That is, when an interpersonal problem arises, the adult is taught to ask the child what his or her thinking is about the nature of the problem, what his or her feelings about it are, what he or she can do about it, what might happen if that particular response is tried, and whether any alternative responses might be more effective.

The results Spivack and Shure report for this brief, focused training program are quite positive. Nearly all children gained in measured ICPS skills, and those rated as more maladjusted to start with gained more than those who were better adjusted initially. The amount of improvement in ICPS skills was related to the amount of behavioral improvement shown by the children. The most important ICPS skills in this regard seemed to be alternative and consequential thinking. At a 2-year follow-up assessment, training effects had been maintained, and children who received the program were rated as more adjusted than control children during the next 2 years of elementary school. At least in some of the studies, the later teachers who rated childrens' adjustment had no knowledge of the training the children received. Spivack and Shure found that these effects were not related to children's IQs or socioeconomic status and that mothers and teachers were about equally effective as trainers.

This program is useful not only as an illustration of the competence-building paradigm but also as a demonstration of how successful mental health interventions can be carried out in natural community settings by natural care givers (i.e., teachers and parents). Several recent replications report finding less clear relationships between the level of ICPS skills in children and their behavioral adjustment, whether assessed by teacher ratings or by direct observation (Gillespie et al., 1982; Winer et al., 1982). Another study (McKim et al., 1982) reports that IQ was more strongly related to both ICPS skill and adjustment than the latter were to each other. Shure and Spivack (1982) suggest that regular practice of the various ICPS skills through "dialoging" in problem situations as they arise is probably necessary to maintain the skills and preserve their link to adjustment. It is becoming apparent, however, that the relationship between learning specific ICPS skills and later reductions in the incidence of psychopathology may not be as simple as we had hoped (Durlak, 1983). Specific links between skills and outcomes may vary among children of different ages and different sociodemographic groups (Gesten et al., 1982); that is, many different "social problem-solving" skills exist. Spivack and Shure and their colleagues are working on identifying additional skills. Not much is known about the natural acquisition of such skills in interaction with key environmental settings during development.

Regarding another area of competence building, millions of Americans have been exposed to sex education in various forms over the past 65 years. Valerio (1985) reviewed the history of sex education and studies evaluating its effectiveness. She found that most studies demonstrated statistically significant increases in factual knowledge about human sexuality. Many studies revealed changes in *attitudes* about the sexual practices of *others*. The studies revealed greater acceptance of masturbation, homosexuality, and variations in sexual practices. In other words, sex education results in greater tolerance of sexual diversity. Clearly, these results could provide the basis for challenges to sex education by groups with different views of the value of sexual diversity. (Part of the widespread acceptance of Spivack and Shure's program may be that its content is noncontroversial.) Among adults, exposure to sex education apparently effects little change in their own sexual behavior. In white male and female and black female teenagers, however, exposure to sex education appears to be associated with lower rates of sexual acitivity. Moreover, exposure to sex education in school has no relationship with the extent to which adolescents discuss sex with their parents (Furstenberg et al., 1985).

Valerio (1985) points out that almost no studies evaluated sex education programs for young children in public schools. This is not to say that young children are not offered sex education in school, but simply that sex education programs have not been subject to controlled study at the elementary school level. That fact probably reflects the social and political difficulties of conducting research on controversial issues. Most of the research has been done with college and medical students, where far less controversy ensues about sex education programs.

Valerio also notes that no long-term studies have evaluated the effect on adult life of exposure to sex education. The potential for long-term positive and negative effects is high, but problems in mounting the research have limited our progress in understanding the possible preventive effects of sex education as a form of competence building.

We share the widespread enthusiasm regarding competence building in high-risk groups as an approach to primary prevention, but would add several additional cautions at this point. First, thorough exploitation of this paradigm will depend on obtaining clearer definitions of what precisely is meant by "competence." To what extent competence is a global, all-purpose "skill" in the form of Mischel's (1973) cognitive and behavioral construction competencies (see Chapter 4) is not clear, for example, nor to what extent it might be better conceptualized as a situation-specific skill. In practice it has been taken both ways. The Spivack and Shure (1974) method and Finkel's (1975) concept of the "trauma-stren conversion" (see Chapter 6) represent attempts to induce or to study widely generalizable and durable cognitive changes. Much of the preventive work with stressful life events (e.g., Bloom, Hodges & Caldwell, 1982) takes a more situation-specific approach. The latter perspective is also illustrated in a study by Sarason and Sarason (1981), who found that training inner-city ninth-graders in specific skills related to finding employment led not only to more and better problem-solving solutions in a test situation in the students who received this training, but also to better performance in actual job-seeking interviews. Bearing in mind the better conceptual connection of incidence to proximal, precipitating events than to distal, predisposing events (Bloom, 1979), and the difficulty some have had in replicating the simple ICPS skill-outcome relationship found by Spivack and Shure, we note that competence building from a situation-specific perspective may rest on sounder empirical footing, at least for the moment (Durlak, 1983).

To the extent that competence turns out to involve a specific set of skills whose value varies from one risk-group/outcome context to another, however, more work is clearly necessary to identify the specific skills in all of the relevant contexts. The generalizability of any one set may not be broad. From the ecological vantage point (presented in Chapter 3; see also Trickett et al., 1985), the problem is one of adaptation. Adaptation is not just an individual feat, but an ongoing process of person-environment fit. In that sense we should ask whether the relevant ICPS skills differ, or even conflict with each other, in key settings such as school, home, workplace, or street. Conditions of adaptation change over time as well, and the relationship between an individual's ICPS performance in childhood and his or her psychological adjustment as an adult has yet to be established. On the other hand, to the extent that competence represents global, widely applicable abilities, one might ask how it is that they are different from the products of ordinary education, and thus whether it is really necessary to expend resources on a special program instead of on the general educational system.

Both kinds of skills, global and situation-specific, may develop out of competence building. Global competencies may reduce the risk related to predisposing causes (e.g., poverty, constitutional vulnerability) while task-specific skills reduce the risks associated with precipitating causes (e.g., divorce and other stressful life events). Assuming that the competencies identified can in fact be learned adequately by the members of high-risk groups, however, one can still ask how the new skills will be maintained across the inevitable changes in time and situation. For example, will cognitive skills taught in a relatively low state of emotional arousal be available and effective in a state of high emotional arousal? More information is needed regarding the nature of behavior-environment continuities across time and place. One day we may wish to teach the ability to assess environments behaviorally and either modify them according to one's needs or select those that naturally provide the best fit (Levine & Perkins, 1980b).

Finally, as practiced, the approach of individual competence building intentionally or unintentionally engages in what some critics (e.g., Albee, 1980; Ryan, 1971) have called "blaming the victim." That is, because the "problem" in these cases is ultimately seen to reside in the existence of specific individual differences between high-risk and low-risk individuals, the inevitable implication is that the only way to rectify the problem is to *change* the high-risk individuals to make them "normal," or acceptable, which leads ultimately to *blaming* the high-risk individual for the predicament (Caplan & Nelson, 1973). Iscoe (1974) and Rappaport (1981) point out that competence building at the community level escapes this moral and political dilemma to a significant degree.

To summarize, the competence-building approach to primary prevention arose out of interest in psychological adaptation as a consequence of acquiring and using certain cognitive behavioral skills. The empirical literature on competence building, while encouraging overall, has nevertheless left us with a complicated picture. From an ecological vantage point, remember that behavioral skills are a property of settings and their "programs" (see Chapter 4), which vary over time and place, and not just of individual people. Still needed are conceptual advances that relate persons and situations in behavioral terms and therefore make it possible to develop competent settings and communities as well as competent individuals. Social setting interventions constituted a second major approach reviewed by the Task Panel on Prevention (1978), and we now turn to this set of ideas.

Social Setting Interventions

Kessler and Albee (1975) point out that even when the goal of an intervention is to reduce the incidence of individual cases of disorder in a population, we have no logical reason why this cannot be accomplished by changing environmental conditions instead of individuals. Full use of preventive interventions based strictly on environmental factors will require considerably better understanding of environmental effects on behavior than we currently possess.

Two questions are particularly useful here. First, what do we know to be the stable, predictable effects of specific environmental changes on behavior? Second, in what sense and to what extent are these influences known to reduce the incidence of psychopathology? Any mechanism of influence must be powerful enough to effect the immediate changes in behavior or reductions in risk, and also must somehow be able to reduce permanently the risk of disorder in at least some proportion of recipients. If we accept the medical analogy to prevention, true preventive effects must of necessity generalize across changes in time and place for the entire period of risk (e.g., until at least middle age for individuals at risk for schizophrenia).

How well can we answer these questions? We see four categories of responses within settings that have implications for an individual's adaptation in the future. First are the affective states induced by different social environments. It is almost a truism to say that settings differ in the degree to which individuals experience positive, negative, or no particular emotional state in them. The Task Panel on Prevention (1978) made no explicit connection between the experience of positive feelings and primary prevention, but its attention to the emotional correlates of settings, particularly the work of Moos (e.g., Trickett & Moos, 1974; see Chapter 4), leads us to infer they were suggesting that the cause of primary prevention would be furthered by creating settings in which people feel comfortable, or experience positive emotions and do not experience negative emotions. If settings are structured to minimize negative feelings, the absence of negative emotions over an extended period is assumed to reduce the incidence of later disorder. (See also the study by Stott et al., 1984, discussed earlier as an example of the accident-prevention model.)

The second category of environmental response falls under the rubric of opportunities for positive development. That is, environments can be judged by the degree to which they provide opportunities to develop the competencies and skills needed at later stages of life. Which settings now provide us with the skills and competencies to come to terms with adolescent sexuality, our emotions, enduring intimate relationships, parenting, separations, or death?

Attempts at primary prevention through a social setting focus can be based on a theoretical concept we introduced in Chapter 4 known as "behavior-environment congruence" (Wicker, 1972). Recall that behavior-environment congruence refers to the process by which an individual's behavior conforms closely and predictably to the demands or programs of the specific settings in which he or she participates. Ecologically speaking, competence thus develops in interaction with the demands of environmental settings instead of as an independent "trait" or personal characteristic. Competence is manifested to the extent that the individual responds to a given situation in an effective, congruent way.

Considering together the first and second categories of environmentally influenced responses, we note that in the first case a practitioner of prevention would try to structure as many settings as possible to elicit positive feelings. In the second the practioner would work to create settings that facilitate mastery over the challenges of everyday life. Thus stated, the behavioral goals sought by these two strategies may be incompatible—trying to modify a setting to elicit *both* relaxed contentment and active coping, for example, may violate the principle of behavior-environment congruence, because a setting uniquely congruent with one behavior may be highly incongruent with another (Price, 1974). Trickett and Moos (1974) found that classrooms high in perceived involvement and clarity were associated with high levels of academic achievement, but these same classrooms were associated with high degrees of competitiveness as well. In competitive situations we have losers as well as winners. Furthermore, we have yet to consider the role of individual differences—that is, an environment providing emotional warmth and support to one individual may suffocate or bore another, while a setting offering constructive challenge to some people may threaten or intimidate others. Successful prevention may require *person*-environment congruence instead of simple environmental manipulation.

A third category of response to environmental conditions might be termed the development of an accurate, confident self-image. Numerous studies (e.g., Sarason et al., 1960; Sarason, Hill, & Zimbardo, 1964; Sadow, 1976) have demonstrated that responses such as test anxiety, reflecting a negative self-evaluation, vary with the situation. Nothing in this research suggests that a temporary increase in negative self-evaluation necessarily has any adverse long-term effects, however. We simply do not yet know enough about environmental settings and how they are related to each other to predict how generalizable the specific learning and experience elicited in one situation will be to the requirements of situations encountered at other times. Nor do we know that a person successful in one setting will necessarily feel confident about succeeding in another setting. Graduate students in psychology, who are selected on the basis of successful performance as undergraduates, sometimes report great anxiety about their ability to compete successfully in the new educational environment, with consequences for their health (Goplerud, 1980).

The fourth dimension of environmental response might be termed the production of deviant statuses based on social responses to the individual's behavior. Chapter 4 reviewed Sarbin's (1970) concept of the "degraded" social identity, and Chapter 5 discussed in detail Scheff's (1966) propositions regarding labeling theory. It follows from this viewpoint that broadening the range of behaviors congruent with key settings (e.g., school classrooms) will widen the available niches, make more acceptable the expression of deviant characteristics, increase person-environment fit, and thus by definition reduce the overall level of maladjustment. To illustrate the implications of these ideas, we examine some research on so-called open classrooms.

Illustration: Preventing Maladjustment through a Social Setting Intervention

As work on the Primary Mental Health Project (reviewed earlier) shows, teachers report a relatively high rate of maladjustment among schoolchildren. Surveys taken since 1922 report that teachers judge as many as 30% of schoolchildren to have some degree of maladjustment and as many as 10% to have problems that are sufficiently severe to justify referral for clinical services (Hochschild, 1976). Although differences exist among judgments made by parents, teachers, and clinicians, teacher judgments of children's maladjustment have some validity when compared with other criteria (Glidewell & Swallow, 1968). From a clinical perspective, variations in maladjustment rates are explained in terms of such person-oriented factors as race, sex,[3] social class, child-rearing practices, and attitudes among the parents of children considered maladjusted.

Thinking ecologically, however, leads us to hypothesize that characteristics of classroom environments may be related to teacher ratings of maladjustment. The social organization of the classroom, the rules governing that social order, and the degree to which that environment provides niches that permit the nondeviant expression of individual differences may also affect pupil adaptation in the school setting. If a child is having difficulty within an organized social setting, characteristics of the setting are assumed to contribute to the problems experienced there.

An exchange took place between American and British educators during the 1970s, in part in response to criticism of U.S. schools and in part in reponse to enthusiastic reports of the success of the British primary school (e.g., Silberman, 1970; Featherstone, 1971). A number of Americans visited England to study British schools, and a number of British educators came to the United States as consultants. By the early 1970s some results of these exchanges were apparent. For example, a mail survey of elementary school teachers in the Buffalo area revealed that as many as 15% said they had modified their own practice toward more informality in teaching, following British methods (Frazitas & Stone, 1974).

The more informal British teaching method represents a considerable change in the organization of the classroom. Informal methods stress giving children some choice in how they spend their day. Within limits, if teachers delegate responsibility in making choices to children, they are sharing power with children. If children have choice, moreover, those in a particular setting may do different things at the same time. Different activities going on simultaneously signify that a number of different behaviors, and thus "ways of being," are legitimate at any given moment. Further, if the environment is arranged to permit different ways of being, the definition of what constitutes deviance, or rule breaking, is less clear than in the situation where only one activity is legitimate at any given moment. The inherent flexibility in the informal methods may promote more positive emotional states and self-images and less anxiety on the part of students, and may also allow the teacher to use additional options in managing and coping with individual differences among children (Levine, 1979). If the teacher has more problem-resolving devices available, presumably the number of problems will diminish, and potential "accidents" leading to school failure and related problems will be prevented.

A test of this hypothesis was conducted by Hochschild (1976), who defined three groups of classrooms based on a brief teacher questionnaire and brief observation of the classroom. These measures included teacher estimates of the extent to which children had choice in how they spent their time, teacher reports of the number of whole-class lessons, and observations of the number of learning materials, the number of activity centers, the number of different activities going on simultaneously, and the number of small groups that were observed. Joy (1977) conducted more intensive and systematic classroom observations and confirmed the validity of the brief screening measure in differentiating classrooms.[4] Based on the classroom measures, seven classrooms were classified as open, ten as transitional, and five as traditional. Hochschild's classrooms were matched for grade and for socioeconomic class of the students. In many instances, the classrooms came from the same school buildings.

Hochschild used a four-point teacher-rating scale to obtain a measure of teacher-rated maladjustment. The four points were: (1) well adjusted, (2) no significant problems, (3) moderately maladjusted, and (4) clinically maladjusted (in need of clinical help for problems). He found the lowest rate of moderate maladjustment in the open classrooms (13.9%), which was significantly lower than the rate he found for the transitional and the traditional classrooms (27.8% and 32.9%, respectively). Levine (1975) used the same measures Hochschild did with British teachers. The most open of the British classrooms were age integrated and team taught. That group had a maladjustment rate of 23.1%, while the rates in classrooms rated lower for openness was about 31%. Weisz and Cowen (1976) had teachers rate their classroom environments and also rate student adjustment. They concluded:

> More time in individualized instruction and work, characteristics that have been linked with "open" classes, correlated (directionally in all cases, and significantly in all but one) with judgments of less serious . . . problems, and fewer judged problems, overall. Conversely, more time in class-oriented instruction and work, characteristic of traditional classes, correlated significantly with knowing and liking children less. Significant correlations between more time spent at specifically assigned desks and more severe problems overall, and between more time in group-oriented instruction and more serious L[earning] problems were consistent with the preceding findings. (p. 186)

Horwitz (1979) summarizes 22 studies dealing with personal adjustment. About a third show evidence of greater adjustment in open classrooms. Most of the other studies show either a mixed pattern of results or no significant differences in adjustment. No study favors the traditional classroom. Neither Hochschild nor Levine found that aggressive children were identified comparatively more often in open classes than in traditional classrooms.

In sum, a body of evidence confirms the hypothesis that teacher-rated maladjustment may well be related to style of classroom management. There may also be important differences among teachers who choose different teaching methods and their attitudes toward children, however. We cannot exclude the hypothesis that the difference is a result of teacher attitude and not of characteristics of the social environment. Hochschild's and Levine's results show no statistically significant differences in the percent of children considered clinically maladjusted in the different types of classrooms. The difference came in the numbers characterized as well adjusted or as moderately maladjusted. These results suggest that some pupil behaviors cannot be absorbed by the classroom environment. On the other hand, a difference of 10–15% in the adjustment ratings due to classroom environment is not trivial. We do not know that greater happiness in school will have a long-term preventive effect. If a child adapts in school, however, letters of complaint to the home decrease, report cards showing deportment improve, trips to the principal's office may be reduced, the need for referral for other services is reduced, and other forms of stigmatization and punishment contributing to the formation of the child's self-image are also reduced. These results are highly interesting in showing that the social characteristics of the school setting may contribute to children's adjustment in school. They suggest the possibility for prevention efforts directed toward aspects of the social environment.

Short-term evidence of preventive potential is thus available for some competence building and some social setting interventions. Is anything comparable over a longer period of time? In trying to answer this question, we will conclude this chapter by reviewing the history and research findings concerning the widely debated Head Start program.

Head Start: An Experiment in Prevention

Head Start, a federally funded program of preschool education, has been called "the most significant and the most comprehensive program ever mounted to serve the nation's economically disadvantaged children and their families" (Richmond, Stipek, & Zigler, 1979, p. 135). It has clearly been the most popular and enduring of the War on Poverty programs. Recent long-term longitudinal data indicate that Head Start may be highly effective as a program for the prevention of school failure and related problems. Because Head Start is the type of program that has affected and will affect millions of children and their families, the theory and the data presented in support of its effectiveness are worth examining.

Head Start originated as one of the War on Poverty programs envisioned by John F. Kennedy and implemented by Lyndon B. Johnson with the Economic Opportunity Act of 1964. The aim of the War on Poverty was to eradicate poverty, a problem that had not received much attention during the 1950s in the aftermath of World War II. Economists and writers for the popular press, however, as well as congressional investigators, began calling attention to the serious problems existing in many parts of the country, especially among black Americans. This attention created a climate of opinion in which public resources could be committed to dealing with the problems of poverty. Kennedy included proposals for a War on Poverty in his planning for 1964. Following Kennedy's death in 1963, Johnson enthusiastically embraced the War on Poverty concept, resulting in the Economic Opportunity Act of 1964. The early stormy history of the antipoverty program is well described by Levitan (1969) and by Moynihan (1969).

Head Start developed in the reform climate that characterized the years when we were beginning to deal with the implications of the 1954 *Brown v. Board of Education* desegregation decision, the larger civil rights movement, and the government's potential role in compensating victimized groups for social and economic inequality and injustice. Theoretical arguments by noted psychologists such as J. McVicker Hunt (1961) and Benjamin Bloom (1964) provided a rationale for early intervention. This school of thought claimed that intelligence was not fixed at birth, but depended on experience and stimulation, especially during the first 5 years of life. Extrapolating from this argument, others hypothesized that if children of poverty (and black children in particular) did poorly on intelligence tests and in school, it was because of "cultural deprivation." Culturally deprived children lacked the experiential background to prepare them for tests and for school. Some argued that there were also important differences between child-rearing practices of lower-income blacks and middle-class whites. Thus poor children were not only less prepared intellectually; they were less prepared behaviorally to cope with the school environment.

Developmental psychologist Urie Bronfenbrenner persisted in arguing that more could be accomplished by taking preventive action and attempting to affect very young children, instead of just dealing with youth and adults already enmeshed in poverty. His arguments were supported by administrators of the Office of Economic Opportunity (OEO), the agency then designated to carry out the War on Poverty. They saw preschool education as innovative, attractive, and likely to gather widespread support (Zigler & Valentine, 1979, pp. 77–80).

The original goals of Head Start were quite broad. They included (1) improving the child's (a) physical health, (b) emotional and social development, and (c) mental processes and skills; (2) raising positive expectations for the child in creating a climate of confidence for subsequent learning efforts; (3) increasing the child's capacity to relate positively to family members and others; (4) developing a responsible attitude toward society; and (5) increasing the sense of dignity and self-worth within the child and its family (Richmond, Stipek, & Zigler, 1979, p. 137).

Thus from the beginning, Head Start's focus was on much more than producing permanent changes in preschoolers' cognitive aptitude. Its specific components included medical and dental examinations, immunizations, involvement of parents, and, perhaps more important than anything else, experiences of success in academic endeavors. Another distinctive characteristic of Head Start from the outset was the flexibility given to individual sponsors in tailoring a given program to meet their own needs, a feature that made the support of local authorities easier to obtain but that hampered the precise definition of Head Start as a single specific intervention. As a result, Head Start represented "not a program but an evolving concept" (Zigler, 1979).

In contrast to the criticism or apathy that greeted many antipoverty programs, Head Start struck a responsive chord in the public and was initiated in 1965 as a summer program. Three hundred individual sites enrolling about 100,000 children were projected for that first year, but such was the enthusiasm that applications for over 3,000 programs covering 560,000 children were ultimately processed (Sugarman, in Zigler & Valentine, 1979, p. 118). The fallacy in assuming that a single 8 week summer experience would somehow inoculate a child against poverty for the rest of his or her life was easily recognized, and Head Start was soon expanded into a year-round program (Levitan, 1969).

Initiated on a crash basis because political leaders believed that continued political support for the overall antipoverty program required rapid results that were popular and visible, Head Start grew, but with little direction. The OEO required community participation and insisted that parents be involved in some fashion. Many parents were offered classes in child care, and many others took jobs as teacher aides, cooks, or playground supervisors. Programs began in public school buildings, in church basements and in other makeshift facilities. Issues regarding the qualifications of teachers, standards for facilities, equipment, curriculum, and quality control soon arose. As the price tag grew, moreover, and riots struck many of our inner cities, demands for evaluation increased.

A study of Head Start's effectiveness was released in 1969 in the context of dismantling OEO programs shortly after Richard Nixon took office. Known as the West-inghouse study (Cicirelli, 1969), it reported that no lasting effect of participation in Head Start programs could be measured. The Westinghouse study reported that mea-sured IQs of Head Start children rose immediately following participation in the pro-gram, but any differences in cognitive ability between children who received Head Start and those who did not disappeared within 3–4 years after entrance into the pub-lic schools. Remember that although IQ was easier to assess than children's health or happiness or parents' involvement in the program, a gain in measured IQ was not the definitive outcome goal in the minds of Head Start's developers (Richmond et al., 1979). Furthermore, recall from earlier in this chapter that an important factor in the stability of behavior over time is stability in the specific demands made by key set-tings, such as those involving education. As Zigler (1979) has pointed out, the failure to maintain cognitive gains produced by Head Start can be interpreted to indicate the failure of the public schools more than the failure of Head Start.

The Westinghouse study itself became the object of much criticism (e.g., Campbell & Erlebacher, 1975) and remains a focus for controversy today (see Cicirelli, 1984; Zigler, 1984). By 1969 Head Start had sufficient popular and political support to sur-vive the attacks made against it. Even when other OEO programs were eliminated or sharply reduced in funding, Head Start continued to receive support through the Car-ter administration and even received modest budgetary increases in the Reagan administration (Berrueta-Clement et al., 1984).

Why has Head Start survived? Many explanations probably exist, including the way nationwide implementation and the deliberate involvement of parents helped politically in building a broad grass-roots constituency (see Chapter 12). More relevant to our focus here is the possibility that professionals, sponsors, parents, and others connected to Head Start recognized the tangible benefits it provided to children and to society. Consistent with the latter explanation, striking long-term evidence for Head Start's success has now accumulated following the earlier politically charged controversy surrounding the Westinghouse study.

Many investigations of Head Start and other preschool programs were undertaken following the Westinghouse report, and by the late 1970s a number of reasonably well-designed studies, many with follow-up evaluations, had been completed. At some sites it was possible to mount true experiments, with random assignment of children to preschool programs. In other places quasi-experimental designs were used because ethical and field conditions made it difficult to initiate or to sustain random assign-ment studies. Social scientists conducting 12 longitudinal studies formed a Consor-tium for Longitudinal Studies to pool their data and subject it to the most rigorous analysis. These pooled data contained information on approximately 3,000 low-income children. In 1976–1977, members of the consortium collected similar data on as many children as they were able to follow. These children ranged in age from 9 to 19 at time of follow-up (Darlington, Royce, Snipper, Murray, & Lazar, 1980; Lazar et al., 1979).

One of the best designed of these studies, and one that has had the greatest success in following all of the children in both the preschool-educated and the nonpreschool-educated groups, was conducted in Ypsilanti, Michigan (Berrueta-Clement et al., 1984). Called the Perry preschool study, it was initiated in the years between 1962 and 1967 and has now followed a cohort of 58 children who had preschool education, and 65 who did not, to age 19. In addition, comparable data on some variables from 11 other studies are available to provide adequate replication. All subjects came from a single pool of families who had indicated an interest in preschool education at the outset. All were black, and all were from lower socioeconomic backgrounds as measured by parents' education, father's or single parent's occupation, and the ratio of rooms in the residence to number of family members. The children's IQs ranged from 60 to 90, and none showed evidence of organic damage. The groups were assigned randomly at the outset, and the research team checked to make sure there were no pretest differences between the two groups on critical variables. Therefore, in keeping with the logic of experimental design, any differences that emerged later were apparently attributable to the differences in preschool education between the two groups.

The conceptual framework underlying this study clearly depicted adaptation as a process of person-environment fit: "Each domain of life may be viewed as a series of interactions between performance and setting. . . . Performance is behavior within a setting. . . . Social bonds develop between persons and settings . . . the internal factors of scholastic achievement and commitment to schooling and the external factor of student role reinforcement" combine to determine how well the individual is able to meet setting criteria for performance (Berrueta-Clement et al., 1984, p. 3). Preschool is here seen as an intervention designed to prevent school failure among children otherwise receiving inadequate preparation for school because of disadvantages resulting from poverty. The child's intellectual and behavioral performance in the earliest phases of schooling becomes the connecting link between early experience and long-term preventive effects. Children who perform better from the earliest days in school are recognized in subtle and not so subtle ways for their performance. They come to believe in their own adequacy and behave accordingly, thus developing stronger bonds to the setting and a stronger commitment to schooling. Once the child exhibits scholastic ability and behaves in keeping with the norms of the setting, he or she is less likely to experience failure and removal from the normal classroom environment to a special class setting. The continuing strength of bonds to the school setting keeps children in school and away from activities in the community that might lead to difficulty. Having obtained credentials in school, links to the world of employment are more readily made, and dependency is reduced.

The Perry project and others like it consistently report that the preschool experience results in improved performance on IQ tests in the early grades. The early increase in IQ score represents more than simply improved cognitive performance. It reflects greater ability to concentrate on schoollike tasks, better ability to communicate verbally, and more successful adaptation to the demands imposed by adults and structured settings. Although the advantage in IQ scores disappears within 2–3 years (Darlington et al., 1980), teachers working with preschool-educated children consistently rate them as better adjusted and more mature than similar children who have not been exposed to preschool education.

One remarkable finding from the Perry project was a difference in the number of children from the two groups ever classified as mentally retarded. Thirty-five percent of those without preschool education received such a classification, compared with only 15% of those with preschool education. Darlington et al. (1980) report a similar finding in the large group of studies they analyzed. Where 45% of children without preschool education had spent some time in special classes, that was true for only 24% of the preschool-educated subjects across all the studies. Although not all studies found this, in the Perry project consistent superiority in performance on academic achievement tests was still apparent at age 14 for those who had been exposed to pre-school education. The Perry project also reported higher high school grade-point averages for the preschool-educated group and more favorable attitudes toward high school. Not surprisingly, a significantly higher number of the preschool group graduated from high school (67% versus 49%) and went on to obtain postsecondary academic or vocational training. Perhaps as a consequence of their better performance in school, by age 19 subjects from the preschool group were more likely to be working and had higher median earnings than did their nonpreschool-educated counterparts. In keeping with their greater academic and vocational success, fewer were receiving public assistance.

The effects of preschool education, such as greater bonding to the school setting as a result of better performance, also showed up in better performance in the community. Fewer of the preschool educated group had ever been arrested as a juvenile or as an adult (31% versus 51%), as indicated in records from the juvenile courts and state police. Females in the preschool-educated group reported 17 pregnancies or births by age 19, while those not in the preschool group reported 28. Using standard methods of economic analysis (i.e., measuring short-term costs and benefits and projecting them to lifetime benefits), the Perry project reported an economic benefit-to-cost ratio of 7.01 for 1 year of preschooling and 3.56 for 2 years. The net projected saving to society was $25,000 per child. In the words of Berrueta-Clement et al.: "The estimated present value of net benefit is positive for both taxpayers (especially potential crime victims) and program participants. No one loses; taxpayers and participants are both better off with early education than without it" (1984, p. 92).

These results are quite remarkable. They give us reason to consider the possibility that time-limited preschool experiences can overcome the serious socioeconomic disadvantages and peer influences that so often pull these children in the opposite direction. Because of this we should look at them more closely. On the surface it makes sense that early success in school leads to later success in school, and that success in school leads to success in the job market. Furthermore, on a behavioral level it seems plausible to assume that there was greater day-to-day continuity in the general performance requirements and conduct demands imposed by settings than in the narrower range of responses tapped by IQ tests. Thus it is not necessary for the IQ gains to persist if the child performs well in school.

One problem, however, has been that neither the Perry group nor Lazar and Darlington (1978) have been able to identify which types of preschool education or curriculum might be superior to others. Although flexibility at the local level in program design and implementation complicates rigorous evaluation using natural science methods, from an ecological vantage point (Trickett et al., 1985; see Chapter 3), such flexibility may be important to the development and maintenance of the intervention. Berrueta-Clement et al. (1984) suggest that what matters is that the program have a definite, consistent quality, that it be implemented consistently and be well supervised. At this point we are not so certain of our educational ideas to be able to justify one approach over another, and we really do not have a clear idea of the effective ingredients of preschool education.

What actually happened thus remains an open question. A clear and consistent finding in the pooled data examined by Darlington et al. (1980) was that fewer preschool-educated children were diagnosed as mentally retarded, and fewer were referred to special classes. These data are consistent with the hypothesis that preschool-educated children actually performed better in their early elementary school years, and that the "head start" they received remained an advantage throughout their school careers. Few differences between the groups at the outset can account for the differences at follow-up.

Were there any possible artifacts to account for the findings? We knew that preschool education improved IQ, at least for a few years afterward, and that the results faded with time. The designers of Head Start were well aware of similar previous findings by developmental psychologists. Enough children may have had their IQs raised sufficiently above the usual minimum for placement in special classes (i.e., IQ of 70) to reduce the number of such placements. Lazar et al. (1978) do not present distributions of IQ scores for children in the first few years, but do show that when IQ at age 6 is covaried, the same results are obtained. Perhaps that analysis effectively controls for the IQ difference at age 6 or perhaps not. Entrance into special education does not vary continuously with IQ. It is an all-or-nothing proposition, in those years frequently determined by statute. If fewer children with IQs below 70 were in the preschool group as a result of preschool education, fewer were eligible for special education. This early effect of disqualifying children from special education placement may in part account for the reported differences in the dependent variable "failed to meet school requirements" in which preschool-educated children were superior (Darlington et al., 1980). Not all children eligible for special classes are placed in them. If post-Head Start children adapted better in the normal classroom, fewer would have been referred for special class placement even if their measured IQs were below 70. Children are often referred for special class placement not only for intellectual difficulties but also for behavioral difficulties.

We note that no other project reported by Lazar et al. (1978) similarly followed up subjects through their high school years and on into the community. Replication of the Perry project's findings at that level has not yet been demonstrated.

Head Start and related programs made varying efforts to involve parents in the preschool as volunteers or in paid positions. The Perry preschool program included weekly home visits with the mothers. The results of Lazar et al. (1978) do not indicate that helping parents learn to teach their children is essential to the success of the preschool programs. Increased contact with preschool staff may have taught parents a great deal about schools and how they work, however, making these parents more sophisticated in interacting with school personnel, more alert in seeking educational advantages and opportunities for their children, and more alert to possible pernicious placements for their children. That the good outcomes described may simply have resulted from increased sophistication about schools is not necessarily bad; it does, however, prevent us from giving full credit to the preschool program alone.

Berrueta-Clement et al. (1984) present case studies of children who were followed in their project. The case studies are interesting and provide capsule pictures of the children, but they are singularly uninformative in tracing the specific mechanisms of preschool education responsible for later outcomes. They also say little about the relationship the project staff developed with parents and children who were in the program.

That the investigators were able to follow all of the children over so many years is really quite remarkable. The report notes only that the staff made heroic efforts: "The interviewers involved in our study are themselves a principal reason for low attrition rates: They have been willing to immerse themselves in the life of the community and to go to extraordinary lengths to locate sample members" (p. 10). The report does not indicate whether the staff intervened in any other way in the lives of the children or their families. Such a "contamination" explanation for the differences in outcome between the groups appears implausible, however. The staff maintained contact with all of the children and families in both groups, and would have had to be heartless to help out one group but not the other.

A Caveat. Because of Head Start eligibility requirements, subjects in the studies reviewed were initially selected from somewhat extreme groups (i.e., all were from poverty-stricken backgrounds, all were black, and most had below average IQs). The significant effects of preschool education on later life outcomes shown for these children thus may not be generalizable to children from different backgrounds (e.g., white middle class) and perhaps not to children from urban backgrounds where there is much more mobility. Jordan, Grallo, Deutsch, and Deutsch (1985) were able to find only 154 of 1,200 students who went through a preschool program in New York City. They were able to report some favorable effects of preschool on the occupational and educational adaptation of males, but not of females. In any event, although they make substantial progress, children coming from deprived backgrounds continue to lag behind their more privileged counterparts despite preschool education. More needs to be done.

In the absence of compelling alternative explanations, however, and given the consistent findings of several studies, we are led to conclude that preschool education may indeed have considerable effectiveness as a preventive program for the misery that befalls at least some of those who fail to do well in school. The earlier assumptions regarding "plasticity" of intelligence have now given way to explanations involving the preschool-educated child's higher aspirations and motivation, better attitudes toward school (Darlington et al., 1980), and increased sense of control over life (Zigler, 1979). Where, then, do these new characteristics come from? Consistent with conceptual points raised earlier in this chapter, we suggest that the development of important cognitive competencies, the continuity present across settings in key behavior patterns, and the repeated successes experienced by preschool-educated children are responsible for their superior "social competence" (Zigler, 1979) later in life. We recommend continued skepticism, however, not just because it is the preferred stance of research-oriented academics, but also because the notion that a year or two of preschool education can overcome many other environmental effects is difficult to accept. Nonetheless, this research is hard to refute, and it stands as a significant landmark in the development of programs in the prevention of psychosocial problems.

Summary

The metaphors of ecology and vulnerability have spawned practical approaches to mental health problems from a preventive orientation. Practice in prevention poses many difficult and unfamiliar ethical and procedural questions regarding the targeted recipients of a program, its goals, and the precise nature and effects of professional intervention. Furthermore, long-standing controversies over the conceptualization of mental health and disorder also apply to prevention activities. Prevention programs require us to take responsibility in advance for the occurrence of conditions we do not fully understand and to adopt a much more extended long-term outlook on the ultimate success of our efforts. We would also note, however, that prevention research is becoming more sophisticated in methodology as well as conceptualization. Several examples of this progress have recently appeared (see especially Durlak, 1985; Rolf, 1985; and Rosenberg & Reppucci, 1985).

One intuitively appealing approach, defined most often as secondary prevention, involves the early identification and prompt treatment of incipient behavioral maladjustment in individuals. Problems exist with both the accuracy of identification and the treatment procedures currently used in secondary prevention. Primary prevention, whose goal is to reduce the incidence of long-term adjustment problems, has attracted an extensive following in community psychology, although here, too, knotty problems in defining such constructs as "positive mental health" and "competence building," as well as the prominent roles played by unfamiliar strategies like public advocacy and political lobbying, have hampered acceptance of primary prevention by the mental health field as a whole.

We examined two areas of prevention research given significant support by the 1978 President's Commission on Mental Health—the building of individual and community competence and the modification of key community settings such as school classrooms. In the area of individual competence building, investigators are currently interested in the generalizability of various cognitive and social skills across settings and over time. Further development of environmentally based prevention programs at the community level will require a concerted effort to identify and systematically describe some of the host of environmental settings influencing behavior in pursuit of a better understanding of the process of behavior-environment congruence. The question of how to help individuals define, select, or create environments optimal for their own well-being needs more consideration, perhaps as a topic related to interpersonal problem solving or competence building. Efforts at primary prevention may also be more successful when focused on a broad range of problems selected from all developmental milestones than when interventions are restricted to early childhood, with effects expected to endure.

Finally, many of the ideas in this chapter were discussed in the context of new findings on the widely discussed Head Start program. Head Start combined both competence building and social setting change to improve the school and community adaptations of disadvantaged children; it had an encouraging preventive impact over a respectably long time frame.

Notes

1. Bloom (1977) makes the ironic point that in some cases, such as that of the disorder phenylketonuria, early detection and prompt intervention actually *increase* prevalence by greatly increasing the life expectancy of individuals carrying the disorder.

2. Contemporary work in psychology conceptualizes detection not so much as a process of objectively sorting "true" cases and noncases, but a process of *making decisions* under conditions of uncertainty. From this vantage point, characteristics of the stimuli involved (i.e., first-grade children in the present example) affect decision making in only a limited, circumscribed way. Of equal or greater importance is the nature of the decision-making process itself and the social and political context in which it occurs. In other words, at best the "case/noncase" status

of a potential target person resides only partly inside his or her skin—to an important degree it is "in the eye of the beholder" as well.

3. We have substantial evidence that boys do far worse than girls in elementary schools. Boys are consistently rated as more maladjusted by their teachers than are girls. This difference holds whether female or male teachers make the ratings, although female teachers tend to rate the behavior of both boys and girls more severely (Levine, 1977). The latter finding fails to support the hypothesis that boys have greater difficulty in a female-dominated environment than do girls. Males are at risk for a variety of school problems, however, and no good explanation of the risk has been put forth.

4. Feeney (1975) and Sadow (1975) studied the same sample of classrooms. They reported significant differences between classroom types in social behavior, in pupil liking of teachers, and in pupil liking of school. Summarizing 57 empirical studies, Horwitz (1979) concludes that almost half the studies report children like open classrooms better, with only two studies favoring traditional classrooms. Hochschild (1975) and Levine (1975) both asked teachers to select classroom management techniques to indicate how they would deal with overly dependent and overly disruptive children. Teachers in the more open classrooms selected techniques such as individualizing instruction, giving the child a choice of activities, and techniques categorized as "including in" versus excluding. The techniques they selected are consistent with descriptions of open-classroom pedagogical theory and consistent with observations of how handicapped children were mainstreamed in British primary schools (Levine, 1979). These studies provide some additional measure of validity for the initial classification of classrooms.

References

Albee, G. W. (1980). A competency model to replace the defect model. In M. Gibbs, J. Lachenmeyer, & J. Sigal (Eds.). *Community psychology: Theoretical and empirical approaches.* New York: Gardner Press.

Anthony, E. J. (1977). Preventive measures for children and adolescents at high risk for psychosis. In G. Albee & J. Joffe (Eds.), *Vermont conference on the primary prevention of psychopathology* (Vol. 1). Hanover, NH: University Press of New England.

Bergin, A. E. (1971). The evaluation of therapeutic outcomes. In A. E. Bergin and S. L. Garfield (Eds.), *Handbook of psychotherapy and behavior change: An empirical analysis.* New York: Wiley.

Berrueta-Clement, J. R., Schweinhart, L. J., Barnett, W. S., Epstein, A. S., & Weikart, D. P. (1984). *Changed lives. The effects of the Perry preschool program on youths through age 19.* Ypsilanti, MI: High/Scope Press.

Bloom, B. L. (1965). The medical model, miasma theory, and community mental health. *Community Mental Health Journal, 1,* 333–338.

Bloom, B. L. (1977). *Community mental health: A general introducton.* Monterey: Brooks-Cole.

Bloom, B. L. (1979). Prevention of mental disorders: Recent advances in theory and practice. *Community Mental Health Journal, 15,* 179–191.

Bloom, B. L. (1984). *Community mental health. A general introduction* (2nd ed.). Monterey: Brooks/Cole.

Bloom, B. L., Hodges, W. F., & Caldwell, R. A. (1982). A preventive intervention program for the newly separated: Initial evaluation. *American Journal of Community Psychology, 10,* 251–264.

Bloom, B. S. (1964). *Stability and change in human characteristics.* New York: Wiley.

Blumberg, M. S. (1957) Evaluating health screening procedures. *Operations Research, 5,* 351–360.

Campbell, D. T., & Erlebacher, A. (1970). How regression artifacts in quasi-experimental evaluation can mistakenly make compensatory education look harmful. In J. Hellmuth (Ed.),

Compensatory education: A national debate. The disadvantaged child (Vol. III). New York: Brunner/Mazel.

Campbell, D. T., & Kimmel, A. J. (1985). *Guiding preventive intervention research centers for research validity* (Contract No. SSN 552-12-4531). Rockville, MD: Department of Health and Human Services.

Caplan, G. (1964). *Principles of preventive psychiatry.* New York: Basic Books.

Caplan, N., & Nelson, S. D. (1973). On being useful: The nature and consequences of psychological research on social problems. *American Psychologist, 28,* 199–211.

Cassel, J. (1976). The contribution of the social environment to host resistance. *American Journal of Epidemiology, 104,* 107–123.

Cicirelli, V. G. (1969). *The impact of Head Start: An evaluation of the effects of Head Start on children's cognitive and affective development.* Washington, DC: National Bureau of Standards, Institute for Applied Technology.

Cicirelli, V. G. (1984). The misinterpretation of the Westinghouse study: A reply to Zigler and Berman. *American Psychologist, 39,* 915–916.

Cowen, E. L. (1973). Social and community interventions. *Annual Review of Psychology, 24,* 423–472.

Cowen, E. L. (1977). Baby steps toward primary prevention. *American Journal of Community Psychology, 5,* 1–22.

Cowen, E. L. (1980). The wooing of primary prevention. *American Journal of Community Psychology, 8,* 258–284.

Cowen, E. L., Izzo, L. D., Miles, H., Telschow, E. F., Trost, M. A., & Zax, M. (1963). A mental health program in the school setting: Description and evaluation. *Journal of Psychology, 56,* 307–356.

Cowen, E. L., Pederson, A., Babigian, H., Izzo, L. D., & Trost, M. A. (1973). Long-term follow-up of early detected vulnerable children. *Journal of Consulting and Clinical Psychology, 41,* 438–446.

Cowen, E. L., Trost, M. A., Lorion, R. P., Dorr, D., Izzo, L. D., & Isaacson, R. V. (1975). *New ways in school mental health.* New York: Human Sciences Press.

Cowen, E. L., Zax, M., Izzo, L. D., & Trost, M. A. (1966). The prevention of emotional disorders in the school setting: A further investigation. *Journal of Consulting Psychology, 30,* 381–387.

Curran, J. W., Morgan, W. M., Hardy, A. M., Jaffe, H. W., Darrow, W. W., & Dowdle, W. R. (1985). The epidemiology of AIDS: Current status and future prospects. *Science, 229,* 1352–1357.

Darlington, R. B., Royce, J. M., Snipper, A. S., Murray, H. W., & Lazar, I. (1980). Preschool programs and later school competence of children from low-income families. *Science, 208,* 202–204.

Dawber, T. R. (1982). *The Framingham study: The epidemiology of atherosclerotic disease.* Cambridge: Harvard University Press.

Durlak, J. A. (1983). Social problem-solving as a primary prevention strategy. In R. Felner et al. (Eds.), *Preventive psychology* (chap. 3). New York: Plenum.

Durlak, J. A. (1985). Primary prevention of school maladjustment. *Journal of Consulting and Clinical Psychology, 53,* 623–630.

Ewing, C. P. (1985). *Schall v. Martin:* Preventive detention and dangerousness through the looking glass. *Buffalo Law Review, 34,* 173–226.

Featherston, J. (1971). *Schools where children learn.* New York: Liveright.

Feeney, M. G. (1975). Attraction and influence in open and traditional classrooms. Unpublished doctoral dissertation, SUNY at Buffalo.

Felner, R. D., Stolberg, A. L., & Cowen, E. L. (1975). Crisis events and the school mental health referral patterns for young children. *Journal of Consulting and Clinical Psychology, 43,* 305–310.

Felner, R. D., Farber, S. S., Ginter, M. A., Boike, M. F., & Cowen, E. L. (1980). Family stress and organization following parental divorce or death. *Journal of Divorce, 4,* 67–76.

Finkel, N. J. (1975). Strens, trauma and trauma resolution. *American Journal of Community Psychology, 3,* 173–178.

Frazita, R., & Stone, R. A. (1977). How Western New York teachers view open education. *Society of Academic Administrators of New York State Journal, 6,* 17–19.

Furstenberg, F. F., Jr., Moore, K. A., & Peterson, J. L. (1985). Sex education and sexual experience among adolescents. *American Journal of Public Health, 75,* 1331–1332.

Garmezy, N. (1971). Vulnerability research and the issue of primary prevention. *American Journal of Orthopsychiatry, 41,* 101–116.

Gesten, E. L., Rains, M. H., Rapkin, B. D., Weissberg, R. P., de Apocada, R. F., Cowen, E. L., & Bowen, R. (1982). Training children in social problem-solving competencies: A first and second look. *American Journal of Community Psychology, 10,* 95–115.

Gillespie, J. F., Durlak, J. A., & Sherman, D. (1982). Relationship between kindergarten children's interpersonal problem-solving skills and other indices of school adjustment: A cautionary note. *American Journal of Community Psychology, 10, 149–153.*

Glidewell, J. C. & Swallow, C. S. (1968). The prevalence of maladjustment in elementary schools. A report prepared for the Joint Commission on the Mental Health of Children, University of Chicago.

Goldston, S. E. (1977). An overview of primary prevention programming. In D. Klein & S. Goldston (Eds). *Primary prevention: An idea whose time has come.* Washington, DC: U.S. Government Printing Office.

Goldston, S. E. (1986). Primary prevention: Historical perspectives and a blueprint for action. *American Psychologist, 41,* 453–460.

Goplerud, E. N. (1980). Social support and stress during the first year of graduate school. *Professional Psychology, 11,* 283–290.

Gottesman, I. I., & Shields, J. (1972). *Schizophrenia and genetics: A twin study vantage point.* New York: Academic Press.

Gruenberg, E. M. (1974). The social breakdown syndrome and its prevention. In S. Arieti (Ed.), *American handbook of psychiatry* (Vol. 2, 2d ed.). New York: Basic Books.

Guerin, D., & MacKinnon, D. P. (1985). An assessment of the California child passenger restraint requirement. *American Journal of Public Health, 75,* 142–144.

Hartman, H. (1958). *Ego psychology and the problem of adaptation.* New York: International Universities Press.

Heller, K., & Monahan, J. (1977). *Psychology and community change.* Homewood, IL: Dorsey Press.

Heller, K., Price, R. H., & Sher, K. J. (1980). Research and evaluation in primary prevention: Issues and guidelines. In R. Price, R. Ketterer, B. Bader, & J. Monahan (Eds.), *Prevention in mental health.* Beverly Hills: Sage.

Holmes, T. R., & Rahe, R. H. (1967). The Social Readjustment Rating Scale. *Journal of Psychosomatic Research, 11,* 213–218.

Hochschild, R. M. (1976). Teacher rated maladjustment in open, transitional, and traditional classroom environments. *Dissertation Abstracts International, 37,* 2508B. (University Microfilms No. DAH 76-26531)

Horwitz, R. A. (1979). Effects of the "open classroom." In H. J. Walberg (Ed.), *Educational environments and effects.* Berkeley: McCutchan.

Hunt, D. E. (1975). Person-environment interaction: A challenge found wanting before it was tried. *Review of Educational Research, 45,* 209–230.

Hunt, J. McV. (1961). *Intelligence and experience.* New York: Ronald Press.

Hunt, J. McV. (1968). Toward the prevention of incompetence. In J. Carter (Ed.), *Research contributions from psychology to community mental health.* New York: Behavioral Publications.

Iscoe, I. (1974). Community psychology and the competent community. *American Psychologist, 29,* 607–613.

Jahoda, M. (1958). *Current concepts of positive mental health.* New York: Basic Books.

Jason, L. A., & Rose T. (1984). Influencing the passage of child passenger restraint legislation. *American Journal of Community Psychology, 12,* 485–495.

Jordan, T. J., Gralle, R., Deutsch, M., & Deutsch, C. P. (1985). Long-term effects of early enrichment: A 20-year perspective on persistence and change. *American Journal of Community Psychology, 13,* 393–415.

Joy, A. (1977). *Classroom organization and classroom behavior: A study of children's behavior in differentially organized classroom types.* Unpublished doctoral dissertation, SUNY at Buffalo.

Kagan, J. (1976). Resilience and continuity in psychological development. In A. M. Clarke & A. D. B. Clarke (Eds.), *Early experience: Myth and evidence.* New York: Free Press.

Kessler, M., & Albee, G. W. (1975). Primary prevention. *Annual Review of Psychology, 26,* 557–591.

Kohlberg, L., LaCrosse, J., & Ricks, D. (1972). The predictability of adult mental health from childhood behavior. In B. Wolman (Ed.), *Manual of child psychopathology,* New York: McGraw-Hill.

Kornberg, M. S., & Caplan, G. (1980). Risk factors and preventive intervention in child psychopathology: A review. *Journal of Prevention, 1,* 71–133.

Lamb, H. R., & Zusman, J. (1979). Primary prevention in perspective. *American Journal of Psychiatry, 136,* 12–17.

Lazar, I., Darlington, R. B., Levenstein, P., Miller, L., Palmer, F., Weikart, D., Woolman, M., Zigler, E., Beller, K., Deutsch, C., Deutsch, M., Gordon, I., Gray, S., & Karnes, M. (1978). *Lasting effects after preschool* (DHEW Publication No. (OHDS) 79–30178). Washington, DC: Office of Human Development Services, Administration for Children, Youth and Families.

Leavitt, J. W. (1982). *The healthiest city: Milwaukee and the politics of health reform.* Princeton, NJ: Princeton University Press.

Levine, M. (1975). Children's adaptation in classrooms differing in complexity. Unpublished manuscript, Department of Psychology, SUNY at Buffalo.

Levine, M. (1977). Sex differences in behavior ratings: Male and female teachers rate male and female pupils. *American Journal of Community Psychology, 5,* 347–353.

Levine, M. (1979). Some observations on the integration of handicapped children in British primary schools. In S. J. Meisels (Ed.), *Special education and development. Perspectives on young children with special needs.* Baltimore: University Park Press.

Levine, M. (1981). *The history and politics of community mental health.* New York: Oxford University Press.

Levine, M., & Graziano, A. M. (1972). Intervention programs in elementary schools. In S. E. Golann & C. Eisdorfer (Eds.), *Handbook of community mental health.* (pp. 541–573) New York: Appleton-Century-Crofts.

Levine, M., & Levine, A. (1970). *A social history of helping services.* New York: Appleton-Century-Crofts.

Levine, M., & Perkins, D. V. (1980a). Tailor-making a life events scale. In D. Perkins (Chair), *New developments in research on life stress and social support.* Symposium presented at the American Psychological Association Convention, Montreal.

Levine, M., & Perkins, D. V. (1980b). Social setting interventions and primary prevention: Comments on the Report of the Task Panel on Prevention to the President's Commission on Mental Health. *American Journal of Community Psychology, 8,* 147–158.

Levitan, S. A. (1969). *The Great Society's poor law. A new approach to poverty.* Baltimore: Johns Hopkins Press.

Lorion, R. P., Cowen, E. L., & Kraus, R. M. (1974). Some hidden "regularities" in a school mental health program and their relation to intended outcomes. *Journal of Consulting and Clinical Psychology, 42,* 346–352.

McKim, B. J., Weissberg, R. P., Cowen, E. L., Gesten, E. L., & Rapkin, B. D. (1980). A comparison of the problem-solving ability and adjustment of suburban and urban third-grade children. *American Journal of Community Psychology, 10,* 155–170.

Mednick, S. A., & McNeil, T. F. (1968). Current methodology in research on the etiology of schizophrenia: Serious difficulties which suggest the use of the high-risk-group method. *Psychological Bulletin, 70,* 681–693.

Mednick, S. A., Schulsinger, F., & Venables, P. H. (1979). Risk research and primary prevention of mental illness. *International Journal of Mental Health, 7,* 150–164.

Miller, H. L., Coombs, D. W., Leeper, J. D., & Barton, S. N. (1984). An analysis of the effects of suicide prevention facilities on suicide rates in the United States. *American Journal of Public Health, 74,* 340–343.

Mischel, W. (1973). Toward a cognitive social learning reconceptualization of personality. *Psychological Review, 80,* 252–283.

Moynihan, D. P. (1969). *Maximum feasible misunderstanding: Community action in the War on Poverty.* New York: Free Press.

Ojemann, R. H., Levitt, E. E., Lyle, W. H., & Whiteside, M. F. (1955). The effects of a "causal" teacher-training program and certain curricular changes on grade school children. *Journal of Experimental Education, 24,* 95–114.

Pedro-Carroll, J. L., & Cowen, E. L. (1985). The children of divorce intervention program: An investigation of the efficacy of a school-based prevention program. *Journal of Consulting and Clinical Psychology, 53,* 603–611.

Peterson, L., & Mori, L. (1985). Prevention of child injury: An overview of targets, methods, and tactics for psychologists. *Journal of Consulting and Clinical Psychology, 53,* 586–594.

Price, R. H. (1974). Etiology, the social environment, and the prevention of psychological dysfunction. In P. Insel & R. Moos (Eds.), *Health and the social environment.* Lexington, MA: D. C. Heath.

President's Commission on Mental Health. (1978). *Report to the President from the President's Commission on Mental Health.* Washington, DC: U.S. Government Printing Office.

Rappaport, J. (1977). *Community psychology: Values, research, and action.* New York: Holt, Rinehart & Winston.

Rappaport, J. (1981). In praise of paradox: A social policy of empowerment over prevention. *American Journal of Community Psychology, 9,* 1–26.

Richmond, J. B., Stipek, D. J., & Zigler, E. (1979). A decade of Head Start. In E. Zigler & J. Valentine (Eds.), *Project Head Start: A legacy of the War on Poverty* (chap. 4). New York: Free Press.

Rolf, J. E. (1985). Evolving adaptive theories and methods for prevention research with children. *Journal of Consulting and Clinical Psychology, 53,* 631–646.

Rosenberg, M. S., & Reppucci, N. D. (1985). Primary prevention of child abuse. *Journal of Consulting and Clinical Psychology, 53,* 576–585.

Ryan, W. (1981). *Blaming the victim.* New York: Random House.

Sadow, J. E. (1975). The effects of open and traditional educational practices on students in nonacademic areas. *Dissertation Abstracts International, 37,* 987B. (University Microfilms No. 76-17,051).

Sarason, S. B. (1981). An asocial psychology and a misdirected clinical psychology. *American Psychologist, 36,* 827–836.

Sarason, S. B., Davison, K. S., Lighthall, F. F., Waite, R. R., & Ruebush, B. K. (1960). *Anxiety in elementary school children.* New York: Wiley.

Sarason, S. B., Hill, K. T., & Zimbardo, P. G. (1964). A longitudinal study of the relation of test anxiety to performance on intelligence and achievement tests. *Monographs of the Society for Research on Child Development,* No. 98.

Sarason, I. G., & Sarason, B. R. (1981). Teaching cognitive and social skills to high school students. *Journal of Consulting and Clinical Psychology, 49,* 908–918.

Sarbin, T. R. (1970). A role theory perspective for community psychology: The structure of social identity. In D. Adelson & B. Kalis (Eds.), *Community psychology and mental health: Perspectives and challenges.* Scranton, PA: Chandler.

Schall v. Martin, 104 S.Ct. 2403 (1984).

Scheff, T. J. (1966). *Being mentally ill: A sociological theory.* Chicago: Aldine.

Shure, M. B., & Spivack, G. (1982). Interpersonal problem-solving in young children: A cognitive approach to prevention. *American Journal of Community Psychology, 10,* 341–355.

Silberman, C. (1970). *Crisis in the classroom.* New York: Random House.

Spaulding, J., & Balch, P. (1983). A brief history of primary prevention in the twentieth century: 1908 to 1980. *American Journal of Community Psychology, 11,* 59–80.

Spivack, G., & Shure, M. B. (1974). *Social adjustment of young children.* San Francisco: Jossey-Bass.

Stott, M. W. R., Gaier, E. L., & Thomas, K. B. (1984). Supervised access: A judicial alternative to noncompliance with visitation arrangements following divorce. *Children and Youth Services Review, 6,* 207–217.

Swift, C. F. (1980). Primary prevention: Policy and practice. In R. Price, R. Ketterer, B. Bader, & J. Monahan (Eds.), *Prevention in mental health.* Beverly Hills: Sage.

Task Panel on Prevention (1978). Report of the Task Panel on Prevention. *Task Panel Reports Submitted to the President's Commission on Mental Health* (Vol. 4). Washington, DC: U.S. Government Printing Office.

Trickett, E. J., Kelley, J. G., & Vincent, T. A. (1985). The spirit of ecological inquiry in community research. In E. C. Susskind & D. C. Klein (Eds.), *Community research: Methods, paradigms, and applications* (pp. 283–333). New York: Praeger.

Trickett, E. J., & Moos, R. H. (1974). Personal correlates of contrasting environments: Student satisfactions in high school classrooms. *American Journal of Community Psychology, 2,* 1–12.

Weiss, M. A., & Scott, K. (1974). Suicide attempters ten years later. *Comprehensive Psychiatry, 15,* 165–171.

Weisz, P. V., & Cowen, E. L. (1976). Relationships between teachers' perceptions of classroom environments and school adjustment problems. *American Journal of Community Psychology, 4,* 181–187.

White, R. W. (1959). Motivation reconsidered: The concept of competence. *Psychological Review, 66,* 297–333.

Wicker, A. W. (1972). Processes which mediate behavior-environment congruence. *Behavioral Science, 17,* 265–277.

Winer, J. I., Hilpert, P. L., Gesten, E. L., Cowen, E. L., & Schubin, W. E. (1982). The evaluation of a kindergarten social problem solving program. *Journal of Primary Prevention, 2,* 205–216.

Zax, M. (1980). History and background of the community mental health movement. In M. Gibbs, J. Lachenmeyer, & J. Sigal (Eds.), *Community psychology: Theoretical and empirical approaches.* New York: Gardner Press.

Zigler, E. (1979). Head Start: Not a program but an evolving concept. In E. Zigler & J. Valentine (Eds.), *Project Head Start: A Legacy of the War on Poverty* (Chap. 16). New York: Free Press.

Zigler, E. (1984). Meeting the critics on their own terms. *American Psychologist, 39,* 916–917.

Zigler, E., & Valentine J. (1979). *Project Head Start: A legacy of the War on Poverty.* New York: Free Press.

8

Self-Help Groups

This chapter will discuss the important and growing self-help movement. The concepts that have been developed in the previous chapters are useful in analyzing the self-help phenomenon. A major purpose of the chapter on prevention was to demonstrate the nature of community psychology in application as well as in theory. We can summarize the key points of this view in a few succinct statements. In community psychology a problem is defined in terms of poor person-environment fit—that is, it involves an individual's relationship to a context, not a medical disease. Natural changes in this context, such as the occurrence of stressful events, occur widely and frequently (see Chapter 1), which theoretically makes everyone vulnerable to maladaptive episodes of behavior. A problem solution is a change in the community context that facilitates adaptation by improving person-environment fit. Interventions, as problem-solving changes in the community context, are designed to be readily available—located spatially and temporally proximate to the problem of poor person-setting fit. These interventions build competence through the acquisition and rehearsal of key responses that enable the individual to expand the range of settings in which he or she can adapt. Ecologically speaking, community psychology interventions become part of the community—they represent a stable, situationally based resource instead of a temporary panacea. Interventions also facilitate adaptation by providing ongoing support and/or arranging meaningful roles and statuses, which ultimately means that in the long run the community itself increases in competence.

Another important response to the "soap opera" of life is the voluntary self-help organization. Self-help groups are among the fastest growing forms of assistance, and no day goes by that any newspaper reader cannot find the announcement of a self-help or support-group meeting. Almost everyone has heard of Alcoholics Anonymous (AA), but fewer are aware of the mushrooming growth of other self-help organizations, many built on the AA model.

Self-help groups are of interest to community psychology for several reasons. They are an important indigenous resource within the private, nonprofessional segment of the community, and they address the current trend toward greater consumer choice and empowerment (see Chapter 12). Even more important may be the fact that some self-help groups seem to serve a clientele different from the young, attractive, verbal, intelligent, successful (YAVIS) individual considered the ideal candidate for traditional psychotherapy. A survey by Knight et al. (1980), for example, found that the average member of major self-help groups like AA or Parents Without Partners is middle-aged, is a homemaker or blue-collar worker, and has little beyond a high school education.

The central themes of this chapter are first that self-help groups are important community resources, and second that they are understandable using the same principles we have used in explaining other interventions, such as prevention; that is, they can be conceptualized as settings that build individual and community competence in pursuit of improved adaptation through person-environment fit. In this chapter we first describe the phenomenon of the self-help group in terms of its nature as a source of help. We next consider the dynamics of self-help groups, including theoretical explanations for how they seem to facilitate adaptation by vulnerable people. Although scientific evaluations of self-help groups as community interventions are not plentiful, information on their effectiveness is increasing, and we direct attention to new evidence on this question involving AA. The chapter closes with a discussion of how community psychologists can directly assist individuals at risk by rationally creating tailor-made self-help groups, versions of which may or may not yet exist. We begin by examining the tremendous growth of self-help groups in recent years.

Growth of Self-Help Organizations

Self-help groups of all kinds are growing rapidly. Tracy and Gussow (1976) and Gartner and Reissman (1977) offer some figures: AA had about 50 groups in 1942; there are now more than 30,000 groups with over 600,000 members. Parents Anonymous began in 1969 with one group and two members; by 1975 it had grown to 450 groups with some 4,000 members. Parents Without Partners had an estimated 30,000 members in 1966; its membership is now estimated at over 100,000 nationally. Recovery, Inc., grew from 850 groups in 1973 to over 1,000 groups in 1976. Tracy and Gussow identified four national groups in existence in 1942, and estimate that by 1975 there were some 2,000 different self-help organizations, many with multiple chapters. Today there are so many self-help organizations that a National Self-Help Clearing House has been formed to disseminate information about the activities of existing groups, the formation of new groups, publications, research findings, funding sources, and ideas and methods for starting new groups. Members of self-help groups often cite this growth in numbers as indicative of the need for such groups and also of their effectiveness.

In counterpoint to the growth of professional mental health disciplines, self-help may appear to be a new phenomenon on the American scene. When Alexis De Tocqueville visited the United States in 1831, he noted the large number of associations of all kinds: "Americans of all ages, all conditions and dispositions, constantly form associations . . . of a thousand . . . kinds—religious, moral, serious, futile, enormous or diminutive. . . . If it be proposed to inculcate some truth or foster some feeling by the encouragement of a great example, they form a society" (De Tocqueville, 1835, p. 198). De Tocqueville believed that associations were peculiarly American, a function of a democratic social order.

In 1902 Kropotkin (1972) argued that cooperation is a basic survival mechanism for human beings. He provided many examples throughout history of spontaneously developing cooperative enterprises and associations that resulted in greater mutual protection and productivity. In medieval guilds, for example, members banded together to regulate their trade. Together the members of a guild constituted a brotherhood, and each was responsible not only for maintaining standards for the trade but also for providing fraternal benefits to the membership—aid in the event of illness, aid to widows and orphans, celebrations of births and marriages. Anticipating today's sociobiologists, Kropotkin argued that a social instinct leads people to help each other: "There is the gist of human psychology. Unless men are maddened in the battlefields, they cannot stand it to hear appeals for help, and not to respond to them. . . . The sophisms of the brain cannot resist the mutual aid feeling, because this feeling has been nurtured by thousands of years of pre-human life in societies" (Kropotkin, 1972, p. 234).

Contemporary Reasons for Growth

People have always organized in response to mutual need, be it out of some social instinct, as Kropotkin argued, or as the manifestation of rational coping capacities (Katz & Bender, 1976; Hurvitz, 1976). If people organize in new ways to fulfill social need, existing means of providing support in time of need have evidently proved insufficient. Many observers link the movement toward self-help and mutual help to a variety of social changes.

For our purposes, we can most usefully link the growth of self-help to changes that reflect problems in existing social organizations and means for providing mutual assistance. Growth in self-help or mutual assistance may reflect changes in other more traditional groups that might at one time have fulfilled human needs. In Chapter 1 we discussed recent changes in the family: the number of single-parent households is increasing, and American society is also very mobile. A large number of people change their addresses each year, many moving long distance and loosening their ties with family and old friends, which forces them to readapt in the sense of making new ties and becoming a part of new social networks. Geographic mobility puts distinct pressures on the nuclear family, and increasing numbers of working mothers may add to that pressure even as their working alleviates economic difficulties. A large number of people live alone and may be unable to call upon friends or family for assistance. In still other cases, the resources of friends and family may not be sufficient to aid the individual in coping with problems in living that are foreign to ordinary experience. In a superb book, the late Raoul Naroll (1983) demonstrated on a worldwide basis that ruptures in what he termed "moralnets"—the largest primary or face-to-face group that serves a given person as a normative reference group—are associated with a wide range of mental health and social problems.

Moreover, changing values have produced a decline in the prominence of some traditional organizations that served mutual need. Despite population growth from 1968 to 1975, Greek letter societies, fraternal, nationality and ethnic societies, and national religious organizations all declined in number (U.S. Bureau of Census, 1976). These traditional groups and associations may well have defined a socially shared outlook helpful to members in making sense of contemporary life and in providing social forms through which that outlook could be expressed. In the same period, national nonprofit organizations concerned with social welfare, public affairs, health, and medicine increased in number (U.S. Bureau of Census, 1976). If we include neighborhood associations and block clubs, hundreds of thousands, if not millions, of new groups exist across the United States (Perlman, 1976). These groups may well be successors to community organizations that served similar purposes in another era.

We have already discussed deficiencies in the medical model of service delivery. Another deficiency of the medical model becomes apparent in examining Kropotkin's view of charity. Writing from an anarchist viewpoint, Kropotkin (1972) argued that the existence of a centralized state interfered with the mutual assistance that would develop spontaneously in the absence of a state. He extended his argument to organized charitable enterprises as well.

> Moreover, while early Christianity, like all other religions, was an appeal to the broadly human feelings of mutual aid and sympathy, the Christian church has aided the State in wrecking all standing institutions of mutual aid and support which were anterior to it, or developed outside of it; and, instead of the *mutual aid* which every savage considers as due to his kinsman, it has preached *charity* which bears a character of inspiration from above, and accordingly implies a certain superiority of the giver upon the receiver. (p. 238)

We need not accept Kropotkin's view regarding the role of the church. Drawing an analogy between organized charity and professional services from a medical model, however, we can argue that it is essentially a "trickle-down" model of assistance. Whatever its other merits, this model limits the possibilities for reciprocity and mutual assistance based on experience with the particular problem in living. Its very professionalism, certainly a strength for many purposes, nonetheless implies the superiority of the giver to the receiver and does not allow for reciprocity in their relationship. We need not repeat other criticisms of the medical model here, but it is important to reemphasize one. Although a professional may have a great deal to offer, he or she usually does not know in great detail what it means to live with a particular problem, nor how one copes with it on a day-to-day basis. Our therapeutic philosophies and approaches tell us to make our clients dependent and not to respond to the plea, "Tell me what to do!" Clients live with the problem of coping on a day-by-day basis, however, and most therapists do not focus on those day-by-day coping techniques. Professional therapists often do not transmit practical, gut-level, tried-and-true methods for handling problems. To the degree that all wisdom is seen to reside in the professional, there is a loss of the wisdom that comes from learning to cope on a day-by-day basis. The self-help model addresses that deficiency.

Anyone who reads the daily paper is also aware of serious and growing problems regarding the cost of health care. Similar problems affect the cost of professional mental health care as well. Insurance companies, wary of the potential high cost of mental health services and the interminability of some mental health treatments, have imposed limits on both inpatient and outpatient care. The argument that psychotherapy and other types of psychological intervention reduce the demand for other medical services and are thus cost-effective has come under more criticism recently than when first advanced (Shackman, 1984).

For those who pay for care directly, the costs of extended treatment are prohibitive for all but the wealthiest. Public agencies with sliding-fee scales take into account the ability to pay, but even these fees can add up. Moreover, most therapists would agree that it is difficult to show an even exchange—that for any unit of fee, a corresponding unit of progress is made. Payment of a fee does not make for an even exchange, nor does it undo the social inequality and lack of reciprocity in the relationship between the client and the professional.

The cost of professional services can be prohibitive, especially if an extended period of assistance is required, while self-help groups provide services indefinitely to substantial numbers of people at very low cost. A telephone survey we did asking self-help groups in the Buffalo metropolitan area about the typical turnout at meetings revealed that as many as 1,000 people a month are being served for little more than coffee money. One thousand people a month is roughly comparable to the case load of the largest mental health center in that area, which provides professional mental health services at a cost of between $2 and $3 million per year. People who attend self-help groups are probably not a representative sample of those in need. Those responding to our survey estimated that more than two-thirds of the participants in most of the organizations are female. It is also our impression that the vast bulk of participants are white, and there are relatively few examples of interracial groups. Another interesting variation from the medical model is that where more than one chapter of a given self-help group exists, a prospective member can "shop around" among them, facilitating an ecological process of mutual selection that acknowledges the diversity among people and has as its goal the improvement of person-setting fit. We have no data on this point but would strongly conjecture that tolerance of such "shopping around" by prospective clients is not nearly so great among professionals. Some patients undoubtedly change therapists from time to time. Is it a matter of resistance, or can such changes be viewed as an attempt by the client to improve the person-environment fit?

Types of Self-Help Groups

So far we have been discussing self-help as if all groups were similar in aims and methods to psychotherapy. Hurvitz (1976), in fact, terms these organizations "peer psychotherapy" groups. In common with psychotherapy, their aim is to assist the individual in coping with the emotions and the dilemmas generated by problems in living. The locus of pathology is within the individual, and the individual is assisted in making a better adaptation to self and to the world.

Sagarin (1969) points out that there are two general types of self-help groups. In one,

> Individuals seek to reduce their deviant behavior and in this way escape from deviance. . . . Such groups paint deviants as worthwhile individuals, souls to be saved; but they view the deviance itself as immoral, sinful and self-defeating. . . . The second type of deviant group, consist[s] of those who are seeking to modify the definition of their conditions as deviant. . . . These groups seek to change the public attitude toward their particular deviance. . . . Groups seeking to change social attitudes thumb their noses at society in order to foster pride in the deviant. (p. 21)

AA is an example of the first type of self-help group. It is directed toward helping members overcome a drinking problem through mutual assistance. AA teaches that for *alcoholics* drinking is self-defeating. AA is not a temperance organization—it takes no position about the drinking of others who are not alcoholics, and it takes no public position on legislation related to drinking. It neither favors nor opposes legislation to raise the drinking age or to introduce stiffer penalties against drunk driving. It makes no effort to create sympathy for the alcoholic or to reduce stigmatization or discrimination directed against former alcoholics. It has no interest in changing society's views of alcoholics, except perhaps in furthering the conception that alcoholism is a disease. Even then it does not speak out as an organization, nor does it allow individual members to speak on such issues in the name of the group.

Notable examples of the second type of self-help organization would be any of the organizations comprising the civil rights movement. Among the most successful movements of our time, civil rights organizations were directed toward the removal of legal barriers against the participation of blacks in almost every public aspect of our society. Segregation and discrimination in public accommodations, schools, employment, housing, and marriage are now barred by law. (We discuss school desegregation in Chapter 11.) The civil rights movement utilized political and social action and adopted a litigative strategy to help create opportunities for blacks and for other minorities and to instill self-esteem. It also served as a model for other oppressed (read "deviant") groups to improve their lives by working to change society's view of and actions toward members of those groups. Milner (1985) describes how the mental patients' rights movement used the civil rights movement as a model in working for change through litigation, legislation, and direct social action. (In the next chapter we describe the women's movement and the use of consciousness raising groups to illustrate how self-help works in helping individuals to adapt and in changing the larger society's views and treatment of those individuals.)

A case in point is the gay rights movement. In recent years, these groups have been active in attempting to change not homosexuals, except perhaps to instill pride in being gay, but aspects of the larger society. For example, these groups were sufficiently active and sufficiently persuasive to affect the nature of psychiatric diagnosis of homosexuality. No longer is the practice of homosexuality officially classified as an illness or a deviation. Although the definition of homosexuality as a psychiatric condition in the official *American Psychiatric Association Diagnostic and Statistical Manual,* 3d edition (DSM-III), now includes symptoms of anxiety about one's sexual orientation, practicing homosexuality is no longer enough to warrant a psychiatric diagnosis. This change in diagnostic usage was the result of social and political action to change the definition of deviance and the world's view of the deviant individual. In the view of gay groups, homosexuality is simply an alternative life-style to heterosexuality and should not be subject to social, economic, or criminal penalties. Gay groups lobby and work for changes in laws that affect their members. They seek to be included in antidiscrimination legislation, and they pursue changes in sodomy laws attaching criminal penalties to sexual acts between consenting adults. Gays do not wish to be barred from having custody of children simply because of their sexual orientations, and some gays would like to have states legalize gay marriages.

None of these goals are achievable simply by helping individuals to cope better with problems in living defined as individual problems. These changes require concerted group action to alter society's views of and actions toward a group commonly defined as deviant and subject to the burdens carried by deviants. The activities of gay organizations would undoubtedly meet Goldenberg's (1978) definition of a social intervention designed to reduce oppression.

This general idea of social and political action to better the lives of certain people suffering with some handicap or feeling some grievance has stimulated the formation of a large number of groups. Some groups have aims as narrow as raising money to stimulate public interest or research on a given disease. Others form spontaneously in relation to a specific problem. The Love Canal Homeowners Association formed when homeowners living in the neighborhood of a hidden toxic-chemical-waste dump site believed they were not getting fair treatment from the state agencies designated to deal with their problem. The homeowners organized and kept fighting for several years, taking their case to the public and in other ways continually making their demands known to public officials. They were successful in seeing their demands met, and in the process raised public consciousness regarding the problems of toxic wastes (Gibbs, 1982; A. Levine, 1982). Their organization also served to alleviate the sense of helplessness experienced by many who felt caught in a severe problem in living that taxed family and community resources (Gibbs, 1983; Stone & Levine, 1985; the example of the Love Canal is discussed further in Chapter 12).

The Nature of Self-Help Groups

We have not yet defined self-help groups in any formal sense. This is difficult to do with any precision because we would like to include many different types of organizations, and many of them have mixed characteristics. Sagarin's twofold classification is insufficient to cover the variety of groups having sufficient characteristics in common to be treated as related phenomena. Many authorities have attempted descriptions and classifications of self-help (both Levy, 1976, and Katz & Bender, 1976, for example, offer fourfold classifications), but no single attempt seems fully satisfactory. We offer our own with the realization that it too is limited in its usefulness. The interested reader may consult Killilea (1976) for a comprehensive review of the characteristics of mutual assistance organizations.

We have found it useful to define five types of self-help groups. The first type involves people whose state or condition leads to some disqualification from being "normal." Members of these groups exhibit behavior or have characteristics that subject them to social isolation, stigmatization, scorn, pity, or social punishment. Although the concept of a degraded social identity (Sarbin, 1970; see Chapter 4) applies more or less here, as does Goldenberg's (1978) concept of oppression, we cannot say that all such persons are necessarily limited to ascribed roles. Examples of those with behavioral characteristics that disqualify them from being "normal" are: alcoholics, persons with diagnoses of mental illness, ex-convicts, gamblers, drug addicts, and gays. Examples of those with physical characteristics or illnesses subjecting the individual to disqualification are: little people (dwarfs), cancer patients, those with colostomies, physically handicapped people (see Hinrichsen, Revenson, & Shinn, 1985), the overweight, and the aged. Although no fault is assigned to persons with these characteristics, they are nonetheless subject to varying degrees of social disapprobation and social disqualification. Some have social characteristics subjecting them to forms of social discrimination that limit opportunity and may affect self-esteem. Blacks, women, gays, and members of other minorities subject to discriminatory treatment fall into this category.

The second type of self-help group is made up of those related to persons with stigmatizing conditions, who themselves may be subject to some secondary stigma or who suffer consequences because of the problems presented by the person related to them. Spouses and children of alcoholics, gamblers, and the mentally ill fall into this category, as do children who are charged with the care of elderly relatives. Parents of those who are mentally retarded, learning disabled, or autistic have much to cope with, as do those who are in extreme conflict with adolescent children and seek the assistance of the courts to help control their children (e.g., York & York, 1980).

A third type of group includes people with common problems that may not be stigmatizing but that do tend to be socially isolating. Public resources may be inadequate, and others who do not have the problem may not understand the individual's or the family's situation. Examples of these are groups for widows (Silverman et al., 1974), groups for single parents such as Parents Without Partners, parents of diabetic children (see the example at the end of this chapter), or parents of children with cancer (Chesler, Barbarin, & Lego-Stein, 1984).

A fourth type are groups organized along ethnic, religious, or racial lines for mutual assistance. These include fraternal organizations that provide education, recreation, cultural preservation, insurance, prepaid medical care, and similar services. Howe (1976) notes that many of these organizations developed among immigrant groups, and many originated as burial societies. In the recent past, we have tended to see fewer multipurpose organizations and more groups organized for single functions, such as women's health collectives, cooperative food services, or day-care centers organized and run by parents.

A fifth type is organized along quasi-political lines for the preservation of specific interests. These include taxpayers' groups seeking to limit taxation, civic organizations designed to preserve the character of neighborhoods, and organizations concerned with community development. Groups such as these may form whenever a common problem arises. The Love Canal Homeowners Association is an example of a spontaneously appearing organization. Groups opposed to school busing for purposes of integration represent another example of this type.

This classification system is difficult to apply because there are rarely pure forms of any one type of group, and most groups fit in more than one category. (A dimensional analysis would be more useful than a categorical analysis, but has yet to be developed in a useful form.) Take as an example a relatively new group showing many mixed characteristics. Equal Rights for Fathers is a group of noncustodial parents dealing with the aftermath of divorce. Members are primarily male, but they include new wives or girlfriends and grandparents who wish to maintain ties with grandchildren following a divorce. Equal Rights for Fathers has political aims as well as self-help aims and believes that the legal system is biased against men. Members also feel stigmatized because some in the public look on them as merely seeking to avoid paying child support. Others feel stigmatized because they report that their masculinity is questioned when they assert their love for their children and their desire to have or to share custody.

Members of this group wish to change aspects of the legal system, and they favor a legal presumption for joint custody. Members agree that men should meet their obligations to pay child support, but argue that the courts do not show nearly the same vigor in protecting visitation rights. The members of this group share information about the legal system, organize to influence legislation, attempt to educate judges and lawyers, help each other understand what to look for in an attorney, and share information about how to use the time they have with their children effectively. They conduct rap sessions to help each other come to terms with their circumstances and their feelings and attitudes about themselves, their ex-spouses, the legal system, and many other problems that require adaptation and for which little or no assistance is otherwise available. Members sometimes assist each other outside of the group meetings, and some core members often find themselves intervening in personal crises of other members.

The Dynamics of Self-Help Groups

Describing self-help in theoretical terms may be helpful in understanding how self-help works to assist members in adapting. (Recall from Chapter 3 that our concept of adaptation did not exclude action to change the environment.) Prospective members of a self-help organization struggle with a problem in living or a life circumstance that departs from some normative ideal. The problem or circumstance will not disappear rapidly no matter what remedies are sought, and as a result the individual faces the problem of adapting over a considerable period of time. Because the core problem represents a departure from a normative ideal, moreover, the individual tends to engage in a process of self-ostracization in perceiving himself or herself as having failed, as abnormal, or as a hapless victim of uncontrollable forces or of fate.

Most important, because the problem is interpreted as a departure from a normative ideal, the individual feels alone, as if his or her problems and feelings and experiences are unique. This feeling of isolation may exist even if the individual is part of a network that may be supportive in many other respects. The individual's difficulties are often exacerbated because the ordinary agencies of assistance have proved insufficient, inadequate, or even punitive. As a consequence, the individual will not have developed a philosophy for viewing the problem, nor had the opportunity to learn, directly or vicariously, useful strategies for coping with the myriad of everyday issues related to the core problem.

What does participation in a self-help group provide that reduces the vulnerability and/or acute stress affecting a person at risk? Like any significant social support system, a self-help group can profitably be compared with the model of an ideal family. Recall from our discussion of social support in Chapter 6 that Caplan (1976) depicts the ideal family as fulfilling several functions for its members. For example, just as older members of the family collect and disseminate information about the world, providing models for younger members to emulate, so more experienced members of the self-help group provide models for less experienced members to emulate. Self-help groups may also serve as a feedback and guidance system to help members understand their reactions to others and the reactions of others to them.

Self-help groups provide a philosophy of life, an outlook on the problem condition. Through repeated discussion of concrete situations with other members, the group's philosophy or ideology comes to serve an organizing function in the lives of self-help group members. By applying the tenets of the ideology to everyday problems, the ideology provides, as Caplan puts it, "prescriptions for wise conduct."

Family members share each other's problems, offer each other advice and guidance, assist in finding external sources of aid, and even make arrangements for such assistance. Much analogous learning occurs in self-help groups. Older members pass on their experiences and help newer members to anticipate changes in their lives. Members of the groups share happy occasions as well. Much laughter goes on, and in some groups members celebrate birthdays, job promotions, and other successful life changes. In many self-help groups members also extend concrete services and material aid to each other.

As a haven for rest and recuperation, the self-help group provides a place where members can be themselves and be assured of understanding and acceptance. There is no need to conceal or to explain the problem to anyone. All understand because all have experienced similar needs and emotions. In many ways, the self-help group also becomes the reference group for its members. Members feel good when they live up to the codes of the self-help group and presumably feel bad when they fail to live up to its standards. The desire to have the approbation and support of fellow group members motivates the individual to live up to the group's standards. Just as in a family, however, difficulty in conquering the core problem does not lead to banishment. The sinner, so to speak, may always return to the fold and be welcomed, if not honored, for being willing to try again.

A foundation for personal identity is established within self-help groups as members share with each other their current problems. In fact, because members are both givers and receivers of help, with the roles changing from moment to moment, sharing of weakness contributes positively to self and to others. An individual member may find himself or herself of value to another simply by sharing a failure. By being of value to another, one's sense of competence and worthwhileness may be enhanced. Finally, sharing problems and feelings within a family enables members to assist each other with the task of emotional mastery. Sharing problems and feelings within a self-help group comes to fulfill similar functions. For some, participation in the self-help group can become critical, not only for the assistance provided in achieving emotional mastery but also because the individual comes to feel like an integral part of a larger social group. In Naroll's (1983) terms, participation in a mutual help group may result in an improved condition because of participation in a protective and restorative "moralnet."

How Self-Help Groups Work

While Caplan's model of the ideal family helps us speculate about the important characteristics of self-help groups, psychological research and thinking have expanded our understanding considerably in the past few years. In light of this, we can identify six aspects of self-help that serve its members' interests. Self-help groups: (1) promote the psychological sense of community; (2) provide an ideology that serves as a philosophical antidote; (3) provide an opportunity for confession, catharsis, and mutual criticism; (4) provide role models: (5) teach effective coping strategies for day-to-day problems; and (6) provide a network of social relationships.

First, bringing together people who face a common dilemma overcomes the problem of self-ostracization. Another way of putting this is that self-help groups promote the psychological sense of community. Sarason (1974) defines the psychological sense of community as:

> The sense that one was part of a readily available, mutually supportive network of relationships upon which one could depend and as a result of which one did not experience sustained feelings of loneliness that impel one to actions or to adopting a style of living masking anxiety and setting the stage for later more destructive anguish. (p. 1)

Discovering that others experience the same problem and feel the same way helps make the personal crisis a social experience. In Sagarin's terms, the odd man is in. Moreover, in those instances where members feel their grievances may be attributed to existing social conditions, the personal becomes not only the social but also the political. Members no longer feel isolated, and the group's ideology provides a program for living with and overcoming the core problem.

Second, self-help groups have more or less articulated ideologies that serve as philosophical antidotes to give meaning to the particular life circumstance that represents a departure from the normative ideal. The dictionary defines ideology as "a system of ideas concerning phenomena, especially those of social life; the manner of thinking characteristic of a class or an individual." Ideologies consist of more or less articulated values that are shared among people and may be used to interpret daily life. Ideologies contribute to a sense of personal identity by defining what an individual is to believe, which reduces ambiguity and uncertainty about the world and provides a basis for making choices in everyday life. Just as every religious group has a body of sacred writings, so many self-help groups have bodies of literature that define the group's beliefs and approach to the common problem. AA's "Twelve Steps" is a primary example of such a core body of sacred writing defining the group's beliefs. Some groups may not have as precisely delineated a set of beliefs as does AA, but generally speaking such a set of beliefs is identifiable even if not fully articulated (Suler, 1980).

Antze (1976) developed a remarkably useful hypothesis about the role of ideologies in self-help. He states that a group's teachings are its very essence and that social scientists have been remiss in examining the role of the specific teachings because some seem contradictory. A group such as AA urges its members to give their problems up to a higher power, arguing that members are powerless to control their situations. On the other hand, a group such as Recovery, Inc., a self-help organization for "nervous people," teaches that members can overcome their problems through an exercise of will power. How can both teachings be correct?

Antze resolves this dilemma by arguing that self-help organizations are specialized. Within this specialization of problem, "It may be possible for a group's ideology to function more precisely, working as a 'cognitive antidote' to basic features of a condition shared by everyone who joins" (p. 327). Given the nature of social organization, anyone having the particular problem is in a

> socially standardized situation. . . . No matter how an individual comes to a given problem, once he arrives he is very much in the same boat with his fellow victims. He comes to cope with life in a similar fashion; he comes to think of himself and others in similar ways; he faces identical problems in trying to change. . . . The ideologies of peer therapy groups may be seen as extremely shrewd and insightful attacks on the most harmful of these standardized implications. If they have therapeutic value, it is because each manages to break some link in the chain of events maintaining a condition and to provide viable defenses against its renewal. (pp. 328–329)

As examples Antze uses the difference in the core problems of alcoholics and of "nervous" persons such as the members of Recovery, Inc. According to Antze, the core problem of the alcoholic is:

> *He exaggerates his own authorship in the events of his life.* Sober or drunk, he tends to perceive his world as fashioned mainly by his own acts; somehow he always finds

himself at center stage. . . . This group of attitudes adds up to *unrealistic voli-tion.* . . . Problem drinkers have an unusually high need to assert power over people and situations. . . . The alcoholic also feels himself to be sole author of his fail-ures. . . . *To absorb the AA message is to see oneself as much less the author of events in life, the active fighter and doer, and much more as a person with the wisdom to accept limitations and wait for things to come.* (pp. 331–332)

Members of Recovery, Inc., are nervous former mental patients. Most experience symptoms that are essentially "ego alien." In the face of an episode of depression or a panic attack, the person feels he or she is not himself or herself. The symptom appears to come from outside the person, and he or she feels powerless in the face of it. The ideology of Recovery, Inc., emphasizes the belief that symptoms, no matter how troublesome, are basically within the individual's mind and are therefore capable of being controlled. Members of Recovery, Inc., learn that the one critical faculty, the "Will," can always be utilized to overcome the ego-alien symptom. Recovery, Inc., emphasizes taking specific actions, no matter how small, to exert will against the symptom (Low, 1950); although "the ideologies of AA and Recovery represent mirror images of one another, . . . their opposition is explained by an equally marked oppo-sition in the phenomenology of the problems they treat" (p. 337).

Self-help groups develop cultures and specialized languages. Recovery, Inc.'s lan-guage includes procedures for identifying the onset of symptoms and taking action to limit the effect of the symptoms. This language is practiced in ritualistic fashion at each meeting, where members are called on to present experiences where they used the Recovery method to overcome a problem. Other members contribute to the anal-ysis of the experience using the Recovery language. Conceptual tags tied to concrete experiences are thus developed, and the members may take these tags away and use them every day on a minute-by-minute basis.

Al-Anon, an organization for people related to alcoholics, follows AA's methods closely. Al-Anon has developed its own ideas, such as "loving detachment," in which the spouse of the alcoholic is taught to love the person but not to protect the alcoholic from the consequences of excessive drinking. Al-Anon also teaches its members to "live one day at a time" and to "learn to let go," meaning that the spouse must learn to live his or her own life, and cannot do anything to control the alcoholic's drinking. These slogans are applied as members discuss their experiences in the group. They take on generalized meaning and may then be used to help the individual decide what to do, if not how to feel, about everyday problems related to the alcoholic spouse and perhaps other problems in living as well.

Third, many groups have a ritualistic format that includes elements of confession, catharsis, and criticism. A sense of group solidarity is developed as members share their feelings and experiences. Members are encouraged to speak of their failures and their problems, experiences that may be associated with lowered self-esteem and guilt. By sharing these experiences with others who have "been there," members essentially unload unwanted baggage and find forgiveness. In some groups, as the feeling of sol-idarity develops, members feel free to confront each other. This mutual criticism (Levine & Bunker, 1975) is a form of deviance control; it is also a method for enhanc-ing self-esteem. If one lives up to the ideals of the group, by definition one has become a better person. During this experience of sharing, moreover, the group helps the indi-vidual learn to use its teachings to overcome the problem.

Fourth, members provide role models for each other. Self-help groups create places and roles for individuals. Those who strive to fulfill the group's teachings and have been more successful at it become role models for others. Because no formal distinctions exist among members, a new member can easily identify with a more experienced member and say, "If she can overcome this problem, so can I." Some persons become active leaders in the organizations and actually build new identities and lifestyles around the membership role. Even though a given individual may not be able to overcome his or her own problems, for example, that individual understands the difficulty of coping with the problem and is aware of mistakes a person is likely to make. Thus in many instances he or she may be able to give another member the benefit of vicarious learning. Something that might have been a matter of shame is transformed into an experience of value for a fellow group member.

The roles of help giver and help receiver are thoroughly interchangeable. Because each member is living with a chronic problem, each will encounter difficulty at one time or another. Even the most successful of members may turn to other members of the group for emotional sustenance or support or for help in solving some new dilemma. Any implication of "inferior" and "superior" positions is reduced because any member may play either role from time to time.

Reissman (1965) developed an idea he called the "helper-therapy" principle. It means that the most effective way of learning is to teach, and those who help may be those who are helped the most. The effectiveness of this principle can be derived from role theory in that a person playing a role tends to meet the requirements of that role.

> In effect, as a helper the individual displays mastery over the afflicting condition—plays the role of a nonaddict, for example—and thereby acquires the appropriate skills, attitudes, behaviors and mental set. Having modeled this for others, the individual may see him or herself as behaving in a new way and may, in effect, take on the new role as his or her own. (Reissman & Gartner, 1977, p. 103)

Fifth, in sharing day-to-day experiences, members discover and share proven coping devices. Because the individuals are in a "standardized situation," their problems are generally recurring, and the solutions that one member passes on to another are pertinent for their respective circumstances. Moreover, the group setting encourages experimentation with new solutions, supports members through any failures, and rejoices even at members' small successes.

Sixth, members provide a network of friends and social relationships not readily available otherwise to the person struggling with social disqualification or with adaptive demands that others who do not share the problem may fail to understand. Members celebrate happy occasions with each other, socialize, have parties, and provide companionship. In some groups they may go further and provide concrete help to each other. For example, members of Reach, a self-help group for relatives of mental patients sponsored by the Buffalo and Erie County chapter of the National Association for Mental Health, have provided respite care for each other. A member who wishes to go away for a short vacation and rest may ask another member, experienced in handling the problems of mental patients, to look after the disturbed family member. Members will of course reciprocate and also provide here-and-now assistance for each other. Many groups have sponsors for new members, who may be called at any time, day or night, for assistance. Help is delivered when and where it is needed, "on call" so to speak, in the situation where the problem arises.

Self-Help and Ecological Concepts. As we noted in introducing this chapter, self-help groups are also understandable using the ecological principles and conceptions discussed in earlier chapters. Self-help groups represent a broadly applicable mode of intervention, for example, yet they address the ecological fact of diversity among people and their needs by providing relatively precise ideological antidotes that can be tailored to any vulnerable condition. In this respect self-help groups illustrate a point we made about social support in Chapter 6: the specific resources provided by a supportive network may be more important to its effectiveness than the size of the group or how it is structured.

Self-help groups are also understandable as ecological settings that improve the degree of behavioral adaptation to the community by improving person-environment fit. In the ideology of self-help groups, improved adaptation follows from concrete, practical changes in behavior. Such concrete behaviors can be understood as joint properties of people and settings. We earlier characterized vulnerability as poor fit between the individual's behavioral repertoire and the demands of settings in his or her life (the outcome of which is alcohol abuse, feelings of oppression, withdrawal and isolation, and so on). Participation in new settings enlarges the individual's behavioral repertoire and expands the community niches available to that person, increasing his or her niche breadth.

Two ecological principles of practice are relevant. By what specific mechanisms does participation in a self-help group produce behavior change? How is change maintained? For specific theoretical answers to these questions, recall the three psychological conceptions of Moos, Barker, and Sarbin that were first examined in Chapter 4. Moos's conception of the psychosocial climate may be used to analyze self-help. One important dimension of a setting is its relationship-oriented qualities. Because membership in most groups is relatively open-ended (the only requirement for membership in AA, for example, is a desire to stop drinking), self-help groups are high in support and acceptance of participants. Support and acceptance serve to reduce self-ostracization and to increase the psychological sense of community among members. Relationship-oriented aspects of the climate are also enhanced by a strengthened and expanded network of friendships involving reversible roles, sponsorship, and other activities or contacts outside the meetings. A second important dimension of settings is the degree to which a setting fosters personal development. Important responsibilities, such as those implied by sponsorship and by Reissman's helper-therapy principle, would strengthen the personal development dimensions of a self-help group's climate. Clear differences would likely exist among groups on specific personal development dimensions, however, reflecting the different directions that personal development ideally takes in different groups (e.g., the importance of taking willful control of one's life in Recovery, Inc., versus acquiring the serenity to accept what one cannot change in AA). Those in groups such as Al-Anon often emphasize how members can come from all walks of life, all socioeconomic and educational backgrounds, and so on, yet within the group they still experience a strong sense of equality and mutual understanding. Moos would explain this by suggesting that the climate defines the group and accounts for its effects, not the specific members as individuals.

In Barker's conception of behavior settings, self-help groups are important community resources in the form of alternative settings within which the individual can structure his or her time. That is, to a certain extent group meetings compete with other settings for the person's time. The standing patterns of behavior they enforce, through the principle of behavior-environment congruence, are incompatible with the maladaptive responses made previously.

As behavior settings, moreover, self-help groups instill the specific coping devices and other adaptive responses necessary to cope successfully with the core problems. Recall Barker's description of the person-environment circuits that define all settings. First, goal circuits represent the member's motivation to change (e.g., to stop drinking). The ritualistic procedures in meetings (e.g., the predictable responses of confession, catharsis, and acceptance) exemplify Barker's notion of a setting "program." Processes such as confrontation serve a corrective, "deviation-countering" function that may or may not be present in other settings in the person's life. The chronic nature of the problem situation provides multiple opportunities for learning, rehearsing, and generalizing the new behavioral responses required to improve the vulnerable individual's fit with key community settings.

Unless the individual's repertoire of responses is permanently changed, however, the recurring nature of most problems increases the chance of relapse into the old maladaptive ways. Clinical treatment, being expensive and thus short-term, often must be repeated, leading to the "revolving-door" syndrome whereby clients must frequently return for another round of care. Self-help groups, on the other hand, are stable, enduring communities—they are permanent fixtures in the community habitat. Thus, while maladaptation is chronic and recurrent, so are meetings of self-help groups.

One limitation of self-help groups when understood in setting terms is that as settings they are bounded in time and space. We can thus ask how widely available a particular self-help group is in spatial and temporal terms. Its existence on paper or in the telephone book does not mean it is actually available to everyone in need. Given the huge numbers implied by the view of life as a soap opera, multiple-setting occasions may be needed weekly in many cases.

In terms of Sarbin's role theory, self-help groups help in certain respects to structure the various ecologies surrounding the vulnerable individual. In the social ecology, a self-help group provides an egalitarian network of peer relationships that reduces isolation and helps to relieve the ambiguity and uncertainty imposed by the real world. Members of a self-help group also give positive esteem to the individual in a normative respect and provide a sense of meaningful integrity to the individual's transcendental needs. In cases where other group members provide material aid, such as a place to stay, outside of group meetings, they enhance even the individual's self-maintenance ecology.

Generally speaking, membership in a self-help group provides important new roles for a person otherwise disqualified from being normal. These roles sidestep the negative aspects of the individual's vulnerable condition and instead offer opportunities for responsibility and leadership that are flexible and open-ended in the degrees of involvement they require. Although these factors improve the individual's self-perceptions, the effects of this role enhancement on the public identities of self-help group members are unclear, because membership is usually a private (and often even anonymous) matter.

In the next chapter we provide an extended analysis of self-help with both personal and political aims: women's consciousness raising groups. The concepts developed in this chapter will be used to enhance our understanding of self-help and any generalizable processes by which people change.

Are Self-Help Groups Effective?

Discussing self-help groups in the same context with professional assistance may imply that professional and self-help services are equally effective in reducing vulnerability. That assumption is untested; the effectiveness of self-help services is difficult to evaluate. For the most part we rely on the testimonials of those who are members. Self-help groups are difficult to study because the membership tends to be shifting and because self-help groups have little interest in cooperating with research on themselves. Members of self-help groups see themselves as there to help themselves and others with similar problems. They point to their growth as adequate evidence of their effectiveness. We rarely hear about the dropouts from self-help organizations or about their failures. Few if any substantial studies have researched comparable populations served by self-help groups and by professional helpers, so we cannot say one mode of treatment is more or less effective than another.

Self-help group members who have had experience with professional helping services frequently assert they get something different from the self-help group than from professional helpers (Videka-Sherman & Lieberman, 1985). For some that difference is striking. Some are willing to assert that professional assistance was no help at all and sometimes even made them feel guilty about having the problem for which they sought help. Others, however, assert that they get something different in a positive sense from professional assistance than they get from participation in self-help groups. The opportunity to work problems through on an individual basis is apparently valued by some. We need not adopt a black-and-white view of the situation, seeing one form of help as all good and another as all bad or one as necessarily superior to the other. Ideally we should examine each form carefully to see what each can learn from the other about the therapeutic process.

AA and Recovery from Alcoholism

Alcoholism is a devastating disorder affecting tens of millions of Americans (see Chapter 1) and costing the United States an estimated $90 billion per year in expenditures for health care and law enforcement and in its general toll on economic productivity (National Institute on Alcohol Abuse and Alcoholism, 1983). The scope and severity of these problems make alcoholism a major challenge to all help-giving professions. Many professionals freely admit that in the area of alcoholism the effectiveness of their services leaves much to be desired. Perhaps as a result, AA groups are frequently welcomed into hospitals and prisons to recruit members. Although alcoholism is correctly perceived as a relatively intransigent problem, and the probability of stable recovery following any given episode of alcoholism is apparently only minimally assisted by formal treatment (Orford & Edwards, 1977; Vaillant, 1983), complete recovery does occur in about half of all cases. Recent evidence suggests that most recovery from alcoholism is attributable to relatively specific "natural healing" processes.

Perhaps the best illustration of this phenomenon comes from the large-scale follow-up studies undertaken by Vaillant (1983). Vaillant's data comprised two large cohorts of initially normal males, one upper middle class (N = 204) and one working class (N = 456), each of which was followed prospectively from the late 1930s until 1980. Comprehensive and sophisticated measures were taken regarding the incidence of alcoholism and other behavioral characteristics in these samples, and the prospective longitudinal research design enabled Vaillant to untangle specific temporal sequences among many often related events (for example, the frequent relationship breakups that occurred among alcoholic subjects were more often found to be an *effect* of prior heavy drinking than its cause).

Conditions found directly to precede stable recovery from alcoholism involved the following specific changes in life-style and/or circumstances: (1) development of a *substitute dependency,* such as candy, tranquilizers, heavy smoking, or compulsive work or hobbies; (2) new *constraints* on drinking, either external (e.g., close supervision from a spouse, employer, or judge), or internal (e.g., threats to health, use of Antabuse); (3) increased involvement in *religion* or some analogous spiritual or ideological experience (such an experience typically helped the alcoholic replace feelings of defeat, worthlessness, helplessness, and guilt with renewed hope, self-esteem, and a powerful new belief system that enabled him to swear off his old maladaptive life-style for a new one); and (4) focused *social support,* often in the form of a new (or renewed) love relationship (e.g., with a spouse or other family member, or another recovering alcoholic).

Many in Vaillant's samples changed their lives and recovered from alcoholism more or less on their own. Given the specific changes required, however, it is not surprising that the single most effective intervention for alcoholism was AA (see also Polich, Armor, & Braiker, 1981). Although it is certainly no panacea, AA does embody all of the natural recovery processes to an extent no contemporary treatment program can. AA facilitates fundamental changes in the alcoholic's belief system, provides an unambiguous conception of the disorder (the so-called disease theory) that is meaningful to him or her, and gives a sense of hope in the possibility of recovery. Thus the alcoholic's previous faith in alcohol as the most dependable source of gratification is turned into the "curse" of alcohol as the cause of all life's pain, and this new attitude is strongly enforced through adherence to total abstinence as the only acknowledged path to recovery.

The fellowship and support provided by other AA members, both during the actual meetings and when needed at other times and places, are powerful reinforcers in the life of the isolated alcoholic and induce strong tendencies to affiliate and identify. As Edwards et al. (1967) point out:

> Identification is not with any one established member so much as with fragments of a whole series of life histories which are synthesized into identification with the group ideal. . . . Identification assumes particular importance in the leaderless group which must have a clear and firmly established picture of the ideal member. (p. 203)

Identification is easier with other recovering alcoholics than with a professional therapist both because of the obvious similarities among those recovering from the same problem and because of the way psychotherapy is structured asymmetrically (i.e., so that personal disclosure and motivation to change flow only from client to therapist, while effective help and support are assumed to flow only from therapist to client). The social support provided by AA's more reversible roles is clearly expressed in this enthusiastic testimonial from one of Vaillant's upper-middle-class alcoholics:

> Most alcoholics, I believe, grow up in a glass isolation booth which they build for themselves to separate themselves from other people. . . . AA shows us how to dis-

solve the glass walls around us and realize that there are other people out there, good loving people. . . . I love the AA meetings and love being able to call people up when I feel tense. Occasionally, someone calls me for help and that makes me feel good. I get much more out of this than I got from decades of psychiatry. My relationship with a psychiatrist always seemed to be distressingly cold. I hated the huge bills. For $50 an hour, one doctor kept assuring me that I was nutty to worry about money, and at the time I couldn't keep up my life insurance. I wish there were some form of Alcoholics Anonymous for troubled people who don't drink. We old drunks are lucky. (p. 208)

AA reaches an estimated 650,000 alcoholics in the United States, twice as many as do all hospitals, clinics, and physicians combined (Baekeland et al., 1975). Thousands of AA groups exist in this country, and in a large city it would be rare not to find a group meeting at almost any hour on any day of the week, making AA much more accessible than formal treatment for alcoholism. This ready availability was important to those of Vaillant's subjects who were already flirting with sobriety for one reason or another (e.g., a health problem, love relationship) and who were able to take advantage of AA's accessibility to help cement the changes in behavior they were already trying to make.

Another important explanation for why AA is more effective than formal treatment is that the duration of participation in AA is generally much longer; it lasts months, years, or even a lifetime as opposed to a few weeks. One consequence is that the whole meaning of one's relationship to AA is different; one "visits" a treatment clinic, and one "belongs" to AA. The lasting impact of AA's communally shared rituals, performed again and again over months or years of participation, is understandable from Barker's ecological conception, since in that view maintaining continuities in an individual's behavior over time is simply a matter of maintaining continuity in the specific settings he or she participates in. Although structuring one's time by frequent attendance at AA meetings may become a new "addiction" substituting for time previously spent with alcohol, the risks associated with active alcoholism presumably far outweigh those involved in addiction to AA.

The very question of an addiction to AA reflects the assumptions of the medical model. Operating with the medical model, we feel we ought to be able to cure and discharge the client so that the client can stand alone, without "crutches." These expectations partly reflect our concern about the cost of treatment and the value that should be returned. AA may reflect another model entirely. We would think it ludicrous if a patient remained in psychoanalysis for an entire adult lifetime, but we might think it admirable if another person remained a member of a church and participated in its activities for an adult lifetime. AA in its underlying model more resembles a church or a fraternal order than it does group therapy. Joining involves little apparent social cost. It is no burden on health insurance. The member makes voluntary donations and can go to a meeting for little more than a donation of coffee money and perhaps the occasional purchase of AA literature. The question of lifetime reliance on AA or enduring membership in other similar groups can only be examined in relation to the assumptions that led us to raise the questions in the first place.

These characteristics make AA a clear illustration of the ecological principle that interventions should take a form that can be maintained as a natural part of the community (see Chapter 3). That is, AA begins with a natural resource, indigenous residents of the community, and defines their involvement as participation in a setting entailing nominal cost over an indefinite length of time. Although the most serious conditions of risk are episodic, the members' basic need for this setting is continuously present, and many in the vulnerable population thus recognize the value of maintaining a relationship with AA similar to the one with their church or fraternal society.

Al-Anon, an offshoot of AA, is a self-help group for spouses or other relatives of alcoholics who are not alcoholic themselves. Al-Anon operates much as AA does. Gillick (1977) conducted a controlled experiment in which wives of patients hospitalized for alcoholism at a VA hospital were randomly assigned to attend an Al-Anon group for 6 weeks or to receive no treatment during that time. More than two-thirds of the spouses of alcoholics attended six or more Al-Anon meetings over the 6-week period of the study. Gillick used the Community Adaptation Scale, a 217-item, self-administered questionnaire that evaluates a person's community activities in a number of different spheres: work, family, personal, civic, commercial, and professional services (see Roen & Burns, 1968). Gillick used the scale because research on the wives of alcoholics had indicated that they were frequently socially isolated.

After 6 weeks the group that had attended Al-Anon meetings showed a number of changes compared to the control group. Spouses who attended Al-Anon reported better and more frequent interaction with family and friends and an overall positive change in community adaptation. The control group showed deterioration on some of the scales over the same period. On posttest interviews, 14 of the 15 Al-Anon attenders rated the experience *very helpful* or *extremely helpful,* and all 15 were able to describe some benefit from attending meetings. Most often they expressed themselves in terms reflecting Al-Anon's ideology: "I liked the idea of living one day at a time and learning to let go." "It made me realize there is practically nothing I can do to stop his drinking once he starts." All but two of the 15 spouses said they planned to continue attending Al-Anon meetings. These short-term results are similar to those claimed for Al-Anon by its long-term members. The controlled experiment demonstrated systematic benefits from attending the groups beyond those resulting simply from the passage of time and treatment of the alcoholic spouse in the hospital.

Vaillant's conclusion that at present natural healing processes involved in recovery from alcoholism are far more significant than what formal treatment can provide should not leave one feeling discouraged. The important finding is that about half of alcoholics do recover eventually, and the power of natural healing has long been used by physicians in the treatment of wounds and other conditions where zealous intervention can do more harm than good. Because apparently *no amount* of formal treatment increases the likelihood of permanent recovery from alcoholism beyond that contributed by natural healing, the most useful role for formal treatment at present is not to pursue evermore intensive and costly services for a limited number of individual clients, but to facilitate the natural healing process in as many alcoholics as possible.

Vaillant's own program, for example, the Cambridge and Somerville Program for Alcohol Rehabilitation (CASPAR), is a comprehensive community-based system set up to lower the incidence and prevalence of alcohol problems by providing an array of medical services, support groups, halfway houses, and educational programs. In a typical year CASPAR receives 20,000 outpatient visits, conducts 2,500 detoxifications, and adds 1,000 new alcoholic clients to its rolls, all at a cost of only about $1 million (Vaillant, 1983). In keeping with the preceding conclusions, the primary long-term goal of CASPAR is to involve alcoholics with AA. A potentially important role for existing alcoholism treatment services thus exists if such efforts are applied as part of a comprehensive effort to reduce incidence and prevalence across the entire community. Gillick's study also showed that professionals can cooperate with self-help programs by making referrals and encouraging their clients to participate. Reasoning from the helper-therapy principle, Gartner and Reissman (1977) suggest that one way of overcoming the "numbers problem" in providing help (see Chapter 1) is by finding ways to:

> transform recipients of help into new dispensers of help, thus reversing their roles, and to structure the situation so that recipients of help will be placed in roles requiring the giving of assistance. The helper-therapy principle operates, of course, in all kinds of peer help situations, in peer counseling in schools, children teaching children or mutual help groups. Therefore, all situations involving human service should be restructured to allow the principle to operate more fully. (p. 106)

The issue of what relationship should exist between professionals and self-help groups has become an important focus of discussion (Katz, 1981). The various alternatives proposed range from essentially no relationship (i.e., where each pursues its helping effort independently) through some degree of formalized cooperation (e.g., mutual referrals, communication regarding community needs and services) to the situation where one directly operates to influence the other. In the latter case, for example, self-help groups are sometimes seen as external agents potentially able to "humanize" the professional system of care (Gartner & Reissman, 1977). More often, however, direct influences probably involve efforts by professionals to create or maintain self-help as one reliable alternative for a particular group at risk. Each chapter of Parents Anonymous, for example, has its own professional sponsor to facilitate the group's functioning. Another option is for professionals simply to stimulate the formation of a group, thereafter leaving its operation largely or entirely in the hands of the members.

One illustration of this latter approach of "seeding" the formation of a self-help group is the work of some graduate students and faculty in the Department of Psychology at the State University of New York at Buffalo in establishing a self-help group for parents of young diabetic children. Diabetes is a serious condition when diagnosed in a child under the age of 4 or 5 and leaves the child at greatly increased risk for weight problems, blindness, and early death. The parents in these cases are usually provided with sufficient medical resources and attention, but given the incomplete state of knowledge about the disease, in many communities the only resource available for dealing with sometimes overwhelming emotional and psychological consequences is short-term individual and family psychotherapy. For many parents this option is less than satisfactory, because it requires them to define their problems in personal terms and to accept what some feel is a stigmatizing label, and because it does not directly combat the day-to-day feelings of stress and isolation brought on by the child's health crisis.

This project began with an initial contact by faculty members with the Juvenile Diabetes Foundation of Western New York, an organization made up of parents of diabetics and others interested in helping to raise money, provide information, and generally improve research and treatment efforts for diabetes. The community psychology representatives offered their services as consultants in an open-ended arrangement. Following additional meetings focused on issues of concern to the parents group, it was decided that the parents of toddlers newly diagnosed as diabetics presented the most compelling focus for consultation. The Children's Hospital of Buffalo served all diabetic children in the metropolitan area, making it possible to contact these parents through the hospital programs and arrange informal group interviews and discussions.

An interested member of the foundation took responsibility for contacting parents of newly diagnosed young children and inviting them to participate in a session involving other parents and the student and faculty consultants. The stated purpose of this meeting was to identify common difficulties faced by parents and evaluate different strategies for coping with these difficulties. It was also expected, however, that simply providing a situation conducive to bringing problems out in the open would reduce the sense of isolation felt by many parents, establish informal communication links among them, and indicate the extent of any unmet need for help in the members of this group.

During these informal sessions the consultants took the position that they were interested in gathering information about situations that posed particular difficulties for these parents, and what emerged was a list of those problems most likely to create psychological stress and exacerbate the new family crisis. One problem area, for example, involved understanding how to manage the child's day-to-day behavioral conduct in the context of diabetes (e.g., using the "correct" mix of discipline and flexibility; understanding what normal "monster" behavior is). Another involved educating other caretakers, such as relatives, baby-sitters, teachers, and other parents about the child's unique dietary needs and restrictions (for example, at birthday parties), his or her ways of manipulating caretakers regarding the diabetes, and how to recognize insulin reactions. Dealing with other children in the family was a third problem common to many parents; coping with the inevitable acute medical crises (for example, severe insulin shock that leaves the child unconscious) was a fourth. Finally, one consistent experience encountered by many families was the so-called predinner crisis, where tensions, fatigue, and irritability among all family members late in the day often build up into more than the usual amount of unwanted conflict and disruption.

The procedure adopted by the consultants for identifying systematic strategies and beliefs that might make up a viable self-help process was similar to that used by Spivack and Shure (see Chapter 7) in developing the ingredients of a competence-building primary prevention program for preschool children. That is, the key to understanding the ingredients of successful coping was assumed to reside in the specific informational, behavioral, and attitudinal differences observed to differentiate parents who were handling their predicament well and those who appeared to be experiencing significant distress. Following the points made by Antze (1976), one particular dimension on which the consultants focused involved the differentiation of "pathological" beliefs (i.e., thoughts and feelings that directly led to emotional upsets and maladaptive responses) from the sort of "cognitive antidotes" that might be used explicitly to counteract these beliefs. For example, one pathological cognition identified was the question, "Why me?" Some parents asked themselves this repetitively, and it made even more acute the perceived loss of prior freedoms and other advantages they might have enjoyed. Another of these maladaptive thoughts was the obsessive reminder, "I must very closely protect and supervise my child." Taken to extremes, this would make the problem even more disruptive for the child, the parents, and other family members. A third pathological belief was the persistent realization, "There's *so much more* I have to do now," leading the parent to perceive an immense new burden of potentially overwhelming proportions.

As Antze would have predicted, however, for each pathological belief expressed by individuals in this vulnerable condition, a corresponding antidote was provided by other members of the group. For the question "Why me?" the successful copers prescribed accepting the situation for what it is, but more important wherever possible relabeling powerful feelings such as anxiety or shame in terms of more constructive emotions, such as anger, which better enable the parent to advocate for the child and also see to it that his or her own needs are met. Concerning the intense new responsibilities to protect and supervise the child, these parents recommended allowing the children to be as normal as possible under the circumstances (e.g., experience normal relationships with other children and with adults), learn how to care for themselves where appropriate (e.g., such as self-administering insulin injections when old enough) and so on. To those overwhelmed by all the new tasks, these parents replied with such useful epigrams as, "Some things are easier to let the child do," "It doesn't have to be done in a day," or, in coping with others' stupidity or insensitivity, "Ignorance wasn't conquered in a day." They were even able to point out a few limited but nonetheless useful advantages to the changes brought about by their child's diabetes, such as the fact that preparing food for the family that is free of sugar offers a much healthier diet for everyone and is usually more economical as well.

These adaptive beliefs and coping strategies generated by the parents were organized and written up as a preliminary body of "sacred writings" along with additional suggestions regarding general ground rules the group might find useful. Among these ground rules, for example, were the recommendations that parents be tolerant of differences among them in parenting styles, ways of expressing feelings, and readiness to disclose personal or otherwise sensitive information, and that all information brought out in meetings concerning personal matters be kept strictly confidential to facilitate frank and open discussion of the problems that most troubled members.

With this level of organized feedback, and periodic contacts with a graduate student consultant, the self-help group made up of parents of diabetic toddlers began holding regular meetings on its own. The meetings continued for about 2 years. The sponsoring organization developed some conflicts which resulted in members affiliating with different factions. One of the leaders seemed to have "burned out" and stopped being active. Another decided to devote her time to fund-raising activities. Both leaders felt the experiences were valuable, and they continued to have an affectionate interest in the graduate student consultant. Involvement of professionals in self-help groups can thus take different forms and in specific cases is best determined by clear communication and careful planning between the two parties. Meaningful professional efforts on a variety of chronic or otherwise intransigent conditions may thus be most promising when they assist the functioning of self-help alternatives and capitalize on nature's own paths to coping and recovery.

Summary

Over roughly the same period of time that community psychology has existed, the number and use of self-help groups have increased tremendously. The many examples now in existence suggest that self-help groups serve a range of important needs. One advantage they have over professional care is that self-help groups are generally indigenous community resources offering help to vulnerable individuals at little or no cost.

We identified five types of self-help groups, each serving one or more of the following populations: (1) people whose social identities disqualify them from being normal because of a defect in conduct (e.g., alcoholism) or physical appearance (e.g., amputees); (2) people who are related to or otherwise involved with those in the first group, and who themselves experience increased stress or a restricted range of available coping options; (3) people who are isolated by some social circumstance, such as divorce or widowhood; (4) individuals organized for mutual assistance along ethnic, racial, or religious lines; and (5) people organized on a more purely political basis who seek to preserve certain special interests (e.g., taxpayers' groups).

From a conceptual vantage point, self-help groups provide a supportive, relationship-oriented social climate that reduces isolation and self-ostracization and promotes a better psychological sense of community. They also function as behavior settings that instill practical, tried-and-true coping techniques through repetitive rehearsal of ritualistic programs and procedures. New roles are provided, allowing members to achieve important opportunities and responsibilities, and the roles are reversible and interchangeable. Most interestingly, perhaps, self-help groups apply specific cognitive antidotes to members' problems, tailored precisely to the maladaptive thoughts making that particular condition of vulnerability so disruptive and distressing.

At least circumstantial evidence now exists on the effectiveness of self-help groups in helping people recover from relatively intransigent difficulties such as alcoholism. We ended the chapter with an example of how the importance of self-help groups and our increasing conceptual understanding of them may enable us to create self-help alternatives that do not yet exist. What we did not cover in this chapter was the way in which social and historical conditions shape specific forms of an intervention such as the self-help group. In the following chapter we will turn to that issue.

References

Antze, P. (1976). The role of ideologies in peer psychotherapy organizations: Some theoretical considerations and three case studies. *Journal of Applied Behavioral Science, 12,* 323–346.

Baekeland, F., Lundwall, L., & Kissin, B. (1975). Methods for the treatment of chronic alcoholism: A critical appraisal. In R. Gibbons et al. (Eds.), *Research advances in alcohol and drug problems* (Vol. 2). New York: Wiley.

Caplan, G. (1976). The family as a support system. In G. Caplan and M. Killilea (Eds.), *Support systems and mutual help: Multidisciplinary explorations.* New York: Grune & Stratton.

Chesler, M., Barbarin, O., & Lego-Stein, J. (1984). Patterns of participation in a self-help group for parents of children with cancer. *Journal of Psychosocial Oncology, 2,* 41–64.

De Tocqueville, A. (1956). *Democracy in America.* New York: Mentor Books.

Edwards, G., Hensman, C., Hawker, A., & Williamson, V. (1967). Alcoholics Anonymous: The anatomy of a self-help group. *Social Psychiatry, 1,* 195–204.

Gartner, A., & Reissman, F. (1977). *Self-help in the human services.* San Francisco: Jossey-Bass.

Gibbs, L. M. (1982). *Love Canal: My story.* Albany: SUNY Press.

Gibbs, L. M. (1983). Community response to an emergency situation: Psychological destruction and the Love Canal. *American Journal of Community Psychology, 11,* 116–125.

Gillick, J. (1977). *Al-Anon: A self help group for co-alcoholics.* Unpublished doctoral dissertation, Department of Psychology, SUNY at Buffalo.

Goldenberg, I. I. (1978). *Oppression and social intervention.* Chicago: Nelson Hall.

Hinrichsen, G. A., Revenson, T. A., & Shinn, M. (1985). Does self-help help? An empirical investigation of scoliosis peer support grups. *Journal of Social Issues, 41,* 65–87.

Howe, I. (1976). *World of our fathers.* New York: Simon & Schuster.

Hurvitz, N. (1976). The origins of the peer self-help psychotherapy group movement. *Journal of Applied Behavioral Science, 12,* 283–294.

Katz, A. H. (1981). Self help and mutual aid: An emerging social movement? *Annual Review of Sociology, 7,* 129–155.

Katz, A. H., & Bender, E. I. (Eds.). (1976). *The strength in us: Self-help groups in the modern world.* New York: New Viewpoints.

Killilea, M. (1976). Mutual help organizations: Interpretations in the literature. In G. Caplan and M. Killilea (Eds.), *Support systems and mutual help. Multidisciplinary explorations.* New York: Grune & Stratton.

Knight, B., Wollert, R. W., Levy, L. H., Frame, C. L., & Padgett, V. P. (1980). Self help groups: The members' perspectives. *American Journal of Community Psychology, 8,* 53–65.

Kropotkin, P. (1972). *Mutual aid. A factor of evolution.* New York: New York University Press (originally published 1902).

Levine, A. G. (1982). *Love Canal: Science, politics, people.* Lexington, MA: Lexington Books.

Levine, M., & Bunker, G. (Eds.). (1975). *Mutual criticism.* Syracuse, NY: Syracuse University Press.

Levy, L. H. (1976). Self-help groups: Types and psychological processes. *Journal of Applied Behavioral Science, 12,* 310–322.

Milner, N. (1985). *Viewing and assessing the mental health patient rights movement.* Paper presented at the meeting of the Law and Society Association, San Diego.

Naroll, R. (1983). *The moral order. An introduction to the human situation.* Beverly Hills: Sage.

National Institute on Alcohol Abuse and Alcoholism. (1983). *Fifth special report to the U.S. Congress on alcohol and health.* Washington, D.C.: U.S. Government Printing Office.

Orford, J., & Edwards, G. (1977). *Alcoholism.* New York: Oxford University Press.

Perlman, J. E. (1976). Grassrooting the system. *Social Policy, 7,* 4–20.

Polich, J. M., Armor, D. J., & Braiker, H. B. (1981). *The course of alcoholism.* New York: Wiley.

Reissman, F. (1965). The "helper-therapy" principle. *Social Work, 10,* 27–32.

Roen, S. R., & Burnes, A. J. (1968). *The community adaptation schedule: Preliminary manual.* New York: Behavioral Publications.

Sagarin, E. (1969). *Odd man in: Societies of deviants in America.* Chicago: Quadrangle Books.

Sarason, S. B. (1974). *The psychological sense of community: Prospects for a community psychology.* San Francisco: Jossey-Bass.

Shackman, S. (1984). *Impact of outpatient alcoholism treatment in a health maintenance organization on drinking and medical services utilization.* Doctoral dissertation, Department of Psychology, SUNY at Buffalo.

Silverman, P. R., et al. (Eds.) (1974). *Helping each other in widowhood.* New York: Health Sciences.

Stone, R. A., & Levine, A. G. (1985–1986). Reactions to collective stress: Correlates of active citizen participation at Love Canal. *Prevention in Human Services, 4,* 153–177.

Suler, J. (1984). The role of ideology in self-help groups. *Social Policy, 14,* 29–36.

Tracy, G. S., & Gussow, Z. (1976). Self-help health groups: A grass-roots response to a need for services. *Journal of Applied Behavioral Science, 12,* 381–396.

U.S. Bureau of the Census. (1976). *Statistical Abstract of the United States* (97th ed.). Washington, DC.

Vaillant, G. E. (1983). *The natural history of alcoholism.* Cambridge: Harvard University Press.

Videka-Sherman, L., & Leiberman, M. (1985). The effects of self help and psychotherapy on child loss: The limits of recovery. *American Journal of Orthopsychiatry, 55,* 70–82.

York, P., & York D. (1980). *Toughlove.* Sellersville, PA: Community Service Foundation.

9

Consciousness Raising as Self-Help

Women's consciousness raising (CR) groups illustrate in an interesting way the nature and life cycle of a specific self-help phenomenon, particularly the powerful role of ideological factors in helping a particular group of people cope with personal or situational disruptions or with rapidly changing external events. In reviewing the consciousness raising phenomenon, readers should keep in mind several of the points raised earlier in this book, such as how the solution to a problem depends on how the problem is defined, how for any problem a number of solutions are possible, and how, more often than we realize, the solutions typically chosen for a problem can be usefully understood as products of a specific time and place in history.

We begin by noting that consciousness raising was a central tool in the organization of the women's movement in the 1960s and 1970s. Consciousness raising in the form of women's groups may still go on, but it has diminished in importance as an organizing tool. Nonetheless, consciousness raising left a historical record that for our purposes is extremely useful. Consciousness raising groups were self-help groups in every sense of that term, and they had both a "therapeutic" and a social action component. We have the benefit of an extensive literature describing these groups. Our discussion is based on that literature and on the comments of friends, colleagues, and students who participated in CR groups.

Although isolating a phenomenon from its context is difficult, consciousness raising can be viewed as a form of self-help for problems in living in addition to the organizing function it served within the women's movement. In its day the CR group was a force for changing women's feelings, attitudes, and behavior, and the group provided social support for many women. Consciousness raising was not viewed as therapy by those who participated (the participants did not view themselves as "sick"), but it proved an important method of providing help for those with problems in living. Many participants achieved changes in attitude and in behavior. Some drastically changed their life-styles as well. We will closely examine descriptions of CR groups in order to understand the process whereby participation produced change and to understand the social dynamics of the self-help process.

Consciousness raising had its origins in the radical politics of the 1960s. "New Left" women, who became increasingly aware of their second-class citizenship within the male-dominated stream of radicalism, split off and began organizing women's groups. One group in New York that had been using a small-group approach in meetings attempted to formalize the method (Hole & Levine, 1971). The concept of CR groups was first described to the nascent women's movement at a 1968 conference involving representatives of many small women's-liberation groups (Sarachild, 1970). Building on the Maoist concept of "speaking bitter," consciousness raising proponents argued that one could find a basis for solidarity if small groups of women shared and analyzed their feelings about themselves and their current life situations. Consciousness raising was not presented as a form of therapy. On the contrary, its aim was to bring women together, to provide a possible organizational unit for a diffuse, widespread movement, and to serve for some as a research method for analyzing and articulating women's roles in society. The small group could serve to support its members and educate them, and it could also provide a unit for political or social action (Jagger, 1983).

The earliest groups began with participants talking about themselves, their individual experiences, and their personal problems. The discovery that different women had common problems and feelings led to the concept that personal problems had social causes. Further, problems with social causes could be attributed to a political or power difference between the sexes. Some groups focused on the idea that men were the enemy. Men were excluded from CR groups from the beginning. Many believed women would be freer to examine their own feelings and would be able to speak more easily in groups composed entirely of women.

A basic ideology emerged: women were a socially oppressed class; women's personal problems were not individual but social, and the personal should be viewed as a political problem. In terms of specific goals, women sought economic and social equality in the job market, in political life, and in the community. Women sought greater equality in sexual relationships and the opportunity to make choices, to discard traditional goals of marriage and motherhood in favor of careers, or to accept those goals, but with greater sharing of responsibilities for housework and child care with their mates. In effect, women sought freedom from the many constraints imposed by a traditional, stereotyped concept of the woman's role. Women wanted greater self-sufficiency and less dependence on males. Eventually the fulfillment of those goals meant that women had to engage in social and political action to overcome formal, legal barriers to equality and in personal action to assert their beliefs in all of their relationships.

The more radical wing of the women's liberation movement encountered internal problems with factions disagreeing (Hole & Levine, 1971; Freeman, 1975). The basic ideas of the women's movement struck responsive chords in many, however. Spread by word of mouth and supported by publications in the underground press and eventually the mass media, a large number of CR groups composed of 4–15 members each sprang up around the country. Carden (1974) estimated that some 15,000 women took part in such groups within a few years, while Cassell (1977) asserted that every block in Manhattan seemed to have a consciousness raising group at that time.

During this period of rapid growth in CR groups, the women's movement was itself growing and differentiating rapidly. Small radical groups sought a women's revolution and eventually a matriarchal society. Some advocated man hating, lesbianism, masturbation, and communal living, among other social changes. Many of the radical groups had meteoric lives. The basic ideas and mode of analysis persisted, however, and captured the attention of many women. The ideas were publicized through the radical underground press. No longer small, an issue of the *Feminist Journal* sold

40,000 copies in 1970 (Hole & Levine, 1971). Feminist ideas engendered interest in the women's movement as a whole through the popular press.

Although the ideas of the radical women's movement were of interest to many women, not everyone was able to find in these ideas a sense of community with all other women. A variety of schisms developed; one of the most publicized was between gay and straight women. Other splits along class and cultural lines had implications for the women's movement in general and for CR groups in particular. A major division was between the women's *rights* group, generally consisting of somewhat older, well-educated, well-established women interested in gaining a more equitable share of the social and economic pie, and women's *liberation* groups consisting of younger, less well-educated, less established women who were in transition and still seeking a basis for personal identity in a changing world. Observers characterized this basic division in different ways, but they tended to agree on its dimensions (Hole & Levine, 1971; Carden, 1974; Freeman, 1975; Cassell, 1977).

The ideas of the women's movement eventually captured the attention of many traditional women's organizations (e.g., YWCA, United Auto Workers Women's Department; National Federation of Business and Professional Women's Clubs; National Council of Jewish Women). The creation of the National Organization for Women (NOW) in 1966, under the leadership of Betty Friedan, was critical for later developments. In 1963 Friedan had written *The Feminine Mystique,* itself a powerful consciousness raising work. Beginning with a charter membership of 300, NOW pressed for change through the traditional tactics of lobbying, education, and publicity. By 1971 there were 150 NOW chapters with an estimated 5,000–10,000 members, and in 1975 there were 750 chapters and 60,000 members (Hole & Levine, 1971; Levine, 1977; Cassell, 1977).

The NOW leadership, at first opposed to "rap" groups and CR groups as antithetical to their action orientation, began to see their usefulness as a method for educating willing, interested, but untutored recruits to the history, philosophy, and objectives of the women's movement. Moreover, NOW chapters around the country found considerable demand for rap or CR groups among potential members (Carden, 1974). The leadership therefore supported the organization of such groups as a means of initiating and socializing women into the movement. Taking advantage of previous experience, CR groups organized by NOW also tended to have a specific form and approach. These groups were constituted somewhat more systematically, and they frequently consisted of women at about the same level of awareness and commitment to the precepts of the movement. These groups also tended to have experienced leaders, some of whom were trained by NOW for this purpose (Cassell, 1977).

The present status of CR groups as an element of the women's movement is uncertain. In 1974, Lieberman and Bond (1976) surveyed some 1,700 women and found CR groups in 37 states. On the basis of an analysis of the contemporary functions of CR groups, Lieberman and Bond predicted they would continue to persist as a vital self-help force. We will return to their data and analysis, but for now we want to state that the women's movement itself has changed, and consciousness raising doesn't have the same attraction it once enjoyed. Moreover, the women's movement has differentiated along a variety of lines, including groups with specialized interests in such topics as rape, health care, women's studies, women alcoholics, spouse abuse, and abortion. Women's centers have sprung up offering psychotherapy, educational courses, recreation, counseling, information and referral services, and crisis-oriented assistance (Women and Mental Health Project, 1976). Women's caucuses developed in many professional organizations. More recently we have seen the development of management-oriented training for women in business and the professions. Courses and workshops in assertiveness training also proliferated, although they are not as common as they once were.

These different self-help modes may fulfill some of the same needs that the CR groups fulfilled at an earlier time. The self-help aspects of the approach are not dead by any means, although the specific organizational forms and sponsorship may have changed over time. Although our analysis is most appropriate to the spontaneously organized CR groups, the terms of the analysis are probably appropriate to the new emerging forms as well, but these forms are not yet as well described in the professional literature as the earlier ones were.

What Is Consciousness Raising?

Consciousness raising was a key concept in the contemporary feminist movement. As Cassell (1977) points out, *consciousness* is a term referring to a personal, subjective experience. The concept of *raising* implies ascending levels.[1] Both of these terms, *consciousness* and *raising,* are ambiguous. Precise meanings are not specified, nor does any set of explicit standards allow one to determine when consciousness has been raised. This ambiguity is advantageous. It allows each group and each member to determine when consciousness raising has been achieved. Given the diversity of class, race, ethnic origins, age, education, occupation, sexual orientation, marital status, and initial interests and concerns in participating, the ambiguity of terminology has the advantage of allowing diverse participants and groups to employ differing denotations and connotations of the terms while unifying around the verbal symbol.

Cassell (1977) stated that consciousness raising generally refers to an increasing acceptance of the proposition that women have inferior social and economic positions in society. Consequently, women have insufficient self-esteem. If one understands that the status of women is low socially and economically and that women suffer from feelings of poor self-esteem, consciousness raising also means that one accepts an imperative to raise women's social and economic status. Feminist ideology includes the concept that the causes of women's inferior positions are not in women's failings, nor inherent in biologically based human nature, but are consequences of the social oppression and exploitation of women. The personal thereby becomes the political (Hanisch, 1978).

This overall ideology provides the social and psychological ground for a profound shift in perspective in the construction of personal and social realities. Participants move toward perceiving women as a degraded or socially oppressed group, toward perceiving themselves as members of this group, and toward committing themselves to personal change, if not to social action in an effort to raise women's status socially, economically, and emotionally. From an organizational viewpoint, the process of learning the ideology, and using the ideology to direct action, provided the basis for the development of solidarity among women.

Participants came to consciousness raising groups with diverse motives and levels of understanding. In the view of those who organized an activist women's movement, CR groups were not meant to be psychotherapeutic. Their participants did not perceive themselves as disturbed or sick. In fact, it was part of the ideology of the movement that psychotherapists, particularly those with a Freudian orientation, contribute to the subjugation of women by asserting a narrow concept of the healthy female social role and of female sexuality. Lieberman and Bond (1976) reported the paradoxical fact that although many women believed psychotherapy in the Freudian mode was antithetical to the women's movement, 54% had been in therapy in the previous 5 years and 17% were in therapy concurrent with their participation in a CR group. The bulk of those with therapeutic experience felt they were aided by their therapy but believed they got something else from consciousness raising. A majority of those currently in therapy were seeing a feminist therapist.[2]

Many participants were discontented and suffered from depression or anxiety, and many did have psychotherapeutic experience prior to or concurrently with participation in consciousness raising groups, but the manifest purpose of consciousness raising groups was not psychotherapy. Consciousness raising groups were designed to change the way participants thought about themselves and their situations. They were intended to result in greater self-acceptance on the one hand and in striving to live up to newly formulated ideals of personal conduct and relationships on the other. Indeed, Cassell (1977) draws an analogy between successful consciousness raising and religious conversion.

Ideally, after consciousness raising was attained, a woman became a feminist, defining herself as a member of the community of women, with others her movement sisters. Feminist analysis, or the ideology of the movement, provided the basis for interpreting the meaning of everyday acts. The ideology provided the cognitive context for feeling and the basis for action in the social world. Work, sexual relationships, parent-child relationships, and other social relationships—indeed, participation in many aspects of the larger culture—were subject to interpretation in terms of feminist principles. Feminist ideology became a core set of constructs defining personal identity. Speech and dress were altered. Relationships with both men and women changed, and increased interaction took place with other members of the community of feminists. Interacting with others whose consciousness had been raised provided a network of mutual support and a community within which ideological precepts were reinforced and extended. For some women commitment to the movement became total. A good portion of waking time was spent in movement activities. Meetings, task forces, fund raising, organizing efforts, demonstrations, lobbying, and similar activities came to be dominant in some women's lives. For others, the changes were far less extensive. They consisted of changed perceptions and interpretations of one's own situation with little behavioral change. Because the term *consciousness raising* is ambiguous and the overarching aim was to create mass support for cultural, social, and personal changes, any degree of change constituted successful consciousness raising.

The Organization of Consciousness Raising Groups

Consciousness raising groups consisted of anywhere from 4–15 women who agreed to meet, usually on a weekly basis, in someone's home. Groups were initiated by anyone who was interested. The impetus often came from one person's personal contact with another who had experienced a consciousness raising group. The groups were relatively easy to organize. They required no facilities, no professional leadership, and cost nothing beyond time and participants' contributions for refreshments. Meetings were advertised by word of mouth through personal networks, through inexpensive or free ads in movement or underground press, and through announcements on college bulletin boards. When NOW adopted sponsorship of groups, the local chapter acted as a broker, bringing together women who had called individually expressing interest. Women's studies programs at some colleges and universities organized around consciousness raising groups. Other women's centers and psychotherapy and self-help health clinics sometimes provided the focus for the organization of groups, which were variously called cells, affinity groups, rap groups, collectives, support groups, small groups, or "my women's liberation group" (Carden, 1974; Women and Mental Health Project, 1976).

Because the groups organized informally and participation was voluntary, the members of a given group tended to be homogeneous along several dimensions. For one, very few black women participated in women's liberation or women's rights groups. Although interest in women's liberation among black women grew later, few black women participated. Originally a sore point among radical leaders, the lack of involvement by black women came to be accepted as part of the contemporary world (Carden, 1974; Hole & Levine, 1971). We simply note that CR groups as such were not usually interracial, just as most other spontaneously organized self-help groups are not.

Observers tended to agree that the women's movement, as reflected initially in loosely organized CR groups, and the women's rights movement as exemplified by the NOW organization, attracted quite different constituencies. Women who belonged to women's rights groups tended to be middle- to upper-middle-class whites, with no more than 10% of lower-class status. The largest number were well educated; 90% had BA degrees, and 30% had professional degrees (Ph.D., M.D., J.D.). Some 60% worked full-time or part-time at professional and higher status white-collar positions. Income (their own or their husband's) exceeded $10,000 (the equivalent of about $30,000 in 1987). Four-fifths were married, and two-thirds of those who were married had children. A minority (estimates varied from 20 to 40%) characterized themselves as housewives. Ages ranged from the teens to the 60s, with a median age somewhere in the late 20s or early 30s. In general, women coming to CR groups who identified with the women's rights branch of the movement tended to be older, better established personally and professionally, and interested less in radical social change than in obtaining greater equity economically, socially, and politically for themselves and for other women.

Women coming to consciousness raising groups through identification with the women's liberation branch of the movement tended to be of the same middle and upper class as measured by origins, life-style, and aspirations, but not as measured by indices of education and occupation. Women's liberation adherents tended to be younger (median age middle to late 20s), were less well educated (far fewer completed college), and were more likely to hold lower status service or clerical positions. Many had aspirations for higher occupational attainment. Women's liberation members were more likely to be single or divorced; only one-fourth were currently married.

Lieberman and Bond (1976) studied a sample of CR group participants obtained by distributing questionnaires to 1,700 women through the existing grass-roots network of the women's movement. They reported that 91% of members lived in urban or suburban areas, and 99% were white. The median age of participants was 31, with

92% in the age range 20 to 40. Approximately 55% were married. A quarter were single, while another 20% were divorced, separated, or widowed. About half the women had children. None of the sources cite data revealing religious origins or affiliations. Only 14% of the women classified themselves as housewives. Ninety percent had attended college, and two-thirds had earned at least a bachelor's degree. These were well-educated, upper-income women.

No one can tell what proportion of groups that began continued and what proportion did not continue. Observers agreed that the groups formed and dissolved rapidly, in many cases within a few weeks or months (Carden, 1974). Some continued for as long as 2 years or more. Carden (1974) estimated that the life of a CR group was typically 9 months. Women may have participated in more than one group, however. Lieberman and Bond (1976) reported that about a third had been in one or more previous CR groups. Of their respondents, 17% had been involved for over 2 years, 25% between 1 and 2 years, 28% between 6 months and 1 year, and 30% less than 6 months. Lieberman and Bond's data suggest that many CR groups served as a long-term support for many members.

The process of forming, disintegrating, and reforming is predictable whenever new settings are created (Sarason, 1972). The tension between maintaining solidarity among members of the group and dealing with individual needs of the members is endemic to groups. In this instance, the dynamics of organizing led to the formation of groups that were relatively homogeneous. This homogeneity is a systematic phenomenon emerging out of the voluntary nature of the organization of groups. Homogeneity of interest, life-style, social position, and social background helps members to identify with each other and to understand and appreciate each other's problems. Groups may be able to tolerate a greater degree of heterogeneity, and members may benefit by the greater diversity. When groups organize informally, however, in the initial stages members who can identify with each other will almost inevitably continue, while those who do not will depart and find other more compatible groups.

Participants express something of themselves in a style of dress and manner of speech that may attract some and repel others. Both Carden (1971) and Cassell (1977), who did participant-observation studies of women's groups, reported that members of women's rights groups were generally more stylishly dressed than were members of women's liberation groups, who favored loose clothing, no cosmetics, and steel-rimmed glasses. Carden modified her dress when meeting with different groups. Cassell carried complete changes of clothing to allow her to blend in with the groups she was observing or interviewing.

Cassell (1977) provides a case study of the organization of one group. The study is instructive in revealing how homogeneity develops and is maintained. Members of a local women's group, noting that they received frequent inquiries about how to get into a consciousness raising group, maintained a pool of names and telephone numbers of potential participants. One woman called the list of potential participants and found six able to attend a meeting on a Tuesday night. Five women came to the initial meeting. All were white, middle class, and Jewish, and they ranged in age from 21 to 35. Only one member had previous consciousness raising experience; four of the five had been in psychotherapy, and the fifth was contemplating entering therapy. Four of the five wore the women's liberation clothing style. None wore bras or cosmetics.

In the initial meeting, in one of the women's apartments, members decided just to talk. After introducing themselves, they found they had mutual friends and other common experiences. Each revealed something about herself and some of her problems in relationships. The initial meeting was wide-ranging, with no particular topical focus. The women decided they liked each other well enough to meet again. They selected "mothers" as a topic for the next meeting and agreed to meet at another member's apartment.

The second meeting was cancelled, but they met the following week and discussed themselves as well as their mothers. A new member attended the third meeting. She decided to return to the CR group to which she already belonged. The following week the group met at the home of the older woman, who had an expensive well-furnished duplex apartment. There was some anticipation of jealousy over her status before the meeting.

Discussions were relatively unfocused in these early meetings. Members began expressing some dissatisfaction with the way the group was going. They exchanged views until they were able to come to some agreement on goals, but they saw that not everyone's purposes would be served by this particular group. The group decided to explore a merger with another group. The merger was unsuccessful. One group was oriented toward exploring what women did themselves to get into trouble. The second group was hostile to this orientation and wished to focus instead on what society did to women. The second group saw the psychotherapeutic orientation as inimical to its purposes. Between meetings members of each group decided it would be futile to attempt a merger. The initiating group, however, gained one member who felt at home within it.

During the process of exchanging introductions and viewpoints, members joined or dropped out until a stable group formed. The abortive attempt to merge two groups with different ideologies, or different levels of consciousness, demonstrated the dynamics of homogenization. Had the two groups been formed as one group initially, they probably would have split much as they did.

The much discussed gay-straight split in the women's movement is a case in point. Some heterosexual women have great difficulty relating to homosexual women, and some homosexual women have difficulty in understanding heterosexual relationships. Ideological aggression might convince some but could well repel others. Cassell (1977), a married woman, belonged to a university action group and stayed with the group for two years. She felt much more comfortable with the group during its first year when there were many older students like herself and more heterosexual women. She was much less comfortable the second year when the group had more undergraduates, more bisexual women, and more lesbians. She wrote: "Attending meetings was a pleasure the first year and an ordeal the second. I probably would have left the group the second year if it had not been part of my dissertation research" (p. 145).

Cassell (1977) pointed out that the initial meeting of a consciousness raising group could be quite unnerving for a novice. If a group had some women with experience in group therapy or encounter and sensitivity groups, or included women with previous consciousness raising experience, initial discussions may have gone on at a very intense emotional level. The fast movement to a deep and intense level of intimate self-revelation and emotional expression might well threaten persons not used to revealing themselves to anyone, much less to strangers. Some may have been put off by the emotional fireworks and may have sought a group in which the level of emotional expression was more congenial.

This process of forming homogeneous groups also occurs in groups such as Alcoholics Anonymous and Al-Anon (see the previous chapter). In any given area there are many chapters meeting in different locations. Prospective members are free to shop around until they find a congenial chapter and can attend as they wish. Compatibility among members is a critical factor for groups just forming or for the recruitment of new members. Pattison et al. (1965) report that 95% of lower-class Appalachian women referred to an Al-Anon meeting composed of middle-class women attended only one meeting. Gillick (1977), observing Al-Anon groups in the Buffalo area, rarely saw a black woman in attendance. Reissman (1976) points to this process of selection as a strength of the self-help movement because it allows each individual to find a group with compatible members and with an ideology and group atmosphere congenial for that member.

If Antze's (1976) viewpoint is correct—that the ideologies of self-help groups are specifically designed to ameliorate members' core problems—shopping around clearly has an important therapeutic purpose as well. The pejorative connotation of "shopping around" or "dropping out" and the fear of duplicating services make sense within a professional frame of reference in which the professional is viewed as offering a specific technical service appropriate to all suffering from a disorder. It makes no sense at all within a self-help framework. In fact, for purposes of developing support networks, redundancy in self-selection may well be much more efficient than single, centralized services.

Why Did Women Join Consciousness Raising Groups?

Lieberman and Bond (1976) obtained ratings of the importance of various motives for joining consciousness raising groups from 1,700 participants using a 33-item scale, which reduced empirically to six factors. Participants in groups rated the six factors in the following order of importance:

1. *Interests in women's issues* (feelings about being a woman; problems with traditional roles).
2. *Help seeking* (obtain relief from troubling feelings; solve current or long-term problems).
3. *Social needs* (loneliness; make friends; find community).
4. *Political activation* (expand awareness; obtain information to be active in movement).
5. *Sexual awareness* (explore sexual feelings about men and women; understand feelings about one's body).
6. *Curiosity.*

Lieberman and Bond also obtained responses to a 41-item life-events stress index and to a 35-item self-report symptom checklist. Women in consciousness raising groups reported a few more stressful life events than did a normative group, but considerably fewer than did women who sought psychotherapy in an outpatient clinic. Similarly, the women had a greater number of self-reported symptoms of psychological distress than a normative sample, but considerably fewer symptoms than women in the psychotherapy sample. Lieberman and Bond concluded that the women in CR groups were dissatisfied with their personal lives and had significantly more symptoms of depression and anxiety than did women in the normative sample. Although many women in their study had sought psychotherapy in the past or were currently in therapy, Lieberman and Bond concluded that the women in attendance in consciousness raising groups were only mildly distressed. Women-to-women services in centers and clinics around the country do not usually accept as clients women exhibiting extremely neurotic or psychotic symptoms. The more severely disturbed women are referred to other mental health services (Women and Mental Health Project, 1976).

Cassell (1977) believed that discontent sometimes stimulated by the movement, or by an acute life crisis, often precipitated women's search for assistance. In her group of five women, one had just ended a relationship with a man after having recently had a second abortion. A second member had been hospitalized after she had "flipped out." A third revealed very little except that she had a lot of fantasies about men and women. A fourth wanted a group where she could discuss her problems as a married student with children. The fifth seemed to have some concerns about her relationship with the man with whom she was living. Later, one of the women confessed that she was ambivalent about an extramarital affair she had had.

Carden (1974) believed that consciousness raising groups helped members to cope with a normless environment. The New Left arrangements for living with a man had brought new problems. Even though not married, women in such relationships frequently found themselves performing the wife's role, reflecting not only their expectations of themselves but also the expectations others had for them. Prohibitions on premarital sex had broken down, and possessive sexual liaisons were viewed as old-fashioned. Still, women who engaged in casual sexual relationships felt hurt when the relationship ended.

Popular attention to the joys of sex and the emphasis on having multiple orgasms brought new feelings of inadequacy to women. According to Hole and Levine (1971), one of the most important works of interest to women in the movement was a paper entitled "The Myth of the Vaginal Orgasm" (Koedt, 1970). The paper opened the topic of sexuality for renewed discussion. The concepts of the women's movement led married women to rethink the nature of the personal distress they were experiencing and to consider whether marriage itself and the traditional role relationships within marriage were the sources of their discontent.

Problems of loneliness and isolation in a large impersonal world and unsatisfying friendships or lack of real friendships with other women led some to seek out a group to develop a sense of community. Young mothers with two or three children felt isolated in suburban tract homes, overburdened with work and responsibility, and disenchanted when reality smashed their romantic ideals. Older women whose children were grown were at a point of transition in their lives. They needed to decide on a life pattern for the future. Others had experienced or were facing divorce and also needed to decide on a future life course. Some tried to enter the work world, but found that either their skills were inadequate or they encountered active discrimination in job seeking or promotions.

These problems in living facing women at various stages in their lives were the immediate sources of the discontent, depression, and anxiety that led women to seek out others with whom to share their problems. The catalog of problems is not unlike those to be found in almost any psychotherapist's office. The consciousness raising group then was not only a means for raising consciousness in the sense of attracting and educating women to the women's movement; it was also an alternative helping service, provided on a mass basis and without professional assistance.

How Do Consciousness Raising Groups Work?

Cassell (1977) described the typical initiation and organization of a group. Once the 4–15 women gathered in someone's home, following the recommendations of published guidelines for organizing and running groups (e.g., *Ms Magazine,* 1972, Vol. 1, No. 1), the women formed a circle. Usually someone with previous consciousness raising experience was present. The experienced member would suggest that members introduce themselves, offer brief biographies, and indicate why they wished to join a group. The groups frequently had an assigned topic for discussion. The topics varied widely; members discussed personal experiences and related the topic on the floor to their position as women. The outline by Sarachild (1970) reported that women "will recall and share bitter experiences," express feelings about those experiences, extend the discussion of feeling to a consideration of self, self in relation to men, and self in relation to other women. Sarachild suggested that women go around the room and talk about their own experiences in relation to the principal topic. All participants were encouraged to speak out as they felt moved by their own feelings. Controls were adopted to prevent more articulate women from dominating the discussion. Members were allowed to question each other as well. An immediate aim was to identify commonalities of experience and to discover and illuminate each member's way of coping as a woman. Ideally, the expression of feelings led to analysis, to theory, and to plans for action.

The topics included such subjects as: Why and how one should dress and use makeup, and how much style of dress is related to attracting men? What should be the relationship between husband and wife, and what sacrifices does a woman make for the comforts of marriage? What are the relative responsibilities of men and women for household work and for child care and child rearing? Should women be more aggressive and assertive? What are the sources of a lack of confidence in women? Why are there male-dominated and female-dominated professions, and should it be that way? Do women like other women? How do women feel about their own bodies? Do husbands and lovers really satisfy them sexually?

Hole and Levine (1971) provided a partial list of topics for use in high school consciousness raising groups. These include such questions as: Did you ever pretend to be dumb? How are women portrayed in books you read? What did you discuss in your sex education classes—lesbianism, masturbation, intercourse, orgasm, abortion? Do you ask boys out, and if not, why not? Is your mother an oppressed woman?

The topics led to the revelation of experiences, often in the mode of confessing. Carden (1974) gave as examples single women describing their anguish at waiting for men to call them for dates; the sense of fury and helplessness when stared at or whistled at in the street; resentment at waiting on husbands; faking orgasms to satisfy men; ambivalence about competing with men; ambivalence about working when they have children, or about marriage itself. Cassell (1977) provided examples of a woman expressing guilt at leaving her child in the evening so she could work in the library, and another woman who felt ambivalent about her husband and her lovers. In one group members confessed feelings of inadequacy about whether their bodies measured up to fashion magazine ideals. They literally bared their breasts, each expressing the feeling that her breasts were somehow deficient, but eventually gaining reassurance that she had perfectly adequate breasts.

Cassell (1977) asserted that within a few months members developed a sense of closeness that was satisfying and even exhilarating. Having confessed, and discovered with surprise and relief that all shared common experiences and common feelings of anger, guilt, or ambivalence, members identified with each other. Because intimacy in a supportive atmosphere was encouraged, members developed trust and a sense of community. The sense of community extended to more than simply confessing. Relationships extended beyond the boundaries of the group meeting. Women frequently dined together before meetings and made an effort to provide refreshments for each other as a symbol of mutual nurturance. Members extended tangible assistance at moments of need. In Cassell's group, when one member decided to divorce her husband, she moved in with another temporarily while apartment hunting. Members provided baby-sitting services for another member during a personal emergency. When one woman's lover was killed and she was fearful of remaining alone, other members kept her company during the week.

Groups were not without their crises. Individuals meeting together in an atmosphere of intimacy inevitably develop feelings of hostility toward each other. These feelings may reflect personal anxiety about specific topics, idiosyncratic antipathies of one member toward another, or anger about lateness, missed meetings, or suppression of personal information. Such a catalog of resistance and hostility is familiar to any group therapist. Within consciousness raising groups, however, members were encouraged to confront anger and hostility in themselves and others in order to learn to handle anger in ways other than dissolving into tears. A tenet of women's movement ideology is that women have not been socialized to deal with angry feelings. This feature of the ideology underlies women's interests in assertiveness training. In other words, the movement provides an ideological rationale for dealing with the hostilities that inevitably emerge in any group and that if left to fester without confrontation could lead to the dissolution of the group (Cassell, 1977).

Sarachild's (1970) original outline listed a great many types of resistance to consciousness raising, defined as becoming aware of women "as abused and oppressed since the beginning of history" (p. 79). Some are well-recognized anxieties about self-revelation: fear of personal exposure; feelings of loyalty to spouses, lovers, bosses, parents, or children; fear of hurting the feelings of other group members; fear that one's feelings or concerns are unique and therefore pathological; fear of feeling the intensity of emotion in the present, despair for the future, or discovering that one's life is meaningless or wasted.

Other feelings, however, are related to resisting consciousness or, as Sarachild (1970) put it: "How to avoid facing the awful truth." This set of resistances is specific to the acceptance of movement ideology. It includes such items as antiwomanism, self-blame, and glorification of, excusing and feeling sorry for, or falsely identifying with the oppressor (males). Difficulty in identifying with one's own group, insistence on the merits of personal solutions, asserting the power of women to get what they want from men, and other forms of self-cultivation or "go-it-aloneism" were viewed as means of maintaining the status quo. Resistances were not only related to the psychological dynamics of relationships within the groups but also to the process of merging with the group, in the sense of adopting an ideology for purposes of analyzing both cosmic and commonplace events.

In the view of many within the movement, it was necessary to understand that the problems women experienced were a function of previous oppression, brainwashing, socialization, and participation in a social order that reinforced women's inferior status. Once having learned to adopt a feminist perspective, many problems were recast in these terms. Action consistent with the terms of analysis could then be taken to alleviate problems. The process of analysis of one's personal and current situation in terms of CR ideology resulted for many in a commitment to change their lives.

Levy (1976) studied several self-help groups, including a CR group, from the perspective of identifying therapeutic elements in terms familiar to psychotherapists. The techniques can be divided into two broad classes, those that focus on and support behavioral change and those that focus on cognitive change. Cognitive change refers to the way members think about their problems, themselves, others, and their relationships, and how critical events in their lives are interpreted.

On the behavioral side, Levy found that group members provided reinforcement for the development of behaviors consistent with the group's objectives and for the elimination of behaviors designated as undesirable. Members received training and support in the use of various forms of self-control and modeled methods of coping with stress and changing behaviors. Moreover, because the group's ideology tended to externalize the source of the problem, it directed members' attention away from themselves. The ideology called for action to modify the social environment in making it less stressful and more supporting. The group's ideology opposed the sense of helplessness or powerlessness individuals felt about changing their environments by providing a rationale, encouragement, and specific methods to deal with commonplace problems.

The groups provided members with a cognitive rationale for their difficulties and a method for dealing with daily problems. Thus feelings of perplexity and helplessness were reduced, while the expectancy for change and for help increased. Moreover, as women's movement proponents and all other self-help groups and group therapists have noted, the discovery that one's problems are not unique or that one is far from alone in having problems is relieving in and of itself. The resulting sense of mutual identification, and participation in rituals (e.g., sitting in a circle; each confessing; using the language of the movement) may well enhance the power of influence of the group on individual members. In the course of revealing problems and solutions, members provide normative information, give advice, and expand the range of possible alternative solutions. Levy suggested that the analysis of problems in the group allowed members to develop generalized analytic and discriminative abilities, improving the possibilities for specific actions appropriate to the desired change outside of the group. Most important, the changes in self-concept and behavior took place within an alternative or substitute culture and social organization providing social support, social validation of new identities, and new values and norms on which to base feelings of self-esteem.

Reissman (1976) described a number of dynamics of the nonprofessional helping role that contribute to personal change. In leaderless CR groups, there is no fixed status differential as there would be between a professional helper and a patient or client. All members fulfill both roles. As members' consciousness rose they moved into the position of contributing to change in others. Anyone could ascend in the fellowship as her understanding of movement ideology increased and as she changed her life in keeping with the ideology. Within the group, all members asked for and received help, and all members gave help. In the process of giving help to others, members advocated the group's position, and in doing so became further committed to that position through a process of dissonance reduction and through clarifying their own thinking in the attempt to explain something to others (Reissman, 1965).

Reissman (1965) identified a number of other mechanisms in the helper-therapy principle. In addition to feeling less dependent, the helper gained some distance from the personal problem by seeing it more objectively in another. Furthermore, the helper enhanced her feeling of social usefulness by playing the helping role and by more intensive involvement with movement activities. In offering help to others, the helper may have found an inner strength of which she was previously unaware.

Professional observers and interpreters of self-help movements have stated that profound changes occurred in some individuals. They have identified powerful social and psychological forces that can account for the changes. We now turn to an examination of the changes reported for participants in consciousness raising groups.

Personal Change Consequent to Participation in Consciousness Raising Groups

Cassell (1977), Carden (1974), and other observers agree that while some women experienced profound changes in their lives, others participated in consciousness raising groups for more limited emotional satisfactions and did not change very much. For some women catharsis and sympathy were sufficient to relieve distress, although discontent sufficient to create change did not emerge. Cassell believes that younger married women with children were less likely to institute profound changes and more likely to use the groups for purposes of catharsis and support. She argues plausibly that the prospects of rearing young children alone were quite alarming for some women. The alternative stemming from confrontation with spouses may be perceived as worse than the current situation. Many other women, particularly those with professional training or other salable skills, perceived their current distressful situations as *temporary* consequences of being locked in with young children. Because the circumstances were viewed as temporary, the woman's situation may have been tolerable simply because it was time limited. The woman whose consciousness was raised could act on the ideology to create changes in her life at some future time.

Emotional changes with relatively small consequences for other relationships did occur. Frequently women renegotiated relationships with husbands or men they were living with. These negotiations involved relatively small changes such as getting a husband to put the children to bed at night, to care for them on weekends, or to share in household chores such as cooking and cleaning. Some women asserted more independence from husbands in their recreational activities or exhibited less emotional dependence on their men. They learned not to become distraught if their husbands became upset with them. With support from their groups, some women learned not to cry when in an argument with a man, but to hold their own (Carden, 1974; Cassell, 1977). Levy (1976) suggests that women used their groups to work out norms for such events as asking for help or accepting the courtesies men extended to women when such actions could be interpreted as violations of movement ideology. The consciousness raising group supported women who were making decisions about job changes, education, or entering the job market when the woman had not worked previously. Groups helped women to relax their self-imposed demands to be superwomen and to stop trying to carry out the roles of wife, mother, and wage earner to the point of exhaustion.

Achieving such changes may not seem profound, but these achievements have implications for a sense of mastery of self and of one's problems when carried through successfully. They also have effects on self-esteem because the changes are viewed as action consistent with a new ego ideal derived from movement ideology. Given the ambiguity of the term, even small changes could be accepted as successfully raised consciousness. A woman reporting any change would have received considerable social reinforcement for this accomplishment.

The component of feminist ideology that views masculine oppression as the source of women's difficulties can lead women to feel anger instead of depression or anxiety and to express that anger toward men. While the release of angry feelings can provide motivation for change, the anger can also have important consequences for male-female relationships. Observers agreed that some marriages dissolved concurrent with women's participation in CR groups. Cassell (1977) states that divorces became epidemic in some circles. In one group four of eight participants divorced, separated, or broke up a previously enduring relationship at some time during the group's existence; in a second group six of twelve severed relationships, and in a third group ten of twelve.

Carden (1974) states that many women who broke up relationships with men went through a process of rethinking whether they wished to develop further relationships with men on the same basis. Some single women made decisions never to marry, to have children only if cooperative day care was available, or, if they married, to do so only under conditions that husband and wife agreed, sometimes contractually, to share equally in housekeeping, child care, and earning a living.

Viewing men as the oppressor and valuing women more, as well as spending more time in the company of women, led some to a rethinking of sexuality and sexual relationships. Sexual activity changed for some. For those who saw heterosexual intercourse as a form of social dominance, celibacy seemed preferable. Others experimented with sexual aggressiveness. Women felt freer to ask men for dates and to initiate sexual overtures, not coyly or seductively but directly. The new sexual aggressiveness posed problems of adaptation for men. At one point there were serious discussions about whether male impotence was a consequence of female sexual aggressiveness. The new sexual aggressiveness posed problems for women as well. Some who experimented with this mode of sexual expression had to deal with rejection of their overtures by men.

Other women felt decreased pressure to participate in a sexual relationship to obtain or to hold a male companion. For those who professed modern sexual values but also held somewhat more traditional views of the sexual relationship, friendships with women provided some of the emotional sustenance for which heterosexual relationships were sought. One reaction was to opt for celibacy. Still others took to fondling or caressing other women to express affection, out of ideological considerations if not to obtain sexual gratification. With the ideological emphasis that vaginal orgasms were myths and that all orgasms derived from clitoral stimulation, some increased their use of masturbation as a sexual outlet. Currently sex therapists recommend masturbation as a prelude to achieving orgasm in intercourse for women with sexual dysfunction or dissatisfaction. Self-help sex manuals include detailed instructions for female masturbation (Heiman, LoPiccolo, & LoPiccolo, 1976).

A number of women experimented with lesbian relationships, some as a matter of ideological commitment, some as a matter of faddishness, and some out of pressure to be correct in the eyes of the women's movement. Observers agree that lesbianism was a prominent issue and that there was pressure to show commitment to the movement by engaging in homosexual activity (Hole & Levine, 1971; Carden, 1974; Cassell, 1977). Cassell is not willing to attribute the adoption of a lesbian life-style only to participation in consciousness raising groups. She believed that other factors were involved in the case of women who became fully lesbian, including deep commitment to radical change and a previous psychological predilection toward lesbianism.

Cassell (1977) believes that the variety of changes in sexual thinking were prompted not only by movement ideology, but also by the fact that many of the women had suffered deep hurt and disappointment in heterosexual relationships based on traditional sex roles. Consciousness raising groups allowed women to express the hurt, "to speak bitterness," and thereby to see alternatives. Carden (1974) notes that some of the concerns of younger women may have been prompted by the large number of women of marriageable age, compared to men, in the 1960s. At some level women may well have become aware that more and more they would be faced with living in a world with many more women than men, particularly as they aged. As we pointed out in Chapter 1, at every age after 35 there are many more widowed women than men and more divorced women than men. A large number of women will inevitably live many years of their lives without the possibility of an exclusive heterosexual relationship. The women's movement ideology may in some fashion be viewed as a means of helping women to cope with a demographic inevitability. In that sense, the ideology of the women's movement may be seen as highly consistent with core problems women face and may be a prime example of Antze's (1976) contention that ideologies attract people because they provide guidelines for solutions to people's core problems.

The larger women's movement provided a social context within which to develop and live out wholly new identities. As with other self-help groups, participation in movement activities and life-styles became central in some people's lives. Cassell (1977) likens such complete changes to religious conversions. Women who became deeply committed to movement ideology changed their appearance and demeanor, the language they used, the people with whom they interacted, their activities, and their goals.

Carden (1974) and Cassell (1977) point out that committed women wore looser, more comfortable clothes, sometimes devising loose-flowing gowns as all-purpose garments. They went braless, and some stopped shaving their legs or underarms. Modes of address changed. Women used the term *sister* or called all by their first names only. Some retained maiden names, and others adopted made-up names as a protest against accepting male-dominated lineage. Many insisted on the use of "Ms," a term as neutral to marital status as "Mr.," instead of "Miss" or "Mrs." Some groups attacked sexist language, insisting on nonsexist terminology and winning out in many quarters (e.g., American Psychological Association, 1977). Thus terms such as *herstory, s/he,* and *chairperson* entered the language. Many women also took to using language formerly reserved to army barracks rooms but now commonplace in New Left rhetoric. Vulgar language was used not only as a symbol of equality but also to show that women could not be shocked, and therefore dominated, by the use of profanity.

Personal aggressiveness increased, particularly in openly opposing anything now perceived as antifemale. Cassell (1977) describes how she stilled a male meeting that had been making jokes about women through using terms with double meanings. She called out loudly and angrily, "This laughter insults women" (p. xii), stopping the laughter. For some women personal aggressiveness included taking lessons in karate for self-protection. For those who became heavily involved with movement action, aggressiveness included participating in demonstrations, confronting officials or supervisors, and acting against sexist institutions and practices.

Those who became heavily involved in movement activities interacted more and more with women who had similar interests. Because there were always causes, and multiple groups and committees, a woman might well use all of her time in promoting movement causes. For others, experience in consciousness raising groups led to awareness of mutual interests that expanded the basis for relationships between women. Thus women could talk to each other about much more than recipes, children, and gardens. Cassell (1977) believes that a primary consequence of participation in groups was a greater bonding between women. Through consciousness raising groups women came to value women more and saw spending time with women as worthwhile, rather than judging time spent with women as secondary to time spent with men.

Observers report broad changes ranging from the relief of distress to profound changes in values, relationships, life goals, aspirations, and sexual orientation. According to Lieberman and Bond's (1976) survey, women felt they would recommend consciousness raising groups for a vast range of problems including unstable marriages, sexual conflicts, and depression. Participants were somewhat less likely to agree that women with deep psychological problems benefited, although women who sought therapy for nervous breakdowns, severe depression, and suicidal tendencies sought help through groups. We have no evidence of the numbers who changed or of the frequencies of types of change.

Equally important, we have no knowledge of possible unintended negative consequences. For example, did women who severed marriages as a result of experiences in consciousness raising groups later come to regret it? Did some who experimented with lesbianism experience enduring guilt feelings? Did some who isolated themselves from men, or who insisted on a relationship compatible with movement ideals, find they were unable to engage in satisfying heterosexual relationships? Did some who sought solutions to dilemmas in an attractive ideology come to be disillusioned, cynical, or bitter as a result of the failure of another god?

Systematic research and follow up were both extremely unlikely in the spontaneous formation of groups with no commitment to a disciplined concern for evaluation of their consequences. We therefore do not have the answers to these questions. All we can do is guess, raise more questions, and rely on such evidence as we can gather from the reports of participants and other observers. Important changes did take place, however, and such groups had profound consequences for individuals and for the culture at large; thus as social scientists we cannot ignore them. We have much to learn from spontaneously formed groups. Consciousness raising groups and related organizations provided a large number of natural experiments in person-to-person helping and efforts at change. As social scientists, we need to develop methods of study that allow us to understand those and similar efforts. As helping professionals, we need to understand such efforts as a means of enlarging our own repertoire of tools and skills and as a basis for developing more powerful and encompassing theory.

The Future

Whether or not women participated in consciousness raising groups, the movement resulted in distinct cultural change with many more women entering law and medical schools and moving into hitherto male-dominated positions in business, industry, and the professions (Levine, 1977). By 1980 women had increased their representation in every category of employment, including those nearly the exclusive province of men, such as engineering, architecture, and law (U.S. Bureau of Census, 1985.) Carden (1974) and Cassell (1977) point to a great many spin-offs and ripple effects. Nonfeminist groups such as the Girl Scouts, the YWCA, and the National Council of Jewish Women have adopted aspects of feminist ideology. The Equal Employment Opportunity Act of 1964 provided a legal base for challenges to employment, promotion, and selection practices in industry and in education (Levine, 1977; Wallace, 1976), and affirmative action programs in industry and in universities have emerged. Women are rethinking their futures in the American economy (Kreps, 1976) and their roles as wives and mothers (Bernard, 1975). All of this activity suggests that cultural change has provided widespread support for varied roles for women. Consciousness raising groups as such seem less necessary.

If Carden (1974) is correct that consciousness raising groups emerged partly in response to a transitional state of normlessness, then with widespread acceptance of components from an ideological movement, normlessness can eventually work itself out in the larger society. A survey (Women and Mental Health Project, 1976) suggests that women moved into more specialized activities such as rape counseling and abortion centers, self-health clinics, and the formation of play groups and day-care centers (Harlow, 1975). The new problem of the feminization of poverty (Harrington, 1984) may lead to a resurgence of women's movement activities, although organizing poorer people is notoriously difficult.

Situation/transition groups have been organized through women's centers or through community mental health centers and other professional service agencies; they have focused on such problems in living as: chronic medical problems; parenting as a new mother, as a single mother, as a stepparent, or as a parent of a child with a special disability; marital disruption; job stress; and maturational crises. These groups form and reform as necessary, serve specific functions of reducing loneliness, provide a supportive forum for expression and catharsis, and give specific and concrete information, advice, and support to assist in coping with the transitional event or situational crisis (Schwartz, 1975).

Groups and their differing ideologies appeal to people in differing circumstances. CR groups with a strong feminist ideology appealed to one class of women. Small-group approaches and a moderate feminist orientation had a strong appeal for suburban housewives. Carden (1974) notes that high school students have not been avid participants in consciousness raising, that black women have not been very much involved, and that advertisements for women's causes through women's magazines such as *McCall's* and *Redbook* were unsuccessful in eliciting responses. The best-selling work by Marabelle Morgan, *Total Woman,* had an ideology emphasizing the benefits to women of devoting themselves to satisfying their men. Some women in different circumstances see their life's problems in quite different dimensions. Women who see it as totally abnormal for others to express support for lesbianism and the use of force against men can hardly identify with those who assert that women are totally abnormal to engage fully in traditional submissive roles as wives and mothers. The error is in insisting that all women share the same circumstances and the same problems and that their problems will give way to the same set of solutions. If we learned anything from consciousness raising groups and from their differing ideological statements, it is that women's situations are quite different. Women needed to find compatible social groups within which an ideology appropriate to their circumstances and designed to help interpret everyday events could be transmitted.

The experience with consciousness raising groups tells us that the emotional stresses associated with normlessness and with a variety of problems of living can be alleviated in groups that are organized spontaneously, do not rely on professional leadership, and cost very little monetarily. Under some circumstances, moreover, ideas that are articulated in small groups can guide and power far-reaching social and political changes. The future of services for people with ordinary problems in living may lie in the direction of self-help groups. Professionals may well be advised to learn how to support the development of such groups as a broader community service.

We have used the ecological perspective to characterize self-help and consciousness raising groups as a new kind of setting. The creation of new settings as an approach to change has a long history in this country and raises a number of important issues. In the next chapter we examine those issues at the level of individual settings and organizations. The subsequent chapter considers an example of change on a national level.

Notes

1. This concept of ascending levels is an interesting one found in many groups organized around an ideology. The Dead Sea Scrolls date to 200 B.C. One of them, the Community Rule (evidently a constitution for the people of Qumran), contains the following passage:

> But when a man enters to Covenant to walk according to all these precepts that he may join the holy congregation, they shall examine his spirit in community with respect to his understanding and practice of the Law, under the authority of the sons of Aaron who have freely pledged themselves in the community to restore His Covenant and to heed all the precepts commanded by Him, and of the multitude of Israel who have freely pledged themselves in the Community to return to His Covenant. They shall inscribe them in order, one after another, according to their understanding and their deeds, that every one may obey his companion, the man of lesser rank obeying his superior. And they shall examine their spirit and deeds yearly, so that each man may be advanced in accordance with his understanding and perfection of way, or moved down in accordance with the offenses committed by him. (Vermes, 1968, p. 80)

The Oneida Community, a religiously based nineteenth-century American commune, had a concept of ascending fellowship in which members of lesser rank were urged to associate with members of higher rank to achieve the state of perfection central to the religious tenets of that community (Levine & Bunker, 1975). Cassell (1977) and others point out that one of the key concepts during one phase of the women's movement was an exaggerated egalitarianism, and "elitists" were sometimes treated cruelly. Consciousness raising groups, however, unquestionably had informal leaders who were differentiated by virtue of personal characteristics and a sophisticated ability to articulate or to employ movement language and concepts. Cassell is astute in pointing out contradictions between ideology and behavior in some women's groups.

2. While women's liberation literature depicts Freudian psychotherapy as detrimental, women still use therapists. Feminists recommend the use of psychotherapists whose viewpoints

are congruent with movement ideology. In some cities women have established clinics operating on a fee-for-service basis, albeit with reduced fees. Referral services have been established to send women to approved therapists whose viewpoints are congruent with the ideology of the organizers of the referral service (Women and Mental Health Project, 1976). If the great majority of these therapists are women, one could see the feminist referral service as an attempt to capture a segment of the psychotherapy market for a particular group sharing certain social and economic interests.

References

American Psychological Association. (1977, June). Guidelines for nonsexist language in APA journals (Publication manual change sheet 2). *American Psychologist, 32,* 487–494.

Antze, P. (1976). The role of ideologies in peer psychotherapy organizations: Some theoretical considerations and three case studies. *Journal of Applied Behavioral Science, 12,* 323–346.

Bernard, J. (1977). *Women, wives and mothers: Values and options.* Chicago: Aldine.

Carden, M. L. (1974). *The new feminist movement.* New York: Russell Sage Foundation.

Cassell, J. (1977). *A group called women: Sisterhood and symbolism in the feminist movement.* New York: David McKay.

Freeman, J. (1975). *The politics of women's liberation.* New York: David McKay.

Gillick, J. (1977). *Al-Anon: A self help group for co-alcoholics.* Unpublished doctoral dissertation, SUNY at Buffalo.

Hanisch, C. (1978). The personal is political. In Redstockings (ed.), *Feminist revolution.* New York: Random House.

Harlow, N. (1975). *Sharing the children. Village child rearing within the city.* New York: Harper & Row.

Harrington, M. (1984). *The new American poverty.* New York: Holt, Rinehart & Winston.

Heiman, J., LoPiccolo, L., & LoPiccolo, J. (1976). *Becoming orgasmic: A sexual growth program for women.* Englewood Cliffs, NJ: Prentice-Hall.

Hole, J., & Levine, E. (1971). *Rebirth of feminism.* New York: Quadrangle Books.

Jagger, A. M. (1983). *Feminist politics and human nature.* Towota, NJ: Rowman & Allanheld.

Koedt, A. (1970). The myth of the vaginal orgasm. In S. Firestone & A. Koedt (Eds.), *Notes from the second year: Women's liberation.* New York: Radical Feminism.

Kreps, J. M. (Ed.). (1976). *Women and the American economy. A look to the 1980's.* Englewood Cliffs, NJ: Prentice-Hall.

Levine, A. (1977). Women at work in America: History, status and prospects. In H. R. Kaplan (Ed.), *American minorities and economic opportunity.* Itasca, IL: F. E. Peacock.

Levine, M., & Bunker, B. B. (Eds.). (1975). *Mutual criticism.* Syracuse, NY: Syracuse University Press.

Levy, L. H. (1976). Self-help groups: Types and psychological processes. *Journal of Applied Behavioral Science, 12,* 310–322.

Lieberman, M. A., & Bond, C. R. (1976). The problem of being a woman: A survey of 1700 women in consciousness raising groups. *Journal of Applied Behavioral Science, 12,* 363–380.

Pattison, E., Courlas, P., Patti, R., Mann, E., & Mullen, D. (1965). Diagnostic therapeutic intake group for wives of alcoholics. *Quarterly Journal Studies on Alcohol, 26,* 606–616.

Reissman, F. (1965). The "helper" therapy principle. *Social Work, 10,* 27–32.

Reissman, F. (1976). How does self-help work? *Social Policy, 7,* 41–45.

Sarachild, K. (1970). A program for feminist "consciousness raising." In S. Firestone & A. Koedt (Eds.), *Notes from the second year: Women's liberation.* New York: Radical Feminism.

Sarason, S. B. (1972). *The creation of settings and the future societies.* San Francisco: Jossey-Bass.

Schwartz, M. D. (1975). Situation/transition groups: A conceptualization and review. *American Journal of Orthopsychiatry, 45,* 744–755.

U.S. Bureau of the Census. (1984). Occupations of the work-experienced civilian labor force, by sex: 1970 and 1980. *Statistical abstract of the United States: 1985* (105th ed.). Washington, DC: U.S. Government Printing Office.

Vermes, G. (1968). *The Dead Sea scrolls in English.* Harmondsworth, Middlesex, England: Penguin Books.

Wallace, P. A. (1976). Impact of equal opportunity laws. In J. M. Kreps (Ed.), *Women and the American economy: A look to the 1980's.* Englewood Cliffs, NJ: Prentice-Hall.

Women and Mental Health Project. (1976). Women-to-women services. *Social Policy, 7,* 21–27.

10

The Problem of Change

Self-help and consciousness raising groups proliferated during the 1960s as informal, situation-specific resources for coping with change. At the same time mental health professionals, saddled with traditional viewpoints of pathology and treatment, were learning how difficult it was to develop their own formal approaches to understanding and dealing with change. The prevailing theories of individual diagnosis and psychotherapy did not deal explicitly with social contexts and were thus of little use in bringing about the changes in service delivery and in other spheres that were necessary to relieve injustice and ameliorate social problems. Those who attempted to introduce new programs or to foster change in existing service agencies often encountered problems, and they soon saw that the compulsive personality of bureaucrats and the anxiety in those faced with impending change were insufficient to account for these problems or inspire solutions to them.

Having an insufficient grasp of system problems, many of us labeled them politics, threw up our hands, and retreated to the safety of our offices. We failed to appreciate the complexities of social organizations, and with inadequate theoretical concepts we were unable to understand the nature of the problems we encountered, estimate the resources required to solve them, or comprehend the time scale of change. In retrospect, however, we may have simply wanted too much too quickly. Many productive efforts during these years did in fact contribute to a theoretical and practical understanding of change. This chapter focuses on those efforts.

Jacobs (1980) reviewed the impact of institutional reform litigation (i.e., suits brought against prisons, hospitals, schools, etc., to change them; see the later discussion of court-ordered change) in bringing about change in prisons. Jacobs thought it an error to view institutional reforms only as the result of a series of discrete litigations, unrelated to each other and to cognate events. In his view institutional reform litigation operated as a social movement over a 20-year period. Seen in this light, the participants in this movement were diverse, and their interactions were scattered diffusely through time. To relate events in simple cause-and-effect fashion is extraordinarily difficult.[1]

Jacobs's views were based on a retrospective examination of efforts to change prisons. Few public-interest lawyers had a clear idea of the process of change at the time they initiated these lawsuits. Similarly, psychologists professing a community orientation also had little by way of articulated theory to guide their efforts at change, although social psychologists such as Bennis (1966) had early called attention to the problems. Psychologists had little idea of what to expect, what would be necessary to bring about and to maintain change, or how long anything would take.

Efforts to develop new programs or interventions based on different concepts and models soon brought psychologists face-to-face with the problem of introducing planned change. To the degree that alternative human-service and educational settings continue to be created today, when social reform is at a low ebb, the knowledge that emerged in the past 20 years is highly pertinent. It is also pertinent in directing our attention to the development of theories that go beyond the individual as the unit of analysis.

One of the most successful and enduring programs that emerged in the 1960s was Rochester's Primary Mental Health Project (PMHP), led by Emory Cowen (Cowen, et al., 1975). PMHP's creators noted, "Although PMHP evolved in part from a felt need to explore such new approaches [in mental health], the project's rationale was not yet clearly developed when it started" (p. 55). In summarizing the project's early history, and with the benefit of a decade's experience, they were able to say:

> The preceding section is essentially an insider's clinical account of some of the vexing moment-to-moment problems and rooting difficulties associated with implementing a new program in new settings. How true it is, to quote Robbie Burns, that "The best laid schemes o' mice and men gang aft a-gley." Establishing a program is not just a matter of developing a good idea or a sound plan. (p. 97)

The project's subsequent successful history is a tribute to the vision and persistence of its leaders and to the effectiveness of their work. A great deal was learned about what it takes to maintain a project, as the following passage (Cowen et al., 1975) indicates:

> Programs that lack a clear identity and those without a "following" that will stand up and be counted at critical moments are especially vulnerable. Fund-allocation decisions by local bodies that disburse public moneys are typically determined, not by a project's abstract theoretical, or scientific merits, but rather by the effectiveness and clout of its lobbying constituency. Distasteful as this fact is to the idealist or the scientist-scholar, it is part of the fabric of reality. (p. 110)

Cowen and his associates were anything but naive when they began the project, and their experiences were not idiosyncratic (see Graziano, 1969, 1974). Their success in maintaining and nurturing PMHP over three decades demonstrates that even if staff members did not understand the problems clearly in the beginning, they quickly learned what they were. That Cowen and his associates saw fit to record their experiences in some detail indicates that they felt they had learned something worthwhile and that their hard-won knowledge would be helpful to others in similar circumstances. For many years they have disseminated their methods to other schools through regular workshops for school and mental health personnel.

If (following the ecological principle of interdependence) everything is connected to everything else, any attempt at planned change is influenced by the existing social organization and context. On the other hand, any form of social organization that is expected to endure has structures and means to ensure continuity despite environmental vicissitudes. The corporation, for example, has a life that exceeds the life of any human being involved with it. It continues to own property even after individual stockholders die. Its contracts bind it no matter who is the chief executive. It cannot be made to disappear easily. The same structures and means that provide for the continuity of a social organization will also create resistance to change when the demand for change arises. In principle, the issues are no different when we discuss change in a single agency or change in the "community" of agencies, although the contexts are different.

The ecological analogy suggests that similar problems of change arise when a new program or organization is introduced into a community and when an attempt is made to change an existing organization. Change stimulates resistance, although the fact that resistance emerges does not mean that change will be stopped. Anything new that survives will likely be changed in some degree by the context, and the context in turn will likely have to make some accommodations. Although these general principles seem self-evident now, they were not then. As we noted earlier, professionals did not realize what kinds of concepts would be necessary to deal adequately with these problems.

Experiences in the 1960s and 1970s thus helped us begin to conceptualize the problem of change. Although, as Cowen et al. (1975) note, the problem of change and the problem of creation of new projects are not in principle different, for analytic purposes we will discuss them separately in the sections that follow.

The Creation of New Settings

Seymour Sarason has been a leader in calling our attention to these problems and in developing conceptual schemas to help us grapple with the issues. In a major creative contribution to the literature on social organization, Sarason (1972) identified what he saw as the core issues in the creation of settings. Claiming that more new settings had been created in the decade of the 1960s than in the entire previous history of the human race[2], he called our attention to the fact that little thought was devoted to the issue of how settings were created.

Creation of settings was a problem, he noted, because too often participants came to believe that the vision motivating the new setting had failed. New settings often were little different from those they were meant to replace. In effect, his work is dedicated to understanding and avoiding the issues implicit in the saying, "The more things change, the more they remain the same."

Sarason (1972) defines a setting as "any instance in which two or more people come together in new relationships over a sustained period of time in order to achieve certain goals" (p. 1). He intends his concepts to be applicable to settings as different as marriage (probably the most frequent example of setting creation) and revolution, or the creation of a new society. His central interest, however, is in the creation of new human-service settings.

A new setting arises when two or more people agree on some need for it and want one that will be different from familiar settings. The agreement is based on a set of abstractions that may reflect either experiences or a vision of what might be. Sarason notes that agreement on abstract values and strong motivation to succeed are insufficient to guarantee agreement on the specific actions that will embody the abstract values. Differences in viewpoint and in opinion cannot be avoided. He describes a common fantasy that a point will be reached in the development of a setting in which all major goals are accomplished and all conflicts resolved. The fantasy interferes with coming to terms with the reality that problems and conflicts will always arise. Agreement on abstract values, strong motivation to succeed, and the fantasy of a problem-free future lead to neglect of critical issues. Drawing on the experience of the U.S. Constitutional Convention of 1787, he argues that setting creation requires an explicit constitution or some set of rules by which individuals agree to be governed, and further that it is necessary to develop means to resolve problems that will inevitably arise. If the safest expectation is that problems will inevitably arise, the organization of settings should include problem-resolving devices.

The universe of alternatives, the recognition that for any problem there is always a range of potential solutions, is an important concept. That concept implies an openness on the part of setting creators and a social climate conducive to the generation of potential solutions, even those that challenge assumptions that are so much a part of us that we rarely question them. The aim is not to question for its own sake, but to allow for the generation of solutions appropriate to the new setting and its context.

Settings are created in contexts that include a history. First is what Sarason calls the "before the beginning" (1972, chap. 2). Settings are not created in vacuums, and there is a limited pool of resources. Therefore, new settings are always in competition with existing settings for shares in a limited pool of resources. Frequently there is an ideological competition as well. The very creation of the new contains an implicit criticism of the old. The new setting is often justified on the explicit assumption that existing settings are not performing well and that the new will perform better. The competition for resources and the implicit if not explicit ideological critique guarantee, if not active conflict with existing settings, then a disinclination on the part of existing agencies to be helpful or supportive of the new (see Graziano, 1969, 1974).

Sarason believes that those involved in setting creation must always "confront history." The new setting will always develop in a context of structured relationships among settings, meaning those relationships include histories and visions of the future that must be understood and taken into account. Because of this history of structured relationships, setting creators have to consider how the context contains vectors that may well move the new setting away from the values or new concepts the setting creators intended to implement.

Sarason focuses carefully on the leader in the beginning context, but not on the leader's personality. He believes the creation-of-settings game is so structured that leaders may deal with the issues differently, but all will confront the same dilemmas. For example, the pressure to meet a timetable to open the new setting while establishing and negotiating relationships with other leaders and subordinates may result in compromises that eventually may lead to unanticipated, if not undesired, changes in the new setting.

Sarason analogizes joining a new setting to entering a relationship based on romantic love. The leader will put the best face on the new position and the new venture in attempting to attract the people the leader believes are the most desirable. The new person, often leaving a situation in which there were disappointments, is prepared to see only the beauty in the new position and to overlook the warts. As Sarason (1972) says, "Time and again I have observed the leader and his core group enter into what is to be an enduring relationship grounded in (if not suffused with) enthusiasm, good will and a problem-free view of their future relationships" (p. 76).

Sarason believes that predictable issues will inevitably arise and will inevitably lead to differences. For example, in an academic setting publications are expected to emerge. All of the differences that can emerge will: authorship order, share of royalties, ownership of the data, responsibility for writing and interpreting data. Goodwill cannot supplant explicit understandings when active conflict occurs (Fairweather & Tornatzky, 1977). Predictable problems will occur between the leader and the members of the core group, and among members of the core group as their relationships to the total enterprise differentiate and as their relationships to the leader change. Such problems are rarely anticipated or discussed, partly because of the tendency for the relationship to begin in an atmosphere of romantic love, and partly because we do not have theories or conceptions that require us to confront problems before they arise. The creation of settings could be discussed in contractual terms, but in the 1960s that was not a prominent psychological concept or analogy.

As an example of a question that goes to core assumptions, Sarason (1972) asks, "For whom does a setting exist?" He is not satisfied with the obvious answer—that it exists to serve its clients. Sarason argues that a service setting should be concerned not only with the welfare of its clients, but also with "the professional and personal growth and change of its members, and the ways in which their mutuality can enhance this growth and change" (p. 86). The issue is important not only for the relationship between the leader and core group members, but also between core group members and those whom they recruit for their departments or divisions. If the problems are not solved for the larger group, the development of differentiated groups will only multiply the difficulties. In part Sarason argues that clients are better served when the setting makes provision for the growth and development of its members. In part he argues that the major purposes of a setting are better maintained when its values, including explicit concern for the development and growth of its members, are maintained. The problem of burnout as well as other consequences may also be averted: "rigidity in function, insularity from changes in the larger society, increased competitiveness for resources within and among settings, decreasing satisfaction in work with a concomitant increase in the need for professional status and money, and the steady loss of the sense of community within the setting" (1972, pp. 124–125). For Sarason (1974) maintaining the sense of community has a high priority.

At some point leaders and others become aware that resources are not unlimited. For the leader, the question arises of whether and how to convey the limitation on resources to the core group and to others in the setting. For core-group members, the question becomes one of competing for resources to promote the growth of each separate component of the setting. The competition for resources brings out differences in values as each subgroup attempts to justify its call on resources and its version of how things should be done. The task of allocating resources including personnel is among the most critical in creating a setting. The choices reflect values that are illuminated in the choices and their consequences. Bypassing consideration of the value questions helps to defeat the purposes of a setting.

Sarason (1972) summarizes the dilemmas of the leadership position:

> Whereas at the beginning he could dream, savor possibilities, indulge the joys of new-found status and power, and see the future as cloudless, he now knows that he has become (or must become) a "realist," that he has become *dependent* on those whom he has attracted, that the surrounding world tends to be indifferent or demanding, or hostile to his setting, that the problems of today and tomorrow

crowd out the future, that there are no isolated problems but rather that everything is potentially related to everything else, and that there is in him a tension between what is and what may be and between his needs and ideas and those of others. (pp. 214–215)

To do justice to the complexity and subtlety of Sarason's ideas in capsule summaries is not easy. He would be the first to recognize that at best he has pointed out some of the common and recurring dilemmas and dynamics that emerge from the situation. His work is a description of issues that will likely be faced by anyone involved in the creation of settings, a task he views as having more kinship with the work of an artist than with that of an engineer. It can therefore be sketched but not blueprinted. These concepts are useful not because they lead directly to solutions, but because the dilemmas are recognizable and replicable because of the common structure of the problem of creating a new setting. We will endeavor to illustrate Sarason's concepts by discussing Goldenberg's book, *Build Me a Mountain* (1971), a description of the creation of a setting, the Residential Youth Center, that was based on concepts discussed by Sarason.

The Residential Youth Center (RYC)

Ira Goldenberg was a member of the Yale Psychoeducational Clinic (Sarason, Levine, Goldenberg, Cherlin, & Bennett, 1966), a Connecticut organization whose creation under Sarason's leadership provided some of the first-hand experiences for Sarason's conceptualization of the problem of the creation of settings. As a staff member of the clinic, Goldenberg had been working as a consultant to the leaders of work crews that were important program components in New Haven's pioneer antipoverty agency, Community Progress, Inc. (CPI). The youths, male and female from ages 16 to 21, unemployable and out of school, lived at home but reported daily to work for a stipend in groups of five to seven, each under the leadership of a leader (called a foreperson). For a part of each day, they went to classes organized by CPI but staffed by teachers employed by the school system. The forepersons were CPI employees. They were indigenous paraprofessionals, people who had come from the same general backgrounds as the youths. None had specialized preparation for the human-service jobs they held. The forepersons were encouraged to develop close working and personal relationships with their charges. (A description of the work crews and their leaders may be found in Sarason, Levine, Goldenberg, Cherlin, and Bennett (1966).) Goldenberg (1971) described the purposes of the work crew program: "Within this framework, then, the work crew program could be described more accurately as a therapeutic experience in living—an experience that utilized the world of work as a therapeutic lever to alter, influence, and redirect styles of life that poverty and despair had already warped and misshaped" (p. 21).

Work crews had been in existence for about 2 years when the federal government announced the Job Corps program. CPI was to participate by selecting youths who would be sent to the Job Corps camps around the country for vocational and educational training. A number of the Job Corps youths maintained contact with their work crew forepersons. After a few months, Goldenberg and a group of the forepersons decided to visit their former charges at a Job Corps camp. Disappointed in what they observed, they returned to New Haven with the thought that if they had had the opportunity to set up a Job Corps program, they would have done it better. Each member of that original core group had also had some dissatisfaction with the work crew program as it operated. The idea that it could be done better and the common bonds the forepersons and Goldenberg had developed represented that combination of strong motivation, dissatisfaction with the past, and a vision of a better future that Sarason described. As Goldenberg (1971) said, "The decision to create a new setting is, in and of itself, a decision born out of the combined feelings of hope and frustration" (p. 43).

The core of credibility that made it possible to proceed was in the program's relationship to CPI, the successful antipoverty program that had sponsored the work crew program. Any funding to be received would be administered by CPI. Goldenberg's proposal for an urban Job Corps received a hostile reception from Job Corps officials who saw it as an ideological competitor and a criticism of their program, for the proposal's justification was based on alleged deficiencies of the existing program. His funding finally came from a rival government agency. He speculated that the rival agency, anticipating potential problems in the Job Corps program, was seeking to establish a position in the field that would enable that agency to mount a new, heavily funded initiative should the Job Corps fail.

Other aspects of the "before the beginning" had to be confronted as well. After it was funded, the RYC core group engaged in a 2-month planning process. One aim of planning was to find a suitable building to house the youths who would participate in the new program. CPI officials, then in the process of expanding, were thinking of leasing a large office building. In order to be able to cover the leasing costs, they wanted the RYC to take several floors of the office building and remodel them. The RYC planners had envisioned a more homelike setting in a real neighborhood. Fortunately the demand was dropped, but it indicates how the prehistory can have its effects on a developing program.

Additional problems emerged in the prehistory. The funding agency wanted Goldenberg to open quickly before the planning, training, and preparatory period was completed. Although he was able to resist, the pressure nonetheless resulted in some hastening of the planning process. Goldenberg also described problems that emerged in relating to existing agencies. For example, the local community mental health center was willing to accept referrals from the RYC, but would not modify its approach in any fashion to take into account the cultural characteristics of the clients who were to be served. Although the community mental health center was located at the edge of New Haven's black ghetto, in Goldenberg's view, the psychological distance between the center and the clients he knew was too great. He also sought to develop an understanding with the local police. The police were willing to talk with him, but because they knew that many of the youths had run-ins with the law, a police official proposed placing an undercover agent on the staff or among the residents. Goldenberg declined the offer.

Sarason's several concepts making up the "before the beginning" phase are illustrated in these experiences. The new center opened in a context that was exerting a force to shape it in directions not envisioned or desired by the program's planners.

The book describing the creation of the RYC is important because it was one of the first to address the question of how a setting should be organized in order to allow those who participate to do the work of the setting. To enhance the sense of community (see Sarason, 1974), Goldenberg proposed an organizational structure that he described as horizontal instead of pyramidal. The horizontal structure had several features. Observing that there was an inverse relationship between the time personnel working in institutions such as hospitals, prisons, or schools for the retarded spent with clients and their decision-making authority, Goldenberg argued that indifferent treatment and a loss of valuable information resulted. He also noted that most in decision-making positions had paper credentials for the job, but did not necessarily have interpersonal competence. He had made a decision to select employees from among the paraprofessional staff. He proposed giving the paraprofessionals decision-making authority in the hope of enhancing their feelings of responsibility for the care of clients.

The rule the group eventually evolved gave the worker with primary responsibility for a client ultimate decision-making authority about that client, but with the limitation that if the decision affected other aspects of RYC life, the worker was obligated to consult with the rest of the staff before finally making the decision. Thus instead of referring the decision to someone higher in the pyramid of authority, as usually happens, decision-making authority was placed at the line level with the line group.

In an effort to overcome the fragmentation that is so common in many organizations organized with separate job descriptions, staff at the RYC had overlapping responsibilities. For example, many administrative duties were rotated so that all obtained some experience and some understanding of administrative problems. All staff took turns at night and weekend duty, no matter what their job description. All workers had primary job responsibilities, but everyone including the secretary and the cook had therapeutic responsibilities as well.

Each worker was encouraged to develop a program of interest to that worker. Thus Jack, who had originally been a neighborhood worker and later became an assistant director and then director of a spinoff RYC, in addition to his work with youth (best but insufficiently described as case management), was encouraged to develop an evening program in karate. Jack was a black belt. He believed that training in martial arts, especially when accompanied by training in its philosophy of self-discipline, would be therapeutic. It also gave him another role at the center, one that enabled him to use a skill that he valued highly. A work crew foreman set up a carpentry class. Another who was interested in cooking took a role in the kitchen. Thus the structure that diffused responsibility also provided for opportunity for staff members to develop themselves and to use skills that were important to them, no matter the job description.

The horizontal structure provided a great deal of satisfaction for staff members. Some inequalities in salary that were related to the funding source's and CPI's views of staffing were never resolved, however. Some of the problems were ameliorated when a successful project opened up opportunity for advancement for several of the paraprofessionals. In these ways, the RYC's organization provided for the development and growth of its members and for their ambitions for themselves.

Internal self-reflection and self-correction were handled by developing an open atmosphere from the outset. During the planning phase, the group initiated a practice that they called sensitivity training. It resembled mutual criticism (see Levine & Bunker, 1975) or Synanon's "hot seat." Goldenberg (1971) describes how the staff conspired to have him selected as the first subject for an individual sensitivity session, and what he and they learned from it (pp. 167ff). They also conducted regular group sensitivity sessions in which any staff member was free to bring up any problem the staff member believed was affecting the group, specific individuals, or the RYC. Special sensitivity sessions were scheduled at 6-month intervals to review where the RYC had been and where it was going. These special sessions were used to work through periodic "crises." The open atmosphere that was built in by the regular use of a problem-resolving device helped to reduce the problems of isolation of the leader that Sarason had noted. The book presents several verbatim accounts that will enable the reader to understand how this self-reflective problem-solving device enabled the workers to continue to be effective despite many stresses and strains.

The problems of leadership were confronted from the beginning. Goldenberg was then an assistant professor of psychology at Yale. He functioned as formal leader for the first 6 months and then as planned became a consultant. The group selected one of the paraprofessional staff to succeed him, and another of the paraprofessionals became assistant director. Those arrangements were worked out in advance, in anticipation of the problem of the succession of leadership. The horizontal and open structure provided the basis for training the successor. Moreover, confronting the problem of succession early on avoided a competition that might have been destructive. Later when an RYC for females was opened, it was planned by the original members, and one of the paraprofessionals became its director.

The same ethos of participation extended to the youths who resided at the center. A house council was given a great deal of responsibility for generating house rules and recreational, educational, and community service programs. The original furnishings of the rooms were built by the participants working in a woodworking class under the direction of one of the work crew foremen. Curtains and other decorations were sewn by members of the families of the youths who were provided with materials and instructions. The text does not describe the rooms, but some would surely not pass muster in many public institutions. For example, one room, including the ceiling, was completely painted in a high-gloss black. The shiny black surface was the background and the frame for a collage that covered most of the ceiling. The collage was made up of *Playboy* centerfolds. The room was striking in appearance: the many nudes provided color and form but did not at all seem prurient. The room reflected the individuality of its occupant.

The first occupants were recruited by going to CPI's neighborhood outreach centers and asking for the most difficult candidates. The youths had extensive records of involvement with the police, and some had histories of psychiatric hospitalization. The first residents were indeed difficult. The staff spent considerable time and effort to work through initial problems of developing an orderly program. The problems are described in vivid detail in the book (Goldenberg, 1971).

Eventually the program did settle down, and the evaluation study reveals considerable success in maintaining employment and educational placements, in attitude change, and in reduced police contact. Because subjects and controls were not assigned at random—the most difficult were selected for treatment—the findings of the study are subject to the technical criticism of regression to the mean. That is, because the worst were selected, there was no place for them to go but up. In addition to that flaw in research design, no long-term follow-up was ever reported.[3]

The RYC provided for the development of its staff members. It provided services to clients who were considered difficult. The group maintained surprisingly high morale over a period of years. While the individual actors in this drama were important because of their personal talents and commitments, their talents do not tell the whole story. Goldenberg's major achievement was in self-consciously thinking through the organizational conditions that would allow those talents to be utilized in creative and satisfying ways.

Change in Existing Organizations

The problem of change is clearly worthy of our attention. Organizations as well as individuals are often required to adapt to change, and efforts at planned change frequently fail (Sarason, 1982; Pressman & Wildavsky, 1979; Fairweather, Sanders, & Tornatzky, 1974). The problem of introducing change is more complex than it appears. Pressman and Wildavsky note that if a change requires positive action by 10 independent actors, the a priori probability that everything will go right and the change be implemented is $1/2^{10}$, or one chance in 1024. Obviously in a change effort not much can be left to chance, but how should we go about conceptualizing this problem?

Systems Theory

Open-systems theory can be applied to the analysis of change in human-service organizations (Schulberg & Baker, 1975). Human-service organizations may be viewed as open systems engaging in resource exchanges with their environments. A psychiatric center receives public funds, takes in people in need, helps to solve a community problem, and presumably returns productive citizens to the community. An open system retains some of the resources it receives for its maintenance and growth. Systems that are highly reactive to variations in the exchange process may direct a considerable portion of their resources toward enhancing the exchange. Publicly supported human-service organizations obtain resources only indirectly from exchanges, however, and therefore they have greater potential for converting resources to the organization's benefit—that is, to use resources to enhance working conditions and rewards for employees rather than to benefit patients. Ideally there should be no conflict, but in practice there is tension between a patient's needs and an organization's needs. Ready responsiveness to the environment may not take place because resources are not directly dependent on an exchange.

An open system is dependent on its environment for a number of factors: (1) the acquisition of "materials" (e.g., clients); (2) capital (annual program and capital budget allocations); (3) production factors (e.g., technology of treatment, trained employees); (4) labor (e.g., hiring of sufficient personnel with sufficient skills, education, or aptitude); (5) output disposal (release of clients back to a receptive community). The terminology, geared to industrial production, is inexact for a discussion of human-service organizations, but the general concepts are useful to direct our attention to pertinent classes of variables that might be involved in a change process.

Because an open system depends on other organizations in its task environment, it will respond to "turbulence." By turbulence, system theorists mean the relationship between the organization and one or more of the factors on which it is dependent is undergoing change. Fairweather et al. (1974) note that little change occurs in mental hospitals, for example, without some form of outside intervention. If the turbulence is created by some other agency with which it is linked and on whom the agency is highly dependent (e.g., a legislature that controls its funds), the organization must adapt to the turbulence in some fashion. The adaptation may be positive in that the organization changes to meet the new demand, or it may freeze and fail to adapt. Whether an organization adapts or freezes in relation to environmental turbulence is in turn a function of other variables such as available resources, knowledge, and leadership. The complex phenomena do not lend themselves to reduction to a handful of readily specified and measurable variables (Mayer, 1979).

Types of Change

Open-systems concepts may be expanded by looking at the change process from a social organization viewpoint as well. Watzlawick, Weakland, and Fisch (1974) classify change into two general classes, one in which the change affects only a portion of the system, while most of the system remains intact; it is called first-order change. The second class is change in the system itself—that is, in the relationships among the component parts. The first two levels we discuss may be considered first-order changes, while the third would classify as second-order change. The simplest form of first-order change may be that of adding something new without taking anything else away. Adding on is not without complications. For example, an additional faculty member requires office and laboratory space and adds to the demand for services and supplies. As we have learned from recent budgets, change can be effected by stopping a program entirely, by eliminating its budget. Many such changes have ramifications that are not directly observed, but from the point of view of a particular organization, the change is comparatively simple even if not painless. A change that requires reorganization or reallocation of resources or functions is more complicated; as we have noted, if any social organization is to continue, it must have structures that ensure its continuity despite environmental vicissitudes. Those structures that provide for organizational continuity also create resistance to change when a demand for change arises.

A change of materials or tools with little change in the structure of relationships may be accomplished readily, with little more than minimal in-service education (e.g., the substitution of a new medication for one used previously). In other instances the change, while apparently simple, requires far more extensive training and preparation of those who will use the new instruments and may require changes by those in other related roles. For example, the introduction of new math into elementary schools involved far more than simply providing new texts and workbooks for teachers. Sarason (1982) notes that in-service preparation was inadequate, and the relationship of the new math to the old math was not sufficiently developed for the teachers and for parents. What was a good idea from the viewpoint of scholars in mathematics proved difficult to implement without an awareness and appreciation of the culture of schools. The introduction of Miranda warnings into police procedure did not require complex change. Preparing the cards and reading them at the time of arrest or interrogation didn't require very much change. The warning did change the power relationship between the policeman and the arrestee and was difficult on that account (Medalie, Zeitz, & Alexander, 1973; Seeburger & Wettick, 1973).

Sometimes what appears to be a simple change encounters unexpected resistance.

A probation department introduced a computerized system of keeping track of alimony and child-support payments. The director found that the backlog of processing information was increased. Upon investigation, the director learned that workers, unfamiliar with computer printouts, continued to keep their records in the old way, in addition to preparing data for the computer. The workers had to present the information to the court, and rather than look stupid before the judge by fumbling with unfamiliar printouts, they continued to keep their handwritten records. Here the change involved the worker's sense of competence and satisfaction in carrying out the job.

A second type of change requires an increase or decrease in the repertoire of behavior within a role. The new behavior may impinge on the activities of others in different roles. If a psychiatric social worker took an active role in soliciting employers for jobs or landlords for living quarters, or advocated for clients with the welfare department, the social worker now in the role of case manager might be doing very different things than before. The new behavior requires changes in other aspects of the work (e.g., reimbursement for mileage charges; time out of the office; less ability to account for time in established reporting categories; loss of income to the agency) impinging on agency structure, complicating the change problem. As another example, teachers who adopted open-classroom methods encountered complaints and resistance from custodians who found their work was increased because the approach created a somewhat higher level of dirt than traditional teaching methods and required more movement of furniture to restore a room's orderly appearance.

Second-order change may affect an organization's goals or structure and often both. Such changes are by far the most complex to implement. Change from an authority-centered to a participatory decisional process, especially if power is really shared, exemplifies a structural change. Change from in-hospital custodial treatment to the provision of care to deinstitutionalized patients, care designed to keep them out of the hospital, represents a considerable change in goals.

Far-reaching changes are difficult but not impossible to achieve. Some forces in the field always push the change back toward the status quo ante, however. The juvenile court was first established in order to emphasize rehabilitation and to deemphasize legal formalism and the criminal prosecution of children and youth. Despite the fact that a few courts managed to maintain the rehabilitative ideal, many did not (Levine & Levine, 1970). Eventually the courts came under criticism and after *In re Gault* (1967), some legal formalism was reintroduced into the juvenile courts. Today we see the paradox of diversion programs—youth being diverted from the juvenile court to social welfare agencies, diverted from the institution initially established to serve youth!

Production and Satisfaction Goals

Change goals may be classified into two types, production and satisfaction. Production goals are those related to the manifest purpose of the setting. Achievement test scores, arrest and conviction rates, recidivist rates, patients released from a hospital, or doctoral students graduated from a Ph.D. program are all examples of items of production. In systems theory, items of production are exchanged for resources. In human service organizations, the relationship between items of production and resources is usually not very clear cut. Administrators have attempted to improve the relationship by tying budget to units of production through contractual arrangements that call for so many client contact hours, or for so many patients discharged from a hospital within a given period of time.[4]

Employees, clients, and other actors exchanging with a human service organization all have satisfaction goals. The satisfaction of members of one group is not necessarily positively correlated with the satisfaction of members of other groups. Production measures and satisfaction measures tend to be orthogonal. It is possible to envision every combination of production achievement and satisfaction. Workers may be very productive in the sense that they are turning out many items of production, but they can be very dissatisfied because they are working too hard, are underpaid, or other working conditions are inadequate. One agency, the mental hospital, may increase "production" by reducing its census, but if the patients still need assistance when discharged to the community, the problem is shifted elsewhere. Thus the achievement of a production goal, halving the population of our mental hospitals, was not greeted with universal acclaim.

Satisfaction goals are more important than we credit in our positivistically oriented society. In the 1960s, the New York City More Effective Schools program was low in production as measured by change in achievement test scores. It was high in satisfaction to employees, however, because of the advantages the program provided for them. The teachers' union fought hard for the program (Levine & Graziano, 1972).

Some policies persist even where there is evidence of inadequacy or evidence the policy creates positive harm. Despite 70 or more years of research showing that it does no good and may do positive harm to leave children back in school (Levine & Graziano, 1972), from time to time school administrations back a get-tough nonpromotion policy. Social promotion solutions are unsatisfying to teachers and others who believe that children will not work unless threatened with nonpromotion. Proposals for retaining children in grade rarely include any program for educating them differently to avoid the failure that occurred the first time. They contain no means for dealing with the blow to self-esteem and the stigma of being retained in grade. When deeply held beliefs are engaged, or when no viable alternatives are in view and the satisfactions of powerful actors are at stake, productivity can take on less importance.

The Social Context of Change

A program targeted for change always functions in a social context defined by the sets of positions and roles within the organization, and outside in agencies, institutions, and constituencies (e.g., parents of schoolchildren) making up the external environment. A change may require a change in relationships among members of groups within the human-service agency, and among and between members of external groups.

Members of role groups stand to gain or to lose in terms of their interests when a change is proposed or implemented. The groups that stand to lose in important interests will oppose change either actively or passively. Opposition may not be sufficient to defeat change, or the opposing groups may not have the power to defeat it or to retard the change significantly. The groups that stand to gain in important interests will support the change.

The set of interests can undoubtedly be categorized in other ways, and there are undoubtedly many subclassifications. For the sake of exposition, we have found it useful to reduce the sets of interests to seven:

I. Energy (money, work time, amount of work).
II. Power (including status or influence).
III. Culture (beliefs, norms, values).
IV. Competence (ability and satisfaction in carrying out work tasks).
V. Relationships (generally satisfactions in social interaction deriving from work relationships).
VI. Legal and administrative considerations.
VII. Information and communication (knowing what's going on).

We will illustrate each of these dimensions before looking at some case studies of how change was brought about in human-service organizations. Because change is usually centered on a single organization and the major actors are the employees, the examples will stress the perspective of employees. The fact that human service agencies have high numbers of professional employees does not change the picture. Professionals in organizations are workers, albeit with different statuses, salaries, and privileges than blue-collar employees.

I. *Energy.* Workers expend characteristic levels of energy on the job. The amount of work, the amount of time, and the amount of money and other benefits are interrelated variables. If a program change requires increased energy output, and there is neither a compensating increase in money or other benefits nor a compensating decrease in hours spent working, the employees will oppose change. The New York City More Effective Schools program was vigorously supported by the teachers' union in part because it provided additional free periods for teachers and teacher aides to assist with classroom work (Levine & Graziano, 1972). On the other hand, anyone who has worked in research in schools can attest that teachers resist filling out research forms that take up their time, and for which they generally receive no compensation. Research workers have taken to building in research funds to pay for teacher time for exactly that reason. Under special conditions, as in Goldenberg's RYC, charismatic leadership, a sense of participation in a mission of importance, or hopes for future rewards may provide intangible compensations that sustain support for change. Emotional highs alone, however, cannot substitute for other tangible rewards for very long.

One can postulate an optimal range of amount of work and argue that changes that require either a marked increase or a marked decrease in work will elicit resistance. A change that removed most functions from a position, even though the person continued to receive full pay, would likely prove distressing. Most people like to feel they are earning their money. Some may not work hard or may take extended coffee or restroom breaks, but the illusion of working is maintained. If one does not have enough work to do, one's feeling of being a useful and worthwhile member of society can be undermined.

II. *Power.* Power is the ability to issue a command with respect to the use of a resource, including the deployment of personnel, accompanied by the authority or strength to enforce the command. Power may be exercised in the control of resources (physical space, materials, supplies), personnel (hire, fire, promote, or determine duties), or territory (control of a variety of prerogatives such as admission to an institution). Power is generally correlated with status (e.g., position in a social organization) and with the expectation of respect or deference from those of lower status. In general, role incumbents relate to programs and to each other through the exercise of power. If an incumbent's power is increased by a change, that person will favor it—and if decreased, oppose it.

Power as a motive has been subject to considerable study. Powerlessness, and efforts to overcome feelings of helplessness and alienation through the sharing of power, and the problems of accommodating to power are well known. The community action aspect of the War on Poverty provides a case in point. The act establishing the War on Poverty and the community action program called for maximum feasible participation of those who were to be affected by its programs. In some cities these provisions of law and the availability of resources stimulated considerable activism. When independent antipoverty agencies took the power the legislature gave them and acted on it, however, they seriously threatened the political power of city halls. Legislation was introduced to reduce the independence of the antipoverty agencies from city government (see Marris & Rein, 1966; Moynihan, 1969). Power struggles and problems stemming from the fragmentation of local, state, federal, and private-sector agencies resulted in delays and difficulties in implementing the Community Mental Health Centers Act (Connery et al., 1968; Levine, 1981).

At the level of a single organization, Jacobs (1980) notes that prison guards felt they had lost power to inmates as a result of the inmates' ability to bring suit. Similarly, hospital personnel lose power to patients if courts recognize the patients' right to refuse treatment. Fairweather et al. (1974) noted that the lodge program encountered resistance to change because it required some basic role changes and to some extent changed the superordinate-subordinate relationship between professional helper and patient. Prison officials and hospital officials have often been resistant to change when the change has been court ordered. Knowledgeable individuals claim that the resistance comes from an unwillingness to be told what to do by outsiders.

On the other hand, increasing power for some actors may have salutory effects in the change process. Goldenberg's RYC program substantially increased the power of line workers, resulting in great support for the program by employees. In some hospital wards, a similar process occurs when the ward shifts from a hierarchical organization to a therapeutic community with shared power and greater role diffusion, in the sense that activities are shared by those in different roles (Colarelli & Siegel, 1966).

III. *Culture.* The term *culture* is a convenient shorthand for the set of beliefs, ideologies, values, and norms characteristic of each group. Note that all of these concepts imply behavior in social relationships. People have expectations of each other, and there are rewards for meeting those expectations and sanctions for failing to meet them. Belief systems or ideologies are important aspects of any culture. Mayer (1979) argues that ideologies are critical in institutional change.

A change may challenge ideologies. Jacobs (1980) states that court orders for change supporting prisoners' rights changed good-guy, bad-guy roles. Where guards had thought of themselves as performing a necessary and valuable service, the courts were saying, in the eyes of the guards, that they were oppressors preventing inmates from exercising legitimate constitutional rights. The *O'Connor v. Donaldson* (1975) decision implies that psychiatrists who retain patients who are psychiatrically "sick," but whose behavior does not meet standards of dangerousness legally required to justify the deprivation of liberty, are not engaging in good psychiatric practice, but are violating patient rights.

Strong commitments to forms of practice (norms) stem from training, cultural conditioning, direct experience, and the need to believe that what is done is right and good. From a distance, we can appreciate the reaction of physicians told by Semmelweiss that they carried germs on their hands, causing the deaths of mothers whose deliveries they had attended. Can we be less sympathetic with the schoolteacher's reaction of rage to the accusations of Kozol's *Death at an Early Age* (1967), or to mental health workers decrying the destructiveness of Rosenhan's (1973) demonstration that admitting personnel cannot detect pseudopatients? Psychotherapists, told by some critics that they do little good, charge high fees, accept for treatment easy, middle-class clients, and could be replaced by paraprofessionals who can do whatever it is they do with a few weeks of training, cannot be expected to react to such propositions by thanking the community psychologist for providing enlightenment. When a practice to which an individual has a deep commitment is challenged, one cannot expect that individual to say gratefully, "Thank you very much for telling me I have been destroying my clients all these years. I never thought about it that way before, and I am now ready to do everything you say."

Requirements for change that affect views about what is right and proper within one's profession or occupation necessarily will encounter resistance. Sometimes, there may be good and sufficient reason to maintain the incumbent's view of what that role and professional status require. Not all resistance is irrational by any means. The principle indicates that we have to understand what the demand for change is asking of others in their contexts and views of themselves and what is right and appropriate for them.

All groups relating to a program are likely to have some beliefs or theories that are as powerful for those who hold them as mental health theories are for mental health workers. The beliefs are learned during the period of professional or occupational socialization, may derive from some experience, or are taken over from figures in authority. "Children won't learn unless you make them." "Inmate self-government will lead to riots or the exploitation of prisoners by each other." "If high fences or walls around an institution for the retarded are taken down, the inmates will wander off." "Sex education leads to promiscuity and a reduction in the authority and influence of the parent." These sentences are all examples of beliefs held very deeply by some people.

The concepts always reflect the data incompletely, but they often have empirical referents, just as there are some empirical referents for concepts professional mental health workers hold. A change agent, especially one without a great deal of experience in a particular setting, can create resistance by advocating programs that have failed in the past or that discount beliefs about reality held by important actors in the social system. A corrections official who had lived through bloody prison riots in the 1930s believed some portion of the troubles then were related to efforts at inmate government. That official is not likely to be receptive to suggestions for inmate self-government proposed by a civil rights attorney or a mental health professional. As another example, school principals are often aware of the difficulty of involving more than a few parents in any program. Such an official will be wary of a social worker who suggests a program of parental participation as a means of solving school problems, no matter how sound the proposal from the point of view of mental health theory. We should also keep in mind Sarason's (1967) observation that receptivity to further innovation is inversely related to the number of previous attempts at innovation in that setting that have failed.

Groups responsible for the care of clients may have beliefs about the characteristics of the client population. Programs for change that are at variance with those views are greeted with less than good cheer. If prison officials believe inmates are untrustworthy and likely to manipulate or to exploit each other, they react poorly to programs that assume the spark of the divine within each inmate, a spark capable of flaming when properly fanned. When teachers believe that children will behave chaotically if not controlled or when managers believe workers will not work unless closely supervised, they will react poorly to proposals that children or workers be given greater responsibility. We have no systematic techniques for determining beliefs about clients prevalent in the various groups concerned with the proposed change. It would be valuable to develop such approaches.

A change agent cannot assume that priorities in the change agent's value system will match priorities in the value systems of other concerned groups. Mental health personnel sometimes assume the primacy of mental health values, failing to realize that others may value different behaviors and outcomes to a greater degree. "He may be happier in school, but he is still 2 years behind in his reading level." "You can't reward bad kids by giving them special treatment, because it is unfair to good kids." "You shouldn't use a reward system that rewards children for doing what they should be doing anyway. That's bribery." "Democratic decision making and participation are all very well, but the result is disrespect for authority." Those familiar statements all reflect value hierarchies. Methods of ascertaining and measuring hierarchies of values are not well developed, but change agents are sometimes insensitive to the issue.

IV. *Competence.* Probably the single most important piece of information about an individual in American society is his or her occupational title. Occupation is central to personal identity and to social existence. Over and beyond the financial and social rewards of an occupation, the mastery and exercise of occupational skills is critical for self-esteem and for individual well-being. The peak experience described by Maslow (1962) often arises during the exercise of occupational skills. One enjoys doing what one does well. A psychotherapist in tune with a client, engaging in an inspired intervention, feels good and enjoys recounting the experience to other professionals. The teacher who delivers a compelling lecture, eliciting a positive response from students, is gratified. The police officer takes pride in the ability to gain an obedient, respectful response to an authoritative, businesslike approach to citizens.

A change may require that an employee no longer exercise skills that provide personal gratification. All of the psychological reactions related to loss may be stimulated by a demand for change. Some teachers had difficulty in adapting to open methods of education because they no longer had the opportunity to perform in front of a large group. Others told us they missed the constant feedback of knowing exactly what the children were doing and learning each day. Psychotherapists trained in long-term therapies with articulate, verbally accessible young people may not feel they are doing anything useful when the patient requires simple support. Physicians who cannot exercise heroic healing sometimes refer to patients with chronic disorders that are uninteresting from the viewpoint of teaching as "crocks." The client who is unresponsive to the care that is offered does not provide the helper with the sense that the helper is exercising skills effectively and contributes to professional burnout (Cherniss, 1980; Farber, 1983).

A change in program requiring that individuals learn new skills or fulfill new functions may be more threatening to an established individual than to a novice. Inequalities in a social order are rationalized on the grounds that differential experience and training justify differences in status and related perquisites of office. When individuals of different statuses in the same organization are required to engage in new learning, there is no guarantee that the competence-based order that emerges will match the status order of the original organization. For this reason, shifts to a therapeutic community orientation where employees with varying statuses and salaries perform the same jobs have led to considerable embarrassment, because competency on the job does not necessarily match the status structure. Goldenberg's (1971) mixed paraprofessional and professional staff took to using the terms *amateur* and *pro* to describe those who were less and more competent, independent of the individual's professional training and formal credentials.

The learning of new skills may be difficult because the demand to learn may well engage deep self-doubts about one's abilities to master new skills and anxiety stemming from the return of repressed feelings of vulnerability as a learner undergoing evaluation by powerful others. The conditioning of years of educational experience may predispose us to expect that learning will be painful, that we will be vulnerable to evaluation, and that our self-esteem will be diminished. We may have insufficient opportunity to obtain training in the new skills, and thus avoid exercising them (Sarason, 1982).

We can assume that individuals enter patterns of occupational functioning consistent with aptitudes, personal style, and perhaps psychological defenses. A change requiring the individual to behave in unfamiliar and uncongenial ways will be threatening. To accept important decisional responsibility when one has been in a dependent role, to interact vigorously and relate closely when one has always kept others at a distance, or to face aggression when one has been timid are all extremely difficult. The demand for change can touch on many such issues and will therefore stimulate resistance to change.

In addition to determining whether persons can exercise new competencies, we must understand whether the social organization will support the exercise of new competencies. For example, teachers who had been trained in methods of life-space interviewing did not use them because of a lack of support from their principals and other teachers in the school not trained in the approach. Poythress (1978) demonstrated that training attorneys in methods of cross-examination of psychiatric expert witnesses was rather easy, but he observed that few used the methods in the courtroom during commitment hearings. They indicated they had reservations about whether their clients should be out of the hospital. Some indicated that the judge was clearly not interested in vigorous advocacy under the circumstances of routine hearings.

Sometimes the clients object to change, and sometimes other staff indirectly involved in the change effort object. In one of our projects, corrections officers who were being trained as paraprofessional counselors reported that some prisoners resented the activity as an attempt to provide them with second-class amateur services. Some fellow officers teased or expressed more active hostility because, in their view, the counseling approach violated their beliefs about the proper behavior for corrections officers and the proper treatment of inmates.

The problem of change in an ongoing service requires an assessment of the new competencies that will be required, an assessment as to whether the target populations of the change effort possess those competencies, consideration of the amount of time and training necessary to acquire new competencies (Fairweather et al., 1974), and consideration of changes in social organization that may be required if the new competencies are to be utilized at all. The problem of change may create a problem of person-environment fit, not only for the clients of a program, but also for the employees who will carry out the new program.

V. *Work relationships.* Work serves many purposes. Social relationships on the job can be a great source of satisfaction and a great source of distress. Most psychotherapists have encountered clients, and almost everyone has one or more friends, whose emotional state is highly dependent on the state of office politics and rivalries. For those who do not have the opportunity or the ambition to be promoted, social relationships on the job are critically important (Kanter, 1977). The police partner system made famous by television is a good example of an intimate working relationship that provides a variety of personal satisfactions as well.

In some settings such as prisons and state mental hospitals located in rural areas, many workers hold second jobs. In other settings, husbands and wives have arrangements for child care that depend on their work shifts. A change that affects changes in shifts can be critically important because from the workers' viewpoint, other aspects of their lives will be affected as well. When a state hospital shifted its program, the change to outpatient care required that workers be reassigned from service to service as needs changed. The leaders were sensitive to the issue of shift changes, and in their planning they took the employee's shift preference into account. Line workers reported a great deal of dissatisfaction with the rapid change of assignments because they felt unable to accommodate to new supervisors and new coworkers so rapidly. Moreover, they reported less willingness to commit themselves emotionally to their work sites, so they brought in fewer personal items to decorate offices and wards (Levine, 1980). A change that requires people to give up attachments to coworkers or to places may well be difficult.

Program changes may require concomitant change between supervisors and supervisors, supervisors and agencies, workers and supervisors, workers and workers, workers and clients, workers and agency, and many other permutations and combinations. A change that may be exciting for one person may be disruptive of many relationships for another. An analysis of relationships that may be changed should probably be undertaken as part of any change effort, taking into account that the change may be a positive factor as well when a conflictful relationship is ended by the change.

VI. *Legal and administrative considerations.* In addition to mutual expectations, stability in a social organization is at least in part dependent on a set of formal regulations mandating certain actions or prohibiting others and on contractual agreements. Efforts to change may encounter restrictions stemming from public laws authorizing the provision of public service. The laws are supplemented by regulations that may have the force of law and are not readily changed. A change agent cannot simply ignore a law or a regulation that impedes change. Bureaucratic structures are usually written into law or regulations. The structure may be an impediment and seem unnecessary, but it is ignored only at the peril of the change effort. Laws governing practice may restrict the personnel who can carry out certain activities. They may require education, training, or licensure.

Examples abound. Laws may restrict or mandate actions. For example, in a mental hospital, only nurses or those attendants who have completed a course of training may pass out medications. Problems arise in treatment relationships when clients who may be accused of sexual abuse are referred for treatment. The psychotherapist may be under a duty to maintain confidentiality, but other laws may undermine the confidential relationship. Laws may require therapists to report their knowledge of acts of abuse to authorities. Police or prosecutors may wish information to help them carry out their duties. Union contracts may restrict the degree of freedom to change. A prison superintendent who wanted to institute a weekend recreation program found that he had to change tours of duty of several of his officers. Restrictions in the union contract required prolonged negotiation before he could achieve his aim.

Regulations are not only restrictive. They may be protective and may be a means through which a change effort is carried out. One can argue that the systematically better conditions in veterans' mental hospitals than in state mental hospitals are a result of the careful regulation of standards of patient care and the enforcement of those standards. In the Wuori case (see later; Levine, 1986), the reforms achieved through litigation were made permanent when they were written into state statutes and regulations.

Legal or administrative rules and structures may represent barriers to change, or they may be used positively. Administrative and legal rules and structures may present challenges to risk-taking leaders willing to "bend but not break" the rules to facilitate program implementation (Levine, 1980; Sarason, 1982). Problems that arise because of formal rule-based constraints cannot be ignored. They should be reviewed as part of the diagnostic and planning effort in introducing change.

VIII. *Information and communication.* People use information to maintain, plan, or reorient their activities or to satisfy curiosity. Information is psychologically important for it undergirds one's ability to exchange information and opinions with others on matters of mutual interest, and it enables individuals to participate with a sense of belonging. Information in advance of actions prevents surprises and may prevent actors from taking action at cross-purposes with each other. Moreover, providing information and explanation in advance is a way of extending deference to people's positions and to them as individuals. Not knowing about events may result in a loss of prestige to those who feel they should know about events affecting their domains.

Some feel that advance knowledge facilitates change. Others say there are circumstances under which advance knowledge serves only to give the opposition time to organize. From the point of view of the change agent, under some circumstances a fait accompli may be preferable. The issue of whether to inform or not may be prominent when an agency wishes to open a group home in the community. One school of thought states that neighbors should be brought into the planning in order to win support, for example, for a group home. Goldenberg (1971) tells how he did make an effort to meet with some concerned citizens and made an attempt to include them.

In other cases, foreknowledge can lead to active opposition. In a case recently decided by the U.S. Supreme Court (*Cleburne Living Center, Inc. v. City of Cleburne, Texas,* 1985), a local zoning ordinance required that the group home get a permit before it could open. Neighbors, notified by law of a proposed home, protested at a zoning hearing, and the city council rejected the permit. The group home protested the prejudicial nature of the ordinance that required a home for the mentally retarded to have a permit in one type of zoning district, but not a nursing home for the elderly or even a group home for delinquent youngsters. The U.S. Supreme Court agreed with the group home operator that the decision denying the permit was prejudiced.

In some states, laws require there be open hearings before a group home opens in a neighborhood, but in other places there are no such restrictions. If a group home is opened despite opposition, or without notice to neighbors if permitted by law, generally the opposition changes to support or to indifference within a reasonably brief period of time. In only a relatively few instances is the opposition prolonged, but no one knows how many group homes were not opened because of community opposition (Lubin, Schwartz, Zigman, & Janicki, 1982).

In sum, a change in any program occurs in a context consisting of social groups relating to programs and to each other through seven groups of interests. Members of the groups evaluate the change by examining the way the proposed changes might affect their interests, and each role representative arrives at a position opposed to or in favor of the change based on a weighing or balancing of those sets of interests. Groups that on balance gain from the changes will support them. Groups that on balance lose from the changes will oppose. The opposition may or may not have the power to block change. Forces in the social context always pull back toward the status quo, however, and a change effort has to recognize that pull, for it may well result in some modification of the planned change. We have no precise measures of the strength of the existing interests or of their relative weights. The schema we have described is a loose set of guidelines for looking at a problem of change. Within each of the variables we have described, it is obviously possible to have a large number of separate dimensions of measurement. Given Pressman and Wildavsky's (1979) concept that change must touch a large number of "switches," and all "switches" have to be lined up properly, the wonder is not that change efforts fail, but that successful change takes place at all. We now turn to an examination of some successful efforts at change.

Changing a Psychiatric Hospital

The Harlem Valley Psychiatric Center, a New York State institution, changed with a period of 4 years from a predominantly custodial institution to a modern psychiatric center (Levine, 1980). Under the leadership of its director, Yoosuf Haveliwala, its census was reduced rapidly, and it developed an elaborate network of outpatient and aftercare services. The change was accomplished with a declining budget by means of reallocating resources, not adding resources, and its patients evidently were being served as well as the state of the art permitted. The changes were accomplished according to a plan and followed recognizable methods.

On July 1, 1974, the hospital had a census of 2,652 patients of which 1,826 (69%) were inpatients averaging 19.5 years of hospitalization. The rest were outpatients. The bulk of full-time staff were assigned to inpatient care. A few part-time clinics provided aftercare services in several of the communities in its catchment area. The hospital's orientation was custodial. The staff had little sense of mission, except to keep patients reasonably clean and involved in routine occupational and recreational programs.

There was nothing to attract well-trained, ambitious professional personnel. There was no research and only perfunctory in-service training. The community was not involved in its programs, and the hospital had no active public relations program.

By 1977, the Joint Commission on the Accreditation of Hospitals (JCAH) had renewed the hospital's accreditation with praise for its progress, for its programs, and for a medical records system that was offered as a model for others. The hospital census was reduced to 590 inpatients, and it carried 2,478 outpatients on its rolls. Thirty separate services were located in seven communities offering programs such as individual, group, and family therapy, day care, day hospitalization, crisis intervention, housing and sheltered living, sheltered workshops and work placement, advocacy services to link clients with other community agencies, and outreach including home visits. Hospital admissions had dropped from about 1,000 in 1974 to about 350 in 1977. A vigorous recruiting program attracted physicians and other mental health professionals, and an extensive in-service education program for professionals and paraprofessionals was in place. Eight psychology interns and 20 students from other disciplines were in training or were doing fieldwork at the hospital.

An extensive monitoring and evaluation system had been put into place and was a key instrument in the change effort. The monitoring devices produced quantitative data on the status of patients and on the quality of service rendered patients. In addition to extensive program evaluation and quality assurance programs, the hospital developed an epidemiological unit used in the assessment of the need for care of different populations within its catchment area. New program development was based in part on data obtained by this unit. The hospital developed a small research department conducting clinical studies. Staff attracted some funding from government agencies and from drug companies and participated in national and international professional meetings.

Community involvement increased strikingly. Community advisory boards were established in each community where a service was located. Regular staff time was devoted to recruiting and working with citizens. Staff participated actively in community mental health boards and in coordinating councils that existed in several of the communities in its catchment area. Volunteer hours at the hospital increased from 7,530 in 1974 to 36,170 in 1977.

Haveliwala took over as director in July of 1974, but there was a "before the beginning." The hospital census had already started to decline in part in response to New York's deinstitutionalization policy. In fact, the hospital's existence was threatened because it was not clear that a rural hospital was needed. The community depended heavily on the institution, however, and would have suffered economically had it closed. Among staff, the idea that one could save the hospital by developing innovative programs was a motivating force. Just prior to Haveliwala's tenure, some reorganization had been accomplished. On one service a group of young professionals had begun a project of discharging patients to communities where they had lived and then sending mobile teams to provide service to them in their home communities.

Haveliwala was among the first generation of state psychiatric center directors formally trained in concepts and practices of community mental health. He had had experience with deinstitutionalization programs as a psychiatric resident and had training in mental health administration in a program emphasizing modern management approaches. He had also been a staff member in the state system and deputy director of a large state facility before he received the appointment as director of Harlem Valley. He was experienced and familiar with the state system.

When he arrived, Haveliwala had clear plans. He was aware that he had some strong staff who would follow his lead. He quickly announced his intention to continue to place patients in the community, but each patient would be placed in accordance with the patient's needs, and excellent care would be provided to all. He pointed out that a deinstitutionalization program accompanied by the development of community-based services would preserve jobs. He thus provided the institution with an ideology that would serve to rationalize change.

He reduced the executive committee of the hospital from 50 to 14 and changed its composition to give much more representation to the unit chiefs than to central staff. He emphasized his intention to strengthen the role of line chiefs in decision making. He thus increased their power. Major decisions were to be made in open discussion in the executive committee, which would be advisory to him. He retained final authority, but once a decision was made, all were to abide by it cheerfully and enthusiastically.

The director had clear goals and objectives, and he was willing to act. His actions were rationally related to the goals he articulated. He gave the unit chiefs more decision-making authority because they were responsible for placing patients and developing community-based services. If they were to be accountable for results, they had to participate in decisions, and they had to be able to deploy personnel as their programs required.

Given civil service and union restrictions, he had little power to hire and fire at will. He therefore used peer pressure instead to move his programs. The executive committee not only became a deliberative and decision-making body; it also became a public forum in which each unit chief's success or failure in meeting objectives was reviewed. Each unit chief consulted with staff and developed a target number of patients for placement in appropriate settings. These targets were discussed in the executive committee and agreed to by the director. Once objectives were assigned, unit chiefs were responsible for meeting them. The program evaluation department produced reports showing each unit's success in meeting targets, and these reports were distributed to all executive committee members. Some unit chiefs met or exceeded their goals, while others failed, but failure was public, putting competitive pressure on the leaders and their units to meet standards. All of the other monitoring devices were used in exactly the same way. Unit chiefs had to explain publicly the reasons for success or failure. The director clearly approved intense performance, and tended to allocate resources and rewards based on performance. Although workloads were increased for many, and work pressures increased, these were matched by a variety of rewards in addition to enhanced prospects of promotion.

His intention was to create a competency-based organization and he used the organization chart to support managerial competency. He built the organizational chart around staff competence rather than formal civil service titles. He made use of his authority to create acting titles when the individual would not qualify for a civil service title, and sometimes assigned lower ranked persons to supervise higher ranked people because the individuals could do the job. They thus enjoyed the rewards of exercising new competencies. Haveliwala developed a core of competent managers who moved from assignment to assignment as program development required their talents. We do not have the space here to describe the non-financial reward system Haveliwala employed, but for those who worked with him, effort and success were repaid.

His program took into account the interests of physicians who lost some status to non-medical personnel. He gave them a line of communication with a physician-supervisor. Their autonomy as physicians was supported even though they were supervised in some aspects of their work by non-physicians. Lower level staff did not always feel their interests were served. Although jobs were saved and no one was fired, line staff felt the changes were made at their expense. Their interests were served, however, by unit chiefs using the same methods of increasing participation and job autonomy and providing opportunity for rapid advancement for those who could produce.

Haveliwala's program was built on the assumption that resources should precede the patient into the community. He provided the resources and more by a creative bending of the rules. He was always careful not to break the rules, thus taking into account the legal and administrative structure of the institution. He provided the resources for developing community programs by temporarily overcrowding a few wards to a slight degree. The overcrowding enabled him to close a few other wards, releasing the personnel that had staffed the now shut-down wards to work in the community to establish community programs. Later, he used his mastery of the state's budgetary procedure to provide the resources. The state's budget for a hospital is based on a ratio of personnel to the patient population, and that ratio is higher for inpatients than for outpatients. The patient population target for the coming fiscal year and thus the number of personnel allocated is set the previous year. Haveliwala encouraged his staff to release patients to the community rapidly, thus creating an excess of personnel that could be deployed to develop the outpatient services and other new projects. He explored the universe of alternatives and developed some new ways of reaching his goals.

Using a situational theory, he said that rehabilitation begins in the community. Arguing that preparatory effort does not predict patient tenure in the community, but that participation in aftercare programs in the community does, he emphasized the development of resources in the community and devoted minimal effort to preparing patients to leave the hospital.

Haveliwala and his staff worked carefully to embed their programs in the community. They encountered many instances of competition for resources with private and county-based programs that already populated the community, but they sought the proper niche for their programs by taking on services the other agencies were not providing. In other instances, the new programs adapted to the existing environment of agencies and needs. Where cooperation in developing programs was possible, the unit chiefs worked closely with existing agencies and sometimes developed jointly sponsored programs.

Harlem Valley's evaluation research, and our own efforts to review its programs, showed that 1 year after discharge, 72% were still in the community. That record is quite good compared to other programs. Visits to patient residences in the community established that patients were by and large content with their community placements, and we could find little evidence that current community placements were substandard, although that might not have been true for all of the earlier placements. Program evaluation also showed that the outpatient centers maintained contact with almost all who were discharged, at least for the first few months after discharge.

A case study cannot pin down causal factors. In this instance, a distinct effort was made to produce change; the approach employed recognizable tools and methods understandable within the systems and social organization viewpoints we described earlier. The consistent application of certain principles produced predictable results[5]—an important fact that tells us that planned change is possible, even in an institution as difficult to change as a bureaucratically organized state hospital. The Harlem Valley story provides a concrete example that static organizations need not remain that way.

Court-Ordered Change in the Care of the Retarded

In the 1970s, a new form of litigation emerged (Chayes, 1976). Working with a variety of legal and constitutional theories, public-interest lawyers along with citizens' organizations began to sue substandard institutions (mental hospitals, institutions for the retarded, prisons) in the federal courts. These suits are highly complex because they bring to the surface the political structure within which human services are embedded. Issues related to the separation of powers (legislative, executive, judicial) and to federalism (state, federal relationships) emerge. In many of the early suits, the violations of standards of care were so egregious that issues of liability (i.e., who was responsible) were rarely important. Once the defendant state agencies lost the suits, they were ordered to remedy the problems, and often the courts retained jurisdiction to oversee implementation of the remedies. In many instances, the cases continued for years. One of the first was *Wyatt v. Stickney* brought in 1972 and still under the court's supervision in 1987 (Levine, 1981). A large legal and social science literature has developed reviewing issues in court-ordered institutional change (see, for example, D. Levine, 1984; Rosenberg & Phillips, 1981–1982).

The change process under court supervision is highly complex. If the defendant state agencies do not or cannot comply with the court's order, the court's prestige and power are challenged. A confrontation between a federal judge and state officials such as governors or legislators contains the potential for creating a political crisis. In institutional reform, all parties are involved in a game where none desire confrontations testing the limits of each other's power. On the other hand, when a court has ordered change, the change process goes on with the threat in the background that the court might use its coercive power.

The 1975 case of *Wuori v. Zitnay cont'd sub nom Wuori v. Concannon* (Levine 1986)[6] was an unusually successful case because the court gave up active supervision within a relatively few years. The court found substantial if not full compliance with an expensive, highly involved, and highly detailed consent decree that called for the improvement of an institution for the retarded and the creation of community facilities and programming as well.

The case was brought as a class action on behalf of Martti Wouri, a resident of the institution, and all others similarly situated, by a public-interest lawyer, Neville Woodruff, who had been working in a state facility for the retarded, the Pineland Center in Maine. The complaint specified a large number of substandard conditions and many instances of poor treatment of residents. Shortly after the suit was initiated, George Zitnay, who had earlier worked with members of the Yale Psychoeducational Clinic (Sarason, Zitnay, & Grossman, 1971), was appointed superintendent. Zitnay, an experienced and gifted administrator, recognized the opportunities provided by the suit to gain resources. When he testified, he told the truth about the institution. At that point the state decided to settle out of court.

Shortly afterward, Zitnay was appointed Commissioner of Mental Health and Corrections in Maine. He and Kevin Concannon, then director of the Bureau of Mental Retardation, began working with the plaintiff's attorney to develop a remediation plan. They had made some progress in developing plans to improve the institution, but that had taken 2 years. Eventually, with the assistance of the Mental Health Law Project, a Washington-based public-interest law firm, they arrived at a comprehensive remediation plan. At the recommendation of Zitnay and Concannon, the state agreed to the plan. U.S. District Court Judge Edward T. Gignoux, a highly respected jurist, entered the plan as the judgment of the court in July 1978.

The plan called for far-reaching changes in the institution and the development of community-based facilities and programming. It was highly detailed, consisting of several hundred specifications covering just about every aspect of living and habilitation (treatment) in the institution and in community programs. It also called for the appointment of a special master (Nathan, 1979; D. Levine, 1984), a court-appointed official given power to monitor the implementation of the order and to recommend necessary steps for complying with the decree.

David Gregory, a law professor with experience in civil rights litigation but none in the care of the retarded, was appointed master for a period of 2 years. Initially, he thought the task of monitoring was straightforward, but he quickly became aware of the organizational and political complexities of introducing change into a public agency. Gregory visited the institution and the community services and interviewed staff and residents to educate himself about the problems. After the first 6 months, he took on a more active role because he discovered that implementation required the cooperation of other state agencies, not named as defendants in the suit. He also came to understand that in order to implement the decree, new resources would be required. Commissioner Zitnay and bureau director Concannon cooperated closely with Gregory by giving him information about deficiencies in the system. Gregory also worked with operators of group homes to encourage them to seek changes in regulations governing community residences and programming that were too limiting. Gregory concluded that only a vigorous and firm position would move the system to action. His semiannual reports to the court on compliance contained graphic descriptions of continued shortcomings and explicit criticism of state officials who were not cooperating. He also made some recommendations for reorganizing the executive branch to give Zitnay greater power over some state programs that were not in his jurisdiction. The threat that the court might use its coercive powers to force change was implicit in his reports. The reports frequently got publicity in Maine and were embarrassing to public officials. Zitnay and Concannon were able to use the reports with the governor and the state legislature to obtain greater budgetary commitment to reform the system of care. They could ask for more resources and point to the special master's reports as the cause for their increased budgetary requests or their requests for other legislative changes.

Zitnay, who had a good working relationship with the governor who appointed him, was unable to sustain the relationship with the next governor. Zitnay returned to Pineland as superintendent. Concannon succeeded him as commissioner. Zitnay now worked closely with Gregory to use the court order to help him improve Pineland. By exercising firm and creative leadership and using the court order to back him when needed, within a relatively short period, Zitnay managed to turn a backward institution into one that could be shown with pride to any visitor. Even the most disabled residents were clean and well dressed, the living quarters were personalized and attractive, and an enlarged and enthusiastic staff was deployed in creative ways to provide good ratios of personnel to residents and thus support active programming.

Gregory had been appointed for a 2-year period. At the end of his tenure, the court order had not yet been fully implemented, although the institution showed much progress under Zitnay. Gregory had recommended that the court retain jurisdiction. The state defendants and the plaintiff's attorneys, recognizing that progress had been made, negotiated a further agreement about how the remainder of the court order was to be implemented. The defendants agreed to continue the office of the special master, but in view of the friction between the defendants and Gregory, they insisted that he be replaced.

Gregory was replaced by Lincoln Clark, a retired professor of marketing, an experienced executive, a skilled mediator, and Judge Gignoux's close personal friend. Noting that Pineland Center, under Zitnay's direction, had come close to complying with the terms of the consent decree, he concentrated on the institution first. He conducted many negotiating sessions between Zitnay, Concannon, other state officials, and the plaintiff's attorney to arrive at still more specific agreements about how the remaining points in the decree were to be met. By July 1981 Zitnay issued a report indicating that his institution was in full compliance with the 315 items in the decree, or mechanisms were in place to ensure compliance. Clark then engaged an experienced consultant to review Zitnay's report and to confirm it by inspecting the institution and its records and interviewing staff and others. When the consultant agreed the institution was in substantial compliance, Clark recommended that the institution be discharged from the court's supervision.

Fulfilling the plan for community programming took 2 more years. Concannon was responsible for providing the leadership that eventually resulted in meeting the decree's requirements for community-based services. Clark met with all parties and worked out plans for correcting the remaining 15 deficiencies in meeting the decree's requirements in the community-based service system. Much went on in a spirit of cooperation, for state officials were basically committed to improving the system of care, but budgetary restraints, bureaucratic inertia, turf problems between agencies of government, and similar difficulties slowed progress. Clark used a mediator's skills, but he was well aware that effectiveness depended on the coercive power of the court in the background. In addition to identifying his actions with the court's wishes, Clark distributed his reports widely to the public, to citizen groups, to state officials, and to state legislators. Clark, who was also head of the state court's mediation service, was able to speak directly to key officials. His reports encouraged citizen groups to lobby directly for resources to implement community-based services.

Eventually the approach combining mediation and pressure moved the state system along. Clark engaged several independent consultants to review progress against the decree's standards and against the subsequent plans for implementation. By 1983, the consultants issued reports agreeing either that the standards had been met or that working mechanisms had been created to ensure that the remaining standards would be met. Before Woodruff, still the plaintiff's attorney, agreed that substantial compliance had been achieved, he insisted that permanent and independent monitoring devices be put into place. A consumer's advisory board was given full access to all programs and records related to the care of the retarded and was authorized to hear any issue concerning client care that was brought to its attention by anyone affected by the system of care. In addition, the state agreed to public hearings and annual independent reviews of compliance by other than employees of the state. The review was to be announced publicly, and specific notice was to be given to advocacy organizations. The auditor's report was to be made public. If it called for corrective action, the Commissioner of Mental Health and Mental Retardation was required to develop a plan for correction and to make that plan public.

At this writing, the monitoring process is in place. Public hearings to identify problems in the service system, the first step in the reviewing process, have taken place. The Consumer Advisory Board was reorganized to handle the work of monitoring continued compliance with the court order. It also recruited and appointed about 130 correspondents, persons to act as friends to those in community facilities who had no families or who had been abandoned by their families. The correspondents are organized into smaller groups reporting to a coordinator. The correspondents are expected to provide "eyes" on the system, by seeing to it that the person they befriended is receiving appropriate care.

Remarkable changes have been brought about in the system of care. The court's order supplied the blueprint and the leverage for change. Skillful and firm leadership, making use of the opportunity provided by the lawsuit and the court's decree, led to substantial improvement and modernization of the system of care. During the course of the litigation and during the implementation phase, Maine changed many of its laws governing the care of the retarded to bring its facilities into compliance with decree requirements, thus making the changes permanent as a matter of state law. So far, the monitoring mechanisms designed to see to it that improvement is maintained appear to be working. Even though the court stopped its active supervision of implementation of the decree, the program seems to be firmly in place.

The change process was long and complex. The leadership provided by Zitnay and Concannon was critical in the change process. The role of special master in the change process is of particular interest. Although they were quasi-judicial officers, the special masters could engage in activities such as indirect lobbying and public relations efforts to create both political pressure and public acceptance of the programs. Those activities would be highly unusual for a judge. The role was "invented" to provide a buffer for the court and avoid critical confrontations of power that threaten political crises.

The change process reveals how much the service system is embedded in our political and governmental system. A close examination of the process of change further reveals that the perspective of no single discipline could suffice to understand or to bring about change. Law, political science, sociology, economics, psychology, medicine, rehabilitation, education, organization and management, mediation and negotiation, evaluation research, and public relations are some of the areas of intellectual endeavor and practice related to the process of bringing about change. The change process calls our attention to the necessity for a perspective that exceeds narrow disciplinary boundaries if we are to understand how to develop effective human services.

Summary

If we are to have different helping services, designed to implement different program concepts, social organizations must be created or modified in order to deliver the new services. The principles that guide planned change, be it the creation of a new setting or the modification of an existing service organization, were forged out of difficult experiences in which change failed or failed to fulfill some of its important purposes. These principles provide general conceptual guidelines; they do not comprise a theory from which predictions can be derived. They help us to understand common problems encountered by those who are creating new settings or who are involved in changing other settings.

New settings must be based on more than a good idea, the agreement on abstract values, and strong motivation to succeed. Because there will never be a time that any setting will be problem-free, settings require constitutions or explicit understandings by which people in the settings will be governed and through which problems will be resolved. New settings are created within contexts, and contexts have histories that need to be confronted. The leader in a new setting faces the problem of allocating scarce resources and of balancing the leader's wishes for the setting with the participants' desires to grow and develop. We illustrated the issues in the creation of settings by showing how the Residential Youth Center was developed.

Change in existing organizations presents other problems. Every new program exists in a context consisting of social groups that relate to the program and to each other in relation to the program. We have identified seven broad sets of interests: energy, power, culture, competence, relationships, legal and administrative considerations, and information and communication. Members of each of the social groups evaluate proposed changes by examining how the proposed change affects their interests. Groups that on balance will gain from the changes will support them. Those groups that on balance stand to lose will oppose the change. Forces in the social context tend to pull the new back toward the status quo ante. Change efforts and change agents have to recognize that pull.

In the chapter, we presented two brief case studies of change in a mental hospital and in a state's system for the care of the retarded. In the first instance, change was brought about by skillful leadership. In the second instance, skillful leadership was enhanced by the power of a court to issue orders correcting wrongs in the delivery of services. In Chapter 12, we illustrate changes brought about by a community organization, the Love Canal Homeowners Association, using techniques of social and political action to create change. Their effort roused national consciousness and indirectly led to changes in legislation governing the cleanup of abandoned toxic-waste dump sites.

In the next chapter, we illustrate change that was brought about on a national scale. The fight against racial segregation in the schools took many years and required courageous and persistent effort by many people. Even after the legal battles were won, the implementation of remedies for school segregation required much effort, for change had to be introduced into one of the most important and complex of social organizations, our school system.

Notes

1. The movement to redefine the status of prisoners is part of an ongoing "democratization" of American society that dates from the end of World War II. The movement depended in part on a change in the federal judiciary's willingness to hear prisoners' grievances. That willingness, Jacobs (1980) argues, heightened the consciousness of prisoners and helped to politicize them. The civil rights movement and its offshoots in such groups as the Black Muslims produced an

agenda and an ideology and created conditions under which several charismatic inmate leaders emerged. Within prisons, jailhouse lawyers achieved new status. Reform sentiment among young lawyers produced a small but formidable prisoners' rights bar. Jacobs notes the symbolic value of the rhetoric in Supreme Court decisions in encouraging and discouraging the several actors and in influencing lower federal courts. The impact spread to state legislatures, and, equally important, the demands of litigation led to improved management of prisons. Professional organizations of corrections officials acted to articulate standards and from their viewpoint to improve prison administration.

2. Sarason was thinking of the large number of antipoverty programs, community mental health centers, Head Start programs, and the myriad of alternative service settings that emerged in the 1960s and early 1970s. The pace of creating settings continues today as new problems emerge or new issues capture our attention. Innumerable abortion clinics with attendant counseling facilities sprang up in the wake of *Roe v. Wade* protecting abortions. Rape crisis centers, havens for battered women, and a large number of health maintenance organizations also emerged. Thousands of self-help organizations have been created in recent years. An example is the citizens' organization opposed to toxic wastes buried in landfills affecting residential neighborhoods and water supplies. A great many were formed after the Love Canal revelation raised our consciousness of the issues and led to national efforts supplemented by state efforts to identify toxic-waste dump sites (Gibbs, 1982; A. Levine, 1982).

3. Although it is not necessary to appreciate the issues in the creation of settings, it is worthwhile recounting a little of the subsequent history. The RYC was sufficiently successful that its sponsor extended its life. A second RYC for women of the same age was established. In the late 1960s the RYC staff formed a third organization to disseminate the RYC concept. The funding difficulties of the War on Poverty limited their opportunities, although they did consult successfully with programs in other cities. The organization had a crisis when Goldenberg left Yale to go to Harvard. Yale had denied him tenure, which became a public issue when a number of Yale students protested the decision. Goldenberg's ability to move while there were no similar career opportunities for many of the paraprofessionals created organizational difficulties and strained relationships. The members of the organization managed to work out their differences. Several continue their relationship with Goldenberg through the external degree program for paraprofessionals that he leads at Hampshire College.

4. Donald T. Campbell (personal communication), in discussing a critical problem in evaluation research, noted that whenever a program is evaluated by some more or less arbitrary criterion, and political or resource allocation consequences depend on the evaluation, one of two results obtain. Either the process becomes corrupted to produce the index or the index becomes corrupted. Thus if a school program is evaluated by achievement test results, the educational process may become corrupted by concentrating on teaching students to perform well on tests. In one notable example, an educational contractor who was to be paid on the basis of achievement test results spent time actually teaching students to do test items that later comprised the criterion.

The concept of index corruption is undoubtedly familiar to anyone who has ever responded to bureaucratic demands for figures. Many people can attest that the reliability of some of the figures offered is highly suspect. For example, in an academic department that was evaluated by administrators in part on the basis of faculty publication productivity, it was common practice to include items that were in press in one year and to count the same item again the following year when the piece had been published, effectively doubling output. No doubt readers can multiply the examples from their own experiences.

5. Shortly after the research for the case study of Harlem Valley was completed, Haveliwala left Harlem Valley and took over the directorship of another larger hospital within the state system. The problems and the task in the new situation were quite different. Haveliwala encountered great conflict with the state bureaucracy, which accused him of mismanagement. The facts on the public record are unclear. Eventually he resigned. Some believe he was forced out because

he had publicly opposed some of the governor's and the commissioner's policies in a letter published in the *New York Times*. At any rate, the circumstances were different at his new post, and it is not clear that he was able to adopt the same approach. The subsequent history indicates that methods must be adopted to the historical situation and to conditions as they exist. As Sarason (1981) notes, psychology is peculiarly ahistorical and focused on contextless principles. The case study is warning that we can ignore history and contexts only at our peril when applying theoretical principles.

6. The research reported here was completed with support from the National Science Foundation Law and Social Science Program, Grant No. SES-8023954. This section is adapted from a longer report published elsewhere (Levine, 1986).

References

Bennis, W. G. (1966). *Changing organizations*. New York: McGraw-Hill.

Chayes, A. (1976). The role of the judge in public law litigation. *Harvard Law Review, 89*, 1281–1316.

Cherniss, C. (1980). *Professional burnout in human service organizations*. New York: Praeger.

City of Cleburne, Texas v. Cleburne Living Center, Inc., 53 L.W. 5022 (1985).

Colarelli, N. J., & Siegel, S. M. (1966). *Ward H. An adventure in innovation*. Princeton, N.J.: Van Nostrand.

Connery, R. H., Backstrom, C. H., Deener, D. R., Friedman, J. R., Kroll, M., Marden, R. H., McCleskey, C., Meekison, P., & Morgan, J. A., Jr. (1968). *The politics of mental health*. New York: Columbia University Press.

Cowen, E. L., Trost, M. A., Izzo, L. D., Lorion, R. P., Dorr, D., & Isaacson, R. V. (1975). *New ways in school mental health*. New York: Human Sciences Press.

Fairweather, G. W., Sanders, D. H., & Tornatzky, L. G. (1974). *Creating change in mental health organizations*. New York: Pergamon Press.

Fairweather, G. W., & Tornatzky, L. G. (1977). *Experimental methods for social policy research*. New York: Pergamon Press.

Farber, B. A. (Ed.). (1983). *Stress and burnout in the human service professions*. New York: Pergamon Press.

Gibbs, L. M. (as told to M. Levine). (1982). *Love Canal: My story*. Albany: SUNY Press.

Goldenberg, I. I. (1971). *Build me a mountain. Youth poverty and the creation of new settings*. Cambridge: MIT Press.

Graziano, A. M. (1969). Clinical innovation and the mental health power structure: A social case history. *American Psychologist, 24*, 10–18.

Graziano, A. M. (1974). *Child without tomorrow*. New York: Pergamon Press.

In re Gault, 387 U.S. 1 (1967).

Jacobs, J. B. (1980). The prisoners' rights movement and its impacts, 1960–1980. In N. Morris & M. Tonry (Eds.), *Crime and justice: An annual review of research*. Chicago: University of Chicago Press.

Kanter, R. M. (1977). *Men and women of the corporation*. New York: Basic Books.

Kozol, J. (1967). *Death at an early age*. New York: Houghton-Mifflin.

Levine, A. G. (1982). *Love Canal: Science, politics, people*. Lexington, MA: Lexington Books.

Levine, D. I. (1984). The authority for the appointment of remedial special masters in federal institutional reform litigation: The history reconsidered. *U.C. Davis Law Review, 17*, 753–805.

Levine, M. (1980). *From state hospital to psychiatric center. The implementation of planned organizational change*. Lexington, MA: Lexington Books.

Levine, M. (1981). *The history and politics of community mental health*. New York: Oxford University Press.

Levine, M. (1986). The role of special master in institutional reform litigation: A case study. *Law & Policy, 8,* 275–321.

Levine, M., & Bunker, B. B. (Eds). (1975). *Mutual criticism.* Syracuse, NY: Syracuse University Press.

Levine, M., & Graziano, A. M. (1972). Intervention programs in elementary schools. In S. E. Golann and C. Eisdorfer (Eds.), *Handbook of community mental health.* New York: Appleton-Century-Crofts.

Levine, M., & Levine, A. (1970). *A social history of helping services.* New York: Appleton-Century-Crofts.

Lubin, R. A., Schwartz, A. A., Zigman, W. B., & Janicki, M. P. (1982). Community acceptance of residential programs for developmentally disabled persons. *Applied Research in Mental Retardation, 3,* 191–200.

Marris, P., & Rein, M. (1967). *Dilemmas of social reform.* New York: Atherton Press.

Maslow, A. H. (1962). *Toward a psychology of being.* Princeton, NJ: Van Nostrand.

Mayer, R. R. (1979). *Social science and institutional change.* (Stock No. 017-024-00868-1). Washington, DC: U.S. Government Printing Office.

Medalie, R. J., Zeitz, L., & Alexander, P. (1973). Custodial police interrogation in our nation's capital: The attempt to implement Miranda. In T. L. Becker & M. M. Feeley (Eds.), *The impact of Supreme Court decisions* (2nd ed.). New York: Oxford University Press.

Moynihan, D. P. (1969). *Maximum feasible misunderstanding.* New York: Free Press.

Nathan, V. M. (1979). The use of masters in institutional reform litigation. *Toledo Law Review, 10,* 419–464.

O'Connor v. Donaldson, 422 U.S. 563 (1975).

Poythress, N. G. (1978). Psychiatric expertise in civil commitment: Training attorneys to cope with expert testimony. *Law and Human Behavior, 2,* 1–24.

Pressman, J. L., & Wildavsky, A. (1979). *Implementation* (2d ed.). Berkeley: University of California Press.

Rosenberg, J., & Phillips, W. R. F. (1981–82). The institutionalization of conflict in the reform of schools: A case study of the PARC decree. *Indiana Law Journal, 57,* 425–449.

Rosenhan, D. L. (1973). On being sane in insane places. *Science, 179,* 250–258.

Sarason, S. B. (1967). Toward a psychology of change and innovation. *American Psychologist, 22,* 227–233.

Sarason, S. B. (1972). *The creation of settings and the future societies.* San Francisco: Jossey-Bass.

Sarason, S. B. (1974). *The psychological sense of community.* San Francisco: Jossey-Bass.

Sarason, S. B. (1982). *The culture of the school and the problem of change* (2d ed.). Boston: Allyn & Bacon.

Sarason, S. B., Levine, M., Goldenberg, I. I., Cherlin, D. L., & Bennett, E. M. (1966). *Psychology in community settings.* New York: Wiley.

Sarason, S. B., Zitnay, G., & Grossman, F. K. (1971). *The creation of a community setting.* Syracuse, NY: Syracuse University and the Center on Human Policy.

Schulberg, H. C., & Baker, F. (1975). *The mental hospital and human services.* New York: Behavioral Publications.

Seeburger, R. H., & Wettick, R. S., Jr. (1973). Miranda in Pittsburgh—A statistical study. In T. L. Becker & M. M. Feeley (Eds.), *The impact of Supreme Court decisions* (2d ed.). New York: Oxford University Press.

Watzlawick, P., Weakland, J. H., & Fisch, R. (1974). *Change: Principles of problem formation and problem resolution.* New York: Norton.

11

School Desegregation:
A Societal-Level Intervention

The desegregation of American society is one of the more profound social changes in our time. We include a discussion of desegregation in part because social scientists played important roles in the desegregation effort, although they were by no means the leaders of the effort to win desegregation, and in part because it is a good example of an intervention that affected the entire nation. Moreover, at the level of individual school districts and individual schools, responsible authorities had to institute a process to accommodate change initiated externally. Another important aspect from community psychology's perspective was that social scientists helped to create a body of knowledge and theory that attributed the plight of black people in the United States not to their individual characteristics, but to the environmental conditions under which they lived—segregation enforced by law. Black and white scholars, literary figures, and social activists developed coherent intellectual rationales to fight racial oppression. Later, especially with regard to the effort to desegregate the schools, social scientists provided important expert testimony in the courts regarding the detrimental psychological effects of segregation. Social scientists also provided theoretical propositions justifying the remedies that were sought.

Social change and social justice were sought via conflict carried out through the legal institutions designed to resolve conflict. Examining the problem of desegregation also shows how psychological and sociological issues are deeply rooted in our history, in our political structure, and in our culture. The involvement of social scientists in the desegregation effort provides a model for the involvement of community psychologists and other social scientists in problems calling for social and community change and alerts us to the complexity of the problems of change affecting the whole society.

Although the desegregation of American society was propelled by many forces, it can be described as a massive, planned, societal-level intervention whose purpose was to solve complex moral, social, economic, and psychological problems. Segregation of the races, a social practice enforced by the power of law, was built on an assumption held by the majority that the black person was inherently inferior and therefore that the interests of both races would be served by rigidly enforcing their separation. This assumption rationalized the exploitation of the black minority who did not share it and who experienced segregation as oppression. Eventually a body of scholarly opinion developed to support the view that segregation was oppression and was the cause of social, economic, and psychological problems found among blacks. Given that segregation was accepted as the cause of the evils associated with it, attacking the cause by getting rid of the formal barriers to full integration made sense.

The theory that segregation as a social and legal practice was the cause of diverse social, economic, and psychological consequences is a situationally oriented theory. The proposition that removing formal barriers to integration would undo the undesirable consequences is a corollary to the theory. To cast the discussion of desegregation as a test of some propositions in social science, however, risks trivializing one of the most admirable and successful battles for social justice that has ever been waged. Desegregation has affected the lives of every American citizen and continues to affect us. The successful fight for civil rights not only transformed race relations in the United States, but also served as the model for other oppressed groups to seek social change. Nonetheless, we note that the theory and the intervention were aimed not at changing persons, but at changing conditions, with the assumption that changes in behavior, attitudes, and self-image would follow.

At the level of our schools, the specific remedy for the evils of segregation—to desegregate them—was based in part on a set of premises drawn from the psychological study of prejudice. Attempting to change a deeply engrained social pattern has revealed both that we know less than we thought we did and that the underlying phenomena are more complex than we thought. The social science propositions were stated most clearly in relation to public education, and we now have a body of evidence testing their validity. Because documentation is strong in the area of school desegregation, we will concentrate on a discussion of those propositions. The reader should bear in mind the larger context of change in American life, however, and the effects of desegregation on every social institution (Brooks, 1974).

Slavery, Segregation, and the Constitution[1]

As we noted in the previous chapter, change occurs in a historical context. No clearer illustration of this principle can be provided than that of school desegregation. Slavery and race relations occupied our attention from the very beginning of our nation. The contradiction in values between the ringing words of political freedom in the Declaration of Independence—"all men are created equal"—and the section of the original Constitution that counted slaves as three-fifths of a person for purposes of representation is clear.[2] This contradiction was solved for many by viewing the black person as less than fully human in intellectual, moral, and social characteristics.

Slavery was an issue at every step in the nation's growth before the Civil War. Whether a new state or territory was to enter the nation as a free or a slave state was a source of political and armed conflict. Eventually that conflict erupted in the Civil War. In the United States, the life of the black person, whether a slave or a free person in a nonslave territory, was difficult. Slaves had few rights and little legal protection. They were denied an education; segregation in public accommodations, churches, and schools was common throughout the nonslave states of the North. For free blacks the right to vote was often denied or was drastically restricted. Free or slave, the black person was viewed and treated as an inferior being.

After the end of the Civil War, in 1865 Lincoln's Emancipation Proclamation became a permanent part of our Constitution as the Thirteenth Amendment, banning involuntary servitude. The Thirteenth Amendment was not sufficient to protect the civil and political rights of the newly freed black. Many southern states passed black codes designed to restore slavery in fact if not in name. The Fourteenth Amendment in 1868 provided all citizens, black and white, with protections against state action that denied the equal protection of the law or that deprived any citizen of life, liberty, or property without due process of law. Although intended to protect the newly freed slave, the Fourteenth Amendment was written in much broader terms to reflect ideals of political freedom and social equality (tenBroek, 1965). The Fifteenth Amendment, protecting the right to vote, became a part of the Constitution in 1870.

For the next 30 years the promise of these amendments was undercut by violence and economic pressure against blacks and by a U.S. Supreme Court that "interpreted away" the protections of the post-Civil War amendments. In 1883, for example, the Supreme Court struck down a federal statute prohibiting the exclusion of blacks from public accommodations. The Court reasoned that although the constitutional amendments protected blacks against action by the state, they provided no protection against the acts of private citizens. Any innkeeper was thus a private citizen who could discriminate against, or for that matter lynch, blacks.[3] Protection was a matter for state law. If the states saw fit to permit private discrimination, or if the states did not enforce their laws against violence, there was no protection.

In 1890 the Louisiana legislature passed a law calling for separate but equal accommodations for white and colored passengers on railroad trains. The "separate but equal" term was designed to meet the requirements of the equal-protection clause of the Fourteenth Amendment. The black citizens of New Orleans, in cooperation with railroad officials who were not pleased with the prospect of having to add extra cars to their trains, tested the law. In 1892 Homer Adolph Plessy, who was seven-eighths Caucasian, boarded a train and refused to move to the segregated car. Arrested and fined, he appealed, and in 1896 his case reached the U.S. Supreme Court.

The Supreme Court then enunciated its notorious separate-but-equal doctrine. Holding that the equal-protection clause of the Fourteenth Amendment did not abolish all social distinctions and could not require that the races commingle "upon terms unsatisfactory to either," the Court went on to say:

> We consider the underlying fallacy of the plaintiff's argument to consist in the assumption that the enforced separation of the two races stamps the colored race with a badge of inferiority. If this be so, it is not by reason of anything found in the act, but solely because the colored race chooses to put that construction upon it. (*Plessy v. Ferguson,* 1896)

In following years the *Plessy* decision was used to support and to sustain discriminatory legislation affecting all of our social institutions.[4] The Supreme Court had grounded its decision in *Plessy* on the social psychological proposition that stigma was not inherent in the action of forced segregation because the law itself contained no stigmatizing words. The problem was in the perceptions of those who were the victims of discrimination. The Court's use of a social psychological proposition was to set the agenda for the next 50 years in the study of race relations. Because the *Plessy* Court used a social psychological concept, the proposition could be challenged with data to show that enforced separation *was* stigmatizing and harmful.

The NAACP and Its Litigative Strategy

The victory for school desegregation in *Brown v. Board of Education* (1954) represented the culmination of a planned self-help effort by a private community organization. The National Association for the Advancement of Colored People (NAACP) was formed in the shadow of virulent and violent antiblack sentiment in 1909. The organization had as its major aim protecting the rights of blacks through social and political action, including litigation (Hughes, 1962). It settled on litigation as the major means to pursue its aims. After 1929 the Howard University Law School became a center for research on civil rights law. Many of the black lawyers who carried the fight trained there, including present U.S. Supreme Court Justice Thurgood Marshall.

Ideology arises in support of the status quo. Some prominent black leaders urged that blacks work to instill black pride and to make black educational institutions first-rate. Booker T. Washington argued that progress for the black depended on improving black education and training blacks in all-black institutions in valuable vocational skills. W. E. B. Du Bois, who grew pessimistic about the possibilities for change in the short run, advocated training black leadership, the "talented tenth," in superior, all-black institutions. This approach implied that blacks lacked self-confidence and did not strive, but that vigorous effort at self-improvement could succeed even under conditions of segregation. Although the black leadership was anything but naive, this approach did tend to attribute blame to the person rather than to the situation. Black and white scholars,[5] however, developed a body of literature arguing that segregation was the evil that resulted in distortions in personal and intellectual development, limiting achievement. The Supreme Court in *Plessy* had explicitly rejected the argument that to segregate was to oppress and to stigmatize. The Court's *Plessy* assertion had never been reexamined by other courts.

The attack on school segregation began as early as 1929, and by 1935 over 100 court cases had challenged school segregation. Direct challenges to segregated schools invariably lost in the courts. The administration of the laws, not desegregation itself, seemed a more promising target to the NAACP legal strategists. If the schools were separate they had to be equal under the *Plessy* doctrine. If black and white schools were not objectively equal in terms of facilities, qualifications and salaries of teachers, and the amount of money spent on black and white children, the states were discriminating against blacks in violation of the equal-protection clause of the Fourteenth Amendment as interpreted in *Plessy*. A review of litigative successes and failures led to a strategy of attacking the myth that, measured objectively, there were separate but equal schools. By insisting that separate schools be equal, the NAACP leadership hoped that segregation would be brought down by the financial weight of maintaining two truly equal school systems.

The years following World War II saw renewed activity in civil rights. President Franklin D. Roosevelt, perhaps influenced by the commitment of his wife, Eleanor, to racial justice, appointed more liberal Supreme Court justices. President Harry S. Truman also took a strong stand on civil rights and desegregated the armed forces by presidential order. In the postwar period, litigation attacking segregation extended to housing, labor law, jury service, and voting. Litigation was accompanied by efforts at legislative change. Social action resulting in the direct confrontation of segregated institutions developed in that period as well (Brooks, 1974).

Thurgood Marshall, later appointed the first black U.S. Supreme Court justice, led the NAACP's legal battles from the late 1930s onward. The postwar attack began with graduate and professional schools. If blacks were not admitted to state schools and no comparable black institutions existed, the requirements of separate but equal were violated. Along with a group of black lawyers centered at Howard University, and with a few white lawyers, Marshall successfully pursued the strategy of insisting on separate but equal at the graduate and professional school levels.[6] These cases resulted in the admission of black students to formerly all-white schools, since the alternatives were to build equal facilities or close down all-white schools. Marshall and the NAACP Legal Defense Fund were also successful in suits for equal pay for black and white teachers.

The struggle against elementary school segregation was renewed in the years following World War II. NAACP legal briefs more and more stressed the stigmatizing and stultifying consequences of segregation, although the basic legal attack continued to center on inequality of facilities. Although the Supreme Court struck down segregation barriers in the higher education cases, it had not confronted the argument that separate educational facilities were inherently unequal. The decisions in the higher education cases provided precedents for many lower courts to order educational authorities at the posthigh-school level to provide truly equal facilities or to admit blacks to formerly all-white institutions.

Marshall and the NAACP thought carefully about how to mount a direct litigative assault on the assumption that separate could be equal. Not only were the legal grounds uncertain; participation in the cases by black plaintiffs was perilous physically and financially. It was also perilous for black civil rights lawyers to bring cases in the South when there was a constant threat of physical violence, but they proceeded with heroic determination. The cultural belief that the low social and economic state of blacks in society was attributable not to segregation but to inherent inferiority was at stake. In the years after *Plessy,* scientific literature, in the sense that it was written by men with scholarly credentials and positions, was published that rationalized the belief in racial inferiority.[7] By the late 1920s other social scientists had developed the opposing position that the social environment was the primary cause of the failure of blacks to achieve. The growing social science literature on the effects of racism provided an intellectual rationale for the argument that segregated facilities were inherently unequal because segregation itself caused severe psychological damage.

Kenneth Clark, a black social psychologist who had been an undergraduate at Howard and later became president of the American Psychological Association, had been experimenting with techniques to show that segregation resulted in impaired self-images in black children. Although not all of his NAACP legal colleagues agreed, Marshall viewed Clark's studies (conducted in collaboration with Clark's wife, Mamie) as an excellent means of demonstrating that segregation damaged the self-esteem of black children.

Cases challenging segregation itself as inherently unequal worked their way through lower courts to the Supreme Court. Clark and other social scientists testified in a number of cases.[8] Testifying in *Brown v. Board of Education of Topeka* (1954), social science expert Louisa P. Holt influenced the trial court's findings of fact on the ill effects of segregation, and this finding of fact was later cited by the Supreme Court in its decision. NAACP attorneys highlighted the social science testimony in their briefs in *Brown* (1954) and in the related cases that were heard with *Brown.* A group of social scientists headed by Isidor Chein, Kenneth Clark, and Stuart Cook prepared a review of the evidence on segregation that was appended to the NAACP brief to the Supreme Court (a footnote now called the Social Science Statement; see later).

The legal arguments in *Brown* dealt with the rational basis for laws that classified whites as different from blacks for purposes of schooling. The equal-protection clause of the Fourteenth Amendment did not prohibit states from making classifications in laws. If the state did classify and the classification was challenged, however, the state was required to show that it had compelling reasons for making the classification. NAACP lawyers argued that the evidence introduced in the cases that were being reviewed, coupled with earlier precedents, showed that classification by race for purposes of schooling was not rational and should not be supported.

When the *Brown* decision was rendered in 1954, the importance of the psychological and sociological premises for the argument were apparent in Chief Justice Earl Warren's opinion for a unanimous Court:

> Segregation of white and colored children in public schools has a detrimental effect upon the colored children. The impact is greater when it has the sanction of law; for the policy of separating the races is usually interpreted as denoting the inferiority of the negro group. A sense of inferiority affects the motivation of the child to learn. Segregation with the sanction of law, therefore, has a tendency to [retard] the educational and mental development of negro children and to deprive them of some of the benefits they would receive in a racial[ly] integrated school system. Whatever may have been the extent of psychological knowledge at the time of *Plessy v. Ferguson,* this finding is amply supported by modern authority.

The Court then cited the ample modern authority, listing social science studies by name and citing their authors in the now-famous footnote 11.[9] Social science evidence directly contradicted the social psychological assertions made by the Court in *Plessy* and thus provided an important part of the rationale for overruling *Plessy.*

Warren's opinion for a unanimous Court declared segregated schools unconstitutional, but the Court waited another year before issuing its word on remedies. The Court was appropriately cautious because what would constitute an effective remedy was not clear. No decision before had affected so many American families and communities directly and personally.

A few communities responded quickly, but in others the decision stimulated talk of massive resistance. The Court spent a long time contemplating remedies and finally returned the problem to local school boards for solution. School boards were to design desegregation programs, and the federal district courts were to oversee their efforts. The Court offered few guidelines, urging that the desegregation of the schools be accomplished "with all deliberate speed" (*Brown v. Board of Education of Topeka,* 1955).

The two *Brown* decisions opposed a few words on paper against 200 years of history and custom. The words of the Supreme Court were law, however, and all of the federal government's power to enforce the law was behind the words. In 1957, when the governor of Arkansas used the National Guard to prevent black children from entering white schools, President Dwight D. Eisenhower sent federal troops to protect the black children's rights (Bickel, 1962). The show of force was not sufficient to end the legal skirmishing as community after community adopted foot-dragging plans.

There was some progress in some rural areas, but in urban areas a simple redrawing of school lines could not accomplish desegregation. In legal terms, desegregation meant that black and white children and black and white teachers and administrators should work side by side in unitary, racially mixed schools. The remedies—busing, busing across school district lines, pairing schools, and affirmative-action hiring— required a departure from the concept of neighborhood schools and from some hiring practices. In 1971 the Supreme Court ruled that in a system segregated by law it was not enough to rely on voluntary choice of schools. The Court approved busing as means of desegregating the schools and indicated that remedies taking race into account were permissible.[10]

Not only southern schools were segregated. Blacks in northern urban areas also attended segregated schools, partly because of the increasing suburbanization of the nation following World War II and the increasing concentration of blacks in the inner cities. Segregation in northern schools was not only due to the "succession" of one population by another (see Chapter 3). In many cities, authorities had drawn school district lines or located new schools in such a way as to ensure segregated schools. In 1973 the Supreme Court ruled (*Keyes v. Denver,* 1973) that if a portion of a school system was segregated as a result of discriminatory practices by school authorities, a systemwide remedy could be imposed even if there was no other history of officially imposed segregation.

Where black students constituted a majority or near majority of the school population, integration could not be achieved without busing students across school district lines. Although the Court had approved cross-district busing in systems that had been segregated by law, it refused to authorize cross-district busing in the absence of evidence that school authorities in the affected suburban districts had acted to cause segregation in the urban district. The Court did approve the plaintiff's request that resources be allocated to remedy educational deficits and to develop programs that facilitated integration within the urban school district (*Milliken v. Bradley,* 1974).

That decision limited the possibilities for desegregation to whatever could be accomplished within a given school district. The decision protecting suburbs against integration might have contributed to so-called white flight (white families moving out of the cities to avoid busing to integrate the schools), but that is debatable (Farley, 1980). Busing undoubtedly contributed to a backlash against integration efforts and to the development of resistance to further efforts at integrating the schools. Moreover, political leaders, sensing the resistance of large numbers of parents to busing programs, articulated those views and turned them into votes (Ravitch, 1983). Although some noteworthy examples of violence took place (e.g., the Boston schools; Smith, 1978; Metcalf, 1983), in other places busing and integration proceeded peacefully (Willie, 1984).

Social Science Theory and Integration

The social science testimony in cases reaching the Supreme Court asserted that segregation was wrong and harmful and that desegregating would undo the harm. There was little discussion of the specific problems of implementing remedies. Cook (1984), a coauthor of what is now called the Social Science Statement, noted that the legal issue in *Brown* (1954) dealt with the effects on children of lifelong de jure segregation and did not require a detailed discussion of remedies. Nonetheless, their testimony and position papers contained a set of implicit situational hypotheses.

Stephan (1978) reviewed the testimony in the several cases. He drew a causal model in which white prejudice toward blacks led to low black self-esteem, low black achievement, and black prejudice toward whites. In turn, the same factors looped back to stimulate and maintain white prejudice against blacks. If enforced segregation, the institutional base for the loop, was interrupted, black self-esteem should improve, black achievement should improve, blacks should develop more positive attitudes toward whites, and whites would have more positive attitudes toward blacks. Stephan's model implies rapid change but did not include time as a variable. Cook (1984) argues that the Social Science Statement anticipated black and white achievement gaps and implied that these would be eliminated gradually, over an indeterminate number of years.

Gerard (1983) notes that the social scientists' views specified several conditions under which real integration, and thus the posited effects, could take place. These include:

> (a) firm and consistent endorsement by those in authority; (b) the absence of competition among representatives of different racial groups; (c) the equivalence of positions and functions among all participants in the desegregated setting; and (d) interracial contacts of a type that permitted learning about one another as individuals. (p. 870)

The statement was drawn from existing knowledge about prejudice extended to the school situation (Cook, 1984).

Busing was a means by which white and black children could be placed in the same schoolrooms working side by side, meeting the fourth condition Gerard cites. The theory received considerable support from the first Coleman report (1966). Based on an elaborate multivariate analysis of data from a huge nationwide sample, Coleman reported that improved school facilities alone did little to improve educational performance. He found, however, that black students in schools with a majority of white students did perform better than black students in segregated schools. He also found that those students had higher levels of self-esteem. Although the study entailed a correlational design and could not unequivocally support a cause-and-effect interpretation, his findings provided a rationale for the busing remedy (Ravich, 1983).

Stephan (1978) reviewed a large number of studies testing hypotheses derived from the Social Science Statement. The results are generally equivocal with respect to improving interracial attitudes. The same number of studies show increases as show decreases in black prejudice toward whites, and more studies than not show an increase in white prejudice toward blacks. Methodological problems make it difficult to interpret the results of most studies, but simply placing blacks and whites in the same physical location is not enough to reduce prejudice, at least not in the short run.

Desegregation has not been shown to have any consistent effect on black self-esteem. Cook (1984) notes that the studies and the measures lack subtlety, but more likely the original hypothesis that simply removing the barrier and increasing contact would increase self-esteem and reduce prejudice was too simple. Cook (1984) states that beginning in the mid-1960s studies were showing that, if anything, black self-esteem in segregated situations was as high as or higher than the self-esteem of whites.

One hypothesis states that widespread cultural change—the civil rights movement, black power, "black is beautiful," and media attention to prominent black political, sports, and entertainment figures—contributed to improved self-esteem. Such attention was associated with the desegregation of American society and the civil rights legislation that followed the *Brown* decision. The changes in black self-esteem sought by the studies of school desegregation were attributable to many powerful social forces, not just to school desegregation.

The consequences of desegregation for school achievement are also complex. According to Stephan's summary, black students in integrated schools may do somewhat better than black students in segregated schools, and white achievement is not adversely affected by black achievement. Gerard (1983) finds little evidence of change in black achievement. Sarason's caveat about giving change a sufficient amount of time to produce an effect is probably relevant here. That is, Cook (1984) argues that the Social Science Statement anticipated favorable effects only over the long run, and said nothing about short-term changes in achievement except to predict what was found—namely, that neither black nor white achievement would be adversely affected by integration. Cook's (1984) review of the literature indicates that the performance of very young black children in desegregated schools showed an advantage over those in segregated schools. He suggests that desegregation may be more effective when children of different races are exposed to each other from the outset and may be less effective when it is necessary to overcome the effects of previous segregation. Moreover, Cook argues that studies examined over an extended period of time show a progressive narrowing of black and white achievement differences. Note that the research is complicated and that simple cause-and-effect statements cannot adequately summarize the interaction of complex, intertwined variables.

Gerard (1983) reviewed the original premises that he identified in the Social Science Statement. He notes that the first condition, firm and consistent endorsement by those in authority, required all authority figures from elected officials to the classroom teacher to endorse desegregation. In Gerard's view, it was shortsighted to expect such consistency, and, in any event, pitting busing against the neighborhood school created anything but consistent endorsement. Cook (1984) defends the social science prediction by noting that in other desegregation situations (e.g., armed forces, industry), forceful leadership overcame the initial disruptions brought by integration.

The second condition for successful desegregation was an absence of competition. Gerard reminds his readers that competition is deeply engrained in American culture, that teachers do not have the skills nor the social characteristics to foster cooperation, and that in any event it was too much to expect of the classroom teacher to homogenize subcultural diversity within the classroom. Cook (1984) responds that there have been many successful experiments in interracial learning teams within the public schools. In many instances, the interventions had been designed by social psychologists building on social science theory and research. It was not that it couldn't be done, but that it was not done enough.

The third condition was the equivalence of functions and positions among all participants. Although affirmative-action programs have resulted in greater numbers of black teachers and administrators within the schools, Gerard claims that the schools have done little to create true equivalence in achievement. In Gerard's data from one city, the gap between black and white achievement widened; in his view, this could only have had an adverse effect on black self-esteem. Cook's (1984) interpretation is that over the long run, and viewed nationally, the gap in achievement may have decreased. Among younger children the gap was much smaller.

As for the fourth condition, interracial contact that permits learning about each other as individuals, Gerard notes that self-segregation occurs within the classroom. For example, his sociometric data show few cross-racial work partnerships or friendship choices. The data do not show whether any specific efforts were made to encourage cooperative working relationships in those particular schools. Gerard sums up his argument by saying that teachers would have to have been social engineering geniuses to have put into operation the conditions social scientists said were necessary to induce the positive effects of integration.

Looking back, Gerard argues that data were not available to warrant the confident predictions he had derived from the Social Science Statement and, moreover, that the social scientists were not fully cognizant of the contexts within which the abstract principles they had culled from the literature would have to be implemented. In effect, he claims that they were unfamiliar with the culture of the schools (see Sarason, 1982). Gerard argues that sufficient *knowledge* was not yet available to legitimize social scientists as "expert witnesses" in school desegregation cases. One issue he raises, for example, concerns the percentage breakdown between white and black students in the optimally "desegregated" school. Between 20% and 40% black is often cited, he says, although there is no empirical basis for this figure.

Cook (1984) is less pessimistic than Gerard about the overall accomplishments of integration. While not denying that many problems emerged, he points to thousands of classrooms where successful interracial learning teams were developed. He reviewed studies showing improved achievement and improved race relations in classrooms where the social structure approximated the conditions called for in the Social Science Statement.

Gerard was chastened by his research findings and experiences, but felt that instead of quitting, social scientists should go back to the drawing board in adopting the kind of "research and development" approach to implementing innovation used by engineering and the physical sciences. That is, in his view there had been insufficient opportunity to experiment with alternative models before an unalterable solution was put into place. He is in favor of smaller and more ecologically valid studies than social scientists usually conduct. Ecologically valid studies might have a better chance of providing the basis for recommendations regarding changes that will produce the sought result. Cook agrees with Gerard on the desirability of small-scale research. In fact, Cook foresees an increased demand for social science contributions.

Deeply held cultural values do not change quickly, even in relation to evidence. We may not see definitive evidence of the benefits of this massive social intervention until several generations of schoolchildren, teachers, and administrators have been exposed to desegregated schools. Perhaps we will not see the full benefits until socioeconomic advantages accrue to parents who have benefited from other aspects of desegregation. Our theories may not have a sufficient historical perspective, as Sarason (1973, 1981) notes.

Some (e.g., Cahn, 1955) argue that it was an error to rely on empirical outcomes to decide moral questions. Should we be able to argue that because all the postulated benefits of desegregation cannot be demonstrated empirically we should again allow states to enforce segregation? Can we afford to wait the many years research and development activities usually take, as Gerard acknowledges, before making policy decisions that have such an impact on people's lives? Certain benefits were implied for forced busing, of course, but if we did not integrate schools and did not integrate faculties, what else would we do, in Justice William Brennan's words (*Green v. County,* 1968), to eliminate discrimination "root and branch"? In other words, the social policy of desegregation can rest on premises other than those pressed by social scientists. Nonetheless, this argument shows that an inevitable tension arises between decision makers who must act to solve social problems, and social scientists who prefer to participate in the public arena only when evidence is available. Another tension exists between those who argue that participation in the public arena is essential, even with imperfect science, and those who wish to wait until firmer data bases are available. The argument forces social scientists to examine the core of their own beliefs and their own values as these affect decisions to participate or not to participate in social action based on social science.

Successful Desegregation of the Schools[11]

We must remember that the organizational changes necessary to support desegregation were not at the forefront of the consciousness of the federal judges who were overseeing desegregation efforts (Kirp & Babcock, 1981). With time judges, plaintiffs, and school board officials did learn to cope with the problems of overseeing desegregation efforts. Although critics of busing have emphasized the difficulties, including the moral questions and dilemmas of discriminating on the basis of race even to effect a remedy (e.g., Glazer, 1975), in at least some cases desegregation efforts have produced overall improvements in the schools. In Buffalo, New York, the judge hearing the case, the plaintiffs, school officials, and other community leaders undertook to desegregate the schools while consciously working to improve them, achieving not just integrated education but a high quality of education as well. Other values were promoted by the desegregation effort in addition to racial integration and the benefits that were to accrue from integration. We now turn to a brief case history of succcessful school desegregation. The reader should consider the case material in light of the principles Gerard (1983) says would be necessary in governing a successful program of school integration and in light of our discussion of change in Chapter 10. The reader should also consider values such as decreased alienation from the schools, pride in the schools, and diversified curriculum offerings when evaluating the results of school desegregation.

In 1976, federal district court judge John T. Curtin found that city school officials, the Common Council, and the mayor had acted to create or to perpetuate segregated schools within the city of Buffalo. The suit, initiated in 1964 by a complaint to the state Commissioner of Education, ended with findings that the school board had redistricted school zones to maintain segregated schools, allowed whites to transfer out of integrated schools, stopped teaching Polish in a high school with many black students (thus encouraging those whites who wanted to study Polish to enroll in other high schools), placed a junior high school in a neighborhood that would guarantee it would be segregated, and fostered discriminatory policies affecting admission to desirable technical high schools. Moreover, the busing plan ordered by the Commissioner of Education after the 1964 complaint was found to be inadequate. The Common Council had tried to block a voluntary busing plan and through its fiscal control had refused to support a new building plan that might have relieved segregation.[12] The U.S. Supreme Court had held in *Keyes* (1973) that if any portion of a school system had been segregated as a result of the action of school officials, a systemwide desegregation remedy was in order.

Once the city schools and the city administration had been found responsible for the degree of segregation that existed, it was necessary to prepare a remedy. The school system initiated one, but the plaintiffs and the judge were not satisfied that it resulted in sufficient desegregation. Because there had been great fear of violence in the city if two-way busing were to be initiated, black children were bused into schools in white neighborhoods. Now the judge insisted that a more comprehensive plan be adopted.

White and black parents were angry, resented the idea of busing for racial balance, and were concerned about their children's safety and opportunities for a good education. The school system was viewed as poor, and school personnel were not credible. Given ethnic prejudice in the largely blue-collar city and the recent example of disorder in Boston (Smith, 1978), many people, including officials of the U.S. Justice Department, expected violence.

By this time there was sufficient understanding of the problems of integration that school officials, led by school superintendent Eugene Reville, and the plaintiffs agreed on the necessity for developing educational programs of high quality to make the schools attractive to parents, along with busing to achieve integration. Judge Curtin insisted that the integration plans be developed in consultation with the community. Associate superintendent Joseph Murray, who had been a highly effective principal of a secondary school in a difficult neighborhood, played an important role in desegregation planning. School officials arranged over 40 open meetings with community groups. After one expensive and fruitless attempt, the school administrators, who were responsible for devising and carrying out the integration plan under the supervision of the court, decided not to use outside consultants who did not know the community. Instead, they sent teams of black and white educators and lawyers into neighborhoods not only to meet with and inform parents that desegregation was going to take place, but also to let parents know this was an opportunity to improve the schools as well. Parents were outspoken, and these meetings were often quite heated. The teams included experienced line educators who were used to working with people in the neighborhoods, however. The U.S. Justice Department also assisted by sending a staff member of its Division of Community Relations to work with community leaders and to monitor the desegregation program. With the cooperation of the ecumenical Buffalo Area Metropolitan Ministries, clergy were also present when trouble was anticipated. In Buffalo, community leadership was unified behind the desegregation plan.

The meetings were intended to bring forward ideas for regional and citywide "magnet" schools[13] and to organize community groups that would contribute to the development of the desegregation plan. The emphasis on education and educational choice was presented to citizens as a means of avoiding forced busing. The outlines for the plans had been developed by school officials, but citizen participation was well utilized. Eventually many of the meetings resulted in parent groups convening to develop constructive plans not only to improve the schools, but also to have schools that reflected diverse educational viewpoints. Much of the strain was relieved once these plans were put into effect, although more work to integrate the schools was necessary.

The 22 regional magnet schools were located in integrated neighborhoods or in inner-city neighborhoods. They were designed to reflect neighborhood interest and to make the schools attractive to white and black parents whose children would be bused to those schools to keep them integrated. The school programs were designed to attract parents to their educational philosophies. One school, for example, operated on Montessori principles. Another was highly structured and traditional. One was formerly an alternative school that had been developed by white parents and was now taken over by the school system. It continued to operate on the same principles of informal and individualized instruction. Still another was located in a new open-plan building suitable for an open-education program. The schools were diverse in emphasis. One had native American programming, while another emphasized education in English and Spanish. One school specialized in programs for gifted children, while another became a prekindergarten through eighth grade school stressing science in all grades.

Neighborhood leaders were identified and in some instances given paid positions within the school programs they helped to design. One grass roots leader, once among the most articulate opponents of busing, subsequently became an advocate of busing. Some might say the school system co-opted potential opposition by such a tactic. Be that as it may, active citizen opposition was avoided. Teams of black and white parents were formed to be troubleshooters in schools that were to be integrated.

The magnet schools accepted children from all over the city. In addition to schools at the elementary level, three citywide magnet schools were developed at the high school level. These included an academy for visual and performing arts, a traditional high school, and City Honors, a school for academically talented youth.[14] Junior high schools that had been criticized for many reasons were replaced with kindergarten-through-eighth-grade schools. At a later phase, early childhood education programs offering excellent care and education for preschool children accommodated the day-care needs of many female-headed households. Arranged in this way, the desegregation plan shifted the balance of power in public education somewhat, giving less power to the mayor and the school board and more to the judge. The school administration also gained more leverage, and although school administrators guarded their professional prerogatives and moved in accordance with their own vision, they also had to be responsive to the interests represented by the plaintiffs and the community. In that sense, ultimately some power shifted to parents and their children as well.

During the period that plans were being developed and implemented, Judge Curtin made himself available on an informal basis to listen to people in the neighborhoods. Curtin received at least his fair share of hate mail, but none of that deterred him in his course. Observers say that although he unequivocally supported the integration program, he also showed his willingness to listen to problems people were experiencing, giving people a feeling that communication was taking place and that plans were not simply being imposed on them from above.

Although they had relinquished some power over public education to the judge and the parents, school administrators became enthusiastic as they realized that the desegregation order now gave them leverage to obtain the financial resources necessary to improve the schools. Judge Curtin backed the city school administrators by ordering the city government, which controlled school finances, to provide funds for desegregation programs when the mayor was reluctant. Moreover, declining enrollments necessitated the closing of some schools. The decision to close a school is always difficult, but the requirements of the desegregation program helped administrators decide which schools to close and helped communities to accept the decisions. Although the positive attitude of school administrators and the school board was critical, the plaintiff group stayed active and continually monitored and pressed for full compliance.

The interests of teachers were not ignored. Teachers were allowed to transfer between schools if the educational philosophy in the school clashed with their own. Parents were actively included. When a program required the busing of preschool children, for example, parents were taken to visit the schools. The school district placed ads in the newspapers and on television. The press also maintained a favorable stance toward the integration program, and school personnel kept Common Council members informed. Although a black candidate was defeated in a three-way race for mayor, a result that local observers claimed reflected racial antipathy in some areas of the city, to the credit of Buffalo politicians, no one overtly exploited feelings about integration for political advantage.

The community was involved at an early date. School superintendent Reville invited the Buffalo Area Metropolitan Ministries to provide support from the clergy for desegregation programs. In addition, a Citizens Commission on Desegregation was formed with representatives from a variety of constituencies. The Citizens Commission was originally intended as a monitoring group, but it proved ineffective and was disbanded. Beginning in 1978 another citizens' organization, Citizens for Quality Education (C4QE), was funded by the Emergency School Assistance Act and by New York State. This project, under the aegis of the Buffalo Area Metropolitan Ministries, was funded to assist community leadership in desegregating the school system. The organization was to work with the school system and the court primarily to develop and assist grass-roots leadership.

The C4QE project was not central to carrying out the desegregation program. Undoubtedly Judge Curtin, school officials, school board members, and the plaintiffs must be given primary credit for the success of this communitywide effort. The C4QE project is worth discussing here, however, because it provides an example of the relationship between a professional change agent and citizens in bringing about change in a complex context.

The project was under the direction of Lewis J. Sinatra, an educational administrator. He had been a teacher in the Buffalo schools and formerly headed a Teacher Corps project housed at State University College at Buffalo. Before that he had worked with a new-teacher project in Buffalo schools (Foster, 1974). Sinatra had also served as a consultant for the State Education Department on school desegregation in Buffalo. School officials and community leaders, including Judge Curtin, knew and respected him. A lifelong Buffalo resident and a product of its schools, he knew the local community well.

C4QE set up a citywide advisory council with representatives from every school board district in the city. It included a representative from the mayor's office and from the school board. Most of the members were parent representatives. The organization adopted a strategy of working with specific projects instead of trying to do something on a citywide basis, and it worked with a strategy of empowerment. C4QE told parents they had a right to be active and then assisted parents in working out their programs. C4QE did the staff work and research, but always stayed in the background when it came to any formal presentation to officials. When there was some need to address the school board, project staff assisted community leaders in preparing to present their problems or their plans to the school board. For example, at one point a school in an integrated neighborhood was scheduled to be closed. C4QE helped the parents involved gain support from a local business group and from the area's councilman. C4QE kept Judge Curtin informed about what they were doing, especially because he had indicated that he desired community input into the desegregation program. Its staff helped the parents to write the proposal, prepare a presentation to the school board, and request that the proposal be heard by the committee of the board that recommended changes in school programming. The school also had a principal who was willing to work with and to support the parent group. Eventually the Board of Education accepted the core of the parents' plan, added a seventh and eighth grade to the school, and kept it open. The court subsequently approved the plan as well. Apparently other principals found that they could get help with programs they felt they needed for their schools by helping to organize and to work with parent groups who would then make the presentation to the Board of Education.

Not all projects worked as successfully for the parent groups as the one described. In one case C4QE assisted a parent group in developing a proposal to keep a school open. The parent group went through the entire process but was unable to gain the court's approval for its plan. Sinatra believed that although the citizens were disappointed, they felt that at least they had had their day in court and were willing to cooperate with the plan that evolved for their children.

The desegregation program in Buffalo has been hailed as a model program (Winerip, 1985). Desegregation took place in peace and relative harmony. The white population of the city has not fled but in fact is highly supportive of its schools. Parental involvement and satisfaction with the schools have increased. Student achievement scores have increased overall, while curriculum options have proliferated. There has also been increased participation of both students and parents in extracurricular school programs (see Baud, 1982). Some observers claim that a level of social interaction between black and white students takes place that would not have been observed 10 years ago.

One cannot say that Buffalo schools are without problems. They have many of the problems of urban school systems. Cutbacks in federal aid to education made financing desegregation more difficult. The conflicts about school finances between the superintendent of schools and the school board on the one hand and the mayor on the other continue. Some claim that schools that were not directly a part of the desegregation plan did not get as many resources as the showcase magnet schools. A new conflict has arisen about a proposed magnet school because opponents claim that it will siphon off talented students from other schools and will result in some degree of resegregation of the schools.

Despite the continuing problems, the same legal mandate to desegregate that led to negative social and educational consequences elsewhere had an opposite impact in Buffalo. We cannot attribute the positive impact only to the approach taken to implement the program, but in examining the approach we observe that officials responsible for desegregation made sensible use of identifiable community processes to produce change that benefited the entire community.

Implications

The history of efforts to desegregate the schools helps us to understand that the social problem of race relations goes back to the beginning of our nation. We have been struggling with the problem for 200 years and more, and only in the last 30 years have we been approaching an open society. The profound social changes that we have seen resulted from a concerted self-help effort to produce change. Social scientists participated in producing the changes by developing data and arguments that permitted an attack on the then-conventional wisdom, as embodied in law, that segregation not only was not harmful, but was positively beneficial. Social science research and theory provided part of the rationale for the desegregation remedy. We do not know whether the theory that ridding ourselves of formal barriers to integration would have beneficial effects was incorrect, or whether instead it was too simply stated. Clearly, no single discipline's perspective is enough to help us to understand as complex a phenomenon as school desegregation. We will have to take fuller cognizance of the complex historical, social, political, legal, and economic contexts within which we work and live.

One might argue, as Gerard (1983) does, that social scientists do not yet have enough to say and should stay out of public affairs until their disciplines are better developed. On the other hand, social scientists do have analytic methods and concepts, and bodies of knowledge exist with some utility for real-world problems. Sarason (1974) issued a call for social scientists not only to engage in relevant research, but also to undertake social action as a vehicle for research. In his view social science would be benefited by "messing in a sustained way with the realities of modern society" (p. 261). In his view social-action research with an uncertain disciplinary base is justified when "one does the best one can and relies on the efforts and criticisms of others to do better the next time" (p. 267). In our view, neither social science nor society has suffered by the immersion of social scientists in desegregation efforts, and a strong argument can be made that both have benefited.

In the next chapter, we will deal further with the rationale for participation in social action, with the problems that arise when science is employed in a politicized context, and with the ethics of participation in social action and intervention in the community.

Notes

1. This chapter owes a great deal to Kluger's magnificent book, *Simple Justice* (1976).

2. Article I, Section 2. The Constitution contained two other provisions with respect to slavery. The importation of slaves could not be prohibited by Congress before 1808 (Article I, Section 9) and runaway slaves could be compelled to return, even if they went to free territory (Article IV, Section 2).

3. *Civil Rights Cases,* 109 U.S. 3 (1883); *U.S. v. Cruickshank,* 92 U.S. 542 (1875).

4. The U.S. Supreme Court cited *Plessy* when it upheld the decision of a Mississippi school board to send a native-born Chinese girl to a segregated school. The court thus found that the state had the power to segregate its citizens (*Gong Lum v. Rice,* 275 U.S. 78, 1927).

5. Among these scholars and literary figures were W. E. B. Du Bois (1903) (Weinberg, 1970, contains a selected bibliography of his writings), E. Franklin Frazier (1969), Davis and Dollard (1940), Dollard (1937), Myrdal (1944), and Ellison (1947). See also Allport (1954) for a summary of the literature on prejudice.

6. *Sipuel v. Oklahoma State Board of Regents,* 332 U.S. 631 (1948); *McLaurin v. Oklahoma State Regents for Higher Education,* 337 U.S. 637 (1950); *Sweatt v. Painter,* 339 U.S. 629 (1950).

7. See Myrdal (1944, chap. 28, Vol. 2) for a discussion of this literature.

8. See *Briggs v. Elliott*, 347 U.S. 497 (1954); *Davis v. County School Board of Prince Edward County*, 347 U.S. 483 (1954); *Belton v. Gebhart*, 347 U.S. 483 (1954).

9. Since *Brown*, the courts at all levels have paid increasing attention to expert social science testimony in a wide variety of cases, although there are many problems to be resolved (see Levine & Howe, 1985; Monahan & Walker, 1986).

10. *Swann v. Charlotte–Mecklenburg Board of Education*, 402 U.S. 1 (1971). Prior to that time there had been question as to whether a remedy that required a state to take into account race would itself be a form of discrimination. The Supreme Court said that to take race into account for purposes of fashioning a remedy was permissible.

11. The information in this section is based on notes taken by Adeline Levine at public lectures given by superintendent Eugene Reville and associate superintendent Joseph Murray, lectures and an interview with Lewis Sinatra conducted by Murray Levine, and Winerip (1985).

12. *Arthur v. Nyquist*, 415 F. Supp. 904 (W.D. N.Y. 1976); see Sellers (1979) for a history of ethnic groups and education in Buffalo.

13. The idea here was to create schools so special that students from all parts of the district were strongly attracted to them (i.e., as if by magnets), even if attending one meant riding a bus.

14. In recent years City Honors has contributed three finalists to the Westinghouse Science Talent Search, bringing national recognition to the city and its schools.

References

Allport, G. W. (1954). *The nature of prejudice.* Garden City, NY: Doubleday.

Baud, R. K. (Ed.). (1982). *Parent power: A handbook for Buffalo public school parents.* Buffalo, NY: Citizens for Quality Education.

Bickel, A. M. (1962). *The least dangerous branch: The Supreme Court at the bar of politics.* Indianapolis: Bobbs-Merrill.

Brooks, T. R. (1974). *Walls come tumbling down.* Englewood Cliffs, NJ: Prentice-Hall.

Brown v. Board of Education, 347 U.S. 483 (1954).

Brown v. Board of Education of Topeka, 349 U.S. 294 (1955).

Cahn, E. (1955). Jurisprudence. *NYU Law Review, 30,* 150–169.

Coleman, J. S., et al. (1966). *Equality of educational opportunity.* Washington, DC: U.S. Government Printing Office.

Cook, S. W. (1984). The 1954 Social Science Statement and school desegregation: A reply to Gerard. *American Psychologist, 39,* 819–832.

Davis, A., & Dollard, J. (1940). *Children of bondage.* Washington, DC: American Council on Education.

Dollard, J. (1937). *Caste and class in a southern town.* New Haven, CT: Yale University Press.

Du Bois, W. E. B. (1903). *The souls of black folk.* Chicago: McClurg.

Ellison, R. (1947). *Invisible man.* New York: Random House.

Farley, R. (1980). School desegregation and white flight: An investigation of competing models and their discrepant findings. *Sociology of Education, 53,* 123–139.

Foster, H. L. (1974). *Ribbin', jivin' and playin' the dozens.* Cambridge: Ballinger.

Frazier, E. F. (1969). *The Negro in the United States* (14th ed.). New York: Macmillan.

Gerard, H. B. (1983). School desegregation: The social science role. *American Psychologist, 38,* 869–877.

Glazer, N. (1975). *Affirmative discrimination: Ethnic inequality and public policy.* New York: Basic Books.

Green v. County School Board, 391 U.S. 430 (1968).

Hughes, L. (1962). *Fight for freedom: The story of the NAACP.* New York: Norton.

Keyes v. Denver School District No. 1, 413 U.S. 189 (1973).

Kirp, D. L., & Babcock, G. (1981). Judge and company: Court-appointed masters, school desegregation, and institutional reform. *Alabama Law Review, 32,* 313–397.

Kluger, R. (1976). *Simple justice.* New York: Knopf.

Levine, M., & Howe, B. (1985). The penetration of social science into legal culture. *Law & Policy, 7,* 173–198.

Metcalf, G. R. (1983). *From Little Rock to Boston. The history of school desegregation.* Westport, CT: Greenwood Press.

Milliken v. Bradley, 418 U.S. 717 (1974).

Monahan, J., & Walker, L. (1986). Social authority: Obtaining, evaluating and establishing social science in law. *University of Pennsylvania Law Review, 134,* 477–517.

Myrdal, G. (1944). *An American dilemma* (2 vols.). New York: Harper & Row.

Plessy v. Ferguson, 163 U.S. 537 (1896).

Ravitch, D. *The troubled crusade: American education, 1945–1980.* New York: Basic Books.

Sarason, S. B. (1973). Jewishness, blackishness, and the nature-nurture controversy. *American Psychologist, 28,* 962–971.

Sarason, S. B. (1974). *The psychological sense of community.* San Francisco: Jossey-Bass.

Sarason, S. B. (1981). *Psychology misdirected.* New York: Free Press.

Sellers, M. S. (1979). *Ethnic communities and education in Buffalo, New York: Politics, power and group identity 1838–1979* (Occasional paper #1). Buffalo Community Studies Graduate Group. Buffalo: SUNY at Buffalo.

Smith, R. R. (1978). Two centuries and twenty-four months: A chronicle of the struggle to desegregate the Boston public schools. In H. Kalodner & J. J. Fishman (Eds.), *Limits of justice: The courts' role in school desegregation.* Cambridge: Ballinger.

Stephan, W. G. (1978). School desegregation: An evaluation of predictions made in *Brown v. Board of Education. Psychological Bulletin, 85,* 217–238.

tenBroek, J. (1965). *Equal under law.* London: Collier.

Weinberg, M. (Ed.). (1970). *W. E. B. Du Bois. A reader.* New York: Harper & Row.

Willie, C. V. (1984). *School desegregation plans that work.* Westport, CT: Greenwood Press.

Winerip, M. (1985, May 13). School integration in Buffalo is hailed as a model for U.S. *New York Times,* pp. A1, B4.

12

Social Action in Community Psychology:
Science, Politics, and the Ethics
of Community Intervention

The preceding chapter on school desegregation illustrated the complexity of community change when looked at from more than one point of view. It also demonstrated the compelling need in many real-world settings for action to achieve change, even when our knowledge regarding change is incomplete. In this chapter, we develop further aspects of this theme in terms of the ecological analogy and other perspectives presented earlier in the book. We showed in Chapter 10 how ecological principles such as adaptation help us to understand change at the level of individual settings, programs, and organizations; these principles are useful on a larger scale as well.

The ecological perspective depicts change as involving units of analysis larger than the individual. A given problem of poor adaptation, and the kind of change called for in response to it, takes place within an interdependent network of relationships among settings and people. The interests of diverse groups are not confined to the background, but become part of the "figure" or issue under consideration. For example, depending on the perspective, the act of reading Miranda rights to a criminal suspect is either a long-overdue constitutional safeguard for the accused or an unreasonable constraint on the legitimate power and authority of law enforcement officers. The principle of interdependence thus says that the context and interests surrounding an issue are to some extent indistinguishable from the issue itself, and that a specific problem definition does not represent an absolute insight as much as a *relative* interpretation of reality.

The context of practice in the community (including both intervention and research) is different from the controlled conditions characterizing traditional clinical practice (e.g., psychotherapy, laboratory research). In the community context a larger number of constituencies surround any given issue, a fact that can complicate the task of reaching a consensus in the definition of a problem.

A second principle of ecology is that change to ameliorate social problems essentially involves creating access to resources. Improved access to resources is not likely to come quickly or permanently without some change in the established system or status quo. Established settings are relatively stable structures that resist change. Intervention to improve access to resources thus requires deliberate action to change the status quo.

Considered together, principles of interdependence and access to resources imply that change in a community may not happen easily, and it may not happen quickly. One basis for community stability (and resistance to change), for example, are the laws and regulations that help to structure the interdependent relationships among interests in the community. Laws and regulations can be repealed or modified, of course, as shown in the examples concerning institutional care of the retarded (the *Wuori v. Zitnay* case) and school desegregation. Recall that in both cases, change did not come without considerable effort by many people over a number of years. The ecological principle of succession, moreover, warns us that even after change is accomplished, we cannot assume that it will be maintained indefinitely.

The view of adaptation we present in this chapter focuses in large part on the condition of powerlessness. One strategy for overcoming powerlessness and victimization involves community organization and participation. We will also consider how information, including media publicity, can sometimes play an essential role in reducing the power discrepancies that contribute to social problems.

We will illustrate many of these points about change using the example of the Love Canal Homeowners' Association, an organization formed in response to a serious community crisis. An additional lesson we will draw from events at the Love Canal is that science, while it is a valuable tool, is also the creation and endeavor of human beings and is thus unable to transcend human biases and self-interest. The chapter concludes with the point that the community psychologist's recognition of his or her place in society as both similar to yet different from the ordinary good citizen imposes several important ethical considerations on his or her professional activity. We begin with the issue of problem definition.

The Politics of Problem Definition

One of the five ecological principles of practice (see Chapter 3) emphasizes the importance of values in community change. Sarason (1972), for example, points out that value conflict occurs often in the creation and dissolution of settings and may even be a necessary condition of change. The central role of values in change was also illustrated in the school desegregation effort where psychologists and other social scientists actively contributed to the debate, more often than not on the side of the plaintiffs.

When should the community psychologist participate in political action? One answer is whenever such means are necessary in advancing the core values of the profession—i.e., adaptive change in individuals and communities, prevention of disorder, enhancement of positive mental health, and protection of the free expression of human differences and cultural diversity. Advancing these values often requires us to undertake new activities not usually within the clinical role. Levine and Levine (1970) point out that turn-of-the-century settlement house workers provided an excellent historical role model for community-oriented practitioners. Social and political action is well within the traditions of the mental health fields.

Graziano (1969) provides an insightful illustration of how organizing against the status quo may become necessary from a practical standpoint when the goal is one of innovation. Drawing a distinction between innovative thinking and talking on the one hand and innovative *action* on the other, Graziano argues that because established systems by their very nature resist innovative action, the only path open in that direction involves organizing an alternative solution outside the system. Graziano found it necessary to develop a facility for the behavioral treatment of autistic children, a new and radical proposal at that time, outside of established mental health agencies.

One reason that pursuing innovation from inside the system is difficult is that established systems are territorial in nature and are also uncritical of other established systems. Different systems tend to be run by interlocking directorates made up of the same professional representatives and influential leaders, a group Graziano called the "mental health power structure." Inside the power structure scientific innovations may be slighted in favor of institutional survival, and so innovation can only come about through organizing an alternative outside the existing power structure.

Rappaport (1977) goes even further in arguing that *all* professional activity is political in nature to the extent that it advances certain values to the detriment of others. Claims that support for traditional mental health interventions reflects their grounding in science, while efforts by those seeking to test alternatives to the status quo are basely "political" in nature, reflect a double standard. Adopting any solution to a social problem, traditional or otherwise, or even choosing to ignore the problem—all represent political choices. The choices implicate only certain values and allocate resources in one direction rather than another. Rappaport concludes that "applied social science is political by definition" (p. 35).

Caplan and Nelson (1973) look closely at the value-laden nature of how social problems are defined, and in particular how the definition structures our whole conception of a problem, including which among the many possible solutions to any problem we decide to choose and which we do not choose. If we try to understand poverty by studying poor people, for example, we will identify certain person-centered explanations for this problem (e.g., lack of education or skills, deficits attributed to cultural or family background, laziness). Defining the problem in the context of the overall political and economic system, however, we could just as easily understand poverty by studying *rich* people, and the explanations (e.g., capitalism as a system) and solutions (e.g., redistribute wealth more equitably) would likely be different.

To summarize what we have said so far, our values often motivate us to stake out a position on one side or another of a particular problem. In so doing we inevitably help to determine the nature of that problem as we see it and also the approach to intervention we consider most likely to solve that problem. That others may not see the problem as we do is shown in the following discussion.

Blaming the Victim

To understand this perspective more fully, consider a position taken by social critics such as Ira Goldenberg (1978) and William Ryan (1971). They begin with the observation that wealth and power form the obvious metric of successful adaptation in our society (at least in the public's perception). Money and power (e.g., in the form of political influence) are finite in availability and are obviously not distributed evenly. Furthermore, people who enjoy a disproportionate share of power and money will naturally resist any attempt to make the distribution more equitable. (We should realize that such feelings are characteristic of virtually everyone in an advantaged position, political liberals as well as conservatives, since all stand to lose their advantage with any shift toward greater economic and political equality.) Because access to wealth and power and control of key community institutions (e.g., education, employment, mental health, and corrections) is restricted, those without access feel powerless, hopeless, and frustrated—emotions intimately connected to the prevalence of social problems and stressful life circumstances. Given that some degree of vulnerability is assumed to be present in everyone, events and circumstances in the soap opera of life have more serious implications for those who lack resources. Because we share common values, moreover, from time to time many advantaged people become appalled at the existence of poverty, crime, mental disorders, and so on, and insist that something be changed.

In Ryan's words, one solution is to "blame the victim" by *defining* the problem in person-centered terms. Primary deviance might be attributed to hypothesized biological malfunctions understood as "mental illness," for example, which leads to labeling and delimiting the problem at the level of individuals. Thus a problem is contained in a way that does not threaten the existing distribution of power and wealth. Once the problem is defined as a pathological characteristic of certain individuals, the range of relevant solutions naturally becomes restricted to interventions that *change* those individuals. We can thus congratulate ourselves that we are a caring society, while at the same time we neatly avoid a definition of social problems in economic and political terms with different implications for change. Putting it simply, blaming the victim enables advantaged citizens to reconcile humanitarian values with their own self-interest.

To the extent that victims accept the definition of social problems in person-centered terms, they reinforce the process of person blame and essentially end up blaming themselves for their predicament. Prior to the U.S. Supreme Court's decision outlawing school segregation, for example, the victim-blaming "separate but equal" doctrine was actually endorsed, for different reasons, by such influential black leaders as Booker T. Washington and W. E. B. Du Bois, legitimizing to some degree the implication that inferior black performance reflected personal deficits in blacks as a group. Goldenberg (1978) argues that the pervasive impact of the commercial media exacerbates self-blame among disadvantaged people by pounding home the message that everyone is expected to be a full-fledged consumer and successful participant in the economic system when clearly this is not possible.

Blaming the victim is inherent in clinical interventions that may simply encourage victims to feel less distressed about their maladaptive circumstances. Even prevention programs implicitly blame the victim. Competence building undertaken with "high-risk" individuals, for example, clearly involves changing these individuals and not the disadvantaged economic and political circumstances that typically surround them. It makes no difference that the alleged deficiency is social or cognitive instead of genetic. Victim blaming thus becomes an inevitable by-product of professional activities *not* directed explicitly at changing circumstances or reallocating resources.

Equity Theory. The social psychological theory of equity provides an interesting analysis of the relationship between victims and exploiters (Adams, 1965; Walster, Berscheid, & Walster, 1973). A central assumption in this theory is that while in any given situation people try to maximize the payoffs or outcomes they achieve, they always endeavor to maintain equity, or what they perceive as equity, between their contributions to the setting and what they achieve as a payoff. A central hypothesis of equity theory is that lack of perceived equity, whether positive (one receives more than one deserves) or negative (one receives less than one deserves), generates psychological distress in people that motivates them to reestablish a sense of equity, either materially or psychologically (e.g., by rationalizing or distorting the inequitable situation so they perceive it as equitable).

Are there general parallels between the laboratory findings of equity theory (e.g., Adams & Jacobsen, 1964) and the social phenomenon of blaming the victim? We focus first on victim blaming as a typical response of positive-inequity individuals (whom we will call "exploiters") toward those experiencing negative inequity (i.e., "victims"). In an experiment where participants' contributions are apparently equal but payoffs are not distributed equally, exploiters do report experiencing psychological distress (Austin & Walster, 1974). Inequity between participants is resolved materially, however, only if the exploiter can do so completely (i.e., material restitution is "all or none"), and complete restitution is likely only when the disparity in payoffs is small. Equity in some form must be maintained, however, so the exploiter resorts to one of three kinds of rationalization to achieve equity psychologically: to minimize the victim's distress (e.g., "It isn't really that much difference"), to deny the responsibility of the *exploiter* (e.g., "*I* didn't create the system"), or to blame the *victim* for the disparity in outcomes (e.g., "He must have done something wrong for it to have turned out that way"). Interestingly, these rationalizations are more likely to occur when the victim is unknown to or isolated from the exploiter, and less likely to occur when the victim is in a position to retaliate against the exploiter (Davis & Jones, 1960; Walster, Berscheid, & Barclay, 1967).

Reactions of the victims themselves are also noteworthy. Initially a victim will try to restore equity by seeking material restitution. If material restitution is denied (as we have seen it will be if "too costly" to the exploiter), the victim will attempt to retaliate if possible, and retaliation is often successful in gaining restitution (Berscheid, Boye, & Walster, 1968). The ability to retaliate requires greater power than most victims probably possess, however. When material restitution is denied and retaliation is not possible, victims are no different from anyone else in needing to maintain equity, and so they tend to achieve equity psychologically by rationalizing the disparity in outcomes (i.e., blaming themselves).

Equity theory suggests that it may be a mistake for victims to accept victimization patiently and stoically. A better alternative might be to cope with the situation actively by organizing to the point where they are able to pressure exploiters into making restitution. Often victims are isolated socially, economically, and geographically from the rest of society, and lack of contact may make it easier for exploiters to rationalize social problems by blaming the victim. (The power of the media to assist victims in gaining public sympathy and pressuring exploiters is considerable, however, as we will show later in this chapter when discussing the Love Canal crisis.) Successful organization will clearly help to make inequity more visible and thus more likely to be resolved through at least some degree of material restitution.

Paradox and Empowerment

Another rationale for political solutions to social problems is the limited validity of existing therapeutic and preventive interventions and the recognition that there may not be a "final" solution to problems such as abnormal behavior, at least not in the sense that these problems will one day disappear forever (Sarason, 1978). Rappaport (1981) argues that far from achieving convergent (i.e., absolute) solutions to social problems, much of what community psychologists have learned from our own work and from observing others leaves us confronting a set of paradoxes (i.e., seemingly contradictory viewpoints, both of which are apparently valid). One paradox, for example, is that professional "experts" with prestigious positions and impressive degrees are still able to learn much about certain behavioral problems from otherwise ordinary people who have managed to overcome these problems, such as members of Alcoholics Anonymous and other self-help groups. Who is really the expert in such cases? Either one can make a valid claim to this role, and therein lies the paradox.

Ideological differences can also lead to paradoxes, such as in the debate over whether the people we help have "needs" (i.e., *deficiencies,* the removal of which makes them "equal" by making them the same as others), or whether instead they have "rights" (i.e., *strengths,* the provision of which makes them "equal" by allowing them to be different from others). Rappaport cites the example of the insanity defense in the criminal justice system. On the one hand, we have the traditional position that some defendants are different from others and thus have certain needs requiring that they be treated with special consideration. Szasz (1963) and others, on the other hand, have championed the position that everyone has a right to behave as they choose, albeit with specific consequences if they violate a law.

Another paradox concerns the conflict between the creation of "alternative settings" for special populations under a needs model and the movement toward mainstreaming diverse groups from a rights position. In this respect, the Head Start program was a distinctly paradoxical creation inasmuch as it reflected a deficit-oriented needs model implemented in the context of an equity-seeking rights policy (the War on Poverty). Head Start's aim was always to integrate children of different racial backgrounds. In fact, Head Start centers sometimes recruited white children to ensure racial balance. If Head Start programs led to the segregation of children, however, the ideologies would clash.

A third (but by no means final) example of paradox arises from the realization that in trying to help people (e.g., through identifying and treating "cases" of psychopathology), we may end up harming them through iatrogenic influences such as labeling and stigma and processes such as blaming the victim. Rather than successfully helping people, Rappaport argues, traditional programs to treat or prevent psychological problems in individuals may represent a kind of paternalistic colonialism by professionals among society's less powerful members. Mental health and other human-service programs generally enjoy a monopoly on publicly supported services. Professionals in effect force the community to accept their goods and services and hold prestigious jobs and good salaries for themselves. Residents of the community end up with the status of dependents who are unable to determine for themselves how best to meet their own needs and goals. Is professional intervention helpful to clients or is it harmful? Although apparently contradictory, these two perspectives both lead to valid observations, to potentially different definitions of problems, and to alternative solutions.

Recognition of the paradoxical nature of social problems and their attendant solutions leads to Sarason's (1978) thought-provoking conclusion: there may not *be* any permanent (i.e., convergent) solutions to social problems. Today's "solution" merely sows the seeds for tomorrow's problem, in the way that Moral Treatment, for example, the solution to a problem in its mid-nineteenth- century heyday, itself later became a problem in the form of large custodial mental hospitals (Levine, 1981). Rappaport raises the possibility that social problems, intertwined as they are with basic human differences that may ultimately be irreconcilable, are not "absolute" in nature and in solution but are *dialectical.* Saying that a problem is dialectical means that it is best understood when viewed from more than one perspective. In a sense, Rappaport accepts the Piagetian definition of objectivity in assuming that phenomena appear different when they are viewed from different perspectives.

One implication of viewing a problem as dialectical is that the solutions should be many and diverse, having in common only that they entail *decentralized* control and *empowerment* of citizens at the local level. Decentralization and empowerment are high in Rappaport's value hierarchy. To empower people is to enhance their ability to control their own lives and entails functioning professionally more as a collaborator than as a symbolic parent. The "best" approach is the one that is most democratic. The paradoxical status of Head Start within the needs-versus-rights dialectic may be one reason why it has far outlived the rest of the War on Poverty. Head Start was both an educationally oriented prevention program for poverty-stricken preschoolers and a vehicle for empowering disadvantaged communities by creating jobs and fostering parents' sense of control over their lives and those of their children. It is a clear example of a divergent solution to the problem of poverty.

To summarize, in Rappaport's judgment community psychologists should pursue and articulate paradoxical definitions of social problems and facilitate the proliferation of multiple solutions to each problem. Recognition of paradoxes and the dialectical nature of problems allows one to see alternatives and exposes one's own basic assumptions to constructive criticism. Neither victim nor environment is blamed (Rappaport et al., 1975). Instead the focus is on creating settings that empower segments of a community to control their own resources rather than on solving problems in a once-and-for-all convergent sense.

Competent Communities

Rappaport's analysis depicts the community psychologist's job as one of helping to build competent communities. How can we understand this task? Using the ecological analogy we assume that change occurs in settings embedded in a preexisting context of interdependent relationships and represents new arrangements in the exchange of resources among settings.

Adapting to the community level the metaphor of primary prevention through competence building, we might begin by asking what characteristics differentiate more competent from less competent communities. Iscoe (1974) identifies three factors: (1) *power* to generate alternatives and opportunities, (2) *knowledge* of where and how to obtain resources of all kinds (i.e., not just money, but also resources such as social support), and (3) *self-esteem* in the form of pride, optimism, and motivation. The adaptation of diverse groups is facilitated in such communities by making a wide ecological niche available.

Community competence building is one response to the theory that inequality, alienation, dependence, and helplessness are attributable to lack of participation and self-determination and to unresponsiveness in government and community institutions (Reiff, 1966). The antidote for alienation and powerlessness is increased citizen involvement in decision making. We can help to define new rights of participation in order to increase citizens' direction and control over bureaucracies. One goal is to humanize the institutions affecting our lives by helping to create independent, critical monitoring of community affairs.

We should note that even these solutions are not without problems. Community participation has not always led to desirable results (Moynihan, 1969). We should also note parenthetically that the ideas, the perspectives, the concepts, and even the language developed during the War on Poverty. In writing as we do, we caution the reader to translate the viewpoint into approaches that are congruent with today's problems, not yesterday's. We should learn from the past, but we should not blindly repeat the approaches of the past.

Community competence building commits us to developing opportunities for self-determination by effecting change through political action. Strategies that pursue competence building at the community level can be broadly organized into two general approaches, called community development and social action, that differ significantly in their basic assumptions (Heller & Monahan, 1977). Community-development techniques assume that the community already has within it the knowledge, resources, and organizational and leadership *potential* to effect constructive community change. In contrast, social action assumes that resources are finite and distributed unequally, differences among various interests in the community are not easily reconcilable, and as a result the solutions to social problems are explicitly political in nature.

Community Development

Rothman (1974) describes community development as a process designed to create conditions of economic and social progress with the active participation of the whole community and the fullest possible reliance on the community's initiative. The community-development approach rests on the assumption that community change can be most effectively accomplished through broad participation of local citizens in goal determination and action. The themes emphasized by community development include democratic procedures, voluntary cooperation, self-help, development of indigenous leadership, and education. The potential present in the local community may not be realized because of forces in the larger society. The local community may appear to be lacking in productive human relationships and problem-solving skills and peopled by isolated individuals suffering from anomie, alienation, disillusionment, and often mental illness. The basic strategy of change is to get people involved in identifying and solving their own problems. Consensus tactics such as discussion and communication are stressed, and cooperative, inclusive techniques are practiced.

The professional's role in this process is to facilitate problem solving by encouraging organization, emphasizing common objectives, and nourishing growth in democratic competence. No clear division is made between members of the community power structure and other citizens; all segments of the community are considered part of the "client" system. The scope of legitimate goals is narrowed to those on which there can be mutual agreement. The interests of various groups and factions in the community are seen as reconcilable and responsive to the influences of rational persuasion, communication, and mutual goodwill. In community development, unitary interests of the whole are asserted over competing lesser interests through deliberative processes involving a cross section of interest groups within the population. Clients are viewed as normal citizens who are valuable, unique, and capable of growth toward greater social sensitivity and responsibility, but who have underdeveloped abilities and need the services of a practitioner to help them actualize these abilities. The preceding chapters offered several examples of the community-development approach, such as Goldenberg's (1971) creation of the Residential Youth Center (Chapter 10) and the work of Lewis Sinatra in the organization Citizens for Quality Education (Chapter 11).

Suppose careful assessment of a community in need indicates that we can accept the assumptions of community development. What forms might specific interventions then take? One general technique is to create new settings, such as citizen advisory boards, block clubs, and self-help groups to increase the degree of participation, responsibility, and knowledge present among residents (Unger & Wandersman, 1985; Wandersman, 1981). Such settings could also be linked into networks to facilitate interpersonal contact and the availability of social support in the community. Another general strategy involves resource exchange through barter networks. Sarason et al. (1977) point out that the traditional concept that solutions to social problems require "more money" has become problematic in an era of shrinking public expenditures; creating new relationships among existing resources can open up a broad range of possible solutions. Many social agencies such as senior centers have the problem of excess unfilled time from members who need stimulation, for example, while others such as day-care centers provide abundant opportunities for people to spend time interacting with special groups such as children. A day-care facility might thus barter supervision time from able-bodied elderly people in exchange for opportunities to interact meaningfully with children and other adults in new settings. No money changes hands, yet both populations are enriched and a key problem for each agency is solved. Networking in this manner provides an excellent illustration of Kelly's (1968) principle of the "cycling of resources" where community interventions take the form of creating new relationships among existing resources instead of bringing in new resources from outside. Goldenberg's RYC and Haveliwala's transformation of the Harlem Valley Psychiatric Center (also discussed in Chapter 10) both illustrate how finding new ways to use indigenous resources, including existing talent and leadership, promotes positive community change.

Community development holds promise as a strategy of change only when its assumptions are met. Creating new settings, for example, requires a sufficient level of social interest and motivation on the part of community residents. Another issue is whether responsibility for change resides only with the local residents, or instead is rightly shared with interests outside the immediate local situation (e.g., government, business). That is, what definition of the community is most accurate (or useful) for these purposes—one that focuses only on local conditions or one that includes a broader array of relationships including possible "exploiters" as well as "victims"?

Social Action

In the social-action perspective, the community is viewed as a hierarchy of privilege and power, with deprived, powerless subgroups suffering social injustice or exploitation imposed by a group of powerful oppressors.[1] Behavioral deviance, where it occurs, is understood as a natural, adaptive response to an oppressive system, not a biological malfunction.

Change will be supported by constituencies that stand to gain from change. One objective in social action, therefore, is increased awareness of problems among those who will gain from change, with problems conceptualized in ways that counteract the self-blaming tendency of victims. The basic strategy of change involves crystallizing issues, thus identifying a legitimate enemy, and organizing group action to bring pressure on selected targets. The practitioner advocates client interests exclusively by creating and manipulating fairly large groups and by influencing political processes. The power structure is seen as a force opposing or oppressing the client system and thus as something that must be coerced or overturned to serve client interests. Over the years, we have discovered that power structures are far from unitary in nature, and the simple assumption that some person or small group exists that can *force* change if persuaded or coerced has not proved useful in most circumstances.

The client group is a disadvantaged segment of the community. Their role is that of employer to the practitioner, as well as participant in mass-action and pressure-group activities. Social action assumes that interests among related parties are in conflict or not easily reconcilable. Thus change tactics often include conflict, confrontation, and direct action. The goal is to change the existing balance of power without resorting to violence. An important assumption is that negotiations leading to greater equity usually succeed only when they involve parties of approximately equal strength. Political organization among society's "victims" is intended to offset the greater influence wielded by those in the community power structure.

The late Saul Alinsky (1971) articulated many of the basic rules of social action. He argued that the key tactic is to organize the victims so that their one advantage, that of sheer numbers, is maximally effective. When a large Chicago retailer did not respond to the support of black consumers with a commensurate number of nonmenial jobs for blacks, for example, Alinsky effected change by organizing the black community to threaten the store's profit margin with a number of disruptive tactics (e.g., overcrowding the store during peak periods tying up the time of sales personnel, ordering merchandise C.O.D. and refusing it when delivered). Breaking no laws, the community organizer nevertheless works outside the normal expectations of the "enemy" to achieve parity in the relationship as a prologue to meaningful negotiation. Violence should never be necessary—Alinsky believed that violence marked a failure of organization—but the organizer must keep the pressure on and at least give the impression of being willing to stop at nothing to achieve an equitable redistribution of political and economic resources.

Criticism can be leveled at social action on several points. The first concerns the validity of social action's basic assumption that redistribution of resources must necessarily occur at the expense of other segments of the community. Are the resources to solve social problems literally finite, in the sense that the only way to obtain more is to reduce those of someone else? Many possible resources may exist in the victimized community itself and in larger units of government and commerce. Sarason's concept of networking and resource exchange provides an example of how redefining resources in noncash terms often makes available much more than was previously thought to exist (although noncash resources are not always relevant to problems such as hunger and severe economic deprivation). Focusing only on the resources held locally also ignores the fact that larger institutions, such as state and federal governments and national or multinational corporations, have a much greater capacity to raise revenues than do local communities and institutions.

All interventions have unwanted side effects as well as intended effects. Regarding social action, for example, Mann (1978) points out that under some conditions the practice of social action can encounter the principle of interdependence. Emphasizing one group's interests may end up threatening the larger fabric holding all interests together. To avoid unproductive divisiveness, it is important to keep the polarization of groups within the community *issue specific* and to maintain good communication with any allies inside the community power structure. Alinsky made it clear that the quarrel between the black community and the large Chicago retailer was strictly over jobs and did not go any deeper.

From an ecological vantage point, further questions are worth asking. Do we understand settings well enough to comprehend adequately the long-term nature and effects of social action? For example, do we understand how settings are related to each other in ways that enable us to predict how organizing one setting will affect other important settings? How will the initial changes made be maintained over time? The ecological emphasis on value congruence between organizer and community residents has clear implications for both achieving and maintaining change. Finally, of course, an added risk is that social-action organizations themselves can evolve into elitist and undemocratic institutions. In this sense they simply sow the seeds of their own demise in a process well described by Kelly's (1968) principle of succession.

In summary, Rappaport's (1981) arguments are again relevant in reminding us that community well-being requires the coexistence of multiple intervention approaches, sometimes dealing with different definitions of the "community." The ecological perspective leads us to a more comprehensive and self-critical approach to problem definition and potentially allows us to contemplate a range of potential solutions to paradoxical social problems.

The insightful writing of people such as Goldenberg, Ryan, and Rappaport makes it clear that social action and empowerment are ideologically compelling approaches to community change. How do they actually work? In the next section we try to answer this question using as an example the community response to the man made disaster at the Love Canal.

The Love Canal Homeowners Assocation: A Grass-Roots Community Organization[2]

The Love Canal Homeowners Association (LCHA) developed spontaneously in response to a community crisis, the discovery that an abandoned toxic-waste dump site was leaking into a residential neighborhood and imperiling the health of residents living nearby. An announcement on August 2, 1978, by New York State's Commissioner of Health that pregnant women and children under age 2 were advised to leave the area galvanized a community that had been getting information from the papers and from officials on the site that something was wrong.

For quite a number of years residents of the affected area had complained from time to time of yawning holes filled with dark, evil-smelling matter on the 16-acre site adjoining their property. A few residents complained of foul-smelling materials seeping into their basements and ruining sump pumps, but local officials took no action. Although an elementary school building was located on the site and hundreds of houses surrounded it, little notice had been taken of the complaints until 1976, when the detection of chemical contaminants in Lake Ontario fish led to a search for the source of the contaminants. This investigation pointed to a disposal site at the Love Canal.[3]

During 1978 the investigation of the disposal site expanded to involve several government agencies, and local news coverage of the problem increased. Lois Gibbs, then a 25-year-old high-school-educated mother of two children, had paid little attention at first to the events around the Love Canal. She lived several blocks away and didn't believe her life was affected. Shortly after her son started to attend kindergarten at the Love Canal school, however, he developed some allergies and kidney and neurological symptoms. Lois Gibbs became concerned that chemical contamination of the school property might be responsible, and the more she read the newspaper reports about the investigation of the Love Canal site, the more alarmed she became. She decided that she wanted her son transferred to another school. School officials, however, would not acknowledge that the school might be dangerous, and they refused her request.

During the summer of 1978, with encouragement from her brother-in-law, a biologist active in the environmental movement, Lois Gibbs went to her neighbors with a petition to close the school. As she went door-to-door during a hot summer, often trailed by her two children, she became aware of the large number and severity of illnesses suffered throughout the neighborhood. By this time the homes and families on streets immediately adjacent to the dump site were under study by the state Health Department and by Department of Environmental Conservation officials. Some community meetings were held that summer to explain what was happening, but these meetings left her with more questions than answers.

By now Lois Gibbs was heavily involved and had made a friend in Debbie Cerrillo, another Love Canal resident who was helping her with the petitions. When the Health Department announced that it was going to have a meeting in Albany, 300 miles from the affected community, to announce its findings, Lois, her husband, Harry, and Debbie Cerrillo decided to go to Albany to attend the meeting. There they heard the commissioner make his fateful announcement that pregnant women and young children should move out of the area, but saw him leave before they could obtain any clarification of the meaning of the announcement.

They drove home despondent, only to find the streets in their neighborhood filled with people who had heard the announcement on television or over the radio. There was no Health Department official in the area who could or would talk with the frightened and angry people. Those living adjacent to the site felt their health and the lives of their children were threatened, while those in the surrounding neighborhoods believed the events would make their houses unsalable and thus worthless. Some in the crowd were burning symbolic mortgages and talking of taking drastic action.

Because Lois Gibbs had met many neighborhood people when she was circulating her petition, and many knew she had been in Albany, she was pushed up to the front of the crowd. There she was asked to mount the makeshift platform and was given the microphone attached to a homemade public-address system. Lois Gibbs, who described herself as painfully shy and who had never addressed an audience before, took the microphone and tried to give the people some hope. That evening plans were announced for a homeowners' group to represent the interests of all, and within a few days the group was organized.

These events of early August 1978 were taking place in the midst of a hotly contested gubernatorial campaign, and because this was the first example of toxic wastes affecting a residential neighborhood, the event took on national and international importance. Then-governor Hugh Carey, desirous of settling the affair in the most satisfactory way and believing that he had federal disaster-relief support, announced that the state would buy the houses immediately adjacent to the Love Canal site and those across the street from it. At that point all that was known was that toxic wastes were indeed seeping into the basements of the adjacent houses, that toxic substances were found in the air, and that an excess of miscarriages occurred among women living in the immediately adjacent area. Homeowners in the surrounding streets, and those who were renting in the low-income project a block away, were still left with questions about the safety of their houses.

The first group of houses was bought, and the people moved out within weeks of the original announcement, although not without considerable stress to individuals and families. The remaining homeowners were given vague promises that investigations would continue. Lois Gibbs had received a great deal of attention from politicians and from the media. She quickly concluded that politicians were not so much interested in what she had to say as they were in giving the appearance that citizens were being allowed to participate in decisions affecting their lives. She also decided that the only way the remaining residents' interests would be taken into consideration was if they remained active and pressed their concerns on officials and through the media.

Plans for remedying the leaks in the canal were going forward, as were additional health and environmental studies to determine the extent of seepage of chemicals into the surrounding areas. Meetings held from time to time with citizens often became shouting matches, as officials gave vague or evasive replies to other neighborhood people who insisted that they also wanted to get out. These meetings and the emotion they generated often made the television news, and that fact kept pressure on governmental officials.

Lois Gibbs and the group of homemakers who had joined her in keeping the LCHA active, kept themselves and the members of their organization informed of changing events. One night, while sitting in her kitchen pondering her next moves, Gibbs hit on the idea of putting pins on a street map to identify the houses where she knew that people had had health problems. When she did that, using her own notes, it seemed as if the pins took on a pattern. Illnesses appeared to follow the paths of what had been identified by long-time residents as underground drainage ditches running off the canal into neighborhoods several blocks away. The underground ditches, called swales, could have provided a preferred path for migration of the chemical leachate. Excited by what she found, she took her map to Beverly Paigen, a biologist employed at the Roswell Park Memorial Cancer Research Center in Buffalo. Dr. Paigen had expressed an interest in the Love Canal situation because she was interested in the interaction between heredity and environment in cancer causation. Paigen was not officially a part of the Health Department team investigating the Love Canal, and she had been warned by her superiors at Roswell Park to limit her involvement in the situation (Roswell Park is funded by the New York State Department of Health). Paigen considered the warning an affront to her academic freedom and continued her involvement.

Paigen trained the Love Canal homemakers to conduct a systematic telephone health survey of the residents in the area. When the survey results were mapped, a concentration of illnesses did appear in what came to be known as "historically wet areas" in the neighborhood. Paigen took her results to Health Department officials, who appeared to listen, but then discounted the research publicly because it was done by "housewives." The publicity attached to this home survey forced the Health Department to review its own data. In February 1979, the Health Department announced that indeed there was an increased risk of miscarriages in the formerly wet underground drainage areas, and that it would be best if pregnant women and children under 2 who were living on those streets also left the area.

This solution was unsatisfactory to the remaining residents, because one implication was that the hazard to unborn children was a hazard to everyone. Another implication was that it was not safe for young couples to conceive while living in the area. Property values had plummeted by then, and people could neither sell nor afford to leave their houses, which often constituted the greater part of their life savings. The homeowners, led by Lois Gibbs, undertook a series of actions designed to keep their cause in the newspapers and thus to keep it alive. In addition to general education efforts, speeches to any audience that would listen, and letters to congressional representatives and state legislators, their more dramatic actions included marches and demonstrations in the Niagara Falls area, taking a child's coffin to Albany to be delivered to the governor, and burning effigies of the governor and the health commissioner. Each of these events received media attention. Lois Gibbs made trips to Albany and to Washington trying to persuade state and federal officials to pay attention to their situation. The officials repeatedly told her there was no definitive evidence of danger that would warrant moving more people.

In the summer of 1979, during remedial construction to cap and partially drain the disposal site, fumes from the canal permeated the neighborhood. Many people reported that they and their children were feeling ill or were subject to asthmatic episodes. As part of an agreement worked out in court between LCHA and the state, residents were to be moved out and housed at state expense if there was evidence of danger to health during the construction period. During this time over 100 families took advantage of that provision and moved into surrounding motels, where the state paid the bill not only for their accommodations but also for their food. This arrangement soon began costing the state several thousand dollars a day, enough to buy many of the houses. After about 8 weeks, the state indicated that it would no longer foot this bill. Some of the residents decided that they would "sit in" at the motels, but by now some competing groups had emerged. The residents were no longer united. They moved back home.

The homeowners kept up the pressure as much as they could. The situation continued to draw media attention. Jane Fonda made a highly publicized visit to the area, for example, capped by an emotional plea for help for the Love Canal people. From time to time, governmental agencies released reports that kept the story alive. Residents continued to confront governmental officials whenever they could. One day when Governor Carey visited Buffalo, a Love Canal resident confronted him on the street and managed to get a statement from him that the state would indeed purchase more houses. In fact, a bill went before the state legislature to authorize the use of some existing funds to buy out the rest of the neighborhood in the interests of "revitalization."

Not much happened from November 1979 until May 1980, when the Love Canal story again became worldwide news. To prepare for an impending lawsuit against the Hooker Chemical Company, the Environmental Protection Agency (EPA) conducted a small study of chromosome damage among Love Canal residents. This study was done without recruiting and testing nonresidents to serve as controls, because EPA did not wish to spend the money to do a thorough study at that time. In May of 1980 this study, which tentatively reported chromosome damage in a number of Love Canal residents, was leaked to the press. The story made headlines, and soon the area was overrun with television and newspaper people from all over the world. At first EPA announced that it would assist in the evacuation of residents based on these new data, but then it backed away from that position. This reversal in policy apparently resulted from pressure by the Office of Management and Budget, which was concerned about the precedent that was being set for purchasing houses in "normal" disasters such as floods or tornadoes by actions taken in this new and unprecedented type of disaster. Although the chromosome study was criticized severely by some, particularly because of its lack of control subjects, it was judged to be scientifically valid by other qualified professionals. At any rate, the inconsistencies frightened and enraged residents, who found themselves learning of matters affecting their health and their families' health from newspaper headlines.

As word spread that the White House had changed its position on evacuating the neighborhood, enraged and distressed residents gathered on the lawn in front of the LCHA office. Someone poured gasoline in the form of the letters "EPA" on a lawn across the street and ignited it. Other residents, who in every other way were law-abiding middle-class citizens, stopped cars in the street, and in one case began rocking a car, threatening to turn it over. By mid-afternoon Lois Gibbs managed to reach two EPA officials who were in town. They agreed to come to the LCHA office to speak with residents. Someone then got the idea that because the homeowners felt they were being held hostage in the neighborhood, they in turn would hold the federal officials hostage when they arrived. (The event took place during the Iranian hostage crisis.) About 100 people were gathered on the lawn when the EPA officials entered the office. Lois Gibbs and several others told the two men they couldn't leave because it wasn't safe for them to go outside into the crowd.

By then the area was crowded with reporters. The telephone in the office was a major link between homeowners, the White House, and other government officials. Police, a SWAT team, and federal marshals stood by watching the crowd. Early in the evening the FBI called and told the group that they had 2 minutes to release the hostages. That threat soon led to the release of the EPA officials, who were escorted through the angry crowd by the police. The residents' point had been made forcefully. A few days later, EPA announced that residents would be temporarily relocated if they wished to be.

No real solution emerged. Residents were told that the government was still studying the problem. The presidential primary campaign was under way, and it was by no means certain that Jimmy Carter would be renominated or that he would win the primary in New York. Subsequent events took place against this political backdrop. Lois Gibbs and many of the other Love Canal residents were invited to appear on the Phil Donahue show. Love Canal residents who had been told they had chromosome damage were interviewed on national television. Love Canal residents went to New York City to picket the Democratic nominating convention in the hope of embarrassing the president. In September Lois Gibbs was interviewed on the Good Morning America show, where in no uncertain terms she blamed the incumbent president for the lack of federal help in the crisis. Two weeks later, an announcement came that

New York State and the federal government had concluded an agreement to purchase the remaining houses and relocate the residents. President Carter was coming to Niagara Falls to make the announcement himself. Eventually all of the residents who wished to sell their homes and move out did so. The LCHA had achieved its major goal. It had fought the state and federal government successfully for 2 years and had finally convinced the government to take action.

Comment. The Love Canal story is important for several reasons. First, it brought the problem of toxic-waste disposal to national consciousness. The Love Canal citizens were fighting for themselves, but in their fight they called attention to a critical national problem. Their efforts have resulted in national legislation to clean up abandoned toxic-waste sites (using the so-called Super Fund) and in increased awareness of the issues of safe disposal. Communities all over the country are now alert to the problem. Hundreds if not thousands of citizen groups have sprung up spontaneously to protest landfills that are too close to homes or schools or that threaten to contaminate water supplies. Industry is concerned that more stringent regulation will increase the costs of disposal, and local industries often use their economic, political, and scientific resources to fight citizen groups. Nonetheless, citizens are making their weight felt in decisions affecting their communities.

Second, Lois Gibbs's personal story demonstrates that ordinary citizens can uncover extraordinary abilities during a crisis, and can emerge much strengthened. From a shy housewife, concerned primarily with her own home and family, she became a folk heroine and national figure who deals with governors, senators, journalists, and governmental officials as an equal. She founded and now heads the Citizens' Clearinghouse for Hazardous Wastes, a Washington, D.C.-based nonprofit corporation supported largely by private foundation funds, which provides organizing help to local groups faced with toxic-waste emergencies in their communities. Others working with Lois Gibbs during the crisis showed similar strength and personal growth. No others went on to a career based directly on their experiences, but many maintain an active interest in community affairs and continue to participate in events around the canal.

Third, the Love Canal Homeowners Association is an example of a spontaneous organization that developed in relation to a community crisis and gave people a means of taking vigorous action on their own behalf. It is all the more interesting as an illustration of how even stable working- and middle-class citizens can take increasingly radical action as their frustration grows. Families in the area were clearly subjected to considerable stress for a prolonged period of time. For many the LCHA provided a means of social support or a sense of community that enabled them to cope with the stressful life events that followed their discovery of the problem (Stone & Levine, 1985). While the homeowners had the benefit of professional assistance from Beverly Paigen (who suffered political reprisals for her participation) and from a few others, the homeowners were always in charge. They welcomed and used professional assistance but were not led by the professionals. The homeowners were receptive to attention by academics who provided some advice from time to time but who were straightforward about their interest in writing about the Love Canal. The homeowners wanted their story told, were pleased with academic attention, and took it as a sign that what they were doing was in fact important.

The homeowners also were wise in focusing their efforts on achieving their narrow goal of relocation. The fact that the story had national significance is a positive side effect of their efforts. They were concerned with saving themselves, but in struggling in their own interest they contributed to the well-being of all of us.

Finally, the story of the Love Canal is not yet over. There is still doubt about the extent of chemical migration and the hazard that such chemicals actually present to those families who still live in the area and to those who might want to move in if the government agency that now owns the houses is permitted to resell them. There is still argument about the scientific data and about their significance for decision making in this kind of situation. The Love Canal story also reveals the problems of doing science in a politicized environment. We turn now to a discussion of the interplay of science and politics in relation to community problems.

Science, Politics, and the Social Context of Research

Throughout this book we have discussed empirical research, and we have directly and indirectly stated our belief that at least in some measure, applications of scientific approaches to social and psychological problems can contribute to the solution of those problems as well as contribute to our knowledge of ourselves and our social world. Given this expression of faith in the scientific approach, however, we must still recognize that every cultural artifact, in this case science, is a compromise product of its social surrounds. We make this point because the social surrounds of the pure science that most of us learn are different from the social surrounds of science in applied contexts.

We can use a simple model to make the point. Films and novels are artistic forms that are shaped in contexts including artists, financial sponsors, publishers, critics, and audiences (Huaco, 1965). Analogous roles surround social science research. In pure research the researchers, funding agencies, journal editors, publishers, critics, and audience all tend to be social scientists who share common frames of reference. When the research has implications for social issues, however, the surrounding roles are filled with people who have different assumptions and different values from those of scientists. Aside from academic social scientists, the actors may include employees of government agencies, private industry, political figures, citizens affected by the particular action, and critics and supporters of the particular position. If a social program is involved, those who are employed in the program also have stakes in it (Levine & Levine, 1977). We are also a rational society. We are unable to say we want something just because we want it and instead must argue on our own behalf by referring to empirical evidence. A political view of this debate sees science as the language of discourse, while the prizes are resources that will be redistributed. As we noted earlier, scientific studies were used on all sides of the Love Canal conflict to undergird the various positions that people took (A. Levine, 1982).

Given limited resources and the obvious fact that one cannot approach all questions at once, the very definition of the problem at hand determines what gets studied and what data are collected. Gouldner (1968) notes that a great deal of research on behavioral deviance has been done from the perspective of the deviant. From this perspective the police officer, welfare worker, schoolteacher, and jail guard become

the villains. Gouldner points out that a long-standing conflict for the control of institutions existed between "cosmopolitans," whose loyalties were to profession and to
discipline and who tended to work at a national level, and "locals," whose loyalties
were to local institutions and communities. Cosmopolitans sponsored the research,
Gouldner notes, and to the degree that the research pointed a critical finger at the
locals, cosmopolitans could argue that limiting locals' control over those institutions
was necessary. He makes the point that financial sponsorship of research is important
because of the restrictive way the specific problem for research inevitably gets defined
and because of the implications of one definition as against another.

One could illustrate this point by asking members of the various constituencies
surrounding schools what should be researched to produce better schools. The
answers one would get from schoolchildren, classroom teachers, school administrators, school board members, city council members responsible for financing schools,
parents, and citizens without children in the schools would surely be quite different.
Researchers typically define a particular problem from their own theoretical viewpoint, but what is interesting to a professional researcher may not be of interest to the
person who is the subject of research. In the Love Canal situation, many parents
resented that questionnaires circulated by the Health Department asked primarily
about illnesses in adults, when residents were more concerned about the health of their
children (A. Levine, 1982). If the problem is primarily defined in one fashion and data
are generated from that viewpoint, those data determine the discourse. The definition
of the problem is often critical.

Other issues that we take for granted in research also have important implications
when decision making is involved. In pure science we generally try to avoid the Type
I error—that is, rejecting the null hypothesis when it should not be rejected. We therefore say we will not accept a finding unless it would not have arisen by chance more
often than 5 times in 100, the familiar .05 standard. We are taught to be less concerned
about the fact that we might miss a potentially important effect by setting a stringent
standard for the rejection of the null hypothesis, and thus rarely worry about accepting
the null hypothesis when we should have rejected it—the Type II error.

In the Love Canal situation, much of the dispute between Health Department scientists and citizens concerned the Type I versus Type II error problem. Health
Department officials, concerned that a decision that the area was unhealthy would
result in costly relocation of many people, wished to avoid the Type I error. They
adopted the usual scientific standard, wanting to have strong evidence before they
concluded that there was an inordinate amount of illness in the area, thus making the
government responsible for moving people. On the other hand, residents wanted to
avoid the Type II error. They took the position that if there was any chance of danger,
they should be moved out of harm's way, whether or not compelling proof of the
danger was present. Where a journal editor might want data indicating an increase in
fetal morbidity and mortality significant at the .05 level before publishing an article,
a pregnant mother is more interested in being relieved of anxiety over the possibility
her baby might be harmed, regardless of whether there was absolute proof that the
chemicals buried in the Love Canal were the cause of the harm. In this case the adoption of the usual scientific decision standard proved to be favorable to the government's position that it did not wish to move people unless it absolutely had to, while
at the same time unfavorable to the residents who wished to avoid any avoidable risk
(A. Levine, 1982).

Details of experimental design can also favor one group over another by making it easier or more difficult to detect effects. The fact that in many situations it is impossible or unfeasible to assign subjects to conditions at random presents such an opportunity. For example, in evaluating a highly politicized experimental school program in New York City during the early 1900s, the evaluator chose to compare experimental schools with a high density of recent immigrant children to control schools with a high density of American-born children. This evaluator was employed by the superintendent of schools, who had objected to the experimental program. The program had been forced on him by school board members who saw features in it that could help the city with its financial problems. Not surprisingly, the results showed that the experimental schools were behind educationally. Even though this study was subjected to intense criticism, it was cited in the debate over the experimental program several years later (Levine & Levine, 1977).

A similar issue of controls affected the Love Canal study. The Health Department research team used as controls the miscarriage rate published for women who were being examined because they had previously borne a defective child. This miscarriage rate was based on the women's self-report. In determining the rate among Love Canal women, however, the Health Department accepted a case of miscarriage only if it was verified in medical records. The comparison of self-report rates with physician-verified rates biased the study in the direction of minimizing the miscarriage effect. The rate in the Love Canal was so high that the difference was still statistically significant, but Health Department officials and others were able to say that the rate of miscarriage among Love Canal women was "only" one and one-half times the control rate when, if compared with a proper control sample, it might actually have been three or four times the control rate (A. Levine, 1982).

A study by Chandler, Weissberg, Cowen, and Guare (1984) reveals a similar problem in the selection of a control group. These investigators were doing a long-term follow-up of children who had been served by the Primary Mental Health Project (PMHP), a widely known secondary prevention program. The children had originally been seen between kindergarten and fourth grade, and at the time of follow-up were in the fourth through sixth grade. The study design did not include as contemporary controls children who, like those in the treated group, were evaluated in the earlier grades and then followed up in the later grades. Instead, one comparison group consisted of children never referred to PMHP who were matched to the treated sample for basic demographic variables. Teachers were also asked at time of follow-up to select the two least well-adjusted children in their classes. Those in this group who were not treated by PMHP and not in the first comparison group provided a second comparison group. The dependent variables included teacher ratings of childrens' adjustment, children's self-ratings, and academic achievement test scores.

Results indicated that on the average, ratings for children in the treated group had improved from the initial ratings taken several years earlier. The treated group was still less well adjusted than the matched sample of never-treated children, but treated children were judged to be superior to the group selected as most poorly adjusted at the time of follow-up. This latter difference was much clearer on the adjustment ratings done by teachers than on childrens' self-ratings and academic achievement scores.

The researchers concluded that early intervention reduced the risk of maladjustment because the treated children were rated as better adjusted than the poorly adjusted children who had never been treated previously. Consider, however, that the treated children were probably at the height of their maladjustment when first referred and that their average level of maladjustment probably would have declined over the next 2–5 years anyway for a variety of reasons (e.g., regression to the mean, loss of the most poorly adjusted children to suspension, expulsion, or special education; in fact, the follow-up sample represented only 21% of the children served by PMHP in those schools 2–5 years earlier). Comparing the treated children to children who were selected for extreme degrees of *current* maladjustment may have given an artifactual advantage to the treated group, thus showing good results for the intervention program. The fact that adjustment data provided by the teachers showed the clearest difference supports this interpretation, because these teachers also identified the "most maladjusted" group in the first place. These criticisms may or may not be valid. Perhaps the treatment program actually did have the effects claimed for it. The method of choosing the control group requires us to question even a study whose results happen to fit our own biases.

An evaluation report and its interpretation may also reflect systematic biases of the investigators or of their sponsors. We have already noted that the characterization of "only" a one and one-half times normal fetal abnormality rate among women living near the Love Canal was designed to minimize the implications of what was in fact a statistically significant difference. It is not unusual for reports to be shaped to meet their sponsor's views or needs. In the Gary schools program, an administrator who wrote a descriptive report based on a site visit to a Gary school was forced by members of the school board to rewrite the report so that it came out more favorable to the program under review (Levine & Levine, 1977). While the assertion of naked power in the mere writing of a report may be unusual, authors of research reports, particularly evaluation reports, probably do take into consideration the positions and sensibilities of their audiences and patrons. Adams (1985) provides a short course in "gamesmanship" for program evaluators to deal with the ethical dilemmas posed by research reports that have significance for the allocation of resources.

The integrity of a scientific effort is not guaranteed by the names and scientific reputations of the participants. We have all heard of instances in which reputable senior research workers had their names on papers that proved to be fraudulent. In many laboratories, the senior scientist's name is included as a coauthor even if he or she had very little to do with the research. Senior people are also subject to a variety of powerful nonscientific influences. In the Love Canal situation, the governor of New York appointed a commission of highly reputable medical scientists to review all research done to that time on the Love Canal. The commission's report was highly critical of all efforts that purported to show any adverse health effect, and it made an ad hominem attack on Beverly Paigen, the Health Department's chief scientific critic. On the other hand, it did not fault the Health Department at all for its failure to conduct well-designed, timely studies, and in fact excused some of the department's public relations ineptitude.

A careful analysis of the report shows that it made statements about health effects for which there was no documentation. Further investigation reveals that Health Department officials had supplied the basic information used by the commission, which was sometimes in the form of memos instead of reports of studies, and that Health Department officials were present at all deliberations of the commission. Paigen, whose work was severely criticized, was not invited to defend her work personally, nor was Stephen Barron, whose study of nerve conduction problems among residents was also discounted. Documents obtained under a Freedom of Information request, submitted when the scientific group refused to respond to inquiries about their sources, showed not only that Health Department officials sat in on all the meetings, but also that aides to the governor had reviewed and commented on the penultimate draft of the committee's report. Of course, nothing in the report itself revealed the extensive participation of Health Department officials and the governor's aides in its preparation. All but one of the five participants in this commission were administrators in medical facilities regulated by the New York Department of Health. Among other powers, the Health Department set reimbursement rates for hospital beds, decided how much would be allotted in the rates for teaching costs, and approved certificates for building or remodeling medical facilities, including laboratories. Although we have no evidence that participants were crudely or directly influenced by such considerations, the appearance of a potential conflict of interest might lead one to look with skepticism on their conclusions (A. Levine, 1982).

The timing of reports is still another matter. In the Gary school situation, there is some reason to believe that the release of a negative report was delayed until after a mayoral election in order not to embarrass the incumbent mayor, who had supported the program (Levine & Levine, 1977). We have already seen how a leaked report in the Love Canal situation led to turmoil that resulted in the eventual relocation of the citizens. If the report had not been leaked, the results might have been buried. If released, the results might have been accompanied by criticism carefully designed to mute their effect.

Research results may have effects on the researcher. Beverly Paigen's employers subjected her to harrassment for her work with Love Canal residents. She eventually left New York State for employment elsewhere (A. Levine, 1982). In the Gary school situation, the office of the research worker who issued the negative findings was subject to reprisal by school board officials. He left his position not too long after the incident (Levine & Levine, 1977). Research may also have effects on the careers of those whose programs are the subject of research. In the Gary school situation, the school administrator who took responsibility for implementing the Gary program in New York was not reappointed to his position after enemies on the school board managed to put together enough votes to block his reappointment. He was reappointed at a subsequent board meeting, but the earlier vote appeared to be in retaliation for his participation in the Gary experiment (Levine & Levine, 1977).

Research can also have direct and indirect effects on those who are the subjects of the research. In the early 1900s a body of scholarly opinion developed that purported to show the inherent inferiority of blacks. That research was used to support segregationist practices and to justify the low social status of blacks in the United States. It required another body of scholarly opinion to assert the opposite position in order to rally efforts to attack segregation (see Chapter 11). Arthur Jensen's (1969) assertions that most of the variance in intelligence is due to heredity, and that the learning styles of blacks and whites are fundamentally different, were used politically to try to justify cutting off aid to education. Who can say what it might mean to a black child to read that a scientist states that he or she is inherently less intelligent than a white classmate?

Because the stakes are high, the actors diverse, and the points of potential influence many, we should recognize that the error is not in the bias in the research but in believing that research can ever be "unbiased." The closed character of a logical system underlying our concepts of research design is inappropriately applied to practical arguments about the real world (Toulmin, 1958). The social context modifies and influences the research process, the inferential process, the report, the participants, and the varied uses to which research may be put. Donald Campbell has been a leading figure in calling our attention to many of the problems in evaluation research and in suggesting solutions to the problems (Campbell, 1969, 1979; Campbell & Kimmel, 1985). The solutions are all in the nature of social inventions that will enable us to understand how the research is being done and how it is being used. Campbell and Kimmel (1985), for example, argue that what society ultimately ends up depending on is not the infallible objectivity of the scientific logic and procedures, but the existence of a self-critical scholarly community of people whose members communicate closely with one another and share a dedicated interest in the honest discovery of knowledge.

We need to recognize in this field that we are as much concerned with fairness as with accuracy and that any approach to research has to be deemed fair by those it affects. We also need to recognize that given the best of intentions, many research efforts will result in ambiguous or disputable conclusions and that, in the end, decisions will often be made on the basis of power, politics, and related values, despite any wishes we may have as social scientists that decisions be grounded entirely on hard evidence.

The Ethics of Community Intervention

The professionally trained individual who lays claim to the mantle of science and who enters the difficult field of social intervention has special problems. One question is simply: "Who asked you?" By what authority does a community psychologist or any other social scientist act to affect other people's lives? Isn't that a political question, and shouldn't the basic decisions be made in the political arena by elected officials who clearly indicate the policies they will pursue? Our democratically elected political officials and their appointees are given authority and legitimacy to allocate public resources and to order our lives. When a professional person does enter this field, claiming some special knowledge or expertise, what obligations does the professional person owe the community at large or the narrower community with whom the professional typically works? Doesn't the professional person have an obligation to be clear about his or her own values and to reveal them? Does the professional have the right to withhold specialized knowledge and services from those with whom he or she disagrees and support only those with whom he or she agrees? Given the limits of knowledge, what obligation does the professional have to be forthcoming about the limits of expertise in a given field or about the limits of knowledge for decision making? Does the professional person have a right to "invade" institutions in order to study them? Does the professional have the right to attempt to intervene in institutions and agencies when the effort is likely to be experimental?

One answer is that all such interventions ought to be undertaken cooperatively, in the interests of all those who participate in the particular setting. Such an answer is overly simple, for it fails to recognize the diverse constituencies and the conflicting interests that are usually represented in any setting. None of these issues is well worked through, and persons of goodwill can take any side of each of the questions at this moment in the development of the field.

We have saved formal consideration of the ethical implications of community intervention until the end of the last chapter not because it is last in importance, but so that discussion of ethics can be based on a comprehensive understanding of community psychology concepts and practices. Our discussion relies heavily on Bermant, Kelman, and Warwick (1978). Certain characteristics peculiar to community interventions create different problems from those in clinical interventions. Because of the focus on large-scale problem definition and solution, for example, any abuses (as well as positive contributions) are magnified far above what might happen at the individual level. As another example, the longitudinal preventive intervention research can subject people to repeated data collection procedures over years or even decades, thus increasing problems involving confidentiality and exploitation.

Berman, Kelman, and Warwick (1978) note important ethical considerations in several aspects of community intervention. The first is the choice of *goals,* or what specifically we choose to change—individuals or relationships among elements of society. The choice is by no means obvious or routine. Scientists must be able to recognize and question their own ideologies and paradigms to be in a position to contribute to solving large-scale problems (Fox, 1985).

A second issue is our definition of *targets*—the "victims" themselves, or some other point of entry into the problem (visible need doesn't always provide the most effective point of intervention). In prevention, for example, a common procedure is to identify individuals who either show incipient signs of being a case of psychopathology (secondary prevention) or else possess certain characteristics known or suspected to leave them at greater risk than the average person of developing psychopathology. Carrying the label prepsychotic (or potentially psychotic), however, is itself a stigmatizing status or condition. Key other people, such as parents, teachers, employers, or perhaps even peers, may become aware of this status or condition because they were told about it or because they participated in the labeling process. The added risk imposed by being labeled publicly comes about largely because of the "person-blame" perspective of contemporary psychology and the larger society that developed it (Caplan & Nelson, 1973). The important ethical question, however, is whether the cumulative damage to the individual's mental health from labeling outweighs the benefit of the preventive intervention.

A third issue is the means of *intervention* we choose: What desirable effects does it have? What undesirable (side) effects? Will participation be compulsory or voluntary? One ethical dilemma sometimes overlooked, for example, is that although full disclosure to participants and voluntary participation have come to be considered mandatory, the apparently weak effects of community interventions make it unclear whether one can actually describe any expected benefits, whether direct or indirect, of participation, especially vis-à-vis the more obvious risks subjects face. Campbell and Kimmel (1985) even raise the possibility that given the doubtful empirical status of any cause-and-effect hypothesis in community intervention, any expectation of direct benefit given to participants might be equivalent to false advertising. They suggest that investigators recognize an obligation to any subjects of their research or professional activity that is equivalent in importance to the obligation they feel toward a granting agency that supports the work monetarily, since the human subjects also contribute in a tangible and indispensable way to the completion of the work.

A final issue is our assessment of *consequences*—our choice of outcome variables and measures will define the nature of our results, including the *un*anticipated consequences. As a matter of ethics, we should always be alert to the possibility of unintended negative as well as positive consequences of any intervention. The literature reporting some long-term longitudinal studies of preventive interventions indicates that some adverse effects of mental health interventions are as likely an outcome for some participants as direct positive effects (Campbell & Kimmel, 1985). Such effects, even if iatrogenic, provide important information about the processes underlying our interventions. They will never even be observed, however, unless investigators are conceptually and methodologically prepared to observe them and ethically obligated to search for them.

On some of these issues the ethical solutions are not absolute, but consist of making our own values known, particularly where they may be different from those of the community we are serving. How do the activities we described in this chapter and the ethical position outlined here differ from those of the ordinary "good citizen"? In part, the answer is that they do *not* differ, and so here we confront yet another paradox of professional activity. Sarason (1976) reminds us that the community psychologist necessarily views problems and solutions from a specific position in time and in social space, but his or her actions should be "more consciously and expertly applied" (p. 328) than are those of "Mr. Everyman." Thus in the end we are left with the reassuring, if still somewhat paradoxical, conclusion that the community psychologist is both similar to *and* different from every other member of the community.

Summary

An important theme developed in the closing chapters of this book has been that even though community change is complex and incompletely understood, complexity and incomplete knowledge about change are not excuses for inaction. The starting point for action to accomplish change, as we emphasized in this chapter, is the step of problem definition. Traditional clinical approaches to problem definition are sometimes said to "blame the victim"—that is, conceptualize the problem as a person-centered characteristic of those individuals who are suffering the most. This approach can create paradoxes or situations where two or more contradictory interpretations, implying radically different approaches to a given problem, both lead to logically convincing and empirically valid solutions. For example, do those at risk need special interventions whose sole purpose is to make them behave in the same way others do, or do they instead deserve additional resources sufficient to guarantee their right to behave differently from others?

Community psychology's ecological approach to problem definition assumes that more than one point of view on an issue can be legitimate, and that problem definitions and solutions are divergent rather than singular. For example, the ecological metaphor enables us to consider the definition of problems and solutions in terms of situations and systems instead of strictly in terms of individuals. It enlarges the scope of potential directions for change, which helps to resolve paradoxes. An intervention such as Head Start, for example, addresses the serious cognitive and nutritional needs of individual children while at the same time providing employment opportunities to their disadvantaged parents as a fundamental economic right.

Community psychology also assumes that the essential path to change and adaptation is empowerment, in the form of increased access to resources for those at risk.

One such resource involves *social organization* (e.g., increased involvement and participation in defining problems and decision making), and another is *information,* including substantive knowledge regarding the strategies and resources necessary for adaptation. For the community psychologist, identifying paradoxes and developing strategies of empowerment also have the salutory effect of placing in a constructively self-critical light his or her own place in the ecological context surrounding a problem.

Community psychology honors a tradition of action outside the established professional system in the service of individual and community adaptation. We discussed two examples of community interventions, each one used most appropriately under relatively specific circumstances. Community development involves identifying and finding new ways to use indigenous community resources, while social action forces a definition (or redefinition) of the problem in terms of an unfair allocation of resources, making the solution one of redistributing those resources.

Many of these points were illustrated using the example of the Love Canal. In this case, as in many situations involving the soap opera of life, a serious community problem came to be defined in terms of situational circumstances instead of individual weaknesses and was ultimately dealt with ecologically through community organization and more direct access to public resources, including media publicity.

The biased self-interest that creeps into established professional viewpoints is often reinforced by the way scientific paradigms and procedures are applied in research on human problems. The idea that all problem definitions and solutions are products of their social and cultural surrounds has important implications for how we understand and use scientific research in the community context. For example, the assumption that scientific research produces the same kind of "hard" evidence in the community that it does in the laboratory is often untenable. Although the choices entailed in defining the problem for study, the specific products of a research endeavor, the values it expresses, and the relationships among participants are never completely free of bias, they often can be made publicly in a way that at least strives to be fair to those affected by the research. Finally, recognition of these issues is also a necessary aspect of ethical practice in the community, where the goals, targets, means, and consequences of intervention are often larger in scope and impact than when working with individuals.

We close with the idea that in many respects the community psychologist is both similar to and different from every other member of the community. Every citizen has the obligation to remain informed about whatever affects the community. The professional community psychologist has the obligation to learn about the community from many vantage points and to disseminate that knowledge in many community forums. In doing our best to promote understanding from many different perspectives, perhaps we can contribute to the development and maintenance of the sense of community that is so important to all of us.

Notes

1. The language of social action implies a "devil theory" or a paranoid view of the world. The processes are not necessarily deliberate, but are more often subtle and rooted in our culture and world view.

2. The material in this section is drawn largely from A. Levine (1982) and Gibbs (1982).

3. The Love Canal was a short waterway used for recreation for about 40 years until 1942, when the Hooker Chemical Company began to dump chemical wastes there. In 1953, when the canal was completely filled, Hooker sold the site for one dollar to the Niagara Falls School Board. The school board needed land for a new school to accommodate the growing population of that area. The deed of sale included a disclaimer that the Hooker Company would be free of responsibility for any injuries or death or damage to property resulting from the chemical waste buried on the site. Deeds of sale to the buyers of modest, low-priced houses adjacent to the attractive new school contained no such warning, of course, and citizens didn't dream that government officials would allow a school and houses to be built in such a dangerous location.

References

Adams, J. S. (1965). Inequity in social exchange. In L. Berkowitz (Ed.), *Advances in experimental social psychology* (Vol. 2). New York: Academic Press.

Adams, J. S., & Jacobsen, P. R. (1964). Effects of wage inequities on work quality. *Journal of Abnormal and Social Psychology, 69,* 19–25.

Adams, K. A. (1985). Gamesmanship for internal evaluators: Knowing when to "hold'em" and when to "fold 'em." *Evaluation and Program Planning, 8,* 53–57.

Alinsky, S. (1971). *Rules for radicals.* New York: Vantage Press.

Austin, W., & Walster, E. (1974). Reactions to confirmations and disconfirmations of expectancies of equity and inequity. *Journal of Personality and Social Psychology, 30,* 208–216.

Bermant, G., Kelman, H. C., & Warwick, D. P. (1978). *The ethics of social intervention.* New York: Halstead Press.

Berscheid, E., Boye, D., & Walster, E. (1968). Retaliation as a means of restoring equity. *Journal of Personality and Social Psychology, 10,* 370–376.

Campbell, D. T. (1969). Reforms as experiments. *American Psychologist, 24,* 409–429.

Campbell, D. T. (1979). Assessing the impact of planned social change. *Evaluation and Program Planning, 2,* 67–90.

Campbell, D. T., & Kimmel, A. (1985). *Guiding preventive intervention research centers for research validity.* Unpublished manuscript, Department of Social Relations, Lehigh University, Bethlehem, PA.

Caplan, N., & Nelson, S. D. (1973). On being useful: The nature and consequences of psychological research on social problems. *American Psychologist, 28,* 199–211.

Chandler, C. L., Weissberg, R. P., Cowen, E. L., & Guare, J. (1984). Long term effects of a school-based secondary prevention program for young maladapting children. *Journal of Consulting and Clinical Psychology, 52,* 165–170.

Davis, K., & Jones, E. (1960). Changes in interpersonal perception as a means of reducing cognitive dissonance. *Journal of Abnormal and Social Psychology, 61,* 402–410.

Fox, D. R. (1985). Psychology, ideology, utopia, and the commons. *American Psychologist, 40,* 48–58.

Gibbs, L. M. (as told to M. Levine). (1982). *Love Canal: My story.* Albany: SUNY Press.

Goldenberg, I. I. (1978). *Oppression and social intervention.* Chicago: Nelson-Hall.

Gouldner, A. W. (1968). The sociologist as partisan: Sociology and the welfare state. *American Sociologist, 3,* 103–116.

Graziano, A. M. (1969). Clinical innovation and the mental health power structure: A social case history. *American Psychologist, 23,* 10–18.

Heller, K., & Monahan, J. (1977). *Psychology and community change.* Homewood, IL: Dorsey Press.

Huaco, G. (1965). *The sociology of film art.* New York: Basic Books.

Iscoe, I. (1974). Community psychology and the competent community. *American Psychologist, 29,* 607–613.

Jensen, A. R. (1969). How much can we boost I.Q. and scholastic achievement? *Harvard Educational Review, 39,* 1–123.

Kelly, J. G. (1968). Toward an ecological conception of preventive interventions. In J. Carter (Ed.), *Research contributions from psychology to community mental health.* New York: Behavioral Publications.

Levine, A. G. (1982). *Love Canal: Science, politics, people.* Lexington, MA: Lexington Books.

Levine, M. (1981). *The history and politics of community mental health.* New York: Oxford University Press.

Levine, M., & Levine, A. G. (1970). *A social history of helping services: Clinic, court, school and community.* New York: Appleton-Century-Crofts.

Levine, M., & Levine, A. (1977). The social context of evaluative research: A case study. *Evaluation Quarterly, 1,* 515–542.

Mann, P. A. (1978). *Community psychology: Concepts and applications.* New York: Free Press.

Moynihan, D. P. (1969). *Maximum feasible misunderstanding.* New York: Free Press.

Rappaport, J. (1977). *Community psychology: Values, research, and action.* New York: Holt, Rinehart & Winston.

Rappaport, J. (1981). In praise of paradox: A social policy of empowerment over prevention. *American Journal of Community Psychology, 9,* 1–26.

Rappaport, J., Davidson, W. W., Wilson, M. N., & Mitchell, A. (1975). Alternatives to blaming the victim or the environment: Our places to stand have not moved the earth. *American Psychologist, 30,* 525–528.

Reiff, R. (1966). Mental health manpower and institutional change. *American Psychologist, 21,* 540–548.

Rothman, J. (1974). Three models of community organization practice. In F. Cox, J. Erlich, J. Rothman, & J. Tropman (Eds.), *Strategies of community organization: A book of readings* (2d ed.). Itasca, IL: Peacock Publishers.

Ryan, R. (1971). *Blaming the victim.* New York: Random House.

Sarason, S. B. (1976). Community psychology, networks, and Mr. Everyman. *American Psychologist, 31,* 317–328.

Sarason, S. B. (1978). The nature of problem solving in social action. *American Psychologist, 33,* 370–380.

Sarason, S. B., Carroll, C., Maton, K., Cohen, S., & Lorentz, E. (1977). *Human services and resource networks.* San Francisco: Jossey-Bass.

Stone, R. A., & Levine, A. G. (in press). Reactions to collective stress: Correlates of active citizen participation at Love Canal. In A. Wandersman & R. Hess (Eds.), *Beyond the individual: Environmental approaches and prevention.* New York: Haworth Press.

Szasz, T. S. (1963). *Law, liberty and psychiatry.* New York: Macmillan.

Toulmin, S. (1958). *The uses of argument.* London: Cambridge University Press.

Unger, D. G., & Wandersman, A. (1985). The importance of neighbors: The social, cognitive, and affective components of neighboring. *American Journal of Community Psychology, 13,* 139–169.

Walster, E., Berscheid, E., & Barclay, A. (1967). A determinant of preference for modes of dissonance reduction. *Journal of Personality and Social Psychology, 7,* 211–215.

Walster, E., Berscheid, E., & Walster, G. W. (1973). New directions in equity research. *Journal of Personality and Social Psychology, 25,* 151–176.

Wandersman, A. (1981). A framework of participation in community organizations. *Journal of Applied Behavioral Science, 17,* 27–58.

Name Index

Subject Index

Abortion, 21, 56, 174, 206, 308*n*
Acquired Immune Deficiency Syndrome (AIDS), 19, 201, 204
Adaptation between persons and situations, 82, 83, 85–87, 89–93, 95, 100, 118, 122, 128, 157–59, 177, 215, 234, 329
  and coping, 172
  as an episodic state, 101, 158
Affirmative action, 275, 317, 319
Aftercare, 55, 124*n*, 299, 302
AIDS. *See* Acquired Immune Deficiency Syndrome
Al-Anon, 184*n*, 245, 247, 252, 253, 266
Alcohol abuse, 14, 15 (table), 32, 117, 249, 250
Alcoholics Anonymous, 148, 234, 235, 238, 247, 266, 334
  ideology in, 244, 245
  public position on alcohol abuse, 238, 239, 250
  and recovery from alcohol abuse, 117, 249–253
  relationship with professionals, 84, 249
Aloneness in American society, 29, 30 (table), 31–33
American Bar Association, standards of, 86–88, 97*n*
American Psychological Association, 8*n*, 273, 315
Arthur v. Nyquist, 327*n*
Assessment
  of communities, 108, 109
  of individuals, 48, 93, 128

Behavior, stability across situations, 121, 123
Behavior therapy, 62, 130, 168, 331
Behavior-environment congruence, 107, 109, 111, 112, 117, 120
  in prevention, 217, 227
  in self-help groups, 248
Belton v. Gebhart, 327*n*
Bereavement, 30, 181
  grief work in, 159

Births out of wedlock, 21, 61, 96*n*, 206, 207 (table)
Blaming the victim, 93, 215, 331–35, 352
Briggs v. Elliott, 327*n*
Brown v. Board of Education of Topeka (1954), 46, 220, 314–16, 318, 319, 327*n*
Brown v. Board of Education of Topeka (1955), 316
Buffalo Area Metropolitan Ministries, 322, 324
Burnout of workers, 90, 105, 283, 296

Cambridge and Somerville Program for Alcohol Rehabilitation, 252
Case management, 286, 290
Change in communities, 93, 95, 124
  "before the beginning" stage, 282, 285, 300
  conflict as essential to, 94, 330
  ethics of, 350–52
  in existing organizations, 288–307
  ideologies in, 293
  in-service preparation for, 289
  leadership in, 282–84, 287, 307
  media publicity in, 330, 333, 339–43, 353
  problems of, 6, 8, 81, 84, 121, 279–309, 329, 330. *See also* Unwanted effects of intervention
  production and satisfaction goals of, 290, 291
  resistance to, 281, 289, 291–94, 330
  social context of, 291–99
  types of, 289, 290
  under court supervision, 303–306
Charity, anarchist view of, 237
Child guidance clinics, 67, 190, 202
Children and adolescents
  due process rights of, 141, 153*n*
  problems of, 16, 17 (table), 218, 228*n*, 347
  sexual and physical abuse of, 62, 204
  as targets of primary prevention activities, 204, 205